Artists of the nineteenth century and their works

A handbook containing two thousand and fifty biographical sketches

(Volume II)

Clara Erskine Clement,

Laurence Hutton

Alpha Editions

This edition published in 2019

ISBN : 9789353862725

Design and Setting By
Alpha Editions
email - alphaedis@gmail.com

ARTISTS

OF THE NINETEENTH CENTURY
AND THEIR WORKS.

A Handbook
CONTAINING TWO THOUSAND AND FIFTY BIOGRAPHICAL
SKETCHES.

BY

CLARA ERSKINE CLEMENT

AND

LAURENCE HUTTON.

VOL. II.

BOSTON:
HOUGHTON, MIFFLIN AND COMPANY.
The Riverside Press, Cambridge.
1883.

CONTENTS.

NAMES OF ARTISTS.

AUTHORITIES CONSULTED.

———◆———

AMERICAN ENGRAVERS AND THEIR WORKS.

BENJAMIN'S CONTEMPORARY ART IN EUROPE.

ENGLISH ARTISTS OF THE PRESENT DAY.

ENGLISH PAINTERS OF THE PRESENT DAY.

GREAT AMERICAN SCULPTORS.

HAMERTON'S THOUGHTS ABOUT ART.

HAMERTON'S PAINTING IN FRANCE.

HAMERTON'S CONTEMPORARY FRENCH PAINTERS.

HAMERTON'S ETCHING AND ETCHERS.

JARVES' ART IDEA.

JARVES' ART THOUGHTS.

MEN OF THE TIME.

MRS. TYTLER'S MODERN PAINTERS.

OTTLEY'S LIVING AND RECENT PAINTERS.

SMITH'S ART EDUCATION.

TUCKERMAN'S BOOK OF THE ARTISTS.

WORNUM'S EPOCHS OF PAINTING.

APPLETONS' ART JOURNAL.

LONDON ART JOURNAL.

THE PORTFOLIO.

MAGAZINE OF ART.

PALGRAVE'S ESSAYS ON ART.

REDGRAVE'S CENTURY OF PAINTERS.

RUSKIN'S ACADEMY NOTES.

RUSKIN'S MODERN PAINTERS.

TAINE'S NOTES ON ENGLAND.

ATLANTIC MONTHLY.

LONDON ATHENÆUM.

ATKINSON'S NORTHERN CAPITALS OF EUROPE.

NICHOLS' ART EDUCATION.

WEIR'S OFFICIAL REPORT OF THE AMERICAN CENTENNIAL EXHIBITION.

REPORT OF THE UNITED STATES COMMISSIONERS AT VIENNA.

MARIO PROTH'S VOYAGE AU PAYS DES PEINTRES.

CHESNEAU'S CHEFS D'ÉCOLE.

L'ILLUSTRATION.

GAZETTE DES BEAUX-ARTS.

L'ART.

GALERIE CONTEMPORAINE, LITTÉRAIRE, ARTISTIQUE.

REVUE DES DEUX MONDES.

CHERBULIEZ' LITTÉRATURE ET ART.

CHARLES BLANC'S LES ARTISTES DE MON TEMPS.

CLARETIE'S ARTISTES CONTEMPORAINS.

T. GAUTIER'S SALON DE 1861.

E. ABOUT'S SALON DE 1864.

ROMA ARTISTICA.

DIE KÜNSTLER ALLER ZEITEN UND VÖLKER, VON PROFESSOR FR. MÜLLER.

ANSICHTEN ÜBER DIE BELDENDEN KÜNSTE VON EINEM DEUTSCHEN KÜNSTLER IN ROM.

DIE DEUTSCHE KUNST IN UNSEREM JAHRHUNDERT, VON DR. HAGEN.

DIE KÖNIGLICHE KUNSTAKADEMIE IN DÜSSELDORF, VON WIEGMANN.

ZEITSCHRIFT FÜR BILDENDE KUNST.

GEGENWART.

BRYAN, VAPEREAU, BITARD, NAGLER, LAROUSSE, AND MANY OTHER DICTIONARIES AND ENCYCLOPÆDIAS.

ARTISTS OF THE NINETEENTH CENTURY.

Jackson, John Adams. (*Am.*) Born in Bath, Me., 1825. Pupil, when quite young, of D. C. Johnston of Boston. After a careful study of linear and geometrical drawing, he gave some time to working in crayons, and later made some successful portraits in this manner. At Paris he studied anatomical drawing from life in the famous school of M. Suisse. In 1851 Jackson executed some fine portrait busts. That of Webster was made from medals and portraits furnished by his family. At Florence, in 1853, he modeled portrait busts of Miss Adelaide Phillips, T. Buchanan Read, etc. In 1854, in Paris, he modeled his bust of Judge Mason, United States Ambassador to France, and during the same year in Boston he made the bust of Wendell Phillips, now in the Boston Athenæum ; that of George S. Hillard, for the New York Historical Society ; and that of Rev. Dr. Lyman Beecher, now owned by Rev. H. W. Beecher. In 1858 Jackson removed to New York, and there modeled ideal subjects as well as those from life, including his bust of T. Buchanan Read, for the Union League Club of Philadelphia. In 1860 he received a commission from the "Kane Monument Association" for a statue of the arctic voyager, to be made in bronze ; his model was unanimously accepted by the committee, and the sculptor went to Florence to attend to the making of the figure. Since that time Florence has been his home. In 1862 Jackson modeled his group of "Eve and the Dead Abel," which (in marble) belongs to Mr. W. G. Morehead of Philadelphia. This work has been much praised by English and Italian art critics. Charles J. Hemans made a careful analysis of it, and Dr. Arrowsmith, an English surgeon, wrote an essay on it, giving the connection in it of anatomy and physiology, and "showing how the artist had in this group expressed the very subtle truths of organization and pathology." Following this work, the artist made a statue of "Autumn," for Mr. Tirrell of Weymouth ; "Cupid stringing his Bow," for Mr. Watson of New York ; "Titania and Nick Bottom," a small group in bronze, for Mr. Thomas Williams of London ; "Cupid on a Swan" (marble), for Mr. H. Clarke of Belmont ; the "Culprit Fay," for Mr. S. D. Warren of Boston, of which several copies have been made for England and the United States ; a bust called "Peace," for Mr. Whidden of Philadelphia, and another called "Dawn," for Mr. Theron Shaw of Boston. The last has been often repeated. Jackson has made many portrait busts (having finished one hundred) and medallions. Among the latter is one called the "Morning-Glory," which has been fourteen times reproduced in marble. In 1867 Jackson visited New York, and modeled for the "Croton Water-Board" a group of figures, and several single figures, to be cast in bronze and placed on the southern gate-house of the Reservoir at Central Park. The design was approved and the contract signed for the work. These statues have not yet been cast, but an engraving of the central group appears on the bonds issued by the Board. In 1869 the artist modeled his statue of the "Reading Girl," belonging to Mr. Aaron Healy of Brooklyn. In the Berlin "Zeitung" Dr. Hans Semper published an article upon this work, which he highly praised. At Vienna, in 1873, was seen the "Musidora," belonging to Mr. Clarke of New York, of which Mr. Gordon McKay of Cambridge has a fine copy, one third reduced in size. This statue was exhibited for a few days in New York, and was as much admired as it had been in Florence before it left the artist's studio. In 1874 the Soldiers' Monument at Lynn was erected. In this Mr. Jackson represented the city as a woman with one hand resting on a shield, while with the other hand she bestowed the laurel wreath ; the shield bearing the city's coat of arms. Below this figure are two others, "Justice" and "War," the latter at rest with arms reversed. The monument is of granite, and the figures of bronze. In 1875 was modeled a "Hylas" ; and following that, "Il Pastorello," which is a group in marble, representing an Abruzzi peasant-boy with his goat. It has been sold to Mr. Nevins of New York. It is very spirited, full of grace as well as life. It has a peculiar interest, since it faithfully represents the artistic Abruzzi costume, which is rapidly disappearing, and is much regretted by all lovers of the picturesque. Of the "Abel and Eve" the Boston Transcript said, —

"The more we study this group the more we find in it to admire. The fine conception is fully carried out in the details. The composition is admirable, viewed from any direction, — a rare accomplishment in a work of this kind. Eve rests on one knee, and on the other she supports the inanimate form of Abel, which she is supposed to have just discovered. Her left hand is under his drooping head, while in her right hangs his lifeless wrist. Her head is bent towards his with a gaze in which curiosity, uncertainty, and anxiety are mingled. The form of Eve is an exquisite piece of modeling. It is full of action, and yet pervaded with grace. The back is especially fine. It would seem as if the very marble itself felt the coming revelation, which is to prostrate the desolate heart of the first mother. The head is also an exquisite piece of chiseling, and we would call particular attention to the hair and the ivy (a happy suggestion of woman's first attempt to adorn herself) which binds it ; the mastery of which sculptors know to be a difficult task. We have rarely seen hair so faithfully and beautifully done. The form of Abel is very bold in its conception. It is dead beyond any hope of recovery ; and yet, through the magic of the sculptor's art, it excites only tender and pleasing emotions. The hand of the boy, and that of Eve which holds it, are worthy the most critical study of both the artist and anatomist. They form a group in themselves. The drooping left arm of Abel is equally successful. The anatomy of the entire group is perfect ; we have heard professional anatomists speak on this point in terms of the highest admiration."

Mr. Jackson is now engaged in modeling another group of " Eve and Abel," in which the form is so changed that it is the same only in name. He intends to make it his *capo d' opera*. It has already been much praised by critics and connoisseurs who have seen the model. [Died, 1879.]

" Mr. J. A. JACKSON'S MUSIDORA. — Several years ago a group in statuary, ' Eve and Abel,' by Mr. J. A. Jackson, was exhibited in this city, and was much admired. It made a real impression. The critics of the day were enthusiastic over it. The artist completed it in Florence, where he had lived some years, and where he now resides. After the Vienna Exposition he sent to this country a life-sized statue, ' Musidora,' which had been exhibited there. For a short time it was shown in New York, and was sold, but not before its superior merits had made for it many friends among the artists and lovers of art. Some time after, Mr. Jackson reproduced this work in marble, two thirds life-size, and this work is now owned by Mr. McKay of Cambridge, who certainly is to be congratulated upon the possession of it. The story of Musidora and her lover Damon, told in the ' Summer' of Thomson's ' Seasons,' gave Mr. Jackson the suggestion. He has taken the moment when Musidora, standing in the lilies by the pool, nude, ready for the bath, is startled by the noise of her retreating lover, who, half angry with her, unaware of her approach, had been musing in a pet under the hazels near by. She leans forward, listening in the attitude of surprise, with left hand and arm uplifted, and the right supporting the drapery. The weight of the body is thrown to the left. The figure is that of a lovely young girl, beautiful in face and form, and graceful in action. The conception is a most fortunate one, and in the embodiment of it the artist has made a gratifying success. He has given the figure a pose which is full of natural grace and charming in its suggested action. The symmetry of a beautiful form is well displayed under conditions where it is easy to offend, and where a hand that was not guided by refinement or was wanting in that confidence in modeling which is the result of conscientious study of anatomy, would have failed. It is altogether a work of great merit, and as a credit to American art ought to be better known."— J. B. MILLET, *in Boston Daily Advertiser,* October 28, 1878.

Jacob, Julius. (*Ger.*) Born at Berlin, 1811. Medals at Paris, Lyons, and Rouen. Member of many artistic societies. Studied under Wach at the Düsseldorf Academy, and later in Paris under Delaroche. He traveled extensively in Europe, and visited Asia and Africa. From all these journeys he brought back twelve hundred sketches of landscapes, and more than three hundred heads, copied from famous pictures. Among his works are a "Scene from the Life of Saint-Louis," "Artist Life," etc. In 1844 he went to England and remained eleven years, — his portraits were much admired, and he made a fortune by them. He afterwards traveled in the South of Europe, and went to Vienna, where he made likenesses of many eminent persons, Metternich, Schwarzenberg, Lichtenstein, etc. He worked with great rapidity, and finished twenty-six portraits in a single year. In 1866, on account of the war, he returned to Berlin. In the National Gallery of Berlin is a study of men's heads by Jacob. At Berlin, in 1876, he exhibited " Steinfeld von Sorrent " and " Aus der Mark."

Jacobs, Jacques-Albert-Michel. (*Belgian.*) Born at Antwerp,

1812. Officer of the Order of Léopold. Member of the Royal Academy of Belgium. Pupil of F. de Braekeleer. Traveled in the East. Paints landscapes and marines. At the National Gallery, Berlin, is his " Grecian Archipelago." [Died, 1879.]

Jacomin, Alfred-Louis. (*Fr.*) Born at Paris. Pupil of his father. Medal at Philadelphia, where he exhibited " Bilboquet and his Companion " and " An Armorer of the Seventeenth Century." At Paris, in 1877, was " A Baptism " ; in 1878, " The Magic Mirror."

Jacquand, Claudius. (*Fr.*) Born at Lyons, 1805. Chevalier of the Legion of Honor and of the Order of Léopold. Pupil of the Academy of Lyons and of Fleury-Richard. His motives are historical. A number of his works have been bought by the Civil List. His " Amende Honorable, — Scene in a Convent " (1853) is in the Luxembourg. His portraits are numerous and excellent. · The " Taking of Jerusalem " is at Versailles. Among his other works are, "Bonaparte at Nice," "The Last Interview of Charles I. and his Children," " The Ransom of a Sicilian Family captured by a Morocco Pirate," "The Death of Joseph," " Christopher Columbus about to die requests his Son to bury with him the Chains which he had worn," etc. His picture of " William the Silent " was exhibited in Boston by Williams & Everett in the winter of 1878.

Jacque, Charles Émile. (*Fr.*) Born at Paris, 1813. Chevalier of the Legion of Honor. When seventeen years old he studied with a geographical engraver, but a little later enlisted as a soldier and remained seven years in the army. He then resumed his engraving, and worked two years in England as a draughtsman on wood. He may be characterized as a rustic artist. His knowledge of sheep and poultry (of which last he is a fancier and breeder) is simply perfect, and he has been called " le Raphael des Pourceaux " from his exact acquaintance with pigs. He has been much in Burgundy, and his pictures of life there are marvelous in their minute representation, not only of the larger objects, but of details ; of the utensils, implements, and all the picturesque peculiarities of that charming country. One cannot always praise the color of this painter, and for this reason many connoisseurs rank his etchings higher than his paintings. A catalogue of Jacque's engravings, numbering four hundred and twenty, was made by M. Guiffrey. Many stories are told of his buying an old shepherd dog for a model, of his giving a new wheelbarrow for a broken, weather-stained one, etc., to the astonishment of the peasantry at Barbizon, where he built a little house and a big studio, and could, in that country, indulge his love for all that the word "rustic" can suggest. His earlier pictures, like his etchings, were small ; but he has painted larger ones ; of which " A Landscape with a Flock of Sheep " (1861) is at the Luxembourg. He has sent nothing to the Salons since 1870 ; then he exhibited " The Border of a Wood with Animals " and " The Interior of a Sheepfold." Jacque has made many designs for book illustrations, and by contributions to "Charivari" has shown himself a good caricaturist. Some of his etchings form delightful series, and are much prized by collectors. The proofs of several of his prints are exceedingly rare. At a Paris sale in 1872 "A Girl Knitting" sold for £164. Several excellent works by this artist, showing the manner of his different periods, are in the Walters Gallery at Baltimore.

" If the word *pittoresque* did not exist in the French language, one would have to invent it for the works of Charles Jacque ; and what is the picturesque, if not the sentiment of life in its most familiar form? When a painter shows me a plow in the fields, a pail near a well, a pot in a kitchen, a lantern in a garret, 1 ought to understand that these are common objects, frequently used, and not brand-new things just out of a shop. Of course the form would be the same, but the expression would be different ; and the expression conveys the charm of a rustic scene by giving us the illusion of reality. Why have Charles Jacque's works such a powerful charm? It is because they always show us things or persons such as they are in nature : because he studies them in the course of their usual life and avocations ; and because this sincerity carries us without effort to the scene that he chooses to represent. Who knows better than he how to paint or draw hens perched on a cart, ducks dabbling in a pond, sheep in search of grass, children rambling about the fields instead of going to school, a servant washing clothes, a plow under a shed? His inns, his farms and poultry yards, his village streets, his skirts of forest ; his old walls, full of crevices, of stains of damp or crumbling plaster ; his barns, with cobwebs hanging from their ceilings, charm us precisely because the painter has not recourse to any tricks, but merely tells us, in his plastic language, the things that he saw, observed, and studied in the country." — René Ménard, *The Portfolio*, September, 1875.

" But it is necessary, in justice, to say that the pictures of Charles Jacque represent him quite unfairly, and that his knowledge of nature and fine artistic sensibility are both neutralized on canvas by his congenital incapacity to see color. His greens are as crude as the worst English greens, and crude, if possible, in a more hopeless way : for English crudity in very many cases is nothing but a vain attempt to render natural brilliance, resulting from an extreme sensitiveness uncontrolled by science ; whereas the crudity of Charles Jacque is not due to sensitiveness at all, but to mere blindness. His ordinary gamut of color — one cannot call it a harmony — is limited to these raw greens, and a set of grays equally raw, passing into lead-color of the most unpleasant hue. When the greens are absent, as they are from some pictures, they are replaced by dirty browns, not less crude in reality, though the crudity of browns is not so generally recognized as that of greens. But when Charles Jacque is free from the embarrassment of color, as in his etchings, or the lithographs and photographs from his pictures, he is often one of the most charming of French artists." — P. G. Hamerton, *Contemporary French Painters.*

Jacquemart, Henri Alfred. (*Fr.*) Born at Paris, 1824. Chevalier of the Legion of Honor. Pupil of Paul Delaroche. This sculptor executed the two Griffons of the Fontaine du Saint Michel. He directed the restoration of the Fontaine de la Victoire, and has done other public works at Paris. At the Salon of 1877 he exhibited "A Camel-Driver of Asia Minor" (group in plaster) and a "Young Wood-Gatherer." His portrait busts and statues are numerous ; among them are several equestrian statues. Many of his subjects represent animal life.

Jacquemart, Jules Ferdinand. (*Fr.*) Born at Paris, 1837.

Chevalier of the Legion of Honor, and of the Order of Francis Joseph. Son of Albert Jacquemart, a man of letters. Some of the best etchings of the son were executed for the illustration of the works of the father. This artist is inimitable as an engraver of still-life ; as a reproducer of pictures he is not remarkable. His *chefs-d'œuvre* are the illustrations of the "History of Porcelain," by his father, and those for "The Gems and Jewels of the Crown." Jacquemart is one of the Committee of Fine Arts of International Expositions.

"I never knew the glory and beauty of noble old work in the precious stones and metals, till Jules Jacquemart taught me. The *joyaux* of the Louvre were familiar to me, but a veil hung between me and their true splendor ; and it was only when Jacquemart had etched them one by one that I learned to know them truly." — P. G. HAMERTON, *Etching and Etchers.*

Jacquemart, Mlle. Nélie. (*Fr.*) Born at Paris. Three medals at Paris, 1868, '69, and '70. Portrait-painter. This artist early showed her talent, has been very successful in her profession, and has the power to make warm friends of her subjects and patrons. At the Salon of 1877 she exhibited a portrait of General d'Aurelle de Paladines, and one of the Viscount Henry G. ; in 1876 those of General de Palikao and of Count de Chambrun ; in 1875, portraits of two gentlemen and one lady ; in 1874, three portraits ; in 1873, portraits of M. Dufaure and of the Marquise A. de C. ; in 1872, M. Thiers, President of the Republic ; in 1870, Marshal Canrobert and a lady.

"One feels that this artist does not take her inspiration alone from the sittings of her subjects, but that she finds the best part of her work in her knowledge of character, and from her close study of the *personelle* of those whom she portrays." — PAUL D'ABREST, *Zeitschrift für bildende Kunst,* 1875.

Jacquesson de la Chevreuse, Louis. (*Fr.*) Born in Toulouse, France, 1840. His family belonged to the ancient French nobility, and their estate in St. Domingo was confiscated by Napoleon I. The young Louis consequently was of necessity educated for an independent career. Having strong musical and artistic tastes, he entered the Conservatory of Toulouse, and carried away the first prize of that institution at the age of fourteen. Later he was sent to Paris to study painting, and entered the studio of Flandrin. Subsequently he became one of the favorite pupils of Ingres. At this time the master was too old to teach in his studio, but gave to Jacquesson the *entrée* into his private chamber, where frequently in his bed Ingres poured into the willing ears of his fortunate pupil the principles and thoughts of his long life and great experience. In consequence of these advantages, Jacquesson is said to have been imbued more deeply with the grand ideas of Ingres than any other artist in France. In 1865 he competed for the grand *prix de Rome*, although quite unprepared for the task. Jacquesson at this time was but twenty-five, and heretofore students of thirty had been admitted to this competition, but a new rule forced him to enter then or never. In addition to this he was disabled by illness, and his picture was not finished in time, although it won the second prize and was purchased by the government for 2,000 francs. Soon after this he opened a studio in Paris for the reception of pupils, of which one of his students writes : " The serious work required, and lofty principles inculcated, have stood in the way of its becoming the resort of the average *rapin*. It is not a popular studio, one to which the masses flock." A number of Americans have been among his pupils. He has so devoted himself to his classes that his own work has seriously suffered, although he has painted a number of fine portraits.

Jacquet, Jean Gustave. (*Fr.*) Born at Paris, 1846. Medals in 1868 and '75. Pupil of Bouguereau. He made his début at the Salon of 1865 with two pictures, " Modesty " and " Sadness." His picture of " The Call to Arms " (1867) attracted much attention. Edmond About said : " Behold an artist, unknown to-day, who will be celebrated to-morrow." His " Sortie de Lansquenets " of 1868 was bought by the State, and is at the château of Blois. Jacquet has traveled in Italy, Germany, and England. His pictures are in demand and bring good prices. He is fond of all the objects which collectors love, and his atelier is rich in tapestry, stuffs, arms, draperies, etc. He took part in the battle of Malmaison, where he saw Cuvelier killed and Leroux grievously wounded. His drawing is spirited, his color pleasing, and the general effect in his pictures is bright and charming. Among his works are, " La pauvrette " (1877), the " Peasant-Woman " (1876), " Reverie," " Halt of Lansquenets," " A Vidette " (1875), etc. He paints many portraits. His " Going to the Races " belongs to Mr. Hawk of New York. At the Paris Salon of 1878 he exhibited " Jeanne d'Arc praying for France."

Jadin, Louis Godefroy. (*Fr.*) Born at Paris, 1805. Chevalier of the Legion of Honor. Pupil of Hersent and Abel de Pujol. He has done some decorative paintings, among which are eight panels of subjects from the chase in the dining-room of the Ministry of State, and a ceiling at the palace of the Luxembourg, representing " Aurora." Many of his pictures are of hunts and animals.

Jadin, Emmanuel Charles. (*Fr.*) Born at Paris. Pupil of his father and of Cabanel. He received a medal at Philadelphia, where he exhibited " The Sheik Salah dead in his Tent." At the Salon of 1877 he exhibited the " Resurrection of Lazarus "; in 1878, " The Return from the Cemetery, Venice."

Jaeger, Gustav. (*Ger.*) Born at Leipsic (1808–1871). Director of the Academy at Leipsic. Pupil of the Academy at Dresden, and of Schnorr von Carolsfeld. Many of his most important works were frescos ; among these the decoration of a salon at the château of the Grand Duke of Weimar. Cartoons of these pictures are in the Museum of Leipsic, where are also two paintings of religious subjects. At Munich he executed one of the frescos of the Grand Hall of the Niebelungen. Among his oil-paintings may be mentioned, "The Death of Moses," bought by the Society of Arts of Saxony, and "The Entombment of Christ." Vapereau says : —

"He enjoyed the reputation of a master of German painting ; he is praised for grandeur of style, clearness of composition, nobleness, expression, boldness of touch, and, with correct drawing, the sentiment of light and color."

Jalabert, Charles François. (*Fr.*) Born at Nîmes, 1819. Officer of the Legion of Honor. Pupil of Paul Delaroche. Passed some time in Italy. Has painted portraits, *genre* and religious subjects. His "Virgil, Horace, and Varius at the House of Mæcenas " (1847) is at the Luxembourg. In 1873 he exhibited at the Salon two portraits of ladies ; in 1872, a portrait and "The Awakening"; in 1870, two portraits. Among his earlier works are, "Christ on the Mount of Olives," "St. Luke," "The Annunciation," "Nymphs listening to Orpheus," "Romeo and Juliet," etc. At the Walters Gallery, Baltimore, is his "Orpheus," of which the Sunday Bulletin, February 12, 1876, says : —

"A most delicately wrought and poetic composition. The grace and beauty of the nymphs, and the soft and dreamy tone that is preserved, betray a peculiarly happy conception and a pretty idea well sustained and fully developed. The picture is in harmony with Orpheus' music, which is sensuous, dreamy, and reposeful, and with nothing too real about it."

Also in the same gallery is a scriptural subject, "Suffer little Children to come unto Me," and another picture of a child.

"The practical work of such a painter as Jalabert depends greatly on the use of the razor. First, the dead-color is laid of about equal thickness throughout, and then scraped down with a very sharp razor till it presents a perfectly smooth and even surface everywhere. On this surface, slightly oiled, the artist proceeds to work, this time in thinner color, and after successive scrapings and repaintings the picture arrives, finally, at a sort of finish remarkable for an extreme equality of surface, which has always a certain charm for the popular mind. And the popular mind is right to some extent, for, although roughness of loading would not signify in the least if the picture were always to be seen by a light equally diffused over the whole of its area, it is true, nevertheless, that since pictures are always seen by a light either coming from above or from one side, many of the rough projections of paint will catch lights and project shadows of their own quite independently of the light and shade of the picture, and often altogether destructive to it. Horace Vernet said, and truly, that light resides in the quality of the tone and not in the thickness of the pigment ; and the love for smoothness of surface which marks Jalabert and some others is perfectly compatible with artistic power, both in color and chiaroscuro, whilst it is more than 'compatible' with drawing, being positively favorable to form. Of Jalabert's works I like his portraits best, and the single figures which resemble portraits, and are, in fact, portraits of models, more or less idealized." — P. G. HAMERTON, *Painting in France.*

Janssen, Peter Johann Theodor. (*Ger.*) Born at Düsseldorf, 1844. Studied at the Düsseldorf Academy, and adopted the manner of E. Bendemann. Visited Munich, Dresden, and Holland. Painted, at the Hotel de Ville in Crefeld, a series of scenes from early German history, and at Bremen, in the Exchange, a picture of "The Commencement of Colonization in the Baltic Provinces." He also painted many smaller pictures, historical subjects and portraits. Recently he has undertaken a series of works in the Hôtel de Ville at Erfurt. In the National Gallery at Berlin he has also painted some decorative works.

Japy, Louis Aimé. *(Fr.)* Born at Berne (Doubs). Pupil of Français. Medals in 1870 and '73. A painter of landscapes. At the Corcoran Gallery, Washington, are "A Spring Landscape" and "Twilight," painted in 1873. At the Salon of 1878 he exhibited " Spring in the Valley of the Somme " and " In the Wood in April."

Jeannin, Georges. *(Fr.)* Born at Paris. Pupil of Vincelet. Medal of the third class in 1878, when he exhibited "A Barrow of Flowers " and " A Basket of Flowers " ; in 1877, "After the Rain" and " In the Flowers " ; in 1876, " The Flower Shop " and " A Quantity of Flowers."

Jeanron, Philippe-Auguste. *(Fr.)* Born at Boulogne-sur-Mer, 1809. Member of the Institute of France and Officer of the Legion of Honor. A writer and painter. His pictures are scenes from every-day life. " The Little Patriots," the first which he exhibited, was purchased by the Luxembourg, and is now at Caen. " The Flight " and "The Repose in Egypt " were bought by the Duke de Luynes. " The Abandoned Port of Ambletense " is at the Luxembourg. Jeanron has made many estimable portraits ; also some engravings with the dry point. In 1848 he was appointed Director of the Louvre and the National Museums. In this position he rendered important services to the world in his classification and arrangement of the art treasures in the Louvre, in the opening of the Egyptian Museum, and many other admirable additions to the conveniences for seeing the little world of wonders and beauties gathered there. Since 1860 he has been the Director of the Museum of Marseilles.

Jenkins, Joseph J. *(Brit.)* Born in London, 1811. He studied under his father, an engraver in London, and began his professional life by designing illustrations for books and magazines. In 1842 he became a member of the New Society of Painters in Water-Colors, resigning, however, in 1845. In 1846 he went to the Continent, spending some time in study and sketching. In 1849 he was elected an Associate of the Old Water-Color Society, full member in 1850, was Secretary for many years, and is at present a Trustee and regular contributor to its exhibitions. Among the better known of his works are, " Going with the Stream," " Going against the Stream," " Hopes and Fears," " Happy Times," " On the Thames at Mill End," "Both Sides of the Channel," " In Sight of Home," " A Creek on the Blyth," " At Caen, Normandy," " A Nook on the Thames," " Mist on the Hillside," and others, many of which have been engraved.

His " En Route " was at the Philadelphia Centennial Exhibition of 1876.

Jenks, Mrs. Phœbe. *(Am.)* Born in Portsmouth, N. H., 1849. Studied art under B. C. Porter and D. T. Kendrick in Boston, spending

1 *

her professional life so far in that city. She paints landscapes, figures, and portraits, and has exhibited frequently of late years in the Boston Art Club and New York Academy of Design. Among her works are, a two-thirds portrait of a lady (owned by Mrs. Alvin Adams of Watertown), portrait of a child (in the possession of W. H. Humphrey, Boston), "Mamma's Comb" (belonging to Robert M. Mason, Boston), "The First Attempt" and "Making Dolly's D'ess" (to Oliver Ames), "Priscilla the Spinner" (to S. L. French), and "Industry" (to Oliver Ditson). Her "Patience" was at the National Academy in 1878.

Jerichau, A. (*Dane.*) Born, 1818. After studying awhile at home, this sculptor went to Rome, where he had for a master his countryman Thorwaldsen. His principal works are, "The Marriage of Alexander and Roxana," a bas-relief for a frieze of the Royal castle at Copenhagen, a colossal group of "Hercules and Hebe," "Penelope" (a *chef-d'œuvre* of this artist), "A Hunter devoured by a Lioness," an "Ascension" (which took the grand prize given by the Princess Albert of Prussia, whose property the statue became), "The Creation of Eve," "Adam and Eve after the Fall," "A Sleeping Woman," "The Panther-Hunter," and the monuments to Oersted and Andersen at Copenhagen, which are much admired. This sculptor is classical in his correctness and purity of form.

Jerichau-Baumann, Mme. Elizabeth. (*Dane.*) Born at Copenhagen about 1825. Pupil of the Academy at Düsseldorf. This painter has been with her husband for a long time in Rome. Her pictures are of *genre* subjects. In 1861 she had an honorable mention at Paris. Her "Reading of the Bible" was a commission from Napoleon III. Mme. Jerichau painted a portrait of the Princess of Wales in her wedding-dress, for the Princess Christian. Among her works are, "The Joys of a Mother," "A Danish Sailor drying his Nets," "The Wounded Soldier," "A Young Girl praying for her Sick Mother," etc. At Berlin, in 1876, she exhibited "A Scene on the Nile," "A Portrait of a Sultana," and "Egyptian Water-Carriers."

Jobbé-Duval, Félix. (*Fr.*) Born at Carhaix, 1821. Chevalier of the Legion of Honor. Pupil of Paul Delaroche. Made his début at the Salon of 1841. In 1875 he exhibited three portraits ; in 1874, the same number ; in 1873, "The Mysteries of Bacchus" and cartoons of frescos in the Palace of Justice at Bordeaux and in the church of Saint-Gervais at Paris ; in 1872, "Wishes" and "Bouquet of Roses." Among his works are, "The Descent from Calvary," some frescos in the church of Saint-Séverin at Paris, and others in the Monastery of the Visitation at Troyes, etc. At the Salon of 1878 he exhibited "The Sea."

Johnson, Horace C. (*Am.*) Born at Oxford, Ct., 1820. Began his art studies under Professor Morse in the city of New York, and during the years 1856, '57, and '58 was a pupil of William Page in

Rome. His professional life has been spent in Italy and in his native State, many of his portraits being in the possession of Connecticut families. He is at present a resident of Waterbury. His " Roman Peasant on the Campagna" belongs to Mr. C. N. Wayland of New York ; " Grape-Gatherers of Gensano," to Mr. D'Aubigny of New York ; and his portrait of Dr. Samuel Elton and " The Roman Mother " are in the possession of Mrs. John P. Elton of Waterbury, Ct.

Johnson, David, N. A. *(Am.)* Born in New York, 1827. At the commencement of his career he received a few lessons from J. F. Cropsey, but has been a close student of Nature, looking upon her as his teacher and master. His professional life has been spent in New York. He has never been abroad. In 1859 Mr. Johnson was one of the founders of the Artists' Fund Society. He was elected an Associate of the National Academy in 1860, and Academician in 1862. In 1867 he exhibited "Echo Lake"; in 1869, "On the Wallkill River"; in 1870, "New Berlin, N. Y."; in 1871, "View at Barrytown, N. Y."; in 1874, "View at Dresden, Lake George" (belonging to Cortland Palmer) ; in 1876, "Near Noroton, Ct."; in 1877, "Greenwood Lake "; in 1878, "Morning at the Harbor Islands, Lake George."

His "Lake George" belongs to Mrs. William H. King, N. Y. ; his "Hudson River," to Mrs. William H. Gerrard ; his "Mount Lafayette," to John J. Cisco ; his "October on the Erie Railway," to E. A. Munson, Utica ; his "Spring at Mount Vernon," to Bryan Smith of Brooklyn. His "Housatonic River," exhibited at the Paris Salon in 1877, belongs to L. A. Lanthier, N. Y.

To the Centennial Exhibition of 1876 he sent "Scenery on the Housatonic" (belonging to Mrs. J. Bullard), "Old Man of the Mountain" (belonging to Richard Taft), and "A Brook Study, Orange County, N. Y.," receiving one of the first awards.

. **Johnson, Eastman,** N. A. *(Am.)* Born in Maine, 1824. As a young man he began the practice of his profession by the execution of portraits in black and white, showing considerable skill, and meeting with some success in that branch of the art. Going abroad, he studied for two years in Düsseldorf, for the first time painting in oil. He subsequently studied in Italy, Paris, Holland, and at The Hague, where he remained four years, and executed his first important works, "Card-Players," "Savoyard Boy," and others. Returning to America, he opened a studio in New York, and was made a member of the National Academy in 1860, painting those original sketches and pictures of American domestic and negro life in which he so decidedly excels. Among the earlier of these works (many of which have been chromoed, lithographed, and engraved) are his "Girls by the Stove," "Boys at the Ragged School," "Post-Boy," "Sunday Morning," "Hard Cider," "Washington's Kitchen, Mt. Vernon," "Old Kentucky Home," "Crossing a Stream," "Chimney-Sweep" (belonging to T. R.

Butler), "The Drummer-Boy," and others illustrative of the life of the American soldier during the Civil War. He sent to the National Academy, in 1869, "The Art-Lover"; in 1871, "The Old Stage-Coach"; in 1873, "The Woodland Bath," "Catching the Bee," and "The Sulky Boy"; in 1874, "The Tea-Party," "Bo-Peep," and "A Prisoner of State"; in 1875, "Milton dictating to his Daughter," "The Toilet," and "The Peddler"; in 1876, "The Husking-Bee" and "The New Bonnet"; in 1877, "Dropping Off" (belonging to R. H. Stoddard) and "The Tramp"; in 1878, portraits of Dr. Patten of Union College, Chief Justice Daly, and "Children playing in a Barn." At the Mechanics' Fair, Boston, 1878, was exhibited "The Lullaby" (belonging to Mr. E. D. Maynard).

His "New England Boy at Breakfast," "Chimney-Corner," and "Wandering Fiddler" were in the Johnston Collection, the last selling for $2,375. His "Old Kentucky Home" (belonging to R. L. Stuart) was in the Paris Exposition of 1867, and the American Centennial Exhibition of 1876. His "Old Stage-Coach" is the property of George Whitney; "Sabbath Morning," of R. L. Stuart; "Bo-Peep," of H. Richmond. "Tender Passion" is in the Walters Collection in Baltimore. His "Corn-Husking" and "What the Sea says" were at the Paris Exposition of 1878. His "Mother and Child" belongs to Abner Mellen, Jr., of New York.

Among Eastman Johnson's portraits is one of A. B. Stone.

"In his delineation of the negro Eastman Johnson has achieved a peculiar fame. One may find in his best pictures of this class a better insight into the normal character of that unfortunate race than ethnological discussion often yields. . . . . 'The Old Kentucky Home' is not only a masterly work of art, full of truth, nature, local significance, and character, but it illustrates a phase of American life which the late war and its consequences will either uproot or essentially modify; and therefore this picture is as valuable as a memorial as it is interesting as an art study." — TUCKERMAN'S *Book of the Artists.*

"In *genre* Mr. Eastman Johnson contributed the 'Prisoner of State,' 'The Old Kentucky Home,' 'Sunday Morning,' and 'The Old Stage-Coach,' which are all representative of the acknowledged excellence of his style. Mr. Johnson's subjects are derived fresh from nature, and are generally illustrative of characteristic traits of American life and customs. They are carefully studied, and always expressive of genuine feeling. They are not altogether free from uncertainty of form and touch and monotony of tone, but no one has more decided individuality and independence in choice and treatment of subject than this artist. His pictures bear the unmistakable stamp of originality. We are never reminded in them of the influence of schools or foreign methods: they rest upon their own merits, and the only comparisons they suggest are those afforded by the truths of nature. 'The Old Kentucky Home' is the picture that first gave him his reputation, which every succeeding work has sustained and increased. 'The Old Stage-Coach' displays greater maturity of method and breadth of treatment, but in accurate delineation of character 'The Old Kentucky Home' is hardly surpassed. The impression made by Mr. Johnson's pictures is a genuine one. We instinctively feel that the artist himself was impressed, and sought to express something that touched his sympathies forcibly. This is their interest and power, and criticism starts from this source rather than from the mere pictorial elements of technical merit that usually, in artists of less character, first engage the attention." — PROF. WEIR'S *Official Report of the American Centennial Exhibition of 1876.*

Johnson, Edward Killingworth. (*Brit.*) Born at Stratford-le-Bow, near London, 1825. He displayed a marked talent for art at an early age, but has never studied under any masters. For some years, however, he copied at the Langham Life School, and has drawn a great deal upon wood. He began painting as a profession about 1863. In 1866 he was elected an Associate of the Society of Painters in Water-Colors, and a full member in 1876. He resided in London until 1871, when he removed to a small ancestral property in North Essex, where his studio still is (1878). Among his more important works are, " The Anxious Mother " (Water-Color Exhibition in 1876, engraved in 1878 and purchased by Birket Foster), "The Reader" (exhibited in London, 1874, Birmingham, 1875, and owned by John Jaffray of the latter city), " A Golden Swarm " (1877), "The Rival Florists " (exhibited in New York in 1873, and belonging to G. B. Warren, Jr., of Troy, N. Y.), "A Peep into the Letter-Bag," and "Going to Bed " (1878). He sent "A Study" to the Philadelphia Exhibition of 1876, and " The Anxious Mother " to the Paris Exposition of 1878.

" We can certainly characterize 'The Rival Floriste' as one of the most remarkable pictures of its kind ever brought to this country."— *New York Times*, February 16, 1873.

" Killingworth Johnson's ' Intruders ' [New York Water-Color Exhibition, 1876] has been received with expressions of the highest praise. The picture is open to criticism perhaps, owing to the absence of positive shadows, but its aim is so high and its motive so charming that it commands admiration in spite of any mere defect." — *Art Journal*, March, 1876.

" Mr. E. K. Johnson sends only one contribution to this exhibition, but in that he seems to have determined to concentrate all the beautiful color and delicacy and brilliancy characteristic of his work. ' A Golden Swarm ' takes us into a garden which is simply a blaze of flowers and sunlight. Of course the women are beautiful women, for Mr. Johnson does not admit the halt and the lame and the blind into these earthly paradises of his. . . . . The action of the female figure in the center of the picture is extremely graceful, and the child beside her is charming in attitude and expression."— *London Daily News*, May 19, 1877.

Johnson, Frost. (*Am.*) Born in New York, 1835. After copying for a short time in Milwaukee he studied for two years under Professor Cummings in the Antique and Life Schools of the Academy of Design, in his native city. He went to Europe in 1859, entering the Art Academy of Düsseldorf, and remaining until 1861, when he became a student of the Academy of St. Luke in Antwerp. In 1863 he went to Paris, drawing in l'École des Beaux-Arts, and from 1865 to '69 he was a pupil of Edward Frère at Écouen. He spent some time in the practice of his profession in London, and is at present a resident of New York. Among Frost Johnson's earlier pictures may be noted, "Grandmother's Spectacles" (belonging to Mr. Morrill of Boston), "The First Whiff," "Caught at It," "The Broken Bottle," and "The Arithmetic Lesson " (owned in Milwaukee, Wis.). His " Les pommes" and a " Study of an Interior " were at the Paris Salon of 1869, and at the National Academy, New York, some years later. His " Roasted Chestnuts " belongs to S. D. Warren of Boston; "Good Night" and a portrait, to G. W. Hollis of the same city. Alvah Hall of New York owns "La petite flaneuse." Menzo Diefendorf of New York owns "Last and Best," which was painted for the Arcadian Club. "The Bouquet," portrait of Lady Helena Blackwood, is in the collection of her father, Earl Dufferin. His "Neglected Lesson," "Does your Mother know you 're out ?" "Love Me, Love Me Not," "Stitch in Time," and others, have been exhibited in New York, Brooklyn, Buffalo, and other cities. To the Philadelphia Centennial Exhibition of 1876 he contributed "Good Night" and "A Thirsty Party."

"Frost Johnson is profitably occupied with several pieces of still-life which are principally remarkable for their rich and subtle contrasts of color. . . . . The artist's studies in heads, mostly taken abroad, are unique. They are simply studies of coloration from Nature, and unite individuality of color with strength of effect." — *New York Herald*, December 12, 1872.

"Mr. Frost Johnson has recently completed a cabinet picture, the central and only figure of which is a portrait of the daughter of the Earl of Dufferin, remarkable not only for artistic treatment, but for the thorough mastery with which conventional laws in regard to color have been controlled and subordinated to the final and most admirable effect." — *Baltimore American*, October 13, 1877.

"Mr. Frost Johnson has just completed a picture which has attracted the attention of connoisseurs, and is of peculiar interest, not only for the admirable finish of the work, but for a certain departure from the recognized conventions of art. The picture is a small one, only cabinet size, and was painted as a portrait of the young daughter of the Earl of Dufferin, but the arrangement of color, the distribution of accessories, and the effect obtained from light through a draperied window is so thoroughly fine, and in some respects original, as to justify the high approval expressed from the most authoritative sources." — *New York Graphic*, October 16, 1877.

Johnston, Alexander. (*Brit.*) Born in Scotland, 1815. Pupil of the Trustees Academy of Edinburgh, and later of the schools of the Royal Academy. Began to exhibit, about 1835, portraits and historical figure pictures. Among his earlier works are, "The Mother's Grave," in 1839; "The Gentle Shepherd," in 1840; "The Covenanter's Marriage," in 1842; "Prince Charley and Flora Macdonald," in 1847; "The Trial of Archbishop Laud," in 1849; "Tyndal translating the Bible," in 1854; "John Bunyan in Bedford Jail," in 1861; and "The Land o' the Leal," in 1863. His "Press-Gang" was in the International Exhibition of 1862, and his "Last Sacrament of Lord Russell in the Tower," painted in 1845 (belonging to the Vernon Collection), is now in the National Gallery of London. In 1868 he sent to the Royal Academy, "The Billet-Doux"; in 1870, "Juliet"; in 1871, "Isaac Watts and his Mother"; in 1873, "The Turning-Point"; in 1874, "Tired"; in 1875, "Ought I to do it ?"; in 1876, "Bonnie Lesley" and "The Kettledrum-Quadrille"; in 1877, "A Waif"; in 1878, "Preparing for Conquest." His "Turning-Point" was at the Paris Exposition of 1878.

"The figure here ['Il Penseroso,' by Alexander Johnston, R. A., 1870] is of a nun, of stately and dignified form, who has walked forth in the evening twilight and stands fixed in contemplation of the heavens. The conception is fine, and the expression of the face, though somewhat severe, is appropriate to the sentiment. . . . . The license taken by the artist in the landscape affects in no degree the excellence of the composition as an example throughout of good and sound painting and of poetic feeling." —*Art Journal,* May, 1873.

Jones, George, R. A. (*Brit.*) (1786 – 1869.) Son of a well-known mezzotint engraver. He entered the Royal Academy in 1801, but he joined the army under Wellington on the breaking out of the Peninsular War, and did not practice art until its close in 1815, when he painted street-scenes of English and Continental cities for some years ; finally turning his attention to war subjects, in which he was very successful. Among the many works of this description, painted during his long career, may be mentioned, "Waterloo," "Lucknow," "Alma," and "Balaklava." He painted also many pictures in water-colors, and pictures of an historical character in oil, the more important being "The Coronation of George IV.," "The Passage of the Reform-Bill," and "The Opening of the New London Bridge." His "Fiery Furnace," "Lady Godiva," and two battle-pieces are in the National Gallery, London. He was made an Associate of the Royal Academy in 1822, and Academician in 1824, Librarian of 1834, and Keeper in 1850. He received from the British Institute, in 1820, a premium of £ 200 for his "Waterloo." Several of his pictures have been engraved.

Jones, Owen. (*Brit.*) Born in Wales (1809 – 1874). Spent some years in the office of a well-known London architect, and later visited the Continent and the East. He was one of the superintending architects of the Crystal Palace at Sydenham, erected in 1851, devoting himself particularly to its decoration, and in 1873 he received a medal for designs furnished for the Exposition buildings at Vienna. He was well known as a writer on subjects connected with his profession, publishing, in 1836, his "Alhambra," containing over a hundred valuable plates ; in 1842, "Views on the Nile"; in 1856, a "Grammar of Ornament," and several handbooks to the various courts of the Crystal Palace, etc. He was architect of St. James' Hall, Piccadilly, probably his most important work.

Jones, Alfred. (*Am.*) Born in Liverpool, 1819. Came to America very early in life. He received the first prize at the National Academy of Design in New York, in 1839, for a drawing from Thorwaldsen's Mercury. "The Proposal," after Durand, and "The Farmer's Nooning," after W. S. Mount, first called attention to him, and his work was sought for the illustrated publications of the day. In 1846 he went to Europe. He there studied in life schools, devoted himself to his profession, and was elected a member of the National Academy, New York, in 1851. He sometimes paints in oil and water-colors. He is one of the foremost American engravers. His plate of the "Image-Breaker," after Leutze, is one of his best. Among his plates are Adoniram Judson (half length, sitting), after Chester Harding ; William Cullen Bryant (head and full bust), after A. B. Durand ; " The Capture of Major André," after Durand ; " Sparking," after Edmonds ; " The New Scholar," after Edmonds ; " Mexican News," after R. C. Woodville ; and several portraits.

Jones, H. Bolton. (*Am.*) Born in Baltimore, receiving his art education and spending the greater part of his professional life in his native city. In 1877 he made a sketching-tour in Brittany and Spain, sending the results of his labors to Baltimore, where several of his pictures were exhibited in 1878. He has been a regular contributor to the National Academy since 1874, where he sent " Summer on the Blue Ridge," followed in other seasons by " September Afternoon," " Hunter's Camp, Maryland," " Old Fort Ticonderoga," " At the Edge of the Moor," " The Parable of the Sower," " After the Shower," " Spring in Brittany," and " Taking Geese to Market." " The Ferry Inn " was at the Centennial Exhibition of 1876 ; " Return of the Cows, Brittany," at the Paris Exposition of 1878 ; and to the Paris Salon of the same year he sent " A Heath in Bloom, Brittany."

Jongkind, Johan Barthold. (*Dutch.*) Born at Latrop, about 1822. He left Holland at an early age, and studied marine-painting under Isabey at Paris. He made his début at the Salon of 1845, and received in 1852 a medal of the third class. Perhaps this artist is more interesting as an etcher than as a painter. Charles Baudelaire, in " L'Art Romantique," calls him a " charming and candid artist," and speaks of his etchings as "abbreviations of his painting " and sketches, which amateurs who are accustomed to find the soul of an artist in his most rapid scrawls (*gribouillages*) will know how to read.

" The purpose of his art as an etcher may be explained in a few words. All landscape-painters make memoranda of impressions, which must of necessity be done very rapidly if they are to be worth anything, because the effects in nature change so fast that they cannot be sketched at all by a slow hand. Jongkind has so far trusted to the intelligence of the public (or of the small cultivated public to which he addresses himself) as to make memoranda of impressions directly upon copper, and print them. This is the whole explanation of his work as an etcher. But now comes the person living outside of art, who, when he sees one of these etchings, feels first puzzled and then offended, and thinks that both artist and laudatory critic must be making fun of him. ' Could not any child of ten years old do as well ? ' The true answer to this question (it is not an imaginary question) is, that, rude as this sketching looks, and imperfect in many respects as it really is, the qualities which belong to it are never attained in art without the combination of talent approaching to genius, and study of a very observant and earnest kind, quite beyond any possible experience of infancy. The right way to estimate work of this nature is to look upon it as the artist's manner of noting down an impression in all its freshness. Jongkind succeeds in doing this, either by an unconsciousness which is itself a great gift, or else by an effort of will strong enough to set himself entirely above the criticism of ignorance. There is something approaching to sublimity in the courage which was needed to send plates of this description to the printer. All landscape-painters have made memoranda of this class, though they rarely make them quite so well, but Jongkind is the first who has had the courage to publish them. It seems like the rashness which tempts Providence to set these things before the French *bourgeois* or the English Philistine, for the only public they are fit for is a public of true amateurs or artists : but whoever can really read them is in a fair way for being able to read all painting that sets itself honestly to the rendering of the mutual impression in its unity." — HAMERTON, *Etching and Etchers.*

Some of the best of these etchings are, " The Town of Maaslins, Holland " (1862), " Entrance to the Port of Honfleur" (1863), "Sortie du Port de Honfleur " (1864), and " View of the Scheldt at Antwerp, — Setting-Sun " (1869). Jongkind has exhibited many pictures of Dutch scenery ; several of them are views in and about Dordrecht.

Jooravlef, F. (*Russian.*) Of St. Petersburg. At Philadelphia he exhibited a picture of " The Dinner after the Funeral," for which he received a medal. The same work was at the Paris Exposition in 1878, together with " The Blessing of the Betrothed."

Jopling, Joseph M. (*Brit.*) Born in London, 1831. Studying in no schools and under no masters, he has spent his professional life in his native city, with the exception of three winters devoted to work and observation in Rome. He was elected an Associate of the New Society of Painters in Water-Colors in 1859, resigning in 1876. He received a silver medal at the Crystal Palace in 1876, and a medal at the International Exhibition at Philadelphia the same year. Among his works may be mentioned, "The Tea-Rose," " The Fair Florist," " Autumn," " Joan of Arc at her Trial," " Baiting the Line," etc. To Philadelphia, in 1876, he sent " Flossy" (belonging to the Right Hon. Cooper Temple), " Winter," and " In the Conservatory." At the Grosvenor Gallery in 1878 was a portrait of M. Rouzaud in armor of the sixteenth century, and several fruit and flower pieces.

Jopling, Mrs. Louise. (*Brit.*) Wife of Joseph M. Jopling. She was born in Manchester, in 1843, and learned to draw for the first time in 1867. She studied in Paris under Charles Chaplin and Alfred Stevens, exhibiting frequently for some years at the Royal Academy, the Dudley and Grosvenor Galleries, and elsewhere in England. Among her more important works are, "Five-o'clock Tea," at the Royal Academy in 1874 (purchased by the Messrs. Agnew), " The Modern Cinderella," " It might have been," etc. Her " Five Sisters of York " was at the Philadelphia Exhibition of 1876 ; " The Modern Cinderella," at the Paris Exhibition of 1878.

" 'The Five-o'clock Tea ' is the largest and most important design we have seen from Mrs. Jopling's hand, and in the disposition of the various figures and the management of color, it certainly exhibits very remarkable technical gifts. Especially do we notice in this lady's work a correct understanding of the laws of tone, very rare to find in the works of English painters, giving the artist power to bring different tints, even if they are not harmonious, into right relations one with another." — *Art Journal*, July, 1874.

Jordan, Rudolf. (*Ger.*) Born at Berlin, 1810. Member of the Academies of Berlin, Dresden, and Amsterdam, and Knight of several Orders. Medal at Philadelphia. Pupil of the Academy of Berlin and of Wach. He at first painted religious subjects, but is most admired in *genre* pictures. At the National Gallery, Berlin, are, " The Offer of Marriage in Heligoland," " Death of a Pilot," "A Scene in Normandy," "An Old Man's Home in Holland," and " The Widow's

B

Consolation" ; the last is in the National Gallery, Berlin, and was sent to the Paris Exposition in 1878. The " Offer of Marriage " is the first work which gave him reputation. Jordan is also a writer on art, and is much interested in its history. At Berlin in 1876 he exhibited "The Boats have all returned ; One alone is wanting."

Jouffroy, François. (*Fr.*) Born at Dijon, 1806. Member of the Institute. Officer of the Legion of Honor. Grand *prix de Rome* in 1832. Professor of Sculpture at l'École des Beaux-Arts. His " Ingenuousness; or, a Young Girl telling her First Secret to Venus " is at the Luxembourg. Jouffroy has executed various busts for private persons, and a " Bénitier" for the church of Saint-Germain-l'Auxerrois, Paris, from the design of Mme. Lamartine. He was charged with the decoration of the new church of Saint-Augustin, and has done many other decorative works for public edifices.

Jourdan, Adolphe. (*Fr.*) Born at Nîmes.' Medals in 1864, '66, and '69. Pupil of Jalabert. At the Salon of 1877 he exhibited "A Breakfast at Saint-Honorat" ; in 1876, " The Good-By " and "The Three Friends." At the Johnston sale, New York, 1876, " A Young Italian Mother" (39 by 31) sold for $ 2,300. At the Salon of 1878 he exhibited a portrait and " The Banks of the Gardon."

Jundt, Guatave. (*Fr.*) Born at Strasbourg, 1830. Medals in 1868 and '73, and at Philadelphia, 1876. Pupil of Guérin, and (at Paris) of Drölling and Biennourry. He traveled somewhat, and made his début at the Paris Salon in 1856 with the "Fête of the Village." Since then he has sent works to nearly every Salon, among which may be named, "Near a Fountain," " Alpine Strawberries," " Mayflowers," " Cutting Hair at the Fair of La Tour in Auvergne " (sent to Philadelphia), " It Rains ! — Swiss Oberland," " The Pence of St. Anne," " Sunday Morning," " The Time of the Wedding," etc.

This artist also makes many caricatures and illustrations for publications, such as " L'Histoire de la Poupée," " Le Poltron," " Polichinelle," etc.

" He draws, as one walks, without seeming thought, and he paints, as one talks, always improvising. Only there are some men who have a good appearance in walking, while they scarcely think of it, and those who talk with wit and humor without making any pretensions. It is precisely in this manner that Jundt paints. His pictures have some piquant improvisations in which malice overflows ; gawky awkwardness takes under his lively and animated touch an air of amusing good-nature. . . . . As a painter he may be reproached with certain defects, but he possesses one very rare quality, he has incontestable originality. Jundt is one of the few who might dispense with signatures on his pictures." — RENÉ MÉNARD, *L'Art en Alsace-Lorraine.*

Kaemmerer, Frederic Henri. (*Dutch.*) Born at the Hague. Medal at Paris in 1874. Pupil of Gérôme. At the Salon of 1877 he exhibited " A Party at Cricket " ; in 1875, " A Winter Day in Holland " ; in 1874, "The Beach at Scheveningen," now in the Corcoran Gallery at Washington. At the Latham sale, New York, 1878, " Autumn, — Terrace of the Tuileries, 1790 " (24 by 16) sold for $1,125. Knoedler & Co. exhibited, in 1878, his "Going to Church in the Olden Time." At the Salon of 1878 he exhibited "A Baptism."

Kalckreuth, Stanislaus, Count of. (*Pole.*) Born at Kozmin, 1821. Professor and member of the Academy of Berlin, and member of the Academies of Amsterdam and Rotterdam. Medals at Berlin, Vienna, and Bordeaux. Studied in Berlin and Polnisch-Lissa. After several years of military life he studied under Krause and Schirmer. His progress attracted the attention of the King, who gave him commissions. In 1860 an art school was established at Weimar by the Grand Duke of Saxony, and Kalckreuth became its conductor. During student travels which he made he visited Switzerland and Spain, saw a large part of Germany, and spent some time in Vienna. In 1876 he gave up his office at Weimar and settled in Kreuznach. His representation of Alpine scenery is especially happy, and remarkable for the effects of light and shade. At the National Gallery, Berlin, are his "Lake of Gaube in the Upper Pyrenees" and "Canagai Valley in the Eastern Pyrenees." At Berlin, in 1876, he exhibited the "Lake of Thun." At the Paris Exposition of 1878 was seen his "Mont Blanc" (belonging to the Emperor of Germany).

Kaufmann, Theodor. (*Ger.-Am.*) Born in Hanover, 1814. Studied art in Hamburg and at Munich, where he was a pupil of Hess. He practiced his profession for a few years in Europe, settling in America in 1850. Among the better known of his pictures painted in this country are, "On to Liberty," "A Railway Train attacked by Indians," and "General Sherman near the Watchfire." In 1871 he published a work entitled "The American Painting-Book." He resided in Boston for some years.

Kaulbach, Wilhelm von. (*Ger.*) Born at Arolsen (1805 - 1874). Officer of the Legion of Honor. Correspondent of the Institute. He received many decorations, and was member of several academies. At the age of seventeen he was placed in the Academy of Düsseldorf, then under the direction of Cornelius. When twenty-one he went to Munich. Six allegorical frescos in the arcade of the Hofgarten were among his earliest works there. Before he was twenty-five he executed "Apollo and the Muses," in the Odeon, and the celebrated design called "The Mad-House." He next painted sixteen illustrations of the story of "Cupid and Psyche," on the walls of the palace of the Duke Maximilian ; then, together with the painter Schnorr and the sculptor Schwanthaler, he worked at the decoration of the new palace of King Ludwig. He completed his design for the "Battle of the Huns" in 1837 ; it was a *chef-d'œuvre.* About the same time he completed the cartoon of the "Destruction of Jerusalem," the painting from which was not made until eight years later, when King Ludwig purchased it. In 1846 his designs illustrative of "Reynard

the Fox" appeared. He also illustrated the Gospels and the Shakspere gallery. Kaulbach devoted many years to the great decorative
paintings of the "Treppenhaus" of the new Museum at Berlin. His
subjects here were, "The Tower of Babel," "Destruction of Jerusalem," and "Battle of the Huns" (reproduced), colossal figures of
Moses, Solon, History, Legend, etc., and "The Reformation," besides
friezes which were designed as borders for the principal works. In
1867 he sent to Paris his "Epoch of the Reformation," a cartoon
of which, belonging to Mr. Durfee of Fall River, was for some time
in the Boston Athenæum. For this painting he received a medal of
honor. Vapereau says : "It united all his qualities of composition,
drawing, and color." In the National Gallery at Berlin are his cartoons of "The Death of the Marquis Posa," and one of a scene from
the "Mary Stuart" of Schiller. Mr. Probasco of Cincinnati has a
beautiful work by Kaulbach called "Mutterliebe" ("Mother-Love").
It was painted for Mr. Probasco, and he claims that it is the only
original painting by Kaulbach in America. It represents a mother
with her four children. She is seated beneath a tree in the midst of
a pleasing landscape. In her right arm she holds one child, whose
face is hidden on her breast ; with her left hand she supports another
tiny one, who stands upon her knee and presses his lips to hers in a
playful baby embrace. Two larger children, one upon the ground
and another climbing up behind and resting on the mother's shoulder,
complete the group, which is well balanced and graceful.

"I have extolled Kaulbach in no stinted terms, yet I know that his mortality is betrayed through his robes of state. His limits are confessed when he rushes towards the
illimitable ; his finality is felt when, in boldest flight, he steals fire from heaven. Kaulbach has many virtues, but moderation is not of their company. Nevertheless, let me,
in fine, recapitulate the claims which Kaulbach lays upon the remembrance of posterity.
His subjects, his styles, and his materials, which are many, are alike worthy of note.
His themes, we have seen, are wide in range and lofty in aspiration. History in epochs
which are landmarks in the world's civilization ; philosophy that teaches through example ; poetry as manifested in the creations of Shakspere and Goethe ; life in its light
and shade, in the climax of its joy and the depths of its sorrow, — such are the subjects
which, in their diversity and import, measure the genius and circumscribe the labors of
Kaulbach. In style, too, as in subject, this painter displays the same versatility ; by
turns he is grave and gay. Like dramatists and actors of first quality, he is great at
once in comedy and in tragedy ; his impersonations, in short, are close upon the models
of Phidias and Raphael, of Dürer and Hogarth. The name of Kaulbach will also be
identified with the most successful efforts to free art from the tyranny of the Church, to
ennoble secular subjects by lofty thought and elevated treatment, and to raise the practice of monumental painting to an equality with the sister arts of sculpture and architecture. Such are the services which Kaulbach has conferred upon his age and country." — J. BEAVINGTON ATKINSON, London Art Journal, December, 1865.

Kaulbach, Hermann. (*Ger.*) Son of the preceding, and a pupil
of Piloty. He is an historical painter who merits attention.

Kaulbach, F. A. (*Ger.*) This painter is a distant relative of the
late William von Kaulbach, and is one of the rising artists of Munich.
Some of his pictures are very pleasing, and show a genuine feeling for

ideal art. At the Exposition of 1878 he exhibited "Reverie," "Portrait of a Young Girl," "Young Woman with her Son," and a "Head of a Woman."

Kemys, Edward. (*Am.*) Born in Savannah, Ga. He lived for some time in New York. By profession a sculptor, he has devoteo himself particularly to the modeling of the more prominent wilo animals of the far West of America ; a collection of groups in plastei by him, which were exhibited in London in 1877, attracted much attention. His "Coyote and Raven," "Playing 'Possum," and "Panther and Deer" were at the Exhibition at Philadelphia in 1876; "Fight between Buffaloes and Wolves," at the Paris Salon of 1878.

"In anatomical knowledge Kemys appears to us little, if at all, behind his predecessor [Barye], and if he be Barye's inferior in audacity and splendor of conception, he partly compensates for this by a subtle perception of delicate shades of character, and a fine discrimination of animal individuality, in which Barye's works are comparatively deficient." — *London Spectator*, December, 1877.

Kensett, J. F., N. A. (*Am.*) Born in Cheshire, Ct. (1818–1873). As a youth he studied bank-note engraving, and practiced art in his leisure hours. He finally went to England, where he worked for some time, sending to the Royal Academy, in 1850, "A View of Windsor Castle," which was highly praised by the London art critics. He remained in Europe seven years, spending two years in Rome, making excursions to Naples, Switzerland, the Rhine, and the Italian lakes, and sending home many cleverly executed paintings and sketches, some of which, exhibited in the Art Union Gallery, New York, established his reputation in America as a landscape-painter of no common merit. His views of American scenery have become justly popular. Among them are, "Sunset on the Coast," "Sunset in the Adirondacks," "Lake George," "Scenes on the Genesee River," "Noon on the Sea-Shore" (engraved by S. V. Hunt), "Beverly Coast," "Bash Bish," "From the Meadows at Cold Spring," "Narragansett," "Lake Conesus" (belonging to Robert Hoe), "Mount Washington," "Keene Flats," "Bass Rock, Newport," etc. His "Morning off the Coast of Massachusetts" (belonging to Shepherd Gandy), "Newport Harbor" (to R. M. Olyphant), "Glimpse of the White Mountains" (to R. S. Stuart), were in the Paris Exposition of 1867. His "View near Northampton" (property of R. S. Stuart), "Lake George" (the property of M. K. Jessup), and his "New Hampshire Scenery" (now in the Century Club), were at the Philadelphia Exhibition of 1876. At the Johnston sale, in 1876, his "Afternoon on the Connecticut Shore" sold for $ 1,500, and his "Secluded Brook" (belonging originally to A. M. Cozzens) brought $ 600. His "White Mountains" (at the Wright sale, some years before) was sold for $ 1,300. His "October Afternoon, Lake George," exhibited in Paris in 1867, and at the Sanitary Fair, New York, in 1864, at the sale of the Olyphant pictures in 1877, found a purchaser at $ 6,300. His "White Mountains " was sent to the Paris Exposition of 1878. Kensett was made a member of the National Academy in 1849.

" Kensett is the Bryant of our painters ; a little sad and monotonous, but sweet, artistic, and unaffected. In his later pictures there is a phantom-like lightness and coldness of touch and tint which gives them asomewhat unreal aspect, but they take all the more hold on the fancy for their lyrical qualities." — JARVES, *Art Idea.*

" Kensett's best pictures exhibit a rare purity of feeling, an accuracy and delicacy, and especially a harmonious treatment, perfectly adapted to the subject. . . . . If we desired to carry abroad genuine memorials of native scenery, to keep alive its impressions in a foreign land, we should select half a dozen of Kensett's landscapes. Other artists may have produced single pictures of more genius, may be in certain instances superior, but on the whole, for average success, Kensett's pictures are, we do not say the most brilliant, effective, or original, but often the most satisfactory." — TUCKERMAN's *Book of the Artists.*

Key, John R. (*Am.*) Native of Baltimore. He studied art in Munich and Paris, painting in Boston for some years, and exhibiting there, in 1877, about one hundred of his pictures, including " Marblehead Beach," " Ochre Point, Newport," " Morning Stroll," and a view of " The Golden Gate, San Francisco," for which he received a medal at the Philadelphia Exhibition of 1876. His " Cloudy Morning, Mount Lafayette " was at the National Academy, New York, in 1878. He has been very successful in his works in black and white.

" Mr. Key's charcoal drawings are among the best ever shown in Boston ; they are firm and masterly in drawing, strong in effect, and graceful in composition. Mr. Key has a fascinating skill in this kind of work, in which he approaches nearer to Allongé than any other American artist The collection of his pictures is highly attractive for the true artistic feeling in all the works on exhibition." — *Boston Saturday Gazette,* 1877.

Keymeulen, Émile. (*Belgian.*) Of Brussels. Medal at Philadelphia, where he exhibited " Landscape in Provence " and " After the . Hurricane."

Keyser, Nicaise de. (*Belgian.*) Born at Santoliet, 1813. President of the Academy of Antwerp, and Chief Director of the Museum of that city. Corresponding member of the Institute of France, and Officer of the Legion of Honor. Chevalier of the Order of Léopold, and that of the Lion of the Netherlands. Medal at Philadelphia. Pupil of the Antwerp Academy under the direction of Van Bree. In 1834 he exhibited " A Crucifixion," which had been painted for a Roman Catholic church in Manchester, England ; it attracted considerable attention. He went soon after to France and England, and returned through Holland. In 1836 his picture of " The Battle of the Golden Spurs in 1302 " was exhibited at Brussels, and won the great gold medal ; this work is now in the Museum of Courtrai. In 1839 he exhibited the " Battle of Woeringen," which took a gold medal in Paris. De Keyser then visited Italy and Germany. The " Battle of Nieuport " and that of " Séneffe " were painted for William II. of Holland. Among his other works are, " Vandyck setting out for Italy," " Memling in the Hospital at Bruges," " Christ and his Disciples," " The Last Moments of Weber," etc. His portraits of royal and distinguished persons are numerous. The courts of Belgium, Sweden, Bavaria, and Würtemberg have conferred decorations upon him, as well as that of France. (The list of honors given in this article is taken from the London Art Journal, of January, 1866.) At the Wolfe sale in New York in 1864, " The Love-Test, — Italian Gleaners " sold for $ 3,100, and " Milton and his Daughters " for $ 2,400. At the Berlin National Gallery are his " Giaour " and " Death of Marie de' Medici." Mr. Probasco of Cincinnati has his "Francis I. at Fontainebleau," painted in 1869.

Kayser, E. (*Am.*) Born in Baltimore, 1850. He received his art education in the Royal Art Academy of Munich, under Professor Widmann, and in the Royal Art Academy of Berlin under Professor Albert Wolff. He went to Munich in 1872, remaining until the autumn of 1876. In Berlin he received " the Michael Beerche Prize " for a life-sized figure, called " Psyche." This prize entitles the successful competitor to one year's study in Rome at government expense. Among his most successful works are the " Psyche," and " The Toying Page " (in bronze), belonging to Dr. O'Donavan of Baltimore, for which he gained the silver medal of the Munich Academy.

Kiers, Peter. (*Dutch.*) Born at Graeneveld, 1807. Member of the Academy of Amsterdam. Pupil of Douwe de Hoop. A *genre* painter. He was specially noted for his effects of light. Among his subjects are, " A Woman going out of her House at Evening " (effect of lanterns), " Woman reading the Bible," " Woman writing a Letter," " Interior of a Dutch House," etc.

King, Charles B. (*Am.*) (1786 – 1862.) Studied with Leslie and Allston in London, living and painting portraits in that city for some years. Finally settled in Washington, D. C., where he died. During his long career many of the celebrities of all countries who visited the capital were among his sitters. His portraits were prized for their accuracy rather than their delicacy of finish.

Kiorboë, Charles Frederic. (*Swede.*) Born at Stockholm (1815 – 1876). Chevalier of the Legion of Honor. Pupil of Henner. In 1874 he exhibited at the Paris Salon, " A Fox surprised by Hunters " and " A Buck coming out of a Wood " ; in 1870, " The Breakfast of the Foxes " ; in 1869, " Hunting Ducks." At a London sale in 1874 his "Inundation " sold for 260 guineas.

Kiss, Augustus. (*Prussian.*) Born at Pless (1802 – 1865). Member of the Berlin Academy, where he was also Professor. Studied at the same Academy under Rauch. In 1839 he exhibited the model of his famous group of " The Amazon struggling with a Panther." This was cast in bronze by means of public subscriptions, which were even taken in the churches, so great was the enthusiasm it excited. It was placed in the Berlin Museum in 1845. A plaster cast of it took the first prize at London in 1851, and was purchased by an American. Among his works are, " The Fox-Hunt ". (Berlin Museum), " St.

Michael and the Dragon," statues of Frederick the Great and Frederick William III., "St. George," etc. At the time of his death a group called "Faith, Hope, and Charity" was unfinished ; this was completed by Bläser, and, with a bust of Kiss, was presented by his widow to the Berlin Museum.

Klein, Johann Adam. (*Ger.*) Born at Nuremberg (1792 – 1875). This artist first studied etching and engraving. He spent some time at the Academy of Vienna, and commenced oil-painting in 1815. Soon after this he went to Rome. He gave his efforts to reproducing the peculiar costumes and habits of different peoples. He had traveled in Northern countries, and his industry and diligent observation made him skillful in his peculiar work. At the National Gallery, Berlin, are his "Hungarian Wagoners" and "The Wallachian Freight-Wagon " ; also, "An Animal-Tamer before a Tyrolese Inn." Klein's engravings are numerous and highly esteemed.

Kloeber, August Karl Friedrich von. (*Ger.*) Born at Breslau (1793 – 1864). Professor and member of the Berlin Academy. Pupil of Berlin Academy. During the war of 1813 Kloeber was a soldier, and afterwards spent nearly four years at Vienna. He affected the manner of Rubens and Correggio. His portraits of Beethoven, Grillparzen, etc., are well spoken of. His first large picture was that of the "Virgin Mary with Jesus and St. John." At the theater of Breslau he painted a frieze and other decorative works. In 1821 he went to Italy, and spent seven years in Rome. Kloeber executed various decorative paintings in the palaces and public buildings of Berlin. Several of his pictures are in the National Gallery, Berlin, — "Education of Bacchus," "Cupid and Psyche," etc.

Knaus, Ludwig. (*Ger.*) Born at Wiesbaden, 1829. Member of the Academies of Berlin, Vienna, Munich, Amsterdam, Antwerp, and Christiana. Officer of the Legion of Honor. Knight of the Order of Merit. Various medals at Paris, Berlin, Weimar, etc. Pupil of Jacobi and the Academy of Düsseldorf, under Sohn and Schadow. He separated himself from their influence, and was allied with Lessing, Leutze, and Webber. From 1853 he lived eight years in Paris, but settled at Düsseldorf in 1866. Among his works are, "The Promenade" (1855), at the Luxembourg, "Peasants reprimanded by their Priest," "A Woman playing with Two Cats," "The Wife of a Shoemaker, her Child, and an Apprentice contemplating a Mouse in a Trap," "The Invalid," "A Woman gathering Flowers," etc. At the Johnston sale, New York, 1876, "The Old Beau," from the Wolfe sale in 1863 (24 by 19), sold for $3,000. In 1874, at Christie's in London, "Thieves at a Fair" sold for 565 guineas. At the Forbes sale, London, 1874, "The Sisters" sold for 1,250 guineas. At the Sedelmeyer sale in Vienna, 1873, "Maternal Kindness" brought £1,440. His "Children's Festival " is at the National Gallery, Berlin. At the Latham sale, New York, 1878, "My Little Brother " (18 by 14) sold for $ 2,200, and "After the Bath" (8½ by 6½), for $ 2,350. His "Priest and Poacher" belongs to Mr. T. R. Butler of New York.

Knight, John Prescott, R. A. (*Brit.*) Born, 1803. He was the son of Edward Knight, a well-known actor, and began life in a merchant's office in London. Displaying a decided taste for art, he studied under Henry Sass, and later under George Clint, entering the schools of the Royal Academy in 1823. His first pictures were at the British Institute in 1827 or '28. He turned his attention to portrait-painting, in which branch of art he has been very successful. He was made an Associate of the Royal Academy in 1836, Academician in 1844. He was Professor of Perspective for many years, and Secretary of the Royal Academy from 1847 to '73, when he resigned with a life pension from the trustees. Among the many portraits of distinguished men painted by Mr. Knight may be mentioned those of the Duke of Cambridge (in Christ's Hospital), F. C. Burnand, Henry L. Holland, the Governor of the Bank of England, Édouard Frère, Arthur Grote, and Sir Titus Salt.

Knight, Daniel Ridgway. (*Am.*) Born at Philadelphia. In 1872 he went abroad, studying for some years in Paris at l'École des Beaux-Arts and under Gleyre. He was in the studio of Meissonier in 1876. To the Paris Salon, in 1873, he sent "The Fugitives"; in 1875, "Washerwomen"; in 1876, "Repast during the Harvest." He has exhibited frequently at the National Academy, New York, contributing, in 1870, "The Veteran" (belonging to Asa Whitney); in 1871, "Othello in the House of Brabantio"; in 1873, "The Antiquary," "The Old Beau," and "Dividing the Profits"; in 1874, "Strolling in the Garden"; in 1876, "Washerwomen"; in 1877, "Market-Place at Poissy" and "Harvest Scene" (belonging to A. J. Drexel); in 1878, "Pot au Feu."

"In 'The French Washerwomen,' by D. R. Knight, the figures are drawn with remarkable spirit, and in their delineation much grace of form is shown. It is without that artificial feeling which belongs to work where the conventional model is called into requisition." — *Art Journal*, May, 1876.

Knille, Otto. (*Ger.*) Born at Osnabrück, 1832. Medal at Berlin. An instructor there, with title of Professor. Pupil at Düsseldorf under K. Sohn, Th. Hildebrandt, and W. von Schadow. Also studied under Conture at Paris. He spent some time in Munich and Italy, and settled in Berlin in 1865. Some of his decorative paintings (the subjects taken from the Thuringian Myths) are in the Castle of Marienburg near Nordstemmen. Others are over the stairway of the University Library at Berlin. In the National Gallery at Berlin is his "Tannhäuser and Venus." At Berlin, in 1876, he exhibited "Athens, — Plato with his Pupils," a portion of a frieze for the Library of the University of Berlin. This was also seen at the Paris Exposition of 1878.

Knowlton, Helen M. (*Am.*) Born at Worcester, Mass. She

has spent her professional life in Boston, where she has classes in painting. She was a pupil of William M. Hunt, and that artist's well-known "Talks about Art" are the result of notes taken by Miss Knowlton during his lessons. She sketches in charcoal, and paints landscapes and portraits in oil, exhibiting at the Boston Art Club, National Academy, and elsewhere.

Knyff, Alfred de. (*Belgian.*) Born at Brussels. Chevalier of the Legion of Honor. Landscape-painter. His pictures represent all kinds of scenery, and he passes easily and gracefully from the beach to the forest, from the banks of the Meuse to the mountains of Scotland. At Paris in April, 1876, several of his pictures were sold. "Setting Sun in the Campine" brought 4,000 francs ; "Moonlight," 2,600 francs ; etc. Among his subjects are, "The Scottish Heather," "The Evening," "Forest of Fontainebleau," "Villiers-sur-Mer." At the Paris Salon of 1877 he exhibited "The Forest of Stolen in the Campine, Belgium" and "The Prairies of Lagrange" ; in 1876, "The Garden of A. Stevens," "The Mouth of the Meuse," and "A Marsh in the Campine in Spring."

Koch, Joseph Anton. (*Ger.*) Born at Obergiebeln am Bach (1768 – 1839). The works of this landscape-painter are seen in various German galleries. At the Museum at Leipsic are three of his pictures, and in the National Gallery, Berlin, is "A View of the Convent of Civitella, in the Sabine Mountains."

Koekkoek, Bernard Cornelius. (*Dutch.*) Born at Middlebourg (1803 – 1862). Chevalier of the Order of the Lion (Netherlands), and of the Order of Léopold (Belgium). Medals at Paris, Amsterdam, and the Hague. Pupil of Schelfhout and Van Os. The landscapes of this painter are much esteemed. He established a Drawing Academy at Cleves. In 1850 he published at Amsterdam a book of his "Souvenirs and Communications" ("Erinnerungen und Mittheilungen eines Landschaftmalers"). At the Johnston sale, New York, 1876, his "Scenery on the Upper Rhine" (32 by 42) sold for $2,800. It was from the Wolfe sale in 1863. A "Winter Scene in Holland," also from the Wolfe sale (20 by 26), sold for $1,550. At a sale in London in 1876, "A Forest Scene" sold for £283. At the Strousberg sale, Paris, 1874, "Interior of a Wood" sold for £1,084. At the Latham sale, New York, 1878, "Landscape with Cattle" (26 by 33) sold for $1,600. In the National Gallery, Berlin, are two of his landscapes, and two others are in the Leipsic Museum. Koekkoek was also a member of the Academies of Rotterdam and St. Petersburg, and of the Society of Arts, London. His "Castle on the Rhine" and "Landscape in Winter" belong to Mr. T. R. Butler of New York.

Koerner, Ernst. (*Ger.*) Of Berlin. Pupil of Eschke and Steffeck. Medal at Philadelphia, where he exhibited "Mahmoudieh Canal near Alexandria." This was "commended for distinguished excellence." At the Paris Salon of 1878 he exhibited "The Mahmoudieh Canal, Egypt" and "Under the Palm-Trees."

Köhler, Christian. (*Ger.*) Born in Werben (1809 – 1861). Professor at Düsseldorf. Studied at Berlin Academy and at Düsseldorf. In 1860 he went to Montpellier for his health, but received no benefit. In the Berlin National Gallery is his "Semiramis."

Koller, Guillaume. (*Aus.*) Born at Vienna, 1829. Followed the course at the Academy of Fine Arts in Vienna, and then studied at Düsseldorf from 1851 to '55. "The Emigrants," "The Asylum," and "Scene from the Peasants' War, 1524" were painted while he was at Düsseldorf, and found their way into the best collections in Vienna. Next Koller resided three years in Antwerp. He first exhibited in that city "The Clandestine Marriage of the Archduke Ferdinand with Philippine Welser at the Château de Meran, in the Tyrol"; it was purchased by Mr. Nieuwenhuys. Koller draws his inspirations from the literature and history of Germany, and as he spends much time on his works they are not numerous; among them are, "The Christening of Martin Luther," purchased by M. Drasche of Vienna; "The First Interview of Marguerite and Faust," purchased by the Chevalier de Knyff of Antwerp; "Albert Dürer receiving a Message from the Archduchess of Parma," purchased by the late Prince Albert of England; "The Coal-Market"; "Philippine Welser demanding Pardon for her Husband from his Father, the Emperor Ferdinand"; "The Departure for the War"; "Almsgiving"; etc.

"In manner of treatment he has grafted upon the comparatively dry style of the German school, acquired in Düsseldorf, the richer and more realistic style of the modern Belgian. His coloring is always good, but he does not strive to produce an impression by this quality so much as by a faithful rendering of his subject. In this his sympathies are more with Leys and his disciples than they are with Gallait, Wappers, and De Keyser. In his choice of subjects he aims high, but certainly not beyond his powers. And as he is still in the early prime of life, a long and prosperous career may be his future, which shall yield more abundant and riper fruit than any he has yet produced." — JAMES DAFFORNE, *London Art Journal*, January, 1867.

Kollock, Mary. (*Am.*) Born in Norfolk, Va., 1840. Studied art in Philadelphia for three years under Robert Wylie, in the Pennsylvania Academy of Fine Arts. Later she took lessons in landscape from J. B. Bristol and A. H. Wyant. The greater part of her professional life has been spent in the city of New York, contributing to the National Academy of Design scenes from the Adirondack regions and Lake George. In 1877 she sent "Morning in the Mountains" and "On the Road to Mt. Marcy"; in 1878, "A November Day" and "An Evening Walk." Her "Midsummer in the Mountains" was at Philadelphia in 1876.

Korzoochin, Alexis. (*Russian.*) Of St. Petersburg. At Philadelphia he exhibited pictures of "A Sunday Tea-Party" and "A Scene in the Wood," and received a medal.

Kotzebue, Alexander von. (*Russian.*) Medal at Paris in 1867. Medal at St. Petersburg. This artist was a soldier in his youth, and understands what he paints. His "Passage of the Devil's Bridge by the Russian Army in 1799" is a well-known picture. He has lived for some time in Munich, and has traveled in various countries of Europe. His pictures in the galleries of Russia are much liked. At St. Petersburg, in 1870, he exhibited "The Battle at Lessnoje" and "The Surrender of Riga in 1710."

Krause, Wilhelm August Leopold Christian. (*Ger.*) Born at Dessau (1803-1864). Member of the Academy, and Royal Professor at Berlin. Founder of the School of Marine Painting at Berlin. Studied at Berlin and Dresden. He was very poor, and did many things to earn money ; among others, he sang in a theater in Berlin. In 1828, never having seen the sea, he painted his first marine picture. He showed great talent in this specialty. In 1830 and '31 he traveled in Northern Europe. At the National Gallery, Berlin, are, "A Storm at Sea," "View on the Coast of Pomerania," and "Scottish Coast Scene in a Storm."

Kröner, Christian Johann. (*Ger.*) Born at Rinteln, in Hesse, 1838. Medal at Berlin in 1876. Pupil of nature, and an artist who, by earnest study, brought himself to a reputable standing in landscape-painting. Many of his pictures are of wild, mountainous scenes. At Düsseldorf he came under the influence of L. H. Becker, who encouraged him to persevere in his art. His pictures are well considered. He has traveled considerably, and visited various parts of Germany, the North Sea, Paris, etc. He has made wood-engravings and etchings. Some of these represent animals as well as landscapes. At the National Gallery, Berlin, is an "Autumn Landscape, with Deer."

Krüger, Franz. (*Ger.*) Born at Radegast (1797-1857). Court painter. Professor and member of the Berlin Academy. Without masters, he became a good portrait-painter, and established himself at Berlin. In 1844 he was invited to visit Russia by the Emperor, and remained there six years. He was called "Pferde-Krüger" from his good painting of horses. He painted many equestrian portraits ; and his parade scenes and other military pictures are excellent. At the National Gallery of Berlin are his "Departure for the Hunt" and "Return from the Hunt," "Emperor Nicholas of Russia," and a "Dead Rabbit."

Krüger, Karl Max. (*Ger.*) Born at Lübbenau, 1834. Studied at Munich Academy, and under Ott and R. Zimmermann ; also at the Art School of Weimar. Traveled in Germany and in Northern Italy. Since 1870 he has lived in Dresden. At the National Gallery at Berlin is a view of "A Forest on the Spree." At Berlin, in 1876, he exhibited "A Hunting-Lodge in the Neighborhood of Lübbenau."

Kühling, Wilhelm. (*Ger.*) Born at Berlin, 1823. Studied at the Berlin Academy, and traveled in Switzerland, France, and Italy. At first he was very successful in portraits. Later, he has painted landscapes, many of which are taken from Upper Bavarian scenery. At the National Gallery, Berlin, is his "Group of Cattle." At Berlin, in 1876, he exhibited four cattle-pictures.

Kunts, Gustav Adolf. (*Ger.*) Born at Wildenfels, 1843. Medal at Philadelphia. Pupil of Schilling at Dresden. In 1869 he went to Italy for two years, and there executed a life-size marble statue of the prophet Daniel for the mausoleum of the late Prince Consort at Frogmore. He then visited Weimar, England, France, Holland, and Belgium, and studied painting. In 1877 he settled in Rome. At the National Berlin Gallery is his "Italian Pilgrim." He sent to Philadelphia "The Nun's Revery."

Kuntze, Edward J. A., N. A. (*Ger.-Am.*) Born in Pomerania (1826-1870). Settled in America in 1844, devoting himself to the practice of his art with some success. He was elected an Associate of the National Academy in 1869, a year before his death. Among his works may be mentioned, statuettes of Shakspere and Lincoln ; a statue of "Psyche" ; bust of "Mirth," in marble ; "Merlin and Vivien," in bas-relief ; and many medallion portraits and busts.

Kurzbauer, E. (*Austrian.*) Born at Vienna, 1846. Pupil of Piloty. We have not been able to obtain a sketch of this artist's life, but he is well considered, and sent to the Paris Exposition of 1878 "The Fugitives" (belonging to the Emperor of Austria) and "La maison mortuaire" (belonging to M. Eggers of Vienna.) [Died, 1879.]

Kuwasseg, Carl-Joseph. (*Austrian.*) Born at Trieste. Naturalized Frenchman. Died, 1876. Medals at Paris in 1845, '61, and '63. He commenced life as a carpenter, but, abandoning this occupation, he went to Vienna, and lived by making water-color drawings. He traveled in South America, and went to Paris in 1830, and there soon earned a good reputation as a landscape-painter. Of late years he has principally exhibited Swiss and French views.

Kuyck, Louis Van. (*Belgian.*) Born at Antwerp (1821-1874). Gold medal at Brussels. Pupil at the Antwerp Academy under Van Bree, and of Baron Wappers. The familiar scenes which he first painted are almost unknown. His first "Interior of a Stable" is in the Museum at Munich ; it is by subjects of this class that he has earned his high European reputation. The names of his different pictures are so much alike that a list is quite useless. They are rural Flemish scenes, most frequently stable interiors, with horses, dogs, poultry, pigeons, etc.

Lacroix, Gaspard Jean. (*Fr.*) Born at Turin (1820-1878). His parents were French, and his professional life was spent in France. He received a medal of the third class in 1842, and medals of the second class in 1843 and '48. He was a pupil of Corot, and proved to be one of his most worthy followers. To the Salon in 1878 he sent a landscape ; in 1877, "Aux Glaises, près de Palaiseau" ; in 1876, "At Palaiseau" ; in 1873, two views in the park of the Gigoux, both belonging to M. Bonnel. One of his landscapes was at the Exposition of 1878.

La Farge, John, N. A. (*Am.*) Figure, flower, and landscape painter, drawing also on wood. He has occupied a studio in New

York for some years. He was elected a member of the National Academy in 1869. Is a member of the American Water-Color Society and of the Society of American Artists. Among his works, in oil, are, " View over Newport," " Sleeping Beauty," " A Gray Day," " A Snowy Day," " A Seaside Study " (belonging to J. F. Kensett), " A Hillside Study," " From the Story of Cupid and Psyche," " New England Pasture-Land," " A Bather," and others, exhibited at the National Academy in different seasons. To the first Exhibition of the Society of American Artists, in 1878, he sent " Autumn Sunset," " Wild Roses," and " Hollyhocks." " Bishop Berkeley's Rock, Newport," " Wreath of Flowers," etc., were at the Philadelphia Exhibition of 1876. To Paris, in 1878, he sent " Paradise Valley, Newport." He executed the frescos in Trinity Church, Boston. Miss Alice Hooper owns La Farge's " New England Pasture-Land," one of his finest works. At Boston, in November, 1878, he exhibited and successfully sold a large number of his pictures.

" La Farge goes to art with earnest devotion, and an ambition for its highest walks, bringing to the American school depth of feeling, subtlety of perception, and a magnificent tone of coloring, united to a fervent imagination, which bestows upon the humblest object a portion of his inmost life. . . . . His landscapes are gems of imaginative, suggestive, and delicate, vital treatment, not pantheistic in sentiment, although the soul of nature breathes in them." — JARVES, *Art Idea.*

" Mr. La Farge sent five pictures, two of figures and three of flowers. The latter are works of peculiar excellence for their purity and charm of color, — flowers forming but the theme for a most delicate and refined harmony that addresses the eye with occult power. Mr. La Farge is learned in his art, working for profound and subtle results, and no one is more sensitive to the value of mystery in tone and color, and of the emission of luminous light through these qualities. His picture of ' St. Paul at Athens ' is stamped with great sincerity of aim, and bears unmistakable evidence of power and thought. His works, however, for the most part give an impression of incompleteness, or suggest a deficiency of form, and the drawing, as of the hands of this picture of St. Paul, is often defective. But these shortcomings are more than compensated by the superior aim which characterizes his work, and renders it highly intellectual, spiritual, and poetical in feeling." — PROF. WEIR'S *Official Report of the American Centennial Exhibition of 1876.*

" All Mr. La Farge's pictures are apt to have that element commonly called ' suggestiveness,' — that sense of progressive fluency, rather than of either loose tremulousness or fixed stability, which once led a clever critic to remark of them that it was always the next picture Mr. La Farge would paint that was the masterpiece. But his sketches — or the pictures he catalogues ' sketches ' — have it eminently, and in them it is especially pleasing. Somehow one learns in time that even in his sketches there is no lack of completeness of motive, and that if it does not seem completely expressed, that may not be so much the fault of the painter as of the observer, if the latter has been accustomed to the stock notion that completeness of expression means a hunting of the motive to its fastnesses." — *New York World*, November 8, 1878.

Laguillermie, August Frédéric. (*Fr.*) Born at Paris. *Prix de Rome*, 1866. Pupil of Flameng and Bouguereau. He has also studied in Madrid, Rome, and Athens. His drawings from the frescos of Michael Angelo in the Sistine Chapel and from the Temple of Erechtheus at Athens are important. He has made some powerful plates after the works of Velasquez. More recently Laguillermie has sent some pictures to the Salons. In 1876 he exhibited a " Portrait of Mme. B." and two etchings, " Ruth and Boaz " and "The Death of Jacob," both after Bida ; in 1875, two portraits (in oil), three water-color sketches for portraits, and an etching of a portrait after Terburg ; in 1874, picture of a " Young Breton Girl winnowing Buckwheat on the Seashore" and an etching, " Fantasy," after Fromentin ; in 1873, " A Spinner " and a portrait (in oil), and an etching of " The Surrender of the City of Breda," by Velasquez ; etc. At the London Academy, 1878, he exhibited an etching after "The Prisoner," by Gérôme.

" The serious and prolonged studies of this artist have resulted in a kind of etching perfectly adapted to the interpretation of such a master as Velasquez, who dwelt in an artistic region elevated very far above the small prettinesses of merely technical mechanical engravers. Few things in the history of the fine arts are more hopeful and encouraging than the emancipation of engraving, and its nearer approach to thoroughly artistic painting, which have been effected by Flameng and his pupils Rajon and Laguillermie." — P. G. HAMERTON, *The Portfolio,* April, 1873.

Lagye, Victor. (*Belgian.*) Of Antwerp. Pupil of Leys. His subjects are taken principally from the fourteenth and fifteenth centuries. " The Antiquaries" is remarkable for its finish of detail. Another of his pictures represents a " Mother putting her Child in the Cradle," and gives a peep at the family life of the olden times in Belgium. It was done for the city of Ghent. He received a medal at Philadelphia, where he exhibited " The Sculptor, — Close of the Fifteenth Century." To the Paris Exposition of 1878 he contributed, " The Gypsies," " The Sculptor," "The Magician," and " The Crossbowman."

Lalanne, Maxime. (*Fr.*) Born at Bordeaux, 1827. Member of the Academies of Bordeaux and Brussels. Medals at the Expositions of Vienna and Philadelphia. Chevalier of the Legion of Honor, of the Order of Christ of Portugal, and of that of St. Gregory the Great. Pupil of M. J. Gigoux. Painter and engraver, and of later years especially devoted to etching. He has published a " Traité de la Gravure à l'Eauforte," and has illustrated it himself in a charming manner. His oil-pictures are landscapes. Among his etchings are, " Rue des Marmousets, Old Paris," " View of Bordeaux," " Demolition for lengthening the Boulevard St. Germain," " Demolition for lengthening the Rue des Écoles," " View from the Bridge of Saint-Michel," " View from the Bridge de la Concorde," " Chez Victor Hugo," — twelve small etchings of the house of Victor Hugo, remarkable for minute delicacy. At the Salon of 1877 he exhibited " View in the Port of Quimper," " Bank of a River," and " In the Fields of Cénon, Gironde "; in 1876, " The Chickens," after Ribot, " The Pool of Ville d'Avray," after Corot, and " Marcoussis," after Corot.

" No one ever etched so gracefully as Maxime Lalanne. The merit of gracefulness is what chiefly distinguishes him ; there have been etchers of greater power, of more striking originality, but there has never been an etcher equal to him in a certain delicate elegance, from the earliest times till now. He is also essentially a *true* etcher ; he knows the use of the free line and boldly employs it on due occasion. So far his work is very right, but it has the fault of too much system." — P. G. HAMERTON, *Etching and Etchers.*

L'Allemande, Fritz. (*Ger.*) Born at Hanau (1812–1866). An excellent painter of military subjects. He never painted a picture until he had visited the scene of the battle. The Emperor Francis Joseph commissioned him to decorate the reception-room of the château of Schönbrunn. After that work, which proved his talent to be good, he was constantly employed upon important commissions. His "Episode in the Combat of Komorn" (seen at London in 1862) attracted attention and admiration.

Lambdin, George Cochran, N. A. (*Am.*) Born in Pittsburg, Pa., 1830, but has lived since childhood in Philadelphia, with the exception of two years, 1868 to '70, spent in New York. He studied under his father, a portrait-painter of some repute. In 1855 he went to Europe, spending two years on the Continent, chiefly in Munich and Paris. In 1858 he sent to the National Academy, New York, a picture called "Our Sweetest Songs are those which tell of Saddest Thoughts," his first exhibited work. The original study of this is now in the Suydam Collection of the National Academy. Two years later he exhibited "The Dead Wife," which was selected by the Committee to go to the Paris Exposition of 1867. This was followed by "Twilight Reverie," "Ask Me No More," and kindred works, of a sentimental cast illustrative of young maidenhood. For some years afterwards he devoted himself exclusively to portraits of children, of which "The Little Knitter" (belonging to Mr. Adams of Boston) is among the best. During his New York residence, in 1868, he was elected a member of the National Academy. After a short visit to Europe, chiefly for the benefit of his health, in 1870, he settled at Germantown, near Philadelphia, cultivating in his garden fine roses and flowers, to the painting of which he has since turned his attention with marked success.

Lambert, Louis Eugène. (*Fr.*) Born at Paris. Chevalier of the Legion of Honor. Pupil of Delacroix. At the Salon of 1877 he exhibited "Portrait of Lido" and "During the Mass " ; in 1876, " En famille " and " Pepito, Toc, d'Artagnan," belonging to the Baroness Nathaniel de Rothschild ; in 1875, "Jack, Sam, Shot," " The Enemy," and " L'Envoi " ; in 1874, "Installation Provisoire " and " The Hour of the Repast." This artist excels in painting small animals, such as kittens, cats, etc. At the Salon of 1878 he exhibited "The Cats of the Cardinal" and " Fallen Greatness."

"The cats of M. Louis Eugène Lambert are as usual the most attractive and characteristic reproductions of animal life to be found at the Salon. One of his contributions this year is probably destined to as widespread a popularity as was obtained by his 'Envoi en Provence,' that basketful of recalcitrant kittens that won such a success a few years ago. This year M. Lambert takes an historic flight, and, remembering the fact that Cardinal Richelieu was passionately fond of cats, he paints for our delectation the pets of the great statesman..... His other contribution is felicitously named ' Fallen Greatness.' A tiger skin is spread upon the floor, and a sober mother cat and her family have taken possession of this relic of the king of the forest The languid dignity of the mother cat, with her glossy fur, pink nose, and reposeful attitude, is well contrasted with the irrepressible vivacity of her offspring." — *Art Journal*, August, 1878.

Lambinet, Émile. (*Fr.*) Born at Versailles (1810 – 1878). Chevalier of the Legion of Honor. Pupil of Drölling. Made his début at the Salon of 1833. "A Landscape" (1855) is at the Luxembourg. His views are those of his own country, such as, "The Seine at Bougeval," "Norman Meadows," "Coasts of Normandy," "The Valley of Arques," etc. At the Salon of 1877 he exhibited "The Village of Quineville"; in 1876, "Summer" and "Le Bas-Prunay." Mrs. H. E. Maynard of Boston has three landscapes by this artist in her collection. Two of his works were exhibited at the Salon of 1878.

" Lambinet is a man of less power, but in his limited choice of lowland scenery natural and simple, having a refined taste and defined execution, suggesting details by emphasis of brush rather than by accurate finish. He fills his pictures with clear, bright light, rivalling Nature's tones as fully as pigments may. But it is a hazardous process, and no way so satisfactory as the lower tone of Corot, whose treatment of light is unequaled. Those who follow Lambinet in this respect would do well to recall Leonardo's maxim in regard to pure white, ' Use it as if it were a gem.' Lambinet's landscape, although ever repeating himself, is fresh and fragrant, like a bouquet of flowers." — JARVES, *Art Thoughts.*

Lami, Louis Eugène. (*Fr.*) Born at Paris, 1800. Chevalier of the Legion of Honor, 1837, officer since 1862. Pupil of Gros, Horace Vernet, and l'École des Beaux-Arts. He has engraved on stone, made lithographs, and painted in water-colors and in oils. "A Supper in the Salle de Spectacle at Versailles" and "An Interior of a Church" (water-colors) are at the Luxembourg. He has given much time to water-colors, and seems most fond of that mode of representation. But he has also painted five or more battle-pieces, in oils, for the Gallery at Versailles, and has a facility of execution in whatever he undertakes.

Lance, George. (*Brit.*) (1802–1864.) Pupil of Haydon and of the School of the Royal Academy. Lance was a very successful painter of still-life, his works being in the possession of many noble families of England. He executed a few historical and figure pieces, but was famous for his fruits and flowers. Among the former may be mentioned, "The Coquette," "The Lady in Waiting," and "Melancthon's First Misgiving of the Church of Rome." In 1860 he exhibited at the Royal Academy, "Full Ripe"; in 1861, "A Sunny Bank"; and in 1862, "A Gleam of Sunshine." Three of his pictures (in the Vernon Collection) are in the National Gallery, London, — "A Basket of Fruit," painted in 1834; "Red Cap," exhibited at the British Institution in 1847; and "Fruit" (a pineapple, grapes, melon, etc.), painted in 1848.

2 *

"Lance was occasionally blamed for exaggeration of color, but his delineation was delicate and his grouping agreeable." — Mrs. Tytler's *Modern Painters.*

Landelle, Charles. (*Fr.*) Born at Laval, 1821. Chevalier of the Legion of Honor. Medal at Philadelphia. Pupil of Delaroche. Historical and religious painter ; has also executed many portraits. "The Presentation of the Virgin" (1859) is at the Luxembourg. His mural paintings are "Law," "Justice," and "Right," in the Palace of the Council of State (destroyed in 1871), six decorative panels for a salon in the Palace Élysée, some works at the Hotel de Ville (also destroyed), and the chapel of Saint-Joseph at Saint-Sulpice. Among his portraits are those of Alfred de Musset, the Countess Fitz-James, Mme. Achille Fould, Stackelberg, Admiral Baudin, Princess of Broglie, and many others. At the Salon of 1877 he exhibited "Salmacis"; in 1875, "The Death of St. Joseph"; in 1874, "A Reverie of Sixteen Years"; in 1873, "A Young Serbian Gypsy" and "The Samaritan Woman"); in 1872, "L'Almée"; etc. At the Johnston sale, New York, 1876, "The Egyptian Girl" (17 by 11) sold for $ 780 ; "The Greek Girl" (18 by 14), for $ 800. At the Salon of 1878 he exhibited a portrait of the Marquis de Saint-M. as an Arab Sheik, and "Ismenis, a Nymph of Diana."

"This distinguished painter has a commonplace facility, which he dispenses in a perpetual repetition of himself. He is consecrated for the rest of his days to what is called character figures, young gypsies, Egyptian women, Moorish women, Ethiopian women. As he knows how to mix the right dose, and in very decent proportions, of the romantic and picturesque with gravity and classic correctness, he never fails to please the public, although he becomes weaker, thinner, and more faded day by day." — Ernest Duveroier de Hauranne, *Revue des Deux Mondes,* June, 1871.

"If, carried away by the sympathy which the artist inspires, one said that the decoration of the chapel of Saint-Joseph was a work of the first order, he might be accused of thoughtless enthusiasm ; but he would be unjust not to see in it one of those works which hold an equilibrium between disparagement and eulogy. M. Landelle, whom the public of the Salons knows so well, has wished to make himself appreciated on a larger scene. Without being presumptuous he had the right to make the attempt, as he has now the right to repeat it. The charming painter of Fellahs and Moors quitted, one fine day, the gallery, already long, of his Oriental beauties. He has elevated his art by ascending the steps of the church. Only an exigency could demand of him to leave forever the voluptuous seraglio that he has created and peopled ; but, now that he has penetrated the temple, he owes it to himself to return there to work and to purify his profane talent. His name, it is true, would not be more celebrated, but it would be more enduring." — Roger Ballu, *Gazette des Beaux-Arts,* February, 1878.

Landseer, John, A. R. A. (*Brit.*) Celebrated engraver. Father of Edwin, Charles, and Thomas Landseer. Born in Lincoln (1761 – 1852). Engraved vignettes for Macklin's Bible published in 1793, for Bowyer's History of England, views in the Isle of Wight after Turner, South of Scotland after James Moore, and a series of engravings of animals after Gilpin, Rubens, Rembrandt, Snyder, etc. In 1807 he was elected an Associate Engraver of the Royal Academy, and exhibited there as late as 1851 several sketches of Druidical temples on the

Channel Isles. In 1806 he delivered a course of lectures on "Engraving" before the Royal Institution, and in 1823 a course on "Engraved Hieroglyphics." He was the author of a book entitled "Sabæan Researches," published in 1823, and of a valuable "Catalogue of the Earliest Pictures in the National Gallery," published in 1834.

Landseer, Thomas, A. R. A., his son and pupil, is a well-known English engraver of the present day. Elected Associate of the Royal Academy in 1868. Among his plates are Rosa Bonheur's "Denizens of the Forest," and (after Edwin Landseer) "Doubtful Crumbs," "The Sanctuary," "The Challenge," "Browsing," "Peace," "The Baptismal Font," and the portrait of the Queen. He has also contributed to the Royal Academy many original drawings in crayon, and (in oil) "A Deluge of Rain," "The Goat without a Beard," "Lion-Hunting," "Cattle," etc.

"That Thomas Landseer the engraver was but an Associate by condescension, sat only at a side-table at state dinners of the Royal Academy, not cheek by jowl with artists [painters] like his brother Edwin and the already forgotten Charles, — this did not deprive him of his faculty as an artist or his right to be recognized as one. The two great Landseers were John Landseer the father, only a 'line engraver,' and Thomas Landseer the son, a mere engraver also."— W. J. LINTON, *in Scribner's Monthly*, June, 1878.

Landseer, Charles, R. A. (*Brit.*) Son of John Landseer, and elder brother of Edwin, born 1799. He was a pupil of his father and of Haydon, entering the Royal Academy at the age of sixteen. His picture was exhibited in 1828. He was elected an Associate of the Royal Academy in 1837, and Academician in 1845. In 1851 he received the appointment of Keeper, a position he held until 1873. While he has never equaled in popularity his younger brother, as an historical painter he has been successful. Among his earlier works, four are in the National Gallery, "The Sacking of Basing House" (R. A., 1836), "The Pillaging of a Jew's House" (R. A., 1839), "Clarissa Harlowe in the Sponging-House" (Society of British Artists, 1833), and "Bloodhounds and Pups" (Brit. Ins., 1839). He is still a regular contributor to the exhibitions of the Royal Academy. In 1860 he sent "Trust"; in 1861, "Births, Marriages, and Deaths"; in 1865, "Savage discovering his Parentage"; in 1867, "Cromwell at the House of Sir Walter Stewart in 1651"; in 1868, "Rustic Gallantry"; in 1870, "Surrender of Arundel Castle in 1643"; in 1871, "Wayfarers"; in 1872, "The Hamlet of St. Martin-in-the-Fields"; in 1875, "Dick"; in 1876, "A Langum Fishwoman, Tenby"; in 1877, "Pamela concealing her Correspondence between the Tiles." [Died, 1879.]

Landseer, Sir Edwin, R. A. (*Brit.*) Born in London (1802 - 1873). Youngest son of John Landseer, a distinguished engraver, from whom his children inherited their decided artistic talent. Edwin received his first lessons in drawing from his father, and at a very early age displayed great abilities as a sketcher and that love of the brute creation which has been displayed in his works. At the South

Kensington Museum are shown some of these wonderfully clever drawings, executed by him when a child of from five to ten years. In 1816 he entered the Royal Academy, contributing at the same time, when only fourteen years of age, pictures to several of the public galleries throughout the country. He subsequently studied under Haydon. His "Dogs Fighting" (engraved by his father) was painted in 1818, and "The Dogs of St. Gothard discovering a Traveler in the Snow" (also engraved by the elder Landseer) was painted in 1820. From that time his success was established, and his popularity as an artist unequaled, until the day of his death, by that of any artist in England of the nineteenth century. In 1826 he was elected Associate of the Royal Academy, and Academician in 1831. He made his first trip to the Highlands of Scotland in 1826, and there acquired that bolder and freer style which distinguishes his maturer works, and there also first evinced his fondness for deer as subjects. Soon after this he painted "Night," "Morning," "The Sanctuary," "Children of the Mist," "The Return from Deer-Stalking" (1827), "The Illicit Whisky-Still" (1829), "Sir Walter Scott and his Dogs" (1833), "Peace" and "War" (1846), "The Dialogue at Waterloo" (1850), "Rough and Ready" (1857), and "The Maid and the Magpie" (1858). He was knighted in 1850. In 1855 at the Paris Exposition he received one of the two large gold medals awarded to Englishmen. The list of his works is very large, and many of them have been engraved. Fourteen of his pictures are in the National Gallery in London, including the "Alexander and Diogenes," "Peace" and "War," "Dignity and Independence" (painted in 1839), "The Sleeping Bloodhound," "Low Life" and "High Life," "Highland Music," "Shoeing the Bay Mare," and "The Dialogue at Waterloo," representing the Duke of Wellington explaining to the Marchioness of Douro, his daughter-in-law, the incidents of the great fight years after it had occurred. This is considered one of the best of the few figure-pieces he has painted. In the Sheepshanks Collection of South Kensington are sixteen of his works,—"Dog and the Shadow," "Suspense," "The Old Shepherd's Chief Mourner," "Comical Dogs," "A Highland Breakfast," "The Drove's Departure," and others. In 1864 he exhibited at the Royal National Academy, "Piper and Pair of Nut-Crackers" (sold for 1,000 guineas) and "Windsor Park"; in 1865, "Prosperity," "Adversity," and "The Connoisseurs"; in 1866, "Lady Godiva's Prayer," "The Chase," and "Odds and Ends"; in 1867, "Her Majesty at Osborne" and "Wild Cattle of Chillingham"; in 1868, "Rent Day in the Wilderness"; in 1869, "Study of a Lion" and "The Swannery invaded by Eagles"; in 1870, "Queen Victoria meeting the Prince Consort on his Return from Deer-Stalking" and "The Doctor's Visit to Poor Relations at the Zoölogical Gardens"; in 1872, "The Baptismal Font" and "The Lion and the Lamb"; in 1873, "Tracker" and a "Sketch of the Queen," which was never finished. His pictures have brought very large prices : "Oxen at the Tank," a small pen-and-ink sketch, was sold after his death for 300 guineas ; "Man proposes and God disposes" brought 2,500 guineas in 1864. A very large and complete exhibition of Landseer's etchings and sketches was held in London in 1875. He designed the sculptured lions at the base of Nelson's Monument, Trafalgar Square, unveiled in 1867, but was not as successful in sculpture as in painting.

"Take, for instance, one of the most perfect poems or pictures (I use the words as synonymous) which modern times have seen, 'The Old Shepherd's Chief Mourner.' Here the exquisite execution of the glossy and crisp hair of the dog, the bright, sharp touching of the green bough beside it, the clear painting of the wood of the coffin, are language,— language clear and expressive in the highest degree. . . . . It ranks as high art, and stamps its author, not as the neat imitator of the texture of a skin or the fold of a drapery, but as the man of mind." — RUSKIN's *Modern Painters.*

"One of Stanfield's landscapes or of Landseer's hunting-pieces is worth all the mystic daubs of all the Germans." — MACAULAY's *Life and Letters,* Vol. II. Chap. XIV.

"Landseer has great merit not only as a painter of deer and dogs and horses, but as an artist most skillful in his delineation of human figures, and of original genius in the representation of vast subjects in small isolated series of individualized parts conceived and wrought out with such powers of comprehension and concentration that in a single episode of 'Peace' and 'War,' all of the blessings of the former, all of the horrors of the latter, are conveyed to the mind of the person who looks on these masterpieces. There is in Landseer's compositions an exquisite delicacy of organization, an acute sense of perception of all that is harmonious in nature or art, a nervous susceptibility of all impressions, pleasing or poetical, such as it would be difficult to find in other artists." — *Memoirs of the Countess of Blessington.*

"Landseer has been distinguished for his masterly handling of his art and the singular expertness with which he has been able to paint. His pictures have been largely engraved, and have commanded a large sale. . . . . Hardly a house which contains an engraving at all is without one of a picture of Landseer." — MRS. TYTLER's *Modern Painters.*

"As monumental sculptures these Lions of Landseer's in Trafalgar Square have been a mistake throughout ; badly planned, badly modeled, and badly cast." — *Saturday Review,* 1867.

"The noble Lions at the foot of Nelson's Column were added by Sir Edwin Landseer in 1867. Only one of them was modeled ; a slight variation in the treatment adapted the others to their pedestals. Their chief grandeur lies in their mighty simplicity." — HARE's *Walks in London,* 1878.

Landseer, George. (*Brit.*) Son of Thomas Landseer. He died in 1878. A portrait-painter of some merit. He also exhibited landscapes from time to time.

Lane, R. J., A. R. A. (*Brit.*) (1800 - 1872.) A grand-nephew of Gainsborough. He was articled in 1818 to Heath, the well-known line-engraver, but soon turned his attention to lithography, in which branch of his profession he was wonderfully successful, practicing it for many years, and reproducing many works of Landseer, Leslie, Lawrence, Gainsborough, and other artists. In 1827 he was made an Associate of the Royal Academy, and in 1837 he was appointed Lithographer to the Queen. He devoted himself particularly to engraving on copper during the last years of his life, and was for some time superintendent of the etching class at the South Kensington Museum.

Lang, Louis, N. A. (*Ger.-Am.*) Born in Würtemberg, 1814. Son of an historical painter. He early showed a taste for art, and between the age of sixteen and twenty executed several hundred pastel portraits of the people among whom he lived. In 1834 he went to Paris for the purpose of study; spent some time at Stuttgart, and sailed for America in 1838, living in Philadelphia several years. He then returned to Europe, passing five or six years in Venice, Rome, Florence, and Paris. In 1852 he was made a member of the National Academy of New York, making that city his home. He visits Europe frequently, and is at present (1878) in Florence. He is a member of the Artists' Fund Society of New York, contributing to its sale in 1878, "Chasing Butterflies," "Fresh Cherries," and "Neapolitan Fisher Family." Lang sent to the National Academy, New York, in 1869, "The Stolen Child" and "Asleep in Prayer"; in 1870, "Fresh Flowers" and "An Old Mill at Greenwich, Ct."; in 1871, "Little Graziosa among the Butterflies," "Blind Nydia," and "Jephthah's Daughter." He sent to the American Centennial Exhibition of 1876 his "Landing of the Market-Boat at Capri." His "Mary Stuart distributing Gifts" and the "Maid of Saragossa" are in the gallery of Robert L. Stuart.

"Lang indulges in brilliant colors, and has executed several large and glowing pictures of our popular holidays: he is fond of delineating female and infantile beauty with gay dresses and flowers, and has adventured somewhat in historic art." — TUCKERMAN's *Book of the Artists.*

"In Lang's studio in Rome are, 'A Bivouac of Circassian Slaves,' 'Mary, Queen of Scots,' 'Cleopatra,' 'Preziosa, or the Stolen Child,' and 'Cinderella.' . . . . The color of 'Cinderella' is very rich and admirably managed, as well as the contrast between the haughty, conquest-anticipating sisters, and the gentle, beautiful one who serves them." — *Art Journal,* September, 1875.

Langerfeldt, T. O. (*Ger.-Am.*) Born in Buckeburg, Principality of Schaumburg-Lippe, Germany, 1841. Studied as an architect at the Polytechnical School of Hanover, and became a landscape-painter upon his removal to England, where he spent five years. He settled in Boston in 1868, and has since resided in that city, making a trip to Germany and the Netherlands in 1874. Some of Langerfeldt's architectural drawings in water-color are in the possession of the Superintending Architect at the Treasury, Washington, D. C., and many of his views of New England scenery, exhibited at Boston and New York, are in the private galleries of those cities. There was an exhibition of his works in the gallery of the Boston Art Club in the winter of 1874, upon his return from Europe. For one of his architectural water-color drawings he was awarded a prize at the Centennial Exhibition of 1876.

"Mr. Langerfeldt's style is refreshing in its freedom and unconventionality. His coloring is bright, harmonious, and agreeable; and his manner combines aerial delicacy of tone with a manly strength. . . . . The collection is remarkable for its architectural features, great towers with queer turrets, gables, and picturesque excrescences breaking out in unexpected places; noble cathedrals, curious street scenes, picturesque roadside shrines, and pretty cottages. There are some admirable landscapes and wood interiors." — *Boston Herald*, November, 1874.

"We particularly noticed a pair of Langerfeldt's water-colors, which were full of nature's spirit. The forest piece struck us as being very happy in its effect of luminosity. Mr. Langerfeldt goes to nature as his master, and while he may not master nature, as no artist can, he masters important features. He secures an out-door effect, which is seen in all his works." — *Boston Transcript*, January 19, 1876.

Lanoue, Félix Hippolyte. (*Fr.*) Born at Versailles (1812-1872). Chevalier of the Legion of Honor. Pupil of V. Bertin and Horace Vernet. Landscape-painter. His "View of a Forest of Pines" is at the Luxembourg. Some of his works are at Versailles, at the church of Saint-Étienne-du-Mont, and in various public places.

Lansil, Walter F. (*Am.*) Born in Bangor, Me., 1846. He studied art in his native city under J. P. Hardy, but has spent the greater part of his professional life in Boston. He was elected a member of the Bangor Art Association in 1876, of the Boston Art Club in 1877. He makes marine views a specialty. Among his most important pictures are, "Crossing the Georges'" (belonging to the Boston Marine Insurance Company), "Abandoned," "Sunset, Boston Harbor," "Fishermen in a Calm," etc.

"Walter F. Lansil's last important painting is still on his easel, awaiting the final touches. It is a view of Charlestown and that portion of the harbor which is embraced in a view from the southeast. The sun is setting in a glowing sky that is varied by fleecy clouds, tinged with crimson and gold. . . . . A shimmering light that is thrown by the sun upon the water is rendered with great success, and the masts of the shipping on the piers, in the middle distance, rising suggestively from the sun-bathed mists, add much to the poetry of the scene." — *Boston Daily Evening Traveller*, May 2, 1878.

Lansyer, Emmanuel. (*Fr.*) Born at l'Ile Bouin (Vendée), 1835. Medals, 1865, '69, and '73. Pupil of Courbet and Harpignies. Painter of marines and landscapes. Many of his motives are from Brittany. He has also painted, in the grand vestibule of the Palace of the Legion of Honor, a large picture called "View of the Palace of the Legion of Honor, taken from the Quai d'Orsay." At the Luxembourg is his "Landscape, — the Château de Pierrefonds" (1869). At the Salon of 1878 he exhibited "Flowering Fields, near Douarnenez" and a "*Vue de la* Cour du May *au XV° siècle*," for a salon in the Palais-de-Justice.

Laoust, André-Louis-Adolphe. (*Fr.*) Born at Douai. Medals in 1873 and '74. Pupil of Jouffroy. At the Salon of 1877 he exhibited "St. John with his Cross" and a portrait bust in bronzed plaster; in 1876, a medallion portrait; in 1875, two portraits; in 1874, "Amphion," a marble statue, a group in plaster, "The Capture," and a bust in plaster; in 1878, "Spes" (a statue in plaster) and a portrait bust.

Lapierre, Louis Émile. (*Fr.*) Born at Paris about 1820. Chevalier of the Legion of Honor. Pupil of Victor Bertin. Among his pictures are, "Twilight," "A Pond in the Forest of Champagne," "Interior of a Forest," "Setting Sun in Winter," etc.

Lapito, Louis-Auguste. (*Fr.*) Born at Saint-Maur (1805 – 1874). Chevalier of the Legion of Honor and of the Order of Belgium. Pupil of Watelet and Heim. He traveled much on the Continent of Europe. Perhaps his water-colors are more admired than his oils. His works are seen in public galleries in France, Holland, and Belgium. They are all landscapes.

Lapostolet, Charles. (*Fr.*) Born at Velars. Pupil of Cogniet. At the Salon of 1877 he exhibited "Rouen" and "The Station at Auteuil." His pictures are all landscapes. At the Royal Academy, in 1872, he exhibited "Low Tide at Trouville." His "View of the Canal Saint-Martin at Paris, Winter, from the Bridge of the Street Buttes-Chaumont" (1870) is in the Luxembourg. At the Salon of 1878 he exhibited "The Canal of the Giudecca, Venice."

Lasch, Karl Johann. (*Ger.*) Born at Leipsic, 1822. Professor at Düsseldorf and member of the Academies at Dresden, Vienna, and St. Petersburg. Medals at Berlin, Dresden, Vienna, and Philadelphia. Studied at the Dresden Academy under E. Bendemann, and at Munich under Schnorr and Kaulbach. In 1847 he visited Italy. Later, he painted portraits at Moscow. In 1857 he settled in Paris. In 1860 he removed to Düsseldorf. His pictures are of *genre* subjects, and he inclines to romantic and idyllic scenes. In the National Gallery at Berlin is the "Master's Birthday."

Lathrop, Francis. (*Am.*) Born on the Pacific Ocean, two days' sail from the Sandwich Islands, in 1849. In 1860 he began the study of art under T. C. Farrar in New York. He went to Germany in 1867, entering the Royal Academy of Dresden. In 1870 he settled in London, remaining three years in the studio of Madox Brown. He was for some time during his London residence with William Morris, in his establishment for the manufactory of artistic household goods, and was also an assistant of Spencer Stanhope. Since 1870 he has lived in the United States. He has painted portraits, furnishing, also, illustrations for Clarence Cook's "House Beautiful," and other publications of Scribner & Co. He is a member of the Society of American Artists, sending to its first exhibition, in 1878, portraits of Thomas and Ross R. Winans. He assisted in the decoration of Trinity Church, Boston, of which he designed the chancel. During the winter of 1878 he was engaged in decorating the interior of Bowdoin College Chapel at Brunswick, Me.

Latouche, Louis. (*Fr.*) Born at Ferté-sous-Jouarre. A marine-painter. At the Cottier sale, New York, 1878, his "Normandy Coast-Scene" sold for $745. At the Paris Salon of 1878 he exhibited "The Beach at Berck" (Pas-de-Calais).

Lauder, Robert Scott. (*Brit.*) Born in Edinburgh (1803 – 1869). He became a student of the Trustees Academy at the age of fifteen. About 1823 he went to London, studying for three years in the British Museum. He visited Italy in 1833, remaining until 1838, in close observation and study, in Rome and Florence. He resided in London until 1850, when he settled in Scotland, and became principal instructor in the Trustees Academy. He exhibited frequently at the Royal Academy and the Royal Scottish Academy, of which latter institution he was made a full member in 1830. He was the author of many popular pictures, illustrative of Scottish history and romance, many of which have been engraved. Among these may be mentioned, "Meg Merrilies," "The Fair Maid of Perth," "The Bride of Lammermoor," and "The Trial of Effie Deans." His "Christ teaching Humility" is in the Scottish National Gallery. By reason of ill-health he did not practice his profession for some years before his death.

Lauder, James E. (*Brit.*) (1812–1869.) He studied under Sir William Allan in Edinburgh, and spent five years in study in Rome. He was made Associate of the Royal Scottish Academy in 1842 and Academician in 1849. In 1847 he received from the Committee for the Decoration of Westminster Hall a prize of £200 for his "Wisdom" and "The Unjust Steward." Among his most popular works may be mentioned, "Ferdinand and Miranda," "Lorenzo and Jessica," "The Toilet," "The Money-Lender," "Time Changes," "Gethsemane," "The Parable of the Ten Virgins," "James Watt and the Steam-Engine," "Walter Scott and Sandy Ormiston," many of which have been engraved.

Laugée, François Désiré. (*Fr.*) Born at Maromme, 1823. Chevalier of the Legion of Honor. Pupil of Picot and l'École des Beaux-Arts. His picture of "Eustache Lesueur chez les Chartreux" (1855) is at the Luxembourg. "St. Elisabeth of France washing the Feet of the Poor" (1867) was purchased by the Emperor. Among his pictures may also be named, "The Candle of the Madonna" and "Going to Matins" (both scenes of the thirteenth century), in 1877; "The Angel who bears the Censer," in 1876; "The Young Housekeeper," in 1875; many portraits and mural paintings at the church of St. Peter and St. Paul at St. Quentin, in the church of the Trinity at Paris (in the chapel of St. Denis). At the Salon of 1878 he exhibited "An Old Man" and "An Old Woman," and a cartoon of his picture of St. Denis in the church of the Trinity.

"The 'Martyrdom of St. Denis' is a drama which Laugée has represented full of action, tumultuous, terrible. Even as a page of history alone, it interests and captivates. Behold the first impression which comes from this painting. The qualities which a further study discloses are purity of design, firmness of lines, clearness of *mise en scène*, and richness of coloring, sustained without weakness."—ROGER BALLU, *Gazette des Beaux-Arts*, February, 1878.

Launitz, Robert E., N. A. (*Am.*) Born in Russia (1806–1870). Studied under his father, a sculptor of some ability. In 1830 he came to America, and was made a member of the National Academy three years later. Among the better known of his works are the Pulaski Monument in Savannah, Ga., the statue of General Thomas at Troy, N. Y., and several fine monnments in Greenwood Cemetery.

Laurens, Jean Paul. (*Fr.*) Born at Fourquevaux, 1838. Chevalier of the Legion of Honor, 1874. Medal of Honor, 1877. Member of the jury for the Exposition of 1878, and for the annual Salon. Pupil of Bida and Léon Cogniet. This painter made his débnt at the Salon of 1863. His most important works are, "The Death of the Duke d'Enghien," at the Museum of Alençon ; "The Excommunication of Robert the Pious" (1875), now at the Luxembourg ; "Francis di Borgia before the Dead Isabella of Portugal" ; "The Austrian Staff-Officers around the Death-Bed of Marceau" (1877), purchased by the city of Ghent for 40,000 francs ; "Death of Sainte-Geneviève" at the Pantheon ; "St. Bruno refusing the Gifts of Roger, Count of Calabria," in the church of Notre-Dame-des-Champs ; "Pope Formosa and Stephen VII."; "The Fishing at Bethsaida," at the Museum of Tonlouse ; "The Interdict," at the Museum of Havre ; "The Funeral of William the Conqueror," at the Museum of Béziers ; etc.

The following extract refers to the picture of the "Death of Marceau" : —

"This magnificent picture is better than an apotheosis ; it is a transfiguration. The drawing of Laurens has never been more firm and well sustained, his arrangement never more perfect, and his execution more masterly. Perhaps he might be a little reproached, this severe and sober colorist, for certain effects of color, — a little bold, — that of the screen, for example, and the red cloak. But time will deaden them, and bring them into a religious harmony with the whole. . . . . But of what import all these minute criticisms ? The universal suffrage, as just in art as in politics, has recognized and proclaimed immediately in this work, not only one of the incontestable glories of the modern school, but still more, one of the most noble pages of history which the immense, eternal, invincible French Revolution inspired." — MARIO PROTH, *Voyage au Pays des Peintres,* 1877.

"The pictures of history, properly so called, become more and more rare at our annual expositions. The *genre,* landscapes, and portraits make up the largest part of the works contributed. So much the more necessary is it to notice the artists who go against the current bravely, and among them is J. P. Laurens, pupil of Bida, who has given two very remarkable pictures to this Salon of 1872. One of them, of a somber tone and of singular energy, represents the terrible and almost fantastic scene in which Stephen VII., having exhumed the body of his predecessor, Pope Formosa, bears it, reclothed with the pontifical vestments, into the Salon of Council ; then, when an advocate had been appointed to reply in the name of the dead Pope, he heaped upon the corpse adjurations and accusations. The scene is fierce and savage, and Laurens has thus treated it. The corpse of the dead Pope, with open mouth, the skin already black, extended on the chair, the red gloves covering the fleshless hands, is as sinister as the dead of Valdès Léal that one sees at Seville. He is not the only Spanish painter this dismal canvas recalls. We might take the members of the Council of Laurens for the bishops or torturers escaped from a picture by Herrera. The face of the advocate of the dead, the menacing gesture of Stephen VII., the corpse itself in which the drama centers, the gray walls with their crosses of blood, the tripod, the sepulchral atmosphere of the scene, add to the impression produced by this picture, — one of the best of the Salon." — JULES CLARETIE, *Peintres et Sculpteurs Contemporains.*

"And one of the most important art movements of the present day is caused by a munificent expenditure of money for the decoration of the entire interior of the Pan-

theon by celebrated French artists, with scenes illustrative of the history of Sainte-Geneviève. The subject is national ; no foreign artist has ever attempted it with success.
To M. Jean Paul Laurens a most important part of this work has been confided, —
a space ten yards in length in the sight of the abside. At the Universal Exhibition
M. Laurens shows nine of his well-known paintings, including the 'Excommunicated,'
the 'Borgia,' the 'Execution of the Duc d'Enghien,' and the 'Death of General Marceau,' which took the medal of honor at the Salon of 1877. The lugubrious themes which
have always inspired the best efforts of this artist prepare one to learn that he has now
chosen to represent the closing scene in the life of the saint. The new work is stamped
with the solemn grandeur of style, the simplicity of effect and broad handling characteristic of all his works, while the realism which has been to some repulsive is refined by a
religious sentiment more elevated, but not less tragic. The dying saint is represented
reclining on a couch. Her hands are raised to bless the company about her. During
eighty years she had prayed and cared for the poor. Her arms, enfeebled by old age and
by privation, are sustained by two young girls, who have reverently interposed a drapery
between their hands and the form which is to them sacred. The numerous company
around them, of every age and condition, is grouped with skill. The dignitaries of the
Church occupy the center. A picturesque assemblage of the costumes of the fifth century indicates that the Greek, Latin, and Pagan religions had all yielded to her influence. Nearer the entrance beggars in their rags contrast with the richness of the
principal group. It is right that this interesting historic composition should be painted
in lasting materials on the very walls of the Pantheon, for it is a masterpiece and deserves to endure." — *London Daily News,* May 15, 1878.

Lauters, Paul. (*Belgian.*) (1806 – 1875.) This artist was distinguished for his excellent landscapes in water-colors. He was a Chevalier of the Order of Léopold, and a Professor in the Academy of
Brussels. He sometimes painted in oil. His works showed a delicate
and refined perception of the beauties of Nature, rather than brilliant
color or powerful execution.

Lawman, Jasper. (*Am.*) Born in Xenia, Ohio, 1825. He began his professional career at Cincinnati when a lad of fourteen. In
1846 he removed to Pittsburg, Pa., where he has since resided. In
1859 he went to Paris to study, remaining for a year under Couture.
His pictures are owned in New York, Baltimore, Chicago, Philadelphia, and elsewhere. Many are in the possession of Capt. William
Ward, John Scott, Judge W. G. Hawkins, John W. Hampton, John
Dalzell, and other residents of Pittsburg.

Lawrie, Alexander, A. N. A. (*Am.*) Born in the city of New
York, 1828. He began his studies in the life and antique classes of
the Academy of Design, and in the Pennsylvania Academy of Fine
Arts. Later he went to Europe, studying under Picot in Paris and
E. Leutze in Düsseldorf, working also in Florence. He occupied a
studio in Philadelphia for some time, but has been a resident of New
York during the better part of his professional life. He is a member
of the Artists' Fund Societies of New York and Philadelphia, and was
elected a member of the National Academy in 1866, to the annual
exhibitions of which he is a constant contributor, sending landscapes,
ideal figure-pieces, and portraits, in crayon and oil. In 1869 he exhibited "Autumn in the Hudson Highlands" (belonging to Henry

Marks) ; in 1870, " A Valley in the Adirondacks " (belonging to N. T. Bailey) ; etc. His portrait of Judge Sutherland belongs to the New York Bar Association ; that of Gen. Z. Tower is in the Library of the United States Military Academy at West Point. He has also painted Gen. John F. Reynolds, Col. Josiah Porter, and other prominent men. He has been particularly successful in his portraits of ladies. Among his crayon heads, numbering in all about a thousand, the best known are those of Richard H. Stoddard, Thomas Buchanan Read, George H. Boker, and other literary men. His " Monk playing the Violoncello " and "Autumn in the Highlands " were at the Centennial Exhibition of 1876.

"Lawrie exhibited a portrait of three-quarters length, which is simply admirable. Admirable in execution, in the rich simplicity of the dress, in the fresh loveliness of the face, and in the union of boldness and strength with gentleness and delicacy." — *Art Journal*, May, 1877.

Lawson, Cecil G. (*Brit.*) Born in Shropshire, 1851. Son of William Lawson a portrait-painter, under whom he studied. He has lived for some years in London. Among his more important works are, "In the Valley, — a Pastoral," at the Royal Academy in 1873, and the Grosvenor Gallery in 1878 ; "The Hop-Gatherers of England," exhibited at the Royal Academy and in Liverpool in 1875 ; "The Minister's Garden " and "Strayed, — a Moonlight Pastoral," at the Grosvenor Gallery in 1878 ; " The Dragon-Flies," never publicly exhibited ; etc. His pictures are in the possession of Viscount Powerscourt, Godfrey Fawsett, Louis Huth, Mrs. P. Flower, and others.

"A distinctive place C. G. Lawson has undoubtedly taken as one of the first to attempt on a large scale the reconciliation of the realistic with the poetic treatment of nature.   In 'The Minister's Garden,' for example, there is no want of painstaking fidelity to nature in the sturdy fir-tree, the roses, the hollyhocks, and the beehives in the foreground, nor in the meadows, swelling uplands, and distant hills, towards which we look from the garden which gives its title to the picture ; but at the same time the artist has thrown such a tender and peaceful sentiment into his work, harmonizing the bright colors of the foreground and choosing a moment of subdued light for the wide expanse of landscape, that he has fully justified himself in describing it as 'a tribute to the memory of Oliver Goldsmith.'   It is just such a garden as fancy would choose for the Vicar of Wakefield to sit in." — *London Examiner*, May 4, 1878.

"Much as we value 'The Minister's Garden,' we prefer to it Mr. Lawson's second and rather less large picture, ' In the Valley, — a Pastoral,' which we remember enjoying some years ago at the Royal Academy.   This is pre-eminently graceful, and poetic in its grace ; it affects one like a snatch of delicate descriptive lyrical verse. . . . . Even had we never before seen any productions by Mr. Lawson, what he now shows in the Grosvenor Gallery would prove to us indisputably his possession of the three precious qualities, — strength, sweetness, and sentiment." — W. M. ROSSETTI *in the Academy*, June 1, 1868.

Lawson, Wilfrid. (*Brit.*) Brother of Cecil G. Lawson. Began his professional career as a designer on wood for the illustrated periodicals, working for some time on the staff of the Graphic. He resides in London, and has exhibited in colors and black and white at the Royal Academy, Dudley Gallery, and elsewhere.

" Mr. Wilfrid Lawson has made himself distinctly the artist of ' The Children of the 'City.' In past years he has shown us at the Academy one canvas in which the little street Arabs are making themselves as merry as may be with shadow figures on the walls, and another in which a boy and a girl of the same pathetic race are looking up wistfully at a tree, whose blossoms, guarded by the iron railings of a garden, suggest, like the children's city-bound lives, ' Imprisoned Spring,' the title of the work. This year the artist exhibits a third of the series in Pall Mall. ' Dawn' represents the interior of a wretched room in a London slum, where a dying girl, supported in her brother's arms, is lying on the floor, watching through the windows the first gleams of light breaking on the city, — symbolic of the heavenly dawn about to beam upon her soul. This picture, like its predecessors, proves that Mr. Wilfrid Lawson is not a mere sentimentalist, but a painter who is also a poet." — *Magazine of Art,* August, 1878.

Lay, Oliver Ingraham, A. N. A. (*Am.*) Born in the city of New York, 1845. A painter of portraits and of *genre* pictures. Devoted himself to art in his early youth ; studied in the schools of the Cooper Institute and of the Academy of Design in his native city, where his entire professional life has been spent. He was also a pupil of Thomas Hicks for three years, and has been a constant exhibitor for some time in the National Academy, of which he was made an Associate Member in 1876. He was elected a member of the Artists' Fund Society the same year. Among his portraits exhibited in different seasons may be mentioned those of James Parton, Mrs. Eliza Riddle Field, Mrs. Jeremiah Hendricks of Red Hook, N. Y., John Rodgers of Albany, N. Y., John Delafield, Winslow Homer, C. C. Colman, C. C. Griswold, and Miss Fidelia Bridges (the last four belonging to the National Academy). Among his *genre* works are, " The Letter," " The Window " (owned by J. M. Toucey), and " The Two Friends " (in the collection of John H. Sherwood).

" ' The Letter,' by O. I. Lay, represents a dark-eyed, dark-haired girl, sitting by an open window, through which is seen an apple-orchard in early bloom. She is engaged in writing upon her lap, in true feminine fashion. The story is not a new one, but it is cleverly told. The face and figure are well and gracefully drawn, the position is natural and unconstrained, and the flesh-tints are admirable. . . . . The drawing of the interior, the bright colors of the Moorish rug on the floor, the little vase of spring flowers in the window, and the old chest of drawers with the quaint brass knobs, is excellent."— *New York Arcadian,* December 15, 1877. .

Lazerges, Jean Raymond Hippolyte. (*Fr.*) Born at Narbonne, 1817. Chevalier of the Legion of Honor. Pupil of David d'Angers and Bouchot. Many of his subjects are religious. A " Descent from the Cross " (1855) is at the Luxembourg ; another representation of the same subject is in the château d'Eu. " The Death of the Virgin " (1853) was painted for the chapel of the Tuileries, and was seen at the Exposition of 1867. Lazerges has executed works at the church of Notre Dame de Bon Secours, near Rouen, at a chapel of the convent of La Providence, in the same city, and the ceiling of the theater of Nantes. In 1877 he exhibited at the Salon, " Falma the Singer " and " The Moors in the Court of the Marabout on Friday, which is their Sunday "; in 1876, " Caravan of Kabyles "; in 1875, " The Resurrection," " Louis XVI. and Marie Antoinette at Versailles,"

and " Jesus led to Prison "; in 1874, " Stabat Mater "; in 1873, " The
Christ of the Nineteenth Century "; etc. Lazerges is a musician, and
has composed several songs. He has also written for journals, and
published some books.

Leader, Benjamin William. (*Brit.*) Born in 1831. Entered
the schools of the Royal Academy in 1854, exhibiting " Cottage Children blowing Bubbles," his first picture, the same year. In 1855 he
sent " A Bird-Trap "; in 1857, a " Stream from the Hills "; in 1860,
"A Worcestershire Lane "; in 1863, "A Welsh Churchyard "; in
1867, " Through the Glen "; in 1871, " The Stream through the Birch-
Wood"; in 1872, " Wild Wales "; in 1874, " The Thames at Streat-
ley "; in 1875, " The Wetterhorn "; in 1876, " An English Hayfield "
and " A November Evening"; in 1877, " Lucerne " and "Lauterbrunnen "; in 1878, " Autumn in Switzerland" and " Summer-Time
in Worcestershire."

" Mr. Leader's ' Country Churchyard ' [R. A., 64], taken apparently at Bettws-y-Coed,
deserves notice for its brilliancy, and for the very truthful style of its architecture." —
PALGRAVE'S *Essays on Art.*

Le Blant, Julien. (*Fr.*) Born at Paris. Medal of the third class
in 1878, when he exhibited the " Death of General d'Elbée." In
1877 he exhibited " La partie de tonneau."

Lechesne, Auguste. (*Fr.*) Born at Caen, 1819. Chevalier of
the Legion of Honor. He went to Paris to study, and first attracted
attention by a frieze which he executed in the Maison d'Or. From
this time he was constantly employed in decorating the hotels of Paris.
He has sent to the Salons several works, and especially excels in the
representation of animals. Larousse says : —

" Lechesne of Caen does not understand animals like Barye, but he models his subjects with so much spirit and taste, and gives them so much animation and nicety, that
their attraction is almost irresistible. It is not grand art, but it is the *genre* sculpture,
appreciable by all, attractive and charming."

At the Salon of 1878 he exhibited " A Dog dying on the Tomb of
his Master."

Le Clear, Thomas, N. A. (*Am.*) Born in Owego, N. Y., 1818.
He displayed a talent for art as a child, and sold ideal heads painted on
rough boards to his neighbors before reaching his teens. In 1832 he
was taken by his family to London, Canada, where he painted portraits,
but met with indifferent success. ·He settled in New York in 1839, and
(with the exception of a few years passed in Buffalo) his professional
life has been spent in that city. He was made a member of the National Academy in 1863. Among his earlier works are the " Marble-
Players " (which belonged to the Art Union), the " Itinerant " (in
the National Academy of 1862), and his " Young America." He has
painted the portrait of Edwin Booth as Hamlet, Gifford and McEntee
the artists, Daniel R. Dickinson, President Fillmore, Dr. Vinton (1870),
Bayard Taylor, E. W. Stoughton (1877), Parke Godwin (at the Na-

tional Academy, 1877, and the Paris Exposition of 1878), George
Bancroft (in the Century Club), and William Page (in the Corcoran
Gallery, Washington). He exhibits occasionally at the Royal Academy, London, and the journals of that city have spoken well of his
works, saying that they are among the best in the Academy, fine in
color, graceful, pleasing in tone, with great individuality, a "sense of
oneness, caused by a subtle rendering of all the parts in their just
relation one with another," and that "they exhibited in a marked
degree many of the rare qualities of great portraiture."

"To the native facility for imitation, Le Clear now unites remarkable power of characterization, a peculiar skill in color, and minute authenticity in the reproduction of
latent, as well as superficial personal traits. In some cases his tints are admirably true
to nature, and his modeling of the head strong and characteristic." — TUCKERMAN'S
Boo': of the Artists.

"The quiet, subdued tones of Le Clear's work [portrait of Page] in middle tint, its fine
finish, and the grave dignity of the head, charm every beholder, so as to make him understand why this noble portrait elicited such marked praise when exhibited in the
British Royal Academy. Le Clear is fortunate in being so well represented in the Corcoran Gallery, alongside of some of the best heads of Stuart, Harding, and Healy." —
Art Journal, July, 1878.

Lecomte Du Nouy, Jules Jean Antoine. (*Fr.*) Born at Paris,
1842. Chevalier of the Legion of Honor. Medals at London and
Vienna. Pupil of Gleyre, Gérôme, and Signol. "The Bearers of
Bad News" (1872) is at the Luxembourg. "The Conversion of the
Galley Slaves by Saint Vincent de Paul" is at the church of the
Trinity at Paris. In 1877 he exhibited at the Salon, "The Door
of the Seraglio" and his own portrait; in 1876, "Homer Begging";
in 1875, "The Honeymoon, Venice, Sixteenth Century" and "The
Dream of Cosron"; in 1874, "Eros" (at the Museum of Tours) and
"The Butchers (*Imacellaj*) of Venice." For private galleries he has
painted, "The Merchant of Pompeii," "Christians at the Tomb of
the Virgin," "The Repose of the Schérif," "Christmas Eve at Jeru-
salem," "Chloe at the Fountain," etc. His portraits are good. Among
them is that of Béranger de la Drôme, for the Museum of Valence.
His "Invocation of Neptune" (1866) is at the Museum of Lille.
The "Love which Passes" (1869) is at the Museum of Boulogne.
At the Salon of 1878 he exhibited "Christians at the Tomb of the
Virgin at Jerusalem" and a portrait.

Lecomte - Vernet, Charles-Hippolyte-Émile. (*Fr.*) Born at
Paris (1821 - 1874). Chevalier of the Legion of Honor. Pupil of
H. Vernet and Cogniet. Made his début at the Salon of 1833. At
the Salon of 1874 he exhibited "Penelope" and "Almée"; in 1870,
"A Young Fellah Girl" and "A Young Girl playing with an Owl";
etc.

Lee, Frederick Richard, R. A. (*Brit.*) A native of Devonshire
(1798 - 1879). He began life as a soldier, seeing some active service. In 1818 he resolved to devote himself to art, and entered the

Royal Academy, exhibiting in its gallery in 1824, and regularly for nearly fifty years. He was elected an Associate of the Academy in 1834, and Academician in 1838, and was placed upon the list of Honorary Retired Academicians in 1872. Among the better known of his earlier works (many of which have been engraved) may be noted "Showery Weather" (exhibited at the British Institute in 1834) ; "Coverside," painted in 1839 (in conjunction with Landseer) ; "Evening in the Meadows" (at the Royal Academy in 1854, the cattle in the stream painted by Thomas Cooper, R. A) ; and a "River Scene," at the Royal Academy in 1855 (in which also the cattle are Cooper's), all of which belong to the National Gallery. His "Distant View of Windsor" and "Gathering Seaweed" are in the Sheepsbanks Collection. In 1856 he sent to the Royal Academy, "Breakwaters at Plymouth" ; in 1858, "The Bay of Biscay" ; in 1860, "Summer" ; in 1865, "Garibaldi's Residence at Caprera" ; in 1867, "The Land we Live in" ; in 1868, "Far from the Busy Haunts of Men" ; in 1869, "Morning in the Meadows" ; in 1870, "The Land's End and Longships Lighthouses," and others, since which his works have not been seen at the Royal Academy.

Leech, John. (*Brit.*) (1817 – 1864.) Was educated at the Charter House School in London, and was also a pupil for some time in the Royal Academy, where he exhibited a few pictures of a *genre* character, which were in no way remarkable. His sketches in "Bell's Life in London" were the first of his works which attracted attention to him as an artist. He was connected with Punch as early as 1841, remaining upon the active staff of that journal for twenty-three years, and receiving for his services, it was estimated, £ 40,000. Many of his sketches, enlarged and colored, were exhibited in London in 1861, drawing crowds of visitors and realizing some £ 5,000. The lithographs of these were very popular and extensively sold, as were his many contributions to Punch, when collected in book form. Among the great number of works illustrated by Leech are, "Jack Bragg," by Theodore Hook ; several novels by Albert Smith ; "The Story of a Feather," by Douglas Jerrold ; "Mrs. Caudle's Curtain Lectures" ; "The Comic Latin Grammar" ; "The Comic English Grammar"; "The Comic History of England" ; "The Comic History of Rome" ; Christmas numbers of the Illustrated London News ; .Bentley's "Miscellany" for many years ; "Jack Hinton" ; "Punch's Pocket-Book," up to 1864 ; the earlier volumes of Once a Week ; "Young Troublesome" ; "Master Jacky in Love" ; "The Book of British Song"; "Puck on Pegasus"; Blaine's "Encyclopædia of British Sports" ; "Paul's Dashes of American Humor" ; "Life of a Foxhound" ; "The Christmas Carol" ; "The Cricket on the Hearth"; "The Chimes."

"John Leech is different from all of these, and taken as a whole surpasses them all, even Cruikshank ; and seats himself next, though below, William Hogarth. Well might

Thackeray, in his delightful notice of his friend and fellow-Carthusian in the Quarterly, say, 'There is no blinking the fact that in Mr. Punch's Cabinet John Leech is the right-hand man. Fancy n number of Punch without Leech's picture ! What would you give for it?' This was said ten years ago (1852). How much more true is it now ! . . . . It is this wholesomeness, and, to use the right word, this goodness, that makes Leech more than a drawer of funny pictures, more even than a great artist. It makes him a teacher and an example of virtue in its widest sense." — DR. JOHN BROWN, *in Spare Hours.*

" Nothing was more characteristic of Leech, and nothing was more enjoyable in his works, than the evident genial sympathy with which he entered into every phase of the many-sided English life of the hunting-field, the seaside, the ballroom, the drawing-room, the nursery. . . . . John Leech had also a fine appreciation of English scenery, and in those bits of it which he introduced into his sketches he did it full justice, while he elevated by their artistic completeness the character of the sketches." — ROSSETTI.

" Very few artists, very few men of any profession, have been privileged to give the amount of pleasure which Leech conferred in very different quarters, and on very different ages. . . . . To the infinite honor of Leech and of the promoters and proprietors of Punch, it was pleasure of the most innocent description." — MRS. TYTLER's *Modern Painters.*

" His [Dickens'] opinion of Leech, in a word, was, that be turned caricature into character ; and would leave behind him not a little of the history of his time and its follies sketched with inimitable grace. . . . . To represent female beauty as Mr. Leech represents it, an artist must have a delicate perception of it ; and the gift of being able to realize it to us with two or three slight, sure touches of the pencil. This power Mr. Leech possessed in an extraordinary degree. . . . . His wit is good-natured, and always the wit of a gentleman." — FORSTER's *Life of Dickens*, Vol. II. Chap. XVIII.

" The out-door sketcher will not fail to remark the excellent fidelity with which Mr. Leech draws the backgrounds of his little pictures. The homely landscape, the sea, the winter wood by which the huntsmen ride, the light and clouds, the birds floating overhead, are indicated by a few strokes which show the artist's untiring watchfulness and love of nature. . . . . No man has ever depicted the little ' snob ' with such delightful touch. Leech fondles and dandles this creature as he does the children. To remember one or two of these gents is to laugh." — THACKERAY, *in the London Times,* June 21, 1862.

Lefebvre, Charles. (*Fr.*) Born at Paris, 1805. Chevalier of the Legion of Honor. Pupil of Gros. At the Salon of 1877 he exhibited " Daïmio, — Costume of the Court of Japan" ; in 1816, " The Separation of SS. Peter and Paul at the Moment when they were led to their Martyrdom" ; in 1875, " St. Anne instructing the Virgin Mary" ; in 1873, " Lucretia," etc. Charles Lefebvre has also painted some portraits.

Lefebvre, Jules Joseph. (*Fr.*) Born at Tournan, 1836. Chevalier of the Legion of Honor. Pupil of Léon Cogniet. He gained the grand *prix de Rome* in 1861, the subject being " The Death of Priam." His " Nymph and Bacchus " (1866) is in the Luxembourg. In 1877 he exhibited at the Salon, " Pandora " ; in 1876, " Mary Magdalene " and a portrait ; in 1875, " Chloe " and a portrait ; in 1874, a portrait of the Prince Imperial ; in 1872, " The Grasshopper" ; in 1870, " Truth " and a portrait, etc. At the Latham sale, New York, 1878, " The Grasshopper " (75 by 35) sold for $ 2,950. At the Salon of 1878 he exhibited " Mignon " and a portrait of Mme. ——. •

Lefuel, Hector Martin. (*Fr.*) Born at Versailles, 1810. Commander of the Legion of Honor. Member of the Institute. This architect was a pupil of Huyot and l'École des Beaux-Arts. He gained the grand *prix de Rome* in 1839. He was architect of the château of Meudon, also of that of Fontainebleau, and in 1854 replaced Visconti at the Louvre. In 1855 he was much occupied with the Exposition. He was soon after appointed Chief Architect of the Louvre and the National Palaces. He is to be noticed for his embellishments of the Tuileries. In 1867 he was a member of the Imperial Commission for the Exposition, and in 1873 was made a member of the Superior Commission of International Expositions. He made one of the jury at Vienna. He is also a member of the Superior Commission of the Fine Arts. He was President of the Institute in 1875.

Legros, Alphonse. (*Fr.*) Born at Dijon. Slade Professor in University College, London. Medals in 1867 and '68. Pupil of M. Lecoq de Boisbaudran. This artist had no assistance in his education, and encountered many hardships before he was able to send a picture to the Salon ; it was a portrait of his father, exhibited in 1857. In 1875 M. Malassis published an account of Legros and his works, from which we give an extract : —

"As it always happens, a literary man was the first to take notice of him. M. Champfleury, — who some years before had pointed out MM. Gustave Courbet and François Bouvin, — with his discriminating curiosity always on the alert, had remarked in the Salon of 1857 the portrait of a man (the artist's father), painted strongly and simply, and signed with the unknown name LEGROS. He wished to become acquainted with the painter ; fancying him as an honest, middle-aged artist, obscure, deserving, and occupied in the production of modest work, he found, to his surprise, a young man under twenty, full of fire and *verve*, already master of a style at once solid and subtle, engaged with justifiable self-reliance upon numerous works in course of execution or preparation. The kind visit of the celebrated writer remains as the pleasantest recollection of the painter's early days. It was like the first smile of fame."

In 1859 "The Angelus" by Legros attracted much attention, especially from artists ; it was purchased by an English amateur artist, Mr. Seymour Haden. Legros has resided nearly fifteen years in England, where he has received the honor and patronage which he failed to obtain in Paris ; and this consideration has at length extended itself to his native country, as will be seen by the fact that his "Ex-Voto" has been purchased for the Gallery at Dijon, "The Stoning of St. Stephen" for the Gallery at Avranches, "Monks at Prayer" for the Gallery at Alençon, a drawing of "St. Sebastian" for the Gallery at Lille, and the "Amende Honorable" (1868) for the Luxembourg. The works of this artist are more frequently exhibited in England than in France. Many of them go directly from his studio to the purchasers. The following are among his more important pictures : "The Pilgrimage," at the Liverpool Gallery ; "The Spanish Cloister" and the "Benediction of the Sea," at Mr. Eustace Smith's ; "The Baptism," belonging to Sir George Howard.

"The Coppersmith," belonging to Mr. Ionides, was at the Salon of 1875, together with the " Demoiselles du Mois de Marie," belonging to M. Miéville. Legros has etched a large number of plates, and his works taken altogether are very numerous. At the Grosvenor Gallery Exhibition, 1877, he exhibited " Four Studies, Portraits " (executed in two hours each) before the pupils of the artist in the Slade School, a Portrait of Thomas Carlyle, " A Landscape," " The Coppersmith," " The Spanish Cloister," and " The Baptism." (The last three are mentioned above.) In 1878 he sent to the Grosvenor ten studies and finished paintings.

" France is a country of very strange contrasts, and this contrast is noticeable amongst others, that whilst many French people spoil themselves by the utmost extreme of affectation, many other French people are just as remarkable for the entire absence of affectation ; so that their simplicity is more simple than ours, and their directness more direct. This contrast has been very strikingly manifested in the French art of the last half-century. Side by side, in the public exhibitions, with art of the most pretentious extravagance, grew up another school of art which discarded pretension altogether. Never was any realism so remarkable for simplicity of purpose as that of the genuine French rustic school. I do not mean the realism of the revolutionary realists, who called themselves so, but of that school which was entirely emancipated from classical authority, and used its liberty for the plain expression of its sentiment, not for the illustration of a theory. These artists were neither influenced by the authority of the classics nor by the force of the reaction against them ; they worked in a calm corner of their own, safe from the flux and reflux of the great currents of their time. M. Legros is one of them ; but instead of going among the oxen and the laborers in the fields, he prefers the solemnity of the village church, or the cathedral aisle, or the quiet monastery ; and there he will watch his models, who know not that they are watched, and who reveal to him the secret of their meditations." — HAMERTON, *in The Portfolio*, August, 1873.

" Bold and strong in his style, sometimes even to brutality, he is a proof that the artist never ceases to be true ; his first attempts testified precisely to that conscientious research, to that obstinate labor which he brings to the interpretation of nature. . . . . M. Legros has never flattered either the taste or the tendencies of his time ; it is thus that he has remained himself, and that in each one of his impressions he has subordinated the form to an original and powerful thought." — CHARLES GUELLETTE, *Gazette des Beaux-Arts*, April, 1876.

Leharivel-Durocher, Victor Edmond. (*Fr.*) Born at Chanu, 1816. Chevalier of the Legion of Honor. Pupil of Belloc, Ramey, and A. Dumont. His " To Be and to Seem to Be " (1861) is at the Luxembourg. Among his works are, " A Group of Angels," on the tomb of Archbishop Pierres in the church of Saint-Sulpice ; " Saints Geneviève and Théodechilde," for the church of Sainte-Clothilde at Paris ; monument to the three brothers Eudes, for the city of Argentan ; " Glory," for the court of the Louvre ; a statue of Visconti for his tomb ; " St. Mary Magdalene," for the church of Saint-Augustin at Paris ; " Tragedy " and " Comedy " (bas-reliefs in stone), for the grand staircase of the Théâtre Français, etc. The list is much too long to be given here. His works are to be seen in many cities, and he has also executed numerous portrait busts and statues as well as other sculptures for private houses. To the Salon of 1878 he contributed a marble statue of " St. Théodechilde."

Lehmann, Charles Ernest Rodolphe Henri. (*Ger.*) Born at Kiel, 1814 (now a naturalized citizen of France). Member of the Institute. Officer of the Legion of Honor. Professor at l'École des Beaux-Arts. Member of the Superior Council of the Fine Arts. Pupil of his father and of Ingres. His subjects are religious and historical, and he has taken many motives from modern poets. His reputation as a portrait-painter is great. His "Grief of the Oceanides at the Foot of the Rock to which Prometheus was chained" (1850) is at the Luxembourg. Among his works are, "An Assumption of the Virgin" for the church of Saint-Louis at Paris, decorative works at the church of Saint-Merri, at the chapel of the Institute for the Young Blind, a chapel at the church of Saint-Louis-en-l'Ile, at the church of Sainte-Clothilde, at the palaces of the Luxembourg and of Justice, etc. His portraits are numerous, and of notable men and women. We may also mention his "Arrival of Sarah at the Home of the Young Tobias," "The Education of Tobias," "Jeremiah," "Venus," "Undine," "Hamlet," "Ophelia," "The Dream of Love," etc.

"He began with the strongest men of the modern French school, — with Ingres, Delacroix, Scheffer, and Delaroche, — and he has always manifested himself at the level of the most conscientious art and the best criticism. He comes directly from Ingres by his style, and with Ingres he made the study of the *brin* his chief care. His point of departure from the spirit of Ingres' work is in his sentiment, which establishes his relation with Scheffer. He is not a typical artist, but for that very reason far less likely to provoke the hostility and depreciation which always accompany the development of a representative and pronounced talent. He is so studied, so conscientious, — he is such a fine draughtsman, and so finished in his manner, — that he has never been exposed to the criticism which made a noise of words, words, words, about the great name of Delacroix, and left the correct and interesting Delaroche undisturbed. Lehmann and Delaroche were fellow-students under Ingres ; but in Lehmann and Ingres classicism was grafted on German mysticism, and it is this union of the positive classic with the poetic sentiment of the North which makes many of his works as strange as they are lovely. Lehmann often gleaned after Delacroix and Scheffer. He followed both in German and English poetry, painting a 'Hamlet' after Delacroix, and painting a 'Mignon' after Scheffer. His 'Hamlet' is described as elegant and contemplative. Greek tragedies and myths and Jewish and Catholic legends have afforded subjects to this most accomplished and indefatigable artist. His portraits are celebrated, and rival those by Ingres and Flandrin. His portrait of the Princess Belgiojosio is one of the most remarkable of modern portrait studies, and has been characterized as a striking and studied work. But *color* is so little sought for, and so little felt by the painter, that the *effect* of the head is described as unreal, — as a head in moonlight or as a scene in dreams, — and it is on this side of elegant and exquisite *fantasie* that Henri Lehmann has been at once the most charming artist, while to some he has seemed feeble in his hold upon nature. His portrait of Liszt is equally celebrated with his portrait of the Princess Belgiojosio, and ranks with Flandrin's heads. It has been called 'a very rare creation, and surprisingly beautiful,' by one of the best French critics. Of late years, Lehmann's style, formed in Rome under Ingres, has changed somewhat ; it has lost its pallor and strangeness, — the charm of his work to his admirers, — and has become suffused with color. Edmond About says it is now warm, like the best examples of Léopold Robert. But we may add that Robert was hardly a colorist, and that what About calls warmth a Venetian probably would call rankly hot." — EUGENE BENSON, *Appletons' Art Journal*, February 26, 1870.

Lehmann, Rudolf. (*Ger.-Brit.*) Born near Hamburg, 1819. Son of a miniature-painter, from whom he inherited his taste for art and received his first instructions, and brother of the preceding. Went to Paris in 1834, studying for two years, and spending a like period in Munich, where, for a time, he was a pupil of Kaulbach. In 1839 he went to Rome, in which city he has passed many winters, sending to the Paris Salon of 1841 a picture for which he received a gold medal. He turned his attention to the painting of the figures of Italian women with considerable success, and won the praise and friendship of Thorwaldsen, Ary Scheffer, Delaroche, and other famous artists. He went to England for the first time in 1850, making many subsequent visits before he finally settled there in 1866. Among his early works are, "Sixtus Quintus blessing the Pontine Marshes" (in the Paris Salon of 1847, and now in the Museum of Lille), "St. Sebastian," "St. Cecilia," "Haidee," "Graziella" (for which he received the gold medal in Paris in 1854), "Early Morning in the Pontine Marshes" (R. A., 1860), "Tasso returning to Sorrento," "Foundling Hospital, Rome," and "A Roman Serenade" (belonging to the Prince of Wales). Since he has lived in England he has sent to the Royal Academy "The Fortune-Teller" and "The Favor of an Answer requested," in 1868 ; "After the Fire," in 1869 ; "Out of the World," in 1870 ; "May we come in ?" (portraits of his own family), in 1871 ; "Confessions," in 1872 ; "Ave Maria," in 1874 ; "Alma and her pet Kittens" and "Robert Browning," in 1875 ; "After the Sitting," in 1876 ; and many portraits.

"Mr. Lehmann's works now take a prominent place, as they deserve, in the exhibitions of the Royal Academy. It is not difficult to recognize in them the influence of his continental training, and especially of his long residence in Rome. His figures always show the feeling they are intended to express, while his coloring is rich yet chastened." — *Art Journal*, June, 1874.

Lehoux, Pierre-Adrien-Pascal. (*Fr.*) Born at Paris. Medals in 1873 and '74. *Prix du Salon*, 1874. Pupil of Cabanel. At the Salon of 1877 he exhibited "St. Stephen, Martyr" ; in 1876, "The Constellation of the Bouvier" ; in 1874, "St. Lawrence, Martyr," now at the Luxembourg. At the Salon of 1878 he exhibited "Surprise" and "The Wrestlers."

Leibl, H. W. (*Ger.*) Munich. This artist is prominent in Munich, and his works can be studied, together with those of his fellow-artists, in the Pinakothek of that city, where are placed the works of the so-called new school to which he belongs. To the Paris Exposition of 1878 he sent "Some Peasants " and a portrait.

"Leibl reveals in painting the rough-featured, roughly clad *Bauerein*, or peasants of the Bavarian hamlets, and the results are sometimes quite marvelous. He can also give you, if he chooses, the delicate beauty of a lady's head with a truth to nature that throws enthusiastic young artists into raptures. But he does not often so choose, and this leads us reluctantly to say that the essential coarseness of his character prevents him from being as great an artist as his abilities might otherwise have made him. The greatest artists generally combine with strength a certain refinement, apparent in their works, if not in their manners. Beauty in the ordinary sense of the term has no attractions for Leibl. Even amidst the homely uncouthness of German peasantry handsome men and comely maidens are to be found. He seems to go out of his way to give us the most repulsive specimens of both sexes that he can find." — BENJAMIN'S *Contemporary Art in Europe.*

Leighton, Frederick, R. A. (*Brit.*) Member of the Academy of Florence. Corresponding Member of the Institute of France. Born at Scarboro', 1830. Studied drawing as a lad in Rome. Student of the Royal Academy of Berlin in 1845, and studied later in Florence, Brussels, Paris, Frankfort, and Rome. He first exhibited, in England, "Cimabue's Madonna carried through the Streets of Florence" (R. A., 1855), which attracted great attention in London, and was purchased by the Queen. He exhibited his "Triumphs of Music," in 1856; "Sunrise, Capri," in 1860; "Star of Bethlehem," in 1862; "Girl feeding Peacocks," in 1863; "Orpheus and Eurydice," in 1864; "David" and "The Widow's Prayer," in 1865; "The Painter's Honeymoon," in 1866; "Venus disrobing for the Bath" and the "Spanish Dancing-Girl," in 1867; "Jonathan's Token to David," in 1868. He was elected Associate of the Royal Academy in 1865, and Academician in 1869, when he contributed "Electra at the Tomb of Agamemnon" and "St. Jerome" (his diploma work). In 1871 he exhibited "Hercules wrestling with Death;"; in 1872, "After Vespers"; in 1873, "Weaving the Wreath" and "The Industrial Arts of Peace"; in 1874, "Old Damascus"; in 1875, "Little Fatima"; in 1876, "The Daphnephoria" and "Teresina"; in 1877, "The Music-Lesson," "Study," and "An Athlete strangling a Python" (in bronze). This last was secured by the Academy authorities for 2,000 guineas, under the Chantrey Bequest, and was pronounced by the London Art Journal (August, 1877), "nobly classic in feeling, yet full of such realistic details as modern anatomical knowledge demands." Mr. Leighton has recently (November, 1878) been elected President of the Royal Academy. He has been knighted by the Queen.

"The 'Dante in Exile' [R. A., 1864] is a piece of refined drawing (with some little mannerism, perhaps, in the proportions), and of carefully studied attitude, and has little to fear from English rivalry. The subject was a noble one to attempt, and we are glad that Mr. Leighton had the courage to undertake it." — PALGRAVE's *Essays on Art.*

"The 'Summer Moon' and 'Interior of a Jew's House,' by Mr. Leighton, are works well deserving of special commendation. The former is exquisitely poetic in sentiment, rich and suggestive in tone, and admirable in grace of composition. The 'Interior of a Jew's House' is a complete poem from the ancient world. . . . . The figures are painted with rare skill and grace, the drawing is admirable, and the archæological learning, which seems to be a matter of special pride in art to-day, is most thorough." — PROF. WEIR's *Official Report of the American Centennial Exhibition of 1876.*

"Mr. Leighton's 'Music-Lesson' [R. A., 1877] is the most striking bit of art work in the whole Exhibition. . . . . What makes this picture valuable in our eyes is, first, the perfect oneness of the conception, the unity of action and sentiment; and, second, the preciousness of the art with which he has carried out the idea." — *Art Journal*, July, 1877.

"Frederick Leighton is distinguishing himself in the treatment of classical subjects as well as portraiture. Such drawing of the human figure divine as in 'Daphnephoria' is rarely excelled." — BENJAMIN's *Contemporary Art in Europe.*

"Leighton's young naked athlete, with his limbs separated and firmly fixed on the ground, struggles with a serpent which is entwined about one of his haunches. With one arm behind he preserves his body from the danger of the formidable clasp, while with the other in front of him he throws out and holds at a distance the terrible head, grasping the neck with his strong hand. The general outline is grand, and it is a beautiful classic study, such as one sees in the drawings of the same artist." — ANATOLE DE MONTAIGLON, *Gazette des Beaux-Arts,* July, 1878.

Leitch, W. L. (*Brit.*) Born in Glasgow, studying there under Knox. He has been for many years a resident of London and member of the Institute of Painters in Water-Colors, of which society he was elected Vice-President, succeeding Louis Haghe in 1870. He was at one time teacher of painting to Queen Victoria, and has furnished illustrations for many well-known books. Among his water-color drawings are, " Peat Moor near Balmoral," " On the Teviot," " Evening," " Distant View of Creffel, Dumfrieshire," " The Valley of the Tweed from Berwick Castle," " Lago Maggiore," " Murano near Venice," etc. At the Loan Exhibition at Glasgow in 1878 were his " Bethlehem," " Church of the Holy Sepulcher," " Highland Raid," and " Windsor Castle."

Le Jeune, Henry, A. R. A. (*Brit.*) Born in London, 1820. Entered the schools of the Royal Academy at the age of fourteen. In 1841 he gained the gold medal for historical painting, his subject being " Samson bursting his Bonds," exhibited at the British Institute in 1842. He first exhibited at the Royal Academy, in 1840, " Joseph interpreting the Dream of Pharaoh's Butler." In 1845 he was appointed Master of the School of Design ; in 1848, Curator of the Royal Academy School of Painting. Among his early works are, " Ruth and Boaz," in 1845 ; " Lear and Cordelia," in 1849 ; " The Sermon on the Mount," in 1851 ; " The Vision of Queen Catherine," in 1857 ; " The Sisters of Lazarus," in 1861 ; and in 1863 (when he was elected Associate of the Royal Academy), " Early Flowers." In 1864 he exhibited " The Wounded Robin " ; in 1867, " The Ride " ; in 1869, " Rather Shy " ; in 1872, " Great Expectations " ; in 1874, " Innocence " ; in 1875, " A Bite " and " My Little Model " ; in 1876, " Cinderella " ; in 1877, " Music " ; in 1878, " The Low-Born Lass " and " Spring Flowers."

"The best performance ever exhibited by Henry Le Jeune is 'Much Ado about Nothing' [R. A., 1878], a fishing-party of three children seated catching minnows on an old river sluice. The color, the grouping, the execution, and the surroundings of this small company entitle it to rank among the most beautiful pieces of art of its kind that have ever been produced." — *Art Journal,* June, 1878.

Le Keux, Henry. (*Brit.*) (1787 – 1869.) Executed a great number of plates ; among others, " Summer Lake " (after Turner), " Venice " (after Prout), " Embarkation of St. Ursula " (after Claude), and illustrations for Britton's " Cathedrals," Rogers' poems, " The

Beauties of England and Wales," etc. He retired from active work
in his profession about 1840.

Leland, Henry. (*Am.*) Born at Walpole, Mass. (1850–1877).
Taken as a child to Boston. He showed a talent for drawing at
an early age, but received no instruction in art in America, although
as an amateur he painted several creditable portraits. He was engaged in mercantile pursuits in Boston until 1874, when he resolved
to become an artist by profession, and went to Paris, entering the
studio of Bonnat. Here his progress was so rapid that in one year
from the commencement of his studies he sent a portrait to the Salon
(1875) which was accepted. In the summer of 1875 he visited Boston,
when he painted portraits of his father and mother, which were sent
to the Centennial Exhibition in 1876. He continued in Bonnat's school
of drawing after his return to Paris, occupying a studio of his own for
painting, and devoting himself closely to his profession. To the Salon
of 1876 he sent a full-length portrait of Mlle. D'Alembert, daughter
of Count D'Alembert, which was highly praised by the Paris press.
To the Salon of 1877 he sent "Italian Girl" and "Chevalier, Time
of Henry III." One of his latest productions, and probably his
best work, "Expectation," was painted for a Boston gentleman. It
represented an interior, furniture of white and gold (time of Louis
XV.), with a lady in white satin costume. It was praised by Bonnat,
and was exhibited in the Gallery of the Society of American Artists
in 1878. In 1877 Leland went to Italy, painting "A Courtyard in
Venice" while in that city. He painted his own portrait and a "Court
Lady" (time of Henry III.), which was left unfinished at the time of
his death ; while at work upon it, December 5, 1877, in his studio,
he met with an accident, dying in a few moments. Mr. Leland's works
show careful and conscientious study, accuracy of drawing, fine coloring, and the strength which might be expected from a constant student
of Bonnat for three years. Shortly after Mr. Leland's death the Boston Transcript said : —

"Mr. Leland's picture is full in the display of artistic genius. In it is a lady in a
white satin dress standing near the center of a room before a piano. She is in the act of
unbuttoning a glove, and her attention has been attracted towards the front and opposite
part of the room from which she stands, so that a full view of the face is obtained as she
turns her head to greet the expected comer. . . . . All the shadows are softly diffused
into the various parts of the room, and are in perfect keeping with the strong high lights.
The face is frankly painted and expressive, the pose of the head easy and natural. The
texture of the dress as it falls in graceful folds and train is, as it should be in order to
give the proper effect, exceedingly well drawn. The painting is in its every part the
most faithful in its appearance of truth of tone and execution that has been exhibited
in this city for some years."

Leleux, Adolphe. (*Fr.*) Born at Paris, 1812. Chevalier of the
Legion of Honor. He studied his art absolutely alone. He traveled
in France and Algiers, and met with remarkable success in his pictures
of manners and customs, which is principally due to his exactness of

representation. His "Wedding in Brittany" (1863) is at the Luxembourg. At the Salon of 1877 he exhibited "A Salon of Crénille" and "The Family of a Maker of Wooden Shoes in Lower Brittany." Among his pictures are, "A Market-Day at Finistère," "Spring Flowers," "A Funeral in Brittany," "Arab Women in the Desert," "Bedouins attacked by Dogs," etc. At the Salon of 1878 he exhibited "Washerwomen in Berry" and "The Departure."

Leleux, Armand. (*Fr.*) Born at Paris, 1820. Chevalier of the Legion of Honor. Brother of Adolphe Leleux. Pupil of Ingres, whom he accompanied to Rome, where he remained two years. A *genre* painter. He had an official mission to Spain in 1846, and has also traveled in Germany and Switzerland. The "Interior of the Pharmacy of the Convent of the Capuchins at Rome" (1863) is at the Luxembourg. Among his works are, "A Village Barber in Switzerland," "The Eve of the Fête" (Swiss), "The Alpine Hunter," "Scenes in the Black Forest," "Gypsies," "Interior of a Forge," etc. At the Salon of 1878 he exhibited "The Letter of Recommendation" and "A Woman winding Skeins."

Leloir, Jean Baptiste Auguste. (*Fr.*) Born at Paris, 1809. Chevalier of the Legion of Honor. Pupil of Picot and l'École des Beaux-Arts. His decorative works are at the churches of Saint-Germain-l'Auxerrois and Saint-Merri at Paris, and at that of Saint-Leu Taverney and the church of Saint-Jean at Belleville. Among his pictures are, "The Holy Family in Egypt," "A Martyr," "Marriage of the Virgin," "Daphnis and Chloe," "Death of Homer," "Marguerite in Prison," "Ruth and Naomi," "Captive Athenians at Syracuse," etc. To the Salon of 1878 he contributed "Horace à Tibur."

Leloir, Alexandre Louis. (*Fr.*) Born at Paris. Chevalier of the Legion of Honor. Pupil of his father. At the Salon of 1875 he exhibited "The Grandfather's Fête"; in 1874, "The Slave." At the Johnston sale, New York, 1876, his "Temptation of St. Anthony" (28 by 39) sold for $2,100. To the Salon of 1878 he contributed "The Betrothal."

Leloir, Maurice. (*Fr.*) Born at Paris. Pupil of his father and brother. Medal of the third class, in 1878, when he exhibited "The Last Journey of Voltaire to Paris"; in 1877, "Robinson Crusoe"; in 1876, "The Marionnettes."

Lemaire, Philippe-Henri. (*Fr.*) Born at Valenciennes, 1798. Member of the Institute. Officer of the Legion of Honor. Pupil of Cartellier. He gained the grand *prix de Rome* in 1821. He made his début at the Salon of 1831. His "Head of the Virgin" (1846) is at the Luxembourg. His *chef-d'œuvre* is the decoration of the front of the Madeleine. The works of Lemaire are seen in many public places. In 1852 he was elected to the Corps Legislatif in the Departement du Nord.

Lemaire, Hector. (*Fr.*) Born at Lille. Pupil of A. Dumont

3*

and Falguière. Medals in 1877 and '78, and *prix du Salon* in 1878, when he exhibited a plaster group of " Samson betrayed by Delilah " ; in 1877, " Maternal Love " and a " Souvenir " (bust, plaster) ; in 1876, a plaster group, " The Bath."

Lematte, Jacques-François-Fernand. (*Fr.*) Born at Saint-Quentin. Medals in 1870, '73, and '76. Pupil of Cabanel. At the Salon of 1877 he exhibited a portrait and " The Widow " ; in 1876, " Orestes and the Furies " and a portrait ; in 1874, " The Rape of Dejanira " ; in 1878, " A Nymph surprised by a Faun " and a portrait of Mlle. S.

Lenbach, Franz. (*Ger.*) Born at Schrobenhausen, a Bavarian village, and the son of a carpenter, whom he assisted in his work ; all the time developing his taste for drawing by making sketches of the men and animals which he saw about him. At length he obtained permission from his father to go to Munich. His allowance was fifteen cents a day ! He presented himself to Piloty, who arranged for him to enter the Academy. When his course was finished he returned to his home, and painted, " with a sort of intoxication," the peasants as in his childhood. His " Sleeping Shepherd " of the gallery of the Baron Schack was painted at this time. Piloty soon sent the young painter to Rome at his own expense. After his return he was made a Professor at Weimar, where he was associated with Reinhold Begas and Böcklin. They all soon resigned their offices, and Lenbach returned to Munich. He went again to Italy and to Spain, and made many fine copies after Titian, Velasquez, and Murillo. At Paris, in 1867, he received a medal of the third class. He is to-day very celebrated, and has become the painter of princes and emperors. His picture of the Emperor of Austria was at the Vienna Exposition of 1873. At the Paris Exposition of 1878 several of his portraits were seen.

" M. Lenbach expresses in a high degree the striking features of a face, the vivacity, the humid depth of the eyes, the accent of the mouth or the ear, the character ; and allows himself to freely rest on such or such a trait which pleases him. His execution is singular, — he is not careful to turn a drawing correctly, and leaves transparencies in his shadows. . . . . But he has a full and profound impression of the man, and of the dominating traits of his face and his whole manner. His portraits of women have much grace, and a charm of sentiment ; although one must seek these qualities beneath a *mélange* of remembrances of Rubens and Jordaens, and under a light which is a little pale. But leaving aside sentiment, and his manner of representing what he sees, he is an artist. . . . . An onion-peel, says one ; a great varnished aquarelle in the manner of Piloty, says another ; painting buttered, garnished with parsley, *à la maître-d'hotel*, shall I add ! All that you wish. The artist who calls himself Lenbach is a personality, a man of the first rank."—DURANTY, *Gazette des Beaux-Arts*, July, 1878.

Lenepveu, Jules-Eugène. (*Fr.*) Born at Angers, 1819. Member of the Institute and Officer of the Legion of Honor. Director of the Academy of France at Rome in 1873. Pupil of Picot. " The Martyrs in the Catacombs," Salon of 1855, is at the Luxembourg. He decorated the chapel of Saint Anne in the church of Saint-Sulpice, Paris. This was completed in 1864. He has also executed decorative works in his native city. His easel-pictures are historical and religious subjects, and portraits. Among them are a "Venetian Wedding," "Pius IX. at the Sistine Chapel," "Moses succoring the Daughters of Midian," etc.

Lepic, Ludovic-Napoléon. (*Fr.*) Born at Paris. Medal in 1877. Pupil of Cabanel and Wappers. His pictures at the Salon of 1877 were, "The Broken Boat" and "The Tempest"; in 1876, "The Inundation of the Quay Bercy, March 16, 1876" and "A Calm in the Bay of Somme"; also, three etchings of "Scenes on the Banks of the Scheldt"; in 1875, "Pêche de nuit an chien de mer" and a "Boat of Boulogne"; in 1874, "Springtime" and "The Deluge" (a triptych); in 1878, "The Departure, — High Tide" and "The Return, — Low Tide."

Lequeane, Eugène-Louis. (*Fr.*) Born at Paris, 1815. Chevalier of the Legion of Honor. Medal at London. Pupil of Pradier, who before his death confided to him the completion of the "Victories" of the Tomb of Napoleon at the Invalides. His portrait statues and busts are numerous. He has executed decorations at the Louvre, and the new church of Saint-Augustin at Paris. His monumental Fountain in the grand Place of Nevers and a "Winged Griffon" at the Museum of Amiens are among his important works. At the Salon of 1876 he exhibited "Gaulois au poteau," plaster statue; in 1874, "That of which the Young Girls dream," plaster statue; etc.

Le Roux, Charles-Marie-Guillaume. (*Fr.*) Born at Nantes, 1814. Officer of the Legion of Honor. Pupil of Corot. At the Salon of 1877 he exhibited "A Farm in Vendée" and "The Banks of the Loire and the Basin of the Basse-Indre at Low Tide"; in 1876, "High Tide at Préfailles" and a "View at the Soulliers"; in 1875, "A Marsh, — Sunrise," "The Bourg of Batz and the Croisic, — Storm," and "The Approach of a Squall on the Coasts of Brittany"; in 1878, "The Vista of the Chestnut-Trees at the Soulliers" and "At the Soulliers, — Morning."

Le Roux, Hector. (*Fr.*) Born at Verdun. Medals in 1863, '64, and '74. Pupil of Picot. At the Salon of 1877 he exhibited "The Danaïdes" and "The Vestal Claudia Quinta"; in 1876, "The Obsequies of Themistocles" and "The Trial of a Vestal"; in 1874, "The Vestal Tuccia." At the Johnston sale, New York, 1876, the "Funeral in the Columbarium" (54 by 39) sold for $725. At the Corcoran Gallery is the "Vestal Tuccia," which gained a second medal at Paris in 1874. His "Funeral in the Columbarium of the House of the Cæsars" (1864) is at the Luxembourg. At the Salon of 1878 was his "Pallas Minerva on the Acropolis of Athens" and "The Little Orphans."

" Hector Le Roux, whose studio is at 12 Rue de Navarin, one of the principal artists in Paris, used to live at Rome. There, in his delightful retirement on the Via Quattro Fontane, in a charming apartment now occupied by Charles Caryll Coleman, the studio of which opened on a beautiful garden full of orange and lemon trees, thick with vines, Le Roux painted some of his most important and beautiful pictures, — the 'Tuccia,' which is in the Corcoran Gallery at Washington ; 'The Vestal Fire relighted by a Miracle,' in Mrs. Herriman's gallery at Rome ; the important and remarkable 'Danaïdes,' which was in the last Salon ; etc. Beside these and other valuable art works, the names of which I cannot recall, he also made, during his long residence in Rome, a number of studies, most poetical and happy subjects for future pictures. . . . . Le Roux has been medaled again and again, and decorated for his beautiful works. His paintings, many of them, have been taken by the government, and are in the various museums of France : one is at the Luxembourg, the beautiful 'Funeral at the Columbarium of the House of the Cæsars, Porta Capena, at Rome' ; it was one of the leading pictures in the Salon of 1864. His 'Messalina in the Suburra,' a terrible but wonderfully strong picture, gained one of his medals some years ago ; it is to be at the Universal Exposition next spring ; when Meissonier, who is on the jury, saw its name in the list Le Roux sent in, he remembered it and expressed much satisfaction. Le Roux sent to the jury a list of six names of pictures for the coming Exposition, — all were admitted, — 1. 'An Ancient Serenade' ; 2. 'Summer Triclinium' ; 3. 'Fire of Vesta relighted by a Miracle' ; 4. 'Messalina in the Suburra' ; 5. 'Toilette of Minerva Pollade' ; 6. 'The Danaïdes.' He is preparing for the spring Salon two new pictures, — one is of two young Roman girls of ancient times visiting the tomb of their parents ; the other is more important in subject, and very interesting and poetical in detail. It is 'The Miracle recorded by Pausanias of the Descent of the Statue of Minerva Poliade from Heaven.' . . . . It is represented most poetically. It is before the great city of Athens and its splendid temples existed. The young Greek virgins are assembled together at sunset on the summit of the hill ; beyond is the sea and the Troad, a lovely bit of landscape, with soft sky ; a grove of olive-trees rises on the second plane ; the tender atmosphere of a Greek sunset pervades the picture. On the front plane to the left is the dark statue of the goddess which has descended from heaven ; the firmly planted, archaic feet are just touching the great stone summit on which her famous temple was afterwards erected. This archaic figure is most impressive. The girls are in various attitudes, expressive of their emotions. You see that it is a solemn and awful moment; to them is being revealed a sacred mystery that they are to reveal to humanity. One girl has thrown herself face downwards on the rocky base below the statue ; others are veiling their faces in awe ; one, a noble, dignified young virgin, stands in front of the olive grove, full of courage and reverence ; she announces and proclaims the marvelous miracle : this one is, of course, the future first high-priestess, and the surrounding girls are her sisterhood or band of vestal virgins. This picture is painted in a moderate size, well fitted for a salon or parlor. I trust some American patron of the arts may secure it at the Salon of next spring." — *Paris Letter of Miss ANNE BREWSTER*, October, 1877.

Le Roux, Eugène. (*Fr.*) Born at Paris. Medals, 1864, '73, and '75. Pupil of Picot. At the Salon of 1876 he exhibited " The Letter of Recommendation " ; in 1875, " An Ambulance during the Siege of Paris " ; in 1874, " An Old Amateur." His " New-Born, — Interior of Lower Brittany " (1864) is at the Luxembourg.

Leslie, Charles Robert, R. A. (*Brit.-Am.*) Born in England (1794 – 1859). Taken to America in 1799, he received an ordinary school education in Philadelphia, and was apprenticed to a bookseller in New York. In 1811 he returned to England, and entered the schools of the Royal Academy, studying also under West and Washington Allston. He painted during his early career in London, " Saul and the Witch of Endor," " Anne Page and Slender," " May-Day in the Reign of Elizabeth," and " Sir Roger de Coverley." He was elected an Associate of the Royal Academy in 1821, and Academician in 1825. In 1831 he accepted the appointment of Professor of Drawing at the Military Academy at West Point, but relinquished it the following year, and returned to England. In 1848 he was made Professor of Painting at the Royal Academy, holding the office until 1851. His lectures were subsequently published. Many of Leslie's works are in the Sheepshanks Collection. His "Uncle Toby and Widow Wadman" (R. A., 1831) and "Sancho Panza in the Apartment of the Duchess" (R. A., 1844) are in the Vernon Collection of the National Gallery, London. His "Columbus and the Egg," "Gulliver introduced to the Queen of Brobdignag," "Library at Holland House," "Queen Victoria receiving the Sacrament at her Coronation," "Jennie Deans and Queen Caroline," "Christ and the Disciples at Capernaum," are well known by the medium of engraving. His "Cooke as Richard III.," "Murder of Rutland by Clifford," and others are in the Philadelphia Academy of Fine Arts. James Lenox owns his portrait of Washington Irving.

"The more I learn of art, the more respect I feel for Mr. Leslie's painting as such and for the way in which it brings out the expressional result he requires. Given a certain quantity of oil color to be laid with one touch of pencil, so as to produce at once the subtlest and largest expressional result possible, and there is no man now living who seems to me to come at all near Mr. Leslie, his work being in places equal to Hogarth for decision, and here and there a little lighter and more graceful." — JOHN RUSKIN.

"From this time [1833] Leslie produced a succession of masterly works, — masterly in every respect, perhaps, except their coloring, in which a dull red or burnt sienna tint is too prevalent. This is, however, not the case with the 'Sancho Panza' and other early works. He is seen to great advantage in the Sheepshanks Collection." — WORNUM's *Epochs of Painting.*

"Leslie's first successful attempt was a likeness of Cooke the tragedian, taken at the theater. He soon copied admirably, and became, like most of his fraternity, early occupied with portraits. After teaching drawing for a short time, he resigned the appointment, returned to England, and enjoyed the liberal encouragement which no other country is so well adapted to yield the kind of genius by which he is distinguished. She claims him as her own, hot, although born there, his parents were American, and his first lessons in art were received on this side the water." — TUCKERMAN's *Book of the Artists.*

Leslie, George D., R. A. (*Brit.*) Born in 1835. Son of Charles R. Leslie of the Royal Academy, whose pupil he was. George D. Leslie entered the schools of the Royal Academy in 1854, and sent his first picture, "Hope" (now the property of Lord Houghton), to the British Institution in 1857. In 1859 he sent to the Royal Academy, "Reminiscences of the Ball," "Matilda" (from Dante); in 1865, "The Defence of Lothian House"; in 1867, "The Cousins"; in 1868 (when he was made Associate of the Royal Academy), he exhibited "Home News," "The Empty Sleeve," and "The Boat-House"; in 1870, "Fortunes"; in 1872, "Lavinia" and "An Elopement"; in 1874, "The Nut-Brown Maid"; in 1876, "Roses" and "Violets"; in 1877 (when he became Academician), he contributed "Cowslips" and "The Lass of Richmond Hill," his diploma work; in 1878, "Home, Sweet Home." His "Celia's Arbor" was at Philadelphia in 1876; "Fortunes," "School Revisited," "Pot-pourri," "Lavinia," and "Celia's Arbor" were in Paris in 1878.

"It must be a great delight to Mr. Leslie to see his son George D. Leslie do such good work as this 'Reminiscence of the Ball.' There is not a prettier piece of painting on the walls, and very few half so pretty. . . . . I shall look anxiously for Leslie's work next year, for he seems to have truly the power of composition, and that is the gift of gifts, if it be rightly used. He colors very well already. — RUSKIN'S *Notes on the Pictures of the Year*, 1875.

"George D. Leslie has painted nothing so complicated in combination of figures and landscape as in this picture ['Fortune,' R. A., 1870]. It illustrates both his merits and defects in a conspicuous way. The purity and beauty of the faces, the taste of the dresses, the grace of the figures, and the felicity of the grouping, with the amenity of the landscape, give a charm to it which was widely and directly felt."—TOM TAYLOR *in English Painters of the Present Day*, 1876.

"It would be difficult, as a rule, to find on the walls of any gallery figures more unaffectedly refined and more winning in their attractiveness than those George D. Leslie places on his canvases. . . . . The painter understands thoroughly the sources of a delicate beauty proper to a refined type of English girlhood ; and he has the power, genuinely artistic of its kind, to bring all of the materials of the composition in accord with the dainty spirit that inspires it ; for even the landscape portions of his pictures seem as if painted under the influence of the same graceful feeling and purity of taste, so as to present a perfect harmony between the outside world, and those who for the time at least occupy the scene." — *Art Journal*, June, 1877.

Leslie, Robert C. (*Brit.*) Son of Charles R. Leslie, and younger brother of George D. Leslie, inheriting much of the artistic talent of his family. He devotes himself particularly to marine views, and has had a studio for some years at Southampton, exhibiting frequently at the Royal Academy, at the Dudley Gallery, and elsewhere. Among his later pictures may be noted, "Beachey Head," "Daybreak on the Atlantic," "A Calm off the Foreland," "A Gale," "A Last Shot at the Spanish Armada in the North Sea," etc.

"All that Robert Leslie has executed of this kind [sailor life, shipping, and the sea] has shown a genuine love and pure feeling for Nature, a thorough mastery of the technical elements of his subjects, and a consistency in all parts of his pictures such as in this particular walk of art only exact knowledge can secure. These qualities give a distinctive value and interest to Robert Leslie's pictures, which as yet [1870] have hardly the recognition their merits entitle them to." — TOM TAYLOR, *in English Painters of the Present Day*, 1870.

"'Daybreak on the Atlantic' [R. A., 1877] is a fine and solid example of true and learned modeling of waves, expressing the movement of a ship with rare felicity, noteworthy for just treatment of the atmosphere and broad sober color." — *London Athenæum*, May, 1877.

Lessing, Charles Frederic. (*Ger.*) Born at Wartenberg, Silesia, 1808. Member of the Academy of Berlin. Knight of the Order of Merit. Medal of first class at Paris. Pupil of the Academy of Berlin under Dähling and Rösel. The father of this artist always objected to his being a painter, but when at seventeen years of age he gained the prize of the Academy by his picture of "The Cemetery in Ruins," he met with no more opposition ; and under the influence of Schadow, who had become interested in him, he rapidly advanced. He read the history of Bohemia, and painted "The Sermon of the

Hussites," which gained him honors in Paris and criticisms at home, where the story of Huss excited violent passions. But the artist only replied by still other pictures, such as "Huss before the Council of Constance," "Huss going to the Funeral-Pile" (in New York), "A Hussite Preaching" (in the National Gallery, Berlin), and others of a similar character. Among his historical subjects are, "Luther burning the Bull of the Pope," "Discussion of Luther and Eck at Leipsic," "Pope Pascal II. Prisoner of Henry V.," etc. Of landscapes we may mention, "The Cloister in the Snow," "View taken in the Eifel," "A Wood-Chapel," "Ritterburg," the famous "Oaks of a Thousand Years" (engraved by Steifensand), and many picturesque views, ruins, convents, Gothic châteaux, and wild forest scenes. The Berlin National Gallery has a large number of his works. The "Luther and Eck" is in the gallery at Carlsruhe, and cost £ 2,333. To the Paris Exposition of 1878 he contributed "A Landscape" (belonging to the Gallery of Berlin).

"A painter vigorous, truth-seeking, and naturalistic as Lessing, might reasonably be supposed to find delight in Nature's ways. Lessing, indeed, has been deemed by some persons greater as the painter of landscape than of history. . . . . All the landscapes I have seen by Lessing have been accentuated with predetermined purpose. The fixed and the forcible intent manifest in the artist's historic compositions speaks out scarcely less decisively and intelligibly in his portraiture of inanimate nature, which thus becomes, as it were, vocal under his touch. . . . . Lessing, it will be seen, is a keen observer of character, an accurate student of physiognomy. He delineates human nature with a breadth which pertains to the species, and in a detail that distinguishes the individual. . . . . And this it is that gives to the works of Lessing their pre-eminent reality ; this it is that endows them with strong power of appeal, and brings them in close correspondence with the pronounced and positive spirit of the age. Lessing's pictures are no unsubstantial visions, no feverish dreams, or ecstatic swoonings : they are real as life, true as nature, and manly as the grand historic characters they seek to honor." — J. BEAVINGTON ATKINSON, *Art Journal,* September, 1865.

Leu, August Wilhelm. (*Ger.*) Born in Münster, 1818. Royal Professor and member of the Academy of Berlin. Member of the Academies of Vienna, Amsterdam, and Brussels. Medals at Berlin. Studied at the Düsseldorf Academy under Schirmer. Traveled in Norway, Switzerland, Bavaria, and Italy. At the National Gallery of Berlin is his "View of a Swiss Lake." At Vienna, in 1871, he exhibited "Am Grundelsee"; and at Berlin, in 1876, "Rocca Bruna, near Nice," "A View of Capri," and a "View near Kandersteg." To the Paris Exposition of 1878 he sent "Lake Oeschinen in the Canton of Berne" (belonging to the National Gallery of Berlin).

Leutze, Emmanuel, N. A. (*Ger.-Am.*) Born in Würtemberg, Bavaria (1816 - 1868). Taken as a child by his parents to Philadelphia, he early displayed artistic talents. By the sale of numerous drawings he realized enough to carry him to Europe in 1841, when he went to Düsseldorf, entered the Academy there, and painted his "Columbus before the Council of Salamanca" (which was purchased by the Düsseldorf Art Union). He also painted, during his stay in

Germany, " News from Lexington," " Mrs. Schuyler firing the Wheat-Fields," and similar works of an ideal or historical character. He also studied in Italy, and returned to America in 1859, after which time he made frequent visits to the art centers of Europe. He was made a member of the National Academy in 1860. He painted many pictures taken from French, German, Spanish, as well as American historical subjects. Among the better known of these are, " Columbus in Chains " (exhibited in Brussels, for which he received from the King of the Belgians a silver medal), " Cromwell and his Daughter," " John Knox and Mary Stuart," and " Western Emigration " (which is in the Capitol at Washington). His " Elaine " was in the National Academy in 1867. After his death, in 1868, were exhibited there the " Mother's Visit " (belonging to H. G. Marquand), the " Storming of Teocalli, Mexico," "Settlement of Maryland by Lord Baltimore," the "Iconoclast " (belonging to R. M. Olyphant), and portraits of General Grant, W. Whittredge, Louis Lang, and himself (the last presented to the Academy by John Taylor Johnston). His " Mary Stuart hearing the First Mass at Holyrood after her Return from France " (belonging to John A. Riston) was at the Paris Exposition of 1867. "Henry VIII. and Anne Boleyn " belongs to W. T. Walters of Baltimore, and his " Christmas Mummeries " to Mrs. Abner Mellen.

" Emanuel Leutze is the representative painter of the American branch of the Düsseldorf school, and stands the highest in popular esteem. He manifests some originality of thought, much vigor, overmuch dramatic force, and has abundance of executive skill, but is spasmodic and unequal. *Tours de force* delight him. He has the vicious coloring of the Düsseldorf school in its fullest extent. The rotunda painting in the Capitol of the ' Star of Empire ' is his most ambitious work. This, the well-known ' Washington crossing the Delaware,' the ' Storming of Teocalli, Mexico,' and the portrait of General Burnside, are striking examples of his epic style." — JARVES, *Art Idea.*

" His admirers are fond of him, and his enemies very severe. The character of Leutze was worked out in his pictures with wonderful exactness. He was a hero-worshiper ; he was fond of adventure, and of wild, gleeful fun ; he was more given to vivid sensation than to sentiment or refinement ; he acted out Emerson's words, ' There is hope in extravagance, there is none in routine ' ; he was brave and cordial, and swept on to his end with a rush, like a spring waterfall, happy in freedom, and in haste for the end of its course. All this is in his pictures, and while we love the works of others more, we may gain much pleasure from his." — MRS. C. E. CLEMENT, *Painters, Sculptors, Architects, and Engravers.*

Lévy, Émile. *(Fr.)* Born at Paris, 1826. Chevalier of the Legion of Honor. Studied at l'École des Beaux-Arts under Abel de Pujol and Picot. He gained the grand *prix de Rome* in 1854. In 1855 he sent to the Exposition a picture of " Noah cursing Canaan," which was purchased by the government. His " Death of Orpheus " (1866) is in the Luxembourg. In 1877 he exhibited the " Meta sudans, or the Fountain where the Wrestlers of the Circus made their Ablutions," and a portrait ; in 1876, "The Willow " and " A Bather " ; in 1875, " The Brook," " The Boat, — an Idyl," and a portrait ; in 1874, "Love and Folly " ; in 1873, "The Path, — an Idyl" and "A Child "; in 1872, "The Letter " and "A Young Girl bearing Fruit "; etc. Lévy has executed decorative works in the church of the Trinity, at the Cercle de l'Union artistique, the ceiling of the theater of the Bouffes Parisiens, and in several hotels, etc. At the Salon of 1878 he exhibited "Caligula."

Lévy, Henri Léopold. (*Fr.*) Born at Nancy, 1840. Chevalier of the Legion of Honor. Pupil of Picot, Cabanel, and Fromentin. In 1865 he exhibited " Hecuba finding the Body of Polydorus on the Seashore "; in 1867, "Joash saved from the Massacre of the King's Sons "; in 1869, "Captive Hebrews weeping over the Ruins of Jerusalem "; in 1872, "Herodias"; in 1873, "Christ in the Tomb "; in 1874, "Sarpedon " (in the Luxembourg); etc. His "Christ in the Tomb" was much remarked. In 1875 and '76 he was engaged in decorative paintings, and has sent nothing to the Salons since 1874.

"The color of Henry Lévy is much praised. To our eyes it is not that of a frank and sincere colorist, it is that of a man of taste who wishes to produce some picturesque effects. Without ever reaching great power he turns easily to mannerism. Thus his angel's wings, instead of being white or of one color, are diversely and brilliantly tinged. In the draperies, in the nude bodies, in the backgrounds, even, one feels an incessant preoccupation with the attempt to avoid the commonplace. Moreover, there is a heaviness, a defect in harmony ; the air does not circulate freely about his personages. Lévy is, in point of color, an intelligent pupil and feeble imitator of Delacroix, as he is in design, composition, and style an eclectic pupil of the great masters. He has neither an inspired genius, nor, perhaps, even the temperament of a painter ; he is, nevertheless, one of the most distinguished representatives of that young, romantic renaissance which essays to revive among us the traditions of the grand school."—ERNEST DUVERGIER DE HAURANNE, *Revue des Deux Mondes*, June, 1873.

Lewis, John Frederick, R. A. (*Brit.*) (1805–1876.) Son of F. C. Lewis the engraver, whose pupil he was. He began his art career by a series of animal studies, which he engraved himself. He painted, in 1822, "Deer-Shooting at Becthns, Essex "; in 1826, "Deer-Shooting in Windsor Forest."; and was elected member of the Society of Painters in Water-Colors in 1828. He subsequently spent some years in study in Spain, Italy, Greece, Turkey, and the East, painting his "Spanish Bull-Fight," "Monks preaching at Seville," "Easter-Day at Rome," and other pictures. He returned to England in 1851. In 1855 he was elected President of the Water-Color Society, an office he held for three years, exhibiting at its gallery, in 1856, his "Frank Halt in the Desert of Mount Sinai," called by Ruskin "the climax of water-color drawing." He exhibited at the Royal Gallery, in oil, in 1856, "The Meeting in the Desert "; in 1859 (when he was made Associate of the Royal Academy) he exhibited "Waiting for the Ferry-Boat, — Upper Egypt"; in 1865, "A Turkish School, — Cairo "; in 1866, "The Door of a Café in Cairo " (his diploma work, deposited on his election as an Academician) ; in 1868 he exhibited "An Armenian Lady "; in 1872, "The Prayer of Faith shall save the Sick"; in 1874, "In-Door Gossip" and "Out-Door Gossip, Cairo ";

E

in 1876, " Midday Meal, Cairo " and "On the Banks of the Nile, —
Upper Egypt." He was made an Honorary Member of the Royal
Scottish Academy in 1853.

" Mr. Lewis' ' Frank Halt in the Desert' [R. A., 1863], substantially a reproduction
in oil of his magnificent drawing in the water-color exhibition a few years back, is
wrought out with such subtle truth of design, and colored with a skill so extraordinary,
that one can hardly help wishing these powers devoted to a subject of larger interest.
Here the whole scene is in shadow, yet full of pervading light." — PALGRAVE's *Essays
on Art.*

" If ' The Frank in the Desert of Mount Sinai ' stands the test of time, it will one day
be among the things which men will come to England from far away to see, and will go
back to their homes, saying, ' I have seen it ! ' as people come back now from Venice,
saying, ' I have seen Titian's " Peter Martyr ! "' " — Mrs. TYTLER's *Modern Painters.*

" There cannot be the slightest doubt that in losing Lewis we have lost one of the
most powerful and original of English artists." — *London Athenæum,* September, 1876. ·

" Lewis' style combined all attainable brilliancy with the utmost finish." — *Art
Journal,* October, 1876.

Lewis, Frederick C. (*Brit.*) (1813 – 1875.) Son of F. C.
Lewis, an eminent English engraver, and younger brother of J. F.
Lewis, R. A. He became an artist at a very early age, studying
under Sir Thomas Lawrence. He went to Persia in 1844, through
Asia Minor and to India, where he remained for many years, painting
the ceremonies and customs of the natives, his pictures being frequently engraved. He was a great traveler, and is said to have visited every quarter of the globe.

Lewis, Edmonia. (*Am.*) Born in the State of New York. She
has in her veins Indian as well as African blood. Displaying a natural genius for sculpture, and comparatively untaught, she first exhibited in Boston, about 1865, a portrait bust of Colonel Shaw, which
attracted much attention. This was followed by " The Freedwoman,"
a statue, after the completion of which, in 1867, she went to Rome,
where she has since resided. Very few of her works have been sent
to America. To the Centennial Exhibition she contributed, in marble,
" The Death of Cleopatra." Her " Old Arrow-Maker and his Daughter," " Asleep," and terra-cotta busts of Sumner, Longfellow, John
Brown, and others, are known to the visitors of her studio in Rome,
but to her own country only by photography. Mrs. Laura Curtis
Bullard of New York owns her " Marriage of Hiawatha." The Marquis of Bute bought her " Madonna with the Infant Christ," an altar-
piece.

" Among Miss Lewis' other works are two small groups illustrating Longfellow's poem
of Hiawatha. Her first, ' Hiawatha's Wooing,' ' represents Minnehaha seated, making a
pair of moccasins, and Hiawatha by her side with a world of love and longing in his eyes.'
In the marriage they stand side by side, with clasped hands. In both, the Indian type
of feature is carefully preserved, and every detail of dress, etc., is true to nature ; the
sentiment is equal to the execution. They are charming bits, poetic, simple, and natural, and no happier illustrations of Longfellow's most original poem were ever made than
these by the Indian sculptor." — *Revolution,* April, 1871.

" This was not a beautiful work [' Cleopatra '], but it was a very original and very striking one, and it deserves particular comment, as its ideal was so radically different from those adopted by Story and Gould in their statues of the Egyptian Queen..... The effects of death are represented with such skill as to be absolutely repellent. Apart from all questions of taste, however, the striking qualities of the work are undeniable, and it could only have been produced by a sculptor of very genuine endowments." — *Great American Sculptors.*

Leys, Baron Jean Auguste Henri. (*Belgian.*) Born at Antwerp (1815 – 1869). Made Baron in 1862. Commander of the Order of Léopold. Officer of the Legion of Honor. Member of the Academy of Antwerp. Originally intended for the Church, this artist was so controlled by his love of art that he entered the studio of F. de Braekeleer, his brother-in-law, in 1830, and three years later brought himself into notice by his picture of "The Pillage of Antwerp in 1576." This was followed by "A Fight between the Citizens of Ghent and a Party of Burgundians" and "The Massacre of the Magistrates of Louvain in 1379." In 1837 his "Rich and Poor," exhibited at Antwerp, was bought by the government. "Rembrandt's Studio" was sent to Brussels the same year, and was purchased for a gallery in Ghent. His "Interior of an Inn Yard" (1842) is in the Museum of Frankfort.. The "Renewal of Public Worship in the Antwerp Cathedral after the Disturbances of the Iconoclasts" is in the Brussels Museum. A picture of the same subject (24 by 31) was sold by Mr. Latham, New York, 1878, for $1,600. After 1846 he exhibited nothing of importance until 1851, when "The Fête given to Rubens by the Gunsmiths of Antwerp" showed the change which his manner had undergone. The absurd name of Pre-Raphaelite is perhaps well enough understood to allow it to be used for the sake of conciseness, in order to give an idea of what this newer manner of Leys is. In 1854, which may be called his best period, he exhibited, at Brussels, "La Promenade de Faust," now in the Brussels Museum ; "New Year's Day in Flanders," bought by M. Fould ; and "Les Trentaines de Bartel de Haze." To the English International Exhibition of 1862 he sent "Luther singing in the Streets of Eisenach." Soon after Baron Leys was commissioned to decorate the great hall of the Hotel de Ville of Antwerp, which he did in a series of pictures illustrative of the eventful history of that city. Want of space forbids a description of these works. Baron Leys has sometimes executed smaller subjects. Among his other works are many excellent etchings. His pictures are very numerous, and are scattered all over Europe. Many have been reproduced by some of the various modes of engraving. "The Promenade without the Walls," "New Year's Day in Flanders" (1855), and "Franz Floris going to a Fête given by the Confrères of St. Luke" are among his *chefs-d'œuvre.* He has also made some lithographs. At the Oppenheim sale, Paris, 1877, "Interieur de Luther à Wittenberg" sold for 23,500 francs. At a sale in London, 1876, "Backgammon Players" sold for £903. At a sale in Brussels, 1874, "The Declaration" sold for £1,060. The same work, one month later, at Christie's, brought 1,110 guineas. At the Paris sale, 1868, "Fêtes in Honor of Rubens" sold for £ 964. At the Sale Wittering, Paris, 1876, "The Studio of Rembrandt," important water-color, brought 1,920 francs. At the Plint sale, London, 1862, "Capestro, the Carpenter of Antwerp, preaching in his Wood-Yard" brought £ 850. In the Berlin National Gallery is a "Religious Service in Holland, Seventeenth Century," "Holland Society in the Seventeenth Century," and "Dürer in Antwerp painting Erasmus."

"Leys is not only this year the grand and illusory colorist we all know ; he reveals himself as a thinker and a poet ; his pictures are not, as some critics insinuate, -- with whom *French gray* is the perfection of art, — laborious copies of the mediæval age ; they are surprising and powerful works, created by a deep knowledge of the epochs he would represent. With Leys one entirely lives in the sixteenth or seventeenth century, and these periods he would not have you understand by the materialism of art, such as costumes, furniture, and architecture. . . . . Leys goes much beyond this ; he searches into the very depths of an epoch : he revives its moral and intellectual life, which he knows how to reflect in the physiognomy of his characters." — *A Critique of the Brussels Exposition of 1854.*

"The genius of Baron Leys, however, is of so diversified a character that he can mold it into any form, and adapt it to any purpose, — to the humorous or the pathetic, to the grandeur of history or the incidents of ordinary social life ; and his pencil portrays, with equal truth, vigor, and delicacy, the art of an age long passed away, and that of his own time." — James Dafforne, *Art Journal,* July, 1866.

Lier, Adolf. (*Ger.*) Born in Herrnhut, 1826. Member of the Academies of Munich and Dresden. Medals at Vienna and Berlin. Studied at Dresden Academy and under Richard Zimmermann in Munich. At Paris he was under Jules Dupré. Has traveled in Italy, England, and Scotland. At the National Gallery, Berlin, is "Evening on the Iser." To the Paris Exposition of 1878 he contributed "An Autumn Evening on the Banks of the Iser" (belonging to the National Gallery, Berlin).

"Adolf Lier is inspired by a subtle sympathy with Nature. He has a true feeling for her various aspects. To him she seems to sing the everlasting minor hymn of the ages that sweeps sadly over the sear fields in the plaintive, melancholy days of October, when the birds are flown, the flowers are faded, and the dying year, drawing to its end, symbolizes the brevity of life below." — Benjamin's *Contemporary Art in Europe.*

Lima, Victor Meirelles de. (*Brazilian.*) Of Rio de Janeiro. Medal at Philadelphia, where he exhibited "The Naval Battle of Riachuelo," "The Brazilian Ironclad Fleet passing by Humaita," and "The First Mass in Brazil."

Lindeneher, Édouard. (*Fr.*) Born at Vaugirard (Seine), 1837. At the age of thirteen this artist entered the atelier of Fannière, a "sculptor in gold," and has remained always with this his first and only instructor. In connection with Fannière, as his *collaborateur,* Lindeneher has received several medals. He has designed for various bronzemakers, has sold his models, and his works have appeared with the signatures of his employers, never with his own. Of late, however, he has become more widely known through the vases and other pieces of Haviland faience which he has made ; these are separately modeled by him and never molded, and each one bears his name. The special excellence of the works of Lindeneher is their truthfulness to Nature. She loses nothing, and is never exaggerated, but is reproduced with her own sweet grace by this earnest student and conscientious artist.

Lindenschmit, Wilhelm. (*Ger.*) Born in Munich, 1829. Professor at the Royal Academy of Munich, and member of the Academy of Berlin. Medal at Berlin, 1870. Historical painter. S. G. W. Benjamin says : —

"He is inspired by noble thought and high artistic qualities in rendering character, especially in historic compositions. His scenes in the career of Luther are marked by singular power, and entitle him to rank among the foremost living artists of Germany."

Among his works are, "Ulrich von Hutten" (now at the Museum at Leipsic), several pictures from the life of Luther, "The Foundation of the Order of the Jesuits," and "The Pleasures of the Convent." At the Berlin Exposition in 1876 he exhibited "Martin Luther before Cardinal Cajetan, Augsbourg, 1518," "Martin Luther brought by his Parents to the School of the Gray Friars at Magdebourg," and "An Episode in the Child-Life of Queen Elizabeth, 1536." There was an exhibition of pictures by Munich artists in Boston in April, 1878, where the "Venus" by this artist was much noticed.

"Lindenschmit struggles and struggles, but cannot get out of the dirty brown tone that he has acquired in Belgium into a healthy, free atmosphere. There is an oppressive heaviness in all his figures which seems to rob them of the use of their limbs. They lack life and motion, they all look jaundiced and ill ; red cheeks and a healthy complexion are unknown in Lindenschmit's pictures, yellow and leather-colored faces are seen on young and old. If we compare Lindenschmit's plain, homely, unpretentious manner with Karl Becker's showy costume pictures, we shall see the intrinsic merit of the works of Lindenschmit in spite of their faults of color." — *Zeitschrift für bildende Kunst,* 1876.

Lindholm, B. (*Russian.*) Of Helsingford, Finland. At Philadelphia he exhibited a picture of "A Steamer in Floating Ice," and received a medal. To the Paris Exposition in 1878 he contributed "Pasturage" and "A Road in the Forest."

Linnell, John. (*Brit.*) Born in 1792. He early evinced a taste for art, and when not more than twelve years of age became a pupil of Benjamin West, studying later under Varley in London. In 1807 he sent his first picture to the Royal Academy, and for a period of seventy years he has been a regular contributor to its exhibitions. He began the practice of his art as a miniature and portrait painter, in later years turning his attention to landscapes, in which branch he has won considerable distinction, painting, during his long career, many hundreds of pictures which are in the public and private collections of England. Among the Vernon pictures in the National Gallery are two specimens of Linnell's work, "Wood-Cutters" (men felling timber in Windsor Forest), and "The Windmill," which was at the Royal Academy in 1847. Among his earlier works are, "The

Timber-Wagon," " Eve of the Deluge," " Barley-Harvest," " Under
the Hawthorn," " Christ and the Woman of Samaria," "The Last
Gleam before the Storm," etc. In 1868 he sent to the Royal Acad-
emy, "Crossing the Brook " ; in 1869, " The Lost Sheep " ; in 1870,
" Sleeping for Sorrow " ; in 1871, " Shelter " ; in 1872, " The Ford " ;
in 1873, "The Coming Storm " ; in 1874, " Wood-Cutters " ; in 1875,
" Woods and Forests " ; in 1876, " The Hollow Tree " ; in 1877,
" Autumn " ; in 1878, "The Heath."

" The forest studies of John Linnell are peculiarly elaborate, and in many points
most skillful." — RUSKIN's *Modern Painters.*

Linnell, James Thomas. (*Brit.*) Son of John Linnell, inheriting not a little of his father's talent. He first exhibited at the Royal
Academy, in 1850, "Temptation in the Wilderness," followed, in
1851, by "Job and the Messengers " ; " Mountain-Path," in 1857 ;
"Wheat-Field," in 1858; " Haymakers," in 1862; " South Coast," in
1864; "Moonlight Road," in 1867; "Plowing," in 1868 ; " Reaping,"
in 1870 ; " Moon is Up," in 1871 ; " A Country Road," in 1873 ; the
" Mower whets his Scythe," in 1874 ; " Sunset over the Moors," in
1875 ; "Dartmoor," in 1876 ; "Cherry Blossoms," in 1877.

Linnell, William. (*Brit.*) Son of John Linnell. He possesses
much of the family genius, and has exhibited regularly landscape
pictures in the Royal Academy for some years. In 1861 he sent
"Collecting the Flock, — Evening"; in 1862, "The Gleaner's Return ";
in 1863, " Over the Muir among the Heather "; in 1864, " Banks and
Braes " ; in 1866, " The Sheep from the Goats " ; in 1867, " The
Heights of Abruzzi " ; in 1869, " Peasants on the Mountains on their
Way to Rome " ; in 1871, " Rest by the Way " ; in 1873, " Over the
Heath " ; in 1874, " Through the Barley " ; in 1875, " Hoppers on
the Road " ; in 1877, " The Hay-Field " and " In the Leafy Month of
June " ; in 1878, "The Peasant's Homestead." In 1862 he went to
Italy, spending his winters until 1867 in Rome. His summer home
is in Surrey.

"This *is* a landscape, however, and if it were more lightly painted, we might be very
happy with it [' Hoppers on the Road ']. William Linnell cares no more than his father
for brush dexterity ; but he does no worse now in that part of the business than every
one else. And what a relief it is for any wholesome human sight, after sickening itself
among the blank horrors of dirt, ditch-water, and malaria, which the imitators of the
French schools have begrimed our various exhibition walls with, to find once more a
bit of blue in the sky and a glow of brown in the coppice, and see that ' Hoppers ' in Kent
can enjoy the scarlet and purple like empresses and emperors." — RUSKIN's *Notes of
the Academy.* 1875.

Linton, William. (*Brit.*) Born in Liverpool, towards the end
of the last century. Died, 1876. Brought up to mercantile pursuits
in his native town, he devoted himself to art in his leisure moments,
and finally decided to adopt it as a profession. He settled in London,
and, traveling extensively, he executed many landscapes and pictures of a *genre* character. He exhibited his first work in 1819, " The

Joiner's Shop," followed by "Italy," "Lake Lugano," "Bay of Naples," "Ruins of Pæstum," "Temple of Minerva at Rome," "Venice," "The Tiber," "Lancaster," "Marius at Carthage," "Jerusalem at the Time of the Crucifixion," and others, many of which have been engraved. "The Temple of Pæstum," bequeathed by Mr. Linton to the British people, is in the National Gallery, London.

Linton, William James. (*Brit.*) Born near London, 1812. He studied under G. W. Bonner, an English engraver, and quickly established for himself a reputation as an excellent draughtsman on wood. During his long career he has furnished many fine illustrations for books and periodicals, both in the United States and in Europe. In 1846 and '47 he illustrated "History of Wood-Engraving" for the Illustrated London News ; in 1860, "Works of Deceased British Painters" for the Art Union of London ; in 1869, Holland's "Katrina" ; in 1877, Bryant's "Flood of Years" ; in 1878, "Thanatopsis," etc. Since 1867 he has been a resident of the United States, living for some years in New York ; he finally settled in New Haven, Ct., where he has opened a large engraving establishment. He is a member of the Artists' Annuity Fund of England, a member of the American Society of Painters in Water-Colors, and an Associate of the National Academy of Design, New York. He paints occasionally in watercolors, but his artistic fame will rest upon his exquisite engraving. Mr. Linton is known also as an editor and author. In 1851, with others, he founded the London Leader ; in 1855 was manager of Pen and Pencil, and has contributed to the Nation, Spectator, Westminster Review, etc. In 1865 he published a volume entitled "Claribel and other Poems" ; he is the author of a Life of Thomas Paine. "The Engraver, his Function and Status," by Linton, appeared in Scribner's Monthly, June, 1878.

Mrs. Linton is the writer of a book called "The Lake Country," published in 1864, which was illustrated by her husband, who furnished both the drawings and engravings.

"Messrs. Ticknor & Fields have also published a pretty little juvenile entitled 'The Flower and the Star,' the joint composition of the pen and pencil of Mr. W. J. Linton, the well-known English engraver, which pen and pencil we are tempted to apostrophize in the words of Milton, viz. 'Blest pair of Sireos.' There are six stories in Mr. Linton's little quarto, all original, ... and there are, we should judge, three or four times as many illustrations as there are stories ; and most exquisite they are. In the first place, they suggest the designs of no other artist, American, English, French, or German ; in the second place, they are wonderfully graceful, fantastic, and airy. Mr. Linton's foliage, and, indeed, his scenery generally, is almost beyond our praise, if only for the reason that we are at a loss whether to bestow it on the artist or the engraver." — *Albion.*

"Mr. Linton is known as the best of living engravers, and as an artist of remarkable ability. The illustration of this charming little story will more than sustain his reputation in this respect, and the story itself ['The Flower and the Star'] ought to make him widely known as a writer who understands just how to write for children." — *New York Citizen.*

"There are several wood-engravers of remarkable talent, but none succeed in giving to the wood-block more than was placed upon it by the draughtsman. Their greatest success is attained in leaving the drawing no worse than they found it   More can be done if you happen to have a little real genius, and Mr. Linton is happy in the possession of that quality." — *Pall Mall Gazette.*

Linton, James D. (*Brit.*) Born in London, 1840. He received his art education in St. Martin's School of Art, Longacre, and under Mr. Leigh on Newman street, spending his professional life in his native city. He has been a member of the Institute of Painters in Water-Colors since 1867, contributing regularly to its annual exhibitions. Among his more important works are, "Washing the Beggars' Feet on Maunday Thursday," in 1874; "Lotus-Eaters" and "Off Guard," in 1875; "The Cardinal Minister," in 1876; "Ave Maria," in 1877; "Émigrés," in 1878; and "The Flag of Truce," never exhibited. His "Washing the Beggars' Feet" was at the Philadelphia Exhibition of 1876; "Off Guard," "The Cardinal Minister," and "Ave Maria," at Paris, in 1878.

"In Linton's 'Volumnia' the figures are well arranged, the face of Volumnia revealing much of the fiery nature ascribed to her, whilst that of Virgilia combines sweetness with grief. 'His Eminence the Cardinal' was one of the most important and striking works in the Exhibition of the Institute of Water-Color Painters last year." — *Art Journal,* May, 1877.

Liparini, Ludovico. (*Ital.*) Born at Bologna (1800–1856). Professor in the Academy of Venice, of which he was also a pupil. He traveled in Italy and studied the old masters. His pictures were portraits and historical subjects, and are seen in the galleries of Italy. Among the most important are, the "Death of Bozzaris," the "Last Hours of Marino Faliero," the "Horatii taking the Oath," and a portrait of Pius VII.

Lippincott, William H. (*Am.*) A native of Philadelphia. He has been for some time a resident of Paris, studying under Bonnat. He devotes himself to portraits and pictures of child-life, exhibiting in the National Academy of New York and the Paris Salons. To the latter in 1878 he sent "Lolotte" (belonging to Dr. G. D. Cochran) and a portrait of "Miss Ethel." To the Philadelphia Exhibition of 1876 he sent "The Duck's Breakfast"; to the Paris Exposition, 1878, two portraits; and in the same year to the Society of American Artists in New York and to the Mechanics' Fair, Boston, he contributed "The Little Prince."

Lloyd, Thomas. (*Brit.*) Contemporary English landscape-artist, residing in London. He contributes to the Royal Academy, and to the Society of Painters in Water-Colors, of which he was elected an Associate in 1878. Among his works, in oil, are, "Nearly Home," "An Hundred Years Ago," "A Pastoral," "Evening," etc. In water-colors he has exhibited, "Fast falls the Eventide," "Up the River," "So Tired," "Shade," "Sunshine," and others.

"In the 'Pastoral' [R. A., 1877] the lighting up of the hill beyond is remarkably like nature, and 'Nearly Home' is very faithful to rural circumstances as well as natural fact. . . . This artist is making rapid strides, and bids fair to become one of our great landscape-painters." — *Art Journal,* August, 1877.

Lockhart, W. H. (*Brit.*) Born in Dumfrieshire, 1846. He entered the Trustees Academy in 1860, studying under Robert Scott Lauder. In 1863 he went to Sydney, and in 1867 to Spain, exhibiting in 1868 his first Spanish picture, "The Lovers' Quarrel." He has made frequent visits to Spain, spending some months in 1875 on the island of Majorca, where he painted his "Orange Harvest." He was elected an Associate of the Royal Scottish Academy in 1871, a full Member in 1878, and also in the latter year an Associate of the Society of Painters in Water-Colors. His studio is in Edinburgh. Among his works may be mentioned, "The Muleteers' Halt," "The Queen's Entry into Edinburgh in 1876," "St. Andrews," "A Scene from the Legend of Montrose," "The Interior of Roslyn Chapel," etc. To the Royal Scottish Academy in 1878 he sent "The Bride of Lammermoor," "Gil Blas and the Archbishop of Granada," "Sunset at St. Andrews," etc. ; to the Water-Color Exhibition, London, 1878, "The Trongate, Glasgow," "Summer Palace at the Hague," "The Jackdaw of Rheims," and others.

Loefftz, Ludwig. Munich. Medal at the National Exhibition, Munich. A few years since this artist was a paper-hanger. He has now a school for drawing. He is one of the important men in the rising German school. His color, drawing, and composition are praised by critics familiar with his works. At the Paris Exposition of 1878 he exhibited "A Cardinal," belonging to Mme. de Gradinger, Munich.

Loison, Pierre. (*Fr.*) Born at Mer, 1821. Chevalier of the Legion of Honor. Pupil of David d'Angers. He made his début at the Salon of 1845. His bronze figure of "Victory, — the Day after the Combat" (1869) is at the Luxembourg. The statue of "Clovis" is at the tower of Saint-Germain-l'Auxerrois. A bas-relief of "Agriculture distributing Crowns to the Children of La Beauce and La Sologne" is at the grain-market of Mer. Several statues by Loison are in the churches of the Trinity and of Saint-Ambrose. "Venus" and "Navigation" are at the Tuileries. He has executed many portraits, and a variety of poetical and mythological subjects. At the Salon of 1877 he exhibited "A Canephora offering Fruits"; in 1875, two portrait busts ; etc.

Lombardini, Gaetano. (*Ital.*) Born at St. Arcangelo, in Romagna (1801 - 1869). A devoted student, he gained prizes in every competition. Canova was his master for a time, and gave his approbation to the "Hercules strangling Antæus," by Lombardini. A fine work, a monument with the figure of an aged paralytic, is in the cemetery of Cesena ; a fine figure of Christ, in the same place, is considered by artists as sufficient to give him fame. This sculptor is a brave patriot, and has served his country well.

Long, Edwin, A. R. A. (*Brit.*) He has resided in London for many years, exhibiting regularly at the Royal Academy, of which he was made Associate in 1876. Among his pictures are, "La Posada," in 1864 ; "Lazarilla and the Blind Beggar," in 1870 ; "The Suppliants," in 1872 ; "Babylonian Marriage Market," in 1875 ; "Bethesda," in 1876 ; "An Egyptian Feast," in 1877 ; "The Gods and their Makers" and "Henry Irving as Gloucester," in 1878.

[No response to circular.]

"'The Babylonian Marriage Market' is a picture of great merit, and well deserving purchase by the Anthropological Society. The varieties of character in the heads are rendered with extreme subtlety, while as a mere piece of painting the work is remarkable in the modern school for its absence of affectation. There is no insolently indulged indolence nor vulgarly asserted dexterity. The painting is good throughout and obtrusively powerful." — RUSKIN's *Notes of the Academy*, 1875.

"'The Egyptian Feast' will at once attract attention as the only subject-picture of the year of great importance, and in this the interest is archæological rather than human. The picture which represents the close of a banquet with the guests seated in a semi-circle, while two slaves drag a mummy round to remind them of death, has many fine qualities, and shows much study and improvement in the painter." — *Saturday Review*, May, 1877.

"Mr. Long's treatment of the human form halts midway between two modes of design not consistent. It is too artificial to have the familiar charm proper to a painting of *genre*, and it is not sufficiently select in its choice of gesture, not serious enough in its conception of beauty, to satisfy the requirements. In depicting upon the faces of the assembled guests [in 'An Egyptian Feast'] the varied emotions aroused by the image of death, the painter's invention sinks still further below the demands of his subject. There is variety of feeling, but it is everywhere expressed with too much emphasis ; and the gravity of the few who closely surround the bier is almost mechanically contrasted with the gayety of others removed from its influence in a manner suggestive of well-planned theatric effect." — *Pall Mall Gazette*, May, 1877.

"Of Mr. Long's work, whether in composition or portrait, only one opinion will be held this year, probably, and this will pronounce that the artist, after the slight weakness of last year's work, has put out all his power of drawing and modeling, and has gained greatly in sureness. The extreme refinement in color in 'The Gods and their Makers' is very pleasing ; different tones of flesh are relieved only by darker or lighter blue-greens, except in the case of the negress who wears a red necklace, the only bit of primary color in the picture. This group of Egyptian girls is full of fun and charm ; the background tones are delicately varied. 'Henry Irving as the Duke of Gloucester' is altogether a noble portrait." — *Magazine of Art*, June, 1878.

Longfellow, Ernest W. (*Am.*) Born in Cambridge, Mass., 1845. Son of Henry W. Longfellow. Landscape and portrait painter. His professional life has been spent in Boston, with frequent visits to Europe. He passed the winter of 1865 and '66 in Paris in work and study, and the summers of 1876 and '77 in Villiers-le-Bel under Couture. A number of his works were exhibited and sold in Boston in 1876. His "Coast Scene, Nahant" was at the National Academy in 1871 ; "A View in Essex County, Mass." in 1875. He sent to the Philadelphia Exhibition, in 1876, "Old Mill at Manchester, Mass." J. Duff owns his "Italian Pines in Cannes." His "John and Priscilla," exhibited at Williams & Everett's, Boston, in 1875, attracted much attention. It represents the Puritan youths strolling on the beach, the water rolling its breakers nearly to their feet, and the sun setting brilliantly in the background. It was one of his earlier efforts at figure-painting, a branch of the art to which of late he has more particularly turned his attention. The Art Journal of July, 1877, says : "Ernest Longfellow is one of our rising young artists. It is evident that his special talent lies in landscape art." Very few of his figure-pieces or portraits have as yet been exhibited.

Loop, Henry A., N. A. (*Am.*) Born at Hillsdale, N. Y., 1831. Settled in New York City in 1850, studying for a year with Henry Peters Gray. In 1856 he went to Paris, where he entered the atelier of Couture, remaining six months, and spending, subsequently, a year in study in Rome, Venice, and Florence. He went abroad again in 1867, visiting the Continental art cities and remaining about eighteen months. With these exceptions his professional life has been spent in New York. He was elected a member of the Academy of Design in 1861. He is a member also of the Artists' Fund Society. Among his ideal works are, "Undine," in the National Academy in 1863 ; "Clytie," in 1865 ; "The Improvisatrice" and "Italian Minstrel," in 1869 ; "Lake Maggiore," in 1870 ; "The White Rose," in 1871 ; "Idle Fancies," in 1874 ; "Venice," in 1875 (belonging to John J. Cisco) ; "Aphrodite" (belonging to C. P. Huntington) and "Ænone" (to Oliver Harriman), in 1877 ; "Hermia," "Marina," and a portrait, in 1878.

Loop's "Italian Minstrel" was in the Paris Salon of 1868 ; his "Aphrodite" in the Centennial Exhibition of 1876. Among his portraits are those of J. M. Ward, W. Whittredge, and Dr. Reisig of New York.

"A picture [by H. A. Loop] of 'Undine' standing by the water, whose child she was, is full of varied loveliness, the ethereality of the sprite being finely given by a luminous quality of flesh which makes the delicate, graceful body half transparent, and by a management of the pale guld:n hair with the shrouded light behind it that almost gives one the sensation of a phosphorescent glow. Few pictures of the supernatural exhibited here have ever exceeded this 'Undine' in sweetness of conception or subtlety of management." — *New York Evening Post*, June 1, 1863.

"Loop's full-length portrait of J. P. Townsend [N. A., 1876] is a firmly painted and expressive work. The likeness is admirable, and in spirit and expression it is not excelled by any work in the Exhibition." — *Art Journal*, May, 1876.

Loop, Mrs. Henry A., A. N. A. (*Am.*) Born in New Haven, 1840. She began her art studies under Prof. Louis Bail, in her native city ; later, entered the studio of her husband in New York, and spent two years at work and in study in Rome, Paris, and Venice. Her professional life has been spent in New Haven and New York. She was elected an Associate of the National Academy in 1875, and has for some years been a frequent contributor to its exhibitions. Among the more important of her works are portraits of Professor Larned and Professor Hadley of New Haven ; of Miss Alexander, Miss Harriman, Mrs. Joseph Low, and others in New York ; and ideal figures, entitled "Baby Belle" (owned in Newburg, N. Y.), "Little Runaway" (owned by Mr. St. John of New York), "A Bouquet for Mamma" (in the possession of a lady in Detroit), etc,

"WE have not many better portrait-painters than this lady [Mrs. Loop] in our country. That she had ability was evident in the first picture she exhibited, and from the first she has steadily and solidly improved. . . . . Mrs. Loop's picture is an honest, unpretending work, well drawn, naturally posed, and clearly, solidly colored.   There is not a trace of affectation about it ; the artistic effects are produced in the most straightforward way. The weak point is the eyes, which, to our thinking, want lighting up a little ; they are good in color and expression, but not liquid enough." — C. C., *in New York Tribune,* April 24, 1874.

"Mrs. Loop is certainly the leading portrait-painter among our lady artists.   Indeed, so highly respected is her brush that she has been chosen to furnish pictures of some of our former chief custom-house officers, whose portraits were voted to hang on the walls of their rotunda.   She is vigorous, conscientious, and perceptive." — *Chicago Times,* May 25, 1875.

Loose, Basile de. (*Ger.*) Born at Zeele, 1809. Studied under his father, and at the Antwerp Academy. In 1835 he went to Paris. Settled at Brussels. In the National Gallery at Berlin are his " Scene at an Inn " and " A Family Scene in Holland." At the Leipsic Museum are " A Dance of Children " and " The Lace-Maker."

Lossow, Arnold Hermann. (*Ger.*) Died at Munich (1805 – 1874). This sculptor was one of Schwanthaler's best pupils, and executed much work for Louis I. of Bavaria. His friezes and statues at the Walhalla and Glyptothek are greatly admired.

Lossow, Friedrich. (*Ger.*) Born at Munich (1838 – 1872). Son of the preceding. He was an animal-painter, and there was a vein of humor running through his pictures which was very attractive. Among his works are, " A Hound with her Young," " A House Dog," several pictures with rats, " A Country Scene," etc. His drawing was better than his color. Perhaps his best works are his illustrations for books and publications, which are numerous.

Lough, John Graham. (*Brit.*) Born in the latter part of the eighteenth century. Died, 1876. Son of a small farmer of Northumberland, apprenticed to a stone-mason in his native country, he became an ornamental sculptor and builder at Newcastle. Studied the Elgin marbles in the British Museum, and first exhibited at the Royal Academy, in 1826, " The Death of Turnus," in bas-relief. " Duncan's Horse," a more famous work, appeared in 1832. In 1834 he went to Italy, spending four years. Among his works are, " Night's Swift Dragon," " The Mourners," " Midsummer Night's Dream," and the statue of the Queen (in the Royal Exchange, London), of Prince Albert (at Lloyd's), the Monument to Southey (at Keswick), and a colossal statue of George Stephenson (in bronze, at Newcastle-on-Tyne). His " Milo and Samson " belonged to the first Duke of Wellington.

Louvrier de Lajolais, Jacques-Auguste-Gaston. (*Fr.*) Born at Paris. Chevalier of the Legion of Honor. Pupil of Gleyre and J. Noël. At the Salon of 1876 he exhibited " For a Fête " and " A Difficult Passage."

Low, Will H. (*Am.*) Born in Albany, N. Y., 1853. A protégé of E. D. Palmer the sculptor, from whom he received encouragement and advice. He worked for the illustrated papers in New York from 1871 to '73, when he went to Paris and entered the studio of Gérôme, remaining a few months. Later, he studied with Carolus Duran for four years, returning to America in 1877. He is a member of the Society of American Artists. Among his most important works are, "Windy Weather" (1875), belonging to Arthur Haseltine, London; "Reverie, — Time of the First Empire" (Paris Salon, 1876, and the National Academy, N. Y., 1877), belonging to J. B. Thatcher of Albany; portrait of Mlle. Albani (Paris Salon, 1877), belonging to Robert Higgins of Albany; "Among the Daisies," belonging to Sir Walter Simpson of Edinburgh (at the Paris Exposition of 1878); etc.

Lucas, John. (*Brit.*) Born in London (1807–1874). As a lad, he was apprenticed to an engraver, but devoted his leisure hours to study, and began the practice of his profession in 1829 as a portrait-painter. Many of the most distinguished people of England were among his subjects. Among his better known works have been four pictures of the Prince Consort, several of the Princess Royal, of the Duke of Wellington, King of Hanover, Rogers the poet, Gladstone, and others. He also painted a portrait group of Stephenson, Locke, Brunel, and other eminent engineers in consultation over the Menai Bridge. Some sixty of John Lucas' portraits have been engraved.

Luccardi, Vincenzo. (*Ital.*) Born at Gemona (1811–1876). Knight of the Orders of St. Gregory the Great, and of the Piano. Chevalier of the Legion of Honor. Professor in the Academy of St. Luke and other Italian institutes. Prizes at Florence and Vienna. Nine medals at Venice. Studied at Venice, and settled at Rome. Among his best works are, "Cain," "The Deluge," "Raphael and the Fornarina," "Hagar and Ishmael," "Cleopatra," and "Aïda." At Munich, in 1870, he exhibited a "Venus" and "The Four Seasons."

Lucy, Charles. (*Brit.*) Born near Herford (about 1804–1873). At an early age he went to London to study art, but, leaving for Paris after a short time, entered l'École des Beaux-Arts, studying also under Paul Delaroche. He subsequently became a pupil of the Royal Academy, London. He was a constant exhibitor at the Royal Academy of original historical paintings, besides making many realistic copies of the old masters, residing for upwards of sixteen years near Fontainebleau. In 1860 he sent to the Royal Academy, London, "Lord Saye and Sele arraigned in 1451 before Jack Cade"; in 1863, "The Reconciliation between Gainsborough and Sir Joshua Reynolds"; in 1865, "Garibaldi at the Tomb of Ugo Foscolo"; in 1867, "The Intercepted Embarkation of John Hampden and his Friends"; in 1868, "The Forced Abdication of Marie Stuart at Lochleven Castle"; in 1869, "Noontide Repose" and a portrait of Mr. Gladstone; in 1871, "Charlotte Corday returning to Prison after her Condemnation"; in 1872, "Columbus at the Monastery of La Rabida"; in 1873, "The Parting of Lord William and Lady Russell in 1683."

"Mr. Lucy's 'Reconciliation of Reynolds and Gainsborough,' like other pictures of this thoughtful and conscientious artist, interesting and unaffected in idea, does not aim at richness or relief, — qualities which, however, a painter can rarely afford to dispense with." — PALGRAVE's *Essays on Art.*

"If Mr. Lucy failed to acquire a distinguished name in the roll of painters, it was not for want of perseverance or from the absence of talent, although it might not have been of the highest order. In noticing his exhibited works during many past years we have endeavored to render justice to the merits of his pictures, which seldom or never failed to be popular, as much for the interest attached to the subjects hs selected as for the pleasing and conscientious manner in which they were carried out." — *Art Journal,* July, 1873.

Luminais, Évariste-Vital. (*Fr.*) Born at Nantes, about 1818. Chevalier of the Legion of Honor. Medal at Philadelphia. Pupil of Cogniet. He paints both in oil and in water colors ; and has painted a few portraits and made many sketches. At the Salon of 1877 he exhibited " À toute volée" and " A Prisoner in Flight " (oils), and " The Tame Bull " and " Pirates " (water-colors) ; in 1876, " The Consequences of a Duel in 1625 " ; in 1875, " King Morvan " and " A Flock carried off to the Enemy." " The Reluctant Bather" is in the collection of Mrs. H. E. Maynard of Boston.

"Formerly Luminais affected the contrasts and the play of light and shade on pictu-resque costumes and uneven ground ; at present he seeks rather the movement and ac-tion of the human figure, and places at the service of bold conscientious drawing the prestige of large execution and brilliant color." — J. GRANGEDOR, *Gazette des Beaux-Arts,* July, 1868.

Lundgren, Egron. (*Swede.*) (1816 – 1875.) Received his art education in Paris, where he lived and studied for four years. He painted also during four years in Italy, and for five years in Spain. Was made a Knight of the Order of Gustavus Vasa by the King of Sweden. Settled in London in 1853, and was upon the staff of Lord Clyde in India, where he made many valuable sketches. He was one of the leading members of the Society of Painters in Water-Colors, contrib-uting to their gallery in London, in 1873, " Italian Music," " The Traveling Companions," and " A Child's Head " ; in 1875 (the year of his death), " Rafaela " and " Children Playing."

Lupton, Thomas Goff. (*Brit.*) (1790 – 1873.) He was appren-ticed to a mezzotint engraver at an early age, and during his career has engraved the portraits of many distinguished men after the lead-ing portrait-painters of his day, besides " Sunrise, — Fishing off Mar-gate " and " Eddystone Lighthouse," after Turner, and other important landscapes of eminent artists.

Lynn, Samuel Ferris. (*Brit.*) Native of Ireland. Died, 1876. Studied in Belfast under his brother, an architect, and in the Royal Academy, London. In 1857 he received the silver medal for the best study from life, and in 1859 the Academy gold medal for the best historical composition. Resided in London until 1875, and was a constant exhibitor of portrait and ideal statues, statuettes, and busts. Among these may be mentioned, " Evangeline," " The Death of Procris," "Master Magrath" (the famous hound of Lord Lurgan), "The First Prayer," and portraits of many eminent contemporary Irishmen.

Macallum, Hamilton. (*Brit.*) Born at the Kyles of Bute, 1843. He entered the Royal Academy, London, in 1865, and has a studio in the English metropolis. Among his works are, "Shrimping," "Waiting for the Ebb," "The Kyles of Bute," etc. His "Gathering Seaweed on the West Coast of Scotland" was at the Paris Exposition of 1878.

Macbeth, Norman. (*Brit.*) A native of Aberdeen. Portrait-painter, spending his professional life in Edinburgh, where his work is highly regarded. He has been for some years an Associate of the Royal Scottish Academy. He has executed many presentation portraits of distinguished clergymen, and others, for the public institutions of Scotland. Among his sitters have been Dr. Guthrie, Dr. John Bruck, Dr. Begg, Dr. Cunningham, etc. He exhibits frequently in London. His portrait of Sir John Steell, R. S. A., was at the Royal Academy in 1877, and at the Royal Scottish Academy the following year. He sent a portrait of William Forrest, A. R. S. A., to the Paris Exposition of 1878.

Macbeth, R. W. (*Brit.*) Born in Glasgow, 1848. Son of Norman Macbeth, A. R. S. A., a Scottish portrait-painter. R. W. Macbeth studied in the Royal Academy, and has since practiced his profession in London. He was elected an Associate of the Society of Painters in Water-Colors in 1871, exhibiting there and in the Royal Academy pictures generally *genre* in character, and relating often to modern life. In 1877 he sent to the Royal Academy, "Potato Harvest in the Fens"; in 1878, "Sedge-Cutting in Wicken Fen, Cambridgeshire, — Early Morning" (both in oil). Among his water-color drawings may be mentioned, "Linked Names," "Land at Last," "News," "A Winter's Walk," "Motherly Indulgence," "The Morning Post," "The Ghost Story," "Lady Bountiful," etc. His "Evening Hour" and "Favorite Customer" were at the Glasgow Loan Exhibition of 1878. To the Paris Exposition of 1878 he sent the "Potato Harvest in the Fens" and his "Lincolnshire Gang."

"R. W. Macbeth's 'Potato Harvest in the Fens' maintains its well-earned prestige as one of the principal attractions of the present Academy Exhibition." — *Art Journal*, August, 1877.

"Macbeth's 'Lincolnshire Gang' is powerfully rendered in color, drawing, and composition." — BENJAMIN's *Contemporary Art in Europe.*

Macbeth, James. (*Brit.*) Son of Norman, and brother of R. W. Macbeth. He is a native of Scotland, but has resided for some time in London, exhibiting his paintings, landscapes, figure-pieces, and portraits at the Royal Academy, the Royal Scottish Academy, the Dudley Gallery, and elsewhere. His "Sunny Day in the Highlands" was at the Royal Academy in 1878. To the Paris Exposition, the same year, he sent "Gareloch on the Clyde" and "The Moor at Whistlefield" (in oil), and " Sunday Evening, Chelsea Hospital Gardens " (in water-colors).

MacCallum, Andrew. (*Brit.*) Born in Nottingham, 1828. Studied in the Government School of Art in his native city, and went to London in 1849, when he became a student in the School of Design in Somerset House. He went to Manchester in 1851 as a teacher, and was sent in 1853 to Italy, visiting Milan, Florence, Venice, Naples, etc., selecting examples of all kinds of mural paintings for the South Kensington Museum. He returned to England in 1858, turning his attention to painting and opening a studio in London. He had previously, however, contributed to the Royal Academy several Venetian sketches. In 1868 he exhibited " The Approach of the Mularia, Ancient Rome," followed in other years by " A Moorland Queen " (bought by John Phillip, R. A.), " The Four Seasons," " The Harvest of the Wood," " The Vanguard of the Forest," " Rheingrafenstein, on the Rhine," " Rome from Monti Mario," " A Sand-Drift, Egypt," " Sunrise, Plain of Thebes," " Charlemagne Oak, Forest of Fontainebleau," a series of views near Balmoral (painted for the Queen), etc. An exhibition of thirty-five of his works in London, in 1866, attracted much attention. His " Sultry Eve " was at the Centennial Exhibition at Philadelphia in 1876.

" The power and weakness of contemporary landscape-painters have never been more strikingly exemplified than in the works of MacCallum. Nobody ever drew the strength of a birch-tree or the lightness of a beech with more entire understanding of the nature of the tree, and the giants of the forest were never celebrated by a hand more faithful or laborious. . . . . But, notwithstanding Mr. MacCallum's great power of observation and memory and realization, he has no spiritual power. Not one of his pictures ever affects us when we stand before it or haunts us when we have left it." — HAMERTON, *English Painters of the Present Day.*

" Although Mr. MacCallum is essentially a tree-painter, and revels in the glories of the wood and the forest, he has produced works that prove his labors have not been limited to such subjects ; his sylvan life has been alternated with glacial mountain scenery, with the architecture of Venice and other places, and with the arid deserts of the East. In some of the latter works we see the influence of poetic feeling which is generally absent in his other pictures : here he is real and naturalistic, material and scientific." — JAMES DAFFORNE, *London Art Journal,* December, 1877.

Maccari, Cesare. (*Ital.*) Born at Siena, 1840. Pupil of Luigi Mussini. He gained the *prix de Rome*, and studied in that city. He affects the coloring of the Venetian school. His first important work, " Fabiola," belongs to Dupré of Florence. His " Melody " followed, and is exceedingly beautiful. The " Descent from the Cross " is a grand composition, and shows a masterly handling of light and shade. The frescos on the ceiling of the royal chapel of the Sudario in Rome add greatly to the fame of Maccari. They were a commission from Victor Emmanuel. For the palace of the Quirinal in Rome he executed a fresco of the " Triumph of the Three Graces," and for the chapel of the cemetery at Campo Veramo, Rome, a lunette, " Tobias burying the Dead." At Philadelphia, in 1876, were two of his works (belonging to J. Raymond Claghorn), "Fond Memories" and "Music hath Charms," for which he received a medal.

MacCulloch, Horatio. (*Brit.*) Born in Glasgow (1805 – 1867). Educated in his native city, studying art under John Knox, a well-known landscape-painter. A picture exhibited in Glasgow, in 1828, first brought him into prominent notice. His "View of the Clyde," painted in 1829, attracted some attention in Edinburgh. He was elected an Associate of the Royal Scottish Academy in 1834, and full member in 1838, exhibiting frequently at the gallery until his death. Among the better known of his works, which are still very popular in his native country, are, "A Deer Forest in Skye," "My Heart's in the Highlands," "Old Bridge over the Avon, near Hamilton," "Druidical Stones by Moonlight," and many other views of Scottish scenery.

MacDonald, James Wilson Alexander. (*Am.*) Born at Steubenville, Ohio. He early developed a taste for art, drawing caricatures of some merit while still a school-boy. In 1840 he saw, for the first time, a bust in plaster, that of General Washington, his admiration and study of which led him to resolve to become a sculptor. In 1844 he settled in St. Louis, spending his days in a business house and his nights in the study of art. Here he received encouragement and some instruction from Alfred Waugh, an artist of that city. He made his first bust in 1846, a portrait of his business partner, in clay. Later, he studied anatomy under Professor McDowell. He went to New York in 1849, where he studied one year. In 1854 he executed his first work in marble, a bust of Thomas H. Benton, said to have been the first likeness in marble, cut from life, west of the Mississippi. Later, he made his first ideal work, a bust of Joan of Arc, followed by a full-length figure, called "Italia." In 1865 he settled permanently in New York. Among his busts are those of Charles O'Conor, ordered by the New York Bar and presented to the Supreme Court of the State ; of John Van Buren ; of James T. Brady (posthumous), in the New York Law Library ; and many more. He is the possessor of Houdin's original model of Washington, from which he has made a heroic-sized bust in bronze, repeated several times. His colossal head of Washington Irving is in Prospect Park, Brooklyn ; his colossal bronze statue of Edward Bates, in Forest Park, St. Louis, was unveiled in 1876 ; the statue of Fitz-Greene Halleck, in Central Park, New York, was unveiled in 1877 by President Hayes ; his colossal equestrian statue of Gen. Nathaniel Lyon is now in the bronze foundry (1878). At present he is engaged on the statue of General Custer, a figure eight feet high, said to be his best work, and to be erected at the Military Academy of West Point. He has also at his studio models for busts of William C. Bryant, Peter Cooper, and Thurlow Weed. Mr. MacDonald has also painted portraits and landscapes in oil, and has written analytical criticisms on some of the most important American artists, besides lecturing upon

4 *   F

artistic and scientific subjects, especially those connected with the proportions of the human form and "artistic anatomy."

MacDowell, Patrick, R. A. (*Brit.*)   Born at Belfast (1799 – 1871). In 1811 he went to London with his mother, where he was apprenticed to a coach-builder for some years. About 1815 fortune placed him as a lodger in the house of a French sculptor, where he turned his natural artistic talents to pleasant account, and began his art career by the modeling of small original figures in clay, which met with a ready sale. Later, he modeled portrait busts and ideal figures of a larger size ; the first of the latter to attract attention being Moore's " Loves of the Angels." This was followed by a " Scene from Ovid," " Bacchus and a Satyr," and a " Girl Reading," which was at the Royal Academy in 1837, and subsequently executed in marble. In 1841, when he was elected Associate of the Royal Academy, he exhibited " Girl going to Bathe " ; in 1842, " Girl at Prayer " ; in 1845 (when he was raised to the rank of Academician) he sent " Cupid " ; in 1850, " Virginius and his Daughter " ; in 1851, " Psyche " ; in 1858, " Day-Dreams " ; in 1865, " Eve " ; and " The Young Mother," in 1867. Among the statues executed by Mac-Dowell are Viscount Exmouth at Greenwich Hospital, Earl of Belfast (in bronze) at Belfast, Earl of Chatham in the House of Parliament, and busts of Lord Dufferin and others.

Macdowell, Susan Hannah. (*Am.*)   Born in Philadelphia, 1851. Received her art education in the Pennsylvania Academy of Fine Arts, and under the instruction of Prof. C. Schusselle and Thomas Eakins. Her pictures, which are portraits, composition portraits, and animals, have been exhibited, and are generally owned in Philadelphia, where her professional life so far has been spent.

MacLeay, Kenneth. (*Brit.*)   Died, 1878. A native of the Highlands of Scotland, he was educated in Edinburgh, and spent the greater part of his professional life in that city. He was for many years a member of the Royal Scottish Academy, and at the time of his death a Trustee and Auditor of that Institution. In his early days, and until the introduction of the photograph, he was very successful and very popular in Scotland as a miniature-painter, numbering many of his distinguished countrymen among his subjects. He painted in water-color for the Queen a large series of portraits of the different Highland clansmen in full costume, which attracted much attention when exhibited. To the exhibitions of the Royal Scottish Academy, in late years, he occasionally contributed miniatures and landscapes.

Maclise, Daniel, R. A. (*Brit.*)   Born in Cork, Ireland (1811–1870). Was for a time a bank clerk in his native city, but began painting as a profession in 1827, studying in the Cork School of Art. In 1828 he entered the Royal Academy, winning, in due course, all its medals for proficiency in the different branches. He went to Paris in 1830. He first exhibited at the Royal Academy, in 1832, " Puck

disenchanting Bottom " ; in 1833, " All Hallow Eve " ; in 1834,
" Captain Rock," and in 1835, " The Vow of the Ladies and the Pea-
cock," when he was elected Associate of the Academy. In 1836 he
exhibited " Macbeth and the Witches " ; in 1840, when he was elected
Academician, he painted " Merrie Christmas in the Baron's Hall "
and " Malvolio and the Countess." Besides his *genre* paintings, in
which his subjects were taken from " Gil Blas," the " Vicar of Wakefield," Scott's novels, etc., and in which his success was decided, he
devoted himself to portraiture and historical painting. His " Death
of Nelson at Trafalgar " and " Meeting of Wellington and Blucher at
Waterloo " (the latter 45 feet by 13 feet) hang in the Royal Gallery
of the New Houses of Parliament, and through the medium of engraving are familiar on both sides of the Atlantic. His " Play Scene
from Hamlet " and " Malvolio and the Countess " are in the National
Gallery, London. His " Scene from Midas," one of his earlier works,
belongs to the Queen. He was not a frequent exhibitor at the Royal
Academy in his later years. He sent, however, in 1866, " Here
Nelson fell " and " Dr. Quain " ; in 1867, " A Winter Night's Tale "
and " Othello, Desdemona, and Emilia " ; in 1868, " The Sleep of
Duncan " and " Madeline after Prayer " ; in 1869, " King Cophetua
and the Beggar-Maid " ; and in 1870, " The Earls of Desmond and
Ormond," his last exhibited work. He was Foreign Member of the
Royal Academy of Arts in Stockholm.

" Of Maclise's genius in his chosen art I will venture to say nothing here, but of his fer-
tility of mind and wealth of intellect I may confidently assert that they would have made
him, if he had been so minded, at least as great a writer as he was a painter. . . . . His
was only the common fate of Englishmen, and when the real story of the fresco-paint-
ing of the Houses of Parliament comes to be written, it will be another chapter added
to our national misadventures and reproaches in everything connected with art and its
hapless cultivators." — FORSTER's *Life of Dickens*, Vol. III. Chap. XX.

" *May 21st,* 1835. — Accompanied Mr. Forster to Mr. Maclise's lodgings, — found him a
young, prepossessing, intelligent man, anxious to paint my picture. Saw his large one
of ' Captain Rock,' and several smaller of great merit. Agreed to sit to him. . . . .

" *March 21st,* 1840. — Called on Maclise, and saw again his grand picture of ' Macbeth.'
The figure of Lady Macbeth, which I had not seen before, I thought the ideal of the
character. It is a noble conception. His picture of Olivia I can look at forever ; it is
beauty, moral and physical, personified." — MACREADY's *Diary and Reminiscences*.

" Young Maclise studied not only in his profession in galleries and studios, but for it
in anatomical schools, and even in dissecting-rooms ; and likewise in libraries he made
himself thoroughly acquainted with the history of art and artists. . . . . The artist who
painted ' Malvolio smiling on Olivia' and the ' Banquet Scene in Macbeth' has condescended to lend his talents to the illustration of magazines and annuals." — *Memoirs of
the Countess of Blessington.*

" Maclise was a man of undoubted original genius, and of an earnest and laborious
life. . . . . He is said to have been very far-sighted, and to have prided himself on
drawing remote objects with a clearness impossible to more restricted eyes. His power
as a draughtsman greatly excelled his power as a colorist." — MRS. TYTLER's *Modern
Painters.*

MacNee, Sir Daniel. (*Brit.*) Born near Stirling, 1805. Educated
at the Trustees Academy in Edinburgh under Sir W. Allan. He

turned his attention particularly to portrait-painting, exhibiting regularly at the Royal Scottish Academy and at the Royal Academy in London, having for his subjects many of the most distinguished of his countrymen, among others, Lord Brougham (in the Parliament House, Edinburgh), Viscount Melville, Norman McLeod, Marquis of Lorne, Duke of Buccleuch, Hugh Blair, etc. For many years he was a resident of Glasgow. He is a member of the Royal Scottish Academy, was elected its President in 1876, and was knighted by the Queen the same year.

Macy, W. S. (*Am.*) He has lived in Munich about four years, studying under Velten. To the National Academy, New York, in 1877, he sent "Lake Stanberg," "Early Winter," etc. ; in 1878, "Hurrying up before the Rain " and "At the Ford." To the first Exhibition of the Society of American Artists, in 1878, he contributed "Forest Scene in Bavaria." His "Meadows near Munich " and "Autumn, Royal Park, Munich " were at the Mechanics' Fair Exhibition, Boston, in 1878. To the Paris Salon of 1878 he sent "Near Munich."

[No response to circular.]

Madou, Jean Baptiste. (*Belgian.*) Born at Brussels (1796-1877). Chevalier of the Legion of Honor, and of the Order of Léopold. Member of the Academies of Brussels and Antwerp. Professor of Drawing in the Military School of Brussels. Pupil of François, and the Brussels Academy of Art. In 1814 Madou was compelled to go into business, but in 1818 he resumed his art studies. He was employed by government in making maps, but in 1820, when lithography was introduced into Belgium, he devoted himself to that art, and in the next twenty years executed an immense amount of work in this department : "Picturesque Views in Belgium " (202 plates), "Scenes in the Life of Napoleon " (144 plates), "Souvenirs of Brussels " (12 plates), "Military Costumes," "Scenes of Society," etc. Of course this work was a preparation for his subsequent painting. His subjects are pure *genre*, and are not numerous, which adds to their value. Among them are, "The Sketch," "Jan Steen and his Friends," "The Stirrup Cup," "The Young Squire of the Village," "The Artist's Amusement at an Inn," "The Bandit," etc. At the Oppenheim sale, London, 1864, "La dame à la ferme" brought 260 guineas. At a sale in London, 1874, "Reading the Gazette" sold for £892. At the Latham sale, New York, 1878, "Interior of a Flemish Cabaret" (18 by 23) sold for $ 1,400. Several of his works were sent to the Paris Exposition of 1878.

"He unquestionably stands at the head of the *genre* painters of Belgium ; his works, whether in lithography, in water-colors, or in oils, show a power of composition, a truthfulness, and a delicacy of touch, combined with solidity, that will bear comparison with the best that have come down to us from the old painters of the Dutch and Flemish schools." — *Art Journal*, February, 1866.

Madrazo, Don Frederic Madrazo Y Kunt. (*Span.*) Born at Madrid, according to the catalogue of the Salons. Vapereau says that he was born at Rome, and baptized at St. Peter's. Officer of the Legion of Honor. He received his earliest instructions from his father, José Madrazo, and studied later at Paris under Winterhalter. Madrazo is court painter at Madrid, and in 1835 he established there an artistic Review. Among his historical portraits are those of "Godfrey de Bouillon," the same "when proclaimed King of Jerusalem" (at Versailles), "Marie-Christine in the dress of a Réligieuse at the Bed of Ferdinand VII.," "Queen Isabella," "The Duchess of Medina-Cœli," and others. His portraits of the Spanish aristocracy are far too numerous to mention. He has sometimes exhibited his pictures at the Royal Academy, London. His portrait of Fortuny, who was his son-in-law, was much admired at the Paris Exposition of 1878, where he also exhibited three other fine portraits.

Madrazo, Louis. (*Span.*) Brother of the above, and also a pupil of his father. At the School of Fine Arts of Madrid he took the grand prize in 1848. His "Burial of St. Cecilia," belonging to the Museum of Madrid, received honorable mention at Paris in 1855.

Madrazo, Ricardo. (*Span.*) Pupil of his father. At the Johnston sale, New York, in 1876, "The Interior of Santa Maria at Rome" (23 by 39) sold for $4,600. At the Paris Salon of 1878 he exhibited "A Well near Venice."

Magaud, Dominique Antoine. (*Fr.*) Born at Marseilles, 1817. Two medals at Paris, and numerous others at the Provincial Expositions. Member of the Academy of Marseilles and Director of l'École des Beaux-Arts of that city. Correspondent of the Institute since 1874. Pupil of the Art School of Marseilles and of Léon Cogniet. His works are very numerous, many of them being in the public galleries and edifices of his native city. At the Salon of 1878 he exhibited a picture called "War."

Magni, Pietro. (*Ital.*) Born at Milan (1816–1877). In his death Italy has lost one of her greatest artists. Among his principal works are, "Angelica Bound," "Sappho," "Reading Girl," and a Napoleon I. The monument to Leonardo da Vinci, in the Piazza della Scala, Milan, was erected in 1872, and is a fine work; the Fontane della Nabresina at Trieste is also much admired; his large group of the "Opening of the Suez Canal" is grand; and his latest works, a statue of "Oristides" and an ideal figure called "Complacency," were intended for the Exposition of this year (1878) at Paris; the last was seen there.

Magnus, Eduard. (*Ger.*) Born at Berlin (1799–1872). Member and Professor of the Academy of Berlin. Medal at Paris in 1855. Pupil of Schlesinger. He traveled in France and Italy. His early pictures of the "Return of the Pirate" and "The Blessing of the Grandson" brought him good reputation. At the National Gallery,

Berlin, are the " Return of the Fisherman " and a " Study of Female Heads." His pictures are of *genre* subjects and portraits.

Magrath, William, N. A. (*Am.*) Has occupied a studio in New York for many years. Devotes himself to landscapes and figure-pieces, generally of Irish peasant life. He was an early member of the American Society of Painters in Water-Colors, and was elected Associate of the National Academy in 1874, and Academician in 1876. He exhibited, in 1869, " Irish Peasantry returning from the Fair "; in 1870, " The Road to Kenmair "; in 1871, " The Reveille "; in 1873, " The Empty Flagon "; in 1874, " Reveries " and " Faltering Foot-steps "; in 1876, " Rustic Courtship " (belonging to Robert Gordon) and " Contentment "; in 1877, " Girl Spinning " and " Paddy's Pets "; in 1878, " Adirondack Slopes " and " A Golden Prospect ": all in oils. In water-colors he has exhibited " Out of the Gloom," " The Wilds of Connemara," " No Place like Home," " The Dairy-Maid," " The Fish-erman's Daughter," " Irish Interior,— Girl winding Yarn," " Gathering Kelp," " On the Threshold," etc. To the Exhibition at Philadelphia, in 1876, he sent, in water-colors, " Mussel-Gatherers " (belonging to Robert Gordon), " Nora " (belonging to J. T. Williams), " An Irish Thatched Cottage," and " On the Hillside."
[No response to circular.]

Maignan, Albert. (*Fr.*) Born at Beaumont. Pupil of J. Nöel and Luminais. At Philadelphia he exhibited " Helen at the Foun-tain " and " The Sentinel," and received a medal. At the Paris Salon of 1877 were his " Frederic Barbarossa at the Feet of the Pope " and a portrait of Mme. F. At the Luxembourg is his " Departure of the Norman Fleet for the Conquest of England " (1874). At the Salon of 1878 he exhibited " Louis IX. consoling a Leper " and " The Admiral Carlo Zeno."

Maillet, Jacques Léonard. (*Fr.*) Born at Paris, about 1827. Chevalier of the Legion of Honor, and of the Order of Léopold. Pupil of l' École des Beaux-Arts and of Feuchère and Pradier. When twenty-four years old he went to Rome, having gained the *prix de Rome.* At the Luxembourg are his " Agrippina and Caligula," sent from Rome in 1853; also "Agrippina bearing the Ashes of Germanicus " (1861). His works may be seen at the Louvre, the Tuileries, and several churches of Paris, while his funeral monuments, his graceful figures, and charming groups are in many places. At the Salon of 1877 he exhibited " Cæsar," a plaster group, and a portrait bust in marble; at the Salon of 1876, " Love and a Satyr " (plaster) and " Eury-dice," statuette in terra-cotta; in 1878, terra-cotta statuettes of young women of Syracuse and Corinth.

Maindron, Étienne-Hippolyte. (*Fr.*) Born at Champtoceau, 1801. Chevalier of the Legion of Honor. Pupil of David d'Angers. His " Velléda " of 1839 was placed in the garden of the Luxembourg, and a repetition of it in 1855 was placed in the Gallery of the Luxem-

bourg. " Sainte Geneviève disarming Attila " is in the church of that
saint at Paris (Pantheon). At the Cathedral of Sens are thirty-two
statues and figures, and a colossal " Christ." A bas-relief is at the
Cathedral of Rheims ; a " Saint Gregory of Valois," at the Madeleine ; etc. At the Salon of 1874, the year in which he was decorated,
he exhibited a marble statue called " France Resigned," and in 1878,
two marble busts.

Maisiat, Joanny. (*Fr.*) Born at Lyons. Medals in 1864, '67,
and '72. Pupil of l'École des Beaux-Arts of Lyons. At the Salon of
1877 he exhibited " The Washerwomen of Vignely " and " A Branch
of Plums " ; in 1876, " On the Banks of the Marne " ; in 1875, " A
Basket of Peaches and Raisins," " Red and White Roses," etc. Two
of his pictures are in the Luxembourg.

Makart, Hans. (*Ger.*) Born at Salzbourg, 1840. Professor at
Vienna. Member of the Munich Academy. Medal at Philadelphia.
Studied at Munich, in the school of Piloty. He has been frequently
in Italy, and sent a picture of " Roman Ruins " to the Exposition of
1867 at Paris. At Vienna, where he settled, he has a large studio,
and here commenced his first historical picture, " Catherine Cornaro,"
now at the Berlin National Gallery, for which 50,000 marks was paid
(£2,500). The reputation of this artist dates from about 1868. At
the International Exposition at Munich in 1869, he exhibited " L'Es-
quisse." Among his earlier works are, " The Seven Capital Sins,"
" The Pest at Florence," " The Dream of a Man of Pleasure," and
" Nymphs coming to touch the Lute of a Sleeping Singer." His
" Romeo by the Body of Juliet " is at the Belvedere in Vienna.
Among his other works are, " Leda," " Modern Cupids," " Cleopatra,"
" Entrance of the young Emperor Charles V. into Antwerp," and
" The Gifts of Sea and Earth." A portrait by this artist, belonging
to E. B. Haskell, was exhibited at the Mechanics' Fair, Boston, 1878.
His " Entrance of Charles V. into Antwerp " and two portraits were
seen at the Paris Exposition of 1878.

"Makart is the Richard Wagner (some say Offenbach) of German painting. His reputation dates back but a year, and already he has enthusiastic partisans and detractors.
I have seen four works of his. . . . . It would be presumptuous to attempt to form a
definite judgment of this artist after four works, following each other so nearly, but it is
allowable to seek in these works the elements of which his system and his success are
composed. The ' Nymphs,' of the Schack Gallery, 1866, have taught the public and the
artist himself that he was incapable of drawing or painting grand figures. ' The Sketch,'
of the present Exposition [International Exposition of Munich, 1869], confirms this observation ; more, it extends it to the figures of smaller dimensions. The torsos, the arms,
the legs, are equally incorrect, and as for the hands, the artist has almost spirited them
away in order to conceal his want of anatomic science. These experiences have clearly
shown the author that he cannot succeed in grand painting. He has bravely chosen his
part upon this conviction. Renouncing the manners of the vulgar, he has sought a kind
of *genre* which demands neither a knowledge of drawing nor of painting, and uniquely a
sort of general taste for the association of colors ; and this *genre* he has found. The
' Sketch ' exhibited helps us to put our finger on all the resorts of this knowing and ingenious mechanism which he has imagined. An architectural framing, in the form of a

buffet, closed in three compartments ; a circle of women and a triumphal cortége, the heroines of which form some very picturesque groups ; various emblems, scientific or artistic instruments, utensils of the *ménage*, etc., are painted on the different parts of the buffet, and testify to a remarkable understanding of the laws of decoration. The golden tone on which the figures are shown, the brown tone of the branches and the flowers, and the tone, sometimes red and again white, of the flesh parts, make a marvelous harmony, of a dazzling richness and a musical charm, — the assemblage offers all the poesy of autumn and the falling leaves. Evidently Makart has his palette to himself, and has imitated no one. He has discovered a precious vein. Will he be able to explore it ? Has he stuff enough in him to make fruitful and to ripen the germs of the first attempts, or will he be blinded by his first success, and believe that he has arrived at the end ? . . . . The forms of these heroines who fluctuate between the softness of childhood and the roundness of ripened age, the forbidding expression of the heads, authorize but too well the reproach of immorality which has been addressed to this art. Not only does Makart debase the human body to the rôle of simple ornament, but he accords to it no more importance than to the hangings and the flowers ; more than this, he changes it, and gives it a dull and cadaverous tint to make it set off the golden or purple tones. This painting is then unhealthy in whatever point of view it is put, and it must be condemned, let the skillfulness of the author and his conviction regarding his system be what it may." — EUGÈNE MÜNTZ, *Gazette des Beaux-Arts*, October, 1869.

"Makart reminds us of certain virtuosos who know everything, but cannot command the technique to express themselves. Nevertheless, we must constantly speak of his brilliant endowment ; we appreciate it, but deplore the want of an elementary training, the absence of a strong, comprehensive design. Flowing verses, rich rhymes, make a poem ; what worth, however, has the most charming poem without that more lovely element which Schiller calls the beautiful soul ? Makart's color is brilliant, satisfying, melting ; shall we ever be able to give the same praise to his conception and drawing ?" — EUGEN OBERMAYER, *Zeitschrift für bildende Kunst*, 1871.

"Taken as a whole, and with due acknowledgment of the courage needed for such an attempt, and the talent with which it has been conducted, the picture seems to me a recall of the manner and the artifice, rather than the essence of the style it affects. What was theatric and grandiose in the art of Veronese has passed into the art of Herr Makart, but the simplicity that made the earlier splendor credible has fled. The laborious invention of costume, the genuine charm of color, do not suffice to take from the work its incurable artificiality. The painter has attempted to reproduce there elements of an epoch that cannot survive. He has let go the permanent truth that was in his master, and has been content to invent what Veronese imitated ; and thus the work is, in the true sense of the term, theatric, for it seeks for the kind of illusion that is desired on the stage. . . . . But although the work of Herr Makart seems to me so far in its essence a failure, it nevertheless deserves consideration for the brilliant technical qualities it displays. There are few painters of the present day who have enough daring to handle such vast material, to dispose fearlessly and with proper relation so large a number of figures ; and there are still fewer who possess the skill in execution which renders Herr Makart's picture a surprising, and in some sense, admirable performance." — J. W. COMYNS CARR (*critique* upon " The Nobles of Venice paying Homage to Catherine Cornaro "), *The Portfolio*, February, 1875.

"Herr Makart, by birth Austrian, but trained under Piloty, is imbued with the romance and voluptuousness of Venezia. He is, in fact, the Veronese of Vienna. It is more than doubtful if Paul Veronese had not enthroned ' Venice crowned by Glory,' whether Herr Makart would have ever painted ' Venice doing Homage to Catarina Cornaro,' a grandiose composition, which, when displayed in London, was looked upon less as grave history than as phantasmagoria. The painter, as seen in the great Exhibition of Paris, becomes still more formless and florid when he emblazons the festive ' Entry of Charles V. into Antwerp.' It may be feared that this triumphant artist is hurrying to his fall. No amount of genius can pardon ill drawing, or excuse an execution which from bravura passes into effrontery. Herr Makart is one of those sensuous painters, nowadays becoming numerous in great cities, who, carrying to fruition the desires of luxurious living, decorate their studios up to the high pitch of their pictures. The door opens, and at once it is seen that the former austerity of German manners has given place to the allurements now permitted in the 'Paris of Eastern Europe.' " —J. BEAVINGTON ATKINSON, *The Portfolio,* 1878.

Malchin, Karl Wilhelm Christian. (*Ger.*) Born at Kröpelin, 1838. Pupil of the Art School at Weimar under Professor Hagen. Since 1874 he has traveled considerably, and paints and etches. At the Berlin National Gallery is his "Northern German Landscape with Sheep " (1877).

Mancinelli, Giuseppe. (*Ital.*) Born at Naples (1813–1875). Member of many academies. He received also many honors. He gained the stipend with which to go to Rome at the Academy of Naples. In 1850 he won the position of Professor in the Academy of Naples, in a *concours,* by his cartoon of "Jacob blessing his Children." Among his best works are, "St. Carlo Borromeo," for the church of St. Carlo all' Arena ; a "St. Francesco di Paolo," for Ferdinand II. ; a "Madonna degli Angeli," for the church of Tripoli ; a "Christ in the Garden," for a church at Syracuse ; a "St. Clara," for the Cathedral of Spoleto ; and a "Death of St. Augustine," at Piedigrotta.

Mancini, Antoine. (*Ital.*) Born at Naples. Pupil of Lista and Morelli. At the Paris Salon of 1877 he exhibited "The Little Mountebank"; in 1876, "The Little Scholar," belonging to Landelle. His picture of "Tired Out" brought $ 210, at the Cottier sale, New York, 1878. At the Salon of 1878 he exhibited "The Fête of St. Januarius at Naples." Several of his works were seen at the Paris Exposition of 1878.

Manet, Édouard. (*Fr.*) Born at Paris, 1833. In spite of his love for art, his family were determined that he should not be an artist, and when seventeen he was forced by them to go to Rio Janeiro ; after this voyage he visited Italy and Holland, and finally entered the atelier of Couture, where he remained six years. In 1860 he painted the "Man drinking Absinthe." For several years his works were refused at the Salons. He exhibited his "Breakfast on the Grass" (which Vapereau says "united, pell-mell, nudities and modern costumes ") at the Salon of refused pictures, and at length, in 1867, made an exhibition of his works alone. By this means he was placed before the public, and was discussed and rediscussed most vigorously. M. Émile Zola published an elaborate biography, study, and critique of Manet, and praised him much. The following works are good examples of his style : "The Dead Man," "Child with a Sword," "Olympia," "A Young Lady" (1868), and "The Spanish Ballet." Manet is also an etcher, and has made plates of "La Vierge au lapin," of Titian, "Portrait of Tintoretto," by himself, and "Les petits cavaliers," by Velasquez, three pictures at the Louvre.

" . . . . Manet, the painter-in-chief of ugliness, which in sincere self-delusion he exalts into a worship. It seems to be a fixed principle with him to make the most promising subjects for beauty—as his ' Olympia ' for instance, which motive a Titian or Correggio would have transformed into a masterpiece of æsthetic joy—the combination of all that is disagreeable in painting. . . . . Olympia was naked, but as her flesh was of the hue of green meat, there was nothing corrupting to the public morals in the gross display of her flaccid charms. She was of no mundane type of feature or figure. Her form was coarser, if possible, than a Terra del Fuegian belle's. A negrese stood grinning in the background, and a witch-cat, with her black back up, in the foreground. These accesories gave a grotesque hideousness to the whole. Yet there were indications of talent and a certain spotty force of splashy contrasts of coloring, which might be trained to better work. Manet is one of the eccentricities of modern art, as Whistler is another but better variety, induced by the popular love of the sensational and extravagant." — JARVES, *Art Thoughts.*

" M. Manet, who is well known to American lovers of art as the leader of the new school of painters and the illustrator of Poe's ' Raven,' exhibits this year two pictures, one at the Salon, the other on the street. Take a look first at ' Nana,' rejected by the jury on the ground of indelicacy. It may be seen in a window at Giroux's, on the Boulevard des Capucines. You will probably be surprised when you see it; it is certainly a remarkable work of the master, and it has become one of the incidents of the day. The other picture, exhibited at the Salon, is a portrait, — that of Faure in ' Hamlet.' In it we see the Danish Prince in the presence of the ghost, and, at the same time, the singer himself. In the picture on the Boulevard he shows his appreciation of grace and elegance; in that of the Salon, that he is the strong master of a noble style." — *American Register,* June, 1877.

Mann, J. H. S. (*Brit.*) Contemporary English painter, residing in London. He is a member of the Society of British Artists, exhibiting cabinet pictures, generally of a *genre* character. Among his later works are, "Nina," "Bosom Friends," "The Pet," "A Quiet Cup of Tea," "Eöthen," "Threatening Weather," "Pleased with a Feather," etc.

" The subject by J. H. S. Mann [R. A., 1873] is larger than he habitually paints. It is catalogued without a name, and represents a lady gazing thoughtfully into the far distance of an open country. . . . . It is painted with all the grace that has characterized Mr. Mann's former productions, but the person has more of intelligence, and carries more of personal importance." — *Art Journal,* June, 1873.

Manson, George. (*Brit.*) Born in Edinburgh (1850 – 1876). He was a wood-engraver of some promise, painting also in water and in oil colors. Among his original works may be mentioned, "The Rhymer's Glen," "The High School Wynd, Edinburgh," "A Sark Fisherman," etc.

Marc, Jean-Auguste. (*Fr.*) Born at Metz, 1818. Chevalier of the Legion of Honor. In 1836 this artist taught drawing in the gymnasium of Diekirch. He went then to Paris, and studied at l'École des Beaux-Arts under Delaroche. He painted *genre* and historic subjects and portraits. Marc also made many designs for illustrated publications. On the death of Paulin, founder of "L'Illustration," he became managing director of that journal, and after 1865 wrote the political bulletin.

Marcellin, Jean-Esprit. (*Fr.*) Born at Gap, about 1822. Chevalier of the Legion of Honor. Pupil of Rude. His " Bacchus giving himself up to Sacrifice " (1869) is at the Luxembourg. The works of this sculptor are seen in Marseilles. Many of his subjects are mythological.

Marchal, Charles François. (*Fr.*) Born at Paris (about 1828 – 1877). Three medals at Paris Salons. Pupil of François Dubois and Drölling. This artist took his own life ; he had felt that he was unjustly estimated, his eyesight was much enfeebled, his cares were many and heavy, and his courage failed him. Among his best works were, " An Interior of an Inn on a Fête Day at Bouxviller, Upper Rhine " (1861) and " Springtime " (1866). At the Salon of 1876 he exhibited " The First Step " ; in 1875, " The Prey " ; in 1873, "The Morning " and " The Evening, in Alsace " ; in 1872, " Alsace ! " ; in 1868, "Penelope " (belonging to Mr. Probasco of Cincinnati) and " Phryne "; etc. His " Choral of Luther, Alsace " (1863) and " The Fair of the Servants at Bouxviller, Alsace " (1864) are in the Luxembourg.

" Charles Marchal offers us an example, rare enough, of an amateur who has arrived in a few years to the rank of a true artist. 1 will not recount to you all the circumstances, more or less romantic, which have led him to live by his labor, nor the difficulties of his début, nor the grand resolve which he one day made to dig to the very bottom of Nature in our dear Alsace. This most gay and truly Parisian of all the painters of Paris confined himself for nearly two years to the little industrious village of Bouxviller, in the midst of a new country where the usages and costumes of the good old times are well enough preserved. The peasant-women there wear the embroidered caps, the bodices glistening with spangles, the red or green petticoats, according to their being Protestants or Catholics. The town itself is as picturesque as one could wish, — it seems a place of the Middle Ages, — you see a beautiful example of it in this picture of the ' Fair of the Servants.' Certainly this young artist owes much to the cordiality and hospitality of Alsace, and above all to those good men of Bouxviller who have cared for him as for a son. But it is necessary to say that he has largely paid his debt in revealing to the Paris public the poesy, half Germanic, of this far-off country, and these manners so little known. . . . . There is, in truth, some little thing wanting in order to make this excellent picture a true chef-d'œuvre; the artist lacks almost nothing to make him a grand painter. But what ?. I cannot say. Perhaps a little more air in the picture. Perhaps a' more free and full effect of light. I am afraid to give advice, especially since it would probably be useless. When an artist walks so firmly in the good path, and makes new progress with each effort, it is best, I believe, that he should consult himself. If he has known how to go so far without the counsel of the critics, he has good eight to discern the end, and good legs to take him to it " — EDMOND ABOUT, *Salon of* 1864.

Marchesi, Pompeo. (*Ital.*) (1790–1858.) Professor in the Academy of Milan, and recipient of many honors. This sculptor was a pupil of Canova. He executed many portrait statues and busts of notable men ; among them, twelve of the Marshals of Italy for the Cathedral of Milan, one of Goethe for the library of Frankfort, one of Francis I. of Austria (now at the castle of Vienna), a colossal statue of Charles Emmanuel III. in Novaro, etc.

Marchesi, Salvatore. (*Ital.*) Of Parma. Medal at Philadelphia, where he exhibited " Interior of the Choir of the Cathedral of Parma," which was one of the pictures most worthy of note in the

Italian exhibit. At the Paris Exposition of 1878 was exhibited his "Interior of the Sacristy of the Church of Saint John at Parma," belonging to the Academy of Milan.

Maréchal, Charles-Laurent. (*Fr.*) Born at Metz, about 1800. Officer of the Legion of Honor, and Correspondent of the Institute. Pupil of Regnault. His pictures are of *genre* subjects. He has gained much reputation by pastels, and more by his glass painting, which is in many of the finest churches and cathedrals of France.

Marilhat, Prosper. (*Fr.*) Born at Vertaizon (1810–1847). Pupil of Roqueplan. His earlier essays gave no promise of the talent which he showed later. He was so fortunate as to have the opportunity of going to the East with Baron Hugel, a rich Prussian, and there found his true inspiration. Gautier says, "Marilhat was a Syrian Arab, he must have had in his veins some blood of the Saracens whom Charles Martel did not kill." Marilhat was invited by his friend to go to the East Indies, but he preferred to remain in Egypt, and passed some time at Alexandria, Cairo, Rosetta, and their environs. He painted a portrait of the Pasha ; he painted other portraits for 300 francs each, in order to support himself. He also decorated a common theater at Alexandria, but whenever he could he made sketches of the country, its environs, costumes, etc. After his return to Paris he sent to the Salons, "Esbekieh Square," "The Tomb of the Sheik Abou-Mandour," "The Valley of the Tombs at Thebes," "The Garden of the Mosque," and "The Ruins of Baalbec." To the Salon of 1844 Marilhat sent eight pictures. Gautier says, that if the expression may be allowed, this exhibition was to him the Song of the Swan, and that these works were eight diamonds. Among them were, "A Souvenir of the Banks of the Nile," "A Village near Rosetta," "An Egyptian City by Twilight," "View near Tripoli," "A Café on a Road in Syria," etc.

The first of these is his *chef-d'œuvre.* He felt that he merited more attention from this Salon than he received, — he was discouraged ; he fell into a state from which death, even at his early age, was a happy deliverance ; and so passed away, leaving two or three hundred pictures in a more or less advanced state. Some of his sketches were very beautiful. M. Camille Marcelle has, at his house at Oisème, a short distance from Chartres, "The Ruins of Baalbec" and three studies. At the Wertheimber sale at Paris (1861), "The Entrance to Jerusalem" (55 by 84 centimeters) sold for 16,000 francs. At the Dubois sale, Paris (1860), "The Passage of the Ford" sold for 7,050 francs. At the Prevost sale, Paris, "A Bazaar near Jerusalem" sold for £640, and "A Turkish Dance near the Bosphorus" for £266. At the Oppenheim sale, Paris, 1877, "Ruins near Cairo" sold for 29,000 francs.

"One of the glories of Marilhat was that he preserved his originality in presence of Decamps. The talents of these two men are parallel lines, it is true, but they do not touch each other; the more fruitful fancy of the one is balanced by the character in the works of the other. If the color of Decamps is more phosphorescent, the drawing of Marilhat is the more elegant. The execution, excellent with both, excels in fineness in the painter who was carried away so young to his glory, and to the long future which should await him." — THÉOPHILE GAUTIER, *Revue des Deux Mondes,* July, 1848.

"Decamps had painted before Marilhat these countries and these figures, and he had impressed on all a strange character and a fierce style, an air of primitive savageness. Marilhat sees them with calmer eyes; he finds in these figures a beauty more human, and perhaps more true. He throws a less oppressive light over his pictures. Regarding this nature on its laughing and magnificent side, he tempers the violence of it, and makes its high colors less pronounced. Marilhat prefers to show us the Happy Arabia." — CHARLES BLANC.

Maris, Jacques. (*Belgian.*) Born at The Hague. Pupil of E. Hébert. At the Paris Salon of 1877 he exhibited "The Plow" and "Baby and the Kitten"; in 1874, "A View of Amsterdam." His "Seaweed-Gatherers" brought $ 1,250 at the Cottier sale, New York, 1878. His "View in Holland" (belonging to B. Schlesinger) was exhibited at the Mechanics' Fair, Boston, in 1878. To the Paris Exposition, same year, he sent "On the Beach" and "A Dutch Landscape."

Maris, Matthias. (*Belgian.*) Born at The Hague. Lives in London. Mr. Cottier has brought the pictures of this artist to America. One of them was called "Where Shadowy Trees their Twilight make."

Marks, Henry Stacy, A. R. A. (*Brit.*) Born in London, 1829. He was a pupil of the Royal Academy in 1851. In 1852, with Calderon, he went to Paris, where he entered the atelier of Picot, becoming later a pupil of l'École des Beaux-Arts. In 1853 he returned to England, and exhibited his first picture at the Royal Academy the same year, entitled "Dogberry." In 1854 he sent "Christopher Sly"; in 1855, "Slender's Courtship"; in 1857, "Bottom as Pyramus"; in 1858, "A Day's Earnings"; in 1859, "Dogberry's Charge to the Watch" (which attracted much attention); in 1860, "The Sexton's Sermon"; in 1861, "The Franciscan Sculptor"; in 1862, "The Jester's Text"; in 1863, "How Shakspere studied"; in 1864, "Doctors Differ"; in 1866, "My Lady's Page in Disgrace"; in 1867, "Falstaff's Own"; in 1868, "Experimental Gunnery in the Middle Ages"; in 1869, "The Minstrel's Gallery"; in 1871 (when he was elected an Associate of the Royal Academy), "The Book-Worm"; in 1872, "Waiting for the Procession"; in 1873, "A Peep of the Avon"; in 1874, "The Latest Fashion"; in 1875, "Jolly Post-Boys" and "A Merrie Jester"; in 1876, "The Apothecary"; in 1877, "A Bit of Blue" and "The Spider and the Fly"; in 1878, "Convocation." He is a member of the Society of Painters in Water-Colors. Among Marks' other pictures, exhibited elsewhere, are, "Jack O'Lantern," "Orpheus," "May-Day in the Olden Time," "The Tinker," "The Princess and the Pelican," and "The Missal Painter." To Philadelphia, in 1876, he sent "The Ornithologist" and "The Three Jolly Post-Boys"; to

Paris, in 1878, "The Apothecary" and "St. Francis and the Birds" (in oil), and "The Princess and the Pelican" (in water-colors).

"Mr. Marks heads the list with a lively and amusing scene of 'The Beggars coming to Town' [R. A. 1865], the best composed and painted work which we remember from his pencil. The humors of the ragged troupe are carefully discriminated." — PALGRAVE's *Essays on Art.*

"The pictorial style of Mr. Marks is expressly mediæval. What middle-age sculptors did in stone, the painter does on canvas. The sly humor, the caustic satire, expended on cathedral stalls in centuries past, this artist now revives on the walls of the Royal Academy." — J. B. ATKINSON, *English Painters of the Present Day.*

"It has been said in the columns of our journal that Mr. Marks can never put brush to canvas without provoking laughter, and yet after a quaint fashion he preserves a certain style of dignity. It is this dignity, mediæval as it generally is in expression, which gives the true value to his works ; one can smile at the artist's humor while acknowledging and respecting the talent and patient labor in which, so to speak, it is clothed, or, in other words, by which it is exemplified." — *Art Journal,* December, 1876.

" 'A Merrie Jest ' is very characteristic of this painter's special gifts. The difficulty of so subtle a rendering as this of the half-checked yet extreme mirth of persons naturally humorous can only be judged of by considering how often aspects of laughter are attempted in pictures and how rarely we feel ourselves inclined to join in the merriment. The piece of accessory landscape is very unaffected and good, and the painting throughout of good standard modern quality." — RUSKIN's *Notes of the Academy,* 1875.

Marochetti, Baron Charles. (*Ital.*) Born at Turin of parents who were naturalized citizens of France (1805 - 1868). Chevalier of the Legion of Honor and Grand Officer of the Order of Saints Maurice and Lazarus. Pupil of Bosio. His "Young Girl playing with a Dog" (1827) won his first medal. His *chef-d'œuvre* is a statue of "Emmanuel Philibert," which he presented to the capital of Sardinia. Among his works are, a bas-relief on the Arc de Triomphe, the Tomb of Bellini, the high altar of the Madeleine, and many other works in public places in France. After the Revolution of 1848 he went to England, where he made the colossal "Richard Cœur de Lion," which adorned the entrance to the Crystal Palace, and was cast in bronze by national subscription ; an equestrian statue of the Queen for the city of Glasgow ; a granite obelisk erected to the memory of the soldiers who fell in the Crimean War ; various ideal subjects, and many portraits, among which was that of Prince Albert. In the country of his adoption he found many powerful friends, and received numerous commissions for both public and private works.

Marshall, Charles. (*Brit.*) Born in London, 1806. Like Stanfield, Bough, and other prominent artists, he began his professional career as a scene-painter, working in that capacity in London for many years. He was articled as a lad to Marinari, the Italian scenic-artist of Drury Lane Theater. He was at the Covent Garden Theater while under the management of Mr. Macready, and at the Haymarket Theater when the same actor first produced Bulwer's "Money." He first introduced the lime light for the illustration of dramatic tableaux, and in his long experience has been associated in the production of many remarkable stage effects in the British metropolis. He illus-

trated by a diorama the interior view of the coronation of William
IV. in Westminster Abbey; assisted at the decoration of the same cathedral at the time of the coronation of Victoria; painted moving
panoramas of the "Naval Victories of Great Britain," "The Battles
of Napoleon I.," "Overland Route to India" (a Christmas pantomime
written by Douglas Jerrold), "Tour of Europe," "The Crimean Campaign," "The Great Gold Fields," etc. He has now retired from
scenographic work, devoting himself to landscape-painting, depicting
chiefly scenes of North Wales, Snowden, etc., also views in War-
wickshire, Derbyshire, Devonshire, and Hampshire. He studied oil-
painting under John Wilson, and when eighteen years of age received
the gold Isis Medal of the Society of Arts for a picture in oil. 'A view
of the Glyddye range of mountains, painted for the Lady Marion
Alford, is now at Ashridge, the seat of Earl Brownlow. His "Evening Lights" was at the Royal Academy in 1878. Mr. Marshall has
contributed to various publications, including Henshall's "Vicinity of
London," "The Gallery of British Artists," etc.

"On a certain occasion when Macready brought out 'The Tempest,' I remember
Leigh Hunt standing up in the box, involuntarily, and murmuring, with tears of rapture
in his eyes, 'O, it is too beautiful!' at the moment the curtain drew up and presented
the seashore of the Enchanted Isle, with the long waves of the tide slowly moving down
towards the spectators, and then bristling into sparkling foam and running onwards in
broad silver ridges and ripples over the yellow sands. . . . . On another occasion, when
Macready brought out 'As You Like It,' the Forest of Arden, where the romantic Duke
had taken up his abode, was represented at his rustic palace, with an entire covering of
tangled boughs and foliage high overhead, among the leaves of which, with their delicate
tints, peeps of sky, and glancing green lights, there was a constant moving and fluttering
as of soft winds and small birds, whose sweet warbling fitfully blended with the subdued
stralus of the orchestra below."— R. H. HORNE, *The Burlesque and the Beautiful,*
Contemporary Review, October, 1871.

Marshall, William C., R. A. (*Brit.*) Born in Edinburgh, 1813.
Went to London at an early age, studying sculpture under Baily and
Chantrey. He first exhibited at the Royal Academy in 1835. The
next year he went to the Continent, spending some time in work and
study at Rome. He opened a studio in London in 1839, and was
elected a member of the Royal Academy in 1852. In 1857 he received a prize for designs for the National Monument to the Duke of
Wellington, to be placed in St. Paul's, London. He executed the
statues of Somers and Clarendon in the Houses of Parliament, of
Sir Robert Peel at Manchester, of Jenner in Trafalgar Square, etc.
Among his ideal works may be mentioned, "The Broken Pitcher," in
1842; "The Dancing-Girl Reposing" (which won the Art Union
Prize), "Fresh from the Bath," "The Carrier-Pigeon," "Jael," in
1867; "Psyche," in 1868; "The Christian Martyr," in 1871; "Ruth,"
in 1872; "The Old Story" and "The New Story" (in terra-cotta), in
1874; "Convalescence," in 1875; "Pygmalion's Statue," in 1876; "The
Prodigal Son," in 1877; "Early Troubles" and "Whispering Vows to
Pan," in 1878.

Marshall, Robert Angelo Kittermaster. (*Brit.*) Born in 1849. Studied under his father, Charles Marshall. Landscape-painter. Member of the Langham Sketching Club, elected in 1872, and of the Artist and Amateur Conversazione Society, elected in 1876. He has spent his professional life in London, exhibiting at the Royal Academy, and elsewhere in the metropolis and in the Provinces. Among his works are, "Looking towards Arthog," "In the late Summer-Time, Hants," "A Shallow, Weedy River, Hants," "Sultry Autumn, Sussex."

Marshall, Thomas W. (*Am.*) (1850 – 1874.) A young landscape and *genre* painter of much promise. Comparatively self-educated as an artist. He exhibited at the National Academy, in 1871, "Near Bellows Falls"; in 1873, "An Interior at Barbison, France"; in 1874, "Late Afternoon in the Forest, Keene Flats."

Marstrand, William Nicolas. (*Dane.*) Born at Copenhagen (1810 – 1873). He spent some time in Germany and Italy, and on his return to his own country, was made Professor and then Director of the Academy of Beaux-Arts, at Copenhagen. Marstrand became very celebrated in Denmark by his portraits and *genre* pictures. He sent works to Paris, where his color was not admired, but seemed false and exaggerated. Several works by this artist were exhibited at Paris in 1878.

Martin, Homer D., N. A. (*Am.*) Native of Albany, N. Y. With the exception of a few weeks' study under William Hart, early in his career, he is entirely self-taught as an artist. For many years he has had a studio in New York. He is a member of the Artists' Fund Society of that city, of the Society of American Artists, and of the National Academy, of which he was elected Associate in 1868 and Academician in 1875. He has been successful as a landscape-painter. Among his works are, "An Equinoctial Day" (belonging to Dr. F. N. Otis), "Brook in the Woods" (belonging to Dr. Mosher), "The Footpath" and "In the Adirondacks" (to John Middleton), "Spring Morning" (to Montgomery Schuyler), "Morning on the Lake," "A Cloudy Day," "Hemlock Woods," "The Thames at Richmond," "Idling," etc. His "Adirondacks" (belonging to the Century Club) was at the Philadelphia Exposition of 1876. During the summer of 1878 he made a series of sketches of the homes of American Poets for Scribner's Monthly.

"Homer Martin is seen in a tenderly and originally treated 'Evening on the Saranac' [Artists' Fund, 1878], with almost gorgeous radiance streaming through and athwart the river ; a genial, vivacious, winning representation, not destitute of truest poetry." — *New York Evening Post*, January 15, 1878.

"'Sand-Dunes on Lake Ontario,' by Homer Martin [Society of American Artists, 1878], is worthy of a place conceived by Dante in his saddest and most lonely hours. A gray sky and an atmosphere loaded with dust envelop some stricken, sear trees, whose torn and shattered limbs are half lost in drifts of white sand. . . . . This painting haunts one like a melancholy dream, and we wonder what sad mood it was in the artist that could have clothed itself in a scene so dreary and hopeless as this. As a purely 'impressionist' picture this takes its place with the dreamy distances of Corot or the 'Silver Nocturnes' of Whistler." — *Art Journal*, April, 1878.

Martineau, Robert B. (*Brit.*) Born in London (1826–1869). Educated at the University of London. He was for four years in the office of a lawyer. In 1846 he turned his attention to art, entered the Royal Academy in 1848, obtaining a medal in 1851. Later he was for a short time a pupil of Holman Hunt. He exhibited for the first time at the Royal Academy, in 1852, " Kit's Writing-Lesson " ; in 1855, " Katherine and Petruchio " ; in 1856, " The Lesson " ; in 1861, " The Allies " ; in 1863, " The Last Chapter " ; in 1866, " The Frog Prince." He sent to the International Exhibition of 1862, " The Last Days of the Old Home," which is perhaps his most important picture, and which attracted much attention. It has since been engraved.

" Mr. Martineau's single picture, a girl, who has knelt down, while she finishes the last chapter [R. A. 1863] of some absorbing book, is one of the most satisfactory pieces of design and execution on the walls ; what we rather miss in it is the sentiment of beauty. Besides the expression of the young lady's face, the skillful gradation of the chiaroscuro as the room recedes from the light, and the skill with which the cool colors have been harmoniously carried into the center of the piece by aid of the cover of the book, deserve especial notice." — PALGRAVE'e *Essays on Art.*

Martinet, Achille-Louis. (*Fr.*) Born at Paris, 1806. Member of the Institute. Officer of the Legion of Honor and Chevalier of the Order of Léopold. Pupil of Heim and Forster. Most of the plates of this celebrated engraver are after the works of the older masters ; a few, however, are from those of the artists of this century. Among these last are the " Charles I." and " Mary in the Desert," after Delaroche ; " The Last Moments of Count Egmont " and " Counts Egmont and Horn," after Gallait ; " The Adulteress," after Signol ; " Tintoretto by the Couch of his Daughter," after Cogniet ; etc.

Marzaroli, Cristoforo. (*Ital.*) Born near Parma (1837–1871). As a boy he attracted much attention by his small plaster figures. He studied under Ferrarini at Parma, and there modeled his " St. Sebastian Bound," which brought him into notice. His statue of Parmigianino is in the Gallery of Parma. By this last work he gained the right to go to Rome, where he modeled his " Nostalgia," or " Home-Sickness." In 1870 he gained the first prize at the National Artistic Exposition. He made a statue of Romagnosi for Piacenza.

Masini, Girolamo. (*Ital.*) Born at Florence, 1840. Professor of Sculpture in Rome. Pupil of Costoli. He won the *prix de Rome* at Florence, and, going there to continue his studies, has remained. His first work was " Cola di Rienzi," which had much merit. His statue of Fabiola has gained him several medals, and is worthy all the praise it has received. Among his other works are a statue of " Cleopatra," one of " Hagar," and one of " Adelaide Cairoli," erected at Gropello.

Mason, George H., A. R. A. (*Brit.*) Born in Staffordshire. Died, 1872. He intended to study for the medical profession, but became an artist while still a young man, studying in Rome, and painting there his " Plowing in the Salt-Marshes of the Campagna," and other pictures. In 1862 he sent to the Royal Academy, London, " Mist on the Moors " ; in 1863, " Catch " ; in 1864, " Return from Plowing " ; in 1865, " The Geese " and " The Gander " ; in 1866, " Yarrow " and " The Young Anglers " ; in 1867, " Evening, Matlock " ; in 1868, " Netley Moor." In 1869 (when he was elected Associate of the Royal Academy) he contributed " Only a Shower " ; in 1870, " Landscape, Derbyshire " ; in 1871, " Blackberry-Gathering " and " The Milkmaid " ; in 1872, " Harvest Moon." Two hundred of his pictures, collected after his death, were exhibited in London in 1873.

"The charm of these pictures does not lie in the realism with which he has painted the scenes, although, according to the Spectator, he has given in them the life of the midlands with a truthfulness which even George Eliot has not exceeded in her writings, but in the idealism that he has put into his fields and commons and country roads, with their peculiar groups, that renders them, while perfectly true, perfectly idyllic." — MRS. TYTLER's *Modern Painters.*

" The colors are uncommonly tender and bright ; the grays are managed with a skill which all who have handled a brush will envy, and every line in the little work [' Catch '] shows that fresh originality of invention or that first-hand recurrence to Nature, which gives an inimitable air of masterliness to landscape. The children and horses, although on a small scale, are studied with a truth and feeling worthy of the fine ' Landscape of the Campagna,' by which Mason won for himself distinction at the International Exhibition." — PALGRAVE's *Essays on Art.*

" Mr. Mason's sources of inspiration have been very humble, but his impersonations are carried out with a refinement above their presumed position. He sets the grammar of Art at defiance in composition, and whether he may or may not have looked at the conceptions embodied on antique vases, we are reminded here and there of the spirit of them. The spirit of Mr. Mason's manner may be signalized as that of the ' Harvest Moon,' and in studying that really admirable picture we are impressed with the amount of learning shown there." — *Art Journal,* March, 1873.

Massaloff, Nicolas. (*Russian.*) Born at Moscow, 1846. Member of the Academy of St. Petersburg. Medal at the Salon of 1873. The father of this engraver, a distinguished connoisseur and collector of works of art, gave his son every advantage and encouragement in his artistic pursuits. He studied at Moscow, then at Dresden under Kriebel, and lastly at Paris under Flameng. He then returned to Russia, and commenced a series of engravings after the masterpieces in the Hermitage at St. Petersburg. He has published sixty plates as the result of this undertaking. Although at first considered an amateur, Massaloff is now recognized as a true artist.

Matejko, Jean Aloysius. (*Pole.*) Born at Cracow, 1838. Chevalier of the Legion of Honor. Studied in Cracow, Munich, and Vienna. He occupies the first rank among modern painters of Polish history. In 1874 he exhibited, at the Paris Salon, " Étienne Bathori, King of Poland, before Pskow, 1582 " ; in 1870, " The Union of Lublin, 1569 " ; in 1865, " The Sermon of Pierre Skarga " ;

etc. In 1875 he exhibited, at Cracow, " The Placing of the Bells in the Cathedral of Cracow in 1521, in Presence of King Sigismond and his Court." He published in 1860 twelve illustrations of Polish costume. Charles Yriarte says : —

"There is in the works of Matejko a vignette appearance which paralyzes the effect which his well-ordered compositions should have. His atmosphere is always violet-colored."

" Matejko, who is especially consecrated to retrace the grand episodes of the history of Poland, has a talent of a singular sort, which enters into no category of the French school. By a certain romantic boldness he reminds us vaguely of Delacroix ; by a certain ugly sincerity he approaches Robert-Fleury ; by a certain brutal realism he sometimes recalls Hogarth ; by a certain systematic barbarity he borders upon Gustave Doré, and the humorous pictures of Vibert, all brought together in enormous canvases, fifteen or twenty feet long, encumbered with people in divers costumes, full of bizarre details, spotted with brilliant colors, which are piled one on the other so that the air and the light cannot play between them. At first the eye suffers from this tumult, then one discovers an original composition, great firmness of drawing, energetic and free attitudes, and figures of surprising rudeness." — ERNEST DUVERGIER DE HAURANNE, *Revue des Deux Mondes,* June. 1874.

Mathieu, Lambert Joseph. (*Belgian.*) Born at Bure (1804 – 1861). Knight of the Order of Léopold. Pupil of Van Bree. A painter of historical, scriptural, and *genre* subjects. Director of the Academy of Louvain. Some of his best works are in the Museums of Louvain and Brussels.

Matout, Louis. (*Fr.*) Born at Charleville, 1813. Chevalier of the Legion of Honor. Pupil of l'École des Beaux-Arts. The principal works of this artist have been cartoons for decorative paintings. Among his easel-pictures are, " A Woman of Boghari killed by a Lion " (1855), at the Luxembourg ; " St. James the Great baptizing the Young Scribe," " Florentine Landscape," " Venus Pandemos," and " Marriage of Bacchus and Ariadne."

Matteson, Tompkins H., A. N. A. (*Am.*) Born in Madison County, N. Y., 1813. As a boy he was an enthusiastic art student, following his profession under many difficulties. He entered the National Academy, and painted portraits in the city and state of New York for some years. His " Spirit of '76," purchased by the American Art Union, first brought him into notice as an artist. Among his early works are his " First Sabbath of the Pilgrims," " Examination of a Witch," " Perils of the Early Colonists," " Eliot preaching to the Indians," " First Sacrament on the American Shores," " Rip Van Winkle's Return from the Mountains," " Rustic Courtship," " First Ride," " Morning Meal," and his portrait of Mayor Havermeyer, in the City Hall, New York. He lived in New York from 1840 to '51, when he removed to Sherbourne, N. Y. Mr. Matteson has been for many years an Associate of the National Academy, but his pictures have not been seen on its walls since 1869, when he exhibited " At the Stile " and " Foddering Cattle."

" Matteson's early groups judiciously avoid extravagance, are often harmonious in color, but sometimes want vigor of handling. . . . . The national and rustic subjects drawn by this pioneer *genre* painter indicate the average taste of the people, and suggest what themes executed with greater finish and more subtle elaboration would most successfully illustrate this branch of art among us." — TUCKERMAN'S *Book of the Artists.*

Maureta, Gabriel. (*Span.*) Medal at the Philadelphia Exposition, where he exhibited "Torquato Tasso retiring to the Monastery of St. Onofrio," which was commended for artistic excellence.

Mauve, Anton. (*Dutch.*) Born at Zaandam. Medal at Philadelphia, where he exhibited "Hauling up the Fishing-Boat," which was especially noted as praiseworthy by Mr. Weir in his report. Mauve is the pupil of P. F. Van Os. At Paris in 1877 he exhibited "Discharging," and in 1876 two pictures with cows. At the Cottier sale, New York, 1878, " Pastures in Holland " sold for $ 1,500. His "Seaweed-Gatherers," belonging to Thomas G. Appleton, and the " Forester's Team, — Frosty Morning, Holland," belonging to B. Schlesinger, were exhibited at the Mechanics' Fair in Boston in 1878. At the Paris Exposition, same year, was his "'Landscape with Sheep, — Winter."

Max, Gabriel. (*Ger.*) This artist is a prominent figure in the present Munich school. We find no note of the more ordinary facts of his life, but whenever his name is mentioned by the writers upon German art of to-day, his power and originality are admitted and admired. Many of his works are tragic in the extreme. That called " Gretchen " seems to show forth the whole experience of Marguerite both in this world and the next ; it is a wonderful conception marvelously carried out, and is said to be a favorite picture with the artist himself. Among his other works are, " The Lion's Bride," " The Young Christian Martyr," " The Anatomist," " The Melancholy Nun," etc. Early in 1878 he exhibited at Vienna " The Infanticide." It represents a mother kneeling on the bank of a stream, and wildly fondling the body of the baby she is about to cast into the water. In " L'Art " we read : —

"The face of the woman is bowed down and half concealed, in a manner that leaves much to be divined, but the impression is none the less painful and profound. Concerning the execution, and especially the color, we are assured that this painting is superior to all those works of this artist which have before made a sensation in Germany."

His " Light " is in the possession of E. B. Haskell of Boston.

" When we come to Gabriel Max we find a genius, to the analysis of whose masterly conceptions we should much prefer devoting a chapter instead of a few meager paragraphs. In respect of mental grasp and imagination, combined with technical ability, we should give the first place in the contemporary Munich school to Max and Böcklin. Artists and public are alike agreed upon the surpassing character of Max's works, although, of course, some prefer one painting to another, while the rather morbid tendency of his subjects makes these paintings better suited, perhaps, to exhibition in a public gallery than in a private drawing-room."—S. G. W. BENJAMIN, *Contemporary Art in Europe.*

May, Edward Harrison, N. A. (*Am.*) Born in England. Was taken to America when a child, and displayed artistic tastes and talents at an early age. As a young man he studied civil engineering, but soon abandoned that profession for the brush. In the beginning of his career he was a portrait-painter, later devoting himself to the production of historical and *genre* pictures. He was a pupil of Huntington in New York, and in 1851 he entered the studio of Couture in Paris. One of his first works was a panorama of "The Pilgrim's Progress," successfully exhibited throughout the United States. Much of Mr. May's professional life has been spent in Europe; at present (1878) he is living in Paris. He was made a member of the National Academy of Design in 1876, but his pictures are rarely exhibited there. In 1869 he sent "Louis XIV. at Marly"; in 1876, "May and December"; in 1878, "Teresina." Among the better known of his earlier works are, "Cardinal Mazarin taking Leave of his Picture in the Louvre," "Michael Angelo leaving the Vatican in Anger," "Lady Jane Grey taking Leave of the Governor of the Tower," "Columbus making his Will," "King Lear and Cordelia," "Young Woman at her Toilet," "Greek Slave," "Esmeralda," "Scene from Waverley," "Death of a Brigand" (which took a gold medal at the Paris Salon of 1855, and was exhibited at the National Academy, New York, a few years later), and "Francis I. lamenting the Death of his Son" (of which Théophile Gautier said, "The whole painting is well executed, the composition very good"). In the Paris Salon of 1866 he exhibited a portrait of M. E. Laboulaye (belonging to the Union Club, New York) and "Amy Robsart et le Colporteur"; in 1868 he sent "Ophelia" and "La Lecture"; in 1869, portrait of Anson Burlingame; in 1870, "Arviragus bearing the Body of Imogen," a scene from Shakspere's "Cymbeline"; in 1872, portrait of Gen. John Meridith Read; in 1873, "Mary Magdalen at the Sepulcher"; in 1874, "Fin de la lecture" and "Souvenir de la Commune"; in 1876, "Une Alsacienne"; and, in 1877, "Antonia." He has painted many portraits, ranking very high in that branch of the profession.

Mayer, Étienne-François-Auguste. (*Fr.*) Born at Brest, 1805. Officer of the Legion of Honor. This painter has treated some *genre* subjects and executed some portraits, but he is essentially a painter of marine views. He has made numerous voyages for the purpose of study. His "Taking of the Island Episcopia" is at Versailles.

Mayer, Karl. (*Ger.*) Born at Vienna (1810–1876). Professor at the Academy of Vienna. Knight of the Orders of Francis Joseph and of Gregory the Great. Studied at the Academy of Vienna under Professor Eselhofer. He made sketching-tours in various parts of Germany and Switzerland, and passed some time in Munich, where he studied diligently. Later, he settled in Vienna. In 1842 he gained a prize at Vienna for his picture of "Prometheus and Pandora," which enabled him to go to Rome, in which city he lived six years, only leaving it for occasional excursions. He was much at the house of Count von

Lützow, where he was an honored guest. Mayer painted portraits, historical subjects, and landscapes.

Mayer, Eduard. (*Ger.*) Born at Asbacher Hutte, 1812. He received the title of Professor from the Grand Duke of Bavaria, and medals at Paris and Berlin. Pupil of the Berlin and Dresden Academies, and of Rauch and Rietschel. He also at Paris was under David d'Angers. In 1842 he settled at Rome. At the National Berlin Gallery is "Mercury attacking Argus," life-size figures in marble.

Mayer, Frank B. (*Am.*) Born in Baltimore, 1827. He studied under Alfred J. Miller of Baltimore, and in Paris under Gleyre and Brion. His professional life has been spent in Baltimore, Paris, and Annapolis, where his studio now is. He has traveled extensively in Europe and the United States, in 1851 visiting the Dacotah Indians in the Territory of Minnesota under peculiarly favorable circumstances for observing their festivals and manners. He made a large collection of life studies of the Indian character, with a journal of his experiences among them, a few of which were published in Schoolcraft's "History of the Indian Tribes." The majority of these sketches, which are still in Mr. Mayer's possession, will no doubt at some future time be of much historic value. During a residence in Paris from 1864 to '69 he exhibited in the Salons there ; before and after that time, in New York, Philadelphia, Washington, and Baltimore. Among his crayon heads are those of Chief Justice Taney, J. V. L. McMahon, Mayor Latrobe of Baltimore, and others. His "Indian Thanksgiving" belongs to S. G. Wyman ; "The Attic Philosopher" and "A Marine Painter," to C. L. Mayer; "The Continentals," to G. B. Coale ; "Waiting Orders," to J. W. McCoy, all of Baltimore ; "Maryland in 1750," to the Peabody Institute of that city. "The Nineteenth Century" belongs to Parke Godwin ; "The Boar's Head," to Edward G. Donelly of New York ; "The King's Jester" was in the collection of the late Copley Greene of Boston ; George Riggs of Washington has "The Cavalier" and "A Lost Letter" ; and W. H. Herriman, Rome, "A Tailor in 1500."

"The Continentals" and "The Attic Philosopher" were at the Centennial Exhibition in Philadelphia in 1876, for which he received a medal and diploma.

Mayer, Constant. (*Fr.-Am.*) Born in Besançon (Doubs), France, 1831. Chevalier of the Legion of Honor. He went to Paris as a youth, entering l'École des Beaux-Arts, and studying under Léon Cogniet for some time. He lived and painted in that city until his removal to New York in 1857, where the rest of his professional life has been spent, with the exception of yearly visits to Paris. His specialty has been life-sized *genre* pictures, which have been exhibited in nearly all the chief cities of America, and have been very popular. Many of them have been chromoed, photographed, and engraved. He is a frequent contributor to the French Salon, of which he is *Hors Con-*

cours. He received the Cross of the Legion of Honor in 1869. Among the better known of Mr. Constant Mayer's works are, " Consolation," painted in 1864 (belonging to Mrs. Frodsham) ; " Recognition," in 1865 (belonging to Joseph Stiner, New York) ; " Good Words," in 1866 (in the collection of MacGregor Adams of Chicago) ; " Love's Melancholy " (the property of Mr. S. M. Scheffer, New York) ; " The Convalescent " (owned in Montreal) ; " Riches and Poverty " ; " Maud Müller " ; " Street Melodies " (belonging to George King, New York) ; "The Organ-Grinder" (to Isaac Van Arden of Brooklyn) ; " The Witch's Daughter" (to Mrs. Bergholz, New Rochelle) ; "The Oracle of the Field" (to M. de Lizardi of New Orleans) ; " The Song of the Shirt " ; " The Dream of Love " ; " Prose and Poetry " ; etc.

In portraiture he has been very successful, painting Mme. de Lizardi, Lady of Honor to the ex-Empress Carlotta, General Grant, General Sheridan, and many people of distinction in this country and France. His " Love's Melancholy " was at the Centennial Exhibition of 1876.

" The whole story of the picture ['Maud Müller '] is of course told in the face of the girl, but so is it completely related in her two eyes only. . . . . The drawing of the picture is true and good, but this is not remarkable in Mr. Mayer's pictures. More noticeable is the skill exhibited in the coloring, — the foliage, running stream, and rock in the foreground, expressly being master strokes of art, — the whole making one of the most pleasing scenes which have left the easels of our painters for a long time." — *Boston Transcript,* October 16, 1867.

" Constant Mayer's ' Orphan's Morning Hymn ' is invested with an expression of sentiment which reflects the highest credit upon his genius. The picture gives no evidence of sentimentalism, but relies for its force upon a simple story drawn from real life, which, though sad, will be studied with interest by all lovers of art." — *Art Journal,* May, 1875.

" Taken as a whole the conception is excellent, the drawing is thoroughly careful, the accessories are painted with rare fidelity, and the color, although low in tone, is so thoroughly pleasing that we should be pained to see a single ' last touch' allowed to disturb the balance. Unquestionably Mr. Mayer has painted in ' The Song of the Shirt ' one of his very best pictures, and illustrated one of the finest poems of the language with infinitely greater faithfulness than he would have shown by slavish adherence to its technicalities." — *Aldine,* November, 1875.

Mayer, Liezen. (*Hungarian.*) Pupil of Piloty, and a resident of Munich. He paints scenic and melodramatic subjects. " Maria Theresa of Austria nursing the Poor Woman's Child " is one of his best-known works. He has made fifty illustrations of " Faust," the cartoons of which were exhibited in London, and there attracted considerable attention. In Munich they received a reward, and many encomiums, when first exhibited. They have been engraved and published in an attractive form.

Maynard, George W. (*Am.*) A native of Washington. He was a pupil of Edwin White in Florence, studying also in Rome and in the Royal Academy of Antwerp. In 1878 he had a studio in Paris. He has turned his attention largely to the painting of portraits. In 1876 he sent to Philadelphia " Vespers at Antwerp " and

" 1776." To the Paris Exposition of 1878 he contributed a portrait, and to the Society of American Artists in New York, in the same year, " The Water-Carriers of Venice." Among his later works exhibited in America may be mentioned " Musical Memories," " Dolce far Niente," and a " Venetian Court."

McCord, G. Herbert. (*Am.*) Born in New York, 1849. He studied art under Col. James Fairman in 1866, and has spent his professional life in his native city and Brooklyn, making sketching-tours through New England, Canada, Florida, and as far west as the Upper Mississippi. He first exhibited at the National Academy about 1870, and frequently since that time. He was made a member of the Artists' Fund Society in 1877. Among his more important works are, " Sunnyside," the home of Washington Irving, exhibited at the Brooklyn Art Association, Philadelphia Academy of Fine Arts, at the Palette Club, New York, in Chicago, and elsewhere ; " The Cave of the Winds, Niagara " (belonging to Mr. Jones, President of the Board of Education, Brooklyn) ; " Twilight Reverie " (N. A., 1878) ; and others.

" ' Sunnyside ' is charming in its lights and shadows. The house is after the Dutch style, and in its lovely hiding-place concealed 'neath the o'ergrowing ivy and surrounded by arching tree-tops, it seems just the spot of all others which the imaginative Irving would select. . . . . Mr. McCord's picture of ' Sunnyside ' derives its noticeable feature of vividness from the fact that it was painted from nature. The road, the trees, the house, are all so real that the observer can but entertain a feeling akin to actual entrance upon the grounds." — *Brooklyn Union*, June 1, 1876.

" The artist [Mr. McCord] has succeeded very creditably in describing the repose of the locality, and at the same time adhering to its literal character [' Sleepy Hollow,' Phil. Acad., 1877]. It is a picture worthy of notice." — *Art Journal*, June, 1877.

McEntee, Jervis, N. A. (*Am.*) Born at Roundout, N. Y., 1828. He began the study of art in the city of New York, in 1850, under F. E. Church. A few years later he opened a studio of his own, and was elected a full member of the National Academy in 1861. In 1869 he visited Europe, spending some months in the galleries of the art centers of the Continent, and making a sketching-tour in Italy and Switzerland.

Among McEntee's earlier works may be mentioned, " Autumn Leaves," " Indian Summer," " October in the Catskills," and " The Melancholy Day," exhibited at the National Academy in 1861 (upon the strength of which he was elected Academician). This picture (purchased by the late James A. Suydam) was bequeathed to the National Academy. In 1867 he sent to the National Academy, " November Afternoon," " Virginia in 1863 " (belonging to Cyrus Butler), and " The Last of October" ; in 1868, " November Landscape " ; in 1869, " The Melancholy Days have come" and "Autumn Twilight" ; in 1870, " Venice" and " October Snow" ; in 1871, " Scribner's Mill " (belonging to Robert Gordon) and " October Afternoon in the Catskill Mountains " ; in 1874, "Cape Ann," " Solitaire,"

"A Wood Path" (belonging to Henry James), and "Dean's River";
in 1875, "Pæstum" (belonging to Henry Holt), "Ginevra," and
"Saturday Afternoon"; in 1876, "The Closing Year," "An Autumn
Idyl," and "A Song of Summer"; in 1877, "And the Year smiles
as it draws near its Death" and "Winter in the Mountains"; in
1878, "Over the Hills and Far Away." McEntee sent to the Paris
Exposition of 1867, "Autumn" (belonging to Robert Hoe) and "The
Last of October." He had several pictures in the Philadelphia Exhibition of 1876, commended by the judges for artistic excellence; and
of his "November," at the Royal Academy, London, in 1872, the
London Times said : —

"This picture shows, what is so rare, an imaginative feeling of the subject. . . . .
The picture is too low in tone and too somber in sentiment to attract much attention,
but it deserves, and will reward, study, and it affixes a mark in the memory to the artist's name."

His "Winter on the Ice" belongs to J. W. Pinchot; his "Autumn
Scene," to Henry G. DeForest. His "Danger Signal" and "November Days" were in the collection of John Taylor Johnston. To Paris,
in 1878, he sent "Falling Leaves" and "An Autumn Idyl."

"Mr. McEntee was represented by 'October Afternoon,' 'November,' 'The Woods
of Ashokan,' 'Frosty Morning,' and 'Late Autumn.' These pictures are all characterized by great sincerity and decided poetic feeling. They evince a subdued yet intense
enjoyment of those phases of nature that are tinctured with melancholy, and which are,
therefore, none the less beautiful. This artist's style is expressive and sensitive, and
within the scope of his stronger sympathies, mature and confident. His pictures evince
a profound insight that is intolerant of that Denner-like portraiture in landscape which
aims at minuteness of imitation. They possess qualities of excellence that in some respects are not surpassed in this branch of art." — PROF. WEIR's *Official Report of the
American Centennial Exhibition of 1876.*

"McEntee manages to give with a few tints a finely felt rendering of nature at a certain season of the year ['A Nipping and an Eager Air,' water-color, N.A., 1877]. — *New
York Times,* January 22, 1877.

"In this picture ['Autumn,' N. A., 1877], as in others of this class, the intensity of Mr.
McEntee's liking for this phase of the year leads him to emphasize his color too much,
to give his landscapes tints which are too freely drawn from his own ideas." — *Art
Journal,* May, 1877.

M'Donald, John B. (*Brit.*) Born in Morayshire, Scotland, 1829.
He entered the schools of the Royal Scottish Academy under Robert
Scott Lauder in 1852, and has since been a resident of Edinburgh.
He has exhibited frequently at the Royal Scottish Academy for the
last quarter of a century (being elected an Associate in 1862, and
a full Member in 1877) pictures in oil and water colors. Among
the better known of his works are, "The Arrest of a Rebel," "In
Venice," "Landscape with Sheep," "Prince Charlie leaving Scotland," "Dougald Dalgetty's Interview with Montrose," "In Hiding,"
"The Falls of the Garry," etc. Several of his works have been
engraved.

"The large canvas 'Strathyre' [R. S. A., 1874], by J. B. M'Donald, takes us by surprise, so grand is it in the sweep of hill and hollow beyond all his previous efforts. This
5 *

noble work, albeit pronounced, in certain circles, hard and deficient in atmospheric depth, makes a powerful impression on the mind." — *Art Journal,* April, 1874.

Meade, Larkin G. (*Am.*) A native of New England. Born in 1835. He displayed artistic talents at an early age, and through the generosity of Mr. Longworth of Cincinnati, who was attracted by his promising work, he was enabled to devote himself to art as a profession. He was a pupil of Henry Kirke Brown in 1853, '54, and '55. In 1862 he went to Italy, settling in Florence. Returning to America at the end of three years, he exhibited in New York, " The Returned Soldier " (life-size), " Echo," " La Contadinella," " The Thought of Freedom," etc. Among the more important of his later works are four bronze groups representing " Infantry," " Cavalry," " Artillery," and " The Navy," of colossal proportion, and the statue of Lincoln for the National Lincoln Monument, at Springfield, Ill. His statue of Ethan Allen is in the National Art Gallery, in the Capitol at Washington. His statue of " Vermont " (19 feet high) is upon the dome of the State House at Montpelier, and his " Columbus appealing to Isabella " (in marble) belongs to D. O. Mills, President of the Bank of California. The greater part of his professional life has been spent in Italy.

" Mr. Lincoln is represented as having just signed the Proclamation of Emancipation, and in his left hand he holds a scroll marked ' Proclamation,' in the right hand he holds a pen. The faithfulness of the portrait in every feature rivets the attention of the observer. The stooping shoulders, the forward inclination of the head, manner of wearing the hair, the protruding eyebrows, the nose, the mouth, with the prominent and slightly drooping lower lip, the mole on the left cheek, the eyes, far back in the head, the calm, earnest, half-sorrowful expression of the face, — all recall to the minds of those who knew him well the same Lincoln who lived and moved among us until called to enter upon his grand career." — *St. Louis Globe,* October 4, 1874.

" The first contribution of Vermont to the National Statuary Hall, being a heroic-sized statue of Col. Ethan Allen of Revolutionary fame, was placed in the hall on Saturday last. It is the production of Larkin G. Meade of Vermont, at present residing in Florence, Italy, where the statue was made. The cost was $ 10,000. It represents Colonel Allen as he appeared when demanding the surrender of Fort Ticonderoga ' in the name of the Great Jehovah and the Continental Congress.' The attitude of the statue is very spirited, much more so than that of any other in the hall." — *Washington Evening Star,* February 28, 1876.

Meissonier, Jean Louis Ernest. (*Fr.*) Born at Lyons about 1813. Commander of the Legion of Honor, 1867. Member of the Institute, 1861. One of the eight grand medals of honor (E. U.), 1867. He went when quite young to Paris, and was for some time a pupil of Léon Cogniet. He is the first French miniaturist of *genre* subjects who has attained celebrity. Perhaps he can receive no higher praise than to be, as he constantly is, compared to Terburg and Metzu. He has been fully appreciated from the commencement of his career, and receives honors and money without stint. His works are too numerous to allow of a complete list here. He first exhibited, in 1836, " The Little Messenger." In the Luxembourg are " Napoleon III. at

Solferino " (45 by 75 centimeters), on wood (1864), and " The Emperor surrounded by his Staff " (12 by 7), also on wood. " La partie des boules " (1848) is regarded as a *chef-d'œuvre;* " A Dream " (1855) was purchased by the Emperor for 20,000 francs, and presented to the late Prince Albert ; the " Cavalry Charge" (1867) was purchased by Mr. Probasco of Cincinnati, and it is said that he paid 150,000 francs for it. At the Johnston sale, New York, 1876, the " Soldiers at Cards," from the Demidoff Collection (8 by 10), painted in 1860, sold for $ 11,500 ; and " Marshal Saxe and Staff " (8 by 9), 1866, for $ 8,600. At the Latham sale, New York, 1878, " The Amused Cavalier " (7¼ by 5) sold for $ 3,100. In " L'Art," January, 1876, there is an article devoted to his picture called " 1807," which was purchased by the late Mr. Stewart of New York for more than 300,000 francs. It is said that the artist worked on it fifteen years, and as regards size it is the most important of his works. At the Salon of 1877 Meissonier exhibited a portrait of Dumas ; small figure, about a foot in height, sitting in a chair, with the legs crossed and the hands folded on the edge of a table, which is covered with books and papers. He has executed some illustrations for books, such as " Les Français Peints par eux-mêmes," " La Comédie Humaine " (Balzac), and, in company with François and Daubigny, an edition of " Paul and Virginia."

" The immense reputation of Meissonier is justified by the perfection attained by him in the kind of art he has chosen. Perfection in art of any kind is so rare, that when we meet with it we are sure to take notice of it ; and, though Meissonier's pictures are very small, they are not likely to be passed over in the most crowded exhibitions. The mere fact of their littleness seems to have helped their reputation by increasing the marvel of the work ; but there is nothing new or exceptional in this : the engravers of book illustrations and the painters of miniatures have long worked on a scale still smaller. What really is new and exceptional in Meissonier is a certain largeness of grasp and vivacity of accent, this vivacity degenerating into excessive *staccato* at times, when *staccato* is not wanted. Meissonier is said to be in the habit of making studies the size of life, in order to keep his breadth of treatment. This, at least, is a proof of his firm belief in a doctrine very generally received amongst artists, — that in order to paint on a small scale really well, you must be able to paint on a larger. Meissonier is a master of the male figure, and has lately studied the horse for his pictures of Solferino and the ' Campagne de France ' ; but he has generally been careful to avoid women, — probably because it is not easy to render a female face with that sharp accentuation which has become habitual with him. I like him best in such pictures as the ' Lecture chez Diderot,' where gentlemen of the last century meet in conversation ; or in such single studies as the ' Smoker,' which, for subtlety of quiet expression, is as good as the best faces of Rembrandt, — as good, for instance, as the portrait of Burgomaster Six. Sometimes the expression is pushed rather far, and slightly verges on caricature, — as in the picture of an officer in the last century giving his orders, called ' L'Ordonnance.' Meissonier is not a man of any grandeur or sublimity of genius, and he has apparently no tenderness, — a defect he shares with Gérôme : but his keen observation, and ready, accurate hand, have made him king of his own realm in art, and his work, I suppose, will never diminish in money value, because such work must always be excessively rare." — HAMERTON, *Contemporary French Painters.*

" Meissonier is, perhaps, the most popular artist of our time. If he has a picture at the Salon, the crowd first ascertain where it is, and the obstruction is such that it is not always easy to approach it. When his works make a part of a public sale, all who occupy themselves with painting rush to the Hotel Drouot. His reputation is European, and volumes could be filled with articles which the reviews and journals have consecrated to him. Edmond About has given in *résumé*, with his usual spirit, the causes which have determined this prodigious success. 'He made his début,' says he, 'by some microscopic pictures : one was obliged to examine them when near by ; it was then only that we perceived Meissonier. The most severe critics, the magnifying-glass in the hand, acknowledged that no one drew better than he, that his figures were irreproachable and his draperies perfect ; that his Liliputian personages wanted neither form, nor dignity, nor elegance. He painted true gentlemen, as distinguished as Lauzun and as alight as scarabei ; he stowed fifty French guards, very life-like and very stirring, on a canvas where two cockchafers would be too crowded. He surmounted so successfully the enormous difficulties that he imposed on himself, that he was soon at ease in the narrowest frame.' Meissonier has painted, in truth, some subjects with several figures, and even some battles, but he oftener makes pictures with a single figure, and he knows how to captivate the attention with scenes so simply conceived that a written description could give no idea of them, and it is absolutely necessary to see them in order to understand their value. . . . . One quality which Meissonier possesses in a rare degree is the research into the intimate character of the time in which he makes his personages move. It is not a man of to-day whom he clothes with the vestments of another time ; there is a perfect accord between the physiognomy, the carriage, the costume of the person represented and the accessories with which he enriches his picture. Above all, he never forgets the principal subject in the decoration, and whatever the charm of the details which make a part of the scene, it is always the man who plays the principal part, and who first attracts attention. Meissonier has found many imitators among our young artists, who think to follow the master in painting microscopic canvases with minute care ; but he has kept for himself the secret of interesting by insignificant subjects, and by painting largely pictures which may be seen through a glass."— RENÉ MÉNARD, *Gazette des Beaux-Arts*, April, 1873.

"This eminent artist has employed in his *genre* painting all the serious qualities of grand painting. He is one of the masters of this day who can count on the future, whose works have an assured place in galleries among the most celebrated ones."— THÉOPHILE GAUTIER, *Gazette des Beaux-Arts*, May, 1862.

"The little and marvelously elaborated pictures, of which Meissonier is still the supreme master in France, were unknown as an object to French painters before Meissonier won so much consideration for his successful efforts to represent Nature, as seen through the small end of a telescope. His aim was a reaction against the dominant masters of his time ; by his indefatigable, tenacious talent, his microscopic vision, he was enabled to surpass the Dutch masters in everything but color. Every form of excellence in art appeared to have been illustrated in French painting but that of the Dutch school : great political tragedies in Delaroche ; military events in Vernet ; the drama of the passions in Delacroix ; classic art in Ingres ; the ideas, fancy, imagination, beauty, pastoral art, — all in a style more or less in direct descent from the great examples of Italian or classic art. Meissonier, without an idea, without a passion, without anything but a wonderfully trained hand, and an uncommon perception of actual objects, applied himself to produce pictures that should 'flabbergast' a public tired of emotions and ideas and revolts, but interested in everything mechanical and laborious and obviously conscientious. He may be said to be a Dutch painter, *plus* the instruction of the photograph. He was not a pupil of l'École des Beaux-Arts : and yet no painter of the imperial school has carried further the science of his art, and none are better instructed in the technical means to reach the object of his work. He contests with Gérôme superiority in the science of representation of Nature on a small scale. His pictures compete with Gérôme's at the picture-dealers' ; their market-value is astounding ; and they interest the mind like clock-work, like the weaving of Egyptian linen, like photographs, like any fine and successful exhibition of the mechanical talent. . . . . Meissonier is an example of a modern artist wholly independent of the actual life of his time, — an artist who has given *no place to woman* in his works, no place to the ideal, no place to the disturbing facts of his own epoch. I know of but one picture in which he represents a woman — and that woman is a dame of the eighteenth century — and her gallant. Consummate as is the executive talent of Meissonier, he cannot be taken as a type of the artist. His aim is too limited, his purpose too material. Absolutely deficient in the ideal, absolutely indifferent to all the consecrating and charming and beautiful elements of Nature and life, he is but a consummate picture-maker, interested in the most prosaic characters and showy costumes of the direct epoch of modern civilization. His works are objects of curiosity. The most stupid lover of pictures can use his ' glass' to magnify the minute merits of Meissonier's pictures, and deepen his sense of wonder at the laborious and skillful hand of the artist ; he can observe his marvelous finish, his masterly drawing, his bold touch, his completeness of representation, and so have the flattering satisfaction of being on a level with the aim and work of one of the most far-famed of modern painters." — EUGENE BENSON, *Appletons' Journal*, September 11, 1869.

Philippe Burty, in the "Gazette des Beaux-Arts," May, 1862, speaks thus : —

"The etchings of Meissonier are few, but the proofs of them are singularly rare. Save the 'Smoker' and that which we publish to-day, and which is unedited ['The Sergeant-Reporter'], there is scarcely a cabinet which offers them to the curiosity of amateurs. They are engraved with an extremely fine point, one would almost say with the point of a needle. But the effect is large, because the niceness of the detail loses itself in the mass, and renders, with most astonishing skill, the appearance of everything, the epidermis of each object."

The following list gives the titles of his principal etchings : " The Holy Table " (or altar), "The Violin," " Preparations for the Duel," "Signor Annibale," " Monsieur Polichinelle," etc. At the Sale Wertheimber in Paris, 1861, a small panel, 27 by 21 centimeters, painted in 1858, representing German cavalrymen in a large salon, playing cards, smoking, etc., brought 28,000 francs, and was purchased by M. Demidoff. From the description this would appear to be the " Soldiers at Cards " of the Johnston sale, but the Wertheimber catalogue date of the picture is 1858, and the Johnston catalogue date is 1860. At the Lehon sale, Paris, 1861, " The Painter at his Easel " sold for 11,200 francs. At a London sale, in 1872, " The Sentinel," an exquisite miniature work, sold for 970 guineas. At the Khalil Bey sale, 1868, " The Amateurs of Painting" was bought by M. Say for £1,272.

Meissonier, Jean Charles. (*Fr.*) Born at Paris. Medal, 1866. Pupil of his father. At the Salon of 1874 he exhibited " Le fripier," " The Convent of Saint-Barthélemy at Nice," and " The Chaplain reading to the Baron " ; in 1866, " In taking Tea " and " Leusen and Rosine."

Melbye, Antoine. (*Dane.*) Born at Copenhagen (about 1822 – 1875). Chevalier of the Legion of Honor. He studied under Eckersberg at Düsseldorf, and, later, in Paris. His subjects are principally marines. In 1867 he exhibited, at the Paris Salon, two marine views ; in 1865, " The Naval Combat of Bothwell on the Coast of Scotland " ; in 1852, " Full Sea " ; etc. At Berlin, in 1876, was exhibited his " Moonlight on the Bosphorus."

Mélingue, Lucien. ' (*Fr.*) Born at Paris. Medal of first class, 1877. Pupil of Cogniet and Gérôme. At the Salon of 1877 he exhibited " The Morning of the 10 Thermidor an II., 1794" and a portrait of the Commandant T.; in 1878, " Mademoiselle de Montpensier at the Bastille."

Mène, Pierre-Jules. (*Fr.*) Born at Arras. Chevalier of the Legion of Honor. Pupil of R. Compare. At Philadelphia he exhibited " A Falconer on Horseback " and " A Hunter and Dogs," both in bronze, and received a medal. At the Salon of 1878 he exhibited "An African Hunter" (group in wax) and " Toréador-matador " (group in bronze). [Died, 1879, aged about 69.]

Menzel, Adolf-Frederic-Erdmann. (*Ger.*) Born at Breslau, 1815. Member of the Academies of Berlin, Vienna, and Munich. Member of the Royal Society of Water-Color Artists of Belgium. Knight of the Order of Merit, of the Legion of Honor, and of Saint Michael of Bavaria. Many of the pictures of this painter are scenes from the life of Frederick the Great. At the National Gallery, Berlin, are " The Round Table of Frederick, 1750 " and a " Flute Concert at Sans-Souci," also " Modern Cyclops." Menzel has also illustrated the works of this monarch. His lithographs are quite numerous, and his water-colors are much admired. Six of his pictures were exhibited at the Paris Exposition of 1878.

A writer in the " Zeitschrift für bildende Kunst," 1866, says of the picture of the " Coronation," by Menzel : —

" He is a decided realist : his attempt is to give the moment as it really existed. Going beyond this, in any measure, he despises, — so despises it, even, that one cannot fail to see his definite intention of doing something unlike others. . . . . Menzel is, judging from the want of transparency, especially in shadows, no real colorist. Although his technique is masterly, and the costumes [except those of the ladies], the mantles of those in orders, the uniforms with their embroideries, and all the furnishing of the apartment, painted with boldness and largeness, he has not given his thought to artistic grouping, or beauty of lines and masses. What, then, are the merits of this work, which we have called remarkable from the beginning, if the painter has ignored all attempt at depicting beauty? Menzel certainly will not allow that art and beauty have any connection ; for him the essence of art lies in characterization. This is a very one-sided view, but when it is illustrated in so masterly a manner it demands respect, and when such an artist opposes his strength to us we can only measure it by itself. Menzel has given us something remarkable in the way of portrait heads, but in these, also, he has fallen short as far as the effect of beauty is concerned, especially in the group of ladies, ... but the masculine heads are all the more true, excellent, and important."

" Very much above these pretentious works it is proper to rank the simple water-colors of Adolf Menzel, an artist of Berlin, — known by a series of pictures and designs consecrated to Frederick II. The Exposition at Munich shows us a dozen charming works, of a more modest sort, representing varied subjects, denoting a suppleness of talent and a reunion of qualities quite exceptional. ' The Return of Troops to Berlin after the War of 1866 ' was the most studied of these compositions. In the middle, through a street, the conquerors defile under a shower of bouquets ; but in the houses on each side the artist has grouped the contrasts which belong to such a day, – at the left all is joy and the intoxication of triumph, while on the right the wounded are received with tenderness and surrounded with careful attentions ; aside, some poor ones, dressed in mourning, steal away from the general joy to weep for their dear ones not here. Let us also mention, as two wonders, the interiors of the churches at Innspruck and Salzbourg, by the same artist. Above, vividly lighted, are white walls, pictures, and altars resplendent with gilding ; then, by insensible degrees, the light decreases, candles lighted burn in a mysterious and lukewarm shade, and below are some faithful ones, women, absorbed in their prayers, with an expression of silence and deep meditation. In place of the heaviness and pretentiousness which, too often, we have pointed out in the works of German painters, we find here a true artist, full of tact and taste, of elegance and easy grace, and who would worthily sustain all comparisons with the best of our French masters."—ÉMILE MICHEL, *Revue des Deux Mondes,* December, 1877.

Mercadé, Benito. (*Span.*) Born at Barcelona. Medal at Paris in 1866, and at Philadelphia, 1876, where he exhibited "The Translation of St. Francis of Assisi," which was also at Paris in 1866. Pupil of the School of Fine Arts at Madrid. In the Official Report of the Judges of the Philadelphia Exhibition, John F. Weir says of this picture : —

"The subject is treated with great purity of feeling, and, indeed, solemnity. The expression of the heads is very fine, and the composition simple and impressive. The picture is cold and monotonous in color, but in the sincerity of its aim it is admirable."

Mercié, Marius-Jean-Antoine. (*Fr.*) Born at Toulouse. Chevalier of the Legion of Honor, 1872. Medal of Honor, 1874. Pupil of Jouffroy and Falguière. At the Salon of 1877 he exhibited a plaster relief of " The Genius of the Arts " (intended for the grand entrance of the Louvre) and a marble statuette of a " Vanquished Juno," which was much praised by Ch. Timbal in the "Gazette des Beaux-Arts"; in 1876, a marble statuette of " David before the Combat " and a bust called " Flowers of May "; in 1875, "Gloria Victis ! " group in bronze, and a bas-relief from La Fontaine. At the Luxembourg is his " David " (1872), a statue in bronze.

Merle, Hugues. (*Fr.*) Born at Saint-Marcellin. Chevalier of the Legion of Honor. Pupil of L. Cogniet. At the Salon of 1876 he exhibited " Day and Night " (a fragment of a decoration) and " Il Bambino "; in 1874, " Pernette the Spinner " (a legend of Dauphiny) and a " Little Bohemian Girl "; in 1873, " The Right Road " and "A Mad Woman " (now in the collection of Mrs. H. E. Maynard of Boston). At the Salon of 1878 he exhibited " Odette and Charles VI." and " Charlotte Corday." His picture of " The Beggar " (1861) is in the Luxembourg. His " Asking Alms " is in the collection of Jeremiah Milbank, New York. " The Young Christian," sold in London for £332, is now in the Belmont Gallery, New York. In the Walters Gallery, Baltimore, are two small pictures by Merle, "A Girl with a Child in her Arms " and a " Group of a Mother and her Children." The latter is an excellent example of this artist's work. " The Scarlet Letter " is also in the same collection. At a sale at Christie's in 1874, were sold " The Mendicant during the Siege of Paris " and " Watching the Crab "; the latter brought 190 guineas.

At the Johnston sale, New York, 1876, " Chasing the Butterfly " (18 by 15) sold for $ 1,615.

" [French Gallery, Pall Mall, No. 164, ' Hagar and Ishmael.'] H. Merle presents a most interesting version of the subject. The figure of Hagar is admirably cast, and is distinctly of the Egyptian type ; the angry expression of her features is her reply to the mockery of Sarah. But the difference between Hagar and Ishmael is remarkable, the pose and action of the boy being both open to improvement ; and we think that if the artist reconsiders the subject, he will arrive at the conclusion that the removal of Abraham from the background would be advantageous." — *Art Journal*, May, 1873.

" Merle shows to more advantage this year at the Salon than he has done for some seasons past : his ' Charlotte Corday,' in particular, being a striking and expressive work. . . . . Painted with Merle's peculiar grace and tender charm, this fine picture daily attracts a crowd of gazers. It goes to America, having been purchased by Mr. William Schans, the well-known dealer." — *Art Journal*, August, 1878.

Merle, Georges. (*Fr.*) Born at Paris. Son and pupil of Hugues Merle. He sent to the Salon of 1878, " The Death of Philip Arte-velde at the Battle of Roosebeke, November 27, 1382 "; in 1877, " Faust and the Three Braves "; in 1876, " Le Pas d'Armes de l'Arbre d'Or."

Merson, Luc-Olivier. (*Fr.*) Born at Paris. Medals at Salons of 1869 and '73. His subjects are generally historical-religious, such as " St. Louis, on coming to the Throne, opens the Jails of the Kingdom " and " St. Louis, in spite of the Supplications of the Barons, condemns the old Enguerrand de Coucy, 1259," both painted for the Gallery of Saint Louis at the Palace of Justice. At the Salon in 1875 he exhibited " The Sacrifice for the Country " and " St. Michael " ; in 1872, " St. Edmond, King and Martyr " ; and in 1878, " The Wolf of Agubbio."

Méryon, Charles. (*Fr.*) Born at Paris (1821 – 1868). Early in life he was a marine, and in New Caledonia, which he visited, he made many very interesting sketches of that country, then so little known ; later, he made engravings from these designs. On his return to France, Méryon devoted himself to engraving, studied under Bléry, and became the best etcher of his day. In spite of his excellence he never felt himself appreciated, and he fell into a misanthropy which at length rendered him insane. He was taken to Charenton, where he slowly died. He wished for no friends or sympathy, and refused to eat. His etchings, especially those of the old parts of Paris, were exquisite. Among those which are highly esteemed are, " The Exchange Bridge," " The Old Morgue," " The Little Bridge," " The Apse of Notre Dame of Paris," " The Turret of Rue Tixeranderie," " The Turret of the Rue de l'École de Medicine," " The New Bridge," and the " Rue de la Pirouette." It is much to be lamented that in a fit of madness Méryon destroyed some of his finest works, among which were etchings of " The College of Henry IV. at Paris."

Mesdag, Hendrik - Willem. (*Dutch.*) Born at Groningen. Medal in Paris and at Philadelphia, where he exhibited " Evening on the Beach." He is a pupil of Alma-Tadema. At Paris in 1877 he exhibited "Summer Evening " and "Twilight " ; in 1876, two pictures, the " Departure and Return of a Life-Boat at Scheveningen " ; at the London Royal Academy in 1872, " A Fishing-Smack " ; and in 1871, "A Fleet of Fishing-Boats at Scheveningen." To the Paris Salon of 1878 he contributed " Ready to weigh Anchor, Scheveningen," and " The Scheldt, — Morning," and to the Exposition, same year, three of his works above named.

Meyer, Ernest. (*Dane.*) Born at Altona (1796 – 1860). Member of the Academy of Copenhagen, at which place he studied. In 1824 he went to Italy ; he passed some time in Naples and Amalfi, and settled at Rome, where he died. At the National Gallery at Berlin is his " Family of Lazzaroni."

Meyer, Jean-Louis-Henri. (*Dutch.*) Born at Amsterdam (1809 – 1866). Chevalier of the Legion of Honor. Pupil of Jean Pienemann. He essayed *genre* and historical subjects before he confined himself to marine pictures, as he did at length. He lived much in Paris, and sent his works to many Salons and to the Exposition of 1855. In 1867 several pictures were exhibited, which were in his studio when he died. His " Shipwreck of William I." is in the Museum at Haarlem.

Meyer, Jean Georges, called **Meyer von Bremen.** (*Ger.*) Born at Bremen about 1813. Member of the Amsterdam Academy. Medals at Berlin and Philadelphia. Pupil of the Düsseldorf school. He at first essayed historical and religious subjects, but afterwards devoted himself to the *genre* subjects which have made him popular in Europe and America. He had, some time ago, executed more than nine hundred pictures in oils and water-colors. At the National Gallery, Berlin, is his " Little Housewife." At the Johnston sale, New York, 1876, " The New Sister" (19 by 15) sold for $ 3,700. Almost all his pictures represent children, so that in Germany he has been called " Kinder-Meyer." The pictures of this artist are so well known, and their place is so well established, that nothing need be said of them. They seem to belong to each person who has looked at them, because they appeal to all hearts and fix themselves in all memories. At the Latham sale, New York, 1878, " What has Mother brought ? " (20 by 16) sold for $ 4,050. His " Water-Girl " is in the collection of Mrs. H. E. Maynard of Boston. Theron R. Butler of New York owns his " Little Coquette," " Leaving Home," " Meditation," and " Prayer," and several very fine specimens of his work were in the collection of the late Alvin Adams of Watertown, Mass.

Meyerheim, Frederic-Eduard. (*Ger.*) Born at Dantzic, 1808. Member of the Academies of Munich, Dresden, and Berlin, and Professor at the last. Medal at Paris in 1855. Pupil of his father and the Academy of Berlin. He joined some young artists in opposition to the Academy, and was obliged to support himself by making lithographs. In 1834 he exhibited the "Blind Beggar," which immediately placed him in the first rank as a *genre* painter. At the National Gallery, Berlin, is his "King of the Shooting-Match."

Meyerheim, Paul Friedrich. (*Ger.*) Born at Berlin, 1842. Member of the Academy of Berlin and of the Belgian Water-Color Society. Medals at Berlin and Paris. *Genre* painter. Pupil of his father, E. M. Meyerheim. Traveled in Belgium and Holland, and remained a year in Paris. He is a skillful water-colorist and lithographer. In the National Gallery at Berlin is his "Antiquary in the Market-Place at Amsterdam." At Berlin in 1876 he exhibited "Two Portraits," "A Landscape with Cows," and a "Harvest Scene."

Meynier, Charles. (*Fr.*) Born at Paris (1768 – 1832). Chevalier of the Legion of Honor. Pupil of Vincent. Meynier took the grand *prix de Rome* in 1789. His picture of the "Entry of the French into Berlin" is at Versailles. "The Infant Œdipus presented to Periboœa" is in the Louvre. This artist decorated the ceiling of the staircase leading to the Museum of Painting, and that of the anteroom to the Great Exhibition Hall at the Louvre.

Meynier, Jules Joseph. (*Fr.*) Born at Paris. Medals in 1867 and '77. Pupil of Delaroche, Gleyre, and Bridoux. At the Salon of 1877 he exhibited "Chrysante and Daria"; at that of 1867, "The First Christians in Prayer at the Entrance to a Crypt"; and in 1878, "Venus chastising Love" and some portraits of children.

Michel, Ernest-Barthélemy. (*Fr.*) Born at Montpellier, where his studio now is. Pupil of Picot and Cabanel. He won the *prix de Rome* in 1860 and a medal in 1870. To the Salon of 1876 he sent "Lisa the Bohemian" and "The Doves"; in 1875, "Fortune and the Child," "Young Girl in the Fields," and "Roman Peasants on the Steps of a Convent"; in 1873, "La Pescivendola." To Philadelphia, in 1876, he sent "Decameron"; to the Paris Exposition of 1878, "The Charity of St. Martin" (belonging to the church of Saint-Nicolas-des-Champs, Paris) and "Daphne."

Miglioretti, Pascal. (*Ital.*) Born at Milan. Medal at Paris in 1855. Pupil of the Academy of Milan, in which city he is known by various religious sculptures and monumental decorations. He exhibited at Paris "The Dying Abel" (1855); and in 1867, "Charlotte Corday," "Neapolitan Piccirello," and "The First Grief."

Mignot, Louis R., N. A. (*Am.*) Born in South Carolina (1831 – 1871). Spent some years in study in Holland. A landscape-painter of much promise, fond of tropical and semi-tropical scenes. He lived in New York, and was made a member of the National Academy in 1859. Upon the secession of his native State from the Federal Union in 1861 he removed to London, where the rest of his life was spent. Among his earlier works painted in this country are his "Twilight in the Tropics," "Southern Harvest" (belonging to R. L. Stuart), "Tropical Scenery" (belonging to M. O. Roberts), and

" Source of the Susquehanna " (in the Wright Collection, belonging
originally to H. W. Derby, exhibited in the Paris Exposition of 1867,
and in the National Academy of New York the following winter).
He first exhibited at the Royal Academy, in 1863, "Lagoon of Guaya-
quil, South America" and " A Winter Morning "; in 1865, "Evening
in the Tropics "; in 1866, " Under the Equator "; in 1867, "Tin-
tern "; in 1870, "Sunset off Hastings "; in 1871, "Mount Chim-
borazo." His collected works were exhibited in London after his
death, and attracted considerable attention.

" At home and abroad Mignot's best landscapes have won admiration. He is a master of color, and some of his atmospheric experiments are wonderful. Compare one of
his winter with one of his tropical scenes, and the absolute truth of his manner and
method becomes impressive." — TUCKERMAN's *Book of the Artists.*

Millais, John Everett, R. A. (*Brit.*) Born in Southampton,
1829. Spent his early years in France, and among the Channel Islands. Received a medal from the Society of Arts in 1838, when only
nine years of age. He entered the Royal Academy two years later,
gaining two silver medals. Exhibited his first picture in the Royal
Academy, in 1846, " Pizarro seizing the Men of Peru "; in 1847 he
received the gold medal for an historical painting, " The Tribe of Benjamin seizing the Daughters of Shiloh "; in 1850 he exhibited " Christ
in the House of his Parents," and his famous " Huguenot Lovers " in
1852; in 1853, when he was elected Associate of the Royal Academy, he sent " The Order of Release " and " The Proscribed Royalist "; in 1855, " The Rescue "; in 1856, " Autumn Leaves "; in 1860,
" The Black Brunswicker "; in 1862, " The Ransom " and " Trust
Me "; in 1863, " My First Sermon," " The Wolf's Den," and " The
Eve of St. Agnes." He was made Academician in 1864, contributing
" My Second Sermon," " Charlie is my Darling," and others; in 1865,
he sent " Joan of Arc," " Esther," and " The Romans leaving Brit-
ain "; in 1867, " The Minuet," " Sleeping," and " Waking "; in 1868,
he sent his diploma work, " A Souvenir of Velasquez," " Pilgrims to
St. Paul's," and " Rosalind and Celia "; in 1869, " The Gambler's
Wife," " The End of the Chapter," and several portraits; in 1870,
" The Knight-Errant," " The Boyhood of Raleigh," and " The Wid-
ow's Mite "; in 1871, " Chill October " and " Yes or No ?"; in 1872,
" Flowing to the River," " Flowing to the Sea," and " Hearts are
Trumps "; in 1873, " Early Days " and " New-Laid Eggs "; in 1874,
" Winter Fuel," " The Northwest Passage," " The Picture of Health,"
and " A Day's Dream "; in 1875, " The Fringe of the Moor," " The
Crown of Love," and " No !"; in 1876, " Forbidden Fruits," " Getting
Better," " Over the Hills and Far Away," and many portraits; in
1877, " A Yeoman of the Guard," " The Sound of many Waters,"
and " Yes !"; in 1878, " The Princes in the Tower," " A Jersey Lily,"
and a portrait of the Earl of Shaftesbury. His " Effie Deans," engraved
by Oldham Barlow, A. R. A., was exhibited in 1877, at a private gal-

lery in London, for the benefit of the Artists' General Benevolent Institution, of which Mr. Millais is the Honorary Secretary. Many of his works have been engraved. He is considered the leading portrait-painter to-day in England, receiving, it is said, two thousand guineas for a single full-length likeness. With Mr. Madox Brown, D. G. Rossetti, Holman Hunt, and a few more (in 1850 or earlier), he founded an association called "The Brotherhood of the Pre-Raphaelites," which was the introduction of what is now known as the "Pre-Raphaelite School of Painting" in England, whose principal theory of action, according to Fairholt, is a rigid adherence to natural forms and effects in contradistinction to the style of rendering of any particular school of art. One of the earliest, and perhaps the most marked of Mr. Millais' pre-Raphaelite pictures, was "The Child Jesus in the Workshop of Joseph the Carpenter," painted in 1850, wonderful in its naturalism and attention to the minutest details. He exhibits at the Grosvenor Gallery. His "Early Days" was at Philadelphia in 1876; "Chill October" and "Hearts are Trumps," at Paris in 1878. Mr. Marsden bought his "Bride of Lammermoor," the same year, for £3,000.

"In 1871 Millais electrified once more the art-loving public by the insurpassable truth of his 'Chill October,' a landscape picture, the exquisite subdued tone of which is one great element of its strength." — Mrs. TYTLER's *Modern Painters.*

"The critics will differ as to the qualities of each composition, but no single individual will venture to question the genius and consummate ability of the artist. Mr. Millais is one of the most powerful painters enrolled in the list of Academicians." — *Art Journal,* June, 1875.

"Millais has placed himself at the head of the living portrait-painters of Great Britain. . . . . As a colorist, it is difficult to see why he should not be assigned to a place among the foremost that Great Britain has produced." — BENJAMIN's *Contemporary Art in Europe.*

"It is simply impossible to render adequate justice to this masterpiece of natural representation ['Over the Hills and Far Away']. It is a very splendid illustration of the author's extraordinary genius, exhibiting consummate draughtsmanship, marvelous power of coloring, and vivid truthfulness of execution." — *Art Journal,* July, 1876.

"Very many of Millais' drawings on wood have all of the qualities of good etchings which the difference of the two processes will permit. His manner of sketching is an excellent manner for an etcher. It is delicate without over-minuteness, and it is rapid and free without neglecting anything essential." — HAMERTON's *Etching and Etchers,* 1876.

Miller, Alfred J. (*Am.*) Born in Baltimore (1810–1874). His first lessons in art were received from Thomas Sully. After painting with success in Baltimore and Washington he went to Europe in 1833, studying in Paris, Rome, and Florence, and living on intimate terms with Thorwaldsen, Greenough, Gibson, and Vernet. He was also a fellow-traveler with Brantz Mayer and N. P. Willis. His works in Europe were chiefly copies of the old masters, but they were considered of great excellence. At New Orleans in 1837 he met Sir William Drummond Stewart, a Scottish Baronet, with whom he visited the Rocky Mountains, making a series of sketches of scenes and incidents of the trip which were the groundwork of the very interesting gallery of Indian pictures now at Murthley Castle, the seat of Sir W. D. Stewart, and probably the most valuable collection of paintings relating to aboriginal American life extant. He spent the winter of 1841 at Taymouth, the guest of the Duke of Breadalbane in the Highlands of Scotland, painting several family portraits. Returning to Baltimore, he practiced his profession there until his death. In portraiture he followed the school of Lawrence. For W. T. Walters of Baltimore he reproduced in water-colors (accompanied by his private journal of the Rocky Mountain expedition) the pictures he had painted for Stewart. His works are in many of the important collections of this country.

Miller, Charles H., N. A. (*Am.*) Born in New York, 1842. Studied medicine, and graduated in 1863. During his medical course he painted occasional pictures, and first exhibited at the National Academy, in 1860, "The Challenge Accepted." In 1864 he went to Europe, and again in 1867, visiting the art centers, and finally settling in Munich, where he remained three years, and became a student of Professor Lier and of the Bavarian Royal Academy. He made frequent excursions to Dresden, Vienna, and Berlin. He exhibited at the National Academy, New York, in 1869, "Near Munich, Bavaria"; in 1870, "Old Mill near Munich" and "Roadside near Munich"; in 1871, "Sunset" and "Twilight at Duchau near Munich"; in 1872, "Old Mill, Springfield" and "Old Bridge, Munich"; in 1874, "Old Oaks at Creedmoor, Long Island"; in 1875, "Sheep-Washing on Long Island" and "High Bridge from Harlem Lane, New York"; in 1876, "Bush-Burning on Long Island" and "New York from Newton Creek"; in 1877, "On the Road to Market, Long Island" and "Autumn"; in 1878, "Sunset, East Hampton, Long Island."

He was elected an Associate of the National Academy in 1873 or '74, and Academician in 1875. Miller's "Sunset at Queen's, New York" belongs to Robert Gordon; his "Road to the Mill," to John L. Melcher. His "Oaks at Creedmoor, Long Island" was at the Paris Exposition of 1878.

"Mr. Miller contributed his 'Returning to the Fold,' 'The Road to the Mill,' and 'High Bridge, New York,' all of which show decided merit with a strong foreign accentuation." — PROF. WEIR'S *Official Report of the American Centennial Exhibition of* 1876.

"Miller's 'Long Island Landscape' is an admirable little picture, full of vigor, but the upper clouds look too heavy. A dark landscape covered by a dark sky which is bright towards the horizon." — *New York Times,* April 3, 1877.

Millet, Jean-François. (*Fr.*) Born at Greville (1814–1875). Chevalier of the Legion of Honor. Pupil of Delaroche. This artist was one of nine children. His father had no means to spare for his education; his grandmother, and an uncle, who was a priest, taught him as well as they could. Very early his vocation for painting declared itself, and in 1834 he went to study with Langlois at Cherbourg. His progress was so remarkable that the municipal council of Cherbourg gave him a small pension in order that he might go to

Paris. In 1837 he became the pupil of Delaroche ; and soon the friend of Corot, Theodore Rousseau, Dupré, and Diaz. He was often hungry and cold, for his pension was very small ; but he had the health of a Normandy peasant, as he often called himself, and he was always courageous and hopeful. For a time he hesitated between historical and *genre* painting, but at length fixed upon representations of pastoral life, that which he knew so well, and with which he was in sympathetic accord. In 1853 he exhibited at the Salon, " The Reapers," "A Shepherd," and "The Sheep-Shearers," and received his first medal ; in 1855, " A Peasant grafting a Tree " ; in 1857, "The Gleaners," which became famous. After this time there was much discussion over his works. " The Woman grazing her Cow " (1859), " The Shepherdess with her Flock " and " Peasants bearing Home a Calf born in the Field " (1864), and the " Knitting-Lesson " (1869), were bitterly criticised on the one hand, and passionately praised on the other. In 1870 he sent works to the Salons for the last time : " November " and " A Woman churning Butter." In the Luxembourg are, " The Church at Greville " (for which 12,200 francs was paid after Millet's death), " The Bathers," and a number of designs or studies in pencil, crayon, and pen drawing. Among his works we would also mention, " A Bit of the Village of Greville," sold at the Faure sale in 1873 for 20,300 francs; "A Woman with a Lamp" at the Laurent-Richard sale, 38,500 francs; " The Evening Angelus " ; " The Potato-Gathering " ; " The Mother cradling her Child "; etc. In the "Harvest of Beans," Millet introduced the portrait of his mother, and the cottage in which he was born. This artist executed only about eighty pictures. When we consider that he painted thirty-one years this is not a large number. He gave much thought to his subjects ; he retained his canvases in his studio, and returned to them from time to time, in order to give to them exactly the sentiment he wished them to express. Millet was in one way extremely remarkable, we might almost say unique ; he never painted from a model. What acuteness of observation was required in order to reproduce from memory, as he did, not only the characteristics of attitude and aspect in his figures, but the details of his landscapes ! He left, besides his pictures, numerous designs and studies in different modes of execution. After his death all that were in his studio (many unfinished) were sold at the Hotel Drouot ; they numbered fifty-six, and brought 321,034 francs. M. Gavet had a collection of designs by Millet, numbering ninety-five, which were also sold at the Hotel Drouot, a short time after the sale above mentioned. Previously, however, M. Gavet had generously placed half his collection on exhibition for one month, for the benefit of the family of the artist. The sale brought 431,050 francs; there were not more than twenty purchasers, and but one who was not French. Millet had also executed quite a number of etchings and a few wood-engravings. The following plates have been made by others from his works:

"The Angelus," engraved by Waltner; "Death and the Wood-Cutter," "Œdipus," and the "Harvest of Beans," by Edmond Hédouin. "The Rustic Labors" and "Les quatre heures du jour" (fourteen pieces) have been copied in wood-cuts by Adrien Lavielle. At the Museum of Fine Arts, Boston, are "An Interior" (unfinished), presented by Martin Brimmer, and "Bergère Assise," gift of S. D. Warren.

"The late M. Millet, besides being a landscape-painter, was a great figure-painter. In the opinion of many, and those not the admirers of the newest phase of French art, the Courbet-Manet-Corot school, he was the first French painter of his time. Certainly the French school has never produced an artist with such thorough devotion to nature, or who has so truthfully rendered scenes and emotions of natural life. His works have nothing theatrical or cynical about them. To an Englishman they are suggestive of the poetry and sentiment of Burns, and the sympathetic feeling for nature of Wordsworth. He had the art of introducing into pictures of modern French pastoral life, while retaining the truthfulness of nature, all the elevated qualities of the best artistic culture to be found in the works of the great masters. Those who remember the 'Angelus du Soir,' in the Exposition of 1867, well know this is no exaggeration. The picture represents a couple of peasants, man and woman, who, while at work in the field, hear the bell of the distant church tolling the *Angelus*. They stop work, reverently bowing their heads in silent prayer. For expression of devotion equally genuine we must go back to the works of the early Italian masters.

"Many of your readers who delighted in Millet's works will probably be interested in hearing of some of the pictures he was last engaged on, but of which few, alas, we may hope, were quite completed. For he kept his works long in the studio, always endeavoring to make them as perfect as possible, not only in their execution but in their sentiment. I remember his showing me a picture of a village church of Normandy, the one in which he was christened. On my speaking of it as completed, 'No,' he said, 'there is an impression of this scene as it struck my imagination when a child which I have not succeeded in rendering, but which I hope to get some day.'

"Barbison is one of those French villages we know so well, a long street of cottages and small farm-houses, with their picturesque *basse-cours*. At the top of the village, approaching the forest of Fontainebleau, is a range of modest buildings, one of which has a large window. This is the residence and studio of Millet. One day last autumn, being at Barbison, I sent my card to M. Millet, and asked permission to see any work he might have finished. He very kindly acceded to my request, and led the way along a shaded alley to his studio. His appearance was decidedly more provincial than Parisian. He wore a straw hat, loose shooting-coat, and *sabots*. His manner was especially courteous and genial, though very quiet. He gave me the impression of being nearer fifty than sixty years of age.

"The picture on his easel represented an old farm-house in Normandy, in which were visible traces of Gothic windows and buttresses: In front was some broken ground with implements of labor; in the distance, the sea. The charm of the picture was in the sentiment of sunny repose in which the old moss and lichen-covered house was steeped. Seeing the respect I had for his work, Millet then produced a series of pictures he had in progress, but which space forbids me to more than briefly notice; the hints will be sufficient for those who know his pictures. Among the figure-subjects were two lovely little idyls, one a shepherd-girl leading home her sheep, girl and sheep and landscape all flushed in rosy light. The second, a boy on a bank blowing his horn to call the cows; the figure was relieved against a sunset sky. A very striking work represented an orchard in springtime; the sun was shining on the near objects and middle distance, over which the rain had just passed; on the dark stormy sky shone a double rainbow. Also a stormy landscape was one subject, with a flock of sheep being driven to shelter under the cover of haystacks. I must not omit a noble composition of which the scene was laid in an autumn field, on a warm sunny afternoon. Women are bringing sheaves of corn to the threshing-ground, around which are ranged a score or so of threshers. This group, for varied and spirited action, is marvelous, and it suggested an orchestra executing an *allegro* motive in a symphony of Beethoven ; behind, straw is being burned, the huge wreath of smoke giving additional impressiveness to the composition.

"There was a series of works that appeared to me deeply touching even then, when their author stood before me in health and vigor. These were some pictures and drawings made during the late war in the neighborhood of his birthplace, a village near Cherbourg. In them was reflected the sadness which must have fallen on every patriotic Frenchman during that terrible period. Its expression was, perhaps, most profoundly given in a landscape representing the seashore, with a long range of low cliffs, the undulating ground and slightly agitated sea being painted in varied tones of gray, exquisitely harmonious, but inexpressibly mournful.

"He seemed to regard with much tenderness a drawing of the house where he was born, very like Burns' cottage, only having an additional story. 'My ancestors were peasants;' said he, 'and I was born a peasant.'

"Herein was the secret of his success, and of his power in reaching the hearts of men. He painted what he had known and loved. He studied and first practiced his art at Paris : latterly, he seems wholly to have lived in the country, and had even given up exhibiting his pictures at the Salon. 'The work there,' he remarked, 'has too much glare and glitter, and too little of the modesty of nature.' " — H. WALLIS, *London Times.*

"At the outset it may be observed that Millet, the greatest painter of humanity seen in France for forty years or more, died last year. None like him survive. To him the human body, with all its exquisite forms and retreating curves, delicate grays and reds, and soft, palpitating flesh, was but a casket, beautiful indeed, but inclosing a still more wonderful and beautiful soul that speaks its volitions and thoughts, its emotions and sensations, with every movement of those limbs, with every parting of those lips, and every glance of those eyes, to whose eloquent and infinite radiance the opals of the Ural or the diamonds of Golconda are but inert matter in comparison. Such was humanity to the searching, divining spirit of Millet." — BENJAMIN's *Contemporary Art in Europe.*

"This picture ['The Gleaners'] attracts you from afar by an air of grandeur and serenity. I might almost say that it announces itself as a religious picture. All is calm there, the drawing is without a fault and the color without glitter. The August sun vigorously warms the canvas, but you find not there those capricious rays which sport themselves in the pictures of M. Diaz, like scholars in vacation-time : the sun of Millet is an earnest sun which ripens the grain, which makes men sweat, and loses no time in trifling." — EDMOND ABOUT, *Salon of* 1857.

"Very different from the mannerists of the ugly, who under a pretext of realism substitute the hideous for the true, he seeks and attains style in the representations of the types and scenes of the country ; he knows how to give them a rare grandeur and nobleness, while he in no sense lessens their rusticity. He understands the inward poesy of the fields, he loves the peasants whom he represents, and in their resigned figures expresses his sympathy for them. The seed-sowing, the harvest, the grafting, are they not virtuous actions having their worth and their grandeur? Why have not peasants style as well as heroes?" — THÉOPHILE GAUTIER.

"The aim of a great painter is not to fly away towards the moon and the stars ; it is to walk with a firm step and a feeling heart in the path which he chooses, always sincere towards himself, towards men, and towards nature. This aim Millet had ; and it was that which made him incomparable and immortal." — THÉOPHILE SILVESTRE.

Millet, Aimé. (*Fr.*) Born at Paris about 1816. Officer of the Legion of Honor. Pupil of his father, of David d'Angers, and Viollet-le-Duc. He studied both painting and sculpture, and made his début as a painter at the Salon of 1842 ; he continued to exhibit pictures until 1852. He is best known and most admired as a sculptor. Among his works may be mentioned, "Ariadne" (at the Luxembourg); " Mercury " (made for the Louvre); " Civil Justice" (made for the Mairie of the first arrondissement of Paris) ; the tomb of Murger, " Youth stripping Leaves from Roses"; " Apollo and the Muses of Poetry and Dancing" (group in bronze for the New Opera at Paris) ; " Vercingétorix " (a statue in copper, *repoussé*), erected at Alise-Sainte-Reine (Côte-d'Or), and " Cassandra placing herself under the Protection of Pallas " (marble group), Salon of 1877. One of the most interesting works of this sculptor is the statue of Chateaubriand, erected at St. Malo (where this author was born) on September 5, 1875. Chateaubriand is represented seated on a rock. His left hand is raised to support the head, but in such a way that the entire face is visible ; in his right hand, which falls on the lap, he holds a crayon. At his feet are exotic plants which recall the travels of Chateaubriand when young. A leaf of the " Genius of Christianity " is held by his elbow on the rock against which he half supports himself ; he is enveloped in a large cloak, which falls gracefully away from the upper part of the figure. The whole effect is most pleasing, and the statue is much admired for its conception and execution. To the Salon of 1878 he contributed two portrait busts in marble.

Millet, Francis D. (*Am.*) Born in Mattapoisett, Mass., 1846. He studied in the Royal Academy of Arts at Antwerp under Van Lerius and De Keyser, gaining the silver and gold medals of honor in 1872 and '73. He has practiced his profession in the United States, Belgium, England, Italy, France, and Austria. He has painted a number of portraits, the most important being those of Charles Francis Adams, Jr., and of Samuel L. Clemens (Mark Twain), both exhibited at the National Academy, New York, in 1877. A large picture called " The Bay of Naples," at the Brussels Salon of 1875, was at the American Centennial Exhibition in Philadelphia in 1876. He was the American Art Juror at the Paris Exposition of 1878, and has distinguished himself as a journalist in America and Europe.

"In the North Room, we first encounter Mr. Millet's portrait of Charles Francis Adams, Jr. This, and the portrait of Mark Twain at the other end of the room, are his only contributions. The latter, owing to its subject, is the more characteristic. Both portraits are excellent, yet with higher 'flesh-tints than the originals : the figures are solid, detach themselves immediately from the background, and are a refreshing contrast to the dim, vapory forms which some portrait-painters give us." — BAYARD TAYLOR, *in New York Tribune,* April 7, 1878.

Mills, Clark. (*Am*) Born in the State of New York, 1815. He learned the trade of a plasterer in Charleston, S. C., beginning about 1835 the modeling of busts in clay, selling his ideal heads for modest prices for some years. His first important work in marble was a bust of John C. Calhoun, finished in 1846, for which he was awarded a gold medal by the City Council of Charleston, in whose possession this work still is. Going thereafter to Washington, D. C., he received a commission from Congress for the equestrian statue of Jackson in that city, cast from cannon captured by that hero, and unveiled on the

8th of January, 1853. For this Congress voted Mills $ 20,000, and $ 50,000 for the Washington statue unveiled in 1860. In 1863 he cast in bronze the statue of " Freedom," designed by Crawford, and now on the dome of the Capitol. A duplicate of the Jackson statue is in New Orleans.

"That Clark Mills possesses genius cannot be doubted, and if his works do not possess all of the conventional graces of European art, he has certainly produced two statues which are original and in perfect keeping with the manly vigor of the Young Republic."— *New York Round Table*, 1866.

" Clark Mills' equestrian statues look like some prodigious Congressional jokes on art."— JARVES' *Art Thoughts.*

Milmore, Martin. (*Am.*) Born in Boston, 1845. He entered the studio of Ball in 1860, and in 1863 he sent to the Sanitary Fair a statuette, entitled " Devotion." He studied and modeled for some time in Rome, executing there busts of Pius IX., Sumner, Wendell Phillips, Emerson, and other noted men. He received the commission for the Soldiers' Monument in Boston, unveiled in 1877, also for the Soldiers' Monument in Forest Hill, Roxbury, Mass. Among his works may be mentioned, busts of Longfellow, Theodore Parker, and of George Ticknor, in the Public Library, Boston ; one of R. W. Emerson, belonging to T. G. Appleton, Boston ; also the ideal figures, of large size, " Ceres," " Flora," and " Pomona," in granite on the Boston Horticultural Hall. His bust of Charles Sumner was presented to George William Curtis by the State of Massachusetts in 1878. He has been happy in representing children. A bust of a young son of ex-Governor Claflin of Massachusetts is notable among his works of this sort.

" The subject is most gracefully treated [Soldiers' Monument, Boston], and the artist is entitled to much credit for the skill with which he has worked out a highly poetic idea."— *Art Journal*, October, 1877.

The Boston Journal of September 18, 1877, in describing the unveiling of the Soldiers' Monument on Boston Common, says : —

" In this, Mr. Milmore's grandest effort, is noted the purity of style which distinguishes him as an artist. . . . . A most striking feature of the monument, and one which will bear the most careful study, is the series of bronze bas-reliefs which are elaborately executed even to the smallest detail. . . . . The statue of ' History ' displays a knowledge and skill which stamp it as the work of genius. . . . . In viewing the monument as a whole the spectator cannot fail to be charmed with the symmetry and completeness of the structure. The immense amount of labor which the sculptor has performed can only be fully realized by a close inspection."

Minardi, Tommaso. (*Ital.*) Born at Faenza (1787 – 1871). This artist was a member of several Academies, and received decorations from several monarchs of Europe. In a *concours* at Milan, Minardi gained the stipend for Rome, where he received from the engraver Longhi a commission for a drawing of the " Last Judgment of Michael Angelo," which is now in the Gallery of the Vatican. While at Rome he was appointed to a professorship in Perugia, where he became so distinguished that he was made professor in the Academy of St. Luke at Rome. His "Vision of St. Stanislaus" is in the Doria Palace; the "Propagation of Faith," a masterly work, is in the Quirinal; "Hector reproving Paris," at Ravenna; the "Supper at Emmaus," at Faenza; and the fresco of "Lost Souls" at Campo Verano in Rome. Minardi made an album containing four hundred representations of the Holy Family. After he was stricken with paralysis he made a lovely crayon drawing of "Hippocrates and his Scholars," which he presented to his physician, Professor Baccelli of Rome.

Minor, Robert C. (*Am.*) Born in New York, 1840. He studied art in Paris under Diaz, and in Antwerp under Van Luppen, Boulanger, and others, traveling through Germany and Italy for some time. His studio is in New York, and he has exhibited at the National Academy, in Brooklyn, Chicago, and elsewhere in America. Among his works are, "Evening," "Dawn," "Studio of Corot," etc. He is a member of the Society of American Artists.

"When we come to the works of our resident artists, who represent what may be called the progressive school of art, we find much to admire. Robert C. Minor's landscapes are always as interesting as they are characteristic. They are strongly impressed with the sentiment of the place and the hour which they represent. . . . . His 'Studio of Corot,' a charming bit of landscape, how it impresses you with just the feeling you would have in the solitude of the country, just after the break of day, and before the sun has burned up the far-reaching mists." — *Boston Transcript*, March, 1878.

"There are those, doubtless, who will blame Mr. Minor for direct imitation in his 'Studio of Corot,' a landscape not surpassed in the Exhibition. But apart from the fact that it is permitted to one artist to see a phase of nature as depicted by another, why should individuality be denied an artist who, seeing and loving one of nature's aspects, endeavors to the best of his ability to acknowledge his indebtedness to the man who has most reverently studied and must adequately expressed that same aspect. In Mr. Minor's other pictures, especially the three smaller ones, 'Autumn Woods,' 'Under the Oaks,' and 'Evening' [Society of American Artists, 1878], no one will miss individuality or force, though prettiness — one of the banes of modern art as of modern literature — will not be found." — *New York Evening Mail*, March 8, 1878.

Mintrop, Theodor. (*Ger.*) Born at Heithausen (1814–1870). This painter was poor, and labored as a peasant until he was thirty years old, when his sketches came under the notice of Geselchap, who introduced him to the art circles of Düsseldorf and secured the recognition of his remarkable powers. He painted but little in oils. His best works are cartoons and friezes, full of his fancies. Such subjects as "Wine," "Occupations of Winter," "Life in the Fields," and the "Apotheosis of Bacchus" were thus rendered by him, and are worthy of much praise.

M'Kay, William D. (*Brit.*) Native of Gifford, East Lothian, Scotland. He began his art studies in 1860, in the Ornamental Class of the School of Design in Edinburgh. Later, he studied under Robert Scott Lauder from the antique, gaining, in 1863, a first prize for the best study in monochrome, and entering the same year the Life Schools of the Royal Scottish Academy. He was elected an Associate of the

Royal Scottish Academy in 1877, exhibiting regularly in its gallery. His specialty is landscapes with cattle and figures. His professional life has been spent in Edinburgh. Among his pictures may be noted, "An October Morning," "Field-Working in Spring, — at the Potato Pits," "Twilight," "Seedtime," etc.

Molteni, Giuseppe. (*Ital.*) Born at Alferi, near Milan (1800 – 1867). Member of the Academy of Milan and Conservator of the Brera Gallery. Pupil of the Academy of Milan. His picture of "The Confession " is in the Vienna Gallery. "A Holy Family ". is at the National Gallery, Berlin. His works are principally in private collections. Molteni gained several medals, and received the decorations of various orders.

Monchablon, Xavier Alphonse. (*Fr.*) Born at Avillers. *Prix de Rome*, 1863. Medals, 1869 and '74. Pupil of Cornu and Gleyre. At the Salon of 1877 he exhibited " The Toilet of Venus "; in 1876, a portrait and " Jeanne d'Arc "; in 1875, " Salvator Mundi " and two portraits; and in 1878, "A Fallen Titan " and " Summer," " August," and " October," three decorative panels.

Montagny, Étienne. (*Fr.*) Born at Saint-Étienne, 1816. Chevalier of the Legion of Honor. Pupil of Rude and David d'Angers. His "Saint Louis de Gonzague " (1864) is at the Luxembourg. In 1877 he exhibited "St. Francis of Assisi," a statue in stone, and " Hope," statue, plaster; in. 1873, " Mater Dei," statue, a font. His portrait busts and statues are numerous, and many have been seen at the Salons.

Montalba, Clara. (*Brit.*) A native of Cheltenham. She studied in Paris under Eugène Isabey, spending her professional life, which began in 1874, in London and Venice. She was elected an Associate of the Society of Painters in Water-Colors in 1874, and has been a member of the Société des Acquarellistes Belges since 1876. Among the more important of her works are, " The Last Journey " (7 by 4½), in oil (R. A., 1878) ; " Clearing the Customs," water-color (never exhibited), 4 by 6 feet (both belonging to W. Ingram, M. P.), " Blackfriars' Bridge," " Fishing-Boats," " Venice," etc. Her " Blessing a Tomb, Westminster," was at the Philadelphia Exhibition of 1876, and her "Corner of St. Mark's, Venice " and " Fishing-Boats, Venice " (all in water-colors) were at Paris in 1878.

" 'Il Guardino Publico' stands foremost among the few redeeming features of the Exhibition [Society of British Artists, 1874]. In delicate perception of natural beauty the picture suggests the example of Corot. Like the great Frenchman, Miss Montalba strives to interpret the sadder moods of Nature, when the wind moves the water a little mournfully, and the outlines of the objects become uncertain in the filmy air." — *Art Journal*, January, 1874.

Monteverde, Giulio. (*Ital.*) Born at Bristagno, near Acqui, about 1836. Professor in the Academy at Rome. The prize of 4,000 lire given at the National Exhibition of Fine Arts at Milan was awarded to the " Genius of Franklin," executed by this sculptor. The work was purchased by the Khédive of Egypt, who conferred on Monteverde the diploma and insignia of Commendatore of Medjié. At the Vienna Exposition his group of "Jenner inoculating his little Daughter," though only in plaster, attracted much attention and gained the gold medal, to which was added the title of Commendatore of the Order of Francis Joseph. One of the latest works of this Roman artist is a colossal monumental group, in honor of Riva of Turin. A statue called "The First Inspirations of Columbus" is in the Boston Art Museum. At Munich in 1870 he exhibited "Children playing with a Cat" (belonging to the King of Würtemberg). Several works by this artist were at the Paris Exposition in 1878, and his model for the monument of Count Massari was much praised by Anatole de Montaiglon in the "Gazette des Beaux-Arts," July, 1878.

Monvel, Louis-Maurice Boutet de. (*Fr.*) Born at Orleans. Pupil of Cabanel, G. Boulanger, J. Lefebvre, and Carolus Duran. Medal of third class in 1878, when he exhibited "The Good Samaritan" and a portrait; in 1877, he sent "The Toilet of Venus" and a portrait ; in 1876, two portraits.

Mooney, Edward, N. A. (*Am.*) Born in New York, 1813. He studied in the National Academy, gaining a gold medal for an original design of a single figure in oil. He was also a pupil of Inman and of William Page. He has spent his professional life in his native city, working, however, during three winters, in Columbus, Ga., and one in Savannah. His summer house is at Red Hook, New York. His specialty has been portrait-painting. He was elected an Associate of the National Academy in 1839 and Academician in 1840. Among the better known of Mr. Mooney's portraits is that of Achmet Ben Aman, Commander of the ship "Sultan," and representative of the Imaum of Muscat to the United States, which was at the National Academy in 1840, and was purchased by the Common Council of New York. His portraits of ex-Mayors Isaac L. Varian, Andrew Mickle, and Jacob R. Westervelt are in the City Hall, New York; that of Judge Edmunds belongs to the New York Bar Association; and that of Governor Seward is in the State House at Albany.

Moore, George B. (*Brit.*) (1806–1876.) Engaged for some years as a teacher of drawing in the University of London and in the Military Academy at Woolwich. Was the author of several useful educational works on art subjects. He has not exhibited at the Royal Academy since 1859.

Moore, Albert. (*Brit.*) A native of York. He studied in the Langham Life Classes in London, and has practiced his profession in the English metropolis for some years. His specialty is the human figure, treated in a decorative style. Among his later pictures are, "Garnets," at the Royal Academy, in 1878; "Birds," at the Grosvenor Gallery, the same year. To the Royal Academy, in 1871, he sent "Battledoor" and "Shuttlecock," companion pictures ; in 1874,

"Shells"; in 1875, "The Flower-Walk"; in 1876, "Beads"; etc. His "Finis," "Beads," and the "Palm Fan" were at the Paris Exposition of 1878.

"Albert Moore is indeed, I think, so far as any contiguity of modern to ancient art may be predicted at all, nearer in spirit to the Greek than any other artist among us. . . . . He stands nearly alone in our day in his realization of an ideal physical nobleness in the human type, and in his power of arranging and combining the lines of the human form into visible rhythm and symmetry, not less delightful than are the audible rhythm and symmetry of music." — SIDNEY COLVIN, *in English Painters of the Present Day.*

"The motives of Albert Moore's art certainly differ widely from that of most of his contemporaries; it differs also from the spirit of much that is great in modern painting. His purpose does not include either sentiment or passion, and the form and color of his work are suggested by the simplest incidents of physical movement." — *Art Journal,* July, 1874.

"'The Reader' is the finest picture in the whole fifteen hundred [Royal Academy, 1877]. . . . . The very essence of the purity of coloring has been introduced by Mr. Albert Moore into this single figure, which, clad in the artistic peculiar shade of red overhung with white, stands engrossed in the pamphlet she easily balances in her hands. All Mr. Moore's works testify to that rare quality of the good effect produced by contrast of color, and the value obtained by placing it judiciously in small quantities." — *London Observer,* May, 1877.

"To a more purely decorative school — for he banishes emotion altogether — belongs Mr. Albert Moore, who has studied the treatment of draperies in the Greek, rather than in the Italian school, and who works in a key of color, or rather of tinting, all his own. He has a way of throwing his flesh into half-shadow, whilst the accessories are brilliant, and the color of this half-shadow is objectionable, — heavy gray with a tinge of violet: this is his one flaw as a colorist, and we have long remarked it. He draws very sufficiently well, but no more than that: and he has an intelligent energy of action, which does not mar decorative repose; of this his 'Birds' is an example. His plan of yellow is exquisitely fanciful and inventive, and in these fine variations he uses as his strongest accent orange-color, the one hue all but universally avoided in art, with happy effect." — *Magazine of Art,* July, 1878.

Moore, Henry. (*Brit.*) A brother of Albert Moore, and a pupil of the Langham Schools. He paints landscapes and marine views, particularly the latter, in oil and water colors. He has a studio in London, exhibiting frequently at the Royal Academy for some years. He was at one time a member of the Society of British Artists, and was elected an Associate of the Society of Painters in Water-Colors in 1876. Among his works in oil may be noted, "Loss of a Barque in Yarmouth Roads," "The Last of the Light," "Mist and Sunshine," "Highland Pastures," "Moonlight," etc. In water-colors he has exhibited "Sunset in the Highlands," "The First Snow of Autumn," "A Fresh Breeze" (marine), "A Salmon Pool," "A Mountain Loch," and others. To the Philadelphia Exhibition of 1876 he sent "A Winter Gale in the Channel" and "Storm coming on at Sunset, Coast of North Wales," both in oil. To Paris, in 1878, he sent (also in oil-colors) "Rough Weather in the Mediterranean" and "A Bright Morning after a Gale."

"'Against the Tide' [water-color] is by an artist, Henry Moore, who describes the different moods of the sea with language peculiarly forcible, and without exhausting his means of effect with exaggerated masses of water." — *Art Journal,* March, 1873.

" H. Moore's ' Loss of a Barque ' is a vessel aground and swamped by breakers. The movement of the waves is powerfully rendered, and the sea is very truly painted ; there is much beauty in the effect of light and local color ; the modeling, though the reverse of smooth, is characteristic of the painter."— *London Athenæum,* May, 1877.

" We must give strong praise to Henry Moore's ' Highland Pastures,' a picture which unites with the artist's invariable mastery of hand and knowledge, a repose and reserve of color which are less usual in his works."— *Magazine of Art,* August, 1878.

Moore, H. Humphrey. (*Am.*) Born in New York, 1844. Displayed a taste for art at an early age; studied in his native city and in San Francisco. In 1865 he went to Munich. After some time spent there and in l'École des Beaux-Arts in Paris, he entered the studio of Gérôme. Later, going to Spain, he met Fortuny at Madrid, whose friend and pupil he became. He devoted two years to the study of Moorish life, and between the years 1873 and '75, he worked in Rome with Fortuny on his " Almeh." In 1875 he returned to the United States. Among his better-known pictures are his "Almeh," " Blind Guitar-Player " (belonging to Robert Graves of Tarrytown), "Gypsy Encampment, Granada," " Moorish Bazaar " (belonging to Charles S. Smith of New York), " Let Me Alone ! " (in the collection of Judge Hilton), " A Bulgarian," "Moorish Merchant," etc. He received a medal for the " Almeh " at the Philadelphia Centennial Exhibition of 1876.

" ' The Moorish Merchant,' by H. H. Moore, is a very strongly painted picture, illustrative of a scene in Tangiers, where the picture was painted. We believe Mr. Moore was once a pupil of Fortuny : at any rate, his art motives and ideas are of the character of that artist. The drawing of this picture deserves marked attention, and the coloring, although necessarily gay, is true to nature. The heads are characteristic both of the race and with reference to the action of the scene."— *Buffalo Courier,* February 7, 1877.

" The figure of the swaying, admirably drawn, and poised woman has the modesty of unconsciousness, associated with gayety ; the abandon of delight in a voluptuous dance without the expression or manner of one impure. The dance, or rather body-swaying, of the ' Almeh ' is located by the artist in one of the gorgeous halls of the Alhambra, frescoed in the intricate and dreamy harmony of Moresque decorations, and over the floor is spread a carpet rich in warm hues. The attitude of the girl leaves the body semi-nude, and, while correct in point of costume, is contrived with consummate judgment for effect in color."— *San Francisco Morning Call,* November 11, 1877.

Moran, Edward, A. N. A. (*Am.*) Born in Lancashire, England, 1829. Elder brother of Peter and Thomas Moran. He arrived in Philadelphia in 1844, and was a pupil of James Hamilton, marine-painter, and of Paul Weber, landscape-artist. He went abroad in 1862, studying in the Royal Academy, London, for a few months. In 1869 he settled in New York, going to Paris in 1877, where he still resides (1878). He is a member of the Philadelphia Academy of Fine Arts, and was elected an Associate of the National Academy in 1873. His first pictures were exhibited in Philadelphia in 1853. Among the better known of his works are, " Mt. Lafayette from Franconia, N. H.," " Bay of New York " (several views), " Liberty enlightening the World," " Launch of the Life-Boat " (owned by Matthew Read of Philadelphia), " The Lord staying the Waters " (owned by Robert Hare Powell, Philadelphia), " Outward Bound " (owned by Charles

Sharpless, Philadelphia), "The Last from the Wreck," "The Tempest, from 'David Copperfield,'" "The Bottom of the Sea," "The Arrival of the Relief Ship at Havre," "Old Fort Dumpling, Newport" (belonging to George L. Thayer, of Boston), etc.

To the Centennial Exhibition of 1876 he sent "The Hawk's Nest" and "Minot Ledge Light" (belonging to Mrs. H. E. Lawrence), "The Winning Yacht" (belonging to W. A. Caldwell), "Moonlight in New York Bay" and "Coming Storm over New York Bay" (belonging to R. E. Moore). Mr. Moran is at present turning his attention particularly to figure-painting in Paris, and with promise of much success.

" Mr. Moran very justly merits the reputation which he enjoys as an eminent landscape and marine painter, for it has been earned by diligent application, combined with close observation of nature. He seems to be constituted peculiarly for an artist, for with quick perceptive faculties and a mind capable of reflection, the task of transcribing and translating with truthfulness the simple beauties and refined grandeur of the land and sea has not been to him an irksome toil, but has proved a pleasure ; consequently, his pictures have in the highest degree the quality of imparting delight to others. An appreciative observer cannot fail to regard them as faithful and intelligent interpretations of the truth and the sentiment of ever-varying nature. . . . . The versatility of this artist is also unusual, for there are few subjects of general interest in the outer world that he has not touched. The willow-copse and the lily-pond, the caves of ocean and the mountain snow-hooded and severe, children busy with nets or playing on the shelly sand, the freshness of spring and the glory of antumn, are among his productions." — *Philadelphia Evening Bulletin,* March 6, 1871.

" ' In the Narrows,' by Edward Moran, is the finest marine we have yet seen from his pencil. Nothing could be simpler in plan or color. . . . . The great charm of the picture is *motion.* That is something far beyond effects of technique. Everything is in swift er beautiful motion. The forms of the water are exquisitely chiseled, so sharp and yet so fleeting, and painted all with two colors, the local color of the water and its shadow color. The drawing shows no random work, but every stroke laid on with consummate knowledge." — *Baltimore Gazette,* July 1, 1878.

Moran, Thomas. (*Am.*) Born in Lancashire, England, 1837. Brother of Edward and Peter Moran. He was taken to America in 1844. Displayed artistic tastes at an early age, and was apprenticed to a wood-engraver in Philadelphia, remaining with him for two years. He turned his attention to water-color painting, studying without a master. In 1860 he began the use of oils, his first picture being an illustration of Shelley's "Alastor." He went to Europe in 1862, and again in 1866, studying and copying on his first visit the works of Turner in London ; on his second, the old masters in France and Italy. In 1871 he accompanied the Exploring Expedition to the Yellowstone Country, and in 1873 went upon a similar expedition under Major Powell, making sketches for his two great works, "The Grand Cañon of the Yellowstone" and "The Chasm of the Colorado," which were purchased by Congress for $ 10,000 each, and are both in the Capitol in Washington. His studio was in Philadelphia until 1872, when he removed to New York. He is an Academician of the Pennsylvania Academy of Fine Arts, a member of the Artists'

Fund Society of Philadelphia, of the Society of American Painters in
Water-Colors, and of the Society of American Artists, organized in
1878. Among the more important of Mr. Moran's works may be men-
tioned, " The Last Arrow " (belonging to Mr. Baird of Philadelphia),
" The Ripening of the Leaf " (to Mr. Drexel), " The Groves were
God's First Temples " (to Dr. J. M. Sommerville of Philadelphia),
" The Remorse of Cain " (to V. Stausse, Philadelphia), " The Children of the Mountain " (at the Paris Exposition of 1867, belonging to
Roswell Smith of New York), " The Cliffs of Green River " (to John
Taylor Johnston of New York), " The First Ship," " Ponce De Leon
in Florida," " A Dream of the Orient," " A Ride for Life," etc. Many
of these have been exhibited in New York, Philadelphia, and other
American cities. He sent to the Centennial, in 1876, " The Mountain of the Holy Cross," and others, for which he received a medal
and diploma.

Besides painting in oil and water-color, Thomas Moran has made
many illustrations for books of travel, history, etc., the original water-
color drawings for Prang's " Yellowstone National Park " (the most
elaborate work of the kind yet produced in this country), and has devoted much time to lithography and other methods of engraving.

"Next to Church's 'Niagara,' Mr. Moran's 'Great Cañon of the Yellowstone' will,
we are sure, be received by the best judges of America as the finest historical landscape
yet painted in this country.' In its original, no less than by its actual achievement, it
deserves to be placed so near to the most famous picture that ever came out of an
American studio. . . . . The composition is arranged with great skill ; the tree drawing
is most satisfactory, and the variety, the richness, the delicacy of the color, must surprise those who have learned from other artists that nature in those regions is dressed
mostly in hodden-gray." — C. C., *in New York Tribune*, May 3, 1872.

" The shrubbery and the foliage are painted with a free but at the same time a careful
hand, and even though occupying a subordinate place in the picture (' The Mountain
of the Holy Cross '), are finished to a high degree. Mr. Moran's touch has greatly improved in firmness, crispness, and certainty, and in this canvas he shows a thorough
command over the technique of his art. The only point in which he seems to have
failed is in giving distance. The picture seems to lack atmosphere. . . . . Beyond this we
have only praise to bestow on the picture." — *Boston Saturday Evening Gazette*, November 14, 1875.

" Of the fidelity of this painting, ' The Mountain of the Holy Cross,' to the special
characteristics of the Rocky Mountains no traveler in the far West can hold one moment
of question. Of the skill in management there can be as little difference of opinion." —
Aldine, April, 1875.

Moran, Peter. (*Am.*) Born in Bolton, Lancashire, England,
1842. He went first to America as a child, and began the study of
art under his brother, Thomas Moran, in Philadelphia. In 1863 he
went to London, and spent some time in studying the English masters, but he has never been connected with any particular school of
painting. He was elected a member of the Artists' Fund Society in
1867, and of the Pennsylvania Academy of Fine Arts in 1868. He
has spent his professional life in Philadelphia, where many of his pic-

tures have been exhibited and are owned. To the Centennial Exhibition of 1876 he sent "The Return of the Herd" (for which he received a medal) and "A Settled Rain" (sheep in a barnyard), which was purchased by a gentleman of New York. He received also a medal for his etchings on copper, — five frames of animal subjects. To the National Academy, in 1875, he sent "A Sunny Slope"; in 1876, "Sand Hills, Atlantic City." His "After the Chase" (rough hounds on the outskirts of a wood in autumn) is owned by P. A. Widner of Philadelphia, and his "Twilight, — Sheep returning Home" (never publicly exhibited) is in the collection of W. H. Whitney of the same city.

"Peter Moran's excellent etchings are very varied in style and subject, and show a thorough mastery over the resources of the etching-needle." — *Art Journal*, June, 1867.

Moreau, Mathurin. (*Fr.*) Born at Dijon about 1824. Chevalier of the Legion of Honor. Pupil of Ramey and Dumont. His "Spinning-Girl" (1861) is at the Luxembourg. This sculptor has usually represented such subjects as "Spring," "Summer," "Meditation," etc., which require single figures. His groups are, "Sleeping Children," "Saltarella," "Primavera," etc. To the Salon of 1878 he sent a statue of "Oceanie" and a statuette of "Phryne."

Moreau, Mathurin-Auguste. (*Fr.*) Born at Dijon. Son and pupil of the preceding. He received a third-class medal in 1874, when he exhibited "Hylas," statue, plaster; "Children," bas-relief, terra-cotta; and "Rita," bust, bronze. In 1877 he exhibited "The Path of Flowers," group, plaster.

Moreau, Adrien. (*Fr.*) Born at Troyes. Medal in 1876. Pupil of Pils. At the Salon of 1877 were "The Tziganes" and "Under the Shrubbery"; in 1876, "Repose at the Farm" and a "Fair in the Middle Ages"; in 1878, "Gypsies of Granada" and "Le menuet."

Moreau, Gustave. (*Fr.*) Born at Paris. Chevalier of the Legion of Honor. Pupil of Picot. At the Salon of 1876 he exhibited, "Hercules and the Hydra of Lernæ," "Salome," and some sketches in water-colors. His picture of "The Swimming Lesson" is a pleasing work. His "Orpheus" (1868) is at the Luxembourg.

Moreau-Vauthier, Augustin Jean. (*Fr.*) Born at Paris. Medals at Paris in 1865 and '75. Pupil of Toussaint. At Philadelphia he exhibited a "Young Italian Shepherd," in bronze, and received a medal. To the Salon of 1878 he contributed "St. Geneviève" (marble statuette) and "Fortune" (plaster statue).

Morelli, Domenico. (*Ital.*) Born at Naples, 1826. Honorary Member of the Academy of St. Fernando of Spain at Madrid; of the Royal Academy of Archæology, Literature, and Fine Arts of Naples; and of all the Academies of Fine Arts of Italy. Commander of the Orders of SS. Maurice and Lazarus, and of the Crown of Italy, and Cavalier of the Order of Civil Merit of Savoy. He resides at Naples, and was sent, when quite young, to Rome by the Neapolitan government. He was the pupil of Prof. Camillo Guerra. In 1855 he took the first prize at the Exposition at Naples ; at the National Exposition of Italy in 1861, and at the Paris Exposition of 1867, he received gold medals. Among his works are, " Cesare Borgia at the Siege of Capua," owned by Count Tosca of Palermo ; " Christian Martyrs," in the Gallery of Capo di Monte ; " The Assumption," in the Royal Chapel at Naples ; " Tasso and Eleonora" ; a " Madonna and Child," in the church of Castellani, which has been praised by Prof. Villari ; a " Christ," painted for the composer Verdi ; an " Odalisque after the Bath " ; etc. The works of Morelli are much praised by Italian critics, and in "Volere and Potere " Sig. Lessona has devoted a chapter to him. At the Paris Exposition of 1878 were his " Odalisque " and " The Temptation of St. Anthony."

"The Neapolitan Morelli paiots sacred subjects iu a less ludicrous, declamatory style, but after a curious manner, equally removed from any profound feeling. He is versatile and clever, but neither sincere nor skillful enough to revive the dubious merits of the Spagnuola school of his native city, whose technical eccentricities he affects. So far as my observation goes, the ' professors' of art, like those of literature, darken knowledge rather than enlighten the people or advance taste. " — JARVES, *Art Thoughts.*

Morgan, William, N. A. (*Am.*) Born in London, 1826. He has spent the greater part of his life in New York, receiving his art education in the schools of the National Academy. Among his more important paintings are, "Emancipation," in the Olyphant Collection (exhibited at the National Academy in 1868) ; " The Legend " (N. A., 1875), belonging to Governor Fairbanks of Vermont ; " Song without Words " (N. A., 1876), belonging to Mr. Dutcher of New York ; " Motherhood " ; " Reverie" ; " The Oracle " ; etc.

"From the easel of William Morgan there is a half-length life-sized figure of a girl, seated in an old library, surrounded by musty books. Tha subject is entitled 'Tha Legend,' and, aside from its unexpressive name, forms a delightful study. The pose is exceedingly graceful, and the modeling of the face, neck, and arms is painted with rare taste." — *Art Journal,* May, 1875.

Morgan, Matthew ("**Matt**"). (*Brit.-Am.*) Born about 1840. He was a pupil of Telbin, with whom he worked for some years. He painted scenery at Drury Lane Theater, and while engaged at that house developed a taste for caricature, which led to his becoming connected with the London Tomahawk, a comic illustrated journal. Later, he went to Spain, making many large designs in water-colors. After his return to London he was engaged by Mr. Frank Leslie, for that publisher's newspaper, and went to America about 1865 or '66, as a rival to Thomas Nast, who was furnishing political caricatures for the Harpers. Later, Mr. Morgan was employed by Jarrett & Palmer and other theatrical managers in New York, besides engaging in certain theatrical ventures of his own. He is at present a resident of Philadelphia, drawing on stone in the Ledger Building there. He is an occasional contributor to the exhibitions of the American Water-Color Society, sending, in 1875, " The Old Home Fading away," of which the Art Journal of March, 1875, said, "The picture is well composed, and is excellent in drawing, but the color is cold and crude."

Morin, François-Gustave. (*Fr.*) Born at Rouen, 1809. Chevalier of the Legion of Honor. Member of the Academy of Rouen. His "Ariosto reading Fragments of his Poem," and other works of his, are in the Museum of Rouen. "Titian preparing his Colors" is at the Museum of Havre. Several of his pictures have been engraved by Sixdeniers.

Morot, Aimé-Nicolas. (*Fr.*) Born at Nancy. *Prix de Rome,* 1873. Medal in 1877. Pupil of Cabanel. At the Salon of 1877 he exhibited "Medea" and a portrait of Mlle. d'Épinay; at that of 1873, "Daphnis and Chloe."

Morrell, Imogene Robinson. (*Am.*) A native of Attleborough, Mass., she studied art in Düsseldorf under Camphausen, and in Paris under Couture, residing in Paris for some years. She paints portrait, *genre,* and historical pictures, gaining a medal at the Mechanics' Fair, Boston, and at the Exhibition of Philadelphia in 1876. Among her more important works are, "The First Battle between the Puritans and the Indians," and "Washington and his Staff welcoming a Provision Train" (both at the Centennial), "David before Saul," and others. Her pictures are still signed by her maiden name, Imogene Robinson.

"In the painting of the horses Mrs. Morrell has shown great knowledge of their action, and the finish is superb. The work is painted with great strength throughout, and its solidity and forcible treatment will be admired by all who take an interest in Revolutionary history. . . . . In the drawing of the figures of Standish, and the chief at his side, and the dead and dying savages, there is a fine display of artistic power, and the grouping of the figures is masterly. As in the companion picture, the utmost care has been taken in the finish. and the painting shows a solidity of treatment and a mastery of a higher standard in art than is often attained by a female artist. In color the works are exceedingly brilliant." — *New York Evening Post,* February 29, 1876.

Morris, P. R., A. R. A. (*Brit.*) Born in 1836. For two years he studied in the British Museum, chiefly the Elgin marbles, entering the Royal Academy in 1855. The same year he won the silver medal of the Royal Academy for best drawing from life; in 1856 he received two medals; in 1858 he won the gold medal for the best historical painting, "The Good Samaritan," and won also the traveling studentship, spending some time in Italy and France. He first exhibited at the Royal Academy, in 1858, "Peaceful Days," a picture purchased by T. R. Creswick, R. A. To the Gallery of the British Institute, in 1860, he sent the "Widow's Harvest"; in 1864, "Where they Crucified Him"; in 1865, "The Battle Scar." His "Voices from the Sea" was at the Royal Academy in 1860; "Captives' Return," in 1861; "Jesu Salvator," in 1865; "Riven Shield," in 1866; "Drift Wreck from the Armada," in 1867; "Ambuscade," in 1869; "The Summit of Calvary," in 1871; "Highland Pastoral," in 1872;

" Whereon• he Died," in 1873.; "Through the Dell," in 1874 ; in
1875, " The Mowers " ; in 1876, " The Sailor's Wedding " ; in 1877,
" The Heir of the Manor " and " The Lost Heir"; in 1878, when
he was elected Associate of the Royal Academy, he contributed
" The First Communion" and " The Tomb." His " Shadow of the
Cross," never exhibited, belongs to the Baroness Burdett-Coutts. " The
Mowers," " The Reaper and the Flowers," and " The Sailor's Wed-
ding " were at the Paris Exposition of 1878.

"Mr. Morris has taken the suggestions for the grace that is in this picture [' End of
the Journey,' R A, 1874] from a simple and earnest style of real life, and the effect he
gains could be got only by close and long observation of figures and landscape seen together. Thus we have no touch of the artificial pose and conscious elegance of the pro-
fessed model. . . . . In the execution of the landscape we note what seems to us to be
the most defective work of the picture. The treatment of twilight wants subtlety and
depth ; passages of color here and there help to give a crude effect to the whole design.
Nevertheless, few works of more delicate and tender sentiment are in the Exhibition." —
Art Journal, July, 1874.

Morse, Samuel F. B., N. A. (*Am.*) Born in Charlestown, Mass.
(1791 – 1872). Graduated at Yale College, 1810. Went to England
the following year with Washington Allston, whose pupil he was,
studying also under Benjamin West. He executed a model of a Dying Hercules, for which he received a gold medal from the Adelphi
Society of Arts. In 1829 he made a second voyage to Europe for the
purpose of completing his art studies. He was one of the founders
of the New York Academy of Design in 1826, and its second president, holding the office from 1829 to '45. At one time he was lecturer on the Fine Arts at the New York Athenæum. As a painter,
he was not very successful, and abandoned art as a profession in
1839. Such of his pictures as still exist are prized rather as the work
of Morse, the inventor of the Electric Telegraph, than on account of
any particular artistic merit of their own. His " House of Representatives in Washington in 1823," belonging to Joseph Ripley, was at
the National Academy in 1869.

Morse, Henry D. (*Am.*) Born in Boston, 1826, where he has since
lived. He had no instruction in art, and cannot be considered a professional artist. Still, in his leisure hours for many years he has
painted pictures, generally of animals and game, which have met with
a ready sale in Boston, and are very highly regarded. He is a member of the Boston Art Club.

Mortemart-Boisse, Baron Enguerrand de. (*Fr.*) Born at
Paris. Medal in 1876. Pupil of A. Johannot and T. Johannot. At
the Salon of 1876 he exhibited " The Bed of an Alpine Torrent near
Nice," and in 1878, " An Oil Mill near Nice."

Moser, Karl Adalbert. (*Ger.*) Born at Berlin, 1832. Medal
at Berlin, 1854. Pupil of the Berlin Academy. Visited France and
Italy. He has executed decorations for various government buildings,
reliefs for the Beuth monument, and the groups on the Belle-Alliance-

Platze. At the National Gallery, Berlin, is his figure called "Kunst-technik."

Moss, Ella A. (*Am.*) Born in New Orleans, 1844. Went to Europe at an early age, became a pupil of the Düsseldorf schools under Professor Sohn, and spent many years in the study and practice of her profession in Belgium and Germany. She returned to the United States in the winter of 1877 – 78, opening a studio in New York. Among her portraits are those of many distinguished people in Europe and America. She exhibited a portrait of Rev. Dr. Morgan at the National Academy in 1878.

Mouchot, Louis. (*Fr.*) Born at Paris. Chevalier of the Legion of Honor. Pupil of Drölling and Belloc. At the Salon of 1877 he exhibited "A Dahabieh on the Nile"; in 1876, "The Ducal Palace at Venice" and "The Grand Canal"; in 1875, "A Shop at Cairo" and "The Shadoof"; in 1874, "Evening Prayer"; and in 1878, "The Grand Canal, Venice" and "A Street in Cairo."

Moulin, Hippolyte. (*Fr.*) Born at Paris. Medals in 1864, '67, and '69. Pupil of Barye. Exhibited at Philadelphia "The Secret" and "A Discovery at Pompeii," both in bronze, for which he received a medal. At the Paris Salon in 1877 he exhibited "Gallia Nostra," statue, plaster, which was praised by Proth in his "Voyage au Pays des Peintres" for that year. "A Discovery at Pompeii" (1864) is at the Luxembourg. To the Salon of 1878 he sent a portrait of M. Duquesne.

Mount, Shepard, A. N. A. (*Am.*) (1804–1868.) Painter of portraits and game pictures. Elected an Associate of the National Academy in 1831, and Academician in 1842. Among his works, exhibited in different seasons, may be named his portrait of Admiral Bailey, U. S. N.; portrait of himself, painted in 1833, and now in the possession of the National Academy; and "Quail," "Brook Trout," "Shell-Fish," "Wood-Robin," "Flowers," etc.

Mount, William S., N. A. (*Am.*) (1806–1868.) Native of Long Island. Began the practice of his profession as an artist in New York in 1829. In 1832 he was elected member of the National Academy. His first picture was "The Daughter of Jairus," but he early turned his attention to the representation of the negro character, in which he was very successful in a quaintly humorous way. During the later years of his life his pictures were rarely exhibited in public. He sent to the National Academy of 1868, "A Portrait of a Lady" (belonging to William H. Wickham) and "The Dawn of Day." He died before the opening of the Exhibition. The next year was seen in the same gallery his "Peach Blossoms" (belonging to J. M. Falconer). His "Turning the Grindstone" and "Farmer's Nooning" were the property of Jonathan Sturges. "The Turn of the Leaf" is in the collection of James Lenox, "Bargaining for a Horse" is in the New York Historical Society, and "Raffling for a Goose" (which has been engraved, and was very popular in its day) belongs to M. O. Roberts.

"Very expressive and clever are Mount's happy delineations of the arch, quaint, gay, and rustic humors seen among the primitive people of his native place ; they are truly American." — TUCKERMAN's *Book of the Artists.*

Mozier, Joseph. (*Am.*) Born in Burlington, Vt. (1812–1870). Was originally a merchant in New York. Having decided artistic tastes and talents, he went to Europe in 1845, opening a studio in Rome, and remaining there until his death. Among the better known of his sculptures are, "Pocahontas," "Wept of the Wish-ton-Wish," "Rizpah," "Rebecca at the Well," "Jephthah's Daughter," "White Lady of Avenel," "Undine," "Queen Esther," and "Truth" and "Silence" (the last two belonging to the Astor Library, New York). His "Prodigal Son" is in the Philadelphia Academy of Fine Arts.

"There is much pathos in this composition [' The Prodigal Son '], which appeals with directness and force to the hearts of those who pause in their rambles through the gallery to gaze on it. The benignity and fatherly tenderness of the old man are expressed in a language that all may read, and that requires no explanation or commentary." — *Great American Sculptors.*

M'Taggart, William. (*Brit.*) Born in Campbeltown. He received his art education in the Trustees Academy, Edinburgh, entering that institution in 1852, and spending his professional life in that city. His specialty is the painting of child-life. He was elected an Associate of the Royal Scottish Academy in 1859, and Academician in 1870. Among his pictures are, "Love lightens Labor," "The Young Travelers," "Followers of the Fine Arts," "An Old Salt," and at the Royal Scottish Academy in 1870, "The Fisher's Landing," "A Day on the Seashore," "Gathering Drift," etc.

"Although M'Taggart is unequal, there is always a fresh geniality about him that commends his pictures ; he takes firm hold of his subject, yet occasionally disregards finish. His ' At the Fair ' has less of this defect ; the girls examining the photograph have each her own idea, and all is natural. 'A Sea-Bird,' where children stretched at ease on the sandy gorse are eagerly examining the wings of a water-fowl, has a fine shimmering motion of the sea which forms the background." — *Art Journal,* April, 1874.

Mücke, Heinrich Karl Anton. (*Ger.*) Born at Breslau, 1806. Medal at Besançon, and a great medal from Portugal. Professor at the Düsseldorf Academy, where he had studied. He traveled in Italy and painted historical and religious subjects. At the National Gallery, Berlin, are "St. Catherine of Alexandria" and "St. Elisabeth of Hungary." He made himself known as a fresco-painter by his work at the castle of Heltorf, and in the Council-Chamber of Elberfeld. Some of his pictures are well known by the engravings from them, especially that of "St. Catherine borne to Heaven by Angels."

Muller, Charles-Louis. (*Fr.*) Born at Paris, 1815. Member of the Institute. Officer of the Legion of Honor. Pupil of Gros and Cogniet. This artist is so well known by his picture of the "Roll-

Call of the Last Victims of the Reign of Terror," that his other works have made but a comparatively small impression. This immense work (at the Luxembourg) contains many figures and seventeen acknowledged portraits. A copy or sketch of it (51 by 94) was sold at the Johnston sale, 1876, for $8,200. Muller has painted many portraits, and among his other subjects are, " Thomas Dialoirus " and " Mater Dolorosa " (1877), " Death of a Gitano " (1876), " Madness of King Lear," " The Waiting," and " One Moment Alone " (1875), " Lanjuinais at the Tribune, June 2, 1793 " (1869), " Desdemona " and " A Scholar " (1868), etc. His picture of " Charlotte Corday in Prison " (1875) is in the Corcoran Gallery, Washington. This work was never exhibited in any other place. To the Salon of 1878 he contributed " Give us Barabbas ! " and a portrait.

" Muller's great picture of the ' Call of the Condemned ' of the Reign of Terror is perhaps the best composed historical painting of our time. None that I know better fulfills the requirements of this branch of art, as a realistic narrative. ·It carries the spectator directly into the scene as it must have appeared on that morning when the last of Robespierre's victims were wantonly hurried to the guillotine. Muller drags it bodily out of the past, and puts it before our eyes in its precise truth, without dramatic exaggeration, or attempt to heighten anguish and despair sufficiently intense in their own naked reality. It is a conscientiously told tale. The officials, at whose action we are aghast, are justly treated ; mada men doing a stern duty, not ensanguined monsters. There are fifty masterly pictures, each a pathetic tale by itself; every separate group and individual action diversified in emotion, but filling its place with appropriate feeling in the harmonious whole : all subdued to an appropriate key of light, in fine gradation, centered outside the prison-door, where waits the cart which is fast filling with its dismal load. There is no attempt at an imaginative treatment, as in Couture's picture, but in place of it a picturesque rendering of the spectacle, based upon a thorough study of incidents, costumes, persons, and locality, with copious variety of action and expression. It is devoid of academic artificiality on the one hand, and of the other extreme of conventional idealism on the other. Sincerity and sympathy are joined to unquestioned skill and rare talent in composition. Delacroix, by his grand manner, writes his autograph all over his work, and we are led to think as much of the artist as his subject. Poussin, Ingres, and like men represent systems or theories, and provoke comparisons. Delaroche excites the sentiments by his poetical sense, but his defective style of painting detracts from the enjoyment. Even the Couture which hangs opposite recalls the studio overmuch as a composition, besides being spotty in high lights, and securing brilliancy at such sacrifice of unity of tone and color as to make it border on the sensational in general effect. Muller attempts nothing that he cannot do thoroughly well, and in a quiet, truth-telling manner. His system gives all to art, regardless of exhibiting the artist. The painting is not the highest effort, but it is a success in high art complete in its way. Muller paints history as Motley writes it, picturesquely, and with insight into its emotions." — JARVES, *Art Thoughts.*

Müller, Carl. (*Ger.*) Born at Darmstadt, 1818. Professor at the Academy of Düsseldorf. Pupil of his father, and of the Academy of Düsseldorf under Professor Sohn. He visited Italy, and when forty years old was Professor in the Academy where he had studied. His pictures are numerous. His " Annunciation," in the Gallery of Düsseldorf, is well known by an engraving. His most important frescos, which are in the church of Saint Apollinarius at Remagen, are deservedly much admired. He sent to Paris, in 1855, "The Last Supper," "The Virgin and Child," and "The Annunciation," before mentioned ; and to the Salon of 1853, "The Holy Family." At the London Royal Academy in 1876 he exhibited "The Virgin and Child before a Grotto" and "The Virgin, Infant Christ, and St. Joseph with an Angel."

Müller, Victor. (*Ger.*) Born at Frankfort (1829 - 1871). Pupil of the Staedel Institute ; studied also at the Antwerp Academy, from which place he went to Paris with a young colony of German and Dutch artists, where he remained for some years and was in the atelier of Couture. He lived awhile at Frankfort, and settled in Munich in 1864. His "Hamlet in the Churchyard," painted in 1869, and exhibited at Munich, first gave him a reputation. In the "Zeitschrift für bildende Kunst," a writer of his obituary says, "No one has more truly comprehended and depicted the inner spirit of this Prince of our first tragedy." Among his works are, "The Muses and Graces," a decorative work in Frankfort, "Hero and Leander," "Bestraften Ehebruch," and several portraits.

Mulready, William, R. A. (*Brit.*) Born in Ireland (1786 - 1863). Entered the schools of the Royal Academy in 1800. He first exhibited, in 1806, "A Cottage"; in 1811, "The Roadside Inn " ; in 1813, "Punch"; in 1815 (when he was elected Associate of the Royal Academy), "Idle Boys." He was made Academician in 1816. Among his earlier works are, "The Wolf and the Lamb," and "An Interior of an English Cottage" (which belonged to George IV.) ; "The Convalescent " ; "The Cousin " ; "The First Voyage " ; "Lending a Bite"; "Blackheath Park"; "The Fight Interrupted"; "The Barber's Shop" and "Fair Time" (1809) ; "The Last Inn " (1835) ; "Crossing the Ford" (1842) ; and "The Young Brother" (1857), which belonged to the Vernon Collection, and is now in the National Gallery, London. After his death a collection of his works was on exhibition for some time at the South Kensington Museum, attracting great attention in London. Some of his drawings were sold at auction about the same time, bringing enormous prices. His last picture, exhibited at the Royal Academy, was "A Toy-Seller," in 1862. Many of his works have been engraved.

"Mulready's ' Sonnet ' has been very justly described as one of the most purely and tenderly poetical of English pictures from common life. . . . . His refinement in form, his great sense of beauty, the poetry and invention of his subjects, combine to give them a peculiarly strong and lasting hold over the memory of those who have studied them." — *Art Journal*, May, 1876.

"Yet Mulready must unhesitatingly be placed among the few really eminent and thorough draughtsmen of the British school. His power over form was almost complete, although not so wide in range when he painted ' The Rattle ' in 1808, as when he drew ' The Bathers ' in 1849. His refinement is not less marked in ' The Gravel Pit ' [1807] than in ' The Toy-Seller ' of 1862. . . . . If Mr. Mulready's earliest aim in his figure-subjects was humor, in his latter it was grace. In its essential purity no English painter can, we think, be set above him. Great as are the claims of Gainsborough, Reynolds, Stothard, and Leslie, none of them equaled Mulready in that refined accuracy which has been noticed as his primary characteristic." — PALGRAVE'S *Essays on Art.*

Mulvany, George F. (*Brit.*) Born in Dublin (1809 – 1869). Son of Thomas Mulvany, who was the first keeper of the Royal Hibernian Academy, and a painter of some repute in Ireland. The son evinced a taste for art at an early age, was educated in Dublin, studied in Italy, and was made an Associate of the Royal Hibernian Academy in 1832. A few years later he was elected Academician, and on the death of his father, in 1845, he succeeded him as keeper. He was also one of the organizers, and as long as he lived a director of the Irish National Academy. He exhibited frequently in his native city, and his works were popular elsewhere. Among his pictures may be mentioned "First Love," "The Peasant's Grave," "The White Man cast on the Red Man's Shore," and a popular portrait of Thomas Moore, which has been frequently engraved. His last work, a portrait of Father Burke, was left unfinished.

Munkacsy, Mihaly. (*Hungarian.*) Born at Munkacs. Medals in Paris in 1870 and '74. Pupil of Knaus. At the Salon of 1877 he exhibited the "Story of a Hunt" and a portrait ; in 1876, "The Interior of a Studio"; in 1875, "The Village Hero, Hungary"; in 1874, the "Mont-de-Piété" and "The Night Prowlers." One of his finest works was the illustration of an old custom in Hungary of exposing a prisoner, who had been condemned, to the public for several hours. In this picture the different expressions of those who have come to see the unfortunate man are very remarkable. Three of his pictures were in the Paris Exposition of 1878.

Munn, George F. (*Am.*) Born in Utica, N. Y., 1852. First studied art under Charles Calverly the sculptor, and later at the schools of the National Academy, New York. He went to Europe to enter the Art Schools at South Kensington, where he received a gold medal, the first awarded to an American, for a model in clay of the Farnese Hercules. In the schools of the Royal Academy he received a silver medal for a life drawing ; and he was subsequently in the studio of George F. Watts in 1876. He has painted and sketched in Brittany, and has exhibited at the Dudley Gallery, London, at Birmingham, and elsewhere. Among his works are, "Wild-Flowers," "Roses," "Meadow-Sweet," "A Sunny Day, Brittany," etc.

"A flower-picture here [Dudley Gallery, 1875], notable for the absence of manufacturing deftness, which goes so far to neutralize the beauties of Fantin's work, is the large and most careful study (wild-flowers, meadow-sweet, the chief) to which is attached a new name, G. F. Munn. This is evidently a labor of love, full of the most minute and loving study, such as a man gives who finds both intense pleasure in his work and the subject of it, such labor as only young men can give, for only they are sustained by such keenness and freshness of delight." — TOM TAYLOR, *in London Graphic*, October, 1875.

Munro, Alexander. (*Brit.*) Born in Scotland (1825 – 1871). Settled in London in 1848. In 1849 he exhibited for the first time at the Royal Academy several portrait busts. His first ideal work,

"Paolo and Francesca," in marble, was at the Royal Academy in 1852, and was purchased by Mr. Gladstone. His "Hippocrates" (R. A., 1857) was presented by John Ruskin to the new Museum at Oxford. Among his ideal works are, "Undine," "The Lover's Walk," "Joan of Arc," "The Young Hunter," and "The Sleeping Boy." He executed busts of Sir Robert Peel, Gladstone, and J. E. Millais, R. A.; a statue of "Mary, Consort of William III." in the House of Parliament, the colossal statue of James Watt at Birmingham, and statues of Galileo, Davy, and Watt at Oxford.

"Though all his works show talent of a high order, Mr. Munro especially excels in female busts, and in his representation of children, both singly and in groups. In all of these is refined and delicate sentiment, a quality which, in the case of the little ones, is often allied with graceful fancy." — *Art Journal*, March, 1871.

Munzig, G. C. (*Am.*) Born in Boston, 1850. He has spent his professional life in his native city. As an artist he was comparatively self-taught. He is a member of the Boston Art Club, and is on the Committee on Design for the "School for Art Needlework" connected with the Museum of Fine Arts, Boston. His specialty is portraits in crayon. Within a few years he has turned his attention somewhat to oils. He has exhibited at Philadelphia, New York, Cleveland, and Boston, and his portraits are in the possession of Dr. Oliver Wendell Holmes, Winthrop Sargent, Frederick R. Sears, Henry D. Parker, George Wheatland, Eben Jordan, Mrs. Oliver Ames, Mrs. Oakes Ames, Mrs. D. B. Van Brunt, Miss Harriet W. Preston, Mr. James Lawrence, Mme. Teresa Careño, the late Mme. Teresa Tietjens, Mme. Rudersdorff, and others.

Murray, Elizabeth. (*Brit.*) Member of the Institute of Painters in Water-Colors of London, and of the American Society of Water-Color Painters in New York. She exhibited at the Institute, in 1878, "A Moorish Saint" and "Music in Morocco"; in 1875, "The White Rose"; in 1873, "The Greek Betrothed"; in 1872, "The Gypsy Queen"; etc. At the National Academy, in 1875, she exhibited, "Spanish Lovers lighting Cigarettes" (in oils).; in 1871, "Dalmatian Peasant"; in 1870, "The Old Story in Spain" (both in water-colors). "The Eleventh Hour" (in water-colors) brought $ 260 at the Johnston sale in New York in 1876.

Murray, David. (*Brit.*) Born in Glasgow, 1849. Brought up to mercantile pursuits, he spent his early youth in a warehouse in his native city, studying art in his leisure hours, but not adopting painting as a profession until within a few years. His studio is now (1878) in Glasgow. To the Royal Scottish Academy, in 1878, he sent "On the Towing-Path, Thames," "The Intruder," "A Sleepy Brook," "The English Yeoman's Dwelling," etc.

Musin, François. (*Belgian.*) Born at Ostende. Medal at Philadelphia, where he exhibited "Seashore at Scheveningen" and the "Harbor of Rotterdam in Rainy Weather." At Paris, in 1877, was "The Dike at Ostende in Heavy Weather."

Mussini, Cesare. (*Ital.*) Born at Berlin, 1808. He early fixed himself in Florence, and has acquired fame in his peculiar branch of painting. His drawing is always correct, and his color excellent. Many of his pictures have been commissions from Russia. Among his works are, "Leonardo da Vinci dying in the Arms of Francis I.," "Tasso reading his Poem to Eleonora d'Este," "Raphael and the Fornarina," the "Death of Atala," and "Stanislaus Poniatowski giving Freedom to the Poles." The portrait of this painter is in the autograph collection of the Uffizi.

Mussini, Luigi. (*Ital.*) Born at Berlin, 1813. Pupil of his brother Cesare. Director of the Academy of Siena. His first work, "Sacred Music," proved him to have unusual merit. In correctness of drawing he is unsurpassed, and his compositions are simple and truthful. They suggest the works of the *cinque-cento* painters. Among his works are, "Eudoro and Cimodocea" (in the gallery of modern paintings in Florence), the "Christian Martyr" (in the Cathedral of Siena), "The Money-Changers in the Temple," the "Last Day of Nero," the "Triumph of Truth," etc. Sig. Luigi Mussini is considered one of the best painters in Italy, and is at the head of his school. Since he has presided over the Academy of Siena, many fine artists have graduated there. His portrait is in the autograph collection in the Uffizi. To the Paris Salon, in 1878, he sent "Page siennois de la Tortue, — XV⁴ siècle."

Mutrie, Martha D. and **Annie F.** (*Brit.*) Natives of Manchester. Settled in London in 1854, exhibiting annually at the Royal Academy flower-pieces, the works of both sisters being very popular. Miss Mutrie sent to the Royal Academy, in 1860, "Fungus"; in 1861, "Wild Roses"; in 1864, "Garden Flowers"; in 1868, "Roses"; in 1872, "In the Flower-Market"; in 1875, "The Cottage Window"; in 1877, "Spring Flowers."

Miss Annie F. Mutrie exhibited, in 1860, "Where the Bee Sucks"; in 1861, "York and Lancaster"; in 1863, "Autumn"; in 1871, "The Balcony"; in 1874, "My First Bouquet"; in 1875, "Farewell, Summer"; in 1876, "The Evening Primrose"; in 1877, "Wild-Flowers of South America."

Both of these ladies were "commended for great merit in *genre* painting" by the judges at the Centennial Exhibition in Philadelphia in 1876.

"These ladies rank as excellent fruit and flower painters. A fault has been found with their subjects that they are too often cultivated flowers, and that whether garden or wild flowers they are apt to be arranged arbitrarily and artificially." — Mrs. Tytler's *Modern Painters.*

"Miss M. D. Mutrie's 'In the Cottage Window' [R. A., 1875], a beautiful study of flowers, is one of the brightest and most truthful little studies from Nature in this year's Exhibition." — *Art Journal*, July, 1875.

M'Whirter, John, A. R. A. (*Brit.*) Born near Edinburgh, 1839. He studied under Robert Scott Lauder, and practiced his profession in

Edinburgh, until 1869, when he opened a studio in London. He devotes himself to landscape-painting, selecting his scenes frequently in the Highlands of the West of Scotland. He exhibits at the Royal Academy and at the Royal Scottish Academy, and is an Associate Member of both these institutions. Among his works are, "The Mail from the North," "Glencoe," "The Falls of Tummell"; etc. To the Royal Scottish Academy, in 1878, he sent "Thunder-Storm on the Prairie" and "Salt Lake City, Utah"; to the Royal Academy, the same year, "The Three Graces" and "The Vanguard." His "Into the Depths of the Forest," "Out in the Cold" and "A Fisherman's Haven" were at the Paris Exposition of 1878.

Naftel, Paul J. (*Brit.*) English water-color artist, for some years a resident of Guernsey, at present living in London. He is a member of the Society of Painters in Water-Colors, sending annually from ten to fifteen pictures to its exhibitions; among others, "Near the Grange, Borrowdale, Cumberland," "Morning at Penllergare, South Wales," "Seaweed-Gathering, Guernsey," "Capri, from the Pine Valley, Sorrento," "First Snow on Blockmount," "The Mole near Twickenham," "Killarney, Ireland," etc. His "Violet-Gathering at Bordighera in December" and "Near Lismore, County Waterford" were at the Grosvenor Gallery in 1878. To the Paris Exposition, the same year, he contributed "Views of the Isle of Arran and of Killarney."

Naish, John George. (*Brit.*) Born in Sussex, 1824. Entered the Royal Academy in 1846, exhibiting the same year his first picture, entitled "Troops departing for India." In 1850 he went to the Continent, studying and working in the galleries of the Louvre, Paris, in Bruges, Antwerp, and elsewhere, returning to England the next year. Among his earlier works are, "Water-Nymphs" and "Hymn to the Rising Sun," in 1849; "Mermaids" and "Titania," in 1850; "The Power of Music," in 1854; "Fairies Returning" and "The Swoon of Endymion," in 1855; "Midsummer Fairies," in 1856 (exhibited both at the Royal Academy and the British Institution); "Influence of the Soul," in 1858; "Ode to the Northeast Wind," in 1860; "Rough Hands and Warm Hearts" and "The Last Tack Home," in 1864; and "Better than Gold," in 1865. About 1860 he altered the style of his paintings, leaving the ideal and classical figures for marine subjects. In 1867 he sent to the Royal Academy, "The Mouth of the Harbor"; in 1870, "Enoch Arden"; in 1871, "A North Devon Cove"; in 1873, "The most Northerly Point of Devon"; in 1874, "Homeward Bound"; in 1876, "The Night-Catch, — on Board a Traveler in Barnstaple Bay"; in 1877, "Life-Boat returning, — a Sea to Starboard"; in 1878, "A Summer Sea" and "The Devonshire Trawlers."

"A grizzled sailor and his son are here seen picturesquely sheltered beneath the rigging of their boat, and looking with fixed, eager eyes on the scattered roofs of the famous village of Clovely ['Last Tack Home,' R. A., 1864]. Everything is drawn with that conscientious fidelity to which Mr. Naish has accustomed us in his work, while ho has given it greater interest by his introduction of the human figure." — PALGRAVE's *Essays on Art.*

"Certainly there was no truer or finer combination of land and ocean among the pictures of that year than the view of the town ['Ilfracombe,' R. A., 1870], in which the painter had been a resident for some time. It afterwards gained a gold medal at the Crystal Palace. . . . Naish disdains to make any compromise with Nature ; he represents her as she appears to his eye, but with something more than mere typographical accuracy, for to this quality must be added, as a general rule, poetic feeling, adapting itself to the circumstances of the subject, and originality of treatment. . . . . As a colorist, moreover, Mr. Naish distinguishes himself." — *Art Journal*, November, 1875.

Nakken, W. C. (*Dutch.*) Of The Hague. Medal at Philadelphia, where he exhibited "Haymaking in Normandy." Mr. Weir especially commends this picture in his report. At the Paris Exposition, 1878, he exhibited "Étalon Normand" and "The Stable of the Inn."

Nanteuil, Celestin. (*Fr.*) Born at Rome, of French parents (1813 - 1873). Chevalier of the Legion of Honor. His family removed to Paris when he was still an infant. He studied under Langlois and Ingres, and then, in 1827, entered l'École des Beaux-Arts, where he became a sort of captain among some turbulent students. When a revolt occurred Nanteuil was expelled from the school, which made him a hero with a class, and he became known as one of the leaders of the reformers of art, as they were called. For some years he was employed in etching for romantic literature. In 1848 he first sent to the Salon a work worthy of notice, "A Ray of Sunshine," which was much admired. He devoted himself to *genre* subjects, and exhibited each year. His "Souvenirs of the Past" and "The Future" are well known from lithographs by himself. Nanteuil executed many plates for artistic publications. He traveled much and made numerous sketches. In 1870 he was placed at the head of the School of Design at Dijon, and appointed Conservator of the Museum of that city. Since his death two of his water-colors, "Hunting-Dogs in Repose" and "The Fawn," have been placed in the Luxembourg.

Nash, Joseph. (*Brit.*) Born about 1812. An artist in water-colors, making as his specialty architectural views and antique exteriors and interiors, English and Continental. He first exhibited in public in 1835. Among the better known of his early drawings are, "The Queen's Visit to Lincoln's Inn Hall," in 1846 ; "The Interior of the Crystal Palace," in 1851 ; "Rochester," "Roman Cathedral," "Charles V. visiting Francis I. during his Confinement," in 1855 ; "Chapel of Edward the Confessor at Westminster," in 1866 ; "Red Room of Louis Philippe at Claremont," in 1867 ;. "The Brown Gallery, Knole, Kent," in 1872 ; ".A Dinner-Party under the early Plantagenets" and "The Thumb Stocks," in 1873.

He has been for some time a member of the Society of Painters in

Water-Colors. In 1838 he published a volume entitled "Architecture in the Middle Ages," with lithographic illustrations, and a few years later, in four series, "The Mansions of England in the Olden Time." He has also furnished illustrations for the works of Shakspere, Scott, and other standard authors. [Died, 1878.]

Nast, Thomas. (*Am.*) Born in Landau, Bavaria, 1840. Taken to America in 1846. Early displayed artistic talents, but, with the exception of a few months' tuition under Kaufmann, is entirely self-taught. He began his professional career as a draughtsman for illustrated journals as early as 1855. In 1860 he went to Europe, followed the army of Garibaldi, sending sketches to London and American pictorial papers ; returned to America in 1862, and during the American Civil War sent many graphic drawings of war scenes to the Harpers' periodicals, attracting great attention on both sides of the Atlantic. He did not develop into a caricaturist until the close of the war, his later work being chiefly in that direction. Although not a member of any academy or society of the country, he is an occasional contributor to the public exhibitions in New York and elsewhere, sending to the National Academy, in 1868, "The Last Drop" ; in 1870, "The Departure of the Seventh Regiment," belonging to James H. Ingersoll.

"Judging from wood-cuts in Harper's Weekly of compositions relating to the various stages of the war, Nast is an artist of uncommon ability. He has composed designs, or rather given hints of his ability to do so, of allegorical, symbolical, or illustrative character, far more worthy to be transferred in paint to the walls of our public buildings than anything that has as yet been placed on them. Although hastily got up for a temporary purpose, they evince originality of conception, freedom of manner, lofty appreciation of national ideas, and action, and a large artistic instinct."—JARVES, *Art Idea.*

"Nast has proved one of the most spirited and authentic draughtsmen of the battles and other scenes incident to the late Civil War. His illustrations for Harper's Weekly show talent and fidelity. He is an original designer, and exhibits a remarkable grasp of the great questions at issue."—TUCKERMAN'S *Book of the Artists.*

"What a gift is this year's volume of Harper's, setting New York and its affairs so wonderfully before us! It would do you good to know, if I could tell you, the enjoyment your great and glorious Nast is giving in this valley. I sent the number to Fox How, when W. E. Forster was there, and they borrowed it again for the Stanleys and Lady Richardson. The favorite, the one supremely extolled, is that of the Romish Crocodile and the children. The Dean [Stanley] was delighted with it."—HARRIET MARTINEAU'S *Autobiography*, Vol. II.

Navez, François Joseph. (*Belgian.*) Born at Charleroi (1787 – 1869). Member and Professor of the Royal Academy of Belgium. Correspondent of the Institutes of France and Holland. Chevalier of the Orders of the Lion of Belgium, of Léopold, of William, and of the Legion of Honor. Member of various academies and important art associations. Pupil of François and David. His "Hagar in the Desert" is at the Brussels Museum ; his "Raising of the Sulamite's Son" and the "Meeting of Isaac and Rebecca" are at The Hague ; an "Italian Mother with a Sick Child" is at the National Gallery, Berlin ; " The Prophet Samuel," in the Museum at Haarlem. His works are also seen in churches in Brussels, Amsterdam, etc. His portraits were much admired. He painted one of William of Holland for the Duke of Wellington.

Neagle, John. (*Am.*) (1799 – 1865.) A portrait-painter, comparatively self-taught. He was apprenticed to a coach-painter in Philadelphia. About 1818 he began the practice of the higher branches of his profession in that city, settling in Lexington, Ky., and subsequently in New Orleans. His best-known work, " Patrick Lyon the Blacksmith," in the Boston Athenæum, was painted in 1826. He was a son-in-law of the artist Sully, from whom, in his early years, he received much encouragement and help. The best part of his professional life was spent in Philadelphia, where are still preserved many of his pictures, notably, the portrait of Washington in Independence Hall, of Henry Clay in the Union League Club, and of Henry Carey in the Academy. He was President of the Philadelphia Artists' Fund Society for many years. A valuable portrait of Gilbert Stuart by Neagle is now in the Boston Athenæum. It was exhibited at the Centennial Exhibition of 1876.

Neal, David. (*Am.*) Born in Lowell, Mass., 1837. He went to Munich in 1861, where he has since lived. In 1862 he entered the Royal Academy of Bavaria, where he studied from the antique for two years, later becoming a pupil of his father-in-law, the Chevalier Ainmuller. In 1869 he entered the studio of Piloty, remaining until 1876, changing his style of work and devoting himself entirely to figure-painting at that master's suggestion. Previous to this, he painted several interiors, the most important being " The Chapel of the Kings, Westminster Abbey " (belonging now to Francis Cutting of Boston) and " St. Mark's, Venice " (now the property of Samuel Nickerson, President of the First National Bank of Chicago) ; both of these were at the International Art Exhibition at Munich in 1869, and later at the National Academy of New York. In 1876 Mr. Neal was awarded the great medal of the Royal Bavarian Academy of Fine Arts for his " First Meeting of Mary Stuart and Rizzio." This medal is the highest in the gift of the Academy, and Mr. Neal the first American upon whom it has been bestowed. This picture was later in the collection of D. O. Mills, President of the Bank of California, and was exhibited at the Munich Art Union, afterwards in London, later in Boston, Lowell, Chicago, and elsewhere in the United States. It has been extensively photographed. Among his works are, " Return from the Chase " (belonging to John Bloodgood of New York), exhibited in Munich for the benefit of the wounded in the Franco-German war, and at the National Academy, New York ; " James Watt," a large historical picture at the Royal Academy, London, in 1874 (belonging to Sir B. S. Phillipps, formerly Lord Mayor of London) ; " The Burgomaster " ; and several portraits and ideal heads.

The " Wartburg," a monthly journal of the Munich Archæological Society, edited by the celebrated art critic, Dr. Förster, says (No. 9, 1876) : —

" The greatest interest was created at the Art Union by a historical picture of considerable dimensions by David Neal. This highly gifted artist, who is still young, an American by birth, and a pupil of Piloty, took as a subject for his picture the first meeting of Merie Stuert, the brilliant and lovely as well as inconstant Queen of Scots, with the singer Rizzio. The artist represents the object of so much poetic lore in the bloom and splendor of her youth ; the period chosen being when she was et the height of her fortunes. . . . . The scene is excellently well conceived and represented in a most masterly manner ; the characters, particularly those of the principal personages, are well carried out with equally as much knowledge of the times, as well as a love and feeling for the subject. In another column we give a notice of the honorable distinction which has been conferred upon Mr. Neal on the part of the Royal Academy for this prominent work."

Referring to a portrait (Mrs. Raymond) exhibited at Munich, the " Zeitschrift für bildende Kunst " says : —

" From David Neal, a pupil of Piloty, we have a lady's portrait which is to so high a degree spirited and fine in the conception, and is executed with so much bravour, that it would do honor to his master, and certainly evinces a finer feeling for color than is possessed by even Piloty himself."

" In England Mr. Neal has earned a place in the high ranks by his 'James Watt,' and his ' Mary Stuert and Rizzin,' that was exhibited in this country, has removed all questions here as to his great merits. Looking at these two paintings, one is impressed with the power of a deep-thinking artist. He has not devised a scene merely to show off his technical skill ; he saw deeper, and represents more than it would be easy to define in words. . . . . It would not be amiss to analyze, also, his ' Mary Stuert end Rizzio.' We should find in it the true elements of historical painting. The Queen, followed by her maids and Darnley, has descended a massive staircase, and has turned on the lower landing, when she sees Rizzio reclining asleep on a carved wood chest, his mandolin by his side. The Queen's fixed look of surprise, her equivocal gesture, are significant. Now we have the clew to all the rest ; since it is known that Rizzio has been taken into the Queen's household service, the love, and the complications, and the murder follow, as night the day. This is high art ! " — *Chicago Tribune*, March 24, 1878.

Neff, Timoleon Charles de. (*Russian.*) Born at Korkulla (1807 – 1877). Court Painter and Member of the Académie des Beaux-Arts at St. Petersburg. Studied at Dresden and Rome. In 1826 he settled in St. Petersburg, and soon became distinguished. Many of his portraits are of the members of the Imperial Family. In the Hermitage at St. Petersburg there are two pictures by Neff of " Nymphs Bathing." There are more copies made of these pictures than of any other works in that gallery.

Nehlig, Victor, N. A. (*Am.*) Born in Paris, 1830. Studied art in his native city under Cogniet and Abel de Pujol, and settled in America in 1850. He opened a studio in New York, was quickly elected an Associate of the National Academy, and made an Academician in 1870, when he exhibited " The Bravo." One of the results of a visit to Cuba was his " Mahogany Cutting " (belonging to John C. Force), which was at the National Academy in 1871, since which time he has not exhibited in that gallery. He visited Europe in 1872.

Among his works are "The Artist's Dream," "The Armorer of the Olden Time," "Gertrude of Wyoming," "Pocahontas," "Hiawatha," "The Captive Huguenot," etc.

Némoz, Jean-Baptiste-Augustin. (*Fr.*) Born at Thodure. Medal in 1877. Pupil of Picot and Cabanel. At the Salon of 1877 he exhibited "Theseus going to fight the Minotaur"; and in 1878, "Paradise Lost."

Neuber, Fritz. (*Ger.*) Born at Cologne, 1837. Pupil of Stephan. He has passed some time in several German cities, and has worked very quietly in a manner quite his own. He lives in Hamburg. Among his works are his statues of Peter Vischer, Gustavus Adolphus, Barbarossa, Handel, Bach, Neander, Schleiermacher, Luther, Twelve Apostles, etc. His works in the Nicolas Church brought him into much notice, and he received numerous commissions for busts and other work from private individuals.

Neuville, Alphonse de. (*Fr.*) Born at Saint-Omer, 1836. Chevalier of the Legion of Honor. Member of a rich family, he had a fine education, and left school with honors. His parents intended him for an official career, but he declared himself only ready to join the army, and in spite of all obstacles he entered the preparatory school of Lorient. The Professor of Design at this school, familiarly known as Papa Dubousset, quickly remarked the astonishing skill of De Neuville in drawing. Naturally the teacher took great pleasure and pride in teaching him, and often declared to the young fellow, "Quoique tu fasses, rappelle-toi que tu ne seras jamais qu'un peintre." He next went to Paris and entered the law school, for the sake of peace with his family. He remained three years, and passed most of his time at the military school or at the Champs-de-Mars, sketching, and making himself intimately familiar with all of a soldier's life which could there be learned. When he next returned home, he declared that he would be a painter or nothing. After a year of opposition his father went with him to Paris to consult some artists on the prospect for the young man. Bellangé, Yvon, Picot, all discouraged him, and advised his return to the home he had left. But the young fellow believed in his "lucky star," and took a small studio and went to work. His first picture, "The Gervais Battery," was accepted at the Salon of 1859 and took a medal of the third class. Just then Delacroix, who was in his decline, became the friend of the artist, and, while his doors were closed to most people, De Neuville spent many hours with him. In 1860 the débutant received a commission to paint "The Taking of Naples by Garibaldi," for the Cercle Artistique. He went to Italy, and the picture which he brought back was bad enough to satisfy a bitter enemy! In 1861 his "Chasseurs of the Guard" took a second medal at the Salon. From this time attention was turned to De Neuville, and he held a place among French military painters. He received, however, but few orders, and was obliged to make wood-cuts for illustrated publications, in order to live. In this department he has been nearly as fruitful as Gustave Doré. His picture of the "Attack of the Streets of Magenta" (1864) was very successful, and was bought by the State for the city of Saint-Omer. His picture of 1868 was purchased for the Museum of Lille, — it was "The Chasseurs crossing the Tchernaïa on Foot." Naturally the war of 1870 – 71 was an inspiration to this painter, and the pictures he has since painted have placed him in the first rank among his fellows. "The Bivouac before Bourget" (1872) is at the Museum of Dijon. "The Last Cartouches at Balan" (1873) was judged worthy of the Cross of the Legion of Honor. In 1874 he exhibited "The Attack by Fire on a Barricaded House at Villersexel." This is considered his best work by many. Paul Mantz calls it a "masterpiece." De Neuville, in his frequent journeys, makes some sketches not "in his line," as one may say, and has painted a few subjects, such as the "Recolte du Varech," which are also excellent pictures. At the Salon of 1877 he exhibited "An Episode in the Battle of Forbach, August 6, 1870" and a portrait ; in 1875, "A Surprise in the Environs of Metz, August, 1870." In the gallery of W. T. Walters of Baltimore is his "Engineer Officer on a Reconnoissance."

"De Neuville has not perhaps the exactness and careful timidity of Detaille ; he is not, like him, the pupil of Meissonier and a miniaturist by profession ; but he has freedom, audacity, movement, truth of physiognomy, truth of gesture, truth of color at the end of his brush, and all without visible effort. In a word, he has the genius of action, that entirely French quality which one cannot exact from a Dutchman like Detaille." — ERNEST DUVERGIER DE HAURANNE, *Revue des Deux Mondes*, June, 1874.

Newell, Hugh. (*Am.*) Born in Ireland. Brought up in Belfast, and educated at Queen's College there. He studied art in Antwerp, also in Paris under Couture, and later, in London, in the South Kensington Schools. At the age of twenty-one he came to the United States, settling in Baltimore, and receiving both the gold and silver medals of the Maryland Institute. His professional life has been spent in Baltimore and Pittsburg, Pa., and his paintings have been exhibited, and are owned in those cities, in Philadelphia and New York. Since 1870 he has been Principal of the Pittsburg School of Design for Women, and was awarded a diploma for the work of this school from the judges of the Centennial Exhibition of 1876 in Philadelphia. His "Smithy" was at the National Academy of New York in 1873; his "In the Cottage Window" and "Basket of Grapes," in 1878.

Newman, Henry R. (*Am.*) A water-color artist, who has lived for many years in Florence. He paints a variety of subjects, and is very happy in his flower-pieces. As a teacher, he has been very successful and fashionable, and well merits the praise bestowed upon his work. He exhibited in Florence, in 1878, "A Study of Pink and White Oleanders" and "Grapes and Olives," and sent to the Grosvenor Gallery, London, the same year, " Flowers" and " An Architectural Study." Several of his Florentine street scenes belong to Lord Spencer. Of a drawing of Santa Maria Novella, Florence, by Mr. Newman, Ruskin wrote to the artist in 1877 : " I have not for many and many a day seen the sense of tenderness and depth of color so united, still less so much fidelity and affection joined with a power of design which seems to me, though latent, very great. To have made a poetic harmony of color out of an omnibus-stand is an achievement all the greater in reality because not likely to have been attempted with all one's strength."

Newton, Sir William John. (*Brit.*) (1785 – 1869.) Miniature-painter to the Queen, receiving the honor of Knighthood in 1837. In his branch of the profession he was popular and much patronized by the Royal and Noble Families. He contributed a large number of works to the Royal Academy yearly, until 1863. " The Christening of the Prince of Wales at Windsor" (which was at the Royal Academy in 1845) was his largest and most important picture. It was painted on ivory, and attracted much attention.

Newton, Mrs. Charles T. (*Brit.*) (1832 – 1866.) Daughter of John Severn, an artist. She displayed remarkable talents for art at an early age, and studied under George Richmond, devoting herself to portrait and figure painting in water and oil. In 1861 she was married to C. T. Newton, Superintendent of Antiquities at the British Museum, and turned her attention, during the few remaining years of her life, to drawing from the Roman and Greek sculptures and vases in that institution. Among her paintings may be mentioned, " Elaine," " Sebaste," " Levantine Lady," " Jewess of Smyrna," " Letty," etc. She exhibited a portrait of herself at the Royal Academy in 1863.

Newton, Alfred P. (*Brit.*) Born in 1835. A graduate of no school of painting, and comparatively self-taught, he has studied directly from nature in Wales, Scotland, and Italy, devoting himself to landscapes, chiefly in water-colors. He was elected a member of the Society of Painters in Water-Colors in 1860, upon the exhibition, in its gallery, of his first works. Among his more important pictures are, " Mountain Gloom," " Mountain Glory," " Mystery and Immensity," " Nature's Merriments" (in oil), " Declining Day," " The First Approach of Winter," etc. His " Mountain Gloom " and " Left by the Tide " were at the Philadelphia Exhibition in 1876, gaining a medal. To Paris, in 1878, he sent " Left by the Tide."

" It is literally certain that no artist whatever, before our day, could have drawn that mountain ['Glencoe'] with such truth. No artist before this century would have understood the mass of granite under the thin and broken turf. Nor would any older artist have felt the loveliness of the natural scene in this half-melancholy, half-pleasurable spirit. The work is impressive because the scene is impressive, and because the artist has trained himself to see and feel enough to reproduce, but not enough to transform nature, and make a new creation of his own." — P. G. HAMERTON, *in English Painters of the Present Day.*

Nevin, Blanche. (*Am.*) Native of Philadelphia. Studied sculpture under J. A. Bailly and at the Pennsylvania Academy of Fine Arts. Executed several portrait and ideal busts, owned principally in her native city. Among her more important works are a full-length statue of " Eve " and a statuette of " Cinderella."

Nicol, Erskine, A. R. A. (*Brit.*) Born near Edinburgh, 1825. Was apprenticed to a house-painter in his native city, in his leisure hours studying in the Trustees Academy, and teaching drawing a few years later in the High School at Leith. After spending three or four years in Dublin, where he gave lessons in drawing and painted portraits, gathering at the same time material for the clever sketches of Irish character in which he has been so successful, he returned to Edinburgh, contributing regularly to the exhibitions of the Royal Scottish Academy, of which he is an Associate Member. He removed to London, where he still resides, in 1862. He sent to the Royal Academy, in 1857, " Did it pout with its Betsy ? "; in 1861, " Toothache " ; in 1862, " Notice to Quit " ; in 1863, " Waiting an Answer " ; in 1864, " Among the Old Masters " ; in 1865, " A Deputation " ; in 1866, " Both Puzzled " ; in 1867, when he was made Associate of the Royal Academy, he sent " Kiss an' make it up " ; in 1868, " A China-Merchant " ; in 1869, " A Disputed Boundary " ; in 1871, " On the Lookout " ; in 1872, " His Babies " ; in 1873, " Steady, Johnny, Steady ! " ; in 1875, " The New Vintage " and " Always tell the Truth ! " ; in 1876, " Storm at Sea " ; in 1877, " Unwillingly to School " ; in 1878, " The Lonely Tenant of the Glen," " Under a Cloud," and " The Missing Boat."

" The Almshouse Nurse," a sketch of Erskine Nicols, was in the National Academy of New York in 1869 ; his " Paying the Rent " (belonging to F. O. Day) was in the Centennial Exhibition of Philadelphia in 1876 ; his " Collecting his Thoughts " brought $ 1,560, and his " Yours to Command " $ 1,575, in the sale of the Latham Collection in New York in 1878 ; both were painted in 1865, and now belong to Theron R. Butler of New York. His works are familiarly known on both sides of the Atlantic through the medium of engraving.

" Erskine Nicol's ' Storm at Sea ' [R. A., 1876] is a picture of great pathetic power, vigorously handled, marvelously well drawn, and abounding in evidences of skill and painstaking study." — *Art Journal*, July, 1876.

" Erskine Nicol is represented by one of his inimitable bits of Irish comedy. Expression could go no further than in his burly farmer who has come into town to consult ' His Legal Adviser ' [R. A., 1877]." — *London Standard*, May, 1877.

" A very broadly painted group [' Unwillingly to School,' R. A., 1877], showing an old Scotch dame doing her best to coax a braw little Hieland laddie, in a kilt and blue bonnet, and with a pair of cheeks like unto two Ribstone pippins, into going to school. The contest of emotions in this work is exquisitely rendered." — *Illustrated London News*, May, 1877.

Nicoll, J. C. (*Am.*) Born in the city of New York in 1845, where the greater part of his professional life has been spent, with the exception of extensive sketching-tours along the coast from the Gulf of St. Lawrence to Florida. Mr. Nicoll painted for two years in the studio of Mr. F. H. De Haas, and has studied in the fields with Mr. De Haas, Kruseman Van Elten, and others, but does not consider himself a pupil of either of these gentlemen, and was not a student of any of the art schools of this country or of Europe. His works, which are of moderate size, have been exhibited in the principal cities of the country. He is not a member of the National Academy, but one of the original members of the Water-Color Society in 1866, holding the position of secretary for nine years, and being better known in that branch of the art, to which a large part of his time has been devoted. His specialty is coast views. He was elected a member of the Artists' Fund Society in 1874.

Among the better known of Nicoll's works in oils are, "Thatcher's Island, Mass." (sold in Syracuse), "Sunset, Bay of Fundy" (now in Chicago), and "A Summer's Resting-Place" (belonging to H. P. Farnham); in water-colors, "Moonlight, Cape Ann" (the property of J. M. Sears of Boston), "Off Portland Harbor," "Shower on the Coast," "Schroon Lake," and "Coast View in Spring." His "Foggy Morning, Grand Menan" and his "Gulf of St. Lawrence" were at the Centennial Exhibition of 1876; "On the Gulf of St. Lawrence" and "Shower on the Coast" (both in water-colors) were at the Paris Exposition of 1878.

"Nicoll's 'Coast View in Spring' [water-color, 1875] is an admirable specimen of his skill. The coast line is rocky, and in giving the texture of the water-worn granite as well as the breaking surf with its shower of spray, the artist shows that his study has been earnest as well as conscientious. In color the work is brilliant, and what is commendable, there is no departure from truth to produce the result."—*Art Journal*, March, 1875.

Nieman, Edmund John. (*Brit.*) Born in Islington, of German parentage (1813–1876). Engaged in mercantile pursuits until the age of twenty-six, when he took up the profession of an artist. He resided in Buckinghamshire, and painted from nature. He first exhibited at the Royal Academy, in 1844, "On the Thames, near Great Marlow," which attracted favorable notice. In 1850 he was elected trustee and honorary secretary of the National Institution, a short-lived association of artists. Among his better known works are, "The Thames at Maidenhead," "Recollections of the Rhine," "Scarborough, — Sunset" (1862), "Moss Troopers," "The Ambush," "Chester Cathedral," "Launch of the Great Eastern," and a view of "Scarborough," his last exhibited work, at the Royal Academy in 1872.

"Nieman's style of painting may lay claim to a certain originality. His coloring is powerful, with often a tendency to heaviness, but at all times it is highly effective. Four of his paintings are in the National Collection at South Kensington."—*Art Journal*, August, 1877.

Niemeyer, John H. (*Am.*) Born in the city of Bremen, 1839. He was taken to the United States at an early age, but returned to Europe as a youth to complete his art education, studying in the School of Fine Arts, Paris, under Gérôme and Yvon, and for some time in the private atelier of Jacquesson de la Chevreusse. From 1866 to '70 he was in the studio of Cornu. He received two medals from the Imperial School of Design in Paris. His professional life in America was spent in New York until 1871, when he was appointed Professor of Drawing in the Yale School of Fine Arts, where are some of his *genre* pictures. Among his important works are, " Guttenberg inventing Movable Type," at the Paris Salon of 1869, and at the Centennial Exhibition at Philadelphia, in 1876. Of late years he has painted portraits and ideal works.

" A picture with a meaning conveys a double satisfaction, and the artist could scarcely have chosen a subject more appreciated by every one. The picture itself ['Guttenberg'] is a product of a master's hand, and Mr. Niemeyer shows so intimate knowledge of detail of the early ages." — *New York Telegram*, March 4, 1871.

Nittis, Giuseppe de. (*Ital.*) Born at Barletta. Medal in 1876. Pupil of Gérôme. At the Salon of 1877 he exhibited " Paris, — View from the Pont Royal " ; in 1876, " On the Road to Castellamare " and " Plâce des Pyramides " ; in 1875, " Plâce de la Concorde " and " At Bougival, on the Seine." At the Glasgow Fine Art Loan Exhibition, 1878, there was a fine picture by De Nittis of the " Arc de Triomphe, Paris," belonging to J. G. Sandeman, Esq. " In the distance the arch, protected by scaffolding and woodwork. In the street, and riding out of the picture, a lady on a black horse and a gentleman on a brown. In the foreground, to the right, a lady in black, accompanied by a nurse with scarlet and black tartan shawl, wait to cross the street. Other figures through the picture."

Nobas, Rosendo. (*Span.*) At Philadelphia he exhibited " A Wounded Bull-Fighter," a portrait of Fortuny, and one of Miguel de Cervantes, all in plaster, and received a medal.

Noble, Matthew. (*Brit.*) (1818 – 1876.) Studied in London, exhibiting there his first work in 1845. He executed the Wellington Monument in Manchester, Oliver Cromwell in the same city (the first statue to the Protector erected in a public place in England), and statues of Sir John Franklin, Sir James Outram, the Earl of Derby, and of Queen Victoria, in different cities of Great Britain. Among his ideal works are, "Amy and her Fawn," " Purity," " The Spirit of Truth," etc.

" This fine bronze statue [Earl of Derby] is an object of great attraction to almost every one who happens to be for the first time in the neighborhood of the Houses of Parliament and Westminster Abbey. The statue is one of Mr. Noble's most successful works. The figure, habited in the costume of the Oxford chancellor, is very dignified, yet easily and gracefully posed ; the expression of the face is rather severe, but highly intellectual. [It was unveiled in 1874.] "— *Art Journal*, August, 1875.

Noël, Edme-Antony-Paul. (*Fr.*) Born at Paris. Medals in 1872 and '74., Pupil of Guillaume, Lequesne, and Cavelier. *Prix de*

Rome in 1868. Chevalier of the Legion of Honor in 1878. At the Salon of 1878 he exhibited a portrait of Baron Taylor (in bronze) and "Meditation" (a statue in marble); in 1876, "After the Bath" (statue, marble); in 1875, "Romeo and Juliet" (group, marble) and "The Retiarius" (statue, bronze); in 1872, "Marguerite" (statue) and "Death" (a bas-relief), both in plaster, etc.

M. Noël is also known by his artistic work in the Haviland faience, a fine specimen of which is a vase in the possession of Mr. Harper of New York. His signature is on his vases, and they are all modeled, never molded.

Norton, William E. (*Am.*) Sprung from a shipbuilding family in Massachusetts, he had, from his infancy, a fondness for the sea, making several voyages before the mast, before he settled in Boston, and began the painting of marine views, which are his specialty, and in which he has met with decided success. In 1877 he went abroad, opening a studio in London. Among his works are, "Gathering Kelp," "Whale-Ships Trying Out," "Early Morning," "Calm Afternoon," etc. His "Fog on the Grand Banks" was at the Philadelphia Exhibition of 1876. To the Royal Academy, London, he sent in 1878, "The Thames near Blackwall," "Twilight on the Banks of Newfoundland," and "Becalmed on the Grand Banks." To the Mechanics' Fair, Boston, the same year, "Midnight Moonlight on the Grand Banks," "Nantasket Beach in November," and "In the Bay."

"William E. Norton's 'Crossing the Grand Banks' is most remarkable for its effective presentation of fine neutral tints of rich deep gray, and soft rich hazy dream-light." — *Art Journal*, May, 1877.

Oakes, John Wright, A. R. A. (*Brit.*) Born in 1822. First sent a picture to the Royal Academy in 1848. In 1860 he exhibited "An Old Sand-Pit"; in 1861, "Water Meadows, Sandwich"; in 1863, "The River in Flood"; in 1865, "Morning at Angera, Lago Maggiore"; in 1869, "Early Spring"; in 1870, "A Summer Morning"; in 1871, "Source of the Thames"; in 1872, "Repairing the Old Boat"; in 1873, "A Mountain Stream, Aberdeenshire"; in 1874, "A Sandy Bit of the Road"; in 1876 (when he was elected an Associate of the Royal Academy), "Fording a Tidal Creek" and "Sheltered"; in 1877, "In the Border Countrie" and "Line-Fishing" (a calm sea on the South Coast); in 1878, "Dirty Weather on the East Coast" and "In the Meadows."

"We remember no landscape of Mr. Oakes' so powerful or so well brought together in effect as his 'Mountain Valley' [R. A., 1864]. Otters catching salmon in the foreground, whilst behind a sudden gleam of angry light, succeeding rain and snow, smites the fractured face of a huge slate-cliff. The work has a real solemnity of effect." — PALGRAVE's *Essays on Art.*

Oakey, Maria R. (*Am.*) Born in New York, 1847. She was educated at the schools of the Cooper Institute and the Academy of Design, and has had the benefit of instruction, at different periods, from

La Farge, William Hunt, Dr. Rimmer, Swain Gifford, George Butler, Edwin Forbes, and Thomas Couture. With the exception of a visit to France and Italy her professional life has been spent in New York. Among her works are a portrait of a boy, life size and full length, exhibited in Boston and New York (belonging to Daniel Oakey); portrait of Miss O. S. Ward; "A Woman Serving," exhibited in New York, Boston, and London (belonging now to Edward Cook); "Violets," a life-size (three-quarter length) figure of a young girl in antique dress, at the Exhibition of the Society of American Artists in 1878 ; "L'Inamorato"; "The Philosopher's Corner" (in oil), belonging to Samuel V. Wright of New York ; and portraits, flowers, still-life, and charcoal drawings, owned by Miss Bartol of Boston, C. W. Woolsey, John P. Townsend, J. Q. A. Ward, Alexander Cochrane, and others.

O'Connell, Mme. Frederic-Emilie-Auguste-Miethe. (*Ger.*) Born at Berlin, 1828. Pupil of Begas of Berlin. Her first picture, the "Day of the Dupes," though far from perfect, was much praised. In 1844 she married and settled in Brussels. Here, by the study of the pictures of the Flemish school, she much improved, and while in Belgium she painted many water-colors, some portraits, and executed most of her etchings. She received at the Salons there all the medals, including that of the first class. About 1853 she went to Paris, where she was also successful, and where she opened an atelier, and received a number of pupils. Among her works are, "Portrait of Rachel," "Peter the Great and Catherine," "Maria Theresa and Frederick the Great." Among her etchings are, "St. Magdalen in the Desert," "Charity surrounded by Children," some busts, portraits, etc.

O'Donovan, William R. (*Am.*) Born in Virginia, 1844. An American sculptor whose professional life has been spent in the city of New York. He sent to the National Academy, in 1874, a bust of the late Peter Gilsey (belonging to Mr. Henry Gilsey). In 1876 he exhibited a bust of the late John A. Kennedy, executed for the monument to be placed over his grave by the Odd Fellows. In 1877 he sent his bust of Thomas Le Clear, N. A., and in 1878, busts of William H. Beard, Winslow Homer, and one of William Page, to be presented by a number of prominent residents of New York to the Academy of Design. He is at present (1878) engaged upon a bust of Theodore Tilton, and many prominent Americans have been among his subjects. He was elected an Associate of the National Academy in 1878.

"In making a bust Mr. O'Donovan, as he should, pays as much attention as a portrait-painter does to the modifying influence of color or form. . . . . One of the best and best-known artists of the country is reported to have said recently of O'Donovan's portrait of the painter Page, that it is executed in the true Phidian spirit. This was only another way of saying that it is in the style of the purest ancient Greek art, and as so little of our modern sculpture deserves such praise, Mr. O'Donovan's bust is a singularly interesting performance." — *Art Journal*, February, 1878.

7 *

Ogilvie, Clinton, A. N. A. (*Am.*) Born in New York, 1838. He has devoted himself to landscape-painting, studying under James Hart, and practicing his profession in his native city. He has twice visited Europe, working for some time in Paris. In 1864 he was elected an Associate of the National Academy, exhibiting there, in different seasons, " The Path by the River," " Valley of the Croton," " Farmington River Scenery," " The Brookside," " Summer Day in Connecticut," " Sunny Summer Time," " The Mountain Brook," " Near Brummer, Switzerland," " Lauterbrunnen," " Lake Como," " Lake of Killarney," etc. His " In the Woods " was at the Centennial Exhibition at Philadelphia in 1876.

Oliva, Alexandre-Joaeph. (*Fr.*) Born at Saillagousse, about 1824. Chevalier of the Legion of Honor. Pupil of Delaistre. Best known by his portrait statues and busts, of which he has made a great number. His "Rembrandt" (1853) and a bust of R. P. Ventura de Raulica are at the Luxembourg.

Olivié, Léon. (*Fr.*) Born at Narbonne. Medal in 1876. Pupil of Cœdes and Cogniet. At the Salon of 1876 he exhibited " The Question " and " A Fisherman of the Seine."

O'Neil, Henry, A. R. A. (*Brit.*) Born in St. Petersburg, 1817. Taken to England as a child, he displayed a taste for art, and entered the Royal Academy in 1867. He exhibited his first picture two years later, since contributing regularly to the exhibitions of the Academy. His " Eastward Ho," in 1858, and (the companion picture) " Home Again," in 1859, attracted great attention in England, and brought him into prominent notice as an artist. Both were engraved. Among the better known of O'Neil's earlier works are, " The Last Moments of Mozart," " Queen Catherine's Dream," " The Return of the Wanderer," and " Ruth and Naomi " (which belonged to Prince Albert). In 1860 (when he was elected an Associate of the Royal Academy) he contributed " The Shipwreck " ; in 1861, " The Parting Cheer " ; in 1862, " Mary Stuart's Farewell to France " ; in 1863, " The Power of Music " ; in 1864, " The Landing of the Princess of Wales at Gravesend " ; in 1866, " The Last Moments of Raffaelle " ; in 1868, " Before Waterloo " ; in 1872, " Rebecca and Ivanhoe " ; in 1873, " Tintoretto painting his Dead Daughter " ; in 1874, " The Path through the Glen " ; in 1875, " An Incident of the Plague of London " ; in 1876, several bits of Scottish landscape ; in 1877, " Shakspere reading ' A Midsummer Night's Dream ' to Queen Elizabeth " ; in 1878, " Loch Leven, 1568 " and " Catherine's Dream." Many of the above have been engraved. To the Philadelphia Exhibition of 1876 he sent " A Volunteer."

O'Neil, G. B. (*Brit.*) A resident of London. He paints *genre* subjects, which appeal to the popular taste. He first exhibited at the Royal Academy in 1851, and continues to send pictures there regularly. Among his earlier works may be mentioned, " A Hearty Welcome," "A Statute Fair," "The Rival Musicians," "A Favorite Tune," etc. To the Royal Academy, in 1868, he sent "Why so late ?" ; in 1869, " New Shoes " ; in 1871, " The Children's Party" ; in 1872, " Nestlings " ; in 1873, " Driving a Pair " ; in 1874, "A Little Better" ; in 1875, " Sympathy " ; in 1876, " Our Boys " ; in 1877, " The Father of the Regiment " ; in 1878, " Reaping Time." One of his first works which attracted public attention, " The Foundling " (R. A., 1852), bequeathed by Jacob Bell, is now in the National Gallery, London. Many of his pictures have been engraved.

Orchardson, William Q., R. A. (Brit.) Born in Edinburgh in 1835, and educated there at the Trustees Academy. He painted portraits in his native city for a few years, exhibiting at the Royal Scottish Academy. In 1863 he removed to London, where he still resides, and sent to the Royal Academy, the same year, " An Old English Song " ; in 1864, " Flowers of the Forest " ; in 1865, " Hamlet and Ophelia " ; in 1866, " Story of a Life " ; in 1867, " Talbot and the Countess of Anvergne " ; in 1868 (when he was elected an Associate of the Royal Academy), a " Scene from Shakspere's Henry IV." ; in 1869, " The Duke's Antechamber " ; in 1871, " On the Grand Canal " and " An Hundred Years Ago " ; in 1872, " Casus Belli " and " The Forest Pet " ; in 1873, " Cinderella " and " The Protector " ; in 1874, " Hamlet and the King " and " Ophelia " ; in 1875, " Too Good to be True " and " Moonlight on the Lagoons " ; in 1876, "The Bill of Sale" and "Flotsam and Jetsam " ; in 1877, "The Queen of the Swords " and " Jessica " ; in 1878, "A Social Eddy" and "Autumn." Elected Royal Academician, 1879.

Among Orchardson's other works are, " Peggy," a scene from " The Gentle Shepherd " (Brit. Inst., 1863), " The Challenge " (Paris Exposition, 1867), " Christopher Sly," " Choosing a Weapon," " The Virtuoso," " The Salutation," etc. He sent to Philadelphia, in 1876, " Prince Henry, Poins, and Falstaff," and " Moonlight on the Lagoons, Venice " ; to Paris, in 1878, " The Queen of the Swords," " The Bill of Sale," " Escaped," and " The Duke's Antechamber."

"Orchardson is an artist of more than ordinary merit."— BENJAMIN's *Contemporary Art in Europe.*

" We look with somewhat mixed feelings on what may, we suppose, be termed the rising school of English and Scottish incident painters. Among the latter Mr. Orchardson has at present the air of losing ground : the less promising qualities in his work of the last two years having obtained in 1865 a certain prominence over the merits visible in his earlier productions. His 'Hamlet and Ophelia' has many clever points, and the scene has been properly imagined as off the stage, but we do not gain so much as might have been expected : the two heads, especially Ophelia's, being poor and unsatisfactory in character." — PALGRAVE's *Essays on Art.*

" 'Two Skye-Terriers ' [R. A., 1873], by Orchardson, are admirably painted. To each dog is given a definition of character which is remarkably impressive. This is, we believe, the only animal picture by this painter that has been exhibited in the Royal Academy. It is not easy to determine whether he deals more favorably with animal or human expression." —*London Art Journal,* June, 1873.

Ordway, Alfred. (*Am.*) A resident of Boston. He was the founder of the Boston Art Club, in 1854, and its first Secretary and Treasurer, its President in 1859, and the Corresponding Secretary in 1866. From 1856 to '63 he was director of the exhibitions of paintings at the Boston Athenæum, and has exhibited regularly at the Art Club. His pictures are owned by Mr. Thomas Wigglesworth of Boston, Colonel Elliot of Baltimore, and other collectors. " On Charles River," " Newton Lower Falls," and " Arline " were at the Mechanics' Fair in Boston in 1878.

Osborn, Miss E. M. (*Brit.*) Residing in London, she had for some years also a studio in Glasgow, painting portraits and occasional subject-pictures. Among her works may be noted, " Olivia," at the Glasgow Loan Exhibition of 1878 ; and " A Golden Day-Dream " and " The Cemetery at Mazorbo, near Venice," at the Royal Academy, London, in 1877.

Oudiné, Eugène-André. (*Fr.*) Born at Paris, 1810. Chevalier of the Legion of Honor. Pupil of André Galle. The works of this sculptor are mostly for public buildings, fountains, etc., and are apparently innumerable. He has also executed a large number of portraits. At the Salon of 1878 he exhibited a portrait of himself, a bust in bronze.

Oudinot, Achille François. (*Fr.*) Born at Damigny (Orne), 1820. Pupil of Huyot in architecture, and of Corot in painting. After visiting Italy, from which country he brought many watercolor sketches, his vocation for painting seemed too *prononcé* to be disregarded, and, although he has since done considerable work as an architect, it is as a painter that he is best known. He has also occupied himself as a designer, especially for the " Magasin pittoresque," and has painted on glass. At the Exposition of 1855 his glass paintings were much admired. In the Art Journal of January, 1876, is the following : —

" At the exhibition of the works commanded by the city of Paris were seen five large and beautiful glass paintings, executed by Oudinot, which are placed on the *chevet* of the church of Saint-Jacques du Haut-Pas, where they make the best effect. It is to be remarked that they are painted in black and white on a ground of mosaic of gold. It has a happy effect, at the same time that it is a progress. M. Oudinot is now occupied in the restoration of the glass of Jean Cousin, at the Sainte-Chapelle at Vincennes."

Oudinot also placed himself in relations with some master-builders, and was charged with the erection of houses in Paris, a hotel at Passy in the style of Louis XIII., and with numerous country-houses, among which was that of the late artist Daubigny, near l'Isle-Adam. During the year 1877 Oudinot took up his residence at Boston, and carried to the United States a large number of pictures, some of which have been exhibited in Boston art galleries and exhibitions. One of these, which wonderfully represents a storm of wind, was purchased by Mr. D. Waldo Lincoln of Worcester. Others have been

bought by Mr. T. G. Appleton, Mr. G. B. Richmond, Mr. Wigglesworth, and others. His subjects are varied. His landscapes
present to us many of the characteristic features of French country
scenes, — thatched cottages, wooded paths, meadows and streams,
are reproduced with the varied effects of shining and lowering
skies, with a charm which written words can scarcely tell, — certainly
not in the space here allotted us. His picture of " Dunes at Dun-
querque " has been much admired.

"Oudinot was long a favorite pupil of Corot, and shows in his works very distinctly
the influence of that master on his manner. While he is versatile, his most successful
labors are landscapes. These are usually at once rich in coloring and imaginative in
temper and quiet. Of the pictures by him recently exhibited those were most attractive which represented pastoral scenes. Several were marine views, however, and
one, representing a land storm, proved that the painter is capable of imaginative work
of a high order." — *Art Journal*, December, 1877.

Ouless, Walter William, A. R. A. (*Brit.*) Born at St. Heliers,
Jersey, 1848. Educated in the Royal Academy, he has devoted him-
self to portrait-painting, spending his professional life in London.
He has exhibited at the Royal Academy since 1873, and was elected
an Associate of that institution in 1877. Among the better known
and more successful of his portraits have been those of Lord Selborne,
Lord Justice Amphlett, Charles Darwin, Admiral Sir Alexander
Milner, Hon. E. P. Bouverie, Hon. Russell Gurney, etc.

"Few artists of greater promise in his line can be found than W. W. Ouless. His
texture, handling, and coloring are of the first order." — BENJAMIN's *Contemporary Art
in Europe.*

"'The Mayor of Newcastle,' by Ouless, is an agreeable and vigorous portrait, highly
creditable to the painter, and honorable to its subject and to its possessors. Mr. Ouless
has adopted from Mr. Millais what was deserving of imitation, and has used the skill he
has learned to better ends. All his portraits are vigorous and interesting." — RUSKIN's
Notes of the Academy, 1875.

"Mr. Ouless' portraits have vast merit. Painted with equal firmness and freedom,
they are invariably life-like and expressive, and display a general grace and brilliancy of
treatment, which imparts to them a distinctive and resistless charm." — *London Morning Post,* May, 1877.

Ouvrié, Pierre Justin. (*Fr.*) Born at Paris, 1810. Chevalier of
the Legion of Honor. Pupil of Abel de Pujol and Châtillon. His
picture of the "Oval Court of the Castle of Fontainebleau" (1840)
and "The Monument to Walter Scott at Edinburgh" (1863) are at
the Luxembourg. The pictures of this artist are numerous, and his
works varied. He paints in both oil and water colors, and makes
lithographs.

Overbeck, Friedrich. (*Ger.*) Born at Lubeck (1789 – 1869).
Associate Member of the Institute of France. After some preliminary
studies this artist settled in Rome in 1810, and remained there during
his life. He became a Roman Catholic, and laid down as the fundamental principle of his art, that it existed only for the service of religion. He drew about him many disciples, who with him under-

took to accomplish the regeneration of painting. He became known through his frescos of the "History of Joseph," at the villa of the Consul-General of Prussia, and "Jerusalem Delivered," at Villa Massini, in which works he was assisted by his brother artists and pupils. The "Miracle of the Rose," in the church of Saint Agnes at Assisi, was almost entirely the work of Overbeck. Among his oil-pictures are, "The Entrance of Christ into Jerusalem," at the church of Notre-Dame in Lubeck; "Christ on the Mount of Olives," at Hamburg; the "Marriage of the Virgin"; several Holy Families; the "Death of Saint Joseph"; etc. Many engravings have been made after the works of Overbeck, and for a time his "new departure" in painting was much talked of, and he apparently had great influence. His pupils, as they returned to Germany, were employed in the decoration of churches and chapels, and these remain to show the fruit of his influence and doctrines. The *chef-d'œuvre* of this painter is the "Triumph of Religion in the Arts," which is at the Staedel Institute in Frankfort. At the National Gallery, Berlin, is his "Jerusalem Delivered."

"The world of modern German art, as that of old, divides itself into two hemispheres: Overbeck rules as the modern Raphael over one; Cornelius, as a German Michael Angelo, bears iron away over the other. Overbeck is the St. John which leant in love on the bosom of our Lord; Cornelius is St. Peter, strong as a rock on which to build the Church. And as with Michael Angelo followers were wanting, so with Cornelius he walks in that *terribile via* wherein few can venture to tread. The lot of Overbeck is more blessed. Like to Raphael, his forerunner, he draws by love all men unto him; near to him, through fellowship of endearing sympathy, warmed by the emotion which beauty, akin to goodness, in the universal heart begets. . . . . Among the oil-paintings of Overbeck, 'The Triumph of Religion in the Arts,' one of the choicest treasures in the Städel Institute, Frankfort, is certainly the most elaborate and ambitious. This grand composition, which may be likened in its intent to Raphael's 'School of Athens,' or to the 'Hemicycle' by Delaroche, has been aptly termed by German critics, 'The Christian Parnassus,' the dawn of light in Europe. I wish that space were left for detailed description of this work, weighty in thought, and loaded with symbolism, — a work meant as a declaration of faith, the programma of a creed, preaching to the world a homily. Yet while pondering on this picture well worthy of veneration, I could not but regret once more, that Overbeck, in maturing his pictorial thoughts, had not shown like diligence in the perfecting of the material instruments, through which alone ideas can be made visible. In the remembrance of the heavenly harmonies of Angelico and Perugino, it is hard to forgive even a spiritual artist for crudeness of tone, and for the use of colors which are of the earth earthy. In the recollection of Italian pictures, lovely in all perfections, it is not easy to bestow unqualified admiration on figures which, whatever be their Christian graces, are severe in outline, ungainly in form, and feeble in bodily frame. Such defects, however, may be perchance but motes that darken the sunbeam; they are, perhaps, but the vapors of earth which the light of heaven has struggled in vain to dispel." — J. BEAVINGTON ATKINSON, *Art Journal*, February, 1865.

"There is also a conservative religious school illustrated by Overbeck, and an eclectic one by Cornelius and Kaulbach, who thought to recast the art of the nineteenth century in old molds, and with about as much permanent success as a new order of Stylites might expect. These artists are ambitious, learned, sincere, and skillful. But the common people wonder, shake their heads, and straightway forgetting the big paintings compounded of defunct foreign systems and feelings, pass on to admire the easel representations of things familiar and domestic. Modern democratic taste, right or wrong, will not tolerate asceticism, allegory, religious or classical idealism, mysticism, romanticism, or other passion of the past, while it can command a plentiful supply of its own loved naturalism. Its idols must talk its own tongue, and have a fellow-feeling. Democracy has hit the right path for a more wholesome art of its own than aristocracy ever worked out for itself. Believe, and *then* be baptized. The habit of church or state is to baptize first, leaving the neophyte to believe if he can, disbelieve if he dare." — JARVES, *Art Thoughts.*

Pabst, Camille Alfred. (*Fr.*) Born at Heiteren. Medal at Paris in 1874. Medal at Philadelphia. Pupil of Comte. At Philadelphia he exhibited "The Alsatian Bride," and at the Paris Salon of 1877, "The Cradle" and "The Album of the War"; and in 1878, "An Apothecary in Alsace" and "A Corner of my Atelier."

Page, William, N. A. (*Am.*) Born in Albany, N. Y., 1811. Removed in 1820 with his family to New York City. Was a pupil in the classical school of Joseph Hoxie. At the age of eleven he gained a premium from the American Institute for an india-ink drawing. He entered the law office of Frederick De Peyster when quite a young man, but soon devoted himself entirely to art, studying under Professor Morse, and in the schools of the National Academy. In 1828 and '29 he painted portraits in Albany. Again settled in New York, and, later, opened a studio in Boston, where he remained until he went abroad. For many years he was considered the leading American portrait-painter in Rome. He was made a full member of the National Academy in 1836. Among Page's earlier works are a "Holy Family" (belonging to the Boston Athenæum), "The Infancy of Henry IV.," and a portrait of Governor Marcy (the last in the City Hall, New York). In 1868 he sent to the National Academy portraits of Robert B. Minturn and Mrs. Theodore Tilton; in 1869, Henry Ward Beecher (belonging to Theodore Tilton); in 1870, Governor Fenton (belonging to the city of New York); in 1874, Col. R. G. Shaw. His "Antique Timbrel-Player" was in the National Academy in 1871; "Farragut's Triumphant Entry into Mobile Bay," in 1872; "Shakspere," in 1874; and "Shakspere, from the German Death Mask," in 1876.

Among his other works may be mentioned, "Ruth and Naomi" (in the possession of the New York Historical Society), "Moses," "Ruth," "Venus," and portraits of Robert Browning, and Charlotte Cushman. A head of Christ, painted by Page for Theodore Tilton, and exhibited at the National Academy and elsewhere, attracted much attention. The lectures which this artist delivered at the National Academy were fine, and much valued by the students who listened to them. A number of Page's pictures were on exhibition in New York in the winter of 1877, including his bust and full-length portrait of Shakspere, his copy of Titian's "Venus," and his own "Venus," painted in Rome in 1859, and exhibited in London in 1860 and in New York in 1867. Mr. Page has for some years occupied a studio in New York.

"There is much in Page to command respect. He experiments boldly in pursuit of the combined splendor and purity of Titian, thinks profoundly, reasons plausibly, and always essays high art. Ever ready to confound or convince, he surprises, delights, confuses, and disappoints all at once. Some of his portraits exhibit nice discrimination of character, while his ideal works, notwithstanding faults of grammar and much want of good taste, when he departs from direct copying, have something grand in suggestion, showing familiarity with great work." — JARVES, *Art Idea.*

"Of all the American portrait-painters, Page is the most originally experimental ; he has studied his art in theory as well as practice. . . . . He seems to unite the conservative instincts of the old-world artists with the bold experimental ambition of the young Republic." — TUCKERMAN's *Book of the Artists.*

"Page's portrait of President Eliot of Harvard College [N. A., 1876] is in many respects the finest work in the Exhibition. It is a striking likeness, and the pose is eminently characteristic of the man. We look upon this work as the highest aim in portraiture. The painting is solid, the drawing firm, and every detail of the work is finished with conscientious care." — *Art Journal*, MAY, 1876.

Palizzi, Joseph. (*Ital.*) Born at Lanciano, 1813. Chevalier of the Legion of Honor. Pupil of the Academy of Naples. He went to Paris in 1844. He paints landscapes, figures, and animals. Naturally, with such endeavors, some things must be good and some bad. It is quite necessary to choose carefully if one buys a Palizzi. At the Salon of 1877 he exhibited "Asses in a Forest" and "Cows in a Pasture"; in 1876, "The Return from the Fair" and "The Road of San Germano, near Mount Cassin"; and in 1875, "An Italian Herdsman descending the Mountain with his Sheep." His "Landscape with Goats" and "A Neapolitan Boy" belong to J. H. Weeks of Boston.

"Joseph Palizzi is a Neapolitan, naturalized Frenchman, even a Parisian by his mind, his talent, his success. I know few artists more fruitful, more varied, more anxious to attempt painting in all phases ; he goes from landscape to figures ; he knows animals by heart ; he leaves one pocket picture in the size and finish of a miniature to undertake a grand canvas of historic dimensions. At times he throws aside his palette to essay charcoal and water-colors. He is a seeker ; an insatiable, an ambitious man in the best sense of the word. We can see that success and failure (there are some heights and depths in his history) stimulate him equally." — EDMOND ABOUT, *Salon de* 1864.

Palmaroli, Vicente. (*Span.*) A medal at the Exposition Universal, Paris, 1867. He is one of the chief painters of his school, and may be compared with Fortuny in certain points, and with Meissonier in others. Two works by Palmaroli, "The Listener" and "The Connoisseur," are in the collection of Mr. Theron R. Butler, New York. When his picture of "The Sermon in the Sistine Chapel" was on exhibition it attracted much attention. The following extract from a writer in the "Gazette des Beaux-Arts" relates to this work : —

"Since the first day of the Exposition the critics, whose enthusiasm was immediately excited, group themselves eagerly before the 'Sermon in the Sistine Chapel.' It is because one is always attracted by works in which effect and style are in unity. The picture of Palmaroli has this merit : it is harmonious, it is tranquil, it is sober, and, moreover, adequately colored : the reds, the blacks, the whites, the browns, are so marvelously mingled that this flourish of trumpets (in color) does not cover up the monotonous voice of the preacher. What is wanting in this picture (but in so small a measure that perhaps I ought not to speak of it) is a more marked character in the physiognomies of the personages. It seems that such an artist as might be named — Meissonier, for example — would have *buriné* with more incisive traits the faces of the cardinals and archbishops. But what we say ought not to hinder the sympathy which is awakened by the picture of Palmaroli. Even after the 'Sistine Chapel' of Ingres, this work is excellent."

Palmer, Samuel. (*Brit.*) Born at Walworth, Surrey, 1805. He studied in the Antique School of the British Museum and elsewhere, and has spent his professional life in London and the counties of Kent and Surrey, passing two years in study and observation in Italy. He has painted in oil and water colors, and turned his attention somewhat to etching. About 1853 he was elected a member of the Etching-Club and a full member of the Society of Painters in Water-Colors. Among his more important drawings sent to the Water-Color Exhibitions in different seasons are, "A Dream on the Apennine," in 1864 ; "The Ballad," in 1860 (belonging to F. Craven) ; "Pompeii" and "St. Paul landing in Italy," in 1868 ; "The Fall of Empire," in 1871 ; "A Golden City," in 1873 ; drawings from "Comus," "L'Allegro," and "Il Penseroso," and "Tityrus restored to his Patrimony," in 1877 ; etc.

" Palmer's studies of foliage are beyond all praise for carefulness. I have never seen a stone-pine or a cypress drawn except by him, and his feeling is as pure and grand as his fidelity is exemplary. I look to him, unless he loses himself in over-reverence for certain conventionalisms of the elder schools, as one of the probable renovators and correctors of whatever is failing and erroneous in the practice of English art." — RUSKIN'S *Modern Painters.*

"Samuel Palmer is one of the few really great English etchers, but as it results from the nature of his work that each plate of his is very costly in time, and as he happens to be a very successful painter in water-colors, the consequence is that his production in etching has been extremely limited. .'. . . If ever a true appreciation of art shall become general among our descendants, they will wonder how it is possible that Samuel Palmer, to whom was given genius and length of days, and who in his time, as they will see, was one of the most accomplished etchers who ever lived, should have left behind him just half a dozen plates." — HAMERTON'S *Etching and Etchers.*

Palmer, Erastus D. (*Am.*) Born in Onondagwa County, N. Y., 1817. He lived in Utica, N. Y., for many years, following his trade, that of a carpenter. In 1846 he settled in Albany, and began his professional career as a cutter of cameos, pursuing this branch of his art with decided success until 1852, when he executed his first important piece of sculpture, " The Infant Ceres," which was exhibited at the National Academy in New York, and attracted much attention. " Ceres " was followed by " The Morning Star," " The Evening Star," and other subjects in bas-relief. Among his ideal busts are, " Spring," " Resignation," etc. His first full-length figure was the " Indian Girl," followed by the " White Captive," " Faith," " The Emigrant's Children," and " Peace in Bondage." Among his other works are, " The Little Peasant," " The Sleeping Peri," and " The Infant Flora." He has executed portrait busts of Moses Taylor, Alexander Hamilton (belonging to Hamilton Fish), Erastus Corning, Governor Morgan, Commodore Perry, and other prominent men.

K

His "Disappointment," at the Johnston sale, in 1876, brought
$ 660. His bronze statue of Robert Livingston was at the Phil-
adelphia Centennial Exhibition of 1876, and was "commended for
artistic excellence," receiving a medal.

Mr. Palmer's professional life has been spent in Albany. ' He made
his first visit to Europe in 1874, observing and studying the masters,
ancient and modern, in the different art centers of the Continent, and
working for some time in Paris.

"Palmer's cameo-cutting was bold, distinct, unevasive ; some of his. works in that
line are perfect gems, and far more satisfactory than most of the cameo portraits for
which travelers pay such exorbitant prices in Rome. . . . . 'Ceres' was idealized with
strict regard to Nature as a basis. The exquisite contour and sublimated infantile expression of the bust attracted a crowd of delighted gazers. The conception proved a
remarkable eye for beauty, while the finish indicated an exactitude and refinement of
chiseling." — TUCKERMAN's *Book of the Artists.*

"Undoubtedly Palmer has a poetic, versatile mind. . . . . His favorite mode of expression is allegory or symbolism. Aiming at original invention, he has attained
a style peculiar to himself. . . . . Perhaps his finest conception is the 'Indian
Maiden finding the Cross in the Wilderness.' It is simple and suggestive, the figure of
the maiden being far more refined than his white women. 'The Ambush Chief' is
forcible and natural. 'The Peri,' ' Spirits' Flight,' ' Peace in Bondage,' ' Resignation,'
'Morning,' ' Evening,' ' Memory,' mostly medallions, although somewhat capriciously
baptized, manifest the varied idealism of his thought." — JARVES, *Art Idea.*

"While noting how thoroughly American the fine head of this angel is ['The Angel
at the Sepulcher'], we are also bound to note that both in face and figure he is
of a very fleshy and unangelical type. Indeed, Palmer has always shown a singular
preference for phlegmatic modes, and his two most important studies from the nude,
' The White Captive '· and 'The Indian Girl,' are lacking in precisely that litheness
which is one of the chief charms of the best antique representations of the nude human
figure. Both of these statues, however, have very admirable qualities." — *Great American Sculptors.*

Palmer, Walter L. (*Am.*) Native of Albany, N. Y. Son of
Erastus D. Palmer. He studied in Paris, returning to New York,
where he opened a studio in 1877, devoting himself to landscape-painting. He sent to the National Academy, in 1878, "An Interior" (belonging to H. G. De Forest) and "Montigny-sur-Loing."

"An ' Interior' with figures is one of the brightest things in the room [Union League
Club, 1878]. Mr. Palmer's sense of light and color is acute, and he has made more than
a faithful transcription in his choice of characteristic accessories, and in the admirably
introduced young gentlewoman who gives to the scene a profoundly human interest." —
New York Evening Post, March 15, 1878.

Pampaloni, Luigi. (*Ital.*) Born at Florence (1791 - 1847). Professor in the Academy of Florence. In 1827 he first attracted attention by a group made for a Polish lady, — a monument, which
represented a little girl sleeping, and a boy kneeling by her side with
upturned face and clasped hands. The figure of the boy, under the
name of the "Praying Samuel," became popular the world over. It
was also called the "Orphan," and as it appeared at about the same
time with the engraving of the Duke of Reichstadt in the same attitude, it added to its popularity in some quarters, where it was believed

that Pampaloni had the son of Napoleon in mind. The plaster copies were sold in immense numbers. He made several other similar representations of children, but the majestic figures of Arnolfo dei Lapi and Brunelleschi on the eastern side of the Cathedral at Florence show more fully the talent of this sculptor. He modeled the Leonardo of the loggia of the Uffizi, and made the colossal Pietro Leopoldo at Pisa, and that of the poet Papi at Lucca.

Pape, Eduard Friedrich. (*Ger.*) Born at Berlin, 1817. Member of the Berlin Academy and Professor there, where he also studied as well as under Gerst. His principal works are landscapes and decorative paintings, of which there are a number in the new Museum at Berlin. He frequently chooses scenes in which there are waterfalls. At the National Gallery, Berlin, are, "The Rhine-Fall at Schaffhausen" and "Erl-Gletscher auf Handeck." At Berlin, in 1876, he exhibited "Lake Maggiore," "A Woody Landscape," and "Chiemsee."

Paris, Camille. (*Fr.*) Born at Paris. Medal in 1874. Pupil of Picot and A. Scheffer. At the Salon of 1876 he exhibited "The Temple of Neptune, in the Latium." His picture of 1874, "A Bull of the Roman Campagna," is at the Luxembourg.

Parker, John A., A. N. A. (*Am.*) Born in New York, 1827. He was brought up to commercial pursuits in his native city. He displayed a marked taste for art as a youth, but did not adopt it as a profession until 1859, when his first picture was exhibited at the National Academy, New York. He studied from nature in the Catskills and elsewhere, and has spent his professional life in Brooklyn, N. Y. He was one of the original members of the Brooklyn Art Association, and was elected an Associate of the National Academy, New York, in 1864. His landscapes are in the possession of Dr. Storrs, H. E. Pierrepont, A. A. Low, Cyrus Butler, and other gentlemen. To the Centennial Exhibition at Philadelphia, in 1876, he sent "Twilight in the Adirondacks," belonging to Charles Baxter.

"A late 'Twilight,' by John A. Parker, with a pathway through a grove, a herdsman and cattle in the foreground, and the church-spire showing through the trees, is suggestive of Gray's elegy. The artist's honesty of purpose is shown in the tenderness with which the several varieties of foliage are suggested. Every leaf is an effort carefully painted. . . . . The sky is painted in rich golden tones, and against it is shown, in delicate relief, the old belfry of the little church, and the interlaced branches of the trees. Usually very little drawing is shown in a landscape picture, but in this it was required in the tree branches, and consequently there is a fine display of it." — *Brooklyn Eagle*, December, 1876.

Parker, Edgar. (*Am.*) Born in Framingham, Mass., 1840. Portrait-painter. He has spent his professional life in Boston, and has received no instruction in painting. Three of his portraits are in Faneuil Hall, namely, those of Charles Sumner, Henry Wilson, and Rear-Admiral John A. Winslow. He has also painted Hon. Charles Hudson, ex-Gov. Onslow Stearns of New Hampshire, Nathaniel Hawthorne, etc. William and Mary Howitt own his portrait of Margaret Foley. Mr. Whittier gave him sittings in 1875 for a portrait, which is the only original likeness of the poet in existence except one, painted when he was a young man, by Hoyt.

Parmentier, Luisa von. (*Aus.*) Of Vienna. Medal at Philadelphia, where she exhibited "Interior of the Castle Ruin, Taufers, in the Tyrol" and "A Landscape." John F. Weir, in his report, says :—

"In landscape Austria did not exhibit works of decided merit : perhaps nothing in this branch of art was more pleasing than the pictures of Luisa von Parmentier."

Parrot, Philippe. (*Fr.*) Born at Excideuil. Medals in 1868, '70, and '72. At the Salon of 1877 he exhibited two portraits ; in 1875, "Judgment of Paris" and two portraits ; in 1874, "The Fountain" and a portrait. Among his other works are "Galatea" and numerous portraits.

Parsons, Charles, A. N. A. (*Am.*) Born in England, 1821. He has spent, however, the better part of his life in the city of New York, studying in the National Academy schools and from nature in the vicinity of the metropolis. He has furnished illustrations for numerous books, magazines, and weekly journals, and since 1862 has been superintendent of the Art Department of the publishing-house of Harper and Brothers. In 1860 he was elected an Associate of the National Academy, is a member of the Artists' Fund Society and of the Society of Painters in Water-Colors, contributing occasionally to the exhibitions of the Academy. He sent, in 1876, to the Water-Color Society, "Salem"; in 1877, "November" (belonging to J. Henry Harper) ; in 1878, "Gravesend Bay."

Parton, Arthur, A. N. A. (*Am.*) Born at Hudson, N. Y., 1842. Pursued his art studies under William T. Richards of Philadelphia, spending his professional life in the city of New York. He went to Europe in 1869, and returned to America the next year. He is a member of the Artists' Fund Society, and was elected an Associate of the National Academy in 1872. Among the more important of his works are, "On the Road to Mount Marcy," exhibited at the National Academy in 1874, and owned by Hon. Charles Farwell of Chicago, "A Mountain Brook," at the National Academy in 1875 (purchased by A. T. Stewart), now in the Stewart Gallery. His "November" is owned by Lord Moncke, formerly Governor-General of Canada ; his "Sycamores in Old Shokan" is in the possession of Amherst College ; "Loch Lomond" is owned by H. P. Cooper. His "Solitude" (belonging to W. D. Judson) and "Stirling Castle" (belonging to Bryce Gray) were at the Centennial Exhibition of 1876.

"Arthur Parton, who is one of our youngest landscape-painters, is finishing a large study from nature on an Adirondack brook. It is a work of rare merit, and the fidelity with which the trees of the forest and undergrowth are painted in detail, together with the running water, merits the highest praise." — *Art Journal,* April, 1875.

"The very name — 'Mountain Brook' — suggests to the imagination just what it is, a quiet, lonely, retired spot, among the recesses of a wooded pass where Nature in her wildest mood has spread out her giant trees, etc. The artist has imparted to the scene the 'still quiet' which seems to reign over all, and the 'weirdness' which ever attaches itself to Nature's forest scenes." — *New York Express*, June, 1875.

Parton, Ernest. (*Am.*) Born in Hudson, N. Y., 1845. Younger brother of Arthur Parton, in whose studio he spent two winters, receiving, however, no instruction in art from regular masters or in any schools. He was elected a member of the Artists' Fund Society of New York in 1873, contributing one work each year to its sales. In 1873 he went to Europe for the purpose of spending a few months in Great Britain, but, meeting with success in London, he has since remained there, exhibiting frequently at the Royal Academy and elsewhere. In 1876 he visited the Swiss Lakes and Northern Italy, making many sketches. Among his most important works are, "Morning Mist" (exhibited in New York in 1873; belonging now to Dr. Lutkins of Jersey City), "Papa's Lunch" (at the Royal Academy in 1875), "The Placid Stream" (R. A., 1876), "Sunny September" and "The Poet's Corner" (R. A., 1877), "The Silent Pool," "Reflections," "Au bord de l'eau," "On the River Loing" (R. A., 1878), "Near Capel Cruig, North Wales," "Borrowdale Meadows," "The Valley of the Derwent" and "The High Hall Garden" (R. A., 1877). The last was purchased by the Art Union of London.

Pasini, Alberto. (*Ital.*) Born at Busseto. Chevalier of the Orders of Saints Maurice and Lazarus, and of the Legion of Honor. Officer of the Orders of Turkey and Persia. Honorary Professor of the Academies of Parma and Turin. Pupil of Ciceri. His pictures are principally of Oriental subjects. There were eleven of them at the Paris Exposition of 1878, and at the Salon, same year, he exhibited "Yechil Turbé, à Brousse (Turkey in Asia)," and "The Door of a Khan at Brousse."

Passini, Ludwig. (*Aus.*) Born at Vienna, 1832. Member of the Academies of Berlin, Vienna, and Venice. Medals at Berlin, Paris, and Vienna. Studied at the Vienna Academy, under Karl Werner, and in Italy. Spent some time in Venice and Rome, and settled in Berlin about 1864, but has made several journeys to Italy. He is very skillful in water-colors. He paints architectural and *genre* subjects, also portraits. In the National Gallery at Berlin is a cartoon by Passini representing the "Choir Men in St. Peter's at Rome." His technique is perfect, and many of his scenes from Roman life are interesting. Among his works are, "A Roman Woman with an Infant," "Prebendaries in the Church," and "Penitence." At the Johnston sale, New York, 1876, a water-color, "The Monk in his Cell" (10 by 8), sold for $ 270. At the Paris Exposition, 1878, he exhibited "A Procession at Venice," "A Bridge at Venice," and "A Public Reader at Chioggia."

" Passini, who should not be confounded with Pasini of Paris, is widely and justly cele-brated as a consummate artist in water-color representations of Italian life."— BENJA-MIN's *Contemporary Art in Europe.*

Paton, Sir Noel. (*Brit.*) Joseph Noel Paton was born in Dunferm-line, Scotland, 1821. He was the son of a designer of patterns, who gave him his first instruction in drawings. He was subsequently a pupil of the Royal Scottish Academy in Edinburgh, and of the Royal Academy in London. In 1845 he received from the Commissioners of Decoration of Westminster Hall a prize of £200 for his cartoon, " The Spirit of Religion," and in 1847 a prize of £300 for his " Recon-ciliation of Oberon and Titania." His " Quarrel of Oberon and Ti-tania " was purchased by the Scottish Academy in 1849, and placed in the National Gallery in Edinburgh, at a cost of £700. Among his works may be mentioned, " Thomas the Rhymer and the Queen of Fairyland," " The Pursuit of Pleasure," " Nicker the Soulless," " The Bluidy Tryste " (1858), " The Fairy Raid " (R. A., 1867), " Caliban " (R. A., 1869), " In Memoriam," and " Home from the Cri-mea," the property of the Queen, and exhibited at the International Exhibition in 1862, engraved, and very popular. Paton was knighted in 1867, upon his appointment as Queen's Limner for Scotland. His " Good Shepherd " (belonging to the Queen) and " Caliban listening to the Music " were at the Paris Exposition of 1878.

" Paton aims always at a higher province of art than the common class of incidents, and his pictures are full of minute detail, not only natural, which he paints with great delicacy, but of that antiquarian character which cannot be obtained without pains and study. All this makes us regret that Mr. Paton persists in attempting subjects which, judging from the results, must be pronounced quite above his abilities. He is an exam-ple of the intellectual illusion which mistakes interest in an art for a power in it." — PALGRAVE's *Essays on Art.*

" Foremost in its class, or rather prominent in that original walk which the painter [Noel Paton] holds exclusively his own. we pause before ' Oskold and the Ellemaids'' [at the Royal Scottish Academy, 1874],— Oskold, the former, being the embodiment of a pilgrim soul, fighting his way through the perils of a false, lying world ; the latter repre-sentative of the five senses, beautiful sirens, bent on the cavalier's ruin through their many glittering temptations. Like most of this artist's allegories, the rigidly poetic con-ception with its thousand dreamy suggestive accessories can find but scant justice in word description. As the whole scene is in a sense spiritually originated, it must be not only materially but spiritually discerned." — *London Art Journal,* April, 1874.

Paton, Waller H. (*Brit.*) A native of Dunfermline, Scotland. Younger brother of Sir Noel Paton and of Mrs. D. O. Hill. He was brought up as a banker. Possessing, however, much of the inherent talent for art which has made his family remarkable, he turned his attention to painting, devoting himself particularly to landscapes. He is an artist comparatively self-taught, and has spent the better part of his professional life in Edinburgh. He has been a member of the Royal Scottish Academy for some years, contributing frequently to its exhibitions, as well as to those of the Royal Academy in Lon-don. Among his later works are, " Old Homes " and " New Tenants," " Decay of the Forest," " Falls of Tummell," and others, at the Royal

Scottish Academy in 1878. His "Lamlash Bay, Isle of Arran " is in the National Gallery of Scotland ; his "Dell without a Name " was at the Philadelphia Exhibition of 1876.

"In all of Waller Paton's landscapes there is a strong leaning to the spiritual above the material, — as little of the human as must be, as much of the divine as may. The 'Summer Evening, Invercloy Arran ' [R. A., 1874], although entirely faithful in feature to the *locale*, is handled with such delicate grace, and is so redolent of the sweet sanctity of perfect peace, that we seem to gaze rather on a fairy region than on any this world can offer." — *Art Journal*, March, 1874.

Patrois, Isidore. (*Fr.*) Born at Noyers. Chevalier of the Legion of Honor. At the Salon of 1877 he exhibited "The Visit " and "The First Suspicion " ; in 1876, " In the Garden " and " Le juge intime " ; in 1874, "The Reading, — Young Russian Girls," "Confidences," and "Fruits." Many of the pictures of Patrois are scenes from Russian life. "The Young Mother " is in the collection of Mrs. H. E. Maynard of Boston. Near St. Petersburg there is annually a procession of Holy Images, which is intended as a memorial of the procession of 1832, when the cholera proved so fatal in Russia. Patrois painted a picture of this procession in 1861, which is in the Luxembourg.

Patten, George. (*Brit.*) (1802 – 1865.) Received his first instruction in art from his father, a miniature-painter of some repute, devoting himself, after studying in the Royal Academy, to that branch of art, but, later, turning his attention to portraits on a larger scale. He was appointed Portrait-Painter to the Prince Consort shortly after the marriage of the Queen, enjoying for many years the patronage of British Court circles. He painted a few ideal pictures, but was more successful in his portraiture of living subjects.

Patten, Alfred Fowler. (*Brit.*) Born in London, 1829. Son of George Patten, pupil of his father, studying also for some time in the Royal Academy. He has exhibited frequently at the Royal Academy, and in the gallery of the Society of British Artists, of which institution he has been a member for some years. Among his later works at the Royal Academy may be noted, " May-Day Revelers fetching forth their Queen," in 1870 ; " Happy Springtime," in 1873; "Reading Robinson Crusoe," in 1878. To the Society of British Artists he sent, in 1877, "Lovers, beware ! " and "Fresh Flowers "; in 1878, " Feeding the Ducks " and " La belle fleuriste."

Pauwels, William F. (*Dutch.*) Born at Eeckeren, 1830. Director of historical painting in the Academy at Weimar. Pupil of Wappers and De Keyser. Painter of historical and *genre* subjects and portraits. Among his works may be mentioned, " The Widow of Van Artevelde," " The Proscribed Victims of the Duke of Alba," and the " Calling of St. Clara." Pauwels has decorated the interior of the Hall at Ypres ; the subjects are historical scenes from 1187 to 1383, such as "The Founding of the First Hospital in Flanders," "The Return of Warriors after the Battle of the Golden Spurs," etc.

One of his later works is a *genre* picture of "Queen Philippa of England succoring the Poor of Ghent." At the Corcoran Gallery, Washington, is his "Justice to Lievin Pyn, 1541."

Pazzi, Enrico. (*Ital.*) Born at Ravenna, 1818. Knighted by Victor Emmanuel, he has received from King Humbert the highest pension of the Commandery of the Order of Saints Maurice and Lazarus. Professor in the Academy of Florence and honorary member of many Italian and foreign academies and societies. He first studied in the Academy of Bologna under Professor Santi; later, in Florence under Dupré. He received a subsidy from the city of Ravenna for six years, to enable him to continue his studies. In 1848 he returned to Bologna. In 1868 his statue of Dante was erected in the Piazza Santa Croce at Florence. Later he modeled a statue of Savonarola (intended for a large hall in the Palazzo Vecchio, Florence) and a group called "Venice Enslaved." He was summoned to Belgrade in Servia, where he received from that government a commission to erect (in bronze) an equestrian statue to Michael Obrenovicht III. About the same time he was charged with the erection of a monument to the illustrious Luigi Carlo Farina, the patriot historian, in the Piazza della Stagione at Ravenna. At the unveiling of this monument Pazzi was made a citizen of the town of Russi, the birthplace of Farini, and it was also upon this occasion that he was so highly honored by King Humbert. One of the earliest works of this sculptor was "The Child Moses trampling on the Crown of Pharaoh," and one of his latest is "Lucretia."

Peale, Rembrandt. (*Am.*) Born in Pennsylvania (1778–1860). He early evinced a taste for art, and in 1795 painted from life a portrait of General Washington, frequently copied by himself and others, and well known through the engravings after it. It was purchased by the United States Government in 1832. Peale studied art under his father Charles W. Peale, one of the early American portrait-painters in Philadelphia, opening a studio of his own in Charleston, S. C., in 1796. In 1801 he went to London, where he was a pupil of Benjamin West until 1804. He lived for three years in Paris, returning to America in 1809. Among the better known of his portraits are those of President Jefferson, Mrs. Madison, Commodores Bainbridge, Perry, and Decatur (in the Gallery of the New York Historical Society) ; of Houdon the sculptor (in the Pennsylvania Academy of Fine Arts) ; of General Armstrong, and an equestrian portrait of Washington (in Independence Hall), and many people of note on both sides the Atlantic. His "Errina" is in the collection of H. C. Carey of Philadelphia. "Wine and Cake" and "Italian Peasant" belong to James L. Claghorn ; "Babes in the Wood," to Marshall O. Roberts ; and "Song of the Shirt," to G. W. Riggs. His "Court of Death" (a large canvas, 13 feet by 24 feet) has been frequently lithographed and engraved, and is probably the best known of his works.

It was exhibited in almost every important city of the United States. Rembrandt Peale was the author of several books : " Notes on Italy," published in 1831 ; " Reminiscences of Art and Artists," published in 1845 ; besides a biography of his father, and occasional papers on art topics.

Peale, Sara M. (*Am.*) Daughter of James Peale. She studied under her father, and under her uncle C. W. Peale (the founder of Peale's Museum), devoting herself to portrait-painting, and working at her profession for some years in Baltimore and Washington, where she had among her sitters Lafayette, Benton, Henry A. Wise, Caleb Cushing, and other distinguished men. She resided in St. Louis from 1847 to '77, painting there, among other portraits, one of Father Mathew. She went to Philadelphia in 1878. Of late years she has turned her attention to fruit-pieces.

Pearce, Charles Sprague. (*Am.*) A native of Boston. He has lived for some time in Europe, painting under Bonnat in Paris, and spending his winters at Nice. He has also made tours in Africa, Algiers, etc. He has devoted himself to portraits and figure-pieces, exhibiting in the Paris Salon. To the Centennial Exhibition at Philadelphia in 1876 he sent " L'Italienne " ; to the exhibition of the Society of American Artists, in 1878, " The Lamentation over the First-Born in Egypt." His " Pet of the Harem " (belonging to R. S. Fay), and the " Lamentation" and others, were exhibited at the Mechanics' Fair, Boston, 1878.

Peduzzi, Renato. (*Ital.*) Of Milan. At Philadelphia he exhibited " A Chimney-Piece with a Boy representing Silence," " A Boy and a Swan," and " A Dancing Fawn," and received a medal.

Peele, John T., A. N. A. (*Brit.-Am.*) Born in Peterboro', England, 1822. Carried to America by his parents in 1824. Began the practice of art in Buffalo, N. Y., under difficulties and with no art education. He painted portraits in New York, Albany, and London, England, settling finally in New York about 1846, where he turned his attention to the painting of ideal subjects, in which children form the principal feature. He went again to England in 1851, to the Isle of Man in 1858, remaining eight years, and finally took up his residence in Kent. He is an Associate of the National Academy of Design, New York, and a member of the Society of British Artists, in whose galleries, as well as in those of the Royal Academy, London, he frequently exhibits. Among his works are, " The Children of the Wood," " Grandma's First Lesson in Knitting," " Music of the Reeds," " The Little Laundress," " Children of Robert Thornton " (R. A., 1874), " Grace before Meat," " Highland Supper," " Sunny Days of Childhood," " Asleep on Duty," " One Tune More," " Blowing Bubbles," " A Monument of Suspense," and " The Prayer for Health," many of which have been engraved. His " Children of the Wood " (purchased by Prince Albert) is in Osborne House, Isle of Wight.

"Peele's method of treating juvenile portraiture is both commendable and pleasant; it retains the individuality while it takes the impersonation out of the category of a mere portrait, dressed and set up for the occasion. . . . . In all of his works Mr. Peele's aim and purpose seem to have been to show as much of the poetic side of nature as is consistent with his subject, to preserve its individuality, while imparting to it something beyond mere naturalism." — *Art Journal*, May, 1876.

Peiffer, Auguste-Joseph. (*Fr.*) Born at Paris. Pupil of Klagmann. Medal of the third class in 1878, when he exhibited "The Swallows," a statue in marble.

Peinte, Henri. (*Fr.*) Born at Cambrai. *Prix du Salon*, 1877. Pupil of Guillaume and Cavelier. The sensation which the "Sarpedon" of this artist made is well shown in the extracts below, and when it is found so artistic and beautiful in plaster what may it be in some more artistic material!

"The 'Sarpedon' of Peinte is one of the statues most justly remarked by all those who have studied the human body and the difficult art of reproducing it with originality. It merits the *prix du Salon* which it received." — CHARLES TIMBAL, *Gazette des Beaux-Arts*, June, 1877.

"The figure is solidly, firmly planted. The attitude and the movement are exact and correct. The design, without angles or *heurts*, is of a rare elegance. The muscles are wisely treated, without exaggeration. The *ensemble* is irreproachable, and the 'Sarpedon,' in bronze, will become classic." — MARIO PROTH, *Voyage au Pays des Peintres*, 1877.

Pellegrin, Louis Antoine Victor. (*Fr.*) Born at Toulon, 1836. Made his début at the Salon of 1864, with a picture of "Louis XIV. making Presents to the Duchess of Bourgogne in the Apartments of Mme. Maintenon." This was followed by "Marie Antoinette waiting to be taken to the Tribunal," "Vert-Vert," "Interior of the Church of Saint-Séverin," "Marie Antoinette conducted to the Scaffold," etc. He exhibited at the London Academy, in 1873, "Saint-Séverin's Church at Paris on Christmas Eve."

Pelouse, Louis Germain. (*Fr.*) Born at Pierrelaye. Medals in 1873 and '76. Landscape-painter. His "Souvenir of Cernay" (1872) is in the Luxembourg. At the Salon of 1877 he exhibited two views in Finistère, one an evening and one a morning effect. They belonged to M. Tabourier and M. Hoschedé.

Penley, Aaron Edwin. (*Brit.*) (1806 – 1870.) Water-color artist, painting landscapes, portraits, and rustic figure-pieces. He was Professor of Drawing at Woolwich Academy, Water-Color Painter to William IV., and author of several valuable books upon art subjects.

Penne, Charles Olivier de. (*Fr.*) Born at Paris. Medal in 1875. Pupil of Cogniet and Jacque. At the Salon of 1877 he exhibited "Dogs of St. Hubert" and "Fox Hounds"; in 1876, "The Cry of the Wild Boar" and "English Dogs"; in 1875, "Norman Dogs" and "Cerf forcé, — tenant les abois." At the Johnston sale in 1876, "The Lost Scent" (12 by 18) sold for $190 (water-color). At the Salon of 1878 he exhibited "English Dogs" and "Dogs of Saint-Germain and Skye."

Pennethorne, Sir James. *(Brit.)* Born in Worcester, England, 1801. At an early age he went to London, studying architecture under Nash, Pugin, and others. About 1825 he visited the Continent, spending some time in study in Rome. In 1840 he was appointed architect and surveyor to the Commissioners of Woods, and turned his attention particularly to the improvement of the streets of London. Among the better known of his architectural works are the new wings of Buckingham Palace and Somerset House, and the new University of London. He also furnished designs for the laying out of Battersea and Victoria Parks. He was knighted by the Queen in 1870.

Pereda, Raimondo. *(Ital.)* Of Milan. At Philadelphia he exhibited, "Love's Net," "A Child's Grief," and "Pretence and Sympathy," in sculpture. At the Paris Exposition of 1878 he exhibited a group in marble, called "Orphelins de mère."

Perigal, Arthur. *(Brit.)* A native of London, residing for many years in Edinburgh. Landscape-painter. Member of the Royal Scottish Academy, exhibiting there and at the Royal Academy in London. Among his later works may be noted, "Loch Assynt, Sutherlandshire," "Vesuvius, from Naples," "At the Pier at Nairn," "Arran," "On the Jed," "A Rough Day," "Evening in Skye," "Loch Tromlie," "Morning in Glen Nevis," etc. His "Moorland near Kinlochewe, Ross-shire" is in the Scottish National Gallery.

Pérignon, Alexis. *(Fr.)* Born at Paris, 1806. Officer of the Legion of Honor. Pupil of Gros. This celebrated portraitist is distinguished by "a true color, a firm and fine *pâte*, with elegance of form, grace in modeling, and a sober and wise execution." Large numbers of his portraits have been exhibited at the Salons. Pérignon became, some years since, the Director of l'École des Beaux-Arts at Dijon. He exhibited two portraits at the Paris Salon of 1878.

Perkins, Charles C. *(Am.)* Born in Boston, 1823. Chevalier of the Legion of Honor, 1867. Corresponding Member of the French Institute, 1868. President of the Boston Art Club since 1871. Member of the American Academy of Arts and Sciences, 1874. Honorary Director of the Museum of Fine Arts, Boston, 1876. Member of the New England Historical Society, 1876. Honorary Member of the Metropolitan Art Museum, New York, for life. President of the Handel and Haydn Society since 1875. Mr. Perkins studied oil-painting under Ary Scheffer, and etching under Bracquemond and Lalanne. Though not a professional artist, he devotes himself to the study of art in various directions, delivers lectures upon subjects connected with etching and other kindred topics, and published "Tuscan Sculptors," two volumes, in 1864, and "Italian Sculptors," one volume, in 1867. The plates in these books were etched by the author, many of them from his own drawings. In 1878 Mr. Perkins published "Raphael and Michael Angelo," a biographical and critical essay.

"'Italian Sculptors; being a History of Sculpture in Northern, Southern, and Eastern Italy.' Mr. Perkins continues, we trust he does not conclude, his valuable popular dissertation on the sculpture of Italy. Having, four years since, given us an excellent account of the arts in marble and bronze as they were practiced in the seats of the old Etruscans and their accessories, he turns to other fields in that peninsula, which, if it was not the birthplace, has been the Capua and the grave of the nobler arts. . . . . The author reviews with much tact, excellent taste, and ample learning, the sculptural schools of Rome, Lombardy, — a very interesting branch of the subject, wherein he points out the error of ascribing the arts of their Italian buildings to the Lombard tribe, rather than to the Maestro Comacini, or freemasons, and traces the whole history of that noble branch of design, — Venice, with a charming school of the greatest wealth, Verona, Vicenza, Padua, Mantua, and Brescia, all of which have marked characteristics, and the cities of Central Italy, Bologna, Ferrara, Modena, Genoa, Carrara, etc. Our verdict on this admirable work is given with pleasure, not only on account of the taste, tact, learning, and comprehensive views of the author, but because his literary style is clear, his research large, and his illustrative power rich." —*London Athenæum*, January 2, 1869.

" In choosing Raphael and Michael Angelo for his subjects, Mr. Perkins sets his feet in a well-worn track. . . . . Next best to new material, however, is a novel and lively presentation of the old. And to so much of originality, Mr. Perkins in this scholarly and refined treatise can lay claim. No one before, if our memory serves, has given a sketch of these two great artists set side by side like the double profile on an antique coin, one shining in the sunshine of youth and love and divine achievement, the other somber with the mighty shadows of his own stormy power." — *Literary World*, March, 1878.

Perraud, Jean Joseph. (*Fr.*) Born at Monay (1821 – 1876). Member of the Institute, 1865. Officer of the Legion of Honor, 1867. Medal of Honor, 1869. This sculptor was the pupil of Ramey and A. A. Dumont, and of l'École des Beaux-Arts. He gained the grand *prix de Rome* in 1847. In 1863 he exhibited "The Infancy of Bacchus," now in the Luxembourg, which reappeared at the Exposition of 1867; in 1869, "Despair," now in the Luxembourg, which was much remarked, and "Sainte-Geneviève," for the church of Saint-Denis-du-Saint-Sacrament. Perraud executed a figure of "Justice" and two caryatides for the Palace of Justice, and a group of the "Lyric Drama" for the New Opera House at Paris. He followed the classical traditions, and has been called cold and mannered. In 1866 he exhibited at the Salon two portrait busts; in 1875, "The Day," a group in marble, for the Avenue de l'Observatoire, and two portrait busts; in 1874, two portrait busts; in 1873, "Galatea," statue in marble.

"'The Infancy of Bacchus' is the work of a sculptor who knows all the secrets of the human form, and excels in expressing them, even in the attitudes, which, like those he has given to these figures, make most prominent the hidden details of the interior structure of the bones. The trunk, the limbs, the shoulders of the fawn, are of superb workmanship; the flesh, although virile and firm, has a supple delicacy and much life; the head is expressive; the little Bacchus is also full of delicacy and force; in fine, the work is marvelously brilliant in all its details. We believe, at the same time, that in the next figure which Perraud cuts in marble he will preoccupy himself more with the beauty of the whole effect and with the eurythmy of the lines. Perraud is a sculptor, he is not yet a statuary." — PAUL MANTZ, *Gazette des Beaux-Arts*, July, 1868.

Perrault, Léon. (*Fr.*) Born at Poitiers. Medals at Paris in 1864 and '76, and one at Philadelphia. Pupil of Picot and Bouguereau.

At Philadelphia he exhibited " The Bather " and " Repose," and at the Salon of 1877, " Jesus Christ in the Tomb " and a portrait ; in 1878, " Maternal Tenderness " and a portrait.

Perret, Aimé. (*Fr.*) Born at Lyons, 1847. Third-class medal in 1877. Pupil of l' École des Beaux-Arts of his native city, and of Vollon at Paris. He exposed several works at Lyons, and had already attracted much attention when he made his début in Paris, at the Salon of 1870, with the " Gossips of the Banks of the Rhone, — in the Fog." This same year he came under the influence of Vollon, who was of great advantage to him. He joined the army in 1870, and after his duties there were ended, he made his journey to La Bresse, the quaint country from which he has drawn so many inspirations. Among his works are, " A Baptism in La Bresse " (1877), " A Wedding in Bourgogne in the Eighteenth Century " (1876), " Between two Fires " and a " Ravine of Bugey " (1875), " The Oriental " and " Young Girls of Mâcon." At the Salon of 1878 he exhibited a portrait and " A Dream on the Grass."

Perry, E. Wood, N. A. (*Am.*) Born in Boston, 1831. Was for some time in a mercantile house in New Orleans. In 1852 went to Europe to study art, visited London and Paris, and settled in Düsseldorf, studying under Leutz for two years and a half, and was in the studio of Couture in Paris for one year. In 1857 he went to Venice, holding the position of United States Consul. In 1860 he returned to the United States, and visited many of the cities of the South and West, where he was well regarded as a portrait-painter. He spent three or four years in San Francisco, and went to the Sandwich Islands ; on his return painting portraits of Brigham Young and other Mormon leaders. He settled in New York in 1866, and contributed to the National Academy, in 1867, " Counting the Spoils." In 1868 he was made Associate of the National Academy, and in 1869, when he exhibited " The Weaver," he was made Academician. In 1870 he exhibited " Huldy," " The Contraband of Peace," and " The Story of the Tiles " ; in 1871, " The Garibaldian," " The Lost Art," " The Clock-Doctor," and " Saturday Afternoon " ; in 1874, " He 's coming, — Anne Hathaway " (belonging to E. E. Dorman) ; in 1875, " The Old Story," " A Good Egg," and " Heart's Ease " ; in 1876, " A Quilting-Party," " A Bit of Gossip," " A Quiet Afternoon," and others ; in 1877, " The Sower," " Sweet Corn," and " A Helping Hand " ; in 1878, " The Story." In 1876 he sent to the Water-Color Exhibition, " A Month's Darning " and " Anne Hathaway's Kitchen " ; in 1877 (when he was elected a member of the Society), he contributed " Spun Out," " A Nice Book," and " The Milkmaid." His " Young Franklin and the Press " belongs to the Buffalo Academy of Fine Arts ; " A Month's Darning," at Philadelphia, in 1876, is in the collection of S. V. Wright.

" Perry at the present time occupies a place very nearly at the head of our American *genre* painters. He was one of the first of them to paint American subjects, and the most lowly are invested with a poetry of feeling and delicacy of expression which are not exceeded by any of his contemporaries. That he is a close student, the wide range of his domestic subjects gives ample evidence. His style is broad, but, in connection with it, there are an apparent mellowness of execution and unity of sentiment, which are so noticeable in the best works of the modern French schools." — *Art Journal*, July, 1875.

"Mr. Perry exhibited three pictures, 'The Weaver,' 'Kept In,' and 'Young Franklin,' all characteristic and distinctively American. This artist has made steady progress, and adhered with commendable strictness to subjects within the scope of his powers and sympathies, and he has gradually, but surely, attained a command over his materials that is worthy of high praise. His pictures are illustrative and pleasing, and evince a conscientious study of his subject. He has not yet attained complete mastery of the figure, nor are his pictures free from labored manipulation and thinness of method, but they evince genuine qualities of merit." — PROF. WEIR'S *Official Report of the American Centennial Exhibition of 1876.*

Perry, Ione. (*Am.*) Born in the city of New York, 1839. She studied in the art schools of the Cooper Institute, New York, and for some months was a pupil in painting of Mr. Henry Loop. Her professional life has been spent in New York, and her works are exhibited in the galleries of Schaus, Goupil, and others. Among her paintings may be mentioned, "Called by the Angels" (belonging to Mrs. Younglove of Cleveland, Ohio), "Fadalma" (belonging to Mrs. A. C. Longstreet of New York), "Hypatia" (belonging to Miss Mary L. Booth of New York), "Romola" (belonging to Miss Bunce), and "Heavenward," "Consuelo," "Aïda," "Zenobia," "Elsa at the Coming of Lohengrin," etc.

"In conception, originality of treatment, and spirited drawing, this work ['Heavenward'] may be regarded as the *chef-d'œuvre* of this gifted lady. It has been reproduced by a Paris artist. Mrs. Perry painted, some years ago, another ideal picture, entitled 'Called by the Angels,' which was similarly reproduced and is now having a large sale in the United States. Both works evince a profound study of the old masters, and are more spiritedly treated than almost any of the subjects of a similar character that we have seen in the American school." — *American Register*, Paris.

"Mrs. Ione Perry is a figure-painter. Her ideal heads are widely known through their lithographic reproductions. She is fond of making studies from great creations in literature. . . . . Her coloring is rich and yet delicate. Her draperies are graceful and conscientiously arranged and completed. Her attitudes are both natural and dignified. Her flesh-tints and textures are tender and natural, but more than all is a superiority of character which she never fails to create for her pictures." — *Chicago Times.*

Perry, John D. (*Am.*) Born at Swanton, Vt., 1845. By profession a sculptor. He is not a graduate of any of the schools of art, but has studied diligently from Nature in his native country, and from the works of the masters on the continent of Europe. He lived in New York in 1869 and '70, but has passed the rest of his professional life in Italy and Boston. A statue for the Soldiers' Monument of Swanton, Vt., his first public work, was unveiled in 1868. He was in Rome in 1872 and again in 1873, and spent the years 1876 to '78 in the same city. He has made many portrait busts, including those of Horace Greeley, C. R. Train, Attorney-General of Massachusetts, Dr. Winslow Lewis, Mr. and Mrs. Thomas Mack, H. D. Parker of Boston,

and others. His bust of Greeley and two ideal works, Tennyson's
"Beggar Maid" and "Christmas Morning," all in marble, are in the
private library of C. Baker of Stanbridge, Canada. He made the
statue of "Morality" (one of the sitting figures of the Plymouth Monument), "Spring" (a marble bust for Mr. Sankenau of Philadelphia),
"The Two Buds" (in bas-relief, plaster, the original of which belongs
to Mrs. H. B. Stowe), statuette of Charles Sumner, etc. His "Widow's
Mite," life-size, is his most important work, not yet in marble. It
has been highly praised in Rome, where it was modeled in 1878. Of
his statuette of Sumner, the late J. T. Sargent wrote in the Boston
Globe : —

"It has the true *otium cum dignitate* which the right treatment of the subject
claims, and withal a sort of home look and familiar social grace and expression which
so many of our statues of public men seem to lack. Its facial truthfulness is admirable,
and as a likeness from head to foot it is without defect. The pose of the figure is fine,
representing Mr. Sumner in an easy sitting posture at a desk, with his right arm resting
thereupon, while the whole person has the dignified aspect so peculiar to him."

"The character study of Charles Sumner, sitting at his desk, will also be remembered
as one of his successful efforts. A bust of a little child, in marble, at the Mechanic Exhibition, is interesting as showing a strong bent of the artist's inclination, his children's
heads being among his most successful realizations of character. He has a decided sympathy with childhood, and their natural ways and unstereotyped expressions are always
attained. We write this especially after having seen a photograph of a semi-ideal bust
of a child, in marble, the original of which has not yet arrived from Rome. It is entitled,
we believe, 'The Butterfly,' and represents a little child looking down at a butterfly that
has alighted on its little bare shoulder, its own bust being lost in a bouquet of roses. The
face of the child is charmingly represented, and the cutting of the marble has been done
so deftly that almost the softness of texture of the skin has been realized."— *Boston
Transcript*, October 29, 1878.

Perugini, Charles Edward. (*Ital.-Brit.*) A native of Italy,
but for many years a resident of England, constantly exhibiting at the
Royal Academy. Among his later pictures are, "Playing at Work," in
1872 ; "Between School-Hours," in 1873 ; "A Cup of Tea" and "A
Labor of Love," in 1874 ; "Gardening," in 1875 ; "Choosing a Nose-
gay," in 1876 ; "Finishing Touches," in 1877 ; "Roses and Butterflies," in 1878. He sent a portrait of his wife to the Philadelphia
Exhibition of 1876, and "The Labor of Love" to Paris, in 1878.

"There is much grace showing itself [in 'A Cup of Tea,' R. A., 1874], as well in the
carefully drawn figure of a young lady who sips the cup of tea as in the general harmony of
color secured for the whole composition. Mr. Perugini understands the sense of rich
effect in setting the creamy tints next the flesh, and in banishing almost entirely the
colder colors."— *Art Journal*, June, 1874.

Perugini, Mrs. C. E. (Kate Dickens). (*Brit.*) Younger daughter of Charles Dickens, and wife of Charles Edward Perugini. She
works in her husband's studio, and sent to the Royal Academy in
1878 "A Competitive Examination" and "In for a Scrape"; the preceding year she contributed "An Impartial Audience." Her "Music
hath Charms" was at the Winter Exhibition of the Dudley Gallery in
1877.

"Mrs. Perugini, who is a daughter of the late Charles Dickens, inherits much of the subtle and delicate humor that characterized her father. A picture near completion, charming in color and feeling, represents a dainty little lady seated on a bench in a garden, with a finger uplifted, reading to, or cross-examining, a grown-up peasant girl, with hands held in orthodox fashion behind her back. On the seat at the child's side are an attentive group of dolls, amongst them a quaint Japanese." — *Magazine of Art,* May, 1878.

Pesenti, Domenico. (*Ital.*) Born at Medole, near Brescia, about 1852. Medal at Naples, 1877. A fine artist, who paints both in oil and water colors. His "Choir of Santa Maria Novella, Florence," in oils, is in the Bodleian Library at Oxford. The "Arch of San Giorgio at Florence," in water-colors, is owned in Boston, and is very fine. It was painted upon a special commission, and has never been duplicated or exhibited in public. The character and costume figures, in water-colors, by this painter are fine, and are very popular among the English and American connoisseurs who visit Italy. Several of these are owned in Boston. "A Violin-Player " belongs to Dr. G. C. Clement.

Peters, Anna. (*Ger.*) Born at Mannheim, 1843. Medals at Vienna, London, Munich, Amsterdam, and Antwerp. Pupil of B. F. Peters in Stuttgart. She has traveled extensively, and has painted some decorative works in several German castles. Her subjects are flowers and fruits. At the National Gallery, Berlin, is her "Roses and Grapes."

Petersen, John E. C. (*Dane.*) Born at Copenhagen (1839-1874). Studied at the Academy of Copenhagen, and under Melbye and Dahl. During the Schleswig-Holstein war he served as an officer of Danish infantry. In 1865 he went to America, where he remained during his life. There was an exhibition of his works at the Boston Art Club, which showed his progress during ten years. Some of these pictures were considered quite remarkable, and the later were far superior to the earlier ones.

Petri, Heinrich. (*Ger.*) Born at Göttingen (1834-1871). Historical painter at Düsseldorf. In 1858 he went to Rome. Among his works are a "Mater Dolorosa" and a large altar-picture, for a church in Portugal ; a mural painting, in a church at Wellbergen in Westphalia ; a decorative work, consisting of three pictures, in a church on the island of Nonnenwert, near Rolandseck ; a "Descent from the Cross " and a "Madonna," which were painted for the Queen of Holland ; a "Madonna at the Cross," for a church in Russia ; etc. Petri also made cartoons for glass paintings, and superintended their execution. His portraits were excellent.

Pettenkofen, Auguste. (*Aus.*) Born at Vienna, 1823. Chevalier of the Order of the Crown of Oak. Studied at the Academy of Vienna at a period when the school was in decadence. At length, after passing the required time in the army, where he became a captain, he laid aside the sword for the brush. He studied Wouvermans, Paul Potter, and Van de Velde, and about 1851 went to Paris.

While there he painted "Soldiers in Wait for a Spy at the Door of a Cottage" and "Marauders in a Field of Grain dividing their Booty." The last was purchased for the collection of Sir Richard Wallace. M. Van Cuyck so admired the "Marauders" that he gave the artist an order for two pictures, "Scene after a Duel" and "Hungarian Volunteers." The last established the reputation of the artist, and was sold to M. Roné, who exhibited it at the Cercle de l'Union Artistique. But M. Van Cuyck regretted the picture so much that at length he repurchased it, saying that only death should separate him from it. After his decease it was sold to a London merchant, who sent it to Vienna. At length it was purchased by M. Sedelmeyer for 16,200 florins. This work was also exhibited at the Palais Bourbon for the benefit of the Alsaciens-Lorraines, and also at Vienna in 1873, at which time the Emperor of Austria decorated the painter of it. Among the works of Pettenkofen may also be mentioned, "A Hungarian Village" (in the Collection Dreyfus), "Gypsies Bathing" (Baron Liebig), "The Market of Sznolnok" (the architect Œtgelt, Vienna), etc. He has also executed numerous drawings and water-colors, which always sell for high prices. He now resides much in Italy, and sends out no pictures. At a Paris sale, in 1871, "A Hungarian Market" sold for £228. At Paris, in 1876, "Hungarian Gypsies" sold to Herr Kolbacher of Frankfort for 5,360 francs. At the Oppenheim sale, Paris, 1877, "Austrian Cavaliers passing a Ford" sold to the Frankfort Museum for 5,400 francs. In 1876, at Vienna, in the yearly exhibition, Pettenkofen exhibited a remarkable picture of a "Market-Scene in Hungary."

Pettie, John, R. A. *(Brit.)* Born in Edinburgh, 1839. Received his art education in the Trustees Academy and in the Life Schools of the Royal Scottish Academy, exhibiting his first picture, "The Prison Pet," in Edinburgh in 1859. Among his early works are, "False Dice," "Distressed Cavaliers," "One of Cromwell's Divines," etc. He first exhibited at the Royal Academy in London in 1860, "The Armorers," followed by "The Trio," "The Tonsure," and "The Drum-Head Court-Martial" (which attracted much attention, and led to his election as an Associate of the Royal Academy in 1867). In 1866 he sent "Arrest for Witchcraft"; in 1868, "The Rehearsal"; in 1869, "The Disgrace of Cardinal Wolsey"; in 1870, "'T is Blythe May-Day"; in 1872, "Terms to the Besieged"; in 1873, "Sanctuary"; in 1874 (when he was elected Academician), "Juliet and Friar Laurence"; in 1875, "Jacobites, 1745" (his diploma work); in 1876, "The Threat" and "Home Ties"; in 1877, "Hunted Down" and "A Sword and Dagger Fight"; in 1878, "A Member of the Long Parliament," "Rob Roy," and "The Laird." ·

Among Pettie's other works are several portraits in modern and ancient costume, and "Battledoor," "Persuading Papa," "Old Mother Hubbard," "The Visit to the Necromancer," etc. He re-

8 *

moved to London in 1863. To Philadelphia, in 1876, he sent "Sanctuary," "Touchstone and Audrey," a portrait of George H. Boughton, and "The Smuggler and Exciseman" (belonging to W. P. Frith, R. A.); to Paris, in 1878, "The Flag of Truce," "Terms to the Besieged," "The Threat," and several portraits.

"Without exaggeration, but with enough of sympathetic treatment, the sentiment of the scene ['The Flag of Truce,' R. A., 1878] is brought home to the spectator. It is a story on canvas, well and clearly told, serious in its import, and tenderly pathetic in its influence." — *Art Journal*, July, 1873.

"I have been examining the painting of the chief Jacobite face very closely. It is. nearly as good as a piece of old William Hunt, but Hunt never loaded his paint, except on sticks and mosses and such like. Now there's a wrinkle, quite essential to the expression, under the Jacobite's eye, got by a projecting ridge of paint, instead of a proper dark line." — RUSKIN's *Notes of the Academy*, 1875.

Pfuhl, Johannes. (*Ger.*) Born in Löwenberg, 1846. Studied under Schievelbein in Berlin. With no hope of success he sent in for approbation sketches for the Uhland, Goethe, and Stein monument erected at Nassau. The decision of the judges gave him the commission. His success was such that he also received a command for an elaborate frieze for the Cadet-house at Lichterfelde. Pfuhl has visited Italy. He has also executed some portrait busts. and a few ideal subjects, among which are "The Inquisitive Girl." In Berlin, in 1876, he exhibited a bust of Goethe made from a mask taken when he was fifty years old, a bust of Prince Otto von Bismarck, and a portrait bust of a woman.

Phelps, W. P. (*Am.*) Born in New Hampshire. Began life as a sign-painter in Lowell, Mass., his work in that line attracting much attention. Later, he devoted himself to landscape art, entirely without a master. Through the kindness of several Lowell gentlemen he was enabled to go to Germany, and he remained three years in Munich under Velten. He returned to Lowell with some twenty of his landscapes, all of which met with ready sale ; two companion pieces, "Morning" and "Evening," being purchased by the Art Association of that city. He is now in Munich, where he is likely to remain. His "Forest Scene near Munich" and "Morning" and "Evening" were at the National Academy, New York, in 1878.

Philippoteaux, Félix-Emmanuel-Henri. (*Fr.*) Born at Paris, 1815. Chevalier of the Legion of Honor. Pupil of Cogniet. The works of this artist are seen in many European galleries. "Louis XV. visiting the Battle-Field of Fontenoy" is at the Luxembourg. Many of his subjects are military, but he has occasionally painted other pictures, such as "Deception," "Return from the Inn," "Moorish Women," etc. His larger works are so numerous that no proper list can be given here. At the Royal Academy, London, 1876, he exhibited, "The Charge of the English Heavy Cavalry at the Battle of Balaklava" ; in 1875, "The Charge of the French Cuirassiers. at Waterloo." Some of his works are at Versailles ; and "The Last

Banquet of the Girondins," at the Museum of Marseilles. Philippoteaux has made many designs for illustrated publications.

Phillip, John, R. A. (*Brit.*) Born in Scotland (1817–1867). Studied and practiced drawing at home under many discouragements until 1834, when he made his first visit to London to see the Exhibition of the Royal Academy. Through the kindness of influential Scottish friends he was enabled to enter the schools of the Royal Academy in 1837, remaining two years. Between 1839 and '41 he painted portraits in Scotland, when he settled permanently in London, exhibiting his first picture, " The Catechism," in the Royal Academy in 1847. Later, he sent " The Free Kirk," " The Baptism," " Drawing for the Militia," and other kindred and clever studies of Scottish character. He went to Spain in 1851, in '52, in '56, and '60, remaining some time at each visit, studying enthusiastically in the Spanish schools, and changing visibly the style of his own work. In 1853 he painted his " Visit to the Gypsy Quarter " ; in 1854, his " Andalusian Letter-Writer " (belonging to the Queen). His " Death of the Contrabandista " was painted in 1858, shortly after his election as Associate of the Royal Academy. He was made Academician in 1859. In 1860 he painted his " Marriage of the Princess Royal," a commission from the Queen. He continued to paint Spanish pictures, of which he was very fond, and in which he was very successful, until his death in 1867. In 1862 he exhibited, at the Royal Academy, " Dolores " and " A Spanish Volunteer " ; in 1863, " Acqua Bendita " ; in 1864, " La Gloria, — a Spanish Wake "; in 1865, " The Early Career of Murillo " ; in 1866, " A Chat round the Brasiers " ; in 1867, " Antonio " and two Scottish figure-pictures ; " O Nannie, wilt thou gang with me ? " and " A Highland Lassie Reading." His " Doubtful Fortune," " Round the Brasiers," " Dolores," and " Wine-Drinkers " were at Paris in 1878.

" Remembering the more delicately executed and more carefully composed scenes with which Mr. Phillip some years ago founded his reputation as a painter of Spanish life, we doubt whether the brilliant ' Early Career of Murillo,' which forms, we suppose, the most popular success of the Exhibition [R. A., 1865], will be valued quite as highly when its first charm has passed. . . . . On the whole, while cordially admiring the work, we feel that this is rather a case in which, according to the old proverb, ' accident helps art' than an example of advancing excellence."— PALGRAVE's *Essays on Art.*

" Phillip's prominent faults were an amount of coarseness and an absence of subtlety in his works. His merits were those of native vigor, and of the acquisition of a rich and mellow, if exaggerated, type of form and color. . . . . The Spectator says, ' Phillip, with a nice discrimination of character, had a subtlety in its expression which belonged to him alone.' "—MRS. TYTLER's *Modern Painters.*

Pickersgill, Henry W., R. A. (*Brit.*) (1782–1875.) Brought up to commercial pursuits, but relinquished business for art while still a young man, and entered the Royal Academy in 1805. In the commencement of his professional career he devoted himself to subjects of historic or ideal character ; later, turning his attention to portrait-painting, in which branch of the profession he was popular and successful. He had among his sitters many distinguished men of Great Britain, including Robert Vernon (painted in 1846, and now in the National Gallery), Sir John Bowring, George Peabody, etc. Mr. Pickersgill was elected an Associate of the Royal Academy in 1822, and Academician in 1826, Librarian in 1856, and in 1873 he was placed on the list of Honorary Retired Academicians. At the National Gallery are his " Nun " and " A Syrian Maid." Among his later works, exclusive of portraits, are, " A Falconer of the Olden Time," in 1861 ; " The Rivals," in 1862 ; " The Murder of Desdemona," in 1864 ; " The First Lesson," in 1871 ; " The Streamlet " (his last exhibited work), in 1872. In 1870 he sent to the Royal Academy his portrait of the Countess Guiccioli, painted from life in 1832, but completed in 1869.

Pickeragill, Henry H. (*Brit.*) Son of Henry W. Pickersgill, and an historical portrait-painter of some promise, who died in 1861. He received his art education in Germany and Italy, and resided for some time in St. Petersburg, spending, however, the later years of his life in England. His portraits were highly regarded.

Pickersgill, Frederick R., R. A. (*Brit.*) Born in 1820. A relative of Henry W. Pickersgill, R. A., and nephew of W. Witherington, whose pupil he was. He entered the Royal Academy in 1840, exhibiting the next year, and regularly for many seasons. He was elected an Associate of the Royal Academy in 1847, and Academician in 1857. Among his early works may be noted, " Amoret delivered from the Enchanter," " Britomartis unveiling Amoret," " Sampson Betrayed," " Christ blessing Little Children," and others. In 1861 he exhibited " Frederick banishing Rosalind " ; in 1862, " The Return of a Crusader " ; in 1863, " Ferdinand and Miranda "; in 1865, " Unfriended " ; in 1868, " Columbus at Lisbon "; in 1875, " Old Letters." He was elected Keeper and Trustee of the Royal Academy in 1874. In 1843 he received a prize at the first Cartoon Exhibition for his " Death of King Lear." His " Burial of Harold " (in the House of Parliament) won a prize in 1847. His " Amoret, Æmelia and Prince Arthur " (R. A., 1845) was purchased by Mr. Vernon, and is in the National Gallery. His " Death of Francesco Foscari " was in the collection of the late Prince Albert.

Picknell, W. L. (*Am.*) Born in the State of Vermont, about 1852. Went to Europe in 1874, studying with Inness in Rome two years, and, later, for a few months, under Gérôme in Paris. He has lived and painted in Brittany, working under Robert Wylie until the time of that artist's death. To the Royal Academy, London, in 1877, he sent, " Breton Peasant-Girl feeding Ducks " ; in 1875, " On the Lande, Brittany." To the Paris Salon, in 1878, he contributed " The Fields of Kerren."

Picot, François-Édouard. (*Fr.*) Born at Paris (1786 – 1868).

Member of the Institute. Officer of the Legion of Honor. Pupil of Vincent and l'École des Beaux-Arts. Soon after his début he was commissioned to decorate two ceilings at the Louvre, where he executed some grand compositions. He has also painted ceilings in the galleries at Versailles. He was associated with Flandrin in the interior decoration of the church of Saint-Vincent de Paul.

Pietrasanta, Angelo. (*Ital.*) Born at Milan (1836–1876). Pupil of Hayez and a pensioner at Rome. On his return to Milan he was made Honorable Member of the Académie des Beaux-Arts. He executed frescos in several churches in the neighborhood of Milan, and, for the gallery of Victor Emmanuel in that city, the allegorical figures of Europe and Science. His drawing was very correct. At the Villa Oppenheim, Florence, he painted "Love and Psyche" and nine figures of women of the time of Louis XIV. These last were so admired that he had several orders to copy them. His frescos were his best works.

Pille, Henri. (*Fr.*) Born at Essommes in l'Aisne. Medals in 1869 and '72. Pupil of François Barrias. Many of his pictures are historical and familiar scenes, but whatever he paints he pays great attention to his costumes and details, and renders all with much skill. He exhibited at the Salon in 1870, "Sancho recounting his Exploits to the Duchess" and "A Cabaret at Todtnau"; in 1872, "Autumn"; in 1873, "Matrimonial Accord" and "The First-Born"; in 1874, "A Pardon near Guémené"; in 1875, "The Reading of the Decree of February 24, 1793, in Brittany," "Market at Antwerp," and "Old Clothes"; in 1876, "The Morning Interview," "Intemperance," and "Sobriety"; in 1877, "An Inn" and "A Portrait." He has also exhibited drawings in pen and ink, which are excellent. Among them are, "Esmeralda," "The Fountain," "The Tithing," etc. At the Salon of 1878 he exhibited a portrait of M. Coquelin as he appears in "l'Ami Fritz."

"We have said that the talent of Henri Pille is eminently *spirituel*. That is not all, his compositions are true, they have style. . . . . Style is a manner of right seeing and true doing, and Henri Pille possesses this manner; and in such a degree that he has known how to make it of value in *genre* painting, where the *savoir-faire* seems sufficient to the great number. More, his painting is fundamentally honest, calm, frank, placid, like himself; for after speaking of the painter it is necessary to speak also of the man. A dreamer, doubled by an observer; a character modest and simple. . . . . Let us say the word, he is a peasant in appearance. But whoever regards him with the attention which he merits will soon see that his small, brilliant eyes reflect a sagacious mind, and that his lips are elegantly *retroussées* with a finely *railleuse* expression. He is endowed with a prodigious memory. One of his friends tells us that having been with him to the theater, he saw him the next day, while making his reflections on the intrigues and the whole effect of the play, design with rigorous exactness the costumes of the actors in their least details, indicating the colors and the shades." — CHARLES FLOR, *Galerie Contemporaine, Litteraire Artistique*, 1877.

Piloty, Carl Theodor von. (*Ger.*) Born at Munich, 1826. Member and Professor of the Academy of Munich. Medal at Paris in 1867. After studying under his father he entered the Academy of Munich, and pursued his studies under the direction of his brother-in-law, Charles Schorn. Piloty visited Paris, England, and Brussels. Upon his return to Munich he was commissioned by Maximilian I. to paint for the Maximilianeum a large historical work, "The Elector Maximilian I. adhering to the Catholic League in 1609." This painting was completed in 1854, and gained Piloty much reputation, to which the seal was set in the following year by his picture of " Seni before the Dead Wallenstein." Among his other works are, " The Battle of the White Mountain, near Prague," " The Murder of Wallenstein," "Galileo in Prison " (1864), "Wallenstein marching against Eger " (seen at the Paris Exposition of 1878), mural paintings on the exterior of the Maximilianeum, portrait of the Baron de Schack, a chef-d'œuvre, a large representation of the " Discovery of America," and "Henry VIII. and Anne Boleyn."

As an instructor, Piloty has been very successful, and large numbers of pupils have gathered about him. He is a prominent representative of the modern, realistic German school. His " Nero walking among the Ruins of Rome " is marvelous in the intensity of its realism. His "Thusnelda at the Triumph of Germanicus " was purchased by the Emperor of Germany for 35,000 florins, and placed in the Pinakothek at Munich. Mr. Probasco of Cincinnati owns his " Elizabeth and Frederick of Bohemia receiving News of the Loss of the Battle of Prague," painted in 1868.

" In even the best paintings of Piloty, who is pre-eminently an historical painter, there is often perceptible a certain theatrical, sensational effect in the composition which takes away from its naturalness. His 'Columbus' offends very strongly in this respect ; 'Thusnelda at the Triumph of Germanicus,' his most ambitious work, is perhaps more satisfactory ; while 'Seni discovering Wallenstein Dead' is more simple, and is undoubtedly a work of great power. . . . . Piloty has founded a school. He achieved his fame and influence early ; but so rapidly has German 'art ripened of late years, that he has lived to see the scepter pass from his hand. Such is the fate of all reformers. The genius which entitles them to our veneration, and increases the world's stock of culture and progress, so tends to educate the rising generation that the very efforts which placed them on so high a point aid to carry their pupils still higher and beyond them. We cannot, perhaps, ascribe to Piloty original powers equal to those of Kaulbach or of some of the rising school. But there is some brilliant work, notwithstanding, in a painting which he is now executing for the new Rathhaus, or City Hall, of Munich, for which he is to receive 50,000 florins ; a large sum for Germany. It is an allegorical representation of the city, and contains portraits of all her citizens who have been distinguished in her past history. It seems thus far to contain more of the good qualities of his style and less of the faults of his other works." — BENJAMIN, Contemporary Art in Europe.

" In Piloty's much-admired picture of 'The Death of Wallenstein,' the truth with which the carpet, the velvet, and all other accessories are painted, is certainly remarkable ; but the falsehood of giving prominence to such details in a picture representing the death of Wallenstein, as if they were the objects which could possibly arrest our attention and excite our sympathies in such a spectacle, is a falsehood of the realistic school. If a man means to paint upholstery, by all means let him paint it so as to delight and deceive an upholsterer ; but if he means to paint a human tragedy, the upholsterer must be subordinate, and velvet must not draw our eyes away from faces." — MR. LEWES, Fortnightly Review.

"In this art, whatever be its worth, Piloty is a master, — what a baton is to the conductor of an orchestra, what a bow is to the leader of violins, such is the brush in the hands of this painter. Manipulation so dexterous, and for detail so minute, does not stop with the delineation of form ; it goes on even to the illusive imitation of surface. Texture is got by loaded solid paint, transparency by thin liquid wash. As an example of the former method, look at the crumbling and calcined ruins of Nero's Golden House. Gaze, too, when next in Munich, on the glitter of that diamond ring which dazzles on the hand of Wallenstein." — J. BEAVINGTON ATKINSON, *Art Journal*, October, 1865.

Pils, Isidore Alexandre Augustin. (*Fr.*) Born at Paris (1813–1875). Member of the Institute. Officer of the Legion of Honor, and Professor in l'École des Beaux-Arts. Pupil of Picot, and a graduate of l'École des Beaux-Arts. In 1838 his picture of " St. Peter healing the Cripple at the Gate of the Temple " won for him the grand *prix de Rome*. After his studies in Rome he traveled considerably, and went to the East during the Crimean war, where he made studies for some of his most notable pictures. That this painter succeeded in addressing himself to popular favor in France cannot be doubted, when we remember the honors bestowed upon him ; but his works are open to severe criticism, and this has not been wanting. His principal works are, " Christ preaching in Simon's boat " (1846); " Death of Mary Magdalene " (1847), purchased by the Minister of the Interior ; " Bacchantes and Satyrs " (1848) ; " Rouget de l'Isle singing the Marseillaise for the first Time " (1849) ; " Death of a Sister of Charity " (1850) ; " The Athenian Slaves at Syracuse " (1852) ; " Prayer at the Hospital " (1853) ; " A Trench before Sebastopol " (1855) ; " Disembarking of French Troops in the Crimea " (1858) ; " Defile of Zouaves in the Trench before Sebastopol "); " School of Musketry at Vincennes " (1859) ; " Battle of Alma " (1861), purchased for the Minister of State, — a *chef-d'œuvre*, the work which in the future will give him the most fame ; " Fête given to the Emperor and Empress at Algiers in 1860 " (1867) ; and many pictures in aquarelle which we have not space to enumerate. The four paintings in the vault over the great staircase in the New Opera House are by Pils.

"The most coarse and truly vulgar of military painters is Pils, whose glaring daubs, of gigantic dimensions, are liberally purchased by the government, whilst their author receives the honors of his profession. The reader may remember a picture by him in the Exhibition of 1867, representing a reception of Algerian chiefs by the Emperor and Empress of the French. I have never seen so perfect an instance of this particular kind of art-degradation. Painters have often before condescended to flatter the pride of powerful sovereigns, but the adulation has been accompanied by art. In this instance the picture was as much painting in the true sense as the reports of the same scene by the government penny-a-liners were literature ; the fierce glare of the colors corresponded to the ardors of the bought journalist. In another picture of nearly equal dimensions are a company of colossal riflemen sprawled on their bellies in the foreground, displaying a row of gaiters and shoes, with odd results to the grace of the composition." — HAMERTON's *Contemporary French Painters*.

"M. Pils paints soldiers with manly simplicity, without bluster and artificial swaggering. He puts a soul under their uniform, and gives each one a character. . . . . You can examine them one by one, they all interest you ; they live, they think, and they act." — THÉOPHILE GAUTIER, *Abécédaire du Salon de 1861*.

" By a singular and rare privilege, that which Pils said of his master can be applied exactly to himself ; and we know not how to better close this notice than to borrow of him the lines which he has consecrated to M. Picot: ' He had neither pride nor vanity ; he never spoke of himself or of his works ; this soul, so honestly born, so sincerely good and instinctively worthy, had no need of any sort of mask in order to make itself respected. He spoke not willingly of art, and took pity on the declaimers on this subject. His love for art was so profound that words seemed to him powerless to express it. All insufficient expression seemed to him a profanation.' I repeat it, Pils is a French artist in the most rigorous acceptation of the term. An artist, he possessed all the beautiful qualities, — the genius, the warmth, the disinterestedness. French he was also, by his eminent qualities as a designer ; his sketching was bold, *spirituel*, very skillful in lightness, and full of freedom . . . . . He never made merchandise of his art, or speculated on his talent. He demanded of his natural gifts only the translations of the conception of his thought, or the dreams of his imagination, without disturbing himself with the demands of fashion or the fondness of the multitude. He was never preoccupied with making a fortune. After having been one of the masters of the French school, after enjoying a fame which to the clever or the complaisant brings infallibly riches, he died poor, very poor. I know no better eulogy to give him. A French painter, his talent had the grand national qualities, — simplicity, neatness, brilliancy. His legitimate ancestors are Lebrun, Jouvenet, Lemoine, Natoire, Gros, Gérard, Géricault. He had the power to take his inspirations or demand his instructions in Germany or Flanders, in Spain or at Genoa. The traditions of his country appeared to be sufficient for him ; he remained indissolubly attached to it, — a merit more rare than one thinks in these times. In studying attentively our contemporaneous art, one discovers some exotic currents, some foreign intrusions, some influences in antipathy to the national temperament ; and this state of things allows us only to reflect sadly enough upon whoever has it at heart to maintain in France the preponderance in works of taste. It is our last superiority ; let us not compromise it ; let us sustain it with all the ardor of filial piety. From this side, perhaps, the rising again and the salvation will come. Pils would have raised a warning finger to those who follow us ; he can take his rest." — L. Clément de Ris, *Gazette des Beaux-Arts*, December, 1875.

" He wished to consecrate the last years of his life of suffering to a work which should class him among the painters of history. . . . . Pils deceived himself ; he was not born for grand mythological painting. He was well able to make his zouaves scale the heights of Alma, but the summits of Olympus are not taken by assault. His figures were too heavy to sustain themselves on the golden clouds of the Homeric heaven. His qualities of life, of movement, of picturesqueness, his lively feeling for the modern military type, which is the characteristic of his talent, only hindered him. To succeed in this new *genre*, it was necessary to become another painter, — to be transformed. That is what he did ; the metamorphosis was sad. He was Isidore Pils ; he was a painter like so many others, skillful, ingenious, experimental, but stripped of originality, of power, of nobility. Happily for this valiant artist, the paintings at the Opera will soon have been forgotten, also the Arab Chiefs and the Holy Thursday ; he will be remembered as the painter of Alma, -- that name which so afflicted Pils, but the only one by which he will be known to posterity." — Henry Houssaye, *Revue des Deux Mondes*, February, 1876.

Pils, Vincenz. (*Bohemian.*)   Born at Warnsdorf, 1819.   Pupil of the Academy of Vienna.   In 1849 he went to Rome, and remained until 1855.   Among his works are a relief of " The Descent from the Cross," in the chapel of the Princess of Lichtenstein ; " Twelve Apostles," for a castle in Grafenegg ; a bronze group of " Wissenschaft und Handel," sent by the Emperor of Austria to Queen Victoria, now at Windsor Castle ; statue of Hannibal, for the Arsenal at Vienna ; and numerous portrait busts and statues.

Pinwell, George John. (*Brit.*) Born in London (1842–1875). Educated at the Heathly, School of Art. Originally devoted his time to wood-engraving for book illustrations, manifesting a decided talent in that branch of art. He was elected an Associate of the Society of Painters in Water-Colors in 1869, contributing frequently to the exhibitions in Dudley Gallery until 1871, when he was made a full member, but failing health prevented his active work after that time. In 1869 he contributed " The Pied Piper of Hamelin " and " A Seat in St. James' Park "; in 1870, " The Elixir of Love "; in 1871, "Away from Town "; in 1872, " The Saracen Maiden " and " The Strolling Player." He illustrated Jean Ingelow's Poems, Buchanan's "Ballads of the Affections," Dalziel's " Wayside Posies," etc. Many of his sketches and studies were exhibited in London in the winter of 1876.

" Pinwell painted some of the most pathetic of modern popular pictures, but we think he did too much to do all things well, and that the shortcomings of his art were in part due to lack of balance in his technical judgment, as well as to his need of severer training than it has been his lot to receive." — *London Athenæum*, September, 1875.

" In all he [Pinwell] has shown himself a man of earnest thought, and an artist who would win the applause of those who think, rather than of those who are attracted by qualities more on the surface than underlying the subject." — *London Art Journal*, July, 1873.

Place, Henri. (*Fr.*) Born at Paris about 1820. Chevalier of the Legion of Honor. A painter of still-life and marines. His " Marine-Cliffs of Dover " (1849) is in the Luxembourg.

Plassan, Antoine Émile. (*Fr.*) Born at Bordeaux. Chevalier of the Legion of Honor. Medal at Philadelphia, where he exhibited " Before the Mirror." At the Wilson Exposition, Brussels, 1873, " The Breakfast " was much admired. At the Walters Gallery, Baltimore, are several of his pictures ; among them the " Bourgeois Gentilhomme " is a spirited and characteristic work, and " A Sleeping Girl " is very charming. At the Salon of 1877 he exhibited " Contemplation " and " A Reading." At the Johnston sale, New York, 1876, " The Physician's Visit " (4 by 3) sold for $ 450, and " The Old Bachelor " (6 by 4) for $ 280. At the Salon of 1878 he exhibited " The Family of Viscount C. " and " Le jour des rameaux." His " Table Supplies " is in the collection of Mr. T. R. Butler of New York.

Plassman, Ernest. (*Ger.-Am.*) Born in Westphalia. Died in 1877. Plassman removed to America about 1850, and followed the occupation of a modeler of statuary for many years in New York. He was the founder of the Society of Art, a flourishing association of German artists and art-lovers in New York. Among the better known of Plassman's works are the statue of Franklin, in Printing-House Square, New York ; the Vanderbilt statue, in the Freight Depots on Hudson Square ; and the statue of Gutenberg, on the building of the New York " Staats Zeitung."

Plockhorst, Bernhard. (*Ger.*) Born at Brunswick, 1825. Medal at Berlin. Professor at Weimar, 1866 – 69. Studied at Munich Academy ; was associated with Piloty ; also studied under Couture at Paris. He painted an altar-piece for the Cathedral at Marienwerder. Most of his historical subjects are religious ; those best known are, " Mary, with St. John," and " St. Michael and Satan struggling for the Body of Moses." These have been engraved. His portraits are his best works. At the National Gallery at Berlin are those of the Emperor and Empress of Germany. At the Leipsic Museum are two of his religious subjects.

Pointelin, Auguste-Emmanuel. (*Fr.*) Born at Arbois. Pupil of Maire. Medal of the third class in 1878, when he exhibited " A Prairie in the Côte-d'Or " ; in 1877, " A Valley in the Jura " ; in 1876, " On a Plateau of the Jura, — Autumn."

Poittevin, Eugène le. (*Fr.*) Born at Paris (1806 – 1870). Chevalier of the Legion of Honor, and of the Belgian Order of Léopold. Pupil of l'École des Beaux-Arts and Louis Hersent. He traveled much on the Continent and in England. His subjects were varied. In the Luxembourg is a " View near Étretat in the Bathing-Season " (1870); at Versailles, " The Capture of Baruth," " Naval Engagement at Embro," " The Battle of Wertingen," and other maritime subjects. Among his works are, " The Turkey-Drover " (1853), " Winter in Holland " (1855), " Dutch Pilots " (1859), etc. At the Johnston sale, 1876, " Lighthouse, Coast of Holland " (48 by 35) sold for $ 1,300. At the Leipsic Museum is his " Fishermen saving a Wreck."

" Upon even his most ordinary subjects M. le Poittevin bestowed the utmost care. His touch is decided, his general manner broad, and in his color the utmost harmony prevails, combined with a brilliancy seldom seen in the works of French landscape and marine painters. Thus his execution may be traced to the works of the Dutch and Flemish artists, while his compositions show more point and anecdote than are generally found in the latter. For his well-earned and duly merited reputation, he was evidently indebted to his close and continual observation of nature ; studying not only in his atelier, but yet more in the green fields and by the open sea, where humanity was busied, and where character was to be found ; for figures, as a rule, play even a more important part in his pictures than do the inanimate objects amid which they are placed." — *Art Journal,* October, 1870.

Pollastrini, Enrico. (*Ital.*) Born at Leghorn (1817 – 1876). Professor in the Academy of Florence, and a member of several other Academies. Pupil of Bezzuoli. He was original in conception, correct in drawing, and a good colorist. Among his best works are, " The Raising of the Son of the Widow of Nain," in the church of the Soccorso at Leghorn ; an " Episode of the Inundation of the Serchio," in the Gallery of Modern Painting at Florence ; the " Death of Ferruccio " ; the " Exiles of Siena " ; " San Lorenzo distributing Alms " ; and the " Battle of Legnano."

Poole, Paul Falconer, R. A. (*Brit.*) Born in 1818. Studied art without a master and in none of the established schools, exhibiting his first picture at the Royal Academy, London, in 1830, "The Well, — a Scene at Naples." In 1837 he sent to the Royal Academy, "The Farewell"; in 1838, "The Emigrants' Departure"; in 1843, "The Great Plague of London." In 1846 (when he was elected Associate) he exhibited "The Surrender of Sion House in the Reign of Henry VIII."; in 1851, "The Goths in Italy"; in 1852, "The May Queen"; in 1860, "The Escape of Glaucus and Ione from Pompeii"; in 1864, "Greek Peasants"; in 1865, "The Eruption of Vesuvius, A. D. 70"; in 1868, "A Border Raid"; in 1869, "The Prodigal Son"; in 1872, "Remorse" (his diploma work); in 1873, "A Lion in the Path"; in 1874, "The Grape-Gatherer"; in 1875, "Ezekiel's Vision"; in 1876, "The Meeting of Oberon and Titania"; in 1877, "Leading the Blind," "The Dragon's Cavern," and "Autumn"; in 1878, "Solitude" and "Harvest-Time." He was elected Academician in 1862. [Died, 1879.]

"Mr. Poole's drawing we fear will be to the end of time a stumbling-stone, not only to his friends, but to his reputation ; but his scene from Pompeii during the eruption [R. A., 1865] is filled with well-imagined incidents, and renders vividly the effect of that lurid and preternatural light which would arise when a midday Southern sun is veiled by clouds of ashes, and reddened by stealthy interminglings from Vesuvian fire." — PALGRAVE's *Essays on Art.*

"There is no artist of our time who has acquired greater success by such realistic pictures as this ['Rest by the Way'] than Mr. Poole. He has produced many of them, but it is not by these that he has won his way into the Royal Academy. The painter of 'Solomon Eagle' ('The London Plague'), of 'The Moors beleaguered by the Spaniards in Valencia,' 'The Visitation and Surrender of Sion House,' and many other pictures of a like high character, takes up, it may be presumed, these pretty rural scenes by way of relief from the more important labors of his studio." — *Art Journal,* November, 1874.

"'The Lion in the Path,' by P. F. Poole [American Centennial Exhibition, 1876], is a landscape of great strength and color. . . . . The colors in it are so strong and deep that it is really a great picture." — *Art Journal,* July, 1876.

"There has always been in Mr. Poole's work some acknowledgment of a supernatural influence in physical phenomena, which gives a nobler character to his storm painting than can belong to any merely literal study of the elements." — RUSKIN's *Notes of the Academy,* 1875.

Porcelli, Antonio. (*Ital.*) (1800 – 1870) Distinguished in landscape and figure painting. He imitated Flemish art with Italian ideality. A fine work of his is "The Fountain Dell Acqua Autosa, close to the Flamminian Way, with a Concourse of People." "The Cobbler's Monday" was purchased by the Emperor of Russia. He painted numerous carnival scenes and kindred subjects, as well as "The Pine Forests of Ravenna" and other fine landscapes. His water-colors and drawings are much prized.

Portaels, Jean François. (*Belgian.*) Born at Vilvorde, 1820. Chevalier of the Order of Léopold. Member of the Antwerp Academy. Director of the Academy of Ghent, and later Professor in that of Brussels. Medal at Paris, 1855. Pupil of Navez at Brussels, and of Delaroche at Paris. At Antwerp, in 1842, he gained the grand *prix de Rome.* Portaels has traveled in Italy, the East, Hungary, Spain, and other European countries. Among his well-known works are, "The Flight into Egypt," "The Drought in Egypt" (in the Corcoran Gallery at Washington), "The Funeral in the Desert," "A Syrian Caravan surprised by the Simoom" and "Leah and Rachel." The pediment of the church of Saint-Jacques at Brussels is adorned by frescos of Portaels, representing Christianity. Another fresco by him is in the chapel of the Brothers of the Christian Doctrine, and in the Tympanum of the Royal Theater at Brussels is another of a dramatic subject. His portraits are famous, among them those of Mehemet-Ali, the Empress of Mexico, the Queen of Holland, etc. His ideal portraits, such as "A Young Girl of Trieste," "Glycine," "An Eastern Girl," and "A Jewess of Asia Minor," are much admired. At the Cottrell sale in London, in 1873, "The Daughter of Zion" sold for 710 guineas. At the Paris Salon, in 1877, he exhibited "Portrait of M. P. D." His picture of "Judith" is a pleasing conception of this well-worn subject.

Porter, Benjamin Curtis, A. N. A. (*Am.*) Born in Melrose, Mass., 1843. As an artist he is comparatively self-educated. He has spent the better part of his professional life in Boston, where of late years he has devoted himself almost exclusively to portrait-painting, and with marked success, numbering among his sitters many prominent people of Boston and vicinity. He went abroad in 1872, and again in 1875, to study, spending some months in Venice and Paris. In 1878 he was elected an Associate of the National Academy in New York. Among his ideal figures are, "The Hour-Glass" and "The Mandolin Player."

"Mr. Porter has placed himself in a high position by close and persistent study of the fundamental principles of his art. The secret of his color, which commands so much admiration, is the tone which governs its value. . . . . But it is not color alone that gives so much importance to this artist's productions, nor is it his general mastery of technique ; there is in his works a depth and purity of sentiment, an undemonstrative thoughtfulness, which gives them a peculiar charm, and which makes of them something much higher than pieces of color. We see in both his portraits and ideal works the painter of refined and poetic feeling, one who can conceive a subject of expressive beauty and so develop it with wealth of palette and richness of impasto, that it shall gain in meaning as the execution progresses. The full-length portrait of a lady which Mr. Porter has sent by invitation to the Paris Exposition [of 1878] is a marked example of his power of combining magnificence of color with chaste design and elevated feeling. Mr. Porter is of no school, and therefore this picture will take its place in the exhibition as essentially an American production." — DARIUS COBB, *Boston Evening Traveller,* May 9, 1878.

Pott, L. J. (*Brit.*) Born in Nottinghamshire, 1837. Displayed phenomenal talents as an artist at an early age, and drew cleverly when not more than five years old. He was articled to an architect when sixteen, but soon left that branch of art for the study of painting in London. He first exhibited at the Royal Academy, in 1860, "Studying from Nature" and "Effie Deans" ; in 1861, "Dark and Fair" ; in 1863, "Puss in Boots" ; in 1864, "Rebecca describes the

Fight to Ivanhoe " ; in 1865, " Old Memories " ; in 1867, " The Defence"; in 1868, "The First Success"; in 1869, " Fire at a Theater " ; in 1871, " Mary Queen of Scots led to Execution "; in 1872, " Charles I. leaving Westminster Hall after his Trial " ; in 1873, " On the March from Moscow " ; in 1874, " Paris in 1793 " ; in 1875, " Don Quixote at the Ball " ; in 1876, " His Highness in Disgrace " ; in 1877, " Waiting for the King's Favorite "; in 1878, " Fallen among Thieves."

" When this picture [' Mary Queen of Scots led to Execution '] was exhibited at the Royal Academy in 1871, very many, if not all of those who had made close acquaintance with the artist's previous works, were satisfied that in it he had accomplished a surprising advance. Pott's ' Defence,' and his ' Fire at a Theater,' showed him to be on the right road, but it was this work which at once gave him something more than an ordinary reputation as a painter of historical subjects." —*Art Journal,* May, 1875.

Powell, William H., A. N. A. (*Am.*) Native of the State of Ohio. He is an Associate Member of the National Academy, and has for some time had a studio in the city of New York. He devotes himself to portrait and historical painting. He is the artist of " The Discovery of the Mississippi by De Soto " (in the rotunda of the Capitol at Washington) and of " The Battle of Lake Erie," painted for the State of Ohio. His "Landing of the Pilgrims " belongs to Marshall O. Roberts. His portraits of General McClellan and of Major Anderson are in the City Hall, New York. [Died, 1879, aged 55 years.]

Powers, Hiram. (*Am.*) Born in Vermont (1805 - 1873). When a boy Powers was taken with his family to Cincinnati, Ohio, where he learned the art of modeling, and acquired some local reputation for his busts and medallions of such men as Calhoun, Webster, Jackson, and Clay. After a short residence in Washington, D. C., he went to Italy in 1837, settling in Florence, where the rest of his life was spent. In 1839 or '40 he completed his " Eve," and the "Fisher-Boy " a little later. " The Greek Slave " (the work upon which much of his fame now rests) was finished in 1843. Of this figure some six or eight copies came from Powers' studio : the first, sold to Captain Grant for $ 4,000, was taken to England, and is now in the gallery of the Duke of Cleveland ; the second, brought to America in 1847, attracted great attention when exhibited in New York, and is now at the Corcoran Gallery in Washington ; the third copy belongs to Earl Dudley ; the fourth, purchased by Prince Demidoff for $ 4,000, was sold at that nobleman's death for $ 11,000 to A. T. Stewart of New York ; the fifth copy is in the possession of Hon. E. W. Stoughton. Other works of Powers have been extensively repeated. Among his ideal subjects are his " Penseroso " (in the Lenox Library, New York ; never copied), " America " (destroyed by fire in Brooklyn), " Eve Disconsolate " (belonging to E. D. Morgan), " Faith," " Hope," " Charity," " Clytie," " Proserpine," ." California," " Christ," and " Paradise Lost." His statues of Washington, Webster, Franklin,

Jefferson, Calhoun, and others are in different American cities. The original Webster, lost at sea, cost $12,000, the duplicate $7,000. Among the distinguished persons who have sat to Powers for their portrait busts, were John Q. Adams, Calhoun, Jackson, Van Buren; Marshall, Abbott Lawrence, Slidell, Grand Duchess of Tuscany, Nicholas Longworth, Winthrop, Sparks, George Peabody, Vanderbilt, Everett, and Dr. Bellows. The Calhoun statue in Charleston, S. C., was taken to Columbia, and destroyed in that city by fire during the Civil War.

Of an exquisitely carved hand, that of an infant daughter of the sculptor, Hawthorne makes Miriam speak very pleasantly in the "Marble Faun." Although small and simple, it is one of the most artistic and touching of Powers' creations. It has been occasionally reproduced. One fine copy is in the possession of Mr. John Erskine of Boston.

"Hiram Powers fitly represents the mechanical proclivities of the nation. His female statues are simply tolerably well-modeled figures, borrowed in conception from the second-rate antiques, and somewhat arbitrarily named. . . . 'California,' 'Eve,' 'America,' 'The Greek Slave,' are the same woman, and each might be called something else with equal felicity of baptism. The 'California' is essentially vulgar in pose and commonplace in allegory." — JARVES, *Art Idea.*

"Powers is an eclectic in the study of nature, and has triumphed over academic dogmas and dictation. Thorwaldsen visited his studio, and pronounced his bust of Webster the best work of the kind executed in modern times. . . . . The genius of Powers is singularly healthful. There is something in the career of this remarkable artist which strikes us as eminently American." — TUCKERMAN's *Book of the Artists*

"Hiram Powers cannot be ranked among the great sculptors of our time. His 'Eve' is undoubtedly his masterpiece among ideal figures, although his 'Greek Slave' has attained larger popularity, simply from being more widely known. The dignity of some of his allegorical statues, such as 'California,' and of some of the portrait statues, as that of Washington, is greatly impaired by the too lavish introduction of accessories or by peculiarities of costume. The statue of Franklin, on the other hand, is simple and thoughtful. Of his busts, particularly those of females, nothing can be said but what is commendatory. . . . . If he made no real advance after the production of 'Eve' and 'The Greek Slave,' he maintained to the last the reputation acquired by these." — *Art Journal*, July, 1873.

> "Appeal, fair stone,
> From God's pure height of beauty against man's wrong:
> Catch up in thy divine face not alone
> East's griefs, but West's, and strike and shame the strong,
> By thunder of white silence overthrown."
> MRS. BROWNING's *Apostrophe to the Greek Slave.*

Powers, Preston. (*Am.*) Born in Florence, 1843. Second son of Hiram Powers, whose only pupil he was, receiving his constant instruction for six years. His professional life has been spent in the United States and in Florence, where his studio, that occupied by his father, now is. Among the better known of the works of Preston Powers are the statue of Senator Jacob Collamer of Vermont (originally ordered of Hiram Powers), to be placed in the Old Hall of Representatives in Washington, D. C.; a bust of Charles Sumner, from photographs and casts taken by Mr. Powers after the statesman's death, and now owned in Washington ; a bust of Agassiz, from a death-mask, exhibited in Boston, the original being in the Cambridge Museum. His bust of J. G. Whittier, from life, is in the Public Library at Haverhill, and a *replica* is to be placed in the Public Library of Boston. His bust of Swedenborg belongs to the New Church Society of Boston ; his bust of Senator Morrill of Vermont belongs to the family of that gentleman ; and his bust of General Grant is for the War Department in Washington. An ideal figure, "Maud Muller," still unfinished, is in his studio in Florence.

" Mr. Powers' style of work reproduces that of his father, and is remarkable for delicacy and finish ; while his devotion to his profession promises an equal amount of work in the future. . . . . The figure of Senator Collamer is distinguished by a quiet dignity and ease which is apparent to the casual observer, but only those who know something of the work can appreciate the difficulties that have been overcome in dealing with our modern costume. " — *Boston Transcript.*

" Mr. Powers is also engaged on an ideal figure and on several portrait busts, and has already crowded his studio with the numerous works he has executed in the ten years of his artistic life. His love for his profession is extreme, and is proved by his careful and delicate modeling of details. Nothing escapes his eye ; every line is turned to account if useful, and the result is the same vivid and life-like look which is so noticeable in his father's work. . . . . His views on the subject of art are essentially the same as his father's, but his mind works in its own way to turn them to the best possible account." — *Boston Advertiser,* October 8, 1877.

Powers, Longworth. Son of Hiram Powers. Resides in Florence.

[No response to circular.]

Poynter, Edward J., R. A. (*Brit.*) Born in Paris, 1836. Son of Ambrose Poynter, an architect, and grandson of Thomas Banks, R. A., an eminent sculptor of the last century. Poynter was taken to England in his infancy, commencing the study of art in 1854. Went to Paris in 1856, studied under Gleyre, and was also a student of l'École des Beaux-Arts. He settled in London in 1860. In 1859 he exhibited in the British Institution, " Two Italian Pifferari " ; in 1861, at the Royal Academy, " Alla Veneziana " ; in 1864, " The Siren " ; in 1865, " Faithful unto Death " ; in 1866, " Offerings to Isis " ; in 1869 (when he was elected an Associate of the Royal Academy) he sent " Proserpine " ; in 1870, " Andromeda"; in 1871, " The Suppliant to Venus " ; in 1872, " Perseus and Andromeda " ; in 1874, " Rhodope " ; in 1876, " Cecil Wedgwood " and " Atalanta's Race " ; in 1877, " The Fortune-Teller " (deposited on his election as an Academician) ; in 1878, " Zenobia Captive " and a portrait of Mrs. Langtry. Poynter was the first " Slade " Professor of Art at the University College, London, and for some time a Director of the Art Schools at South Kensington Museum. His " Ibis Girl," " The Golden Age," and " The Festival " were at Philadelphia in 1876. " Israel in Egypt," " Proserpine," and " The Catapult " were at Paris in 1878. He is also a contributor to the Grosvenor exhibitions.

"Among the younger painters of England whose work departs from traditions exclusively English, and is such as to take its place in the general stock of trained European art, Mr. Poynter is one of the most noteworthy. . . . Were one to try to analyze the characteristics of this central example of Mr. Poynter's talent [' Israel in Egypt'], one would have to speak first of a clear and determined practical sense, showing itself in the carefully rational and probable arrangement of the general scene, and the effective realization and solution of every problem, whether of archæology or mechanics, which it suggests." — SIDNEY COLVIN, *in English Painters of the Present Day*, 1871.

"The figure, although somewhat statuesque, is striking and graceful, and the birds are most picturesquely grouped, but the composition as a whole [' Feeding the Sacred Ibis in the Halls of Karnac '] loses much of its harmony in the engraving by the obtrusiveness of the background of Egyptian architecture with its redundancy of varied and prominent ornamentation." — *Art Journal*, January, 1874.

"I wonder how long Mr. Poynter thinks a young lady could stand barefoot on a round-runged ladder [' The Festival '], or that a sensible Greek girl would take her sandals off to try, on an occasion when she had festive arrangements to make with care. The ladders themselves, here and in No. 236 [' The Golden Age '], appear to me not so classical or so rude in type as might have been expected, but to savor somewhat of expeditious gas-lighting. . . . Both these pictures are merely studies of decorative composition, and have far too much pains taken with them for that purpose." — RUSKIN's *Notes of the Academy*, 1875.

Pozzi, Francesco. (*Ital.*) Born at Portoferraio (1790 – 1844). The colossal statue of Ferdinand III. at Leghorn, and the Farinata degli Uberti of the loggia of the Uffizi at Florence are fine works by Pozzi. His " Dancing-Girl," " Bacchante," " Mercury," and " Ciparisso " have been frequently repeated.

Pradilla, F. (*Span.*) Of Madrid. At the Paris Exposition of 1878 this painter was awarded the medal of honor for his picture of " Doña Juana La Loca." She was the daughter of Ferdinand and Isabella and the mother of Charles V. She is represented upon one of the occasions when the funeral cortége of her husband halts for the night. It will be remembered that she followed this sad procession to the place of burial. The atmosphere in this picture speaks of chill and desolation, and the whole effect is that of strength and sincerity on the part of the artist.

Pratère, Edmond de. (*Belgian.*) Born at Courtrai. Medal at Philadelphia, where he exhibited " Animals, — a Halt." At Paris, in 1877, were " Dog-Keepers at the Rendezvous of the Hunt " and " Dogs at Bay."

Préault, Antoine-Augustin. (*Fr.*) Born at Paris, 1809. Pupil of David d'Angers. Made his début at the Salon of 1833, but was excluded from the Salons during fifteen years. At length, in 1849, his works were admitted for exhibition, and he gained reputation rapidly. His works are seen in churches and other public places. In 1877 he exhibited a " Funeral Bas-Relief," belonging to Carolus Duran ; in 1876, a portrait, medallion, plaster, and " Ophelia," bas-relief in bronze, bought by the Ministry of the Beaux-Arts ; in 1875, " Jacques-Cœur," statue, marble, bought by the Ministry of the Beaux-Arts, and two medallion portraits in bronze ; in 1874, funeral medallions in bronze ; etc.

Preller, Friedrich Johann Christian Ernst. (*Ger.*) Born at Eisenach, 1804. Professor of Drawing in the School of Fine Arts at Weimar. Court painter. Studied under various masters at Weimar and Dresden, and at the Academy of Antwerp. Goethe was the friend of Preller, and through his influence the Grand Duke Karl August became interested in the young artist, and took him on a journey. Preller was very ill, and the Grand Duke cared for him most tenderly. In 1825 the artist went to Milan, where he studied in the Academy. He went to Rome in 1828; there Joseph Anton Koch influenced his studies, and directed his attention to the study of drawing, as he was inclined to regard only the grand effects of nature, to the injury of the whole effect of his composition. In 1831 he went to Weimar, and was employed from 1835 to '37 in decorating the Wieland Hall in the museum of that city. In the Castle of Weimar he executed six historical Thuringian landscapes. In 1840 he visited Norway, and afterwards painted Northern landscapes and marine views. He had already painted in Leipsic his series of Odyssey pictures which seemed to be his one entrancing thought; he repeated them three times. The Grand Duke gave him a commission to repaint them, and he went to Italy for the purpose of making studies for them. This occupied two years, and the sixteen cartoons are in the Museum at Leipsic. Two of his works, "Calypso" and "Leucothea," are at Munich. At the National Gallery of Berlin are his "Styrian Landscape" and a "Norwegian Coast Scene." About 1830, at Weimar, he became interested in etching, and for a long time was very active in an etching-club which he had established. His own works of this sort are much prized by collectors.

"In Preller's representations we find energy and conscientiousness which surpass, not only in execution, but in the whole spirit, the works ordinarily considered as up to the required level. The peculiarity of historical representation — that peculiarity of it which makes the figures appear as if molded from nature — he has forcibly presented to us once more. Nothing in Nature is hidden from him, — her beauty is naked to his observation. The remarkable knowledge of forms and their organic connection which he has gained by unceasing study and an industry never satisfied by itself, shows him outlines through any and every covering. In his landscapes he renders justly both the vegetation and the outlines or undulations which it conceals, and takes from the spirit of neither by over attention to details. He has not thus mastered Nature by prying and digging : she has been revealed to him spiritually, and has become his through a devotion of thought and an inexorable earnestness of contemplation. This, far from making him a slave to trivial things, makes him a ruler with a sort of loving authority." DR. MAX JORDAN, *Zeitschrift für bildende Kunst*, 1866.

Preyer, Johann Wilhelm. (*Ger.*) Born at Rheydt, 1803. Studied in Düsseldorf Academy. Passed some years at Munich and settled at Düsseldorf. Traveled extensively in Europe. His pictures are of flowers and fruit. Several are in the Berlin National Gallery. At the Johnston sale in New York in 1876, "Fruit" (21 by 20), from the old Düsseldorf Gallery in New York, sold for $1,400.

At the Leipsic Museum is one of his fruit-pieces. Mr. T. R. Butler of New York has his " Fruit and Wine."

Princeteau, René. (*Fr.*) Born at Libourne. Pupil of l'École des Beaux-Arts. Medal at Philadelphia, where he exhibited a portrait of Washington and " Horses frightened by a Railway-Train." At Paris, in the Salon of 1875, he exhibited the preceding picture and "Halte!" and a group in plaster, "The Punishment of Brunehaut"; in 1872, " A Patrol of Uhlans surprised by French Sharp-Shooters " ; in 1878, a picture of " The Return from the Promenade " and an equestrian portrait of Count T. L.

Prinsep, Val. C., A. R. A. (*Brit.*) Born in India, 1836. He was originally intended for the Indian Civil Service, but, resolved to devote himself to art, he went to England to study, exhibiting at the Royal Academy in 1862, " How Bianca Capello sought to poison the Cardinal de' Medici" ; in 1864, " My Lady Betty " ; in 1865, " Belinda " (from Pope's " Rape of the Lock ") ; in 1867, " Miriam watching the Infant Moses " ; in 1868, " A Venetian Lover " ; in 1869, " Bacchus and Ariadne " ; in 1870, " The Death of Cleopatra"; in 1871, "News from Abroad " ; in 1872, " The Harvest of Spring " ; in 1873, " Lady Teazle "; in 1874, " Newmarket Heath, — the Morning of the Race "; in 1875, " A Minuet " ; in 1876, " The Linen-Gatherers " ; in 1878, " A Kashmiree Nautch-Girl " ; and many more, besides an occasional portrait. His " Minuet " and " Death of Cleopatra " were at the Centennial Exhibition at Philadelphia in 1876 ; " Reading Grandison," " Linen-Gatherers," and " À Bientôt," at Paris, in 1878.

" Mr. Princep, if he does not this year try any subject of powerful interest, has gained in mastery over his art. His ' Berenice,' although not exactly the lady of whom Mr. Browning speaks in the verse quoted, is a grand piece of decorative coloring, although rather coarse in design. This same artist's ' Lady of the Last Century,' in her full court dress and fan, sweeping gracefully by, shows command over motion, color, and life." — PALGRAVE'S *Essays on Art.*

"'À Bientôt ' [R. A., 1876] is by Val. C. Princep. He is always exceptionally strong in these charming little pieces of drawing-room incident, and this picture is an admirable illustration of the care and skill with which he handles such subjects." — *Art Journal*, July, 1876.

Priou, Louis. (*Fr.*) Born at Toulouse. Medals in Paris in 1869 and '74, and at Philadelphia, 1876. Pupil of l'École Municipale of Bordeaux, and of Cabanel. At Philadelphia he exhibited the " Education of Young Satyrs," and at Paris, in 1877, the same picture and a " Venetian Duo " ; in 1876, " Nymph of the Wood " and " A Souvenir " ; and in 1874, " A Family of Satyrs," now at the Corcoran Gallery in Washington. The catalogue says : —

" The prodigious vigor of the composition and its fine color are equal to the artist's thorough classical conception of the subject. The whole scene is replete with the spirit of the wild, joyous sylvan life, associated with those imaginary wood deities of the ancients."

To the Salon of 1878 he contributed " The First Miseries of a Young Satyr " and a portrait.

Probst, Karl. (*Austrian.*) Of Vienna. Medal at Philadelphia, where he exhibited a " Portrait Study, — Female Figure," of which Weir says : —

" A portrait study by Charles Probst has exceptional merit. The expression and attitude are very natural, and the technical treatment skillful. It was one of the best portraits of the Exhibition."

Protais, Paul Alexandre. (*Fr.*) Born at Paris, 1826. Chevalier of the Legion of Honor. Pupil of Desmoulins. He followed the French armies in the Crimea and in Italy, and devoted himself almost entirely to military subjects. He received his first medal in 1863, and his decoration in 1865. Among his works the following are the most important : " Battle of Inkermann," " Death of Colonel Brancion," " Taking of a Battery of the Mamelukes " (1857), " Attack and Taking of the Mamelukes," " The Last Thought " (1859), " Brigade of General Cler on the Route to Magenta," " Passage of the Sezia," " An Evening March," " A Sentinel " (1861), " The Morning before the Attack " and " The Evening after the Combat " (1863), — the last two are his most admired works, and were in the Exposition of 1867, — " The End of the Halt," " Passage of the Mincio," " An Interment in the Crimea," " The Conquerors, — Return to the Camp " (1865), — the last was also in the Exposition of 1867, and was purchased by Count W. de la Valette, — " A Wounded Soldier," " A Bivouac " (1866), " The Grand Halt," purchased by the Princess Mathilde (1868), " En Marche ! " and " The Night of Solferino " (1870), " The Separation," " Army of Metz," October 29, 1870, and " Prisoners," near Metz, November 1, 1870 (1872), " The Repose " (1873), " An Alert," " Metz," (1874), " French Guards " and " Swiss Guards " (1875), " La garde du drapeau " (1876), " Passage of a River " (1877).

" Protais has discovered new material in warfare, leaving to others the purely military spirit, and studying soldiers, for the first time in the history of art, simply as human beings, placed in circumstances of great interest. . . . . The picture called ' Morning before the Attack ' represents a small body of Chasseurs de Vincennes, marching warily towards the enemy, on hilly ground, in the cold light of early morning. There is no glare of color ; but the dark uniforms harmonize pleasantly with the gray sky and dewy green mountain ground. The execution is modest and simple, a little too methodical perhaps, but without dash or bravura : and the spectator is made to understand that the artist would rather he felt the awfulness of the moment than wandered from the matter to admire pretty tricks of execution or clever bits of detail." — HAMERTON, *Contemporary French Painters.*

" He paints soldiers as a comrade ; we see that he knows them, understands them, and loves them. He knows war to the bottom in all familiar aspects, heroic and melancholy. He will tell you how the men lie down and shield themselves during a halt, and how they replace themselves en route. If you reproach him with having exhibited in 1864 the same troopers as in 1863 and '62, he will reply to you, not without reason, that the troopers change little, that they resemble each other more or less : that the army, like the convent and the prison, and all institutions outside of nature, is a mold, a gauffer-iron, in which man models and forms himself anew on a uniform type. From this comes that uniformity which penetrates, whatever happens, through the most varied episodes." — EDMOND ABOUT, *Salon de 1864.*

It was said that the Emperor paid £5,000 for two pictures, " The Morning and Evening of the Soldier," at the Salon of 1863.

Prout, Samuel. (*Brit.*) Born at Plymouth (1785 – 1852). He evinced a decided talent for water-color painting as a youth, and, going to London early in the century, he found a ready sale for his works. About 1820 he visited the Continent, making many sketches of the scenery of the Rhine, the Alps, etc., which were subsequently engraved. He was made a member of the Society of Painters in Water-Colors very early in his career, and contributed regularly to its exhibitions for many years. He turned his attention particularly to architectural drawings, and his works were very popular, and by collectors are still highly prized. Among the better known of his pictures are, " Chartres Cathedral," " City of Venice," and the drawings illustrating " Views in the North and West of England," " The Continental Annual," " The Landscape Annual," and other volumes of a similar character.

" We owe to Samuel Prout, I believe, the first perception, and certainly the only expression, of precisely the characters which were wanting to old art, of that feeling which results from the influence among the noble lines of architecture, of the rent and the rust, the fissures, the lichen, and the weed, and from the writings upon the pages of ancient walls of the confused hieroglyphics of human history. . . . . For numerous as have been his imitators, extended as his influence, and simple as his means and manner, there has as yet appeared nothing at all to equal him. There is *no* stone drawing, *no* vitality of architecture, like Prout's." — RUSKIN's *Modern Painters.*

Pugin, Edward W. (*Brit.*) Born in 1834. Pupil of his father, a well-known English architect, whom in 1852 he succeeded. He has designed and completed many important buildings, principally church edifices, in all parts of Great Britain and Ireland.

Puvis de Chavannes, Pierre. (*Fr.*) Born at Lyons. Died, 1871. Chevalier of the Legion of Honor. Pupil of Henri Scheffer and Couture. He has devoted himself to mural and decorative painting. His " Peace " and " War " were immense symbolical works ; small reproductions of them were seen at the great Exposition of 1867, and they were much noticed and discussed. In 1865 he executed for the Museum at Amiens "Ave Picardia nutrix," a monumental work with eight figures, for Le Cercle de l'Union Artistique. He painted a decorative figure called " Sport " for the grand staircase of the Museum of Marseilles, " Massilia, a Greek Colony," and " Marseilles, — the Gate of the Orient " (1869). At the Salon of 1870 he exhibited " The Beheading of St. John the Baptist " and " Mary Magdalene in the Desert " ; in 1872, " Hope " ; in 1873, " Summer " ; in 1874, " The Year 732, — Charles Martel saved Christianity by his Victory over the Saracens near Poitiers," and a design for " The Sixth Century, — Radegonde, retired to the Convent of Sainte-Croix, gives an Asylum to Poets, and protects Letters from the Barbarity of the Age," — both of these subjects were for the decoration of the Hotel de Ville at Poitiers ; in 1876, one painting and one sketch for his scenes in the life of St. Geneviève, which he was commissioned to execute in the Pantheon, now the church of Sainte-Geneviève, by the Ministry of Public Instruction and Beaux-Arts.

" The artist so long disputed is henceforth in full favor in public opinion ; he seems to have disarmed criticism, triumphed over the most rebellious, and rallied the most frivolous among the worldlings who felt themselves much affected by this epic simplicity and this profound sincerity. He has not a useless gesture, not a line which has not its value ; all the words are ideas, and the poem is accessible to all. M. de Chavannes had his public restraint, he isolated himself in his intellectual aristocracy, and people remember that curious inauguration of frescos at the Museum of Amiens presided over by Théophile Gautier, where only a few of the initiated had a place. To-day, after having so long suffered, he is honored, and his hour is decidedly come." — CHARLES YRIARTE, *Gazette des Beaux-Arts,* June, 1876.

" The truth is that, for intensely poetical sentiment, few living painters may be compared to Puvis de Chavannes. His art is a poetical abstraction ; the region that he paints is not the world, but a painter's dreamland, and the figures that dwell in it are not men and women, but the phantoms of a powerful yet tranquil imagination. To enjoy works of this kind thoroughly, we must surrender ourselves to them, and live an hour in this world of strange beings, — so strong, so stately, so magnificent in irresistible action, so calm in their everlasting rest." — HAMERTON'S *Painting in France.*

Pye, John. (*Brit.*) (1782 – 1874.) Settled in London in 1800, and was an apprentice of Heath. He engraved Turner's "Pope's Villa," one of his earliest works, in 1808, and later, Turner's "Temple of Jupiter," and the paintings of Claude, Michael Angelo, and other prominent British and Continental artists, ancient and modern.

Pyne, James B. (*Brit.*) (1800 – 1870.) Spent the early part of his life in Bristol, his native city, painting and teaching drawing. He removed to London in 1835, exhibiting for the first time at the Royal Academy the next year. His works, however, have not been seen at the Royal Academy since 1841. He was elected a member of the Society of British Artists in 1839, and was for some years its Vice-President. In 1841 he went to Italy, where he painted many attractive Venetian landscapes. In 1848, for the Agnews, he painted a series of twenty-four pictures of English landscapes, which were subsequently lithographed. In 1851 he visited Italy and the Rhine.

" Pyne has very accurate knowledge of limestone-rock, and expresses it clearly and forcibly ; but it is much to be regretted that this clever artist appears to be losing all sense of color, and is getting more and more mannered in execution, evidently never studying from nature except with the previous determination to Pynize everything." — RUSKIN'S *Modern Painters.*

" As a rule, Pyne's pictures are not popular. Like Turner's, they are not generally intelligible. . . . . But he has left works behind him which, if the colors are found to be permanent, will be valued hereafter as among the best of our modern school of landscape-painting." — *Art Journal,* September, 1870.

Quarnström, Carl Gustav. (*Swede.*) Born at Stockholm (1810 – 1867). Member and Director of the Academy of Stockholm. Pupil of the same under Hasselgren. He at length studied sculpture under Byström. In 1836, by means of a stipend from the King, he went to Rome. Since then he has visited Paris, and been again to Italy. Among his works are, " Martyrs in the Amphitheater," " Neapolitan Fishermen " (in the Museum of Stockholm), busts of Wasa, Frederika Bremer, and other notable people. Some of his motives are drawn from Northern mythology, such as " Höder von Loke," etc.

Quartley, Arthur, A. N. A. (*Fr.-Am.*) Born in Paris, 1839. As an artist, he is self-taught, having studied in no schools and under no masters. His professional life has been spent in Baltimore and New York, opening a studio in the latter city in 1875 or '76. He first exhibited at the Royal National Academy, in 1875, "Calm Days, Isles of Shoals," and "Evening at Narragansett." Among the more important of his works are, "Low Tide" (N. A., 1876) and "Making the Landing, White Island, Isles of Shoals," both owned by John B. Thoms of Baltimore; "Morning Effect, North River" (N. A., 1877), the property of John Taylor Johnston; "An Afternoon in August, Coast of Maine" (N. A., 1878), belonging to Mr. Colgate. He was elected a member of the Artists' Fund Society in 1876. His "Morning Effect in New York Harbor" was sent to the Paris Exposition of 1878.

"'The Close of a Stormy Day' is the strongest thing Arthur Quartley has yet done, and it admits him without demur into the front rank of our marine-painters." — *Art Journal*, May, 1877.

"Among the most progressive landscape-painters in this country is Arthur Quartley, whose 'Afternoon in August' is, so far as we know, the best marine he has yet painted. . . . . With its exquisitely soft and beautiful far distances and skies it contains several special bits of decoration that are absolutely tinsel. But what especially interests one in him is the rapidity of his growth. Even now he is almost, if not quite, at the head of American marine-painters; and the creditable appearance which he is making is one of the distinct and bright features of the Academy Exhibition." — *New York Evening Post*, April 20, 1878.

Raabe, Joseph. (*Ger.*) Born at Deutsch Wartenberg (1780 – 1849). Painter to the Court of Hesse-Darmstadt. Professor at the Academy of Bonn. Member of the Académie des Beaux-Arts at Dresden. Painter to the Court of Saxony and Professor at l'École des Beaux-Arts at Breslau. He had a varied talent, a sure hand, and exquisite taste. He made a large number of fine copies in Italy. His "St. Peter and St. Paul" is in the principal church of Naumbourg-sur-la-Queiss, Silesia. In the Dresden Gallery there is a series of sketches and paintings, illustrating "L'antique histoire de la Germanie et de l'Allemagne au moyen âge."

Radclyffe, Edward. (*Brit.*) (1810 – 1863.) Son of William Radclyffe, a noted English engraver, whose pupil and assistant he was for some years in Birmingham, his native town. He went to London about 1842, where he became associated with the Art Journal, and other illustrated periodicals, furnishing many fine plates after the leading artists of the day. "Kenilworth Castle," "Peat-Gatherers," "Outskirts of the Forest," "Changing the Pasture," and others, after David Cox, were among his later works.

Radford, Edward. (*Brit.*) Born at Plymouth, 1831. At the age of fifteen he was articled as a pupil to a civil engineer, practicing as an architect in Canada and the United States from 1854 to '61. He was some months a lieutenant in an Ohio battery in the American Civil War, and was engaged upon ordinance until 1862. In

1863 he commenced painting as a profession, in Cincinnati, Ohio, returning to England the same year, and becoming a subscriber to the Artists' Society, Langham Chambers. He was elected an Associate of the Society of Painters in Water-Colors in 1875, and is also a member of the Adelphi Society of Arts. Among his more important works are, "The Soldier of the Cross," at the Royal Academy in 1868 (owned in New York) ; "Flora," at the Dudley Gallery in 1873 ; and "Weary," at the Water-Color Exhibition of 1875 ; "The Convalescent" (belonging to Mr. Baring, M. P.) ; "Footprints" and "Caveas Emptor," in 1876 ; "A Little Chilly" (belonging to Collingwood Smith) ; "The Introduction" and "Godiva," in 1877 ; "In Consultation" and "The Critics," in 1878.

"Edward Radford's 'Weary' is a picture painted with much care and attention to detail, especially in the imitation of the textile fabrics ; the figure of the woman is excellently modeled, and the pose easy and natural." — *Art Journal*, March, 1877.

Raffet, Denis-Auguste-Marie. (*Fr.*) Born at Paris (1804 – 1860). Chevalier of the Legion of Honor. Pupil of Charlet, l'École des Beaux-Arts, and of Gros. At the time of his studies it was quite the custom for artists to publish an annual album of lithographs. Raffet's first album was dated 1826, and his success was more than usual for a young man. The subjects which he drew from military life have, with good reason, remained celebrated. Raffet early resolved to be a painter of soldiers and the incidents of their lives. He studied hard, and neglected no means to fit himself for his chosen specialty. It is said that at one time he obtained the head of a young soldier who had died in the hospital, shut himself up with his ghastly treasure, and made repeated pictures of it in order to master the strange pallor and painful mysteries of death. He still wished to see war itself, and in 1832, at the siege of Antwerp, he made many sketches. At the Salon of 1835 the lithographs of these scenes were exhibited ; they gave promise of the future success of the artist, and attracted much attention to him. Prince Demidoff became his friend, and took him on a long journey in Russia, Moldavia, Wallachia, the Crimea, Smyrna, etc. During this time Raffet had always the pencil in hand, and his lithographs illustrating this journey are most valuable, and are a perfect reflection, as in a mirror, of the scenes represented. Raffet was often asked to paint an historical picture for the Gallery at Versailles ; this he intended to do, but his lithographs were so much sought, and his series of plates (especially that of 92, for the "Journal de l'Expédition des Portes-de-Fer," for the Duke of Orleans) so important, that the painting was always deferred. Raffet visited Belgium, and in 1849 he went to Italy to study the motley soldiers. The troops of Garibaldi, the Swiss Papal Guards, the Austrian, the Piedmontese, the French armies, and the picturesque costumes of the Italian women, afforded great scope to the painter. He sketched much in water-colors, and his picture of "The Evening of the Battle of Navara," where all were seeking and burying their dead, is a splendid example of his art. After the siege of Rome Raffet divided his time between Paris, where his family were, and Florence, or San Donato, where Prince Demidoff always wished for him. In 1853 these two friends went to Spain, and Raffet had not completed at the time of his death the album of his Spanish sketches, which is much to be regretted, but at the same time he had in train his illustrations of the siege of Rome, and was so suddenly cut off that much was left unfinished. His works are far too numerous to be mentioned, but his sketches show the true heroism, the sad, tender, and brave elements, of the soldier's life, and in them one will find harmonized history and poetry.

Rahl, Charles. (*Ger.*) Born at Vienna (1812–1865). Pupil of the Academy of Vienna. He had an extensive atelier in Vienna, and received many pupils. His works are numerous, and some of them are important. They are seen in the galleries and churches of his native city. He executed some frescos and monumental painting, and four hundred portraits. His picture of "Christians surprised in the Catacombs" is in the National Gallery, Berlin.

Rajon, Paul-Adolphe. (*Fr.*) Born at Dijon. Medals in 1869, '70, and '73. Pupil of Gaucherel and Flameng. The etchings of this artist are fine. Hamerton says that he "never issues slovenly or careless work." He is a painter as well as an etcher, and has consequently a certain understanding which is of service to him, but which is wanting in one who is only an engraver. His engravings are very numerous, and are principally (in late years entirely) etchings.

Ramsay, Milne. (*Am.*) A native of Philadelphia, he has lived for some time in Paris, studying under Bonnat, and contributing to the first exhibition of the Society of American Artists in New York, in 1878, "The Bird-Fanciers." To the Paris Salon he sent, in 1876, "The Home of a Naturalist"; in 1878, "Cromwell and his Daughter Elizabeth." Several of his *genre* pictures have been purchased and photographed by Goupil & Co. Among them are "A Moral Lesson" and "Douce Béatitude," which have been highly praised for fineness and finish of detail.

Rankley, Alfred. (*Brit.*) (1820–1873.) A *genre* painter of considerable reputation in England. Among his works are, "The Village School," "Old Schoolfellows," "The Benediction," "The Farewell Sermon," "After Work," "The Doctor's Coming," "The Hearth of his Home," "The Lonely Hearth," "Eugene Aram," "Dr. Watts visiting some of his Little Friends," "George Stephenson at Darlington," "Milton's First Meeting with Mary Powell." He last exhibited at the Royal Academy, in 1871, "The Benediction."

"Rankley's pictures are carefully painted. The story, whatever it may be, is attractively set out, and for the most part conveys some good and wholesome moral, and without any forced or vapid sentiment. They were hung in the Academy in various years; all were directed to awaken dormant sympathy in favor of what is kindly in feeling and of good report." — *Art Journal*, February, 1873.

Ranvier, Victor Joseph. (*Fr.*) Born at Lyons. Medals in 1865 and '73. Pupil of Jannuot and J. Richard. At the Salon of 1876 he exhibited "The Morning"; in 1874, "The Deliverance of Prometheus"; in 1873, "Echo" and "The Exiled Virtues" (water-color). His "La chasse au filet" (1864) and "The Infancy of Bacchus" (1865) are in the Luxembourg.

Rapin, Alexandre. (*Fr.*) Born at Noroy-le-Bourg. Medals in 1875 and '77. Pupil of Gérôme and Français. Landscape-painter. At the Salon of 1878 he exhibited "Le Valbois (Doubs) in November."

Raven, J. S. (*Brit.*) He was the son of the Rev. J. Raven of Preston, an amateur painter. As an artist J. S. Raven was comparatively self-taught. He exhibited at the Royal Academy, the Dudley Gallery, and elsewhere. He was drowned while bathing at Harlich in 1877. Among his pictures are, "Midsummer Moonlight" (R. A., 1866), "A View of the Tay near Dunkeld," "Baiff and Lord's Seat from the Slopes of Skiddaw," "Summer Haze," and "Part of the Land-Slip, Chapel Rock, Lyme-Regis," etc. After his death a collection of his works were on exhibition in the Gallery of the Burlington Fine Art Club, in London, of which the London Times said : —

"The loss to art will be felt with the more regret now that we have brought before us the whole work of his life, and see such fine poetic endowments and strong develnpment of long-cherished aspirations, with such vigorous and energetic application of a most observant study of Nature."

Read, Thomas Buchanan. (*Am.*) Born in Chester County, Pa. (1822 - 1872). In 1839 he entered the studio of a Cincinnati sculptor, intending to learn that branch of art. He quickly relinquished it for painting, however, and opened a studio of his own in New York, two years later. In 1846 he settled in Philadelphia, and in 1850 he went to Europe, working and studying in Florence and Rome. He made the latter city his home, with occasional visits to America, upon one of which, in 1872, he died in New York. Among the better known of his works are, "The Water-Sprite," "The Lost Pleiad," "The Star of Bethlehem," "Sheridan and his Horse." He began his career as a portrait-painter with some success. His portrait of George Peabody is in the Peabody Institute, Baltimore. Mr. Claghorn of Philadelphia, an early friend of Mr. Read's, purchased a number of his pictures, painted at different periods, illustrating his progress from time to time. His was a very versatile genius. He occasionally turned his attention to sculpture in his maturity, and executed a bust of General Sheridan, which proved how successful he might have been with his chisel, had he so elected in his youth. By his poems, perhaps, he will be best known in the future. His "Sheridan's Ride" is one of the most popular productions of the minor poets of America. His first book of "Poems" was published in 1847 ; his "Lays and Ballads" in 1848, "The New Pastoral" in 1855,

"The Home by the Sea" in 1856. A collected edition of his works was published in 1860.

Ream, Vinnie (Mrs. Hoxie). (Am.) American sculptress, residing for some years in Washington, D. C. She went to Italy in 1869 or '70, executing in Rome her statue of Lincoln (for the United States government), now in the Capitol at Washington. Among her works are busts of Lincoln, Thaddeus Stevens, Reverdy Johnson, etc. ; and medallions of Father Hyacinthe, Gustave Doré, and Kaulbach. She is at present (1878) at work upon statues of General Custer and Admiral Farragut. Her "Spirit of the Carnival," "The West," "Miriam," a bust of Senator Morrell, and a bust of a child were at the Philadelphia Exhibition in 1876.

[No response to circular.]

Redgrave, Richard, R. A. (Brit.) Born in 1804. Brought up to commercial pursuits. Studied from the Elgin Marbles in the British Museum in 1823 or '24. Sent his first picture to the Royal Academy, "The Brent, near Hartwell," in 1825. In 1831 he sent his "Commencement of the Massacre of the Innocents"; in 1833, "Cymbeline"; in 1840 (when he was elected Associate of the Royal Academy), "The Reduced Gentleman's Daughter." Among his early works may be mentioned, "Quintin Matsy's First Picture" (1839), "The Poor Teacher" (1843), "The Seamstress" (1844), "Fashion's Slaves" (1847), "The Lost Path," "The Old English Homestead," "The Flight into Egypt" (1851), and other well-known pictures. He was elected Academician in 1850, and has held several high official positions under the government in the different art institutions of the country. His "Olivia's Return to her Parents" and "Country Cousins" are in the National Gallery, London, and his "Gulliver on the Farmer's Table" belongs to the Sheepshanks Collection. He exhibited at the Royal Academy, in 1861, "The Strayed Flock"; in 1863, "The Way through the Woods"; in 1864, "Jane Shore doing Penance"; in 1866, "The Woodman's Dinner"; in 1868, "Eugene Aram"; in 1869, "From Autumn to Winter"; in 1870, "Jack-o' Lanthorn"; in 1871, "The Charcoal-Burners"; in 1872, "Expectation"; in 1873, "The Lady of the Manor"; in 1874, "Sermons in Stones"; in 1875, "The Mill Pool" and "Starting for a Holiday"; in 1876, "Calling the Sheep to Fold" and "The Oak of the Millhead"; in 1877, "Deserted," "Help at Hand," and "A Well-Spring in the Forest"; in 1878, "The Heir come of Age" and "Friday Street." To Paris, in 1878, he sent "Deserted" and "Starting for a Holiday." He is a member of the Society of British Artists.

"'Sunday Morning' is one of those avenues which Mr. Redgrave now paints with so much grace and truth. When we remember the very highly finished figure-pictures which he was accustomed to exhibit in former years, it is at least remarkable that he should have forsaken a very fascinating manner of minute execution for the free but by no means ineffective method he now professes." — *Art Journal*, September, 1873.

"Mr. Redgrave, the now veteran painter and writer upon art, has been a contributor to the publications of the Etching Club, The temper of his work is always studious and sincere ; and, besides these qualities, it has a certain tenderness of sentiment ; but, from the technical point of view, it has been injured by a striving after finish, which was due in part to the habit of working on a small scale." — HAMERTON's *Etching and Etchers.*

Reed, Helen. (*Am.*) A Boston artist. She began her professional career in that city by the drawing of portraits in crayon. Later, she went to Florence, where she studied sculpture under Preston Powers, sending to America bas-reliefs in marble, which have been exhibited at the Boston Art Club, in New York, and elsewhere.

Regnault, Alexandre - Georges - Henri. (*Fr.*) Born at Paris (1843 – 1871). *Prix de Rome*, 1866. Medal, 1869. Son of the academician who was director of the manufactory at Sèvres. Pupil of Lamothe and Cabanel. Regnault contended for the *prix de Rome* in 1863, and was much disappointed at not winning it. In 1864 he sent two portraits to the Salon, which were coldly received. At length in 1866 the prize was his, and he went to Italy. Soon after he returned to Paris for the Exposition. After he was again in Rome he made twenty-seven designs for the illustration of " Wey's Rome." These designs are excellent. In 1867 he sent to the Salon a decorative panel ; in 1868, one painted portrait and the sketches of two other portraits. In the autumn of 1868, not being well, this artist went to Spain, and saw General Prim, from which resulted the portrait of the Salon of 1869, which is now so well known ; it is in the Luxembourg. From Spain Regnault went to Tangiers, and even in the short time he was able to spend there, fell so in love with the life of that country that he determined to return when at liberty to do so. In 1869 he painted his " Judith," and in 18— sent to the Salon the " Salome," which is a remarkable work. In summer of 1870 he went again to Tangiers, and painted " The E. on with Judgment under the Moorish Kings of Granada," now mbourg. Hearing of the war, Regnault returned to Pari part in the defence of his country. On the 19th of Janu he left Paris with a spirited party who made a sortie attempting to join the expected army of succor. He was killed towards evening on the field of Buzenval. No friend saw him die, but the next day an ambulance-driver found his body and read his name on the lining of his capote. In the confusion the traces of him were again lost, and it was not until the 25th that his friends recovered his remains. His funeral took place at the church of Saint-Augustin, just at the sad moment when the capitulation of Paris was made known. Paul Mantz closes his account of Regnault thus : —

" It will soon be a year since these fatal things occurred ; but the remembrance of Regnault remains as fresh as on the day of his death, and yesterday, when at the exhibition of the works of the pensioners at Rome, we saw in the place where his contribution for the fourth year should have been, an easel draped in black and decorated with green boughs, each one felt an oppression at the heart at this spectacle, which told too well of human injustice, and of the cruelty of the times. Regnault, crowned already with a precocious glory, was scarcely at the first chapter of his book ; his art was young, like his soul ; he knew little of painful experiences, and in the constant holiday of his life could not yet understand them. He would without doubt have advanced in the sentiment of manner, as in that of the drama. But the dream is ended : the present and the future, both have perished together. There remains to us only his work, which is but a radiant beginning, and the example of his death, which plainly shows that the culture of art extinguishes not the religion of patriotism in the soul. Let us guard faithfully the memory of the artist and the citizen, and on this tomb, where so many hopes are buried, let us read, with our regrets for the departed master, our hatred for those who killed him " — *Gazette des Beaux-Arts*, January, 1872.

In the Luxembourg, besides the works already named, there are four water-colors of Spanish subjects (executed in 1868 and '69), and fifteen sketches, presented to the gallery by V. Regnault, member of the Institute. At a Paris sale of 1872, "'A Morocco Soldier at the Gate of a Pasha, Tangiers " sold for £ 960.

" Henri Regnault, who was killed at the battle of Buzenval in 1871, when but twenty-eight years of age, was the most remarkable painter of the contemporary school in point of promise, and had he lived until maturity would have attained a pre-eminent position. The works he left behind him remind one, in fire and force, of Géricault's paintings or Schiller's Robbers. . . . . Winning the *prix de Rome* at twenty-three, he sent home during his absence such works as ' Judith and Holofernes,' ' Salome,' the famous ' Portrait of General Prim,' and an ' Execution under the Moors at Granada,' the last two painted during a trip to Madrid and Tangiers In the portrait of Prim the horse is of the Andalusian type ; the *motif* of the composition represents the arrival of General Prim before Madrid, with the revolutionary forces, October 8, 1868. The execution scene aroused a profound sensation on the part of both critics and public, as well it might, from the startling character of the subject and the tremendous power of the treatment, greatly assisted by that simplicity which indicates large reserve strength in the artist and wonderfully stimulates the imagination of the observer. It is marvelous that artists so rarely avail themselves of this master weapon of simplicity. A marble stairway with two or three steps leads to a Moorish court in the style of the Alhambra, which is suffused with a glowing light suggesting the warming heat of a Southern noon. In the immediate foreground are the two figures composing the awful drama : executioner and his victim. The former, erect, massive, infl..., a statue, draws his cimetar across his tunic to wipe off the blood ; gled trunk of what was once a man has fallen heavily down the steps, and a pool of blood It is not too much to say that this blood mantling . slab is one of the finest bits of color in modern art . . This painting is hung in the Luxembourg, and persons have been so overcome by its horrible realism as to be seized with faintness when gazing upon it. There see ms to be an impropriety in admitting such a work to a public national gallery . . . , Either it is bad as a work of art, and should therefore be excluded, or it is good as a work of art, and should therefore be forbidden, on exactly the same grounds that the public are guarded from the demoralizing influence of a public execution This, however, would not prevent its more private exhibition, purely as a work of art, to those who would study it only from such a point of view." — Benjamin's *Contemporary Art in Europe*

Reid, George. (*Brit.*) Born at Aberdeen. A portrait-painter, executing occasional landscapes, generally in the manner of the Dutch school, of which he is a disciple. He was a pupil of Mollinger. He has spent the greater part of his professional life in his native city, where his studio now is. He was elected a full member of the Royal Scottish Academy in 1878. Among his works are, " The Washing-Day," " Whins in Bloom," etc. To the Royal Scottish Academy in

1878 he contributed " Dornoch," " A Highland Kitchen," and several portraits.

" A more uopretending theme could scarcely have been selected than a stretch of common with masses of blooming freeze, a bare pathway, down which sheep are wending, and a cool, gray sky overhead. Yet out of these Mr. Reid has constructed a charming landscape [' Whins in Bloom ']. — *Art Journal,* April, 1874.

Reid, Archibald D. (*Brit.*) Native of Aberdeen, where he still resides. He is a brother of George Reid, R. S. A., and devotes himself to landscape-painting. " A Harvest Scene," by A. D. Reid, was at the Glasgow Fine Arts Loan Exhibition of 1878 ; the same year he sent to the Royal Scottish Academy, " Boys and Buoys," " An East Coast Fishing Village," " Guessing the Catch," and " On the Findhorn, — Autumn."

Reinhart, Benjamin Franklin, A. N. A. (*Am.*) Born near Waynesburg, Pa., 1829. He displayed a talent for art as a child, and notwithstanding many obstacles, decided to follow it as a profession. At the age of fifteen he found himself at Pittsburg, Pa., receiving there a few lessons in the mixing and application of oil-colors, beginning his career untutored and alone by the painting of portraits. Later, he went to New York, where he spent three years, studying in the schools of the National Academy. In 1849 he visited Ohio and several cities of the West, painting many notable men of that section. In the course of a year or two he was enabled to go to Europe, settling first in Düsseldorf, and later in Paris. He availed himself of the best schools, studying grand composition and design with a view to becoming an historical painter. At the end of three years he returned to America, following his profession in New York, Ohio, and New Orleans. At the outbreak of the American Civil War he went to England, and lived seven years in London, where he met with decided success as a painter of English *genre* subjects. In 1868 he came again to New York, where he has since resided, devoting himself to cabinet-sized pictures, *genre* and historical. He is an Associate of the National Academy. About forty-five of his pictures have been engraved. Among his more important works are, " Cleopatra " (the studies for which were made in Egypt, and which is now in England, where it was painted), " Evangeline," " The Nymphs of the Wood," " Katrina Van Tassel," " Pocahontas," " Washington receiving the News of Arnold's Treason," " Consolation," " The Entombment," " Young Franklin and Sir William Keith," " The Regatta," and " The Pride of the Village." all painted since his last return to New York. Among his portraits are those of the Princess of Wales, the Duchess of Newcastle, the Countess of Portsmouth, Lady Vane Tempest, Lord Brougham, John Phillip, R. A., Thomas Carlyle, Tennyson, Mark Lemon, Chief Justice Daly, Charles O'Conor, Dr. Marcy, George M. Dallas, James Buchanan, E. M. Stanton, Winfield Scott, S. P. Chase, Bishops McElvaine and Polk, Elliott, J. C. Breckinridge, Stephen A. Douglas, Samuel Houston, and many more.

Reinhart, Charles S. (*Am.*) Born at Pittsburg, Pa., 1844. Was engaged upon the United States military railroads in Virginia, during the Civil War, for a period of three years, and, later, spent four years in a steel manufactory at Pittsburg. In 1868 he began the study of art in Paris, going subsequently to Munich, where he entered the Royal Academy, and studied drawing under Professor Streyhüber, and etching and painting under Professor Otto. The greater part of his professional life has been spent in New York. For six and a half years he was in the employ of Harper and Brothers, opening a studio of his own in the summer of 1876. He is a member of the American Art Club in Munich, the Pittsburg Art Association, New York Etching Club, and was elected a member of the Water-Color Society in 1876. He has contributed illustrations to various publications of the Scribners', Harpers', Appletons', and of Osgood's, and exhibits frequently at the National Academy, oil and water-color paintings, as well as sketches in pen and ink. "Caught Napping" and "Clearing Up" in 1875, "Reconnoitering" in 1876, "The Rebuke" in 1877, are among his oil-pictures. To the Water-Color Exhibitions he sent, in 1877, the "Close of Day" and "Gathering Wood"; in 1878, "At the Ferry." His "No Trespassing" belongs to Fletcher Harper, Jr., and his "Noon and Midnight" (both in black and white), to J. Abner Harper.

"C. S. Reinhart's 'Gathering Wood' is composed in his happiest mood, the least ambitious but best water-color he has to show, being remarkable, not only in figures, where his strength lies, but in color as well." — *New York Times*, January 22, 1877.

Reinherz, Conrad. (*Prussian.*) Born at Breslau. Pupil of the Academy of Munich and of Dietz. His pictures are landscapes, and have been exhibited in the prominent German exhibitions for some years. He ranks high among the artists of his country.

Rethel, Alfred. (*Fr.*) Born at Aix-la-Chapelle (1816 – 1859). When thirteen years old this artist executed a design, which gained him admission to the Academy of Düsseldorf. At twenty he took up his residence in Frankfort. The subjects of his works are very varied. His historic portraits are famous. He executed many frescos. In 1844 he went to Rome, and two years later commenced, in the Council Chamber at Aix, a series of scenes illustrative of the life of Charlemagne. But his mind became diseased, he imagined and suffered more than we have space to recount, and his life was all the more sad for its early promise of brilliancy unfulfilled.

Among his works may be mentioned, "The Massacre of St. Boniface," "The Swiss in Prayer before the Battle of Sempach, 1386," "Death coming as a Friend," "The Dance of Death," "Death as an Avenger," etc. In the Berlin National Gallery is his picture of "St. Boniface," and several cartoons of his pictures at Aix. At the Leipsic Museum is his picture of "Peter and John healing the Lame Man at the Door of the Temple."

Reusch, Friedrich. (*Ger.*) Of Berlin. At Philadelphia he exhibited "A Group for a Fountain," in bronze, and received a medal.

Riviere, Briton, A. R. A. (*Brit.*) Born in London, 1840. Son of an artist of considerable ability, from whom his early art-training was received. After graduating at the University of Oxford he settled in the neighborhood of London in 1867, devoting himself to painting as a profession. He first exhibited at the Royal Academy, in 1858, "Rest from Labor"; in 1859, "On the Road to Gloucester Fair"; in 1864, "Iron Bars" and "Romeo and Juliet"; in 1866, "The Poacher's Nurse"; in 1867, "Strayed from the Flock" and "The Long Sleep," which first attracted popular attention to his work. In 1868 he sent the "Last of the Garrison"; in 1870, "A Midsummer Night's Dream"; in 1872, "Daniel"; in 1873, "Argus"; in 1874, "Apollo"; in 1876, "A Stern Chase"; in 1877, "A Legend of St. Patrick" and "Lazarus." He was elected an Associate of the National Academy in 1878, contributing "Sympathy" and "An Anxious Moment." Among his water-color paintings may be mentioned "Fox and Geese" (in the South Kensington Collection). His "Charity" (engraved by F. Stackpole) received a medal at the Vienna Exposition, and his "Circe and the Companions of Ulysses" (engraved by the same artist) and "War-Time" (R. A., 1875) were at the Philadelphia Exhibition of 1876; "The Last of the Garrison," "Charity," and "Daniel" were at Paris in 1878.

"There is a pathos in this composition ['War-Time'] so touching as to make one turn sadly away to search after more cheery work, before examining with any minuteness the other contributions of the same excellent artist" — *Art Journal*, June, 1875.

"'Circe and the Companions of Ulysses,' by Mr. B. Riviere, is conceived and executed with that rare skill which deservedly entitles this artist to the high reputation he enjoys. The humor is admirably rendered, and exhibits a keen appreciation of the possibilities of expression in swinish physiognomy." — Prof. Weir's *Official Report of the American Centennial Exhibition of 1876.*

Rhomberg, Hanno. (*Ger.*) Born at Munich (1820 - 1869). Studied under Schnorr and Bernhard. He was much associated with Enhuber, who influenced him. His fame dated from his "Traveling Students," which Louis I. bought for the Pinakothek. Among his earlier works are, "The Work of a Village Painter," "The Votive Tablet," "The Tight Shoe," "The Best Scholar." In 1869 he painted "An Inn Scene."

Ribera, Carlos Louis. (*Span.-Fr.*) Born at Roma, of Spanish parents, about 1812. Two medals at Paris. Pupil of his father and of Paul Delaroche. This painter has lived much at Paris, and has exhibited at many Salons. Among his works are, the "Origin of the Family of Los Girones," "Battle against the Moors of the Sagra of Toledo," "Don Rodrigo de Calderon led to Execution," and "Mary Magdalene at the Sepulcher."

Ricard, Gustave. (*Fr.*) Born at Marseilles (1824 - 1873). Two medals at the Salons. This painter studied in his native city until

1844, when he went to Paris and exhibited the portrait of Mme. Sabatier, which was much admired. He studied under Cogniet, and made many copies at the Louvre. Three years later he went to Rome, where he continued to make copies and also original works. He visited Florence, Venice, and England. He made his début at the Salon of 1850, and continued to exhibit nine years ; he then appeared no more until 1872, when he sent the portrait of Paul de Musset. He found the Salons decidedly against his ideas. His portraits, however, were much sought. In 1863 the decoration of the Legion of Honor was tendered him, but he replied, " It is too late," and could not be prevailed upon to change his decision. He lived as simply after his fortune was made as before, and admitted but few to his home or heart. So sudden was his death that his model knocked at his door as he breathed his ·last. At the Wilson Exhibition at Brussels, in 1873, was seen his own portrait, painted by himself in his earlier years.

Richards, T. Addison, N. A. (*Am.*) Born in London, 1820. In his youth he resided in the State of Georgia. In 1845 he removed to the city of New York, where, with the exception of occasional American and European tours, the rest of his professional life has.been spent. In 1848 he was elected an Associate of the National Academy, Academician in 1851, and Corresponding Secretary in 1852. He was the first Director of the Cooper Union School of Design for Women, in 1858 to '60, and since 1867 he has been Professor of Art in the University of New York. Among the better known of Mr. Richards' early paintings may be mentioned, " Alastor, or the Spirit of Solitude" (from Shelley's poem), at the National Academy in 1854 (belonging to Mr. Wolsey of New Haven) ; " The Indian Paradise, — a Dream of the Happy Hunting-Ground," at the National Academy in 1854 ; " The Edisto River, S. C." ; " Live-Oaks of the South " ; ": The French Broad River, N. C.," at the National Academy in 1859 ; " The River Rhine" and " Warwick Castle," in 1869 (belonging to N. Jarvis). In 1871 a collection of one hundred of his works was on exhibition at the Somerville Gallery in New York, including American, Canadian, tropical, Swiss, and English landscapes, and a number of fruit and flower subjects, which were afterwards sold.

His " Chatsworth, England " and " Lake Thun, Switzerland " belong to A. Jenkins of New York; " Italian Lake Scene," to A. Aiken, New York; " Lake Winnipiseogee," to Mrs. M. B. Young, Fall River ; " Sunnyside," to James S. Virtue, London. Mr. Richards has furnished illustrations for many books and magazines. The first of these was the " American Artist," treating of flower-painting, published in Baltimore as early as 1838 ; followed by " Georgia, Illustrated," steel-plates, published in 1842 ; " The Romance of American Landscape," quarto, in 1854 ; " Summer Stories of the South," in 1853 ; " Pictures and Painters," in 1870. He was also engaged on the Appletons' " Hand-Books of Travel," Illustrated Guide-Books

to the Hudson, to Saratoga, to Central Park, etc. ; as well as many
illustrated papers for Harper's Magazine, including " Sunnyside, the
Home of Irving," " Idlewild, the Home of Willis," " Lake George,"
" The Connecticut River," " The Rice-Lands of the South," and so on,
in a great many instances furnishing the letter-press as well as the
plates.

" At various times Mr. Richards has visited all sections of the country, and through
the medium of the magazines has presented to his countrymen careful and accurate
pictures of the scenery of the country, from the sunny valleys of New England to the
wide savannahs and rolling prairies of the South and West. In addition to his art
labors Mr. Richards has also devoted much time to literary study, and many of the
papers that have appeared in Harper and the Knickerbocker are the products alike of
his pen and pencil." — *New York Evening Express,* February 29, 1868.

" Richards' landscapes range through a considerable variety of subjects, the most of ·
them being views studied by the artist from choice portions of American and European
scenery. Some are compositions, and all show that sure artistic sense of the elements
of beauty in scenery, which has heretofore given the artist his rank in the art-pro-
ductions of the country. Of the artist's methods of technical execution it is needless to
speak at this day, his style probably being as familiar to the public as that of any
of the veteran exhibitors on the walls of the National Academy." — *Home Journal,*
March 22, 1871.

Richards, William T., N. A. (*Am.*) Born in Philadelphia, 1833.
At an early age he turned his attention to the study of art, and be-
came a painter by profession in 1853. In 1855 he went to Europe,
spending a year in study and observation in Florence, Rome, and
Paris. In 1856 he opened a studio in Philadelphia, and in 1866 re-
turned to Europe for a short visit. He is an Honorary Member of
the National Academy of Design and an Associate Member of the
Water-Color Society. His summers of late years have been spent at
Newport, R. I. Among his works in oil are " Mid-Ocean," " New
England Coast," " At Atlantic City," " Midsummer," " June Woods,"
" Wood Scene," " Spring," " Summer Afternoon," " Ebb Tide," " Old
Orchards at Newport," " The Inlet near Newport," and " Out in the
Country." In 1871 he sent to the Water-Color Exhibition, " Mount
Desert," " Pulpit Rock, Nahant " ; in 1874, " Off the Spar Buoy,
Atlantic City " ; in 1875, " Lake Squam " and " The Third Beach,
Newport " ; in 1876, " Almy's Pond " and " Gooseberry Island,"
near Newport ; in 1877, " Autumn, near Newport" ; in 1878, " So'-
west Point, Conanicut " and " Almy's Pond, Newport." He sent
to the Paris Exposition of 1867 his " Foggy Day at Nantucket"
(belonging to George Whitney) and his " Woods in June " (belonging
to Robert L. Stuart). To the American Centennial Exhibition of
1876 he contributed " The Wissahickon " (in oil) and " Old Trees at
Atlantic City " and " Paradise, Newport " (in water-colors), for which
he was commended by the judges. His " Going to the Spring" and
" First Beach, Newport " belonged to John Taylor Johnston, and his
" Sunset on the Ocean," to S. J. Harriot. His " Spring," at the
Blodgett sale, brought $ 1,610. To Paris, in 1878, he sent " South-

N

west Point, Conanicut," in water-color, and three pictures in oil, —
" In the Woods," " Spring," and " The Forest."

" So carefully painted in some of Richards' landscapes are the leaves, grasses, grain-stalks, weeds, stones, and flowers, that we seem not to be looking at a distant prospect, but lying on the ground with herbage and blossoms directly under our eyes." — TUCKER-MAN's *Book of the Artists.*

" Mr. W. T. Richards contributed but a single oil-painting, ' The Wissahickon,' not one of his best pictures. This artist is a careful, conscientious student of Nature, but it is only recently that he has permitted himself to exercise that freedom and largeness of vision characteristic of mature art ; his later works manifest this in a marked degree. No painter is more thoroughly master of the sea and waves in motion than is this art-ist." — PROF. WEIR's *Official Report of the American Centennial Exhibition of 1876.*

" William T. Richards' ' Gull Rock, Newport, — Fog coming in ' [in oil, N. A., 1877] shows water without life or transparency, and rocks wanting in character. The picture is quite without depth or originality." — *New York Times,* April 8, 1877.

" There is no storm [' Gull Rock,' N. A., 1877], but the dark green sea lifts with a deep pulsation, and dashes over the rock with a resistless motion that is very suggestive of latent power. It is a picture full of large simplicity and quiet truth that study cannot easily exhaust." — *Art Journal,* May, 1877.

" Richards is one of the first American painters who adopted the pre-Raphaelite style of treatment in their pictures ; this was in 1858, and since that time no artist in this country has achieved greater success in the profession. . . . . His drawing is never at fault, and the crispness of his touch is charming." — *Art Journal,* August, 1877.

Richards, Orren C. (*Am.*) Born in South Boston, 1842. In 1857 he began the study of decoration with Thomas Savory in Boston. In 1860 he studied under George Inness at Medfield, Mass. He entered the army at the outbreak of the Civil War. He has painted scenery at nearly all of the Boston theaters, and easel-pictures of still-life, in oil. His " Peonies " (belonging to Mrs. E. E. Slack) was at the Mechanics' Fair, Boston, in 1878.

Richardson, T. M. (*Brit.*) Contemporary English water-color artist, residing in London, and for many years a member of the Old Water-Color Society. He paints landscapes, generally of the High-lands of Scotland and the Continent. Among his works, exhibited in different seasons, are, " Loch Tulla," " Loch Awe," " Glen Nevis," " Look-ing towards Glencoe," " Argyleshire," " On the River Oran," " Bone Church, Isle of Wight," " Lago Maggiore," " Via Mala," " Market-Boats, Lake Como," etc.

" In No. 36 [Society of Painters in Water-Colors, 1873], by T. M. Richardson, we have one of those luxuriously colored and elaborately worked drawings on which this artist has built his reputation. It is entitled ' In the Neighborhood of the Town of Cozenzos, Northern Calabria.' The mountains, of which a mass closes the middle distance, are most skillfully drawn and richly colored, and in the entire composition there is a complete-ness which almost bespeaks a scenic study." — *Art Journal,* June, 1873.

Richet, Léon. (*Fr.*) Born at Solesmes. Pupil of Diaz, whose style he has adopted. His pictures are charming. In the collection of Mrs. H. E. Maynard of Boston is " Near Nouvion, in Picardy." His works are rare in America. At the Salon of 1877 he exhibited " Aurora " and " Route of the Artists, Forest of Fontainebleau " ; in 1876, " The Boundaries of Barbison, Forest of Fontainebleau " and " After the Storm "; in 1878, " A Scene near Evreux " and " The Gleaners."

Richmond, George, R. A. (*Brit.*) Born in 1809. Entered the schools of the Royal Academy in 1824. He made his most decided success as a portrait-painter, at first in water-colors and crayon, later in oils. He was elected an Associate of the Royal Academy in 1859, and Academician in 1867. Among his later portraits may be mentioned, "The Earl of Elgin," in 1860 ; "Edward M. Ward, R. A.," in 1861 ; "The Duke of Buccleuch," in 1865 ; "Sir Moses Montefiore," in 1875 ; and many prominent people of church and state. Among his paintings of another class are, "The Agony in the Garden," in 1858 ; "Sunset from Hyde Park," in 1861 ; and "A Scene from 'Comus,'—the Measure," in 1864.

"The art of George Richmond is studious and painstaking to almost too great a degree, leaving upon the mind not a very vivid sense of freshness of vision in the painter. The work is often overlabored, the necessary impression of spontaneous vitality drawn unfairly out by hard and cautious style. Still in everything from this painter's hands we have work that carries with it a conviction of conscientious and well-directed effort, oftentimes yielding a cultured and satisfying result." — *Art Journal*, July, 1878.

Richomme, Jules. (*Fr.*) Born at Paris, 1818. Chevalier of the Legion of Honor. Pupil of Drölling. Made his début as a portrait-painter in 1839. Richomme has executed mural paintings in the church of Saint-Séverin at Paris, and in several provincial churches. His picture of "St. Peter of Alcantara healing a Sick Child" (1864) is at the Luxembourg. In 1877 he exhibited "An Arab Woman" and "The Chinese Doll"; in 1876, "The Dove" and a portrait of the Marquise Ginori ; in 1875, "The Shower," "The Little Idle One," and the "First Lesson on the Violin."

Richter, Adrien-Louis. (*Ger.*) Born at Dresden, 1803. This artist was, in early life, a painter and designer, as well as an engraver. But his labors as a designer were the most important, and occasioned his traveling quite extensively. In 1828 he was appointed to the School of Design of the porcelain factory at Meissen, and later he became professor and president of the landscape studio in the Academy of Dresden, and also a member of the Council of that Academy. His oil-paintings are few in comparison with his designs and engravings, but they are such as give him good rank among German landscape-painters.

Richter, Gustav. (*Ger.*) Born at Berlin about 1822. Professor and member of the Senate of the Royal Academy of Arts in Berlin, and member of the Academies of Munich and Vienna. Grand medal in Berlin, 1864, and other medals at Paris, Brussels, Vienna, and Philadelphia. This artist is known in America by chromos from his pictures, which are brilliant in color, and charming to the public generally. His Oriental scenes are very rich in effect. His portraits are excellent. Among his works are, the "Odalisque," "The Raising of Jairus' Daughter" (at the National Gallery, Berlin), and many portraits. He sent to the Philadelphia Exposition a portrait of the Hon. George Bancroft. At the Exposition at the Academy at Berlin, in

1876, he exhibited three portraits and the "Löwenritt," and at the Paris Exposition, 1878, three portraits.

"In spite of the artificial arrangement of his works his excellence is chiefly shown in his delicate painting, his well-balanced parts, his careful and often corrected modeling, and the beautiful coloring in the principal lights, while his shadows so round the flesh parts that they are softened to an ivory-like smoothness." — R. D. *in Zeitschrift für bildende Kunst*, 1875.

Riedel, August. (*Ger.*) Born at Bayreuth, 1800. Professor of St. Luke's Academy at Rome. Member of the Academies of Berlin, Munich, Vienna, and St. Petersburg. Pupil of the Academy of Munich. His pictures are landscapes and *genre* scenes, and are in many galleries, both public and private. The "Albanian Girls" and "Bathing Girls" are in the National Gallery, Berlin.

Riefstahl, Wilhelm Ludwig Friedrich. (*Ger.*) Born at Neu-Strellitz, 1827. Director of the Art School at Carlsruhe. Medals at Berlin; and member of Berlin Academy, at which place he studied. In 1848 he made the designs for illustrating "Kugler's History of Art." He traveled much in mountainous countries, and was passionately fond of their scenery. In 1869 he went to Rome. At the National Gallery at Berlin are his "Mountain Chapel with Herdsmen at Devotion" and "All Souls' Day in Bregenz." In Berlin, in 1876, he exhibited "A Convent on the Inn"; and at the Paris Exposition of 1878, "The Pantheon of Agrippa at Rome" and "Attendant le cercueil."

Eugène Müntz says of Riefstahl : "He sees justly, feels profoundly, and knows how to express what he feels."

Riésener, Louis-Antoine-Léon. (*Fr.*) Born at Paris, 1808. Chevalier of the Legion of Honor. Pupil of David and Gros. His picture of "Erigone" (1864) is at the Luxembourg. Among his works are, "Roses," "Bacchus and Ariadne," "The Awaking," "The Toilette," "Country Pleasures," "The Brook in the Wood," and "Le doux sommeil secoue sur lui ses pavots."

Rimmer, William. (*Am.*) Born in Boston, 1821. He was educated for the medical profession, devoting himself particularly to anatomy. Later, he turned his attention to sculpture and to art instruction. He has delivered a valuable course of lectures on art anatomy at the Lowell Institute, Boston, at the University at Cambridge, Mass., before the National Academy, New York, and elsewhere. He was Director of the School of Design of the Cooper Institute, New York, for some years. He published, in 1864, a volume entitled "The Elements of Design." Among his sculptured works are statues of Alexander Hamilton, "Falling Gladiator," etc., and a colossal head of "St. Stephen," in granite. [Died, 1879.]

"This artist [Dr. Rimmer] has wrought a figure of the most rare anatomical power and truth : and a group which was mistaken for Bunyan's 'Great-Heart and Giant Grim' in mortal struggle, but which was intended to represent 'Union and Secession.'" — TUCKERMAN'S *Book of the Artists.*

"Dr. Rimmer, an accomplished teacher of design, of much original mental force, destined to do good service to American art, has given a striking example of his capacity for realistic sculpture in the model of an athlete reeling under the force of a death-blow. The knowledge of anatomical science displayed is wonderful. . . . . In a head of 'St. Stephen,' carved by himself from granite, Dr. Rimmer has shown a fine capacity for lofty expression." — JARVES, *Art Idea.*

Rinehart, William Henry. (*Am.*) Born in Frederick, Md. (1825–1874). In his youth he was apprenticed to a stone-cutter in Baltimore, studying in the night schools of the Maryland Institute. He went to Italy in 1855, studying and working at sculpture in Florence for three years. He returned to Baltimore in 1858, but after a short stay, went again to Italy, opening a studio in Rome, where the rest of his life was spent. Among his works may be mentioned, "The Woodman" (one of the earliest), "Leander," "Night," "Morning," "Woman of Samaria," "Indian Maiden," "Rebecca," "A Nymph," "Endymion," "Hero," "Atalanta," and "Clytie" (in the Peabody Institute, Baltimore). He executed many portrait busts. His statue of Chief Justice Taney, ordered by the State of Maryland, was unveiled at Annapolis in 1872.

"Rinehart's 'Woman of Samaria' is admired for the deep and pure thoughtfulness of her expression, as if the words of Christ had sunk into her soul. He has charmingly illustrated maternal affection in his 'Latona and her Iofant,' while two sleeping babes on one pillow are full of nature and beauty." —TUCKERMAN's *Book of the Artists.*

Ritchie, Alexander H., N. A. (*Brit.-Am.*) Born in Glasgow, 1822. He studied drawing in the Royal Institution at Edinburgh, under Sir William Allan, and during his first year received four premiums. He has been a resident of New York for many years. In 1871 he was elected a member of the National Academy. He is a painter and engraver, and is highly regarded in both branches of his profession. Among his works in oils are, "Mercy knocking at the Gate," "Fitting out Moses for the Fair," "Death of Lincoln," "Baby, who's that?" (portraits), and portraits of Dr. McCosh of Princeton, Prof. Charles Hodge of Princeton, etc., all exhibited at the National Academy. He engraved "Washington and his Generals" and "Mercy at the Gate," after his own pictures; "Contemplation," after S. J. Guy; "Washington entering New York," "The First Blow for Liberty," and "The March to the Sea," after Darley; "Lady Washington's Reception," after Huntington; etc.

Rivalta, Augusto. (*Ital.*) Born at Genoa, 1837. Professor in the Academy of Florence. He has received many medals. His early inclination for art was cultivated, and he soon became known for his taste in composition and his skill in execution. He went to Florence, and there modeled his statue of "Clinzia," which he sent to the Accademia Ligure. His most famous work is called "An Episode of War," and represents a wounded soldier supported by a brother soldier and a Sister of Charity. It is full of feeling, and admirably executed. The subject was suggested to the artist by his own experience as a volunteer. His statues of Niccolini the poet for Florence, and Cavour for Naples, are very fine. For the Hospital for the Poor in Genoa he made the statue of Palleri and the monument to the Marchesa Corsi Pallavicini. For the celebrated Cemetery of Stagheno he has made several monuments; those of Giuseppina Croce and Bartolomeo Savi deserve mention.

Robbe, Louis-Marie-Dominique-Romain. (*Belgian.*) Born at Courtrai, 1807. Chevalier of the Legion of Honor, of the Order of Léopold, and of that of Charles III. of Spain. His pictures are of animals, and much admired. His " Shepherd and Flock " is in the collection of Mrs. H. E. Maynard, Boston.

Robbe, Henri. (*Belgian.*) Brother of the preceding. He is a painter of fruits and flowers, and has received several medals.

Robbins, Horace W., N. A. (*Am.*) Born in Mobile, Ala., 1842. When about twenty-one years of age he entered the studio of James M. Hart in New York, where he spent a few months. Later, he opened a studio of his own. In 1865 he visited Jamaica with F. E. Church, going thence directly to Europe. He worked in Paris during three winters, from that of 1865, making sketching-tours during the summer months in Switzerland and elsewhere. He returned to New York in the fall of 1867, and has since resided principally in that city. He was elected an Associate of the National Academy in 1864, and Academician in 1878. He is Secretary of the Artists' Fund Society, and has been a member of the Water-Color Society for some years. To the National Academy in 1869 he sent, " The Close of a Cloudy Day " ; in 1870, " A Tropical View " (belonging to Dr. F. N. Otis); in 1871, " An Autumnal Morning " (belonging to D. C. Blodgett) ; in 1873, " A Morning View in Switzerland " ; in 1874, " Morning in Jamaica " ; in 1875, " Passing Shower, Jamaica " (belonging to J. Vanderpoel of New York) ; in 1876, " Flooded Meadows " ; in 1877, " Harbor Islands, Lake George" ; in 1878, " Morning in the Adirondacks " and " Sunny Banks of the Ausable." Among his contributions to the Exhibitions of the Water-Color Society may be mentioned, " A New England Road Scene," in 1877, and " A New England Homestead," in 1878.

To the Centennial Exhibition at Philadelphia, in 1876, he contributed " New England, — Autumn " and " Farmington River, Ct."; to the Paris Exposition of 1878, " Harbor Islands, Lake George." His " White Mountain Scenery " belongs to W. S. G. Baker of Baltimore ; " Mount Madison," to H. W. Robbins ; " Roadside Elms," to Mrs. Attwood of Poughkeepsie ; " Mount Philip, from the Farmington River," to G. D. Phelps of New York ; and " The Freshet," to Mrs. A. R. Phelps of Hartford.

Röber, Ernst. (*Ger.*) Born at Elberfeld, 1849. Pupil of the Düsseldorf Academy and of E. Bendemann. At the National Gallery of Berlin are some of his decorative paintings in the Halle von der Nische.

Röber, Fritz. (*Ger.*) Born at Elberfeld, 1851. Brother and pupil of the preceding. He also painted in the National Gallery at Berlin.

Robert, Léo-Paul. (*Swiss.*) Born at Bienne. Medal in 1877. Pupil of his father and Gérôme. At the Salon of 1877 he exhibited " The Zephyrs of a Beautiful Evening."

Robert-Fleury, Joseph-Nicolas. (*Fr.*) Born at Cologne, of French parents, 1797. Member of the Institute. Commander of the Legion of Honor. He studied in Paris under Girodet, Gros, and Horace Vernet. Visited Italy, and remained there several years. Made his début at the Salon of 1824. At the Luxembourg are his " Conference at Poissy in 1561 " (1840), " Jane Shore " (1850), and the " Pillage of a House in the Jews' Quarter at Venice in the Middle Ages " (1855). " The Entrance of Clovis into Tours " is at Versailles. This painter has been Professor at l'École des Beaux-Arts in Paris and at the Villa Medici at Rome. In 1864 he was a member of the Municipal Council of Paris. The following important works were executed by Robert-Fleury for the decoration of the Audience Hall in the new palace of the Tribunal of Commerce : " The Institution of the Juges consuls, in 1563," " The Promulgation of the Ordinance of Commerce in 1673," " Napoleon receiving the Code of Commerce presented to him by President Vignon in 1807," and " Napoleon III. visiting the New Palace of the Tribunal of Commerce in 1865." Concerning these works Réne Ménard wrote in the " Gazette des Beaux-Arts," February, 1869, a long article, which closes thus : —

" As a whole, these great canvases are an honor to Robert-Fleury, and prove what veritable power there is in that talent which holds its superiority despite the most unfavorable conditions. Robert-Fleury had never attempted works of grand dimensions, and his début is the work of a master ; he had never painted official subjects, and in this difficult and thankless style he takes a first rank. All that is wanting to make his work complete is a greater freedom of inspiration. A man of talent is always master of his execution, because he rules it with all the superiority of his science ; but inspiration demands that it shall not be shackled by restrictions which straiten it. It is only able to soar when it is personal, and has the fundamental laws of art alone for its guide."

At the Pereire sale in Paris, 1872, " Charles V. in the Monastery of St. Just " sold for £1,600. At the Oppenheim sale, Paris, 1877, " The Sack of Rome " sold for 12,700 francs.

Robert-Fleury, Tony. (*Fr.*) Born at Paris. Chevalier of the Legion of Honor. Son of Joseph-Nicolas Robert-Fleury. Pupil of Delaroche and Cogniet. Painter of historical subjects and portraits. In the Luxembourg are his " Les vieilles de la Place Navona, Rome " (1867), and " The Last Day of Corinth " (1870). In 1866 he exhibited " Varsovie, the 8th of April, 1861," and received for it his first medal ; in 1873, " The Danaides " ; in 1874, " Charlotte Corday at Caen, 1793 " ; in 1876, " Pinel, Chief Physician at the Salpêtrière in 1795 " ; in 1877, two portraits.

Roberts, David, R. A. (*Brit.*) Born in Edinburgh (1796 – 1864). He served an apprenticeship of seven years in his native city, as house-painter and decorator, and was engaged for some time as a scene-painter, with a company of strolling players. He received no regular instruction in art. He painted scenes for the theaters of Edinburgh and Glasgow, and for Drury Lane Theater in London in 1822. He exhibited pictures in Scotland, and in several provincial cities of England, sending his first work to the Royal Academy, in 1826, "A View of Rouen Cathedral." In 1838 he was elected an Associate of the Royal Academy, and Academician in 1841. He traveled extensively on the Continent and in the East, painting out of England some of his best-known works, "Jerusalem from the Mount of Olives," "The Church of the Holy Nativity, Bethlehem," "The Gateway of the Great Temple, Baalbec," etc. Later, he studied in Italy, and in his own country, exhibiting at the Royal Academy, in 1860, "Venice, the Piazza of St. Mark's," "A Street in Antwerp," "The Interior of the Cathedral of Pisa," and "The Coliseum, Rome, — Evening"; in 1861 he sent "Ruins of the Temple of the Sun at Baalbec" and "A Fête-Day at St. Peter's"; in 1862, "A Chapel of the Cathedral of Notre Dame, Bruges," and a series of views on the river Thames, from Chelsea to Greenwich, which were continued the following year, and upon which he was at work at the time of his sudden death in 1864. His "Chancel of the Church of St. Paul, Antwerp" (1848) and "The Interior of Burgos Cathedral, North Transept" (1835, belonging to the Vernon Collection) are in the National Gallery, London. His "Crypt, Roslin Castle," "The Gate of Cairo" (1843), and "Old Buildings on the Darro, Granada" are in the Cruikshank Collection. Many of his works have been engraved, and £16,000 was raised by the exhibition and sale of some of his sketches and paintings in 1865. He was an Honorary Member of the Royal Scottish Academy, and of several continental institutions of a similar kind.

"From his early occupation as scene-painter, Roberts borrowed broad effects which saved him alike from trifling minuteness and servile imitation. . . . . His work was uniformly scenic, made up of buildings and street scenes, and, although he knew how to vary and animate these by the introduction of numerous characteristic figures, they were apt to partake of the groupings of stage processions. . . . . But he loved the buildings which he was content to paint, loved every vaulted arch and wreathed pillar, down to the individual atoms of the pavement, and rendered them all with rare fidelity and grace." — Mrs. Tytler's *Modern Painters and Paintings.*

"Among the members of the Academy we have at present only one professedly architectural draughtsman of note, David Roberts, whose reputation is probably further extended on the Continent than that of any other of our artists except Landseer. . . . . The fidelity of intention and honesty of system of Roberts have been, however, always meritorious; his drawing of architecture is dependent on no unintelligible lines, or blots, or substituted types: the main lines of the real design are always there, and its hollowness and undercutting given with exquisite feeling. His sense of solidity of form is peculiar, leading him to dwell with great delight on the roundings of edges and angles; his execution is dexterous and delicate, singularly so, in oil; and his sense of chiaroscuro refined." — Ruskin's *Modern Painters.*

Roberts, Edward J. (*Brit.*) (1797–1865.) An engraver. Pupil and for some years an assistant of Heath in London, doing much fine work in the illustrating of gift-books and elaborate editions of standard authors. His etchings are still highly regarded by critics and connoisseurs. He executed but few large plates.

Roberts, Thomas. (*Brit.*) Born in 1820. Educated as an engraver, he followed that branch of the profession for some time, devoting himself to the brush when about twenty-five years of age. He was made a member of the Society of British Artists in 1855, and has been its secretary for upwards of twenty years. Among his later works are, "The Image of his Father," in 1877 ; and "The Missing Curl," in 1878. To the Philadelphia Exhibition, in 1876, he sent "The Night before Bosworth."

Roberts, Howard. (*Am.*) Born in Philadelphia, 1843. He began his art studies under J. A. Bailly, in the Pennsylvania Academy of Fine Arts. At the age of twenty-three he went to Europe, entering l'École des Beaux-Arts in Paris, and spending some years in that city in study under Dumont and Gumery. Returning to America, he opened a studio in Philadelphia, and modeled his first important work, a statuette of "Hester and Pearl," from the "Scarlet Letter," exhibited at the Academy of Fine Arts, and attracting much attention. This was followed by "Hypatia," "Lucille," and other ideal and portrait busts. He went again to Paris in 1873, remaining a year at work in that city, and modeling there "La Première Pose," which was at the Centennial Exhibition of 1876, receiving a medal. His latest work is a statuette of "Lot's Wife." On the strength of the "Hester and Pearl" he was elected a member of the Philadelphia Academy.

" 'Lot's Wife' is a very singular creation, which could only have been imagined by the artist in a grotesque mood. It cannot be called beautiful, but it is most original in conception and execution ; and in spite of its grotesqueness, it is full of power and impressiveness. . . . . Roberts' busts are charming, those representing childhood and womanhood especially. His ideal busts are the inspirations of a most rare fancy, while his portraits have that inestimable quality in all portraits, of showing their subjects at their best, while losing none of their resemblance." — WILLIAM J. CLARKE, JR., *Great American Sculptors.*

" Roberts is one of the most careful and conscientious of young American sculptors, and one of the best trained. All his works show very careful study and real knowledge, gained by patient endeavor. His ' La Première Pose' was one of the three works of American sculptors to which medals were awarded at the Centennial Exhibition of 1876." — *Art Journal,* April, 1877.

Robie, Jean-Baptiste. (*Belgian.*) Born at Brussels, 1821. He has received medals at Paris and The Hague, and is Chevalier of the Order of Léopold. His fine pictures of flowers and fruits are well known in Europe and America. At the Johnston sale, New York, 1876, "The Massacre of the Innocents " (18 by 24) sold for $ 550. His "Flowers and Objects of Art " is in the collection of Mr. T. R. Butler of New York.

Robinson, John Henry, R. A. (*Brit.*) (1796 - 1871.) Went to

London in his youth, and was articled to James Heath. One of the first of his engravings which attracted attention was "The Wolf and the Lamb," after Mulready. Among other plates are, "Napoleon and Pius VII." (after Wilkie), "Little Red Riding-Hood" (after Landseer), portrait of Sir Walter Scott (after Lawrence),. Vandyck's portrait of Rubens, Murillo's "Spanish Flower-Girl," Leslie's "Mother and Child," and many more. He was elected Associate Engraver of the Royal Academy in 1856, and Academician in 1867.

Robinson, Thomas. (*Am.*) Born in Nova Scotia, 1835. He studied in Paris under Courbet, and received also instructions from August Bonheur, although he was not a regular pupil of the latter artist. He has lived and painted in Providence, R. I., in Boston, and in France. A number of his works were sold in Boston in the spring of 1878. He sent to the Centennial Exhibition of 1876, "A Bull's Head" (belonging to Dr. Angell of Boston), "Dog's Head," "Sheep in Pasture," and "A New England Farmer" (belonging to John Foster of Boston). He painted a portrait group of five dogs (belonging to William Sprague), and his pictures are owned by Amasa Sprague, Mrs. Charles Ames, and others. His "Sprague's String Team," painted for Amasa Sprague, attracted much attention. One of his earlier works, a fruit-piece, is in the possession of Thomas J. Flagg of New York.

Rodakowski, Henri. (*Ger.*) Born at Leopol, 1823. Chevalier of the Legion of Honor. Pupil of Cogniet. Among his works are many portraits, and some historical subjects, such as "Sigismond I. of Poland, conquered by the Seditions of the Nobles and the Intrigues of Queen Bona Sforza, making Proclamation, etc.," "The Battle of Choczim," "Peasants of Gallicia at Church," etc.

Rogers, Randolph. (*Am.*) Born in the State of New York, about 1825. Brought up to mercantile pursuits, but turned his attention to sculpture at an early age, going to Italy for the purpose of study, and remaining for some time in Rome. Returning to America, he opened a studio in New York. Among his earlier works are, "Nydia," "Boy and Dog," and statue of John Adams at Mount Auburn, Mass. In 1858 he designed the doors of the Capitol at Washington, representing the chief events in the career of Columbus, which were cast in bronze at Munich. He finished the Washington Monument at Richmond, Va., which was left uncompleted by Crawford at his death, adding the statues of Mason, Marshall, and Nelson, and many of the allegorical figures for which Crawford made no designs. Since the Civil War he has executed the Memorial Monument erected at Providence, R. I., in 1871, and that in Detroit, Mich., unveiled in 1873. His statue of Lincoln, in Philadelphia, was completed in 1871 ; that of Seward, in New York, in 1876. His "Angel of the Resurrection," on the monument of Colonel Colt in Hartford, Ct., is one of the most satisfactory of his works. Among his ideal heads those of "Isaac" and "Ruth" have been greatly admired. To the Centennial Exhibition of 1876 he sent "Atala," "Ruth," and "Nydia, the Blind Girl of Pompeii" (the last two belonging to James Douglas). His colossal figure of the "Genius of Connecticut" was placed on the new Capitol at Hartford in 1877. His studio is still in Rome ; his professional commissions bring him occasionally to his native country.

"Rogers was commissioned to create doors for the Capitol at Washington. In the light of symbolic portals to a Temple of Freedom, the idea partakes of the sublime ; but the American is too impatient for original inspiration, and has no adequate conception of his opportunity for noble work. Borrowing his general ideas from Ghiberti, he hurriedly elaborates a prosaic historical composition of the ' Discovery of America by Columbus,' clever and interesting as illustration, but far beneath the requirements of creative art or the dignity of the occasion." — JARVES, *Art Idea.*

"The statue representing ' Michigan ' is a warlike figure, moving forward, with shield aloft, and sword drawn back for the thrust. In the girdle which binds the coat of mail appears the Indian tomahawk, and in the hair the Indian ornaments of shells and feathers, indicating the youth of the State, whose lands within the memory of living men were the home of the savage. There is nothing else, however, savage in the representation, which is full of grace and life." — TUCKERMAN's *Book of the Artists.*

"The Seward statue [Madison Square, New York], although open to criticism in a few details, is, as a whole, an excellent piece of work, worthy of its conspicuous position in one of the great centers of the metropolis." — *Art Journal,* September, 1877.

Rogers, John, N. A. (*Am.*) Born at Salem, Mass. As a young man he studied civil engineering, but was compelled to abandon that profession on account of the weakness of his eyes. He entered a machine-shop in Manchester, N. H., where he remained for eight years, modeling in clay during his leisure moments. He visited Europe in 1858, but soon returned to America, and in 1859 executed the first of his small plaster groups, called "The Slave Auction." Quickly following this were "The Picket-Guard," "Taking the Oath," "The Wounded Scout," "One More Shot," and other war subjects, which met with a degree of popular success never equaled in its way in America. He was elected a full member of the National Academy in 1863. In 1869 he sent to the National Academy, "The Fugitive's Story"; in 1870, "The Foundling"; in 1874, "Hide and Seek"; in 1877, "The Mock Trial" and "School Days." To the Paris Exposition of 1867 he sent, in bronze, "One More Shot," "Taking the Oath," and "The Wounded Scout," and twenty-nine groups to the American Centennial Exhibition of 1876, for which he was commended by the judges "for excellence in the fine art of sculpture."

"We now come to a high order of ability ; indeed, we may call it genius, in its peculiar province, as original as it is varied and graphic, pure in sentiment, clever in execution, and thoroughly American, in the best sense of the word, in everything. . . . . We know of no sculptor like John Rogers of New York in the Old World, and he stands alone in his chosen field, heretofore in all ages appropriated by painting ; a genuine production of our soil, enlivening the fancy, enkindling patriotism, and warming the affections by his lovely, well-balanced groups in plaster and bronze. Although discriminative, they possess real elements of greatness. In their execution there is no littleness, artifice, or affectation. The handling is masterly, betraying a knowledge of design and anatomy not common, and a thoroughness of work refreshing to note." — JARVES, *Art Idea.*

Rogers, Frank Whiting. (*Am.*) Born at Cambridge, Mass., 1854. He became a pupil of J. Foxcroft Cole in 1873, and, later, was in the studio of Thomas Robinson of Boston. His specialty is animal-painting. Among the better known of his pictures are, "The Two Friends" (belonging to William F. Morgan of New York), "Resignation" and "Steady!" (belonging to Thomas Wigglesworth of Boston), "Mischief" (belonging to S. L. Brackett, Boston), and "Loo," a portrait of a dog, in possession of Charles Turner of St. Louis. He exhibits in Boston and New York.

"Mr. Rogers has had from the first a good measure of success with his paintings of dogs. He seems to have talent in plenty for this work, and to make the best use of it. His painting of a setter which was hung at the last Art Club Exhibition was much admired and judiciously praised, for it appeared to be somewhat of a surprise to the public from so young an artist. . . . . There are not many dog-painters in this country, and there are none known to us in Boston, who devote themselves as Mr. Rogers does to this subject. He attempts a great deal, and succeeds better than any one would reasonably expect of him." — *Boston Advertiser.*

Rolfe, H. L. (*Brit.*) A well-known fish-painter, of the English school, exhibiting frequently for many years, in London and the Provinces, works in his peculiar line, which are very popular. He sent to the gallery of the Society of British Artists in 1877, "On a Visit to the Upper Proprietors"; in 1878, "The Last Struggle."

"'Perch, Roach, and Dace' [by H. L. Rolfe, R. A., 1873] exhibits really the perfection of fish-painting. Indeed, this artist paints river fish as they never before appeared on canvas, — an enviable immortality, which must certainly reconcile them to the hook!" — *Art Journal,* June, 1878.

Roll, Alfred-Philippe. (*Fr.*) Born at Paris. Medals in 1875 and '77. Pupil of Gérôme and Bonnat. At the Salon of 1877 he exhibited "The Inundation in the Suburbs of Toulouse in June, 1875"; in 1876, "The Huntress" and a portrait; in 1875, "Halte-là!"; in 1873, "A Bacchante"; in 1872, "A Wounded Fugitive"; in 1870, "The Environs of Baccarat" and "Evening."

"His inundated ones are not models. They do not pose themselves, nor regard them public. They live, each one his own life, all brought into the powerful unity of action. The groups are well arranged, the faces varied; all are understood. The action is just; the nude is well treated, well modeled; and the anatomy observed. That of the boy who holds his mother, half fallen over, by the middle of the body, is a bit of masterwork. The water is muddy, — it surges. The values are exact, the color vigorous, the perspective vast. Roll, in fine, copies not nature photographically, in the fashion of the skillful ones of to-day, corrupting the public, and corrupted by it. He interprets nature, and grandly, because his art is grand. The place we gave him a year ago among the débutants he has kept. It is the first." — MARIO PROTH, *Voyage au Pays des Peintres,* 1877.

Romanelli, P. (*Ital.*) Professor at Florence. Pupil of Bartolini. Among his principal works are, "Monumental Statue of Count Fossombroni," "A Boy Bacchus treading the Grapes," "The Betrayed," "William Tell's Son" (executed in marble for Mr. Vanderbilt of New

York), a fine portrait bust of Bartolini, "The Genius of Italy," "The Nymph of the Arno," etc. To the Paris Exposition of 1878 he contributed a statue in marble, " The Rose of Sharon."

Romberg, Arthur Georg. (*Ger.*) Born at Vienna (1819 – 1875). Professor of Painting at Munich. Member of the Academy of Berlin. Studied at the Academy of Dresden and under Hübner. Went to Munich in 1850, where he soon became distinguished as a *genre* painter. His drawing is correct, and his personages all have marked characteristics. He usually combines some mirth with his representations. Among his pictures are, " Peasant-Women of Dachau on Sunday," " The Bouquet," " The Walk with the Hofmeister," " Hiding," and " After the Masked Ball." In 1860 he went to Weimar, and there executed his " History of Civilization " for the Maximilaneum at Munich. His designs for the Schiller and Goethe Galleries added to his fame. In connection with Pauwels he executed frescos at the Wartburg in the part where Luther had lived. In 1865 he removed to Munich, where, in 1870, he exhibited " Frederick II. holding Court in Palermo."

Ronner, Mme. Henriette. (*Dutch.*) Born at Amsterdam. Member of the Academy of Rotterdam. She has resided more than twenty years in Brussels, and has gained many medals in her own country and in others. She paints principally subjects in which domestic animals are introduced. At the Glasgow Fine Art Loan Exhibition in 1878 was her " Boy and Dog," loaned by J. Stevenson. " Exterior of a house. The door is open, but guarded by a big, surly red and white dog. A boy in a blue overall, and with a basket on his arm, hesitates to enter from fear of the dog."

Ronot, Charles. (*Fr.*) Born at Belan-sur-Ource. Pupil of A. Glaize. Medals in 1876 and '78, when he exhibited " The Charities of St. Elizabeth of Hungary "; in 1877, " The Anger of the Pharisees "; in 1876, " The Workmen of the Last Hour."

Roqueplan, Joseph-Étienne-Camille. (*Fr.*) Born at Malemort (1802 – 1855). Officer of the Legion of Honor. Pupil of Gros and of Abel de Pujol. This artist belonged to the romantic school. His pictures are landscapes and *genre* subjects. He also painted battlepieces for the Gallery at Versailles, and decorated several ceilings for the palace of the Luxembourg.

Rosales, Édouard. (*Span.*) Died at Rome, 1873. Chevalier of the Legion of Honor. Corresponding Member of the Institute. Director of the Spanish Academie des Beaux-Arts. The picture of " Isabella the Catholic dictating her Will " was the most important Spanish picture at the Paris Exposition of 1867. After the death of Rosales, " The Death of Lucretia," another grand work, was exhibited in Paris. Larousse says of this : —

" In a subject so often repeated, and which may be well made emphatic and melodramatic, the Spanish artist has understood how to be original and simple, to unite the nobility and pathos of tragedy with the gravity of history ; his figures have an antique character inspired by study of celebrated masters, and the costumes are arranged with science and taste. A rich and vigorous color adds to the merits of this work ; the light, largely concentrated on one arm of Lucretia, and on the face of the old Lucretius, has great brilliancy, and makes a somewhat violent contrast with the shadows in the work."

Rosen, George, Count von. (*Swede.*) Professor of the Royal Academy of Stockholm. At Philadelphia he exhibited " A Portrait " and received a medal. To the Paris Exposition of 1878 he contributed " The Flower-Market " and a portrait of a painter.

Rosenthal, Toby E. (*Am.*) Born in Hessen, Germany, and taken to America as an infant. He began the study of art in the public schools of San Francisco, taking lessons there also from a Spanish painter, under whom he made rapid progress. At the age of seventeen he went to Munich, and entered the Royal Academy, remaining two years in that institution, and spending three years longer in Munich as a private pupil of Professor Raupp. Again entering the Academy, he remained about seven years under Piloty, painting, during that time, " Morning Prayers in the Family of Bach " (purchased by the city of Leipsic, and now in the museum there). Among his works may be mentioned, " Elaine " (at the Philadelphia Exhibition in 1876), " Love's Last Offering," and a study of the head of Mrs. Greatorex, painted in Munich in 1871, and exhibited at the National Academy in New York in 1875. Very few of his works have been exhibited in America.

"Toby Rosenthal's ' Elaine ' in illustration of Tennyson's lines, ' And the dead, steered by the dumb, went upward with the flood,' attracted great attention in Boston when it was recently exhibited there. The critics all concede that the picture is well painted, and embodies great dramatic force, but the wisdom of choosing so sad a subject is doubtful." — *Art Journal*, April, 1875.

" Mr. Rosenthal's picture of the ' Young Monk ' in the refectory of a convent was one of the most poetic in sentiment to be found in the whole Exhibition. It is pure and delicate in feeling, and skillfully painted." — Prof. Weir's *Official Report of the American Centennial Exhibition of* 1876.

Rosier, Amedée. (*Fr.*) Born at Meaux. Medal at Paris in 1876, and at Philadelphia the same year. Pupil of Cogniet and Durand-Brager. At Philadelphia he exhibited " Evening in the Harbor of Venice " and " Morning on the Lagoons of Venice " ; at Paris, in 1877, " On the Lagoons of Venice, — Setting Sun " and " The Canal of St. Mark's, Venice." " A Landscape " by this artist is in the collection of Mrs. H. E. Maynard of Boston. To the Salon of 1878 he sent two Venetian views.

Ross, Sir William, R. A. (*Brit.*) (1794 – 1860.) Displayed remarkable talents as a child, painting portraits before he reached his teens, and winning many valuable medals and prizes for his work in London and the Provinces, while still a lad. He entered the Royal Academy in 1805, when only ten years of age, exhibiting regularly at its gallery after that period for many years. He was elected an Associate of the Royal Academy in 1838, and Academician in 1839. He executed several important figure-pieces of a scriptural and historical character, but his specialty was portraiture in miniature, in which branch of art he was wonderfully successful, no artist of the English school of any century ranking higher. He numbered among his sitters the Queen and Prince Consort of England, with many members of English royal and aristocratic families, Louis Philippe, Louis Napoleon, Léopold of Belgium and his family, etc. He was knighted by Queen Victoria in 1839.

Ross, Robert Thorburn. (*Brit.*) Born in Edinburgh, 1816. Student of the Trustees Academy for three years, when he opened a studio in Glasgow, painting portraits for some time. In 1842 he went to Bewick, remaining for ten years, and for the first time turning his attention to ideal subjects, contributing to the Royal Scottish Academy, in 1845, "The Spinning-Wheel." In 1852, when he was elected an Associate of that Academy, he removed to Edinburgh. He was made an Academician in 1869. Among his works, many of which have been engraved, are, "The Dead Robin," "The Mote in the Eye," "Hide and Seek," "The Thorn in the Foot," "The Dancing-Lesson," "The Broken Pitcher," "Leaving Home," "Highland Pets," "Asleep," and "The Highland Shepherd's Fireside."

" This artist [Ross] has evidently studied Scottish life in the cottage, on the sea-coast, and by the river-side. His pictures are all of this class of subject, which he renders with fidelity, and under most attractive aspects. He is an excellent colorist, and shows true feeling for the picturesque, both in his figures and their surroundings, whether in or out of doors." — *Art Journal*, 1871.

Ross, Alfred. (*Fr.*) Born at Tillières-sur-Arve. Pupil of Jonffroy. Exhibited at Philadelphia a statue (in bronze) of " A Bohemian at the Spring," and received a medal.

Rosseels, Jacques. (*Belgian.*) Of Antwerp. Medal at Philadelphia, where he exhibited "A Mill on the Scheldt."

Rossetti, Dante Gabriel. (*Brit.*) Born in 1828. Educated at King's College, London, contributing illustrations as a young man for a fine edition of Tennyson's poems. His "Girlhood of the Virgin," exhibited in London in 1849, first attracted attention to him as an artist in colors ; it appeared simultaneously with Millais' "Isabella" and Holman Hunt's "Rienzi," and introduced with them what is known as the pre-Raphaelite school to England. To the Liverpool Academy, in 1856, he sent three pictures in water-color, "The Wedding of St. George," "Dante's Dream on the Death of Beatrice," and "A Christmas Carol." To the Royal Scottish Academy, in 1860, he contributed "Fair Rosamond." Of late years his pictures have not been shown to the public. He is better known as a writer than as an artist. His "Early Italian Poets," translations from Dante and others, was published in London in 1861 ; a revised edition, called "Dante and his Circle," appearing in 1874. He also gave to the world a volume of original "Poems" in 1870.

"As a figure-painter his drawings, such as I have seen, are far above the strictly real-istic work produced by acolytes of his order . . . . Rossetti, a man of genius, has lighted his canvas and his pages with a quality that is ennobling." — STEDMAN's *Victorian Poets.*

"D. G. Rossetti was the founder and for some years the vital force of the pre-Raphael-ite school. ' He was the first assertor in painting, as I believe I was myself in art liter-ature (Goldsmith and Molière having given the first general statements of it), of the great distinctive principle of that school that things should be painted as they probably did look and happen, and not as by rules of art developed under Raphael, Correggio, and Mi-chael Angelo they might be supposed gracefully, deliciously, or sublimely to have hap-pened." — RUSKIN's *Notes of the Academy,* 1875.

"There are few more intense and perfect poems in the English tongue than the ' Blessed Damozel,' by Dante Gabriel Rossetti, and there must be thousands of persons who feel something more than mere curiosity to see the picture, founded on the poem and bear-ing its name, painted by the poet himself for Mr. William Graham. An opportunity to do so is not, however, likely to occur, at least for some years : and all but a favored few must be content to know it by inadequate verbal description. The damozel is leaning ' from the gold bar of heaven,' surrounded by groups of happy reunited lovers. Below is a predella just added by the artist ; the bereaved lover stands amid the fall of leaves with his eyes fixed on heaven. The cerulean, rose, and delicate green tints of the upper can-vas are brought out into beautiful contrast by the autumnal tints and the black grays of the predella. Mr. Rossetti has more than one new work in hand." — *Magazine of Art,* June, 1878.

Rossiter, Thomas P., N. A. (*Am.*) Born at New Haven, Ct. (1818 – 1871). He studied in his native city, and in 1838 began the practice of his profession there as a portrait-painter. In 1840 he vis-ited Europe, studying in London for six months, and in Paris for a year. In 1841 he settled in Rome, remaining five years, spending his summers in sketching-tours in Germany, Switzerland, and Italy. In 1846 he opened a studio in New York, painting an occasional portrait, but devoting himself chiefly to the illustration of scriptural and his-torical subjects. In 1853 he returned to Europe, remaining in Paris until 1856. Spending a few years in New York, he removed in 1860 to Cold Spring, on the Hudson. He was elected an Associate of the National Academy in 1840, and Academician in 1849. Among his works, some of which have been engraved, are, " The Last Hours of Tasso," " Puritans reading the Bible," " Miriam," " The Ascension," " Return of the Dove to the Ark," " The Wise and Foolish Virgins," "Noah," " Italy in the Olden Times," "Home of Washington," " Washington in his Library," " Washington's First Cabinet," " Prince of Wales at the Tomb of Washington," " Palmy Days at Mount Ver-non," " Representative Merchants," etc.

Rossiter, Charles. (*Brit.*) Born in 1827. A pupil of Mr. Leigh's school, in Newman street, London, he did not turn his attention to art as a profession until about 1850, making his specialty small *genre* pictures. For a quarter of a century he has exhibited at the Royal Academy and the Gallery of the Society of British Artists. Among his earlier works, which were very popular with all classes of people, were, " The Song of the Shirt," " The Protector," " Puritan Purifiers," " The Return of Olivia," etc. He sent to the Royal Academy, in

1866, " The First Lesson " ; in 1867, " The Little Singer " ; in 1868, " Il Penseroso " ; in 1870, " A Gleam of Hope " ; in 1871, " Memories of the Past " ; in 1872, " The Necklace " ; in 1875, " Rival Anglers " ; and in 1877, " Rough Weather."

Rossiter, Mrs. Charles, wife of the foregoing, exhibited for some years attractive pictures of birds at the Royal Academy, but her name has not been seen in its catalogues since 1873.

Roth, Christian. (*Ger.*) Professor at Munich. This sculptor has studied anatomy with great thoroughness, and he has done much to enable the students of sculpture about him to pursue this necessary branch. Among his works are a fountain at Munich representing a " Faun with the Mask of Jupiter." His " Kampf um das Frühstück " (now belonging to Duke Charles Theodore of Bavaria) gained a prize. It represents a boy and goose struggling over a piece of bread. Roth's best works are those above the *genre* subjects. His perfect knowledge of the human form should be employed in monumental sculpture. His " Wacht am Rhein " is a work of strength, but not of high art. His colossal bust of the late Prince Charles of Bavaria, for the park of the castle of Tergernsee, is without doubt his master-work in portraiture, and perhaps the verdict of years will make his portrait busts his *chefs-d'œuvre.*

Rothermel, Peter F. (*Am.*) Born in the State of Pennsylvania in 1817. He was brought up as a surveyor, and did not devote himself to the study of art until he was twenty-one years of age. In 1840 he began the active practice of his profession by the painting of portraits. In 1856 he went to Europe, spending some time in the art centers of the Continent, painting his first historical picture, and later making that class of subjects a specialty. Among the better known of his works are " St. Agnes " (painted in 1858, and now in Russia), " The Foscari," " Patrick Henry before the Virginia House of Burgesses," " Cromwell breaking up the Service in an English Church," " Columbus before Isabella," " De Soto discovering the Mississippi," " St. Paul on Mars Hill," " The Battle of Gettysburg " (in the Capitol at Harrisburg, Pa.), " Christian Martyrs in the Coliseum," and others, many of which have been engraved. To the Centennial Exhibition at Philadelphia, in 1876, he sent " The Battle of Gettysburg," " Amy Robsart interceding for Leicester," " The Trial of Sir Henry Vane " (belonging to J. L. Claghorn), " Macbeth meditating the Murder of Duncan " (belonging to Thomas Dolan), " Hypatia stripped and torn to Pieces by the Christian Mob of Alexandria," " The Landsknecht " (belonging to Matthew Baird), and " The Christian Martyrs." He was " commended for excellence in historical painting."

" With unequal power, but frequent fidelity to the conventional requirements of his historical painting, Rothermel's career, in view of the department he illustrates, has been remarkably prosperous. The pictures he has exhibited abroad have gained him honorable mention, though confessedly unfinished." — TUCKERMAN'S *Book of the Artists.*

Rousseau, Philippe. (*Fr.*) Born at Paris about 1808. Officer of the Legion of Honor. Pupil of Gros and Victor Bertin. At first Rousseau painted landscapes, and made his début in 1831. Since his earlier works he has painted numerous subjects which may be termed animal *genre.* They are very much admired. "The Importunate" (1850), "Storks taking a Siesta," and "A Kid feeding on Flowers" (1855) are in the Luxembourg. In 1866, "The Monkey Photograph" and "Flowers," remarkable works, were purchased by the Princess Mathilde. In 1877 he exhibited "The Breakfast" and "O ma tendre musette!"; in 1876, "Oysters" and "Poppies"; in 1875, "The Wolf and the Lamb" and "Cheeses"; in 1874, "La Fête-Dieu" and "The Salad"; in 1872, "The Sweetmeats" and "Springtime"; in 1870, "The Flowery Fountain" and "The First Plums and the Last Cherries," etc.

"M. Philippe Rousseau is not only a man of genius, he is also, unfortunately, a seeker of genius. Curiosity and surprise make a portion of the interest which his works inspire. One sometimes studies them as the subscribers to 'L'Illustration' meditate upon the rebus. Animals are wise little personages to Rousseau ; each of his frames resembles an outlandish theater in which the beasts play a comedy. . . . . I recognize with the public the originality and the attraction of his works, but I am not able to approve of all the talent which he expends in order to lower painting to the level of the vignette." — EDMOND ABOUT, *Nos Artistes au Salon de* 1857.

Rousseau, Théodore. (*Fr.*) Born at Paris (1812–1867). Chevalier of the Legion of Honor. Pupil of Guillou-Lethière. A landscape-painter. Made his début in 1834. In 1867 he exhibited "A View of Mont Blanc" and "The Interior of a Forest"; in 1866, "Sunset, Forest of Fontainebleau," and "Boundaries of the Forest of Fontainebleau at Barbison"; in 1864, "A Village,—Cottages under the Trees"; in 1863, "A Pool beneath some Oaks"; etc. At the Hôtel Pereire in Paris there is an exquisite landscape by Théodore Rousseau which was purchased at the Demidoff sale for 3,250 francs. At the Strousberg sale, Paris, 1874, "A Fisherman" sold for £832. At the Laurent-Richard sale, Paris, 1873, "Watercourse at Sologne" sold for £1,600; "Hoar-Frost," £2,404.

"This artist, in truth, has varied prodigiously, and his work sometimes shows us vivid impressions expressed with rare happiness, but the execution will not bear the attentive examination of amateurs who seek to analyze it and judge it in detail : at other times he executes pictures treated with scrupulous care, but which have not as a whole the charm and the unaffected simplicity which artists admire in the first." — RENÉ MÉNARD, *Gazette des Beaux-Arts,* March, 1873.

"Théodore Rousseau has been for twenty-five years the first apostle of truth in landscape. He made a breach in the wall of the historic school, which had lost the habit of regarding nature, and servilely copied the bad copyists of Poussin. This audacious innovator opened an enormous door by which many others have followed him. He emancipated the landscape-painters as Moses formerly liberated the Hebrews, 'in exitu Israel de Ægypto.' He led them into a land of promise, where the trees had leaves, where the rivers were liquid, where the men and the animals were not of wood. On the return of this truant school the young landscapists forced the entrance of the Salon, and it was still Théodore Rousseau who broke down the door. In that time Rousseau occupied the first rank in landscape, above all as a colorist ; but neither the Institute nor the public wished to confess it. His incontestable talent was contested by all the world. It is only to-day that his reputation is made. He can become remiss with impunity without its being seen, etc." — EDMOND ABOUT, *Nos Artistes au Salon de* 1857.

Rowbotham, Thomas L. *(Brit.)* (1823–1875.) Active member of the Institute of Painters in Water-Colors, painting landscapes with skill and taste. His works were pleasing and popular ; among them may be mentioned, "The Sacred City of Benares on the Ganges," "Mill in Surrey," "On the Thames, — Evening," "A Winter Sunset," "The Impérieuse, — Breaking up at Woolwich in 1867," "Castellamare, Bay of Naples," and "Sisteron, South of France."

Rowse, Samuel W. *(Am.)* A native of the State of Maine. Recently this artist has spent some time in New York, but the greater part of his professional life has been passed in Boston. He devotes himself particularly to drawing in black and white. His work is seldom publicly exhibited, although he has been for some years one of the most successful of American artists. Photographs of his lighter works, chiefly ideal pictures of children in crayon, have been very common throughout the United States. While in the sun copies justice has not been done to the originals, each one, no matter how slight and sketchy, has something of the peculiar charm of manner which in his drawing of children is irresistible. One well-known connoisseur writes : —

"The apparent simplicity and real subtlety of Rowse's portraits of children is beyond analysis. They constantly remind one of Sir Joshua ; but Sir Joshua in only a few instances attained such completeness, such unity in purpose and in execution, as is shown by Rowse. Herein his work possesses a quality seldom reached in modern art, — that of harmony. Whatever he undertakes, the result is a *picture.* It is not an effort, a fragment, not the exhibition of some school or method ; it is a whole, and it is beautiful."

While Mr. Rowse has had few pupils, in the ordinary sense of the term, he has had many followers, disciples, and imitators, and has had a decided and beneficial influence upon his peculiar branch of art. Among the many illustrious men whose portraits he has drawn in crayon, have been James Russell Lowell, R. W. Emerson (belonging to Charles E. Norton), and Hawthorne (the property of James T. Fields). Recently he has given more attention to painting in oil, and devoted the year 1877 (in New York) to the producing of portraits in that medium. His "Head of a Child" (belonging to Morris K. Jessup) was at the Loan Exhibition of the Society of Decorative Art at the National Academy in 1877.

"Rowse is one of the most delicate and true crayon limners in this country ; some of his heads are unsurpassed for fine feeling and exquisite drawing." — TUCKERMAN's *Book of the Artists.*

"'Even in England,' writes Mrs. Elizabeth Murray to a London art journal, 'there are none to compare with Rowse in crayon portraits, for refinement and beauty in idealizing a portrait, while the likeness is wonderful in its identity.'"— *Boston Advertiser,* May 23, 1868.

Rubio, Louis. *(Ital.)* Born at Rome in 1797. After studying in Italy he passed some time at Paris under Cogniet. He finally settled in Geneva. He gained several medals at Paris and Rome, and was made member of the Academy of St. Luke. His works are seen occasionally in public galleries.

Rudder, Louis-Henri de. (*Fr.*) Born at Paris, 1807. Chevalier of the Legion of Honor. Pupil of Gros and Charlet. Many of his pictures are of historical and religious subjects. At the Luxembourg is " Nicolas Flamel, an Alchemist of the Fifteenth Century." Rudder painted considerably in water-colors. At the Salon of 1878 he exhibited " Ecce Homo " and a " View on the Banks of the Douet at Benzeval (Calvados)."

Ruskin, John. (*Brit.*) Born in London, 1819. He graduated at the University of Oxford, and gained the Newdigate Prize for Poetry in 1839. Later, he studied art under Fielding and J. D. Harding, attaining no ordinary proficiency as a draughtsman, but never becoming a professional artist. Ruskin is known, however, throughout the English-speaking world as an art critic, and a brilliant and prolific, as well as original, writer upon art subjects. Not always temperate in his strictures upon existing art and contemporary artists, he has frequently been the subject of severe criticism from rival critics ; but, unquestionably, no work of its kind has been more widely read than Ruskin's " Modern Painters," and to no single work and to no single author does the world of art owe so much. An ardent and enthusiastic admirer of Turner, Ruskin's first literary effort was a small pamphlet, the avowed object of which was the defence of that artist. It was subsequently enlarged, and was published in 1843 as the first volume of " Modern Painters: by a Graduate of Oxford." It attracted much attention in England. The second volume, to which the author's name was not attached, appeared in 1846; the third volume was not published until some ten years later; the fourth, and perhaps the ablest, followed more quickly; and the fifth and last was given to the public in 1860. During the irregular and desultory appearance of this work Mr. Ruskin's pen was by no means idle. He published " The Seven Lamps of Architecture," in 1849 ; the first volume of " The Stones of Venice," in 1851; " Lectures on Architecture and Painting," in 1854; " Giotto and his Works in Padua," in 1855; " Notes on the Turner Collection," in 1859; etc. Besides these, he is the author of many other volumes, and has written interesting and valuable " Notes on the Pictures of the Royal Academy," for several seasons (the last in 1875), and has contributed articles to the London Times, Art Journal, Quarterly Review, Cornhill Magazine, and other periodicals. In 1867 Mr. Ruskin was appointed Rede Lecturer at Cambridge, and in 1869, Slade Professor of Fine Arts at Oxford. In 1871 he endowed the Taylor Gallery at Oxford with £5,000 for the maintenance of a Master of Drawing, and he has generally spent the greater part of his private fortune in other schemes for art education and the public good. Mr. Ruskin has furnished illustrations for " The Stones of Venice," and for the later volumes of " Modern Painters." His original drawings are rarely seen by the public. In 1878, however, was exhibited in London one hundred and twenty-six drawings by Turner, together with nearly eighty sketches, drawings, and photographs executed or collected by Ruskin. Of these F. R. Conder wrote, in the October number of the Art Journal of that year, as follows : —

"The collection under review gives a rare proof of the possession by Ruskin of an indispensable qualification for the thorough judge of art, namely, the hand to create, as well as the eye to see. It may not be true that none but a painter can truly be a judge of painting. It may even be urged that a painter is not the most reliable judge or critic of the works of his brothers of the pencil. But we think that it must be admitted that none but an artist in some field or branch of art can be a thorough judge of art in any of its branches. The education of the hand is needed in order to give a reflected power and accuracy to the education of the eye. There is an unfinished pencil sketch of an ' Outline from the Fresco of the Sacrifice of Job in the Campo Santo of Pisa,' from the hand of Mr. Ruskin, which might have been placed without discredit in the exquisite collection of drawings by old masters exhibited last autumn in the Grosvenor Gallery. In refined delicacy and graceful truth of touch, combined with depth and tender sense of feeling, it almost leads us to echo the half-suppressed sigh of the draughtsman, ' Had I been able to keep myself clear of literature ! ' Some of the architectural sketches give a feeling of Gothic tracery akin to that which must have been possessed by the great artists of our cathedrals."

If the world is not familiar with the work of Mr. Ruskin's pencil, the work of his pen has made him a power wherever art is known. Of his " Stones of Venice," Charlotte Brontë wrote to Mrs. Gaskell in 1851 : —

"'The Stones of Venice' seem nobly laid and chiseled. How grandly the quarry of vast marbles is disclosed ! Mr. Ruskin seems to me one of the few genuine writers, as distinguished from book-makers, of this age. His earnestness even amuses me in some passages, for I cannot help laughing to think how utilitarians will fume and fret over his deep, serious (and as they will think), fanatical reverence for art. That pure and severe mind you ascribe to him speaks in every line. He writes like a consecrated priest of the Abstract and Ideal."

" This book [' Modern Painters'] contains more true philosophy, more information of a strictly scientific kind, more original thought and exact observation of nature, more enlightened and serious enthusiasm, and more eloquent writing than it would be easy to match, not merely in works of its own class, but in those of any class whatever. It gives us a new, and, we think, the only true theory of beauty and sublimity : it asserts and proves the existence of a new element in landscape-painting, placing its prince upon his rightful throne ; it unfolds and illustrates, with singular force, variety, and beauty, the laws of art ; it explains and enforces the true nature and specific functions of the imagination with the precision and fullness of one having authority, — and all this is delivered in language which, for purity and strength and native richness, would not have dishonored the early manhood of Jeremy Taylor, of Edmund Burke, or of the author's own favorite Richard Hooker." — DR. JOHN BROWN, *in North British Review.*

" There is one man among us who has done more to breathe the breath of life into the literature and the philosophy of art, who has encouraged it ten thousand times more effectually than all our industrious Coles and anxious Art Unions, and that is the author of ' Modern Painters.' I do not know that there is anything in our literature, or in any literature, to compare with the effect of this one man's writings. He has, by his sheer force of mind and fervor of nature, the depth and exactness of his knowledge, and the amazing beauty and power of language, raised the subject of art from being subordinate and technical, to the same level with poetry and philosophy. He has lived to see an entire change in the public mind and eye, and, what is better, in the public heart, on all that pertains to the literature and philosophy of representative genius. He combines its body and its soul. Many before him wrote about its body, and some well ; a few, as Charles Lamb and our own 'Titmarsh,' touched its soul ; it was left to John Ruskin to do both." — *Notes on Art in Horæ Subsecivæ.*

"Unquestionably one of the most remarkable men of this or any age is Mr. Ruskin. He is, if you like, not seldom dogmatic, self-contradictory, conceited, arrogant, absurd, but he is a great and wonderful writer, he has created a new literature, the literature of art." — *Fraser's Magazine.*

"Yet in his book ['Modern Painters'] there was a bold originality, an uncompromising independence, quite startling to the lovers of the old beaten track, the devotees to precedent. The daring champion of Turner, not content with asserting the painter's claims to universal admiration, announced, somewhat authoritatively, certain principles of art neither derived from Alison or the Royal Academy. . . . . Indefatigable in the pursuit of that branch of art, which is all his loving is *the* love, Mr. Ruskin has lately written a book for young persons, entitled ' The Elements of Drawing, in Three Letters to Beginners.' He always writes *con amore,* but never more so than in this valuable little treatise. Mr. Ruskin is not only a practical artist, but he has also had much experience in teaching, being employed at present as head-teacher of a class in drawing in the Working-Men's College, 45 Great Ormond street, London." — *Introduction to* MRS. TUTHILL'S *Beauties of Ruskin,* 1865.

"A man has arisen among them [British artists] to justify and elevate their practice into theory, namely, John Ruskin, an admirer and friend of Turner ; an earnest, impassioned, and original writer, perfectly competent, very studious, very popular, and possessing a thoroughly English intellect. Nothing is more precious than personal, independent, and well-ordered impressions. Especially when, like his, they are boldly expressed, they lead us to reconsider our own. There is no one to whom Ruskin's works, such as ' Modern Painters ' and ' The Stones of Venice,' fail to suggest subjects for thought. His first principle is that the literal truth and the characteristic detail must be loved with enthusiasm." — TAINE'S *Notes on England.*

Sain, Edouard-Alexandre. (*Fr.*) Born at Cluny. Medals at Paris in 1866 and '75, and at Philadelphia in 1876. Pupil of Picot. At Philadelphia was exhibited an " Italian Girl " by this painter (owned by Theodore Lyman of Boston), " A Family Scene in the Pyrenees " (medal), and " The Convalescent." At the Salon of 1877 he exhibited " Andromeda " and a portrait of T. Lambrecht. At the Luxembourg is his " Excavations at Pompeii " (1866).

Saint-Gaudens, Augustus. (*Am.*) Born in New York. He began his professional career as a cameo-cutter in his native city, and upon the proceeds of the sales of his work in that branch of art he went to Paris, where he spent some years modeling and drawing in the Academy, and the School of Medicine, gaining a medal in the latter institution. He also studied sculpture in Rome. Among his works are a statue of " Hiawatha " (belonging to E. D. Morgan of New York), a statue of Farragut for the city of New York (now in course of execution), and busts of President Woolsey of Yale, William M. Evarts, etc. He executed the bas-reliefs in St. Thomas Church, New York, and assisted La Farge in the decoration of Trinity Church, Boston. He is the Vice-President of the Society of American Artists.

Saintin, Jules Émile. (*Fr.*) Born at Leïné. Chevalier of the Legion of Honor. Medals in 1866 and '70. Pupil of Drölling, Picot, and Leboucher. At the Salon of 1877 he exhibited "The First Engagement" and "Self-Satisfied"; in 1876, "The Last Ornament" and "The Thoughtless Soubrette." One of his pictures, called "The Tomb without Flowers," represents a young woman standing on the shore and gazing out at the sea. To the Salon of 1878 he sent "Jeanne" and "Will he return?"

Saint-Jean, Simon. (*Fr.*) Born at Lyons (1812 – 1860). Chevalier of the Legion of Honor. Pupil of François Lepage. This painter was made famous by his pictures of flowers, fruits, birds, etc. He has sometimes painted in water-colors. At the Johnston sale, New York, 1876, "A Fruit-Piece" (19 by 26) sold for $ 1,350; and at the Latham sale, New York, 1878, "Fruit and Flowers" (32 by 24) sold for $ 1,400. At the Corcoran Gallery, Washington, is a picture of "Fruit" (1855).

Salentin, Hubert. (*Ger.*) Born at Zülpich, 1822. Medals at Vienna and Besançon. Commenced his studies late in life at the Academy of Düsseldorf. *Genre* painter. His scenery is well done and he has a pleasing manner. At the National Gallery at Berlin is his "Pilgrim at the Chapel." In Berlin, in 1876, he exhibited "The Praying Maiden," "Hol'über," and "The Return from the Wood." His "Foundling" belongs to Mr. S. D. Warren of Boston.

Salmson, Hugo. (*Swede.*) Born at Stockholm. Pupil of the Academy of his native city, and of Comte of Paris, where, at the Salon of 1878, he received honorable mention. This artist paints *genre* subjects. At the Paris Salon of 1875 he exhibited "The Little Swedish Girl." The child, dressed in the peculiar costume and cap of her country, holds a pigeon in her arms, while the flock are on the ground beside her; the background is good, and well expresses the character of Swedish scenery. In the Corcoran Gallery at Washington is the "Fête of St. John in Dalecarlia." This picture was in the Salon of 1874, and selected by the Ministry of Beaux-Arts for purchase; but as their appropriation was insufficient, it was secured for the Corcoran Gallery.

Salter, William. (*Brit.*) Born in Devonshire (1804 – 1875). Went to London in 1822, studying under Northcote for five years. In 1827 he went to Florence, where he painted his "Socrates before the Court of Areopagos," a picture that at once established his reputation as an artist, and led to his being elected a member of the Academy of Fine Arts, and Professor of the First Class of History in Florence. He went to Rome in 1832, studying there and in Parma, returning to London the next year. For over a quarter of a century he was a prominent member, and for some time Vice-President, of the Society of British Artists. Among his works (many of which have been engraved) are, "The Annual Banquet given by the Duke of Wellington at Apsley House to the Veterans of Waterloo "; " Jephthah's Rash Vow " ; " Interview of Charles I. with his Children in the Presence of Cromwell " (1863) ; " Queen Elizabeth reproving Dean Noel, in the Vestry of St. Paul's " (1865) ; " Desdemona and Othello before the Senate " (1869) ; " The Last Sacrament " (1874) ; " The Merchant of Venice " ; etc.

"Salter's best works are his portraits, both male and female. These are numerous, and as a rule show brilliant and harmonious coloring." — *Art Journal*, March, 1876.

Sand, Maurice, real name, **Dudevant.** (*Fr.*) Born at Paris, about 1825. Chevalier of the Legion of Honor. Son of Mme. Dudevant, (George Sand). This artist has also a name as a man of letters. His pictures are of such subjects as, " Muleteers," "A Market at Pompeii," " Leander and Isabella," etc.

Sanderson, Charles Wesley. (*Am.*) Born at Brandon, Vt., 1838. A music-teacher by profession, Mr. Sanderson has from boyhood prac- ticed and studied drawing and painting. His first teacher was James Hope, a Scotchman who settled in Vermont. Later, he studied oil- painting under S. L. Gerry. In Paris he practiced drawing from life in the atelier of Julien, where he took two prizes and was admitted to l'École des Beaux-Arts for excellence in drawing from the nude. He afterwards gave some attention to water-color painting in England, and has continued the practice of this art. Of late his pictures have attracted attention, and several of them have been sold for good prices. Among them are, " Lana Cascade, near Lake Dunmore, Vermont " (purchased by Mr. Turner of Brooklyn), " The Afterglow, Wetter- horn " (Mrs. S. D. Warren of Boston), " Otter Creek Meadows, Ver- mont " (Mr. Wright of Boston), etc.

" In the same gallery there is a water-color by Mr. C. W. Sanderson, whose paintings should be more frequently exhibited. The painting is a study of the ' Lana Cascade,' near Lake Dunmore, Vt., and is in most respects an excellent picture. There is noth- ing at all conventional about it, and one can easily see that the artist has attempted to make an accurate, careful, and truthful interpretation of the scene before him. The handling of the colors is a clear indication that the artist has skill in manipulating the brush, and it is this disclosure of reserved strength that arouses the desire to know the artist better through his paintings. The scene in itself is a charming one, very familiar to be sure, but of that sort which one is never tired of seeing."—*Boston Daily Adver- tiser.*

Sandys, Frederick K. (*Brit.*) Born in 1832. First exhibited at the Royal Academy in 1854. A painter of portraits, in which he has been very successful, and occasionally an exhibitor of ideal sub- jects. Among the latter may be mentioned, " Oriana " (R. A., 1861), " La Belle Ysonde " (1863), " Morgan-le-fay " (1864), " Cassandra " (1865), and " Medea " (1869). This artist also furnishes wood-cuts for the publishers of illustrated books from time to time. His " Medea " was at the Paris Exposition of 1878.

" Mr. Sandys, though we believe known as the author of some noteworthy drawings, must be also reckoned as a painter among the men of promise in which this Exhibition

[R. A., 1863] has been unusually fertile. His head of Mrs. Rose has struck every one as a remarkable example of execution, in which careful drawing and characteristic expression are set off to the best advantage by significance in the accessories and care in the finish." — PALGRAVE's *Essays on Art.*

" Neither in his portraits nor in his pictures does Frederick K. Sandys always attain ideal grace and harmony, but he is always closely in contact with his subject. There is never any want of reality in the impression given by his paintings, rather perhaps there is sometimes a want of reserve in the emphasis and vivid power displayed. But when these powers do find a complete embodiment in the treatment of some worthy theme, the effect is as strong as anything to be found in the art of our time. The picture of ' Medea,' exhibited some time ago, is a remarkable example in this direction. There the ideal was kept supreme, and yet the influence of the picture was intense in its reality." — *Art Journal*, August, 1873.

Sangster, Samuel. (*Brit.*) (1804 – 1872.) A line-engraver of considerable reputation. Among the better known of his works are, " The Gentle Student " and " Forsaken," after G. S. Newton ; " The Syrian Maid," after Pickersgill ; " The Victim," after A. L. Egg ; " Juliet and the Nurse," after Briggs ; " The Sepulcher," after Etty ; and " A Scene from Midas," after Maclise. Sangster retired from the active practice of his profession some time before his death.

Sanguinetti, Francesco. (*Ital.*) Born at Carrara. Died 1870. Pupil of his father and of Rauch of Berlin. After visiting Italy he returned to the studio of Rauch in 1831. He executed several busts and a statue of Hylas in marble. He then settled in Munich, where he died. He there executed many portrait busts of distinguished individuals, and at the time of his death was engaged upon a statue of Maximilian II., intended for the National Museum. He carried out the models of Schwanthaler for the figures in the State Library and the Asylum for the Blind.

"Sanguinetti's private life seems to have been particularly unfortunate. First, he lost, it has been stated, by mismanagement, a property he had bought with the savings of many years ; next, his daughter was assassinated at the age of nineteen by a jealous lover ; then he was swindled by a dealer out of a valuable collection of pictures ; and, lastly, lost what money he had latterly accumulated by the bursting of a bubble company, and was even compelled to sell the little house in which he resided." — *Art Journal*, May, 1870.

Sanson, Justin-Chrysostome. (*Fr.*) Born at Nemours. Chevalier of the Legion of Honor. Pupil of Jouffroy. His " Pietà " (group, marble, 1876) was bought by the Ministry of Fine Arts. This sculptor has been much employed upon public monuments and buildings, such as the Palace of Justice at Amiens, the New Opera, etc.

Sant, James, R. A. (*Brit.*) Born in London, 1820. Became a pupil of Varley, and entered the Royal Academy in 1840, shortly after beginning his career as a painter of portraits, in which art he has been very successful. Among his sitters have been the Prince Consort, and several members of the Royal Family, the Duc d'Aumale, the Lord Bishop of London (1865), and the Queen and the children of the Prince of Wales (1872), shortly after which he was appointed Principal Painter in Ordinary to Her Majesty. Among his figure-pictures may be mentioned, "Samuel" (1853); "Children of the Wood" (1854); "Infancy" (1857); "Little Red Riding-Hood" (1860); "The First Sense of Sorrow" (when he was elected Associate of the Royal Academy in 1862); in 1863, "Taking Notes"; in 1864, "Turn again, Whittington"; in 1866, "Light in Dark Places"; in 1869, "Mentonese Children"; in 1870, "Alone"; in 1871, "The Schoolmaster's Daughter" (his diploma work, deposited on his election as Academician); in 1874, "Peaches"; in 1875, "The Early Post"; in 1877, "Gleanings"; in 1878, "Little Zàra."

His "Young Whittington" was at Philadelphia in 1876; "The Early Post" and "Adversity," at Paris in 1878.

"Mr. Sant has given us everything in this painting ['Early Post,' R. A., 1875]: youth, beauty, life, sympathy, a charming story, and a very pleasant reminiscence of an English country-house, without our ever having been there. As an example of careful art-work and purity of tone in coloring, this composition of itself is excellent, but as an incident of every-day life, depicted on canvas, it is one of the very best pictures of the Academy." — *Art Journal*, July, 1875.

Santarelli, Emilio. (*Ital.*) Born at Florence, 1801. Professor of the Academy of Fine Arts at Florence. Son of an artist, he was early instructed in design, and went to Rome, where he was a pupil of Thorwaldsen. He has not attained great fame, although he has executed many works by which he will be honorably remembered. One glorious act of his merits the gratitude of coming generations. He has collected a marvelous number of original drawings by the old masters, and these he presents to the city of Florence, in order that they may never be dispersed or fall into mercenary hands; among them are some *chefs-d'œuvre*. Among the works of Santarelli are a statue of Michael Angelo, placed under the loggia of the Uffizi, many portrait busts, a series of bas-reliefs of mythological subjects, a statue called "The Good Shepherd," a "Kneeling Magdalen," a "Bacchante," "The Prayer of Innocence," "Cupid in Mischief," a half-colossal statue of St. Francis, etc.

Sargent, John S. (*Am.*) A native of Philadelphia, he has lived for some years in Europe, painting in Paris under Carolus Duran. His "Fishing for Oysters at Cancale," at the Exhibition of the Society of American Artists in New York in 1878, was purchased by Samuel Colman. To the Paris Salon, in 1878, he had "En route pour la Pêche." At the Paris Exhibition of 1878 he exhibited a portrait.

Sarrocchi, Tito. (*Ital.*) Born in Siena about 1825. Professor at the Academy of Siena. Pupil of this Academy and of Dupré in Florence. He has been successful as an artist, showing much imagination, great fidelity to nature, and great skill in execution. Among the works by which he is known we may mention the "Finding of the Cross by Queen Helena," an alto-relievo on the façade of Santa Croce, Florence; a very beautiful Bacchante, exhibited at the Exposition in Paris in 1867 ; a fine group for the Campo Santo of Siena ; a group of a little girl teaching a young child his first prayer ; a beautiful figure of Hope, and several portrait statues, all fine in conception and execution. The restorations of the statues of the Cathedral of Siena and of the Fonte Gaia in the Piazza Victor Emmanuel are by Sarrocchi.

Sartain, John. (*Brit.-Am.*) Born in London, 1808. Academician and member of the Philadelphia Academy of Fine Arts. Trustee and Member of the Committee on Instruction in the Pennsylvania Museum and School of Industrial Art. Controller of the Artists' Fund Society, Philadelphia. Vice-President of the School of Design for Women, Philadelphia. Chief Administrator of Fine Arts at the Philadelphia Centennial Exhibition of 1876. Honorary Member of the Art and Amicital Society of Amsterdam. In 1878 he received the Cross of Officer of the Equestrian grade of the Order of the Crown of Italy from King Umberto. He removed to America in 1830, having already made a reputation as an engraver. In 1842 – 43 he was proprietor of Campbell's Magazine and editor of Sartain's Union Magazine. He was the first engraver in mezzo-tinto of any account. He has, it is said, produced more works than any other living engraver. His " Christ Rejected," after Benjamin West, and " The Iron-Worker and King Solomon," after C. Schussele, are the largest and most important as well as the finest mezzo-tinto plates ever made in America. His portraits of Sir Thomas Lawrence and others are fine ; that of Professor Mapes was made from his own drawing. His " Battle of Gettysburg," after the picture by Peter F. Rothermel, is a very interesting work. Among his plates are, William Penn (full length), after H. Inman ; Henry Clay (full length, in the act of speaking), after John Nagle ; Martin Van Buren (full length), after Inman, and other portraits, which we have not space to name. Also, " Adam and Eve," after Marc Antonio's celebrated print ; " Zeisberger preaching to the Indians," after Schussele ; " County Election in Missouri," after C. C. Bingham ; " Eugenie, Empress of France, and the Ladies of her Court," after Winterhalter ; " The Return from Market," after J. L. Krimmel ; " The Valley of the Battenkill," after Boutelle ; etc. He has been for many years a resident of Philadelphia.

Sartain, William. (*Am.*) Born in Philadelphia, 1843. Son of the preceding. He spent six months in the Pennsylvania Academy of Fine Arts and seven years under Léon Bonnat at Paris, studying also at the Academie Nationale des Beaux-Arts, and making excursions to Algiers and elsewhere. He passed one winter in Rome, one in Seville, and the winter of 1877 and '78 in New York, joining the Society of American Painters on its organization in 1877, and contributing to its first exhibition, " A Court-Yard, Paris," " Italian Girl," and other pictures. His " View in the Street of Algiers " was in the Paris Exposition of 1878. His " Italian Head," at the National Academy of 1876, was purchased on the opening day of the Exhibition by Samuel Colman, N. A. To the National Academy, in 1878, he contributed "Young Italy" and "A Street in Algiers."

"For a female figure in life-scale, however, if we wish to go to one which easily over-comes everything else in the Exhibition, whether portraits or invented characters, we must approach William Sartain's simple head of a Contadina [N. A., 1876]. No other study of life compares with it in the most distant way, and from the standpoint of its intentions and problems it may be called a perfect work. It is a beautiful, plaintive Italian face, looking upward in prayer. The lifting of the brows over the forehead ; the sockets of the black, hollow eyes ; the dark, yet transparent, olive of the cheek ; and the flesh shadows, so deep, yet not opaque, show the great promise and present success of this pupil of Bonnat." — *New York Nation*, April 6, 1876.

"The colors are so grave and the modeling so delicate that it reminds one of the Spanish pictures in the Louvre or the Pitti. This is W. Sartain's 'Italian Head,' something wholly quaint and unusual for an American painter. Artists admire it for its exquisite relations of light, and the excellent manipulation of the paint." — *Art Journal*, April, 1876.

Sartain, Emily. (*Am.*) Born in Philadelphia, 1841. Daughter of John Sartain, the well-known American engraver, from whom she acquired the art of engraving on steel. She was a pupil of the Pennsylvania Academy of Fine Arts, Philadelphia, and, going to Europe, she studied in Paris four years with Evariste Luminais. Her work has been portraits and *genre* pictures. She has exhibited in the Salon in Paris, and at different local academies throughout the United States. The greater part of her professional life has been spent in Philadelphia, where she has practiced both painting and engraving. She worked for some time in Paris, and in Parma, Italy. To the Centennial Exhibition in Philadelphia, in 1876, she contributed "The Reproof," for which in the official report she was "commended for merit in *genre* painting."

Satterlee, Walter, A. N. A. (*Am.*) Born in Brooklyn, 1844. A graduate of Columbia College. He studied art in the schools of the Academy of Design, spent some time in the studio of Edwin White in New York, and, going abroad, was a pupil of Léon Bonnat in Paris. He began to exhibit at the National Academy about 1868, sending to the gallery in that year, "Autumn turning the Leaves" and "Count Fosco." In 1870 he contributed "Morning among the Flowers" ; in 1871, "Feeding the Pets" ; in 1873, "A Coquette of the Olden Time" ; in 1874, when he was in Rome, he sent "Out for a Ride" (belonging to H. C. Howell) ; in 1876, "The Arrow and Song" ; in 1877, "His Eminence the Cardinal" ; in 1878, "Contemplation" and "The Captive." He was elected a member of the American Society of Painters in Water-Colors in 1873 or '74, exhibiting, in 1875, "The Young Bohemians" and "Cinderella" ; in 1876, "The Evening Prayer on the Lake" ; in 1877, "The Fortune-Teller" ; in 1878, "Old Ballads," "The Belle of the Village," etc. Among his most important works are, "Contemplation," "Come, ye Disconsolate," "The Peacemaker," "Marguerite," "Love in Sunshine," "Love in Shade," and "Love-Making in Capri" (the last belonging to Samuel V. Wright of New York). To the Centennial Exhibition at Philadelphia, in 1876, he sent "Marguerite" (in oil), and "Far-Away Thoughts" and "One Hundred Years Ago" (in water-colors).

Scaramuzza, Francesoo. (*Ital.*) This artist's illustrations of the "Divine Comedy" are much praised. His subjects have been varied; historical, poetical, and mythological themes have all come under his brush. He has boldness and energy, and his effects of light are astonishing. His representations of "The Assumption of the Virgin," "Eve," "Sarah," and "Rachel" are admirable.

Schadow, Friedrich Wilhelm. (*Ger.*) Born at Berlin (1789–1862). Doctor of the University of Bonn. Knight of the Red Eagle and other orders. Member of the Academy of Berlin and the Institute of France. Professor at Berlin and at Düsseldorf. Went in 1810 to Rome with his brother Rudolph, and joined the German artists there, who were called "Nazarites." Two years later both brothers entered the Roman Catholic Church. The "Wise and Foolish Virgins" of the Städel Institute, Frankfort, is a fair work from which to judge this painter. He was not a great master, and he holds higher rank as a professor than as an artist. Scholars crowded to him from Berlin, and at Düsseldorf he numbered Hildebrandt, Sohn, and Lessing among his pupils. He lived, however, to see even this glory shadowed. He was accused of sectarianism or over-zeal for religious art ; he was called weak and superficial, and he resigned his position as a leader. He received many honors, but he paid the necessary penalty in this age, for desiring every picture to be sanctified by crucifixes, Virgins, and other symbols, forgetting that truth and beauty simply rendered must lead the mind to the source of truth, and need not the aids of artificial or formal signs. At the National Gallery, Berlin, are his "Christ at Emmaus" and a portrait of a woman.

Schampheleer, Edmond de. (*Belgian.*) Born at Brussels. Medal at Philadelphia, where he exhibited "Nimuegen on the River Wahal." At Paris, 1877, were his "Dordrecht and the Meuse" and "The Road of Loosdricht at Hilversum." He has also exhibited some of the above pictures at the Royal Academy, London, and at the Paris Exposition, 1878, to which he sent "Near Gonda" and "Between Witteren and Zèle."

Schaus, Prof. Ferdinand. (*Ger.*) Of Weimar. Medal at Philadelphia, where he exhibited "Saint John" and "A Dryad," which were commended. To Paris, in 1878, he sent "Calisto."

Scheffer, Ary. Born at Dordrecht (1795–1858). Officer of the Legion of Honor. This artist was French before the civil law, because, under the name of the Bavarian Republic, his birthplace was within the limits of the new French Departments. His father, an artist, died young, and his mother superintended his education. As early as 1807 a picture of Scheffer's attracted attention. His mother took him to Paris, and placed him under the instruction of Guérin. For several years after his début he painted small *genre* subjects, including "The Soldier's Widow," "A Sister of Charity," etc. At length he occupied himself with scenes from works of great poets, such as Goethe, Burger, Schiller, Dante, and Byron. "Beatrice" and "Francesca di Rimini," which appeared at the Salon of 1835, were his crowning works in this department. Later, he devoted himself to religious subjects, as "Christ bearing his Cross," "Temptation of Christ," "Christ the Consolator," "Ruth and Naomi," etc. Many of his works are well known from the engravings of Bernardi, Blanchard, Calamatta, Dupont, Louis, Thevenin, etc. Scheffer may be called a romanticist. He was extravagantly fond of music, and, in truth, had the soul of a poet. After the death of his mother he wished to execute a funeral monument for her, not being willing that any hand but his own should do this work. He essayed sculpture for the first time, and, for a novice, the work was creditable. The sentiment which prompted this act is most touching to the hearts of all mothers. At the Johnston sale, New York, 1876, "Love Celestial and Terrestrial" (13 by 8, sepia) sold for $ 200. At the Corcoran Gallery, Washington, is his picture of "Count Eberhard."

"All the circumstances of Scheffer's life were favorable to his artistic development. His father had been a respectable artist, with a competent private fortune ; . . . . Madame Scheffer herself was an amateur painter of some ability, and both respected artists and understood the aims of their existence. . . . . Scheffer, like David, led an ardent political life by the side of his artistic one ; but whereas David's political career lowers him in the opinion even of his own party, that of Scheffer is always honorable, and its greatest fault is nothing worse than that want of prudence inseparable from all private political action. . . . . Scheffer will be remembered as a friend of the Orleans family. He was introduced to them by Gérard in 1826, and became their drawing-master, and soon afterwards their friend. . . . . It is very curious that Scheffer was one of the two persons [Thiers being the other] who, in 1830, rode to Neuilly to tell Louis Philippe that he was to be king, and that Scheffer should have been also one of the sad group that quitted the Tuileries in 1848, when he assisted Louis Philippe into his cab. . . . . The affectionate relation which existed between Scheffer and the Princess Marie reminds us of Roger Ascham and Lady Jane Grey. . . . . Scheffer, as an artist, owes his rank almost entirely to the elevation of his feeling. His drawing is usually correct and his taste refined ; but his color is bad, and though his handling is neat, from much practice, it has no artistic subtlety. The excellence of his personal character had some concern in his success. . . . . I have a great difficulty in admitting that any artist is a great painter who is not also a colorist, and Scheffer, by uniting bad color with considerable artistic merits of other kinds, has done positive harm to the art of painting. . . . . Of landscape he was wholly ignorant, and, like most figure-painters, could not understand that there were fields of study in that department of art lying outside the limits of his knowledge. He was a cultivated gentleman and man of the world, and had the habits of one, so far as they were compatible with the industrious pursuit of art. His great interest in politics gave him a common ground on which he habitually met men of distinction who were more or less indifferent to painting. In this respect Scheffer enjoyed an advantage somewhat rare among artists, whose own pursuit is so engrossing that they are liable to be entirely absorbed by it. . . . . He will be remembered as an artist of high aim and pure sentiment, and a man of more than common political conviction and fidelity, but his influence upon art has been slight, and will not be durable." — HAMERTON's *Contemporary French Painters.*

" However, Ary Scheffer was not alone an artist, he was a mind, a heart, a character: a mind open to all culture, all graces, all enthusiasms; a heart tender, generous, devoted, under an envelope somewhat rude and harsh; a character imbued with stoicism, with inflexible uprightness, austere probity, which has lived in our time (it is to say all) without pollution, without weakness or faltering. Have I told how sweet and true were his friendships, how solid and charming his conversations, how sincere, indulgent, and faithful his affection? To enjoy them was the privilege of his friends and associates. Did I tell of his unbounded generosity, his prodigal benevolence, so inexpressible that after a fruitful, laborious life and many well-paid labors, Scheffer had only wherewith to live from day to day, and left not the least saving? He would tell me that the left hand should not know that which the right gives. Shall I tell, in fine, the immovable constancy of his opinions and of the attachments which he formed? . . . . I wish only among a hundred equally honorable acts to cite one, not well known, and which a late confidence revealed to me. Ary Scheffer was for a long time an Officer of the Legion of Honor. After the terrible and fatal days of June, 1848, when he bravely led the battalion of the National Guard, of which he was chief, the cross of a commander was offered him. ' If this distinction,' replied he, 'were accorded to me in my career as an artist, and as a prize for my works, I should receive it with deference and satisfaction; but to adorn myself with a collar which would recall to me the horrible combats of civil war, — never!' He was inflexible. This instance suffices to paint the man, and we can terminate this sketch of his life with the last words of the preface to the Book of Job, in which the eminent interpreter of this old Hebrew poet deplores that Ary Scheffer was not able to finish his compositions on this subject. 'Alas! what lessons of moral elevation, what a source of profound emotions and high thoughts, have disappeared from our age, an poor in great souls, with the last sigh of this man of heart and genius.' " — LOUIS VIARDOT, *Gazette des Beaux-Arts*, February, 1859.

Schelfhout, Andrew. (*Dutch.*) Born at The Hague (1787–1870). Member of all the academies of Holland. Medals at Antwerp, Brussels, Ghent, and The Hague. This landscape-painter was especially successful in representing winter scenes. His pictures are in the Munich and other galleries. They are usually small, although he has sometimes painted large works. They show skillful drawing, with fine knowledge of perspective, and are good in color and careful in execution. At the Johnston sale, " A Winter Landscape " (21 by 27) sold for $610. It was from the Wolfe sale in 1863. At a sale in Utrecht, 1873, " The Mountain Landscape " brought £758. Mr. Probasco of Cincinnati has in his collection " A Skating Scene " by Schelfhout, painted in 1849, which is a fine example of this master's style.

Schenck, August-Frederic-Albrecht. (*Ger.*) Born at Gluckstadt, 1828. Chevalier of the Orders of Christ of Portugal and of Isabella the Catholic. Medal at Philadelphia. He passed some time in business in England and Portugal before he became a pupil of Cogniet. He made his début at the Salon of 1855. His " Repose on the Seashore " (1864) and " The Awakening " (1865) were bought by the State. His pictures are much admired, and his reputation is, perhaps, greater in England, Portugal, and America than in France. His exhibit of 1877, " The Return to the Park " and " A Bit of Auvergne," was much praised. Soon after his début he lost his fortune.

At Philadelphia he exhibited "Sheep in a Storm." Mr. D. Waldo Lincoln has a very fine work by Schenck with the same title. Among his more famous pictures are " Autour de l'ange," belonging to Count Castellani ; " Perdus," to Miss Wolfe of New York ; " The last Hour," to Mr. Gibson of Philadelphia. Mrs. Eliza Sutton of Peabody, Mass., has a fine example of his brighter manner, where the flock are beneath a bright sky, in the midst of gay flowers and fresh pasturage. The " Awakening" is at the Museum of Bordeaux ; and "In the Dale," at the Museum of Lille, — in short, Schenck's pictures are in many galleries in Europe and America. At the Salon of 1878 he exhibited " Anguish " and " The Neighboring Mill."

" Albert Schenck is certainly one of the most original figures of the contemporaneous artistic gallery : I should like to have the time to paint in full this robust companion, born in Holstein, annexed by Prussia without asking, and adopted by France because he wished it. All the world to-day regards Schenck as one of our first animal-painters. He is one of those originals, of a species not yet extinct, who prefer dogs to men, and find more sweetness in sheep than in women. With such fancies one leaves the city for the fields, and has only to do with animals. Our artist has taken this part after having profoundly studied his fellow-creatures. Retired to Écouen, to a farm, he lives in the midst of oxen, dogs, goats, asses, horses, and sheep of all types, races, and species ; cares for them, cultivates them, loves them, and above all studies them, as never artist studied his models. He knows better than any one their habitual behavior, their favorite poses, their preferred attitudes, and the mobile play of their physiognomies. By means of studying closely the joys and griefs of these modest companions and humble servants of man, he has penetrated the inmost recesses of their souls, which he knows how to show us in pictures of striking truth. His animals' heads are portraits particularized with all the care which Cabanel, Dubufe, and Bonnat gave to the human mask. The picture which he exhibits to-day under the title of ' Angoisses ' is pathetic to the last degree. A lamb is wounded, lying on the ground, losing its blood, which pours out of a horrible wound. The ravens, with their infallible instinct, scent the approaching death, and await their prey ; their sinister circle is closed in, — the unfortunate little beast cannot escape them. The mother is there; she comprehends it, the poor creature! the fate which awaits her dear nursling, and broken-hearted, full of anguish [it is the title of the picture, and it is just], she bleats for the shepherd who comes not. It is a little drama, this picture, and as poignant as if it had men for actors and victims." — *Supplement of the Figaro,* June 5, 1878.

" There are few artists more popular than Schenck, and the crowd which goes from year to year to the Palace of Industry has quickly discovered, among the innumerable pictures, his works with a touch so *spirituelle* and a dramatism so powerful in their simplicity. The reflected judgment of the connoisseurs confirms the instantaneous impression of the multitude, and this artist is able to please equally the difficult and the naïfs." — ÉDOUARD DRUMONT, *Galérie Contemporaine, Litteraire, Artistique,* 1871.

Schendel, Petrus van. (*Dutch.*) Born at Ter Heyden (1806 – 1870). Medals at Paris, in Holland and Brussels. Studied in Amsterdam, Rotterdam, and Antwerp. His earlier works included a variety of subjects. After a time he devoted himself to scenes by lamplight and firelight, which were very popular. At the National Gallery at Berlin are two of his market-scenes, " A Woman selling Fish " and another with vegetables. At the Leipsic Museum are " The Return from the Hunt " and "A Scene in a Fish-Market."

Schetky, John Christian. (*Brit.*) Born in Scotland (1778 – 1874). Educated at the High School of Edinburgh, with Brougham, Scott, and Horner. In 1825 and previously he exhibited marine-pictures of an historical character, and was marine-painter successively to George IV., William IV., and Victoria. He exhibited at the Royal Academy, London, as late as 1871, "A Gallant Rescue" and "Coming to Anchor in Portland Roads"; in 1872, he sent "Wreck of the Frigate Anson," "Shipping in the Olden Time," and "A Trial of Speed off the Dodman."

"As a marine-painter Mr. Schetky's pictures were always held in estimation for their truthfulness; this quality appears to have been his great aim. A gallery of his works would contain among them some of the most stirring naval actions that occurred during the long wars of the early part of this century, besides others of a later time." — *Art Journal,* February, 1874.

Schievelbein, Friedrich Anton Hermann. (*Ger.*) Born in Berlin (1817 – 1867). Pupil of the Berlin Academy and of Professsor Ludwig Wichmann. He early received a commission at St. Petersburg, where he was employed in the rebuilding of the Winter Palace and on the St. Isaac's Church. At that time he had taken the grand prize at Berlin. Before he left for Rome he sent in his drawing for the group for the Castle Bridge. The choice fell on his design, and he soon returned from Rome in order to execute it. At Berlin he was very active and much employed in public works. The Stein memorial was completed from his designs, by his pupils, after his death (it was not erected until 1875). He also made the statues of Luther and Melancthon for the University of Königsberg. At the National Gallery, Berlin, is the model of a frieze in relief, subject, the "Destruction of Pompeii." Among his other works are, "The Muses," "Raphael," "The Months" (at Sans-souci), "Colossal Statue of Hermann von Salza," "A Despised Christ," "A Winter Evening," "A Protecting Angel," etc.

Schilling, Johannes. (*Ger.*) Born at Mittweida, 1828. At the Leipsic Museum are his reliefs of "Jupiter and Ganymede" and "Aphrodite and Eros." At the Brühl Terrace in Dresden are his groups of "Evening" and "Night." Among his latest productions is the National Monument in the Niederwald, — a great work, combining a representation of "Father Rhine," nymphs, and other designs.

Schinkel, Karl Friedrich. (*Ger.*) Born at Neu-Ruppin (1781 – 1841). Studied at the Academy of Berlin under David and Friedrich Gilly. Traveled in Italy and visited Paris. He was for a while obliged to support himself by painting, at which time he became associated with Karl Gropius, for whom he later composed his famous panoramas. In 1824 and '26 he again visited Italy and France, and also England. In 1839 he received a high official position as an architect in Prussia. His decorative works were remarkable for their grandeur of conception and grace of composition. He was somewhat wanting in technique; but his sentiment and rich imagination gave a spirit to his works which more than compensated for this. At the National Gallery of Berlin are, "An Ideal Landscape at Sunset," "An Italian Landscape," and several others.

Schirmer, Guillaume. (*Ger.*) Born at Berlin (1804 – 1866). Professor and Member of the Academy of Berlin. He executed decorative works in the Castle of Prince Albert of Prussia, and in the New Museum of Berlin. In the National Gallery, Berlin, are his pictures of "Tasso's House at Sorrento" and a "Scene at Sans-Souci."

Schleich, Eduard. (*Ger.*) Born in Castle Haarbach near Landshut (1812 – 1874). Royal Professor of Bavaria. Pupil of the Munich Academy, but essentially taught by the old masters and nature, which he studied lovingly. His pictures are landscapes. He traveled considerably in Europe. His "Evening Landscape" is in the National Gallery, Berlin. His "Beach at Scheveningen" (belonging to the Royal Museum at Munich) was at the Paris Exposition of 1878.

Schlesinger, Henri Guillaume. (*Fr.*) Born at Frankfort. (Naturalized Frenchman.) Chevalier of the Legion of Honor. Pupil of the Academy of Vienna. He made his début at the Salon of 1840. At the Salon of 1875 he exhibited "The Dove-Cot" and "Jehanne"; in 1874, "Brother and Sister"; in 1872, "Lost Labor"; in 1869, "The Good Friends," etc. He has exhibited many portraits. At the Royal Academy, in 1873, he had "Ce n'est pas moi!" To the Salon of 1878 he sent "A Good Kiss" and "Correggio drawing some Pictures of Children."

Schloesser, Karl. (*Ger.*) Born at Darmstadt. Painter of the Düsseldorf school. Resides in London. Knight of the Order of Merit. Medal at Vienna. At the Exhibition of 1876, at the Royal Academy, he exhibited "The Village Lawyer"; at the first exhibition of the Grosvenor Gallery (1877), "The Refectory." His "Forbidden Fruit" was bought by Napoleon III. Among his other works are, "The Reprimand" and "Reading the News," — the last is a small picture (only 12 by 9) and was sold at the Johnston sale in 1876 for $310. "The Political Opponents" was much remarked at the Berlin Exposition of 1871. In 1875 he exhibited "Obligatory Instruction" (two children sent off to school, one going very unwillingly). At the London Academy in 1878 he exhibited "Reprimand," and at Paris, same year, "Seeking Advice."

Schmid, Mattias. Pupil of Piloty. Paints the same sort of subjects as Defregger, and has nearly always a political or religious motive behind his representations. One of his most powerful works represents priests playing cards before a Tyrolese inn; an old man comes forward and beseeches the holy fathers to buy his crucifixes which he carries in his arms; his wife with her infant remains a little behind. The priests roughly repulse him, but a young girl who is serving them with beer regards the old man with pity.

Schmidt, Max (*Ger.*) Born in Berlin, 1818. Professor at Königsberg. Member of the Academy of Berlin. Medals at Berlin and Vienna. Studied at the Berlin Academy. Traveled extensively in Europe and in the East. Landscape-painter. Some of his decorative works are in the New Museum at Berlin. In the National Gallery, Berlin, is his "Wood and Mountain." His "Banks of the Spree, — Dull Weather" was at the Paris Exposition of 1878.

Schnorr von Carolsfeld, Julius Veit Hans. (*Ger.*) Born at Leipsic (1794 – 1872). Member of the Institute of France. Professor at the Academy of Munich, and later at the Academy of Dresden, where he was also Director of the Royal Museum. Pupil of his father and of the Academy of Vienna. In 1817 he went to Rome and remained ten years. After his return to Germany he was commissioned by King Louis to execute decorative works at the new Residence. They consisted of five pictures from the story of the Nibelungenlied. He also executed other important works of the same sort, such as scenes from the lives of Charlemagne, Barbarossa, and Rudolf of Hapsburg. The cartoons of the Nibelungen series and a picture of "St. Roch distributing Alms" are in the Museum of Leipsic. At the National Gallery, Berlin, are two other cartoons of scenes from the Nibelungenlied. Among his other pictures are, "The Three Christian Cavaliers" and "The Three Pagan Cavaliers," a "Holy Family," frescos of scenes from the works of Ariosto, the "Marriage of Cana," "Jacob and Rachel," the "Annunciation," and other religious subjects.

Schœnewerk, Alexandre. (*Fr.*) Born at Paris. Chevalier of the Legion of Honor. Pupil of David d'Angers, Jollivet, and Triqueti. At the Salon of 1877 he exhibited the "Mime-dompteur," a group in plaster ; in 1876, "Hesitation," a marble statue ; in 1875, "A Young Girl at the Fountain," in terra-cotta, being a reduction of the marble statue of 1873 ; in 1874, "Lulli," plaster statue (model of a work intended for the New Opera), "St. Thomas Aquinas," statue in stone (for the façade of the Sarbonne), and "The Upper Portion of a Monument to E. Ortolan, Professor at Law," bronze ; and, in 1872, a statue of the "Young Tarentine," a subject suggested by the words of Chénier, —

> "Elle a vécu, Myrto, la jeune Tarentine,
> Son beau corps a roulé sous la vague marine !"

Scholtz, Julius. (*Ger.*) Born at Breslau, 1825. Professor in the Academy of Dresden, and Member of the Academy of Berlin. Studied at Dresden Academy and under J. Hübner. He is an historical painter. In the National Gallery at Berlin is his "Volunteers of 1813 before Frederick William III."

Schorn, Charles. (*Ger.*) Born at Düsseldorf (1803 – 1850). Pupil of Cornelius at Munich, and of Gros and Ingres at Paris. When he returned to Munich he assisted Cornelius in some of his great works. Schorn made the cartoon for a painted glass window for the Cathedral of Ratisbon, representing "The Conversion of Slaves by St. Benno." He was employed by the King of Bavaria to assist in forming the Munich Gallery. He visited many continental cities to collect pictures, and in London purchased Wilkie's "Reading of the Will." His own pictures are of the historical *genre* style, such as "Paul III. contemplating the Portrait of Luther," "Salvator Rosa among Brigands," etc.

Schrader, Jules. (*Ger.*) Born at Berlin, 1815. Professor and Member of the Academic Senate of the Academy of Berlin. Medal at Paris, 1855. Pupil of his father and the Academy of Berlin, where he obtained several prizes, but failed of that which would take him to Rome. He also studied at Düsseldorf under Hildebrandt and Guillaume Schadow. At Berlin in 1844 he gained the grand prize, and went to Rome in 1845, where he remained three years. He there painted the "Capitulation of Calais," which was much admired, and gained him his election to the Academy of Berlin. His best works are, "Frederick the Great after the Battle of Kallin," at the Museum of Leipsic ; "Jephthah's Daughter," in the Museum of Königsberg ; "The Consecration of the Church of St. Sophia at Constantinople by the Emperor Justinian" (1853), a grand mural painting at the Museum of Berlin ; and "Cromwell at the Death-Bed of his Daughter" (1864), in the Museum of Cologne. At the Exposition in the Royal Academy at Berlin, in 1876, he exhibited "The Flight" and two portraits ; and to Paris, in 1878, he sent a portrait of Dr. Becker.

"Schrader is, moreover, one of the best painters of *genre* and of portraits of our time, and his portraits of Alexander von Humboldt and Peter de Cornelius may be mentioned, above all, as veritable *chefs-d'œuvre*. His principal qualities are a profound science of colors, an inimitable talent in the drawing of the nude and of draperies, and a consummate knowledge of the costumes of all times." — LAROUSSE, *Dictionnaire Universel.*

Schreyer, Adolphe. (*Ger.*) Born at Frankfort-on-the-Main, 1828. Medals at Paris, 1864, '65, and '67 ; at Vienna, in 1873 ; at Brussels, in 1863 ; and the Cross of the Order of Léopold in 1864. In 1862 he was made Painter to the Court of the Grand Duke of Mecklenbourg-Schwerin, and is Member of the Academies of Antwerp and Rotterdam, and Honorary Member of the Deutsches Nochstift. Belonging to a distinguished family, this artist received every advantage that travel and instruction can give. In 1855 he followed the regiment commanded by Prince Taxis to the Crimea. He has visited Algiers, and other Eastern countries, as well as all the principal countries of Europe, and everywhere has diligently studied his subjects. Among his best works are the "Battle of Waghensel," belonging to the Duke of Mecklenbourg ; the "Battle of Comorn," belonging to the Count of Bouilly-Mensdorf ; "An Attack of Cavalry," belonging to

M. Ravenet of Berlin ; the " Prince of Taxis wounded at Temeswar," belonging to the family of the Prince. His "Horses of the Irregular Cossacks," snow-scene (1864), and a " Charge of the Artillery of the Imperial Guard in the Crimea " (1865) are in the Luxembourg. At the Johnston sale, New York, 1876, " Wallachian Peasants crossing a Ford " (21 by 42) sold for $ 2,700 ; and " Arabs Retreating " (45 by 69) for $ 6,700. At the Latham sale, New York, 1878, "Traveling in Russia " (18 by 42) sold for $ 2,150 ; " A Wet Day in Moldavia " (18 by 42) for $ 2,050, and a " Wallachian Stable on Fire " (47 by 79) for $ 3,500. " The Watering-Place " is in the Corcoran Gallery at Washington. At the Museum of Fine Arts in Boston is the " Flight of the Standard-Bearer," belonging to John C. Phillips. At the Walters Gallery, Baltimore, are the " Winter Scene in Poland " and an " Arab Horseman." A fine picture called " Winter " is in the collection of Mrs. H. E. Maynard of Boston, and " Coming to Camp " belongs to Mr. Frank R. Kimball of the same city. It is a very fine specimen of Schreyer's work, and is a Wallachian winter scene.

"Schreyer joins to a grand and bold conception a profoundly poetic sentiment ; this makes him both German and French. His manner, as well as his talent, has two natures ; it recalls both Delacroix and Fromentin. His color is a happy mingling of the dreamy tones of the one and the powerful colors of the other. And one should above all admire it for the incontestable originality thus manifested in this mingling, — a quality one does not look for in a man whose character and manner have different aspects. All that I say of the color of Schreyer may be also applied to his drawing. His lines, clear and vague at the same time, are, in spite of these two distinct qualities, strangely personal with this artist. From all this the great talent of Schreyer seems like something much more than talent." — *Courrier Artistique*, February, 1864.

In the " Moniteur Universel," February 18, 1864, Théophile Gautier praised in the most exalted terms the works of this artist, and compared him to Delacroix, Decamps, and Fromentin, saying at the same time that he was an imitator of no one. The following is a translation of a charming letter to Schreyer from the same critic : —

"MY DEAR SCHREYER, — I came with Hert and Martinet to see you. You are gone out, but your genius remains at home. We have admired this marvelous picture of ' Chasse-Neige,' — so true, so picturesque, so dramatic. I am egotistic enough to be a good judge in this matter. I have been myself enveloped in a snowy whirlwind near Kowno, and your canvas makes me shiver ; I seem to be still in Russia. We hope that you will be willing to send this masterpiece to our exposition. I dare not believe in such a happiness, and I thank you in my name and in the name of the Société nationale des Beaux-Arts.   Your admirer and President,
                                        " THÉOPHILE GAUTIER."

Schrœdter, Adolf. (*Ger.*) Born at Schwedt (1805 – 1875). Member of the Academy of Berlin. Professor of the Polytechnic School at Carlsruhe. Pupil of the Düsseldorf Academy. His pictures were *genre* subjects, with a comic element, such as scenes from " Don Quixote," " Falstaff," etc., " The Wine-Taster," " The May Tree," and others. At the Wolfe sale, New York, 1863, " Falstaff thrown into the Thames " sold for $ 975.

Schulz, Moritz. (*Ger.*) Born in Leobschütz, 1825. Honorary

Member of the Polytechnic School at Rotterdam. Studied at the Academy of Berlin. Was in Rome from 1854 to '70, when he established himself in Berlin. One of the bas-reliefs on the column of Victory is by Schulz, and he has executed two groups illustrative of Instruction in the Arts, which are in the National Gallery at Berlin. At Berlin, in 1871, he exhibited "Cupid and Psyche," "Love's Dream," and " Rape of Ganymede "; in 1876, " Night as a Charity " and " Bacchantes, a Faun, etc."

Schutzenberger, Louis-Frederic. (*Fr.*) Born at Strasbourg. Chevalier of the Legion of Honor. Pupil of Gleyre. At the Salon of 1877 he exhibited, " The Harvest, — Souvenir of Italy " and " Diana at the Bath"; in 1876, a portrait and "Joan of Arc hearing her Voices"; in 1875, "The Seven Capital Sins," "The Flight of Nero," and " A Marsh in the Gombo of Pisa," etc. At the Luxembourg are " Terpsichore " (1861) and "Centaurs hunting a Wild Boar" (1864).

Schwarz, Albert. (*Ger.*) Of Berlin. Medal at Philadelphia, where he exhibited " Broken Flowers."

Schweinitz, Rudolf. (*Ger.*) Born at Charlottenburg, 1839. Studied at the Berlin Academy under Professor Schievelbein. In 1865 he visited Paris and Italy, and has also traveled in the North of Europe. Among his works are the Soldiers' Monument for Gera, eight colossal groups for the Royal Bridge at Berlin, monument to Frederick William III. at Cologne, nine reliefs for the balcony of the Hotel de Ville at Berlin, and a group, the " Fine Arts," in the National Gallery of that city.

Schwind, Moritz Ludwig (Ritter von). (*Ger.*) Born at Vienna (1804-1871). Professor at the Academy of Munich. Pupil of Schnorr and Cornelius. This painter executed many frescos which brought him reputation. At the National Gallery, Berlin, is his "Rose, a Wedding Scene." At the Leipsic Museum is a cartoon, "Symphony," which is a representation of various scenes in the love of a young couple; they are called " Andante," " Allegretto," etc., like parts of a symphony in music, — several portraits are introduced. Among his other works are scenes from " Cinderella," the " War of the Singers at Wartburg," etc.

"That original and genial artist, Maurice von Schwind of Munich, has just exhibited his last completed work, — the story of the water-nymph Melusina. Like his 'Cinderella' and 'The Seven Ravens,' known to English readers by the fairy-tale of Andersen, the drawing is in water-color, about two feet high, and divided into a series of compartments, six or eight or more feet long. Schwind's particular taste has always led him to choose old German tales of fairy or of folk lore for the subject of his pictures, and, so completely does he identify himself with the story, that all those representations of his are surrounded by an atmosphere wholly their own. . . . . The delicacy with which Herr von Schwind manages such subjects is decidedly a marked feature in all his compositions. Yet everything is natural, and seemingly as if it could not possibly have been otherwise." — *Art Journal*, May 7, 1870.

" Schwind was taken away from all other interests of life by his devotion to his art. Art permeated his whole being, and he ever strove for perfection. His desire to create never allowed him to rest. His poetic conception enabled him to render the most ordinary and prosaic scenes attractive. Schwind's peculiarity can only be comprehended by seeing his representations of the antique and of old German art. A rich vein of humor runs through all his work. There is and has been, perhaps, no artist to whom the entire beauty of the antique has been more fully revealed, but while he has been so utterly occupied with the beauties of the past, he seems never to have been oblivious to the immense gap which intervenes between the old and the new. His understanding of modern, in contradistinction to classic, art, was plainly shown by Schwind in his practice of his art, and he was not the man to lessen his individuality by studying *and copying* the old masters ; he used the knowledge gained from them in his own manner. So, in 1833, he went often to the Sistine and observed the works of Michael Angelo, and then, as he himself said, returned home to go on with his Ritter Kurt. His use of Grecian myths was not incompatible with this, for he copied not the dead academical forms, but he brought them down to the minds of his time by giving them the warmth of his own imagination." — CARL ALBERT REGNET, *Zeitschrift für bildende Kunst,* 1872.

Scifoni, Anatolio. (*Ital.*) Of Rome. Medal at Philadelphia, where he exhibited " Offerings to the Lares " and " Preparations for a Feast at Pompeii," which last was especially commended in the report of Mr. Weir.

Scott, Sir George Gilbert, R. A. (*Brit.*) (1811 – 1878.) Son of the Bible commentator. Was placed at an early age in an architect's office, and designed the Martyrs' Memorial in Oxford in 1842. Later, he furnished designs for churches in Camberwell, Croydon, Leeds, Liverpool, Doncaster, and elsewhere. In 1855 he obtained a medal of the second class for designs exhibited in the Paris Exposition of that year. In 1861 he was elected Academician of the Royal Academy in London, sending " Views illustrative of Gothic Designs of Government Offices." His drawings of the Memorial Window to the Prince Consort for the Chapel Royal, Windsor, were at the Royal Academy in 1862 ; view of the New Leeds Infirmary, in 1863 ; the Midland Railway terminus and hotel, in 1865 ; a new building for the University of Glasgow, in 1869. In 1873 he received the honor of Knighthood, contributing the same year, to the Royal Academy, designs for the Cathedral of St. Mary's, Edinburgh. In 1875 he exhibited Premiated Designs for the new German Parliament House, prepared in conjunction with his son, J. O. Scott.

"Scott's merit as a designer lies rather in the whole than in the details. Carefully and correctly drawn, the main outlines of his more important buildings are sometimes satisfactory. But a nearer approach reveals that the ornament is cold and unimaginative ; compared with what the higher Gothic demands, it is dead decoration." — PALGRAVE's *Essays on Art.*

Scott, Julian, A. N. A. (*Am.*) Born in the State of Vermont. During the American Civil War he was attached to a Vermont regiment, where his rough charcoal sketches of war-scenes attracted the attention of art-lovers in the army. He opened a studio in New York at the close of the war, and began to exhibit at the National Academy in 1870, sending " Gen. O. B. Wilcox in Libby Prison " (belonging to William T. Blodgett) and " The Rear-Guard at White Oak Swamp " (the property of the Union League Club). He was elected an Associate of the National Academy in 1871. In 1873 he exhibited "Complacency" (belonging to William E. Dodge, Jr.) ; in 1874, "Prison Life" (belonging to John Rogers), "Near the Outposts" (belonging to Judge J. R. Brady), "Cavalry Charge near Ashby's Gap, Va., in 1862" (to Col. Joel B. Erhardt), and "On Board the Hartford" (belonging to Loyall Farragut) ; in 1875, "Old Records" (belonging to William E. Dodge) ; in 1876, "The Duel of Burr and Hamilton" and "The Capture of André" (belonging to J. Abner Harper), and "A Camp Raid" (the property of Fletcher Harper, Jr.) ; in 1877, "Reserves awaiting Orders" (belonging to R. B. Livermore) : in 1878, "Meditation" (belonging to J. W. Casilear) and "Poke o' Moonshine." To the Water-Color Exhibition he has sent "Changing Guard, 1776," "New England Turkey-Shoot" (belonging to N. T. Bailey), and "On Guard, 1861."

[No response to circular.]

Seel, Adolf. (*Ger.*) Born at Wiesbaden, 1829. Member of the Royal Society of Water-Color Artists of Belgium. Studied at Düsseldorf Academy, and was a disciple of K. Sohn. Resided in Paris for two years, and passed two other years in Italy ; traveled also in Spain, Portugal, Africa, and the Orient. On these journeys he made many sketches. At the National Gallery, Berlin, is his "Arabian Court-Yard in Cairo," which was sent to the Paris Exposition of 1878.

Ségé, Alexandre. (*Fr.*) Born at Paris. Chevalier of the Legion of Honor. Pupil of Flers and Cogniet. Painter of landscapes. His "Oaks of Kertregonnec" is in the Luxembourg. To the Salon of 1878 he sent "The Green Road" (Seine et Marne), belonging to M. Hédé.

Seiffert, Karl Friedrich. (*Ger.*) Born in 1809. Pupil of the Berlin Academy and of Biermann. He paints landscapes and portraits. He has spent some time in Italy, but lives now in Berlin. His picture of the "Blue Grotto of Capri" is in the Berlin National Gallery.

Seiaser, Martin B. (*Am.*) Born in Pittsburg, Pa., 1845. He went to Europe in 1868, studying under Carl Otto in Munich. In 1869 he entered the Royal Academy of Bavaria, receiving corrections from Piloty, Schwind, and others. He remained in Munich until 1871, when he returned to Pittsburg, where his professional life has since been spent. Among his works are portraits of Francis Murphy, Rev. Carl Lorch, Col. Henry Hays, and others ; and a picture entitled "The Crusaders," painted in 1875, which was stolen in 1878 at an auction sale in Philadelphia.

Sell, Christian. (*Dane.*) Born at Altona, 1831. Studied at Düsseldorf Academy. He is a disciple of Th. Hildebrandt and W. von Schadow. Traveled in Germany and Belgium, and followed the Prussian army in the wars of 1866 and '70. Paints military *genre* subjects and scenes from the older German wars. In the National

Gallery at Berlin is his "Scene at the Battle of Königgrätz." At the Leipsic Museum is his "Soldiers in the Thirty-Years' War dividing Booty."

Sellier, Charles Auguste. (*Fr.*) Born at Nancy. *Prix de Rome* in 1857. Medals in 1865 and '72. Pupil of Leborne and Cogniet. At the Salon of 1875 he exhibited "The Return of the Mendicant Friar" and "Christ in the Tomb"; in 1872, "A Nereid." This artist paints many portraits, two of which were at the Salon of 1878.

Sellstedt, Lars Gustaf, N. A. (*Am.*) Born in Sweden, 1819. Began life as a sailor, following the sea for some years. In 1842 he settled in Buffalo, N. Y., where the better part of his professional life has been spent. Here he began to study art without a master, and made portraiture his specialty. In 1846 he met Thomas Le Clear, and profited much by the association. In 1858 he began to exhibit in the National Academy, New York. In 1859 he sent the head of a Jewish Rabbi, which attracted some attention. In 1871, when he was elected an Associate of the National Academy, he contributed his own portrait, which is now owned by the Buffalo Fine Art Academy. He exhibited a portrait of William G. Fargo in 1874, and was elected Academician. From 1862 to '76 he was Corresponding Secretary and Superintendent of the Buffalo Fine Art Academy, an institution which, with Le Clear, William H. Beard, and others, he was instrumental in founding. He was its President in 1876 and '77, and, from preference became again its Superintendent in 1878. Among Mr. Sellstedt's portraits may be mentioned those of Judge Verplanck and Mrs. Fargo (belonging to William G. Fargo), Millard Fillmore (belonging to the Buffalo Club), E. G. Spaulding and wife, Dr. William Shelton, George W. Clinton, LL. D., in the Natural Science Rooms, Buffalo, and others, including eleven "kit kat" portraits of distinguished citizens of Buffalo, — mayors, judges, lawyers, etc., in the City Hall of that city. His "Abandoned," a marine picture, is in the possession of David Gray of Buffalo, and other *genre* and marine pictures of more or less importance are owned in Buffalo and elsewhere.

"One of the very best portraits of the year is that of Mr. L. G. Sellstedt, painted by himself. It is not possible to conceive a more unaffected piece of realism." — *New York Tribune*, April, 1871.

"The half-length of an artist — probably himself — by Mr. Sellstedt of Buffalo, turning from his easel to speak to a friend or to look at a sitter, is the finest portrait in this year's Exhibition; gravely strong in color, while the head is painted with wonderful roundness and reality." — *New York Leader*, April, 1871.

Semper, Gottfried. (*Ger.*) Born at Hamburg, 1804. Professor of the Academy at Dresden. Member of the Academy of Marlborough House. Professor of Architecture at Zurich. Medal at Paris, 1867. This architect studied at Munich and Paris, and visited Italy, Sicily, and Greece. He acquired at Dresden a great reputation as an instructor, and was charged with the decoration of the antique cabinet of the Royal Museum. He also superintended the construction of the Hos-

11 *

pital of the Ladies of Saint-Maternité, and in 1839, by order of the King, constructed the new theater, which proved a great success. He was also architect of the new synagogue, the Villa Oppenheim, and the new Royal Museum, commenced in 1847, which·he conducted only to the first floor. It was finished after his designs, with the exception of the cupola. He reconstructed the church of St. Nicolas at Hamburg. On account of political troubles he left Germany for England in 1848, and soon became a member of the Academy of Marlborough House. In 1856 he was called to Zurich, where he has been Professor of Architecture and Director of the School of Architecture of the Polytechnic Academy of the Confederation. [Died at Rome, May, 1879.]

Settegast, Josef. (*Ger.*) Born at Coblenz, 1813. Studied in Düsseldorf and Frankfort, and went to Rome. Upon his return to Germany he executed frescos in the Maximilian Church at Düsseldorf, which established his reputation as a painter.

Shaldere, George. (*Brit.*) (1825 – 1873.) Landscape-painter. He introduced animals into his pictures, and executed many pictures of the scenery of Surrey and Hampshire, besides views in Ireland.

Shapleigh, F. H. (*Am.*) Born in Boston, 1842. He has spent his professional life in his native city, and was elected a member of the Boston Art Club in 1874, but received his art education in the studio of Lambinet in Paris. A landscape-painter. Among his more important pictures are, "Venice" (belonging to A. F. Harvey, Boston), French landscape (belonging to J. C. Howe), "Cathedral Rocks" (to C. O. Foster), "Mount Washington" (to W. F. Robinson), "Yosemite Valley" (in the possession of Henry C. Bacon, San Francisco), "Mirror Lake" (owned by David Dudley Field, New York), "Cohasset Harbor" (owned by Martin Bates), etc.

"Shapleigh is engaged on a winter subject, already nearly finished, the composition of which is novel and decidedly pleasing. . . . . The snow is represented with great fidelity, and the cold atmosphere of winter, the dark and brittle foliage, and so forth, are also rendered capitally." — *Boston Post*, March 14, 1878.

Shattuck, Aaron D., N. A. (*Am.*) Born in the State of New Hampshire, in 1832. In 1850 he entered the studio of Alexander Ransom in Boston, and painted portraits. Later, he became a pupil of the National Academy of New York, settling finally in that city. He first exhibited, at the National Academy in 1856, a study of wildflowers and grasses. In 1861 he was elected Academician. Among his earlier works are, "Glimpses of Lake Champlain," "Autumnal View of Androscoggin Scenery," "Sunset on the Lake," and others. In 1869 he sent to the National Academy, "Hillside, Lake Champlain" and "Morning Light"; in 1870, "Lake Champlain" and "A Study of Rocks"; in 1871, "The New England Farm" and "A Group of Sheep"; in 1872, "White Hills in October"; in 1873, "Sheep"; in 1874, "Sheep and Cattle in Landscape" (belonging to

J. H. Sherwood); in 1875, "The Old Homestead" and "Haying-Time"; in 1876, "The Road to Simsbury; Ct." and "Autumn near Stockbridge, Mass."; in 1877, "Granbury Pastures" and "Cattle Grazing." His "Stockbridge Scenery" (25 by 42) brought $ 660 at the Johnston sale in 1876.

"Shattuck is exact, graceful, and often effective; there is a true pastoral vein in him. His best cattle and water scenes, with meadows and trees, are eloquent of repose and of nature." — TUCKERMAN'S *Book of the Artists*.

Shaw, Richard Norman, R. A. (*Brit.*) Student of the Royal Academy. Received silver medal for architectural drawings in 1852, gold medal in 1853, and traveling studentship in 1854. He has furnished designs for many public and private buildings throughout Great Britain, turning his attention chiefly to country-houses. He was elected an Associate of the Royal Academy in 1872, and Academician in 1878.

Shaw, Annie C. (*Am.*) Born at Troy, N. Y., 1852. She has lived for some years in Chicago, studying art under H. C. Ford of that city. She was elected an Associate of the Chicago Academy of Design in 1873, and Academician in 1876, the first woman upon whom the distinction has been conferred. Among her paintings are, "On the Calumet" (1874), belonging to J. H. Dole; "Willow Island" (1875), belonging to C. L. Hutchinson; "Keene Valley, N. Y." (1875), to A. A. Munger; "Ebb-Tide on the Coast of Maine" (1876), to William Butterfield; "Head of a Jersey Bull" (1877), to Mrs. Jenny F. Kempton; "Returning from the Fair" (1878), exhibited in Chicago, Boston, New York, and elsewhere. Her "Illinois Prairie" was at the Centennial Exhibition at Philadelphia in 1876.

"Annie C. Shaw has steadily advanced in the profession, and has achieved decided success in painting landscapes, having studied from nature in successive summers at Mackinac, the Adirondacks, the Rock River region, the coast of Maine, and in the quiet nooks of Massachusetts. . . . . Her latest painting is a study from life of an Alderney bull, which is a marked departure from her previous attempts, and is faithful to nature. It is a bold, strong picture, good in form, and filled with vigorous characteristics of animal life." — *Milwaukee Evening Wisconsin*, 1877.

"Annie C. Shaw has finished her upright landscape, of medium size, combining the best results of her studies for many years. It bears the title 'Returning from the Fair,' from the group of Alderney cattle in the road curving through the forest. The eye of the spectator is struck with the rich mass of foliage passing from the light green of the birches in the foreground, where the light breaks through, to the dark green of the dense forest, shading into the brownish tints of the early September-tinged leaves. Farther on, the eye is carried back through a beautiful vista formed by the road leading through the center of the picture, giving a fine perspective and distance through a leafy archway of elms and other forest-trees, that gracefully mingle their branches overhead, through which one catches a glimpse of deep-blue sky. As the eye follows this roadway to its distant portion, the sun lights up the sky, tingeing with a mellow light the group of small trees and willows, contrasting beautifully with the almost somber tones of the dense forest in the middle distance." — *Chicago Times*, April, 1878.

Shirlaw, Walter. (*Am.*) Born in Paisley, Scotland, 1837. He was taken to America in 1840, and has spent his professional life in Chicago, Munich (Bavaria), and New York, studying in Munich for some years under Professors Rabb, Wagner, Ramberg, and Lindenschmidt, eminent men of the various schools there. He was elected Academician of the Chicago Academy of Design in 1868, Associate of the National Academy, New York, in 1878, and is at present (1878) a professor in the Art Students' League in the latter city. His "Toning of the Bell," a number of "Heads," and minor works are owned in Chicago. To the Society of American Artists, of which he was one of the original members and first President, he sent, in 1878, "Good Morning," "The Young Patrician," "Sleep," and a study of a "Head." To the National Academy, in 1877, he sent "Sheep-Shearing in the Bavarian Highlands"; in 1878, "The Bather" and a portrait.

His "Toning of the Bell" and "Feeding the Poultry" were at the Centennial Exhibition in Philadelphia in 1876; "Sheep-Shearing in the Bavarian Highlands," at the Paris Exposition of 1878.

"Mr. Shirlaw, a student of Munich, exhibited two exceptionally strong and admirable works, evincing remarkably dexterous powers of manipulation." — PROF. WEIR's *Official Report of the American Centennial Exhibition of 1876.*

Shumway, Henry C., N. A. (*Am.*) Born in Middletown, Ct., 1807. He settled in New York at an early age, and during his long professional career has been a resident of that city. He was a student of the American Academy of Fine Arts in 1828 and '29, and one of the early members of the National Academy of Design, having been elected Academician in 1832. In 1829 he began his career as an artist by painting on ivory, exhibiting his work annually at the National Academy for many years. As a portrait-painter he was popular and successful, and has numbered among his sitters many prominent citizens of New York and other places. In 1838 he was commissioned to go to Washington, D. C., to paint Henry Clay, the picture being owned at present by Mrs. Gideon Lee of New York.

Shurtleff, R. M. (*Am.*) Born at Rindge, N. H. After studying drawing at the Lowell Institute, Boston, and at the National Academy, New-York, he settled in the latter city, where most of his professional life has been spent. Among his pictures are, "A Race for Life," "The American Panther," "The Still Hunter" (belonging to George Dwight, Jr., of Springfield, Mass.), and the "Wolf at the Door," owned in Utica, N. Y.

"'A Race for Life' [N. A., 1877] is the most remarkable animal picture in the Exhibition. It will surprise every one who overlooked the artist's 'Panther' of last year, and who only remember him by his landscapes. Scene and subject are equally grim and terrific. A weird winter forest; gleams of a coppery sunset burning low behind the trees; prints of flying feet on the crisp, livid snow; and a horde of ravenous gray wolves dashing forward in an animal frenzy of pursuit, the foremost seeming to spring bodily from the canvas. . . . . The open, slavering mouths, the swift vigor of the legs and paws, the hair bristling into knotty points and rising along the back, are all repre-

ARTISTS OF THE NINETEENTH CENTURY. 253

sented with a power which makes the spectator's flesh creep. "It is rather a ghastly subject which Mr. Shurtleff has chosen, but he has succeeded in giving it the necessary tragic dignity." — *New York Tribune,* April 28, 1878.

"Mr. Shurtleff has executed a grimly humorous painting, 'The Wolf at the Door,' representing an open studio door, with the easel and hand of the artist just dimly visible within, and hungrily waiting outside a lone gaunt wolf, evidently just at the point of starvation or he would not call at that unpromising abode." — *Springfield Republican.*

Siegert, August. (*Ger.*) Born at Nenwied, 1820. Studied at Düsseldorf and paints historical subjects, among which are, "The Entrance of Luther into Worms," "Frederick defending his Son pressed upon by the Soldiers of the Emperor," etc. He also paints *genre* scenes, such as "Hospitality," "Children in an Artist's Studio," and "The Service of Love," in the Museum of Hamburg.

Siemiradsky, Henri. (*Pole.*) Born at Kharkow, 1843. Gold medal at St. Petersburg. Medal at Philadelphia. Pupil of the Academy of St. Petersburg. *Prix de Rome.* His picture of "The Confidence of Alexander the Great in his Physician" (1870) attracted much attention. At Philadelphia he exhibited "The Amulet Seller." His picture of "The Christians burning for Torches before Nero" excited an unusual interest in Rome. It combines remarkable effects of magnificence and horror. The architecture, the pomp of the Emperor with his Empress, courtiers, and attendants, would well befit a scene of peace and happiness. But the horrible effect of placing in the midst of all this splendor these Christian martyrs, bound and ready for the burning, with the executioners waiting to apply the torches, can only be realized in seeing it ; for so well is the reality made to appear in this picture, that one feels by turns horror and pity, as fully as if in a life scene of the same character. The wonder is great that so young an artist could have grasped the thought or its execution. This picture is to be permanently in St. Petersburg.

To the Paris Exposition (1878) he sent the above-described picture, "The Cup or the Woman," and "The Shipwrecked Beggar."

Signol, Émile (*Fr.*) Born at Paris, 1804. Member of the Institute, and Officer of the Legion of Honor. Pupil of Blondel, Gros, and l'École des Beaux-Arts. He gained the *prix de Rome* in 1830. His picture of "The Adulteress" (1840) is at the Luxembourg, and gained much fame for the artist by reproductions in engraving which are widely known. Several works by this master are at Versailles. His "Death of Sapphira" is at the Madeleine. He has executed much decorative work in other churches of Paris, the last of which was that of Saint-Augustin. He has also painted many portraits.

Silva, Francis A. (*Am.*) Born in New York, 1835. He inherited his taste for art from his grandfather, Col. François Jean of the French army, who was exiled during the first Revolution, went to Lisbon, devoted himself to his brush, and became Painter to the Spanish Court. Young Silva, whose father opposed his studying art, after trying several trades, was finally apprenticed to a sign-painter in

New York, remaining until the outbreak of the Civil War. He served in the army as an officer until 1866, when he returned to his native city. In 1868 he began his professional career as an artist. He is entirely self-taught. He was elected a Member of the Water-Color Society in 1872, of the Artists' Fund Society in 1873. He devotes himself particularly to marine views. Among his more important works are, "Moonrise" (belonging to Eugene Van Rensselaer), "On the Hudson" (to Dr. Judson of St. Petersburg, Russia), "Sunrise in Boston Harbor" (to H. P. Cooper), "A Gray Day at Cape Ann" (to R. G. Dun), "Bass Rocks" (to George C. Waldo), "Sunset on the Coast" and "Moonrise, Hudson River" (to J. A. Jameson), "New London Light" (to Cortlandt Palmer), "The Twilight Hour" (to Jackson Schultz), "Hudson River" (to Cyrus Butler), "The Yacht Magic" (to W. T. Garner), and "Moonlight on the Chesapeake" (to W. J. Best).

Simart, Pierre Charles. (*Fr.*) Born at Troyes (1806 – 1857). Member of the Institute. He wished to be a sculptor from his earliest years ; but he met with positive persecution from his family on account of this desire, and at seventeen he went to Paris with a pension of only 300 francs a year from his native city. It is easy to see that on this sum he could only live in misery, and his trials had such an effect on him that one of his friends says of him, that he entered on life with a broken heart. He was always a prey to intense sadness, as may be seen from his letters (Étude sur sa vie et son œuvre par M. Gustave Eyriès). In 1833 Simart obtained the grand *prix de Rome*, and went there at about the same time as Ingres, who replaced Horace Vernet. His first notable work was the "Disk-Thrower," models of which, in plaster, are at the Louvre and at the Museum of Troyes. His "Orestes taking Refuge at the Altar of Pallas" was called by Ingres the most beautiful statue of modern times. It was seen at the Salon of 1840. The plaster model is at the château of Vendreuve, and the marble is at the Museum of Rouen. He next executed two bas-reliefs, "Sculpture" and "Architecture," which were placed on the right wing of the Hotel de Ville at Paris; two large figures, "Justice" and "Abundance," attached to the columns of the Barrière du Trône; the bust of a Prince of the House of Orleans, at Versailles; "Philosophy," a marble statue in the library of the Luxembourg; a bust of M. Jourdan at the Museum of Troyes ; and "An Angel consoling Tobias," belonging to Daguet, a molder at Paris. All these works were executed between 1840 and '43. In 1841 Simart married, and from that time his life was happier. He then undertook a "Virgin and Child" for the altar of the Virgin in the Cathedral of Troyes. It is now in its place, — a marble group, — both figures are standing, but the position seems to separate too much the mother and child ; altogether, it is not satisfactory in sentiment. Simart next executed the bas-reliefs for the château of the Duke de

Luynes at Dampierre ; they are among his best works. For several years previous to 1857 he was occupied with the decoration of the tomb of Napoleon I. at the Invalides, and the ceiling of the Salon Carré at the Louvre. These works are not likely to increase his fame. In 1857 he composed the charming group of " Art demanding Inspiration. from Poesy " (in marble), in the Salle du Trône at the palace of the Luxembourg. This was completed from his model after his death. At the Museum of Troyes is a collection of models from his works.

Simler, Friedrich Karl Josef. (*Ger.*) Born at Hanau (1801 – 1872). Studied at Munich. Landscape and animal painter. He remained some time at Vienna, and traveled in Upper Austria and Styria ; later, in France and Italy. He was for a time at Hanover, where he had been commissioned to paint a number of portraits. In 1862 he settled at Aschaffenburg. At the National Gallery, Berlin, is his picture of a " Wild Bull." The three sons of Simler all studied art.

Simmons, William Henry. (*Brit.*) Born in 1811. Received his art education in London, and gained a medal of the Society of Arts while still a young man. Among the more important of Simmons' plates are, " The Queen in the Highlands," after Landseer ; "The Marriage of the Prince of Wales," after Frith ; " A Wee Bit Fractious," " His Only Pair," " Daddy 's Coming," " The Poor Man's Friend," " Baith Faither and Mither," and others, after Thomas Faed; "Christ and his Disciples " and " The Light of the World," after Holman Hunt ; " The Proscribed Royalist " and "Rosalind and Celia," after Millais ; " Not Guilty," after Abraham Solomon ; " Both Puzzled" and " Steady, Johnny !" after Erskine Nicol; " Luff Boy," after Hook ; " Great Expectations," after Henry Le Jeune ; " The Shepherd of Jerusalem," after P. R. Morris ; and many more.

Simmons, Franklin. (*Am.*) Born in Maine, 1841. He devoted his leisure time as a boy to drawing and painting, and finally to modeling, executing portrait busts as soon as he graduated from college. In Washington, during the Civil War, he found ample employment in the cutting of busts of statesmen and soldiers, and the execution in bronze of several statues for public monuments. He settled in Rome about 1867. Among his works executed there are the statues of Roger Williams and Governor King, in Washington ; "Jochebed," for Mr. W. S. Appleton ; " Roger Williams," in bronze, in Providence, R. I., unveiled in 1877 ; and the Naval Monument in front of the National Capitol.

" The general expression of the principal figure [Jochebed] is the union of mental activity with external repose. This is well contrasted with the restless playfulness of the smiling boy, Moses. The design of Jochebed's figure would almost amount to grandeur were not its simplicity lessened in a degree by the exuberance of the drapery, or rather by its being cut up into numberless folds." — *Art Journal,* October, 1873.

" The story tells itself with all-sufficient completeness, but the merits of the statue

[' Jochebed '] do not by any means exhaust themselves with a satisfactory exposition of the subject. The face is full of expression, and the draperies, while broadly massed, as draperies in sculpture always should be, are minutely and admirably studied in a manner that is suggestive of some of the best antique work." — *Great American Sculptors.*

Simonetti, Cavaliere Attilio. (*Ital.*) Born at Rome. Professor at Naples. Pupil of Fortuny. At the Paris Salon of 1875 he exhibited " The First Fable " ; in 1876, "After the Ball " ; in 1878, at the Exposition, " Via Giuseppe Mancinelli, at Palazzolo." At the Johnston sale, New York, 1876, his " Proclamation in Front of the Pantheon " (32 by 63) sold for $ 2,725.

Simonsen, Niels. (*Dane.*) Born in Copenhagen, 1807. Member of the Academy of Copenhagen. Studied first in Copenhagen under Professor Lund. Went then to Munich. He traveled in Algeria, and, by a picture of " Lord Byron's Corsair," won considerable fame. His best works are sea-views, among which may be mentioned " Fishermen rescuing a Ship in the North Sea." " A Betrothal, Sweden " may be commended for its representation of national customs.

Simpson, William. (*Brit.*) Born in Glasgow. He commenced his career as an artist in his native city, where he was apprenticed to a firm of lithographers. Later, he removed to London, entering the employment of the Messrs. Day. He went to the Crimea in 1854, and during the Russian war sent home sketches which were published in book form. He was in India in 1859, and has visited many countries on the staff of the Illustrated London News. He is a member of the Royal Geographical Society, and exhibits occasionally sketches in water-colors, as well as in black and white.

Sinding, Otto. (*Norwegian.*) Medal at Philadelphia, where he exhibited " Ruth and Boaz," which Weir pronounced the most important work in the exhibit of Norway, and says, in his report, " This picture is a production of mature art, admirable in sentiment, in breadth and freedom of execution, and fine in color. The figures are thoroughly well drawn, and the landscape skillfully rendered."

" Otto Sinding is a coast-painter who makes one actually hear the roar of the breakers as they chase each other in tumultuous masses, and lash the rocks with a power that may be felt." — BENJAMIN's *Contemporary Art in Europe.*

Skill, F. John. (*Brit.*) Contemporary English water-color artist. Member of the Institute, living in London. Devotes himself to landscape and marine views, with occasional figure-pieces. Among his works are, " Rising Tide," " By the Sea," " A Shrimper," " Thames Lock in June," " Sheep, South Devon," " Little Cow-Keeper," " Her First Ball," etc. To the Paris Exposition he contributed, " View on the Tiber " and " San Lorenzo, Genoa."

"The tints are so delicately chosen, are so skillfully combined, that we must look upon this little sketch [F. J. Skill's ' Sunrise on the Grand Canal, Venice,' 1875] as equal in effect to anything in the Exhibition. It is conceived and executed in the true spirit of water-color art." — *Art Journal,* February, 1875.

Skovgaard, Peter Christian. (*Dane.*) (1817 – 1876.) Professnr at the Academy of Copenhagen, where he studied and won medals. He is one of the most celebrated landscape-painters of Denmark. Few northern artists have so nearly approached Claude Lorraine. His drawing is better than his color. His pictures of wood-scenes and of gently flowing streams are especially good. Several of his best works are at Christiansborg. His portraits are also good. Eight of his Danish landscapes were exhibited at the Paris Exposition of 1878.

Slingineyer, Ernest. (*Belgian.*) Born at Loochristi, 1823. Chevalier of the Order of Léopold. He won several medals. Pupil of Wappers. He sent to the Brussels Exposition of 1842 "The Avenger," afterwards seen at Paris and The Hague, and sold in Cologne. His "Death of Classicus" was purchased by the King of Holland ; the "Death of Jacobsen," by the King of Belgium ; "Camoens," by the King of Portugal. He has painted several battle-pieces, which have been much praised. Among his other works are, "The Christian Martyr," "An Episode of St. Bartholomew's," and "The Physician Vesalius following the Army of Charles V.," a *chef-d'œuvre,* now at the Museum of Brussels.

Small, William. (*Brit.*) Contemporary English landscape-artist, residing in London. Member of the Institute of Painters in Water-Colors. Among his works in that medium are, "The Fallen Monarch," "Going to Market," "Connemara," "Early Spring," "The Harvest-Field," "The Last Offer," "At Hampstead," etc. In oil he has exhibited of late years, at the Royal Academy, "After the Storm," "The Highland Harvest-Home," and others. To the Paris Exposition of 1878 he sent "The Wreck " (in oil), and "Beech-Trees " and "Poplars " (in water-colors).

" 'The Wreck ' [R. A., 1876], by William Small, is a noble specimen of grandly painted seascape, certainly one of the masterpieces of the year." — *Art Journal,* July, 1876.

Smart, John. (*Brit.*) Born in Edinburgh. Educated in his native city, spending the greater part of his professional life there. A landscape-painter, he devotes himself particularly to the wild and barren scenery of the Highlands of Scotland, frequently introducing cattle into his pictures. For some years Associate of the Royal Scottish Academy, he was elected Academician in 1877. Among his later works may be noted, "Autumn, Glen Lyons," "Drumbarry," "Head of Glen Ogle," "Hill Frank, — Clipping-Day," "A Feeding Storm," "In the Pass of Lyon," "Far from the Busy World," "When Hilltops a' were White," "Halt of the Herd," etc., exhibited at the Royal Academy and the Royal Scottish Academy. His "Gloom of Glen Ogle" was at the Philadelphia Exhibition of 1876 ; "Among the Yellow Corn," at Paris in 1878.

" Perhaps John Smart has risen more rapidly into deserved esteem than most of his compeers. He has certainly never achieved greater success than in ' The First of Winter's Snaws ' [R. S. A., 1874]. The chill from the whitened hillside creeps into our blood, and we feel that none but a veritable scion of canld Caledonia could have expounded a theme of such thoroughly bleak nationality." — *Art Journal,* March, 1874.

Q

Smillie, James. (*Brit.-Am.*) Born at Edinburgh, 1807. When about eleven years old he was apprenticed to a silver-engraver. This master died soon, and Smillie was for a short time with Edward Mitchell, an engraver of pictures. When he was less than fourteen he was taken to America. His father and brothers established themselves as jewelers in Quebec, and James worked for them. His skill attracted the notice of Lord Dalhousie, who gave him a passage to London, with letters of introduction. This proved an injury, for the engravers to whom he applied demanded large prices for his instruction, supposing him to be a protégé of Lord Dalhousie. He therefore went to Edinburgh, and remained five months with Andrew Wilson, and then returned to Quebec. He went to New York City in 1829, and has since resided there. He has been much connected with banknote engraving. He was made a member of the National Academy in 1851. His plate of "The Convent Gate," after R. W. Weir, first attracted public attention to his work. His series after Cole's "Voyage of Life" and Bierstadt's "Rocky Mountains" are too well known to require praise. Among his best plates are, "The Bay and Harbor of New York," after John J. Chapman; "Dover Plains," after A. B.· Durand; "Evening, in the New York Highlands," after Weir; "Mount Washington, from Conway Valley," after John F. Kensett; "American Harvesting," after J. F. Cropsey; "The Land of the Cypress," after D. Huntingdon; etc.

"James Smillie, conceded to be the best landscape engraver in America, is altogether a self-educated man, overcoming every obstacle by patient, persistent effort. His plates, the most important in this particular branch of the art yet produced in this country, executed with great taste and ability, are replete with fine artistic feeling, and are truthful translations of the originals." — W. S. BAKER, *American Engravers and their Works.*

Smillie, James D., N. A. (*Am.*) Born in New York, 1833. Son of James Smillie, N. A., by whom he was educated as an engraver on steel, devoting all his time to that profession, until 1864, when he turned his attention to drawing and painting, without, however, the benefit of schools or masters. He has spent his professional life in New York, studying also among the great mountain-ranges of the United States, the Sierras, the Adirondacks, the Rocky, White, and Catskill Mountains. He made a short visit to Europe in 1862. He was elected an Associate of the National Academy in 1868, Academician in 1876, and member of the Council the next year. He was one of the original members of the American Society of Painters in Water-Colors, in 1866, was its first Treasurer, and its President from 1873 to '78, contributing regularly to its exhibitions as well as to those of the Academy of Design. Among the more important of his works may be mentioned, "Evening among the Sierras of California" (owned by S. T. Williams of New York), "The Lifting of the Clouds, White Mountains" (belonging to George Hearne of New York), and "Dark against Day's Golden Death" (belonging to William M. Smillie of

New York), all in oil; in water, "A Scrub-Race on the Western Prairies" (owned by W. Wilson of New York) and "The Track of the Torrent, Adirondacks" (in the collection of F. W. Lewis of Philadelphia). "The Scrub-Race" and "A Study from Nature, Ausable River" were at the Centennial Exhibition at Philadelphia in 1876. For Appletons' "Picturesque America" he illustrated "The Saguenay," and furnished the letter-press description as well as the illustration for the article on the Yosemite in the same work.

"In the coloring the tones on the mountain side, in shadow, are almost opalescent in effect, and are brought together and harmonized in the most artistic way ['Evening, High Sierras, Cal.,' N. A., 1876]." -- *Art Journal*, June, 1876.

Smillie, George H., A. N. A. (*Am.*) Born in the city of New York, 1840. Son of James Smillie, line-engraver, and younger brother of J. D. Smillie, N. A. He entered the studio of James M. Hart at an early age, spending the greater part of his professional life in New York. In 1871 he made a trip to the Rocky Mountains and the Yosemite Valley for the purpose of study and sketching, and in 1874 he visited Florida. He was elected an Associate of the National Academy in 1864, and member of the American Water-Color Society in 1868, contributing regularly to the annual exhibitions of both institutions. Among his more important works are, "Boquet River and Hills" (N. A., 1869), belonging to A. Van Valkenburg, New York; "Under the Pines of the Yosemite" (water-color, 1872), owned by James Smillie; "A Lake in the Woods" (N. A., 1872), the property of Touro Robertson, New York; "A Florida Lagoon" (N. A., 1875), owned in Utica. To the Centennial Exhibition he sent (in oil) his "Lake in the Woods" and (in water-color) "Sentinel Rock, Yosemite Valley" and "Study on the Ausable River, N. Y."

"George H. Smillie's sketches do infinite credit to him in their carefully finished execution and in the understanding of the subject. . . . . A certain refinement runs through all his artistic work, no matter what be the subject. It enhances the charm of his more quiet scenes, and modifies, without losing the character of bolder, wilder views. His sketches in detail show a careful study which form most promising and valuable means for important works."— *New York Herald*, November, 1870.

"There is a charming picture of good size by George H. Smillie, 'Under the Pines of the Yosemite.' Two large, brown pine trunks rise about thirty or forty feet to the top of the picture. Indians are camping beneath, etc. . . . . The work is full of artistic skill and of poetical feeling, and gives us delightful associations with this romantic and unexplored region." — *Atlantic Monthly*, March, 1872.

Smirke, Sir Robert, R. A. (*Brit.*) (1780-1867.) Son of Robert Smirke, a prominent painter and member of the Royal Academy. He studied architecture in Italy, and elsewhere on the Continent, and upon his return to England was employed upon the British Museum and the new London Post-Office. He designed many buildings in Great Britain, public and private, and was knighted by William IV. in 1831. He was elected an Associate of the Royal Academy in 1813, Academician in 1823, and for many years was Treasurer to the Academy, resigning that position in 1850.

Smirke, Sydney, R. A. (*Brit.*) Born in the early part of the present century. Younger brother of Sir Robert Smirke. He entered the schools of the Royal Academy as a youth, gaining the gold medal in 1819. In 1848 he was elected an Associate of the Royal Academy, Academician in 1860, Professor of Architecture in 1861. Treasurer in 1862, Trustee in 1867, and was placed upon the list of Honorary Retired Academicians in 1877. Among the better known of the London buildings designed by Sydney Smirke are the Carleton Club, the Conservative Club, the Reading-Room and other portions of the British Museum, and the new Royal Academy, Burlington House, completed in 1874. He was also engaged in the restoration of the Temple Church, London, York Minster, Lichfield Cathedral, and many fine edifices throughout the kingdom.

Smith, Colvin. (*Brit.*) (1793 – 1875.) Began his art career at an early age, entering the schools of the Royal Academy in London, and studying and painting in Italy. He settled in Edinburgh in 1827, and became a member of the Scottish Academy in 1829. He exhibited as late as 1871. A portrait-painter, having many of his distinguished fellow-countrymen for his subjects ; among these, Mackenzie ("The Man of Feeling"), Jeffrey, Sir Walter Scott, and others. His portrait of Scott was very successful, has been engraved, and it is said that over twenty copies of it were painted by the artist, for many of which Sir Walter gave sittings.

Smith, T. L., A. N. A. (*Am.*) Born in Glasgow, 1835. He emigrated to America at an early age, and studied for a short time under George H. Boughton, in Albany, N. Y. He opened a studio in that city in 1859, remaining there three years. In 1862 he removed to New York, where the rest of his professional life has been spent. He has been a frequent contributor to the exhibitions of the National Academy, and was elected an Associate of that institution in 1870. He began his career as a painter of winter scenes, with a strong love for the season itself, and has devoted himself almost exclusively to the delineation of landscapes of that character, with marked success. Among his more important works are, " The Homestead in Winter," at the National Academy in 1871 ; "The Grove in Winter," at the National Academy in 1872 (owned in Albany, N. Y., by Captain Sweeney) ; " The Deserted House," at the National Academy in 1873 (now in the collection of W. H. Hamilton of New York); " The Eve of St. Agnes," exhibited at the Boston Art Club in 1873 (now in the Saville Collection of that city) ; and " Woods in Winter " and " Woods in Autumn," his two largest works, belonging to J. H. White of Boston. "The Deserted House " and " The Eve of St. Agnes " were at the Centennial Exhibition at Philadelphia in 1876.

" Mr. Smith paints, conscientiously, winter trees and snow, a farmer's cosy home, out-buildings, and wood-piles ; the calm, warm glow of a winter sky and clouds, truly and faithfully, according to his own inspiration. . . . . The merit of this picture [' Winter

Homestead '], as far as style is concerned, is the art, which conceals art, an individuality of thought and expression by which we recognize and sympathize with a fresh local inspiration from nature." — *New York Evening Post,* April, 1870.

Smith, George. (*Brit.*) Born in London, 1829. He entered the schools of the Royal Academy in 1845, and was also for some time a pupil of Cope. He first exhibited at the Royal Academy about 1850, and regularly since. Among his early works are, " The Launch " and " The Bird-Trap." In 1861 he exhibited " The Seven Ages "; in 1862, " Searching for the Well "; in 1864, " Beware of the Dog "; in 1865, " Light and Darkness "; in 1867, " The Valentine "; in 1869, " A Game of Speculation "; in 1870, " In the Study "; in 1872, " Paying the Legacies "; in 1873, " Who comes here ? "; in 1875, " A Scrap of Nature "; in 1876, " Out in the Cold World "; in 1878, " The Soldier's Wife."

Smith, A. Cary. (*Am.*) Born in New York, 1837. He studied under M. F. H. De Haas, and has spent his professional life in his native city, devoting himself to marine views. He has been a frequent exhibitor at the National Academy for some years, sending, in 1867, " Off Little Gull "; " The Yacht Eva " (belonging to L. L. Lorillard), in 1868; " Sunrise," in 1869; " The Last of the Old Ship " and " Nor'-wester, Coast of Maine," in 1871; " Windy Day," in 1876 ; " The Yacht Dauntless " (belonging to Philip Schuyler), in 1877 ; and " Perils of the Sea," in 1878. He has also painted the yacht " Columbia," for Lester Wallack; the " Sappho," for William P. Douglas; the " Wanderer," for James Stillman; and many more.

Smith, F. Hopkinson. (*Am.*) Born in Baltimore, 1838. A self-educated artist, and prominent member of the Water-Color Society, of which he was elected member in 1871, and Treasurer in 1873, a position he still holds (1878). He is a constant contributor to its exhibitions, sending, in 1871, " Summer in the Woods, White Mountains "; in 1874, " The Old Man of the Mountains "; in 1875, " Overlook Falls " and " Walker's Falls, Franconia Notch, N. H."; in 1876, " A Summer's Day " and " Grandfather's Home "; in 1877, " In the Darkling Woods " (belonging to William D. Irwin, Chicago), " Under the Leaves " (belonging to William D. Sloane, New York), and " Deserted " (the property of Charles F. Havermeyer); in 1878, " The Old Smithy," " Looking Seaward," etc. His professional life has been spent in New York. His " Old Cedars, Franconia Mountains " and " In the Darkling Wood " were at the Centennial Exhibition of 1876. His " Profile Notch " (in charcoal) is in the collection of Samuel V. Wright; " A Cool Spot " (in water-color), in the collection of John Jacob Astor.

" ' Walker's Falls, Franconia Notch ' [N. A., 1875], by F. Hopkinson Smith, is remarkably successful in the delineation of the falling water and the moss-covered rocks which line the ravine. The tree foliage is fresh, and shows some clever gradations from the dark tones in shadow to the topmost branches, which are under the influence of the noonday sunlight." — *Art Journal,* March, 1875.

"Smith belongs much to the same set of landscapists as Bellows, Durand, and in certain respects, Bristol and Whittredge ; painters who represent American scenes of cheerful vegetation, usually under bright skies. Mr. Smith is succeeding very well in water-colors, a branch that neither of the other men we have named, except Bellows, has affected much : and in the recent Water-Color Exhibition of the Academy, if the eye rested upon a clear brook, whose clean amber-colored bed reflected green forest-trees that nodded about it ; or if the visitor espied some rustic bridge that connected two sides of a country village, with gray-white church-steeple ; or where a couple of lovers reposed upon a bank thick grown with wild-flowers — it was quite probable that each of them was painted by this artist. . . . . Mr. Smith's paintings are all of a summer-like character ; and, although the arrangement of his compositions is sometimes a little formal, the detailed objects are well handled ; and whether it be rocks, water, or wood-land glades, all indicate a very genuine lover of Nature, and that a hard and enthusiastic-student is diligently seeking to transcribe her moods." — *Art Journal*, March 11, 1876.

Smith, Frank Hill. (*Am.*) Born in Boston, 1841. He received his early training in the schools of that city, and studied architecture there with Hammatt Billings. Later, he entered the Atelier Suisse in Paris, and was also a pupil of Bonnat, and other masters in Paris and Italy. His professional life has been spent largely abroad, in Belgium, Holland, Italy, the interior of France, and four or five years in Paris. For some time he has been a resident of Boston. He was a Judge of Fine Arts at the Philadelphia Exhibition of 1876, and is a Director of the School of the Boston Museum of Fine Arts. He has painted portraits, figure-pieces, and landscapes ; and his works are in public and private collections in Boston and elsewhere in the United States. " Venice," one of the most important of his landscapes, belongs to the Boston Somerset Club ; another view of " Venice," to Hon. William Claflin of Massachusetts. Within the last two years Mr. Smith has given special attention to fine interior decoration, his study and observations in Europe being in some degree directed with a view to this work. He made many drawings and sketches of famous Continental interiors which he brought to America. He decorated the Windsor Hotel and Opera House, Holyoke, Mass., and several private and public buildings in Boston and Cambridge. In this work he has been assisted by a large corps of artists who have had more or less training under him, but the principal part of the labor he has performed himself.

" Among the notable pictures at Doll and Richards' are the portraits of two children, by Frank H. Smith, which we think will prove more generally attractive than such pictures usually do ; inasmuch as, besides containing excellent likenesses of the originals, it is a charmingly arranged and painted interior, with figures such as any lover of good pictures might enjoy. . . . . The painting of these accessories is worthy of much praise. The characteristics of the different materials, and particularly of the vase, are very skillfully and admirably rendered, while the values of color and tone are managed with fine artistic skill and feeling. Although we have spoken first of the painting of the accessories, they by no means occupy a place of undue prominence, but are subserved with much good taste and forbearance to the figures." — *Boston Transcript*, February 17, 1878.

" Mr. Smith has by no means abandoned the production of oil-paintings, yet much of his time is now occupied in drawing designs for the adorning of the walls of buildings, both public and private. The movement that he has had the honor of inaugurating in this city is now moving rapidly on to success. He has recently completed the drawing-rooms of a residence on Commonwealth Avenue, giving to each detail a careful treatment that has made the walls veritable works of art." — *Boston Post,* July 3, 1878.

Smith, William Russell. (*Am.*) A native of Scotland. He was taken to America at an early age by his family, who settled in Pittsburg, Pa., and apprenticed the lad to Lambdin in Philadelphia, under whom he learned to draw. Returning to Pittsburg, he became a scene-painter in the theater there, and held a similar position in the Walnut Street Theater, Philadelphia, where he is said to have displayed uncommon proficiency in the higher kinds of scenic art. Subsequently he became painter of landscapes of a smaller and more elaborate style in Philadelphia, where his studio still is, and where his pictures are highly prized and many of them owned. His "Cave at Chelton Hills" was at the Centennial Exhibition of 1876.

"We have seldom found landscapes more cherished by their owners or more enjoyed by those intimately acquainted with their authentic charms than are Russell Smith's. . . . . In the happiest efforts of this artist we find the fresh and free impression of nature reproduced with singular vitality." — TUCKERMAN's *Book of the Artists.*

Sohn, Karl Ferdinand. (*Ger.*) Born at Berlin (1805 – 1867). Professor at the Düsseldorf Academy. Studied at the Berlin Academy. In 1826 he followed Schadow to Düsseldorf. In 1830 he went to Italy, and afterwards traveled in France, Belgium, and Holland. In 1832 he became Professor at Düsseldorf, where he takes high rank among the artists of that school, and has instructed many of its best men. At the National Gallery, Berlin, are his "Lute-Players," "The Rape of Hylas," and "Portrait of a Woman." At the Leipsic Museum is his "Donna Diana." Among his other works are, "The Lorelei," "Vanity," "The Sisters," "Tasso and the Two Leonoras," "Romeo and Juliet," "The Judgment of Paris," "Diana at the Bath" (a *chef-d'œuvre*), etc. At the Johnston sale, New York, 1876, "Diana surprised by Acteon" (28 by 23) sold for $ 575.

Solomon, Abraham. (*Brit.*) Born in London (1824 – 1862). He entered the schools of the Royal Academy at the age of fifteen, and was considered a very promising pupil. His first work, "The Courtship of Ditchen" was exhibited at the Royal Academy in 1843, followed by others in a similar vein. His best-known pictures, which have become popular on both sides of the Atlantic by means of the engravings of them, are, "Third Class, — the Parting" and "First Class, — the Return," exhibited in 1854 ; "Waiting for the Verdict," in 1857 ; and "Not Guilty," in 1859. His last exhibited works were, "Le malade imaginaire" and "Consolation," in 1861 ; and "The Lost, Found," in 1862, the year of his death.

Sonntag, William Louis, N. A. (*Am.*) Born in Western Pennsylvania, 1822. His professional life has been spent in Cincinnati, Ohio, in Italy, where he studied and painted for some time, and in the city of New York, which has been his home during the last twenty years. He is a member of the Artists' Fund Society, and was in 1861 elected a full member of the New York Academy of Design. As an artist he is entirely self-taught. His first work of importance was entitled "The Progress of Civilization," comprising four paintings; his second, "Alastor, or the Spirit of Solitude," from Shelley; his third, "The Eagle's Home," painted for Charles M. Stewart of Baltimore; his fourth, "The Dream of Italy," property of Mr. Dinsmore of New York; his fifth, "The Spirit of the Alleghanies," a large canvas, purchased by the Marquis of Chandos, now Duke of Buckingham; sixth, "A View of the Shenandoah," lately in the possession of Jay Cooke of Philadelphia; seventh, "Recollections of Italy," belonging to Abram Adams of Boston. Among his later works exhibited at the National Academy may be mentioned, "Sunset near Bethlehem, N. H.," in 1871; "Sunset in the Swamp, near the Coast of Maine," in 1873; "The East River in February," in 1874; "A View in Vermont," in 1875; "The Gulf" (belonging to John H. Sherwood), in 1876; "Deserted," in 1877; "A Passing Shower" and "Clement's Brook, N. H.," in 1878. His "Hour after Sunset" and "Hour before Sunrise," on the Susquehanna, companion pictures, belong to Mrs. E. D. Kimball of Salem; and "A View near Harper's Ferry, Va.," to Mr. C. H. Miller of the same city. His "Sunset in the Wilderness" he sent to the Centennial Exhibition in Philadelphia in 1876.

Sörensen, C. F. (*Dane.*) Member of the Academy of Copenhagen. Medal at Philadelphia, where he exhibited "Sunset on the Atlantic, — an Old Frigate in a Gale." To Paris, in 1878, he sent, "Vessels of War leaving the Faroe Islands," "Fishers on the Coast of Norway," and "Navigators passing Kinn Sound on the Way to Bergen." [Died, 1879.]

Soumy, Joseph-Paul-Marius. (*Fr.*) Born at Puy Amblay (1831 – 1863) Student at l'École Impériale at Lyons, where he gained the first prize. In 1852 he entered l'École des Beaux-Arts at Paris, and studied under Henriquel Dupont. In 1854 he took the grand *prix de Rome*, and soon went to Italy. Not long after he painted the portrait called "La Carolina," at the Museum of Marseilles. He made designs after the masters; one from a portrait by Giorgione in the Doria Palace, and from it he made an engraving. This was his *chef-d'œuvre*. Could he have lived he would have had an influence on the engraving of his time. But his life was a sad one, and, after having become nearly blind, he threw himself from the window of a *maison de santé*, and was killed.

Spangenberg, Gustav Adolf. (*Ger.*) Born at Hamburg, 1828. Royal Professor and member of the Berlin Academy, also member of Vienna and Hanau. Medals at Cologne, Berlin, and Vienna. Studied in Hanau under Pelissier. In 1849 went to the Antwerp

Academy for a short time. In 1851 went to Paris, where he remained six years; he there studied a short time under Couture, and spent a year in the atelier of the Triqueti. He visited Italy, England, and Holland, and settled in Berlin. His subjects are principally illustrative of German history and literature. At the National Gallery, Berlin, are his "Luther translating the Bible" and the "Procession of the Dead." His picture of "Luther with his Family" is at the Museum at Leipsic, and has become well known from the engraving by Louis Schulz. He occupied himself for some years in a series of pictures from the life of Luther, whom he has depicted with his companions and occupations in a very graphic manner. He has thoroughly studied their habits and customs, he represents much in detail, and, in short, gives an elevated and charming idea of a cultured, pure, and refined life. One of these works, "Luther, his Wife, Children, and Melancthon," painted in 1867, is in the collection of Mr. Probasco of Cincinnati, and is, perhaps, the only work by Spangenberg in the United States. His "Death and its Cortége" (belonging to the National Gallery, Berlin) was at the Paris Exposition, 1878.

Spartali, Marie (Mrs. William J. Stillman). (*Brit.*) Daughter of a well-known Greek merchant, who has been for many years a resident of London. Miss Spartali was a pupil of Ford Madox Brown, and is one of the most prominent disciples of that artist's peculiar school. She exhibited, for the first time in public, at the Dudley Gallery in 1867, "Lady Pray's Desire," followed by "Christiana," in 1868; "Burning the Love-Philter," in 1869. To the Royal Academy, in 1870, she sent "St. Barbara" and "The Mystic Tryst"; in 1873, "The Finding of Sir Launcelot disguised as a Fool"; in 1875, "Mona Lisa"; in 1876, "The Last Sight of Fiammetta"; in 1877, "Roses and Lilies." To the Exhibition of the Water-Color Society at the National Academy, New York, she sent "Lilacs and Roses," "Launcelot and Elaine," "On a Balcony," "Tristram and Isolde," in 1875; "Roses," in 1877; and "Bloom-Time," in 1878. To the Centennial Exhibition at Philadelphia in 1876 she contributed, "Sir Tristram and Queen Yseult." "On the Balcony" belongs to Col. John Hay, and "Mona Lisa" to Mrs. Charles Fairchild of Boston.

"Miss Spartali has a fine power of fusing the emotion of her subject into its color, and of giving aspiration to both; beyond what is actually achieved one sees a reaching towards something ulterior. As one pauses before her work a film in that or in the mind lifts, or seems meant to lift, and a subtler essence from within the picture quickens the sense. In short, Miss Spartali, having a keen perception of the poetry which resides in beauty and in the means of art for embodying beauty, succeeds in infusing that perception into the spectator of her handiwork." — W. M. ROSSETTI, *in English Painters of the Present Day*, 1871.

"'The Finding of Sir Launcelot disguised as a Fool' and 'Sir Tristram and La Belle Fonde' [R. A., 1873, both in water-color] are two illustrations of the 'Mort d'Arthur' which have many commendable artistic qualities. Mrs. Stillman has brought imagina-

12*

tion to her work. These vistas of garden landscape are conceived in the true spirit of romantic luxuriance, when the beauty of each separate flower was a delight. The figures, too, have a grace that belongs properly to art, and which has been well fitted to the condition of pictorial expression. The least satisfactory part of these clever drawings is their color. There is an evident feeling of harmony, but the effect is confused, and the prevailing tones are uncomfortably warm." — *Art Journal*, July, 1878.

Spencer, Frederick R., N. A. (*Am.*) (1805 – 1875.) Studied without a master in his native village, Canistota, N. Y., where he practiced his profession as a portrait-painter until he settled in New York about 1830. He was elected Associate of the National Academy in 1837, and Academician in 1846, painting the portraits of many distinguished men. He retired to Canistota in 1853. His name rarely appeared in the catalogues of the metropolitan exhibitions after that year, although he continued to paint until the time of his death.

"Mr. Spencer carried his work to a high degree of finish, and in his style resembled, in a measure, that of the late Henry Inman. He was generally successful in procuring the likeness of a sitter." — *Art Journal*, May, 1875.

Spertini, Giovanni. (*Ital.*) Of Milan. At Philadelphia he exhibited a bas-relief in terra-cotta, "The Modern Cain," "Love's Messenger," and a portrait of Giuseppe Dassi, Vice-President of the Italian Centennial Commission. He received a medal.

Spread, Henry F. (*Brit.-Am.*) Born at Kinsale, Ireland, 1844. He studied art for four or five years at the schools of South Kensington, gaining several prizes. Later, he studied painting in water-colors under Riviere and Warren. In 1863 he went to Brussels, and became a pupil of Slingineyer. The next year he visited Australia, settling in Melbourne, where he painted many portraits, making sketching-tours in New Zealand and Tasmania. He removed to the United States in 1870, spent a few months in New York, and settled in Chicago, where his studio now is. He is a member of the Chicago Academy of Design. Among his more important works are, "The Bard," in the collection of Mr. St. Clair, London; "Thoughts of Home," now in Melbourne; "Chicago rising from her Ashes," belonging to Morris Martin; "The Roman Honey-Girl," also owned in Chicago, and many portraits.

Spring, Edward A. (*Am.*) Born in the city of New York in 1837. His first visit to Europe was made in 1846 – 47, when, at the age of nine years, he modeled a head of "Medusa" in the studio of Hiram Powers. In 1852 he drew from casts in the studio of H. K. Brown, the winter of 1861 – 62 he spent in the studio of J. Q. A. Ward, and he studied under Dr. Rimmer in 1864 and '65. Besides these, he has spent five years in study in England and France. In 1862 Mr. Spring occupied a large studio with William Page, N. A., at Eagleswood, N. J. In 1868 he discovered in the neighborhood fine modeling clay, peculiarly suitable for terra-cotta work, and turned his attention to that branch of art, establishing the Eagleswood Art Pottery Company in 1877. He exhibited at the National Academy, N. Y., a bust of Mazzini in 1873, and a number of terra-cotta works in 1878. In 1876 he exhibited over two hundred objects in clay in Washington, illustrating many branches of scientific and art study, which now belong to the National Museum of Education. Mr. Spring has been favorably known as a lecturer in different American cities, and is successful as an instructor. Of his lectures in Boston, in 1875, the Advertiser of that city said : —

"His genuine enthusiasm for art in every form, and generous aid in endeavoring to spread the art idea by his practical lectures on modeling and instructive conversations, will be long remembered by those who have enjoyed them. We hope Mr. Spring may find it to his advantage to return to Boston and make it his home."

Sprosse, Carl. (*Ger.*) Born in Leipsic (1819 - 1874). He was a very poor boy, and struggled for the merest existence. Water-color painter of architectural subjects. His views at Venice and those of Roman ruins are among his best works. Later, he painted some Grecian views. At the Museum at Leipsic are, " The Interior of a Gothic Church," " View of an Ancient Cemetery," " View of the Cathedral at Regensburg."

Stacquet, N. Lives at Brussels. We only know this artist by his small water-color pictures, exhibited in America of late by Mr. Daniel Cottier. Two of them, belonging to Mr. W. L. Andrews, were in the Exhibition of the Water-Color Society of New York, early in the winter of 1878. Mr. Clarence Cook spoke of them as worthy of the admiration they received, and said they were " expressive of the artist's love for what is tenderest and most evanescent in natural beauty."

Staigg, Richard M., N. A. (*Brit.-Am.*) Native of Leeds, England, but taken to America in his youth, having previously received no art education, except such as was gathered during a short season of employment as a draughtsman in an architect's office, and a few evenings' instruction at the Leeds Mechanical Institute. He began the practice of art at Newport, R. I., as a miniaturist, receiving there encouragement and valuable assistance from Allston. His excellent miniatures of Allston, Everett, Webster, and others are well known through the engraved copies of them. Some of his portraits on ivory, exhibited at the Royal Academy, excited considerable attention from English art critics and connoisseurs. He was elected a member of the National Academy, N. Y., in 1861, and has been a member of the Boston Art Club for some years. He went to Paris in 1867, remaining until 1869, and exhibiting at the Salon of 1868 portraits of the sons of John Munroe the banker and of the daughter of Richard Greenough. He went to Europe again in 1872, and spent two years. Since his return he has painted portraits in Boston and Newport, with an occasional *genre* picture and landscape study. Among his earlier works are, " The Crossing-Sweeper," " The Sailor's Grave," " Cat's Cradle," " News from the War," " By the Sad Sea Waves," " Beach at Newport," "Moonlight," "Gathering Fagots," and "Going Home in the Snow." He exhibited at the National Academy, N. Y., in 1870, "First Steps," " St. Jerome," "The Lesson," and several portraits ; in 1875, "The Italian Chestnut-Gatherer" ; in 1876, "Italian Peasant Knitting" ; in 1877, "Italian Girl's Head" ; in 1878, "Boy's Head" and "Margaret." His "Empty Nest" and "Cornice Road, Italy" were at the Philadelphia Exhibition of 1876.

"Staigg has painted several remarkable portraits, wherein the character and tone are masterly, and the skill exhibited as delicate as it is truthful. . . . . He has a fine feeling and delicate insight ; there is nothing crude or exaggerated in his style, and he comprehends the refinements of his art, of which his ideal is exalted, and to which his devotion has been single and earnest." — TUCKERMAN's *Book of the Artists.*

Stallaert, Joseph. (*Belgian.*) Medal at Philadelphia, where he exhibited "Palm Sunday, Albano, Italy," "The Fan," and "The Cellar of Diomede, — Scene at the Destruction of Pompeii." At Paris, in 1877, was his "Polyxena sacrificed to the Manes of Achilles." To the Exposition of 1878 he sent "The Death of Dido," "The Sacrifice of Polyxena," and "The Last Combat of the Gladiators."

Stanfield, Clarkson, R. A. (*Brit.*) (1793 – 1867.) Began life as a sailor. With a decided taste for art from his youth, and fondness for the drama, he became a scene-painter, exhibiting his first pictures of a smaller character in the galleries of the Society of British Artists, of which he was an original member in 1823. His "Wreckers off Fort Rouge," one of the earliest of his important works, was at the British Institute in 1827. He first exhibited at the Royal Academy about the same year, and was elected an Associate in 1832, and Academician in 1835. He traveled extensively on the Continent, painting many landscapes, but his most successful works were his marine views, many of which have been engraved. His "Battle of Trafalgar" belongs to the United Service Club in London ; his "Wind against Tide" (in the Paris Exposition of 1855) was painted for Robert Stephenson. "The Victory towed into Gibraltar after Trafalgar" and the "Siege of St. Sebastian" were in the collection of Sir Morton Peto. In the National Gallery, London, are his "Entrance to the Zuyder Zee" (R. A., 1844), a sketch of his "Battle of Trafalgar," his "Lake of Como," and "The Canal of the Giudecca." His pictures are very popular and command very high prices. At the sale of the collection of Charles Dickens, in 1871, a thousand guineas were given for a view of "Eddystone Lighthouse," a scene painted by Stanfield in the course of a few hours for one of the famous amateur plays organized by Dickens and his friends.

Stanfield, George C. (*Brit.*) Son of Clarkson Stanfield. Has exhibited frequently at the Royal Academy for some years, sending, in 1860, "The Church of St. Michael, Ghent"; in 1861, "Saarburg Castle"; in 1863, "On the Lahn" ; in 1864, "The Amphitheater, Verona"; in 1867, "At Luzern" ; in 1868, "Angers" ; in 1871, "A view in

Brittany " ; in 1872, " Dunbar Castle, Scotland " ; in 1873, " Holy Island, Northumberland " ; in 1875, " Entrance to the Harbor of La Rochelle, France " ; in 1876, " On the Banks of the Nile, Upper Egypt."

Stanhope, R. Spencer. (*Brit.*) An English artist, belonging to the pre-Raphaelite school. He first exhibited at the Royal Academy about 1860. In 1862 he sent " The Flight into Egypt " ; in 1864, " Rizpah " ; in 1865, " Beauty and the Beast " ; in 1868, " The Footsteps of the Flock " ; in 1869, " The Rape of Proserpine " ; etc. The more important of his later works have appeared in the Grosvenor Gallery, including " Eve Tempted," " Love and the Maiden," and " On the Banks of the Styx," in 1877 ; and " Night," " Morning," " The Sulamite," and " Cupid and Psyche," the following year. His " Water-Gate " and " On the Banks of the Styx " were at the Paris Exposition of 1878.

Stebbins, Emma. (*Am.*) A native of New York, where, as an amateur, she distinguished herself by her drawings in black and white, and her paintings in oil. Going to Italy some years ago, she settled in Rome, where she worked and studied assiduously as a sculptor. Her earliest important work was a statuette of " Joseph," followed by " Columbus," " Satan descending to tempt Mankind," etc. She executed for the Central Park, New York, a large fountain, the subject of which is " The Angel of the Waters." She is the author of the biography of her friend, Charlotte Cushman.

[No response to circular.]

Steell, Sir John. (*Brit.*) Born in Aberdeen in 1804. He studied art in Edinburgh, and later in Italy, remaining in Rome until 1833, when he opened a studio in Edinburgh, where he has since resided. His statue of Sir Walter Scott, in Carrara marble, in the well-known Scott monument, on Princess street, Edinburgh, first brought him into prominent notice as a sculptor. A duplicate in bronze of this figure, cast in 1873, is now in the Central Park, New York, and a companion statue of Robert Burns is at present (1878) in course of construction. Among the better known of Sir John Steell's works are the statues of Wellington, Professor Wilson, Allan Ramsay, and Thomas Chalmers, all in bronze, and in the public streets of Edinburgh, and the statue of the Queen in the Royal Institution in the same city. He executed the monument to the 42d Highland Regiment at the Cathedral of Dunkeld ; the monument to the 93d Highlanders in Glasgow Cathedral ; statues of Lord Melville and Jeffrey ; busts of the Queen, Prince Albert, Duke of Wellington, Duke of Edinburgh, Florence Nightingale (the only portrait of any kind for which she ever sat), and many more. His last and perhaps most important work is the Scottish National Memorial to the Prince Consort, in Charlotte Square, Edinburgh, upon the unveiling of which by the Queen, in the summer of 1876, the sculptor received the honor of knighthood. Early in his career he was appointed Her Majesty's Sculptor for Scotland ; he has been a member of the Royal Scottish Academy for many years.

"The memorial has been for twelve years in course of design and construction. It was proposed soon after Prince Albert's death, and has been paid for by public subscription. It is a colossal equestrian statue in bronze, upon a pedestal of Aberdeen granite, the whole about thirty feet in height. The Prince is in military costume, and his handsome German face and figure are said by persons who knew him well to be faithfully portrayed. Horse and rider are gracefully and naturally posed, and the effect is artistically fine." — *New York Evening Post,* September 2, 1876.

Steell, Gourlay. (*Brit.*) Born in Edinburgh, where he was educated, and where his professional life has been spent. He is a younger brother of Sir John Steell. A painter of animals and of scenes in humble Scottish life. He is a member of the Royal Scottish Academy, exhibiting there and at the Royal Academy in London. On the death of Landseer, in 1873, he was appointed Animal Painter for Scotland to the Queen. Among his later works are, "A Challenge" (Highland bulls), "On the Trail of the Deer," "Noble, Waldman, and Corran" (favorite dogs of the Queen, to whom the picture belongs), "The Open Window" (water-color), "Rough Art-Critics," "When Greek meets Greek," "Death of Old Mortality," etc. His "Spring in the Highlands" belongs to J. H. Sherwood. His "Robbie Burns and the Field Mouse," "Visit of the Queen to a Highland Cottage," and others have been engraved.

Steffeck, Karl Constantin Heinrich. (*Ger.*) Born at Berlin, 1818. Professor and member of the Berlin Academy ; also member of the Vienna Academy. Medals at Berlin, Paris, and Philadelphia. Studied at Berlin Academy under Franz Krüger and Karl Begas, and then at Paris under Delaroche. Visited Rome, and in 1842 returned to Berlin. At first he painted historical subjects ; later, animals and sporting scenes. He has executed a quantity of lithographs and etchings, — many of these are studies of horses. At the National Gallery, Berlin, is his "Albert Achilles in the Struggle with the Nurembergers, 1450," painted in 1848. At Berlin, in 1876, he exhibited a portrait of the Emperor and a "Gypsy Scene" ; and at Paris, in 1878, "Attrape!!" belonging to the Emperor of Germany, and "Chez l'accouchée," belonging to Baron von Arnim.

Steinbrück, Eduard. (*Ger.*) Born at Magdebourg, 1802. Member and Professor of the Berlin Academy. Pupil of Wach. He has painted "Mary kneeling before her Son," for the church of St. Jacques at Magdebourg, and a few landscapes, but most of his subjects may be called romantic *genre*. At the Berlin National Gallery are, "Children Bathing" and "Marie with the Elves." Among his works are, "The Elves," "The Nymphs," "Red Riding-Hood," "Undine in a Boat," etc.

Steinheil, Louis-Charles-Auguste. (*Fr.*) Born at Strasbourg, 1814. Chevalier of the Legion of Honor. Pupil of Decaisne. This artist has gained a large part of his reputation by his mural and glass painting. He has executed pictures in almost every kind of style, and works in water-colors as well as oils. In 1876 he received the commission to execute some frescos in the Cathedral of Strasbourg.

Steinle, Eduard. Born at Vienna, 1810. Member of the Academies of Berlin, Vienna, Munich, and Hanau. Medals at Berlin and Paris. Pupil of the Academy of Vienna and of Cornelius at Rome. Professor at Frankfort. His decorative paintings are at the Château Reineck, the Cathedral of Cologne, the Museum of Cologne, the Imperial Hall of Frankfort, at Riga, in the church of Saint Ægidius at Münster, and in other places. The cartoons of the last named are in the Leipsic Museum. In the Berlin National Gallery there are also cartoons from the " World's History," and some scenes from Shakspere's " Twelfth Night " or " What You Will." To the Paris Exposition, 1878, he sent " The Virgin and Child," in water-color, belonging to the Princess Marie de Lichtenstein, and cartoons of nine frescos in the chapel of the Princes of Löwenstein at Heubach-sur-Mein, and ten others from frescos at the Museum of Cologne.

Stephens, Edward B., A. R. A. (*Brit.*) A native of Exeter. He entered the schools of the Royal Academy at an early age, and in 1843 gained the gold medal for a work in alto-relievo. Later, he went to the Continent, remaining three years in the study of sculpture at Rome. To the Great Exhibition in London, in 1851, he sent " Satan Vanquished " and " Satan tempting Eve." Among his earlier works are, " Eve contemplating Death," " Angel of the Resurrection," etc. To the Royal Academy, in 1861, he contributed, " Evening, — Going to the Bath," a group in marble ; in 1863, " Alfred the Great in the Neatherd's Cottage " (purchased by the Corporation of the City of London, and now in the Mansion House) ; in 1865, when he was elected an Associate of the Royal Academy, " Euphrosyne and Cupid " ; in 1867, " Lady Godiva " ; in 1868, " Coaxing " ; in 1869, " Saved from the Wreck " ; in 1871, " Zingari " ; in 1873, " A Deer-Stalker " ; in 1874, " Leander " ; in 1875, " Evening " and " Morning " ; in 1876, " The Bathers " ; in 1878, " The Little Carpenter." He has also executed many statues and busts.

Stevens, John. (*Brit.*) Born in Ayr (about 1793 - 1868). Entered the schools of the Royal Academy in London in 1815, gaining in 1818 two silver medals. He practiced portrait-painting in his native town for a few years, when he went to Italy, settling in Rome, and making that city his home for many winters. He was a member of the Royal Scottish Academy. His " Standard-Bearer " is in the Scottish National Gallery.

Stevens, Alfred. (*Brit.*) Born in Blandford, Dorsetshire (1817 - 1875). He displayed marked talent for painting as a child, and at the age of sixteen he went to Italy, studying the works of Salvator Rosa in Florence. Later, he entered the studio of Thorwaldsen in Rome, turning his attention to plastic art, and remaining with that master for some years. He returned to England in 1843, when he settled in London, and connected himself with the Art Schools of Somerset House. In 1850 he removed to Sheffield, executing what is known as "decorative work," in iron and silver, for manufacturing firms of that city. He received in 1857 the commission from government for the great work of his life, the monument to the Duke of Wellington in St. Paul's Cathedral, London. The sum voted by Parliament (£14,000) for the execution of this commission was utterly insufficient and exhausted long before its completion. He expended upon it much of his private means, was censured for his delays in the work, and suffered much grief and disappointment during its progress, leaving it unfinished at his death, eighteen years after the commission was given him. It has nevertheless added greatly to his fame as a sculptor. He was the author of several admirable portrait busts of the members of the family of his friend, Mr. Collman, and others. He executed the mosaic "Isaiah" in the arch of the dome of St. Paul's, turning his attention also to painting and architecture.

"Stevens' figures were always (like nearly all first-rate sculpture in the best times) part and parcel of something else. Sculpture was to him as intimately related to architecture as was his own flesh to his own bones, and so we find that his noblest sculptured works, — the life-sized marble figures in Dorchester House, and the bronze figures of the Wellington memorial, — are, like the best sculpture of which the world knows, integral and essential parts of architectural compositions. Since Michael Angelo made the monument to Lorenzo de Medici, no stronger nor more vigorous work has been made in marble than these Dorchester House figures. The pose of them, the manner in which the heads and shoulders are related to the cornice over them, the modeling of the flesh, all speak of an artist greater than our modern scale of measurement can by any possibility gauge. These figures belong to the culminating period of Stevens' career, and are contemporary with the groups of the Wellington monument, his last and crowning work." — EDWARD W. GODWIN, F. S. A., *Art Monthly Review.*

"Those interested in such matters, however, were well aware that Stevens had designed some of the finest works of the day : innumerable decorative objects of daily use, distinguished by the finest taste, decorations proper in metal, stone, and marble, to say nothing of works of higher pretensions, with which the names of manufacturers, rather than of the real designer, were associated. A fine example of his peculiar skill is seen by those who pass the British Museum, and admire, probably without knowing to whom they are indebted for them, the excellent designs of the little sejant lions on the iron posts before the grille, and, we believe, the very handsome grille itself. In fact, his works are numerous, yet they rarely bear his name." — *Athenæum,* May 8, 1875.

Stevens, Joseph. (*Belgian.*) Born at Brussels, 1819. Chevalier of the Orders of Léopold and of the Legion of Honor. After studying at Paris, he made his début at the Salon at Brussels in 1844 and at Paris in 1847. He continued to exhibit at Paris until 1863, since which time he has appeared at but one Salon, that of 1870, with "The Intervention." He paints *genre* subjects, very frequently with animals, and holds a high rank among artists of this type. Among his works are, "The Surprise," "An Episode in the Dog-Market at Paris," "The Dog and the Fly" (at Paris in 1878), "A Philosopher without knowing it," "The Kitchen," "The Corner of the Fire," etc.

"Rarely have the Dutch or Flemish artists done better than Joseph Stevens in his 'Kitchen.' It is an interior animated by no figure ; no interesting cook paring the vegetables while listening to a lover leaning on the window-sill ; no scullion in a white cap licking the sauce from his fingers. Joseph Stevens has disdained these vulgar artifices ; he has painted, with masterly dexterity, the chimney in brown tones, the stove backed with faience, without other objects than the great iron fire-dogs, the toothed turnspit, the stewpans polished like antique shields, the kettles glittering, the coffee-pots prattling ; all this is of a color so true, strong, and beautiful, and so broadly and at the same time so exactly rendered, that we arrest ourselves before the ' Kitchen ' as before a Peter de Hooge." — THÉOPHILE GAUTIER, *Abécédaire du Salon de* 1861.

Stevens, Alfred. (*Belgian.*) Born at Brussels, 1828. Officer of the Order of Léopold. Commander of the Order of St. Michael of Bavaria, Commander of the Order of Ferdinand of Austria, and Officer of the Legion of Honor. Pupil of Navez in Belgium, and of Roqueplan at Paris. This painter represents scenes from modern life, and reproduces with great exactness the costumes, furniture, etc., of the time. He has exhibited his works in Brussels and Paris since 1849, and in reality belongs to the schools of two countries. Stevens sent eighteen pictures to the Exposition of 1867 ; among them were, "The Visit " (purchased by the King of Belgium), "La Dame Rose " (purchased for the Museum at Brussels), "Consolation," "Innocence," "Ophelia," "A Duchess," "A Morning in the Country," "A Good Letter," etc. At a sale in Brussels, in 1874, "The New Year's Gift" sold for £840. Among his later works are "The Bath " and "The Japanese Woman." At the Latham sale, New York, 1878, "Springtime of Life " (49 by 19) sold for $ 1,050.

"We have been able to follow this painter (who has grown in France, and who belongs to two schools) since his début. With pleasure we have seen him absudon, little by little, his first manner, in which solidity degenerated into heaviness, in which the strong tones too nearly approached black. Stevens has been transformed under our eyes, and, while remaining earnest, he has become one of the best of the painters of modern elegances. . . . . In 'La dame rose,' in 'Une bonne lettre,' the faces of the charming little women painted by Stevens are veiled by an obscure tint, which threatens, by the action of time, to become darker. To tell the truth, it is the only fault which troubles us in these pictures, so well done, so charming to see, and which, taking in the daily realities of modern life, will always tell of its costumes, furniture, and elegances." — PAUL MANTZ, *Gazette des Beaux-Arts*, July, 1867.

Stever, Gustav Curt. (*Russian.*) Born at Riga (1823–1877). Honorary Cross of the Order of the House of Mecklenburg. Studied at the Academy of Berlin. In 1850 he went to Stockholm to paint portraits and execute other commissions. In 1854 he went to Paris and studied under Couture. Among his works are, "The Death of Gottschalk, King of the Wendens," "King David and Abishag, the Shunamite," "The Angel of Prayer," "The Last Supper," and "The Transfiguration." In 1859 he settled at Hamburg, where he was much employed. In 1865 he removed to Düsseldorf, and there painted more religious pictures as well as *genre* subjects, such as "Vandyck at his Easel," "Jean Mabuse painting his Dead Child," etc. He was a successful instructor, and executed some excellent portraits. His picture

12 *

B

of "Master Adam van Noort surprising his Pupil Rubens at his Secret Studies" attracted much attention at the Exposition at Berlin in 1871.

Stocks, Lumb, R. A. (*Brit.*) Born in 1812. He began his career as a line-engraver when about twenty-one years of age, furnishing illustrations for fine editions of English books ; and, later, plates of a larger and more important character, such as Webster's "Dame School," Paton's "Olivia and Viola," Maclise's "Fitting Moses for the Fair" and the "Meeting of Wellington and Blucher on the Field of Waterloo," Wilkie's "Gentle Shepherd," T. Faed's "Silken Gown," Mulready's "Fight Interrupted," Horsley's "Deserted," E. M. Ward's "Marie Antoinette in Prison" and "Charlotte Corday in the Conciergerie." He was elected an Associate Engraver of the Royal Academy in 1853, and Academician in 1872.

Stone, Frank, A. R. A. (*Brit.*) Born in Manchester (1800 – 1859). He had no instruction in art, and did not adopt it as a profession until 1825, devoting himself in the beginning of his career to water-color drawing. He joined the Old Water-Color Society in London in 1832, remaining a member about fifteen years. His first picture appeared on the walls of the Royal Academy in 1837. In 1840 he exhibited "The Legend of Montrose," his first important work in oil, followed by the "Stolen Interview between Prince Charles and the Infanta of Spain," in 1841 ; "The Last Appeal," in 1843 ; "The Course of True Love," in 1844 ; "Ophelia and the Queen," in 1845 ; "The Impending Mate" and "Mated," in 1847 ; "The Gardener's Daughter," in 1850 ; "A Scene from the Merchant of Venice," in 1851, when he was elected Associate of the Royal Academy ; "The Old Old Story," in 1854 ; "Bon jour, messieurs," in 1857 ; and the "Missing Boat," in 1858 : many of which have been engraved.

"Frank Stone was one of the most graceful of English *genre* painters. His subjects are commonly of a sentimental character, and distinguished for their delicate allusions to the 'gentle passion,' and his young women certainly seem very lovable persons. In later years he turned his attention much to French subjects, illustrating local manners and customs." — WORNUM's *Epochs of Painting.*

Stone, Horatio. (*Am.*) (1810 – 1875.) He was a native of New England, and a practicing physician in New York for some time. He went to Washington about 1848, devoting, after that period, his entire attention to sculpture, executing several statues and busts of public men, — Chief Justice Taney, Thomas Jefferson, John Hancock (in the Senate Chamber), Thomas Benton, and others. About 1856 he made his first visit to Italy, remaining several years.

"Dr. Stone was very enthusiastic in his nature, and had he given his attention earlier to the study of art, under a competent master, he might have achieved lasting fame." — *Art Journal.* November, 1875.

Stone, William Oliver, N. A. (*Am.*) Born at Derby, Ct. (1830 – 1875). Studied art in New Haven, and painted portraits there, as a young man, with considerable success. He settled in New

York about 1858, and was made a member of the Academy of Design in 1859, exhibiting annually until the year of his death. As a portrait-painter he was very popular, and among his sitters have been Howell L. Williams (in the Union Club, New York), Daniel Le Roy, Mrs. Hoey, James Gordon Bennett, and others.

"Mr. Stone was an admirable painter of women and children, and some of his pictures of this class have never been equaled in America. . . . . In his handling of these subjects he threw around them an expression of ideality which was artistic in the highest degree, and raised his art far above the level usually attained in portrait pictures. He was a prolific painter, and one year sent nine pictures to the Academy." — *Art Journal,* November, 1875.

Stone, Marcus, A. R. A. (*Brit.*) Son of Frank Stone, A. R. A., an artist of much repute. Marcus Stone was born in London in 1840. He worked in his father's studio, inheriting some of his father's genius, but receiving little instruction in art. He exhibited his first picture, "Rest," at the Royal Academy in 1858. In 1859 he sent "Silent Pleadings"; in 1860, "The·Sword of the Lord and Gideon"; in 1861, "Claude accuses Hero"; in 1862, "The Painter's First Work"; in 1863, "On the Road from Waterloo to Paris" (a picture containing a portrait of Bonaparte, which attracted some attention). In 1864 he exhibited "Working and Shirking"; in 1865, "Old Letters"; in 1866, "Stealing" and "Nell Gwynn"; in 1868, "The Interrupted Duel"; in 1870, "Henry VIII. and Anne Boleyn observed by Queen Katherine"; in 1871, "The Royal Nursery in 1838"; in 1872, "Edward II. and Piers Gaveston"; in 1874, "My Lady is a Widow and Childless"; in 1875, "Sain et Sauf"; in 1876, "Rejected"; in 1877 (when he was elected an Associate of the Royal Academy), "The Sacrifice" and "Waiting at the Gate"; in 1878, "The Post-Boy" and "The Time of Roses." His "Childless Widow" was at Philadelphia in 1876, and at Paris in 1878.

"This picture ['Claude accuses Hero,' R. A., 1861], instead of looking like the work of a very young man, has rather the appearance of being painted with a decision and breadth of touch bespeaking one who has painted on from vigorous style into facile manner. The ripe facility of pencil is at least equaled by adroit dexterity of grouping and disposition of color, so that, as a whole, this is a most winning and attractive picture." — *Art Journal,* June, 1861.

"Marcus Stone stands at the head of his craft as a skilful designer and admirable painter of pieces of historic *genre.*" — *Art Journal,* April, 1877.

Stone, J. M. (*Am.*) Born in Dana, Mass., 1841. He received his art education in Munich, under Professor Seitz and Professor Lindenschmidt. He has spent his professional life in Boston, where he is an instructor in the School of the Museum of Fine Arts. He was elected a member of the Boston Art Club in 1876, exhibiting there his "Tuning of the·Violin," the same year, considered his most important work. Among his portraits are those of Frank Dengler the sculptor, belonging to F. X. Dengler, Covington, Ky., and of F. W. Tilton of Newport, painted for Phillips Academy at Andover.

"The portrait of Mr. Tilton is not only an admirable likeness, but the best portrait Mr. Stone has yet done, and ought to rank him among the first portrait-painters of Boston. The artist's thorough knowledge of drawing is shown in the certainty of the lines and the firm, vigorous modeling. The execution manifests both strength and nice perception; not a feature is neglected or slurred over, and, at the same time, there is no suggestion of higgling. . . . . The expression and pose are finely conceived, having that quality which in portraiture is most difficult to catch, — action. This is particularly evident in the rendering of the eyes, which are not set or fixed in gaze, which have a peculiarly animated and, at the same time, contemplative glance, — a striking something which may be expressed in the word 'intelligence.' " — *Boston Advertiser,* June, 1878.

Storelli, Felix-Marie-Ferdinand. (*Ital.*) Born at Turin (1778 – 1854). Medal at Paris. This landscape-painter exhibited works at Paris many times. Some of them were at the palace of Saint-Cloud ; others are at the Trianon ; and his portrait of Marshal Schomberg is at Versailles.

Storey, George Adolphus, A. R. A. (*Brit.*) Born in London, 1834. Displayed a love of art as a child, and won a prize at school for painting in oil when not more than twelve years of age. Between. 1848 and '50 he studied mathematics in Paris, painting in the Louvre in his leisure moments. Later, he studied art in London, entering the Royal Academy in 1854. In 1852, however, he had sent to the Royal Academy his first picture, " A Family Portrait " ; in 1853, " Madonna and Child " ; in 1854, " Holy Family," which attracted considerable attention. He visited Spain for the purpose of painting and study in 1863. Among his earlier works are, " Sacred Music," " The Widowed Bride " (1858), " The Bride's Burial," and " The Annunciation." His " Meeting of William Seymour and Lady Arabella Stuart in 1609 " (which first brought him prominently into public notice) was exhibited in 1864. In 1865 he sent " The Royal Challenge " ; in 1867, " After You ! "; in 1868, " The Shy Pupil " and " Saying Grace "; in 1869, " Going to School " and " The Old Soldier " ; in 1870, " The Duet " and " Only a Rabbit "; in 1871, " Rosy Cheeks " and " Lessons "; in 1872, " Little Buttercups " and " The Course of True Love " ; in 1878, " Love in a Maze " and " Mistress Dorothy " ; in 1874, " Grandma's Christmas Visitors " ; in 1875, " Caught " and " The Whiphand " ; in 1876 (when he was elected Associate of the Academy), " A Dancing-Lesson " and " My Lady Belle " ; in 1877, " The Old Pump-Room at Bath," " The Judgment of Paris," and " Christmas Eve " ; in 1878, " Sweet Margery." He sent to the Paris Exposition of 1878, " Scandal " and " The Old Soldier."

"George A. Storey has still to acquire more finish, delicacy, and completeness of execution to fit his pleasant class of subjects ; and he will then fill a place of his own in which he will not find many competitors. . . . . Mr. Storey, too, may for the moment almost claim a monopoly of pretty, playful *vaudeville.* His portraits of children and girls are particularly pleasing and happy in arrangement." — TOM TAYLOR, *in English Artists of the Present Day.*

"Among the younger men of our living school of painters we cannot point to a more conscientious worker than Mr. Storey. His principal characters are, as they should be, his chief study, but the accessories are not neglected. . . . . His canvases are never overloaded, and on the other hand they are never wanting in subject-matter of more or less interest. The domestic life of a past generation affords him an ample field for the display of many of the best qualities one desires to see in a picture." —*Art Journal*, June, 1875.

Story, William W. (*Am.*) Born at Salem, Mass., 1819. Graduated at Harvard College, 1844. Studied law, and published several law treatises considered valuable in that profession. He published a volume of Poems in 1847, a Life of his father, Judge Story, in 1851, and a second volume of Poems in 1856. Adopting sculpture as a profession, he went to Rome, one of his earliest works being a statue of his father, now at Mount Auburn Cemetery, in Cambridge, Mass. His "Cleopatra" (bought by John T. Johnston), and his "Sibyl," exhibited at the London International Exhibition of 1862, were highly praised by critics and connoisseurs. Among his works are, "Saul," "Sappho," "Delilah," "Moses," "Judith," "Infant Bacchus," "Little Red Riding-Hood," and "Jerusalem in her Desolation" (presented by the purchasers of it to the Academy of Arts in Philadelphia). His "Medea" was at the Philadelphia Centennial Exhibition in 1876. He is the author of the statues of George Peabody, in London, and of Edward Everett, in the Public Garden at Boston, both in bronze. At present (1878) he is engaged on a National Monument to be placed in Independence Square, Philadelphia.

"'Jerusalem in her Desolation' is the title given by W. W. Story to a colossal statue [exhibited in London in 1873]. It is a noble female figure clad in flowing drapery: the head, crowned with a kind of phylactery, is finely modeled, the Hebrew face having an expression of mingled distress and contempt. . . . . The general impression of the design is that of majestic sorrow, and the execution of the work throughout is most careful." —*Art Journal*, August, 1873.

"The two conceptions, 'Cleopatra' and the 'Libyan Sibyl,' have placed Mr. Story in European estimation at the head of American sculptors. . . . . Profiting by the knowledge of the old masters, and forming his tastes upon the best styles, Story has had the independence to seek out an unused field. In this he confers honor on our school, and gives it an impetus as new as it is refreshing." — JARVES, *Art Idea*.

"In a word, all Cleopatra — fierce, voluptuous, passionate, tender, wicked, terrible, and full of poisonous and rapturous enchantment — was kneaded into what, only a week or two before, had been a lump of wet clay from the Tiber. Soon apotheosized in an indestructible material, she would be one of the images that men keep forever, finding a heat in them that does not cool down through the centuries." — HAWTHORNE, *in The Marble Faun*.

Story, George H., A. N. A. (*Am.*) Born in New Haven, Ct., 1835. He began his art studies, at the age of fifteen, under Professor Bail of New Haven ; later, spending two years in the studio of Charles Hine, a portrait-painter, in that city. Going to the Continent of Europe, he passed a year in general observation and study. He then resided two years in Portland, Me., gaining, in 1858, the State Medal of Maine for the best oil-painting. He painted for two years in Washington, D. C., passed a year in Cuba, and for some time has been a resident of New York. In 1875 he was elected an Associate of the National Academy, and is a member of the Artists' Fund Society. His pictures are exhibited frequently in New York and elsewhere. Among the better known of them are, "The Testy Old Squire's Complaint" (the property of Charles Rogers), "The Young Mother" (owned by J. F. Nash, Yonkers), "The Student of Nature" (owned by E. B. Warren, Philadelphia), "The Young Student" (owned by David Grosbeck, Suffern, N. Y.), a full-length life-sized portrait of H. J. Kimball, a portrait of Whitelaw Reid (belonging to the Lotus Club), "The Winter School," "Uncle Peter in his Castle," "The Return of the Forager," "Freeing the Butterfly," "Prayer," "A New England Professor of Psalmody," "Making his Mark," "The Clock-Tinkers," a large portrait group of the Governor of Villa-Clara, in his gallery at Madrid, Spain, and others. His "Young Mother," "Echoes of the Sea," and "The Young Student" were at the Centennial Exhibition of Philadelphia in 1876.

"No artist in this country has made such a decided advance in his profession during the last five years as George H. Story ; and he invests his works with so much refinement of feeling that they at once arrest attention in whatever position they may be placed." — *Art Journal*, May, 1875.

Strazza, Giovanni. (*Ital.*) Born at Milan (1818 – 1875). Professor in the Academy of the Brera. He received many medals. When but twenty years old he had modeled, in Rome, his statue of "Ishmael," which won him much fame. His works are seen in many cities. His bust of Manzoni was greatly admired at Vienna in 1873. One of his last works was the statue of Donizetti placed in the atrium of the Theater of the Scala at Milan in 1874.

Street, George Edmund, R. A. (*Brit.*) Born in Essex, 1824. He studied architecture for some years under Sir George G. Scott. In 1866 he was elected an Associate of the Royal Academy, Academician in 1871, and Auditor in 1873. He has designed many important buildings throughout Great Britain, particularly turning his attention to country-houses and church edifices. He was instrumental in the restoration of Bristol Cathedral and Christ Church Cathedral, Dublin, among others, and was appointed Architect to the new Courts of Justice, London.

Stroebel, J. A. B. (*Dutch.*) Of The Hague. Medal at Philadelphia, where he exhibited "The Deacons of the Silversmiths' Guild conferring a Certificate," of which John F. Weir says, "while tending towards the conventional it is nevertheless admirable in many estimable qualities, broad and simple in treatment, and pure in tone."

Stroobant, François. (*Belgian.*) Born at Brussels, 1819. Chevalier of the Order of Léopold. Medal at Paris, 1855. Pupil of Lauters. An artist of good reputation as a landscape-painter. He used water-colors and pastels, and made numerous lithographs.

Sturm, Friedrich Ludwig Christian. (*Ger.*) Born at Rostock, 1834. Medal at London. Pupil of Berlin Academy under Eschky; later, under Professor Gude, at Carlsruhe, he finished his studies. Traveled in the North of Europe and Italy. At the National Gallery, Berlin, are his pictures of the " Baltic Sea " and the " Mediterranean Sea."

Sully, Thomas. (*Am.*) Born in England (1783 - 1872). Taken to America at the age of nine years, he studied art in Charleston, S. C., where he began the practice of his profession as a portrait-painter. He lived for some time in Richmond, Va., and in New York, settling finally in Philadelphia. He made several visits to Europe; in 1838 painting from life a portrait of Queen Victoria, now in the possession of the St. George's Society of Philadelphia. Among his portraits are those of Lafayette, in Independence Hall ; Fanny Kemble; Charles Kemble ; George Frederick Cooke, and others, in the Academy of Fine Arts, Philadelphia. His portrait of Jefferson belongs to the Military Academy at West Point ; that of Commodore Decatur (at Philadelphia Exhibition in 1876) is in the City Hall, New York ; those of Reverdy Johnson and Charles Carroll are in Baltimore. His " Washington crossing the Delaware " (so familiar in America by the engraving) is in the Boston Museum. In the gallery of M. O. Roberts are his " Woman at the Well " and " A Girl offering Flowers at a Shrine."

" Sully's organization fits him to sympathize with the fair and lovely rather than the grand or comic. He is keenly alive to the more refined phases of life and nature. His pencil follows with instinctive truth the principles of genuine taste. His *forte* is the graceful. Whatever faults the critics may detect in his works they are never those of awkwardness or constraint. He exhibits the freedom of touch and the airiness of outline which belong to spontaneous emanations. . . . . The series of illustrations that Sully commenced are happily, but not forcibly conceived. Portia is fair and dignified, but not sufficiently vigorous. Isabella is as chaste and nun-like as Shakspere made her, but her dormant and high enthusiasm does not enough appear; Miranda, a character better adapted than either to Sully's pencil, has an arch simplicity caught from Nature herself." — TUCKERMAN's *Book of the Artists.*

Sunol, Geronimo. (*Span.*) Medal at Paris in 1867. At Philadelphia he exhibited " Dante," in bronze, and received a medal. [No further authoritative information could be obtained.]

Sussmann, Hellborn Louis. (*Ger.*) Born at Berlin, 1828. Member of the Academy of Rotterdam. Medals at Berlin, Brussels, Munich, Paris, and the Bavarian medal of Louis. Pupil of Berlin Academy and of Professor Wredow. He has spent much time in Italy, and has traveled considerably in Europe. Among his important works are the statues of " Frederick the Great " and " Frederick William III.," for the grand salon of the Berlin Rathhaus ; a statue of " Frederick the Great in Youth," and a copy of " Frederick William III.," for the city of Breslau; and a statue of " Frederick the Great as a Warrior," in bronze, for Brieg (erected in 1878). His " Drunken Faun " is at the National Gallery, Berlin. To the Paris Exposition, 1878, he contributed a group, in marble, called " Lyric Poetry and Popular Song."

Suydam, James A., N. A. (*Am.*) Born in New York (1817 -

1865). He traveled through Greece, Turkey, and other parts of the East with Minor C. Kellogg, and from him received the first rudiments of art. On his return to America he painted for some time with Kellogg, and later with Durand and Kensett, executing in the studio of the last named some of his best pictures. The most satisfactory of his works were coast views, although at times he was very happy in his views of the White Mountains, etc. He was a full member of the Academy of Design, elected about 1856. When the building of the present Academy in New York was projected Mr. Suydam was instrumental in procuring large subscriptions towards that object, and took a very prominent part in its construction. He was made Treasurer of the Academy, a position he held until his death. He bequeathed to it the pictures now in its possession, known as the "Suydam Collection," as well as a large sum of money. He was devoted to his art. One of his most agreeable pictures was a twilight with the New London lighthouse in the distance (in the Olyphant Collection). A "View on Long Island," with harvesting of salt hay, (one of his most important works), is now in the possession of his nephew, William A. Reese. His "Hook Mountain on the Hudson" belongs to S. Clift.

Swertchkow, Nicolas. (*Russian.*) Born at St. Petersburg. Chevalier of the Legion of Honor. Professor at the Academy of St. Petersburg. Studied in his native city, and paints *genre* subjects and animals, such as "The Kabitka in the Snow," "The Village Wedding," "Travelers Astray," "Landscape in Winter," etc. This artist has exhibited his works in Paris, London, and Brussels. In 1863, the year of his decoration, he sent to Paris, "A Horse Fair in the Interior of Russia," "Station for Post-Horses," and "The Return from the Bear-Hunt"; in 1864, "A Child fallen from a Sleigh during the Night, found in the Morning safe and well, in the midst of Wolves" and "Russian Travelers in Sleighs meeting in the midst of the Woods."

Sylvestre, Joseph-Noël. (*Fr.*) Born at Béziers, 1847. Medals, 1875 and '76. *Prix du Salon,* 1876. Pupil of Cabanel. In 1876 he exhibited a very remarkable picture of "Locuste testing, in the Presence of Nero, the Poison prepared for Britannicus." Much has been written and said of this picture. It is called "horrible," "wonderful," "magnificent," and "detestable," and all these epithets may be legitimately used. It is, in a word, a powerful, realistic representation of a scene without a trace of anything good or pleasing, but a scene which gives an opportunity for the display of artistic skill and knowledge. It is in the Luxembourg. In 1875 Sylvester exhibited "The Death of Seneca"; in 1873, "Jeu de Bergers"; in 1878, "The Last Moments of Vitellus Cæsar."

Tadolini, Adam Scipione. (*Ital.*) Born at Bologna (1789 – 1870). Professor of the Academy of Bologna. Pupil of Canova. Among the works of this celebrated sculptor are, "Venus and Love,"

for Prince Hercolani ; "The Rape of Ganymëde," for Prince Ester-
hazy ; the Tomb of Cardinal Laute, for the city of Bologna ; statue
of "St. Francis de Sales," for St. Peter's at Rome ; a colossal "St.
Michael," for the late Mr. Gardner Brewer of Boston (for which Vapereau says the artist received 200,000 francs).

Signora Tadolini, wife of this artist, made a reputation as an engraver of cameos.

Tait, Arthur F., N. A. (*Brit.-Am.*) Born in Liverpool, 1819. In 1850
he removed to America, settling in New York, where his professional life
has been spent. He has studied from nature in the Adirondack regions
and elsewhere during the summer months, but has had no regular instruction in art from any teacher, and belongs to no school of painting.
He is a member of the Artists' Fund Society, and was elected member of the National Academy in 1858. He spent four months in Europe in 1874, never painting professionally out of America. To the
National Academy, in 1868, he contributed "A Duck and her Young";
in 1869, "Ruffled Grouse"; in 1870, "Our Pets" (painted in part
by James M. Hart); in 1871, "Woodcock Shooting" (belonging to
John C. Force) and "The Halt on the Carry" (belonging to Henry
D. Polhemus) ; in 1873, "Racquette Lake"; in 1874, "The Bogert
Homestead, Eagleswood, N. J."; in 1876, "There's a Good Time
coming"; in 1878, "A Good Point" and "Lake Trout" (belonging
to John E. Sidman). To the Centennial at Philadelphia, in 1876, he
sent "The Portage, — Waiting for the Boats," also painted in conjunction with James M. Hart. His "Snowed In" is owned by Judge
Hilton of New York, and other works are in the possession of John
Osborn, James B. Blossom, Charles Blossom of Brooklyn, and others.

Tait, John R. (*Am.*) Born in Cincinnati, 1834. He displayed
artistic talents as a child, but did not follow painting as a profession
until somewhat advanced in manhood. He went abroad in 1852,
painting as an amateur in Florence and Rome for a few years, but
devoting himself chiefly to literature, publishing a book of travels,
and later, in 1859, a volume of poems entitled "Dolce Far Niente,"
both of which were very favorably received. He went again to Europe in 1859, and spent some twelve years in Düsseldorf, broken by
occasional visits to America, and by sketching-tours in nearly every
country of Europe. In Düsseldorf and Munich his teachers were
Professors A. Weber and Andreas Achenbach, but since 1870 he has
pursued his studies independently in a direction diverging from the
Düsseldorf school. In 1871 and '72 he received the first-class medals
of the Art Department of the Cincinnati Industrial Exhibition. Comparatively few of Mr. Tait's pictures have found their way to America.
They have been exhibited in the Salons of Paris, in London, Vienna,
Berlin, etc., and have been sold in those cities. His first picture was
bought by Major, afterwards General, Philip Kearney, U. S. A. His
"Waterfall, Pyrenees" is in the collection of James Caird, Gourock

House, near Greenock on the Clyde ; his "Meyringen" belongs to James Staats Forbes, Wickenham Hall, Kent ; Prince Heinrich XVIII. of Reuss owns his "Waterfall" ; Hon. William S. Groesbeck of Cincinnati, his "Lake of Wallenstadt" ; Hon. George Vickers of Baltimore, his "Solitude." His "Evening on the Lake" and "Tyrolese Idyl" were at the Paris Salon of 1876 ; to the Centennial Exhibition, Philadelphia, 1876, he sent "Summer." Recently he has been a resident of Baltimore, Md.

"John R. Tait exhibits a large landscape with cattle which reminds one of the best examples of the old Dutch painters, without any sacrifice, however, of the artist's individuality. Foliage, water, air, and the figures are treated with equal success, and a breath of the most charming lyric poetry pervades the whole, so that the picture belongs among the best of the present Exhibition." — *Munich News (Bavaria),* April, 1873.

"Mr. Tait exhibited here, several years ago, a few pictures which showed a decided force and originality ; but they were touched with a savage gloom which rendered them not altogether pleasing. In his more recent style he has chosen the sweeter and gentler moods of nature. . . . . The landscapes are in the main well drawn. In color they are not brilliant ; we should say that the aim of Mr. Tait is chiaroscuro rather than color. His skies are nearly always luminous, full of space and air ; he sets a tree against the sky with a very felicitous relief." — *Baltimore Gazette,* July, 1876.

Tantardini, Antonio, Commander. (*Ital.*) Medals at London, Berlin, Oporto, and Vienna. He resides at Milan, and is one of the first sculptors of the Lombard school, and shows by his work a careful study of Greek masters and of the best examples of the *cinque-cento.* His statues of the "Bagnante" and the "Pompeiana" were exhibited at Philadelphia, where he was one of the art judges. His statues, "Il primo dolore," "La Schiava," "La Leggitrice," and "La Vanità," are among his best. His statue of Arnoldo da Brescia was put in marble for Antonio Traversi, and was erected in Desio near Milan. To the Paris Exposition, 1878, he sent "The Kiss" (a group with a pedestal in marble). His "Leggitrice" (Reading Girl) is now in the collection of Mr. Probasco of Cincinnati. [Died, 1879.]

Tardieu, Pierre-Alexandre. (*Fr.*) Born at Paris (1756 – 1844). Member of the Institute, and Chevalier of the Legion of Honor. This celebrated engraver was descended from a family in which there had been several artists. His works were excellent from his early years, and some of them are now valuable. He was skilled in the processes of Audran, Edelinck, and Nanteuil, and, having the gift of imparting knowledge, was a successful instructor. Among his pupils were Desnoyers, Bertonnier, and Aubert. Among his plates are, "St. Michael," after Raphael ; "The Communion of St. Jerome," after Domenichino ; "Judith and Holofernes," after Allori ; the portraits of Henry IV. of France, after Janet and Pourbus ; two of Voltaire, after Lagillière and Houdon ; Marie Antoinette, after Dumont ; the Earl of Arundel, after Vandyck ; etc. His plates number ninety. After his death Mme. Tardieu refused large offers from merchants for the plates of her husband, and in order to preserve them intact, she gave to the Calcographie of the Louvre all those which she possessed.

Tatkeleff, Vogisny. (*Russian.*) Born about 1813. The father of this painter was the serf of a nobleman in the Borissov Government, who, seeing the rude charcoal sketches made by Vogisny when a child, determined to educate him. When fourteen years old he painted a good portrait of his benefactor, who unfortunately lost his fortune when the artist was but nineteen. The new owner of the estate forced him into the army, where he was obliged to serve fifteen weary years. In all this time he had no opportunity to display his talent until, during the last two years, being stationed at Tiflis, he was allowed to fresco the walls of the dining-room of the house of a relative of his colonel. He was too poor to dream of buying materials for his work. In 1849 he was discharged, and went home to find his parents dead. His master was also dead, and in his widow he found a cultivated and liberal woman. Tatkeleff asked of her the position of teacher in the village school. When she discovered his talent she furnished him with means to complete his studies, but stipulated that he should not leave Russia, and that she should have her choice of his works. The artist was now happy, and made many pictures which were hung on the walls of the château of his mistress. In 1854 he went with her son to the Crimean war, and there partially lost his eyesight. His benefactress died; the son would do nothing for the painter, who, by making designs for a publishing-house at Kiev, managed to exist. About 1870 a tourist, who saw the sketch-book of Tatkeleff, exacted a promise from him to send some works to Moscow for exhibition. For months he could not buy the paints and canvas necessary, but at last two pictures were finished, and sent to the Art Exposition in Moscow of 1873. They represented scenes in the Crimean war, and made the artist famous in a day. They were purchased for the gallery of the Winter Palace of St. Petersburg for 60,000 roubles. The Moscow Gazette said of them : —

"The impression which they produce upon the beholder is almost overwhelming, — such terrible reality, such wonderful grouping, such superb coloring, truly Horace Vernet never painted anything better in his palmiest days, if his productions are at all worthy to be mentioned side by side with those of the Russian, whose two paintings have suddenly made him famous and raised him from poverty and obscurity to wealth."

As no one had ever heard of this artist, the editor of the Gazette sent some one to Borissov for information about him, and Tatkeleff himself went to Moscow, where, on March 6, 1873, Count Baranowicz, the president of the Art Exhibition, presented him to an assembly attended by many of the élite of Russian society. He is described as follows, in the Baltic Gazette of that time : —

"Imagine a little slender man of sixty, with the head of a child, almost beardless, only a few tufts of silver-gray hair on his scalp, with small, elegant hands and feet, plainly clad in the national costume of the middle classes, with the timid manners of a little girl, and you have before your eyes the man who henceforth will number with the great painters of modern times."

Tayler, Frederick. (*Brit.*) Born in 1804. Was a pupil of the Royal Academy, studying also in Italy and Paris. In 1828 or '30 he was made Associate of the Society of Painters in Water-Colors, a full Member in 1835, and President in 1857. He has taken an active part in its affairs, and contributed regularly to its exhibitions. Among his later works are, " Taking in the Game," " Otter-Hunting in the Highlands," " After the Battue," " Waiting for the Hounds," " A Hawking-Party," " A Meet in the Forest," " Business and Pleasure," " Rustic Surgery," " A Hunting Morning, — Time, George II.," " Sherwood Forest, — Hounds in Full Cry," etc. His "Gamekeeper's Daughter," " Cattle Ferry-Boat," and " Woodland-Hunting " were at Paris in 1878.

"For instance, there are few drawings of the present day that involve greater sensations of power than those of Frederick Tayler. Every dash tells, and the quantity of effect obtained is enormous in proportion to the apparent means. Brilliant, beautiful, and bright, as a sketch, the work is still far from perfection as a drawing." — RUSKIN'S *Modern Painters.*

" I should say, judging from Mr. Tayler's skillful and rapid manner in water-color sketching, and from the ability displayed in the few etchings of his that have been published, that he had all of the natural gifts of a first-rate etcher, and nearly all the knowledge; nothing having been wanting to the full development of his powers in that direction, but their culture on a larger scale in works issued independently." — HAMERTON'S *Etching and Etchers.*

Tayler, Norman. (*Brit.*) Son of Frederick Tayler. He was elected an Associate Member of the Society of Painters in Water-Colors in 1878, when he exhibited " In the Valley where the Daisies Grow," " Rainy Weather," and " The Nearest Way to the Farm."

Tenerani, Pietro. (*Ital.*) Born at Tarrano, near Carrara (1798 – 1870). General Director of the Museums and Galleries of Rome. Member of many Academies and Knight of several Orders. He also received honors from various Royal personages. He was in effect a Roman. He was an indefatigable worker, often passing the night with chisel in hand. His art was his life, his love, his religion, and it brought him riches and honors. No adequate list of his works can be given here. At Rome, in the Via Nazionale, in 1876, a museum was opened containing more than four hundred and fifty works and studies of Tenerani's. His " Psyche " was a famous work ; a model of it is in the Leipsic Museum. He was much influenced by Thorwaldsen, and with him executed the monument to Eugène Beauharnais, erected at Munich.

Ten Kate, Hermann Frederic Karl. (*Dutch.*) Born at The Hague, 1822. Ten Kate was a Commissioner of the Netherlands to the Exposition of 1878. Medals at The Hague, Philadelphia, and other places. Pupil of Kruseman at Amsterdam. He spent a year in Paris. He lives at The Hague. His " Fishers of Marken " (1857) is at the Museum of Bordeaux. Among his works are, " The Military Enrollment," " Une fête champêtre," " Political Discussions," " The Paternal Benediction," and "Calvinist Prisoners under Louis XIV." "The Wood-Gatherers" is in the collection of Mrs. H. E. Maynard of Boston. To Paris in 1878 he sent three pictures in oil and two in water-colors.

Tennant, John. (*Brit.*) (1796–1873.) Originally a merchant's clerk, his decided talent for art was made so manifest that he entered the studio of a landscape-painter when still a young man, and made for himself a fair, if not high, reputation in the profession. He was a member of the Society of British Artists for many years, and for a long time its Honorary Secretary. He visited and painted during a large portion of his life in Wales and Devonshire, many of his works being scenes of those sections.

"Tennant's landscapes are of a character which could not fail to invite attention for picturesqueness and appropriate treatment, if not for higher qualities of art." — *Art Journal*, June, 1873.

Tenniel, John. (*Brit.*) Born in London, 1820. He displayed a taste for art at an early age, and had a picture on exhibition at the Gallery of British Artists while he was still a lad. He had little or no instruction. In the cartoon competition for the decoration of Westminster Hall, in 1845, he won a prize, and executed one of the frescos in the Palace of Westminster. His most successful work has been done in black and white. He paints only occasionally, and rarely exhibits. In 1851 he joined the staff of Punch, and has contributed many illustrations to that journal. He has also illustrated Once a Week, "The Ingoldsby Legends," "Lalla Rookh," and other books and magazines.

"When Mr. Tenniel first associated himself with Punch it was thought generally that his abilities were of too classic an order for the duty he had undertaken, ... but he had too much confidence in the pictorial strength he possessed to feel that he need limit himself to a particular sphere, and hence he persevered with his pencil until in time he became inoculated, as it were, with a sense of humor which has not been subordinate to, but has served to stimulate, his graphic powers." — HODDER's *Memoir of my Time.*

Terry, Luther. (*Am.*) American painter resident for many years in Rome, where he has executed historical, portrait, and *genre* compositions, following closely, it is said, the manner of the old masters. He visited the United States in 1874, but his pictures are rarely seen in his native country.

Teschendorff, Emil. (*Ger.*) A young artist of Berlin, where his studio now is, and where he exhibited, in 1877, "Troubled Days" and "A Nymph and Satyr," besides two water-color drawings which attracted much attention. His works are as yet but little known out of his native country, but he is a young painter of promise.

Thackeray, William M. (*Brit.*) Born in India (1811–1863). Was educated at the Charter-House School and at Cambridge University. Traveled upon the Continent, and for some time resided in Paris, studying art, and copying the pictures of the Louvre. The practical following of the profession he abandoned for literature, illus-

trating, however, and very cleverly, his " Comic Tales and Sketches,"
" Irish Sketch-Book," " Vanity Fair," "Pendennis," etc., besides drawing for Punch.   A volume entitled " Thackerayana," published by
Chatto and Windus, London, in 1875, contains nearly six hundred of
his original drawings and sketches, and fully establishes his claims to
an honorable position among the artists of the nineteenth century.

" We can hardly agree with those who hold that Thackeray failed as an artist and
then took to his pen.   There is no proof of failure.   His art accomplishes all he
set it to.   Had he, instead of being a gentleman's son, been born in the pariah of St.
Bartholomew the Great, and apprenticed, let us say, to Raimbach the engraver, we
might have had another, and, in some ways, a subtler Hogarth.   He draws well ; his
mouths and noses, his feet, his children's heads, all his ugly and queer ' mugs,' are
wonderful for expression and good drawing.   With beauty of man or woman he is not so
happy : but his fun is, we think, even more abounding in his cuts than in his words." —
Dr. JOHN BROWN, *in Spare Hours.*

" If it was one of Thackeray's few fanciful griefs that he was not destined for a painter
of the grand order, it doubtless consoled him to find that the happier gift of embodying
that abstract creation, an idea, in a few strokes of the pencil, was his beyond all question, and this graceful faculty he was accustomed to exercise so industriously that
myriad examples survive of the originality of his invention as an artist." — *Introduction
to Thackerayana.*

" Thackeray, in reply, sent a caricature portrait of himself, drawn by his own hand,
and representing a winged spirit, in a flowing robe and spectacles on nose.   Thackeray,
in early life, had taken to painting, and, perhaps, if he had pursued his first vocation,
he might have come in time to handle the brush as well as he afterwards handled the
pen.   At any rate the drawing in question, as I can bear witness, was enough to bring
tears into your eyes for laughing." — TAYLOR's *Thackeray the Humorist, etc.*

" If he had had his choice he would rather have been famous as an artist than as a
writer ; but it was destined that he should paint in colors which will never crack and
never need restoration.   All his artist experience did him just as much good in literature as it could have in any other way, and in traveling through Europe to see pictures
he learned not only them, but men, manners, and languages." — JAMES HANNAY, in *the
Edinburgh Courant.*

Thayer, Abbott H. (*Am.*) Born in Boston, 1849, and brought
up in the country, where he became familiar with the brute creation,
the painting of which has been his specialty.   He began to paint
from nature without instruction when a child of eight years.   Later,
he studied under Henry D. Morse.   In 1867 he settled in Brooklyn,
studying under J. B. Whittaker in the Brooklyn Academy of Design,
gaining, in 1868, the gold medal for the best drawing from the antique.   After a few years he took a studio in New York, drawing in
the Antique Life Schools of the National Academy, under L. E. Wilmarth.   He went to Paris in 1875, where he entered l'École des
Beaux-Arts, working with Lehmann, and afterwards in the studio of
Gérôme.   Among his more important pictures are, " Young Lions of
Central Park," life size (belonging to W. H. Thayer, M. D., of Brooklyn), "Gray Wolf" (belonging to A. J. C. Skene, M. D.), " Ice in
the River " (to G. C. Brackett), "Cows coming from Pasture " (to
Dr. H. P. Farnham), " Feeding the Cows " (to Mrs. J. O. Stone),
" Boy and Dog " (to Rev. A. P. Putnam), "Shamming Sick " (to

J. O. Low), "Autumn Cornfield," (to Mrs. Bullard of New York), "Hunter waiting for Game" (to F. A. Faulknér, Keene, N. H.), "View on the Seine," "Cloudy Day in the Pasture," "Alderney Herd in Guernsey," "Mountain Pasture," "Sleep," and "Childhood" (Paris Salon of 1878), exhibited in Brooklyn, New York, and Paris. His "Shamming Sick," a pair of pictures representing a terrier dog forgetting feigned illness at the cry of "Rats!" was drawn by the artist on the block for the Aldine in 1874, and copied in the London Sporting and Dramatic News in 1876.

"Mr. Thayer's 'Sleep' loses nothing by near study or distant view. It would be hypercritical to find fault with it on any technical grounds. In conception it is most poetic. . . . . Delicate gradings of gray and white carry the eye far back behind the perfectly relieved little head, with its tender tones of pearl and rose, and the dark spot of color (and that not very dark) is the little brown puppy that sleeps beneath the unconscious hand of the child. Mr. Thayer has been studying with Gérôme, but his manner is not mannered, as many of the rest of the Beaux-Arts students." — *New York Independent,* April 18, 1878.

Theed, William. (*Brit.*) Born in 1804. Highly regarded as a sculptor of portrait busts and statues, executing during his long career many of the most distinguished people of Great Britain. Among the better known of his works are the statues of Sir Isaac Newton, in bronze, at Grentham; and in marble, group of the Queen and Prince Albert, in early Saxon costume, at Windsor; statue of the Prince Consort, at Balmoral; Duchess of Kent, at Frogmore; Burke, in the House of Lords; Sir William Peel, at Greenwich Hospital; the late Lord Derby, at St. George's Hall, Liverpool; Sir Robert Peel, at Huddersfield; Hallam the historian, at St. Paul's Cathedral; Mackintosh the historian, at Westminster Abbey; and busts of John Bright, Sir Henry Holland, and many more. He is also sculptor of the statue representing "Africa," on the Albert Memorial, London.

Thirion, Eugène-Romain. (*Fr.*) Born at Paris. Chevalier of the Legion of Honor. Pupil of Picot, Cabanel, and Fromentin. In 1872 this artist decorated the chapel of Saint-Joseph in the church of the Trinity at Paris, and he also worked with Baudry in the decoration of the Hotel Païva. His painting in the above chapel is praised by the critic, Roger Ballu, in the "Gazette des Beaux-Arts," February, 1878. At the Salon of 1876 he exhibited "Jeanne d'Arc." She is represented as a young girl, listening to the voices she is said to have heard bidding her go to the aid of the King of France. In 1875 he exhibited "St. Sebastian" and "St. Theresa"; in 1874, "Rebecca at the Fountain" and "Field-Flowers"; etc. This painter has also exhibited many portraits.

Thom, James Crawford. (*Brit.-Am.*) A native of America, of Scottish descent. He was a pupil of Edward Frère in Paris. He has lived and practiced his profession in England and in the United States. He first exhibited in London, at the Royal Academy, in 1864, "Returning from the Wood," followed by "Tired of Waiting," "Going to School," and "The Monk's Walk." In the French Gallery, London, he has exhibited, at different seasons, "Household Duties," "Children returning from Church," "Love in the Kitchen," "The Farmyard," "Return of the Conscript," etc. He sent to the National Academy, New York, in 1878, a winter landscape with figures, and "Le jour de la Toussaint." His "Summer" and "Winter" belong to Henry P. Cooper; "Kitten and Strawberries," to Samuel V. Wright. His "Day" and "Night" (panels), and "Going to Church, Christmas Eve," the property of J. M. Burt, were at Philadelphia in 1876. A number of his landscapes were at the Mechanics' Fair, Boston, in 1878.

Thomas, John Evan. (*Brit.*) Native of Wales. Died in 1873 at an advanced age. Was a pupil of Chantrey, and exhibited at the Royal Academy, for many years, portrait busts and statues, as well as ideal figures; among the latter, "Music," in 1852, and the "Racket-Player," in 1856. He is the author of the statue in bronze to the Marquis of Bute at Cardiff, of the statue of Wellington at Brecon, of that of the Prince Consort at Tenby, and other works in Wales and other parts of Great Britain.

Thomas, William Cave. (*Brit.*) Born in London, 1820. He at first turned his attention to sculpture, and entered the Royal Academy in 1838, drawing and modeling for two years. In 1840 he went to Munich, where he studied drawing, and executed several cartoons. He returned to England in 1843, and devoted himself for a time to oil-painting, exhibiting at the Royal Academy, in 1850, "Alfred giving his last Loaf to the Pilgrims"; followed in different years by "Alfred visiting Churches at Early Dawn," "Rivalry," "The Protestant Lady," "Petrarch's First Sight of Laura," "The Heir cast out of the Vineyard." In water-color he has painted "The Lord of the Harvest," "The Fruit-Bearer," "Morning," "Dante and Beatrice," "Sunset on Calvary," and an "Ecce Homo" (belonging to the late Prince Consort). He received a prize of £100 for a cartoon of Westminster Hall, "St. Augustine preaching to the Saxons," and £400 for the execution of "The Spirit of Justice," in the South Kensington Museum. He designed also several decorations for the International Exhibition of 1862 in London, and is the author of several valuable books upon mural decoration and social economy.

"If we examine Mr. Cave Thomas' works we shall find them characterized by a remarkable solidity of grouping, which contrasts favorably with the somewhat sparse disposition of members prevailing in paintings that aspire to be historical, and which, irrespective of this weakness, are not contemptible."—J. L. TUPPER, *in English Artists of the Present Day.*

Thomas, Gabriel-Jules. (*Fr.*) Born at Paris, 1821. Member of the Institute. Chevalier of the Legion of Honor. Pupil of Dumont and l'École des Beaux-Arts. *Prix de Rome* in 1848. His statue of "Virgil" (1861) is in the Luxembourg. In 1876 he exhibited at the Salon, "Christ on the Cross," in bronze; in 1872, four figures in wood, representing the four quarters of the globe, commanded for the gallery of the Hotel of Toulouse by the Bank of France ; in 1870, " Thought " (statue, marble) ; etc.

Thomas, George H. (*Brit.*) (1824 – 1868.) After serving an apprenticeship to G. Bonner, a wood-engraver in London, he went to Paris, where he made designs for illustrated books. He subsequently spent two years in New York, upon the staff of a pictorial journal, making also some graceful drawings for the engraving of American bank-notes. Returning to Europe in 1848, he went to Italy to complete his art studies, and furnished many vivid sketches of the Garibaldi campaign of 1849 for the London Illustrated News. He visited the Crimea for the same paper in 1854, the original of many of his drawings being in possession of the Queen. Among his oil-paintings are, " Rotten-Row," " The Ball at the Camp of Boulogne," " Parade at Potsdam in Honor of Queen Victoria in 1858," " Happy Days," " Coronation of the King of Prussia " (painted by command), " Marriage of the Princess Alice," " The Queen and Prince Consort at Aldershot in 1859," and " The Investing of the Sultan with the Order of the Garter," many of which belong to the Queen. His " Apple-Blossoms " and " Masterless " were at the Royal Academy in 1868, the year of his death. His happiest book illustrations were those for Wilkie Collins' " Armadale," and the delineations of negro character for " Uncle Tom's Cabin."

Thompson, Cephas G., A. N. A. (*Am.*) Born in Middleborough, Mass., 1809. He obtained something of the mechanism of art from his father, Cephas Thompson, an artist who painted a great deal in Southern Italy, but he was comparatively self-taught, studying and observing closely nature, and the many masters he has known intimately on both sides of the Atlantic. He began his professional career in Plymouth, Mass., when nineteen years of age, finding his way to Boston, and working in Bristol, Providence, and Philadelphia. He spent ten years (1837 to '47) in the city of New York, painted some forty portraits in New Bedford, many in Boston, and went to Europe in 1852, visiting London, Paris, Florence, and Rome. He made his home for seven years in the latter city. Since 1860 he has had a studio in New York. He is an Associate Member of the National Academy, and of several prominent art societies of Europe. Mr. Thompson's works are owned throughout America, and many specimens are in England, Russia, France, etc. Before going abroad, he painted a series of portraits of American authors, including Hoffman (belonging to the New York Historical Society), Dr. Francis, and others. His portrait of Hawthorne, with whom in Italy he was on intimate terms, was engraved, and is in the edition of " Twice-Told Tales " published by Ticknor and Fields. His full-length portrait of Dr. Matthews, the first President of the New York University, is in the president's room of that institution. His portraits of William C.

Bryant and Mrs. Bryant, and a copy of the "Staffa Madonna of Raphael," belonged to the venerable poet. C. H. Rogers of New York has his "Guardian Angel"; Mr. Wales of Boston, "Prospero and Miranda"; Ex-Governor Padelford, of Providence, R. I., "St. Peter delivered from Prison"; Charles Sprague, the banker-poet, owned his "Spring and Autumn"; and others of his pictures belong to the family of Hawthorne, to Mr. Longfellow, to E. H. Miller, to George Bliss of New York, and to Mrs. Lee Smith of Ravenswood, N. Y.

"It is certainly a beautiful picture, full of genius and spirit ['St. Peter led from the Prison by an Angel']. It is very rarely you see a production so effective in all its parts. The background equals, without rivaling or forcing attention from the prominent and principal objects in the foreground. The depth of shadow in the one does not prevent its distinctness and accuracy of outline from telling a striking tale, while the brightness and vividness of the figures in the other lastingly impress themselves on the eye and the memory." — Mrs. Gibson, *in the Richmond (Va.) Enquirer*, 1859.

"Not one of our artists has brought back with him from Italy a more thorough knowledge and appreciation of the old masters, technically, historically, and authentically, than Cephas G. Thompson. He conscientiously endeavors to infuse their lofty feeling and motives into his own refined manner." — Jarves, *Art Idea*.

". . . . Or we might bow before an artist who has wrought too sincerely, too religiously, with too earnest feeling and too delicate a touch, for the world at once to recognize how much toil and thought are compressed into the stately brow of Prospero and Miranda's maids in loveliness; or from what a depth within this painter's heart the angel is leading forth St. Peter." — Hawthorne, *in the Marble Faun.*

Thompson, Jerome, A. N. A. (*Am.*) Born in Middleborough, Mass., 1814. Son of Cephas, and younger brother of Cephas G. Thompson, N. A. He early displayed artistic tastes, and began his career as a sign-painter in the neighborhood of his native town. After painting portraits for some years on Cape Cod, he went to New York at the age of seventeen, devoting himself from that period to the study and practice of his art. He had no masters, and is a graduate of no schools. His professional life has been spent in New York. In 1852 he went to Europe, spending two years. He was elected an Associate of the National Academy about 1850, but has not exhibited in its gallery since 1863 or '64. Although still painting, his pictures are not shown by him to the public, and his life of late years has been very retired. Among the better known of his works are, "Reminiscences of Mount Mansfield," "The Old Oaken Bucket," "Home, Sweet Home," "Woodman, spare that Tree," "Hiawatha's Homeward Journey with Minnehaha," "The Home of my Childhood," "Coming thro' the Rye," "The Land of Beulah," "The Voice of the Great Spirit," and many others, none of which have been exhibited by Mr. Thompson, although a few have been sent to different galleries by their owners. Many of them have been engraved and chromoed.

"Mr. Jerome Thompson has painted a very beautiful and attractive picture illustrating 'The Old Oaken Bucket.' It is at once an illustration of these well-known verses, and a portrait of the early home of their author in Scituate, Mass. While he has made a picture that is very agreeable to look at, the artist has not attempted to secure the pleasure of the eyes at the expense of truth, by dressing his subject in charms that do not belong to it. He has done us all good by painting this unpretending, truthful picture." — *New York Tribune*, May 14, 1868.

"Jerome Thompson, whose pictures so charm the natural feelings of the heart, has gratified the public with another work from his easel, 'Home, Sweet Home,' a companion to the 'Old Oaken Bucket.' It is an ideal creation, and so truthful to nature that all ideality is lost, ... and herein lies the charm of Jerome Thompson's pencil and brush. Stand before the picture, and the longer you look, the more vividly will you recall some half-forgotten scene, or detect the unexplained growth from a counterpart from out the wilderness, bounded by the silvery lines of memory." — *New York Turf, Field, and Farm*, October 8, 1868.

"The 'Beacon Fire,' another work by the same artist, Jerome Thompson, gives a striking picture of the region of Lake Pepin. .... The composition is quite picturesque and effective, and in all these works Mr. Thompson shows the pleasing charm that so endears his ballads of the pencil to ingenuous hearts and simple tastes." — *New York Home Journal*, January 8, 1872.

Thompson, Launt, N. A. (*Brit.-Am.*) Born in Ireland, 1833. Removed to America in 1847. Settled in Albany, N. Y. Entered the office of a professor of anatomy in that city, and subsequently became a student of the medical college. He early displayed a talent for drawing, occupying his leisure hours with his pencil. He abandoned medicine to become a pupil of the sculptor Palmer, and worked in his studio in Albany for nine years. In 1858 he moved to New York, was made an Associate of the National Academy in 1861, and Academician in 1862. In 1875 he took a studio in Florence, where he still remains (1878). Among his works are portrait busts of William C. Bryant (for Central Park), of James Gordon Bennett, Robert B. Minturn, Captain Charles Marshall, Edwin Booth as "Hamlet," Professor Morse, Dr. Tyng (1870), Parke Godwin, and C. L. Elliott, N. A. (1871). Among his ideal works are, "Elaine," "The Trapper," "Morning Glory," and "Lily Maid." His statue of Napoleon (bronze) and a bust of a "Rocky Mountain Trapper" were at the Paris Exposition of 1867.

Thompson, A. Wordsworth, N. A. (*Am.*) Born in Baltimore, 1840. In 1861 he went to Paris, and began the study of art under Charles Gleyre in 1862, and, later, was, for a time, a pupil of Émile Lambinet. In 1864 he entered the studio of Albert Pasini, working there one year. His first publicly exhibited picture, "Moorlands of Au-Fargi," was at the Paris Salon of 1865. In 1868 he settled in New York, since then his home, with the exception of occasional visits to Paris. In 1873 he sent to the National Academy "Desolation," upon the strength of which he was made an Associate of that institution ; he was elected Academician in 1875. In 1878 he joined the Society of American Artists, sending to their first exhibition, the same year, "The Road to the Saw-Mill." Among the better known of Wordsworth Thompson's works are, "The Port of Menazzio, Lake Como " (owned by William H. Davis of New York), "Desolation " (now in Buffalo), "Steamboat-Landing at Menenazzio " (owned by Mr. Fairbanks of St. Johnsbury, Vt.), "Virginia in the Olden Times " (belonging to D. H. McAlpine, N. Y.), "The Vesper Hour" (to William Brookfield, N. Y.), "Annapolis in 1776" (to the Academy of Fine Arts in Buffalo, N. Y.), "Traveling in Corsica" (to Isaac S. Platt). To the Exhibitions of the National Academy he has been a regular contributor for some years, sending, in 1869, "View of Mount Etna"; in 1870, "Reminiscence of the Potomac"; in 1871, "Evening on the Moor"; in 1874, "A Picnic on the Rocks, Lake George"; in 1875, "Gathering Apples"; in 1876, "A Midsummer's Day on Long Island"; in 1877, "Pursuit of Knowledge under Difficulties" and "By the Sea, Mentone"; and, in 1878, "A Review at Philadelphia in 1777." He sent several works to Philadelphia in 1876, and "The School-House on the Hill" to the Paris Exposition of 1878.

"Mr. Thompson has caught the sorrowful sentiment of the scene ['Desolation'], and embodied all its poetry and romance. Apart from its merits as a work of art, the picture will be valuable as an historical souvenir, for doubtless the ruins of St. Cloud will before long be cleared away, and there is no probability of the palace being rebuilt. We learned afterwards, as we guessed from his work, that Mr. Thompson, starting with a genuine vocation for art, had studied it with rare fidelity, had passed years in the ateliers of the best artists of Paris, had devoted his days and nights to careful drawing of the human figure, from the marble and from life, that in pursuit of the picturesque he had made the tour of Europe on foot, etc., and also that he devoted fully as much time to American scenery, making not merely drawings, but elaborate pictures in the fields." — *Boston Daily Globe,* May 7, 1873.

"A. W. Thompson exhibited 'On the Sands, East Hampton' and 'Virginia in the Olden Times,' both works showing marked evidence of discipline and careful study. There is a tendency towards the adoption of the French manner in this artist's work, which shows whence he derived this discipline. It is a question whether a better manner may not be derived directly from nature without the interposition of another's method of viewing things." — PROF. WEIR's *Official Report of the American Centennial Exhibition of 1876.*

Thompson, Elizabeth (Mrs. Butler). (*Brit.*) Born about 1844. As a child she evinced a decided taste for drawing soldiers and horses. Entered the South Kensington schools; painted for some years as an amateur, and did not exhibit in public until 1873, when she sent to the Royal Academy "Missing," a picture which attracted great attention. In 1874 she exhibited her famous "Roll-Call" (purchased by the Queen), which achieved a popularity for itself and for its painter almost without precedent in the history of art in England. Her picture of "The 28th Regiment at Quatre-Bras" was at the Royal Academy, 1875, since which she has exhibited at private galleries, "Balaklava," in 1876, and "The Return from Inkerman" (purchased for £3,000 by the Fine Art Society in 1877). Her latest work (still on the easel) is "'Listed for the Connaught Rangers." Among her other works is "The Magnificat," a religious picture painted in 1869.

In water-colors Miss Thompson has painted "On Duty," a trooper of the Scot's Grays (1875); "Scot's Grays Advancing," "Cavalry at a Gallop," "Sketches in Tuscany" (1877), etc. "The Return from Inkerman" was at the Paris Exposition of 1878.

"I never approachsd a picture with more iniquitous prejudice against it than I did Miss Thompson's ['Quatre-Bras'], partly because I have always said that no woman could paint, and secondly because I thought what the public made such a fuss about *must* be good for nothing. But it is Amazon's work this, no doubt of it, and the first fine pre-Raphaelite picture of battle we have had ; profoundly interesting, and showing all manner of illustrative and realistic faculty. . . . . But actually here, what I suppose few people would think of looking at, the sky is most tenderly painted, and with the truest outline of cloud of all in the Exhibition; and the terrific piece of gallant wrath and ruin on the extreme left, when the cuirassier is catching round the neck of his horse as he falls, and the convulsed fallen horse, seen through the smoke below, is wrought through all the truth of its frantic passion, with gradations of color and shade which I have not seen the like of since Turner's death." — RUSKIN's *Notes of the Academy*, 1875.

"'Inkerman' is simply a marvelous production when considered as the work of a young woman who was never on the field of battle. . . . . No matter how many figures she brings into the scene, or how few, you may notice character in each figure ; each is a supreme study." — *Art Journal*, August, 1877.

"It would be natural for some errors to appear in them ['Roll-Call,' 'Quatre-Bras,' and 'Balaklava']; the wonder is, considering the circumstances, that they are so few. As works of art we should say that they display real pathos and dramatic power in parts, often with effective drawing of the horses. But the power is too scattered, the composition lacks simplicity, breadth, concentration. While isolated groups are very well conceived, and would appear well as separate paintings or episodes, they do not sufficiently harmonize to form the unity of one great composition. The coloring is also sometimes very good, and then again is impaired by crude unnatural yellows or other tints out of tone with the rest. Miss Thompson's genius seems to be lyrical rather than epic." — BENJAMIN's *Contemporary Art in Europe.*

Thompson, Albert. (*Am.*) Born at Woburn, Mass., 1853. He received his early art education in Boston. In 1872 he spent six months in European travel, going abroad again in 1874, with J. F. Cole and E. L. Weeks, when he visited Great Britain, France, and Italy, and studied in the continental galleries. In 1873 he became a pupil of W. E. Norton. He paints landscapes and figures, exhibiting at the Boston Art Club and other galleries. He is the author of a work entitled "Elementary Perspective," published in 1878.

"Mr. Albert Thompson has a number of truly fine pictures in this collection. In an 'Apple-Orchard, — Summer,' are purity of atmosphere and fine contrasts of color. His 'Cattle on a Hillside' is a sweet composition, and Mr. Thompson's knowledge of the anatomy is here conspicuous. . . . . His 'Landscape and Cattle,' 'Summer Afternoon,' and 'Lake Winnipiseogee from Wolfborough,' all attest Mr. Thompson's power in selection of subject, and nice gray qualities, as well as for tone and quality of rich color." — *Boston Transcript.*

"At Noyes and Blakeslee's gallery a number of Albert Thompson's paintings are now on exhibition. One is a very life-like study of an Italian boy, two or three are picturesque scenes in Normandy, and among the smaller pictures is a wood interior and a bit of pasture-land, with lowering clouds above, that will attract especial notice. The cattle which Mr. Thompson so freely introduces into his landscapes are excellently drawn, and, like J. Foxcroft Cole, he knows just where to place them. All of the pictures are fresh in tone, broad in treatment, and, while representing a variety of subjects, show at the same time a marked individuality." — *Boston Advertiser.*

Thorburn, Robert, A. R. A. (*Brit.*) Born in Dumfries, 1818. Entered the Drawing Academy of the Royal Institution, Edinburgh, in 1833, and the Royal Academy, London, in 1836. He first exhibited at the Royal Academy in 1837.   Until the introduction of photography he devoted himself to the painting of miniatures, in which he met with decided success.   Among his sitters were the Queen and several of her children, the Prince Consort, and other distinguished people.   He was admitted to the Academy as an Associate in 1848, and received a first-class gold medal at the Paris Exposition of 1855. In later years he has painted life-size portraits in crayon and oil, and ideal figure-pictures, exhibiting at the Royal Academy, in 1864, "Where shall I take Refuge?"; in 1865, "Asleep" and "On the Esk"; in 1866, "The Orphans"; in 1867, "Scotch Stream"; in 1868, "Forecasting"; in 1869, "Undine" and "Country Life"; in 1870, "John the Baptist" and "Catherine of Aragon"; in 1871, "Summer" and "The Concealment of Moses"; in 1872, "The Widow's Stay"; in 1873, "Rebecca at the Well"; in 1874, "In the Meadow" and "On the Hillside"; in 1875, "On the West Coast of Scotland"; in 1876, "Christian descending the Hill Difficulty"; in 1878, "The Slough of Despond" and "Out in the Cold."

"Thornburn's miniatures combine truth and spirit with graceful grouping and delicacy of execution." — Mrs. Tytler's *Modern Painters.*

Thorndike, G. Quincy. (*Am.*) Born in Boston, about 1825. Graduated at Harvard University in 1847, when he visited Europe, studying for some time in Paris.   Returning to America, he settled in Newport, R. I., devoting himself to landscapes and marine views. Among the better known of his pictures are, "The Wayside Inn," "Swans in the Central Park," "The Lily Pond," "The Dumplings, Newport," and "View near Stockbridge, Mass."

"Thorndike is so thoroughly French in style and motive that his pictures require naturalization before being popularly welcomed at home." — Jarves, *Art Idea.*

Thornycroft, Mary. (*Brit.*) Born in 1814.   Daughter of John Francis the sculptor, whose pupil she was.   She evinced decided taste for art as a young girl, modeling busts and ideal subjects, and exhibiting at the Royal Academy at an early age.   Her first important work was a life-sized figure, entitled "The Flower-Girl," which attracted some attention.   In 1840 she married T. Thornycroft, one of her father's pupils, and with her husband went to Rome in 1842, spending a year in that city at work and in study.   A few years later she was commissioned by the Queen to execute statues of the children of the Royal Family, which were designed in character, as the "Four Seasons," were exhibited at the Royal Academy, and were much praised.   To the Paris Exposition of 1855 she contributed, "A Girl Skipping."   In 1861 she exhibited, at the Royal Academy, "Princess Beatrice" (belonging to the Queen); in 1863, "The Princess of Wales" and "Princess Louis of Hesse"; in 1869, "A Young Cricketer"; in 1871, "The Princess Louise"; in 1872, "Melpomene"; in 1875, "Princess Christian"; in 1877, "The Duchess of Edinburgh."

" Sculpture has at no time numbered many successful followers among women. We have, however, in Mrs. Thornycroft, one such artist, who, by some recent advance and by the degrees of success which she has already reached, promises fairly for the art. Some of this lady's busts have refinement and feeling." -- PALGRAVE's *Essays on Art*, 1863.

Thornycroft, Thomas. (*Brit.*) A contemporary English sculptor. He was a pupil of John Francis. Among his works are, " James I." and " Charles I." (in marble), in the Royal Gallery of the palace of Westminster, " The Prince Consort," " Melpomene," " Thalia," " Clio," etc. (in bronze), and many portrait busts and statues.

Thornycroft, Hamo (sculptor) and **Helen** and **Theresa Thornycroft** (painters), children of the two preceding artists, have inherited the family tastes and talents for art. They all exhibit their works at the Royal Academy, London.

Tidemand, Adolphe. (*Norwegian.*) Born at Mandal (1814–1876). Chevalier of the Orders of Saint Olaf and the Legion of Honor. Court painter in Norway. Member of the Academies of Berlin, Amsterdam, Copenhagen, and Stockholm. Studied first at the Academy of Copenhagen, then at that of Düsseldorf under Hildebrandt and Schadow. Tidemand decorated the château of Oscarshall, near Christiana. He painted landscapes and historic *genre* subjects. His most important work is " The Baptism of Christ," which is in a church in Christiana. Among his pictures may be mentioned, " The Distribution of the Sacrament to the Aged and Infirm, according to the Lutheran Form," " Single Combat in Ancient Times," " Village Funeral in Norway," " Farewell of Emigrants leaving for America," and " Young Man Preaching." His picture of " The Assembly of the Haugiens," a very important work, is in the Düsseldorf Gallery; it has been reproduced several times by the artist. Tidemand has vigor of conception, vivacity of expression, and the power of harmonizing his groups, and giving a characteristic expression to each face and figure.

" It was in studying the manners and the costumes of the peasants of his country and reproducing them on his canvas, that he made an original and merited reputation. Tidemand had not the temperament of a colorist; but his color, a little cold and dull, failed not to harmonize with his compositions, intelligently arranged, and frequently of a remarkable character. . . . . He was, above all, a painter of *genre*, or rather a painter of manners, and one of the more distinguished; a conscientious and learned artist, with a talent severe and elevated." — *L'Art*, 1876.

" The primeval strength of the Norwegian peasant would never have been so well known if this artist had not represented it by academical idealization. His feeling, conception, and masterly individualization transfigure most of his personages, even when they are not correct according to the accepted idea of beauty. His color is fresh, strong, and of great harmony; his drawing broad and bold, but without pretension. Free from forced contrasts, his pictures have the simplicity of nature, and are distinguished for careful and conscientious study, and a proper adaptation of parts." — *Unsere Zeit*, October, 1876.

Tidey, Arthur. (*Brit.*) Born in 1808. Brother of Henry Tidey. He was a fashionable painter of portraits in miniature, before the invention of photography, and still exhibits at the Royal Academy. He is a resident of London.

Tidey, Henry. (*Brit.*) (1814 – 1872.) Received his first instruction in art from his father, John Tidey, and began the practice of his profession as a painter of portraits in oil, having among his sitters members of the aristocracy and of the Royal Family, and exhibiting frequently at the Royal Academy. In the later years of his life, however, he devoted himself entirely to water-colors, and was made a member of the Institute in 1858, contributing to its gallery in the same year, " The Feast of Roses " (purchased by the Queen) ; in 1860 he painted " Queen Mab," for which he received two medals ; in 1863, " Christ blessing Little Children " ; in 1864, " The Night of the Betrayal." Among his later works are, " Sardanapalus," in 1870 ; " Seaweeds," in 1871 ; and " Castles in the Air," in 1872.

Tieck, Christian Frederic. (*Ger.*) Born at Berlin (1776 – 1851). Member of the Academy of Berlin, and Director of the division of Statues of the Museum of that city. Pupil of Schadow in Germany and of David in France. This sculptor traveled much, and remained a long time at Carrara, where he became the intimate friend of Rauch. Tieck was more successful in portrait busts than in embodying imaginary conceptions. He had many sitters among people of mark. Among his busts may be mentioned those of the Emperor of Germany (in the Salle des États at Berlin), the King of Bavaria, Schelling, Schinkel, Goethe, Lessing, etc. He assisted in the decoration of the new château at Weimar ; he was charged with the decoration of the new theater at Berlin ; the portal of the Cathedral, Berlin ; and the models of the Genii for the monument of Saalfeld and that of Kreuzberg. Tieck was very active in establishing a gallery of models from antique statues and monuments at the Museum of Berlin, and, together with Beuth, Schinkel, and Rauch, he executed a large number of these copies.

Tiffany, Louis C., A. N. A. (*Am.*) Born in the city of New York in 1848. Was a pupil of George Inness for some time, studying subsequently in Paris and under Léon Bailly. He has traveled extensively in France, Africa, Spain, and other countries, painting many characteristic pictures of Eastern life. He was made a member of the Water-Color Society in 1870, an Associate of the National Academy in 1871, and Treasurer of the Society of American Artists in 1878. To the National Academy (in oil) he has sent " A Dock Scene, Yonkers," in 1869 ; " Fruit-Vender, under the Sea-Wall at Nassau," in 1870 ; " Hunter's Dinner " and " Street Scene in Tangiers," in 1872 ; " Market-Day outside the Wall, Tangiers," in 1873 ; " Clouds on the Hudson," in 1874 ; " Ceramic Wares " and a " Study at Quimper, Brittany," in 1877 ; " A Laborious Rest " and several street scenes, in 1878. To the Water-Color Exhibition in 1869 he contributed " Venice " ; in 1872, " Meditation " ; in 1874, " A Merchant of the East " ; in 1876, " A Shop in Switzerland " ; in 1877, " An Old Shop at Algiers " and " The Palace of the Pasha Ali Ben Haessein, at Algiers " ; in 1878, " The Cobblers of Boufarik." To Philadelphia, in 1876, he contributed (in water-color), " Old and New Mosques at Cairo," " Lazy Life in the East," and " A Street Scene in Cairo " (belonging to George D. Morgan). To Paris in 1878 he sent, " Duane Street, New York " (in oil), and " Market-Day, Morlaix " and " The Cobblers of Boufarik " (in water-colors). His " Life in the East," a view of the old Sub-Treasury Building, Tangiers, in the Johnston Collection, is now in the possession of Mrs. John C. Green. His " Citadel at Cairo " belongs to Charles Storrs of Brooklyn ; his " Old Second-Hand Shop at Geneva," to Joseph Millbank ; his " New London Harbor " (water-color), to Samuel V. Wright.

Tilton, John Rollin. (*Am.*) Born in Loudon, N. H., 1833. He has been a close student of the Venetian school of painting, especially of Titian, but is a graduate of no art academy, and has studied under no master. His professional life has been spent in Italy, chiefly in Rome. Many of his landscapes are in the collections of the Marquis of Sligo, Sir William Drummond Stuart, Lord Amberly, Lady Ashburton, and others in England. Marshall O. Roberts of New York owns his " Kem Ombres." He exhibited at the Royal Academy, London, in 1873, " The Palace of Thebes," etc. Mrs. A. Mitchell of Milwaukee owns an Egyptian view ; Martin Brimmer of Boston, " Como " and " Venice " ; Fletcher Adams of New York, " Venetian Fishing-Boats." He has exhibited at the Royal Academy, London, National Academy, New York, Boston Athenæum, etc. To the Centennial in Philadelphia, in 1876, he sent " The Lagoons of Venice " and " Kem Ombres."

" Of the American artists who have won fame for themselves by persevering industry. Mr. Tilton is a prominent example. He is the first American painter since Benjamin West whose works have received special commendation from the President of the Royal Academy, who, as some of our readers will recollect, at the annual dinner last year, complimented Mr. Tilton, in the most flattering terms, on the success of his picture of ' Kem Ombres,' Upper Egypt, which was placed ' on the line' at the last Exhibition." — *London Daily News*, 1874.

" A long and loving observation of Nature in many climes and in all her moods has enabled this artist [John R. Tilton] to do by Nature as an experienced portrait-painter does by his sitters, to select each subject at its best, at the most favorable moment of the day, and of the year, and under the most favorable circumstances of light and atmosphere ; and the result is that this little view of Orvieto makes a singular contrast of tone to that of the ' Thebes.' The Valley of the Nile in the latter is at its greenest, and yet it is a very different greenery from that of the Valley of the Tiber. . . . . The solidity of the painting and at the same time the transparency of the work are truly remarkable in this little titbit of a landscape." — T. ADOLPHUS TROLLOPE, *London Standard*, February 5, 1874.

" He [Mr. Tilton] was born on the other side of the Atlantic, but he has studied life and nature in all countries, and his paintings of Naples and Venice, of Greece and Egypt, are as well known in Italy, in England, and all over Europe, as they are in his own country. . . . . He values his picture not so much as a masterpiece of landscape

13 *

painting, as it is, but for the importance it will have in after times as a faithful historical memorial of Rome as it was, and as, if he had his way, it should never cease to be. Few men have, by a quarter of a century of loving familiarity, made themselves more minutely acquainted, not only with every inch of its ground, and every stone of its buildings, but what is much more, with every phase, shade, and *nuance* of its ever-changing, ever-charming atmosphere. There can be nothing more true, yet nothing more exquisitely got up, more genially idealized, than this long-meditated picture of ' Rome from the Aventine.' " — *London Times,* January 8, 1878.

Timbal, Louis Charles. (*Fr.*) Born at Paris, about 1822. Chevalier of the Legion of Honor. Painter and art-critic. Pupil of Drölling. He sent his first contribution to the Salons in 1847. He has painted a variety of subjects, and some portraits, but the larger number of his works are religious subjects. He has also decorated a chapel at St. Sulpice, and executed a " Theology " in the church of the Sarbonne. In the Luxembourg are his " Muse and Poet " (1866) and " Christ's Agony in the Garden " (1867). Timbal contributes many articles to the " Gazette des Beaux-Arts." He is a man of fortune, and art is his passion. He has a fine collection of Italian objects of art of the Middle Ages and of the Renaissance.

" M. Timbal pretends not to occupy a considerable place in the contemporaneous school ; he holds the rank assigned to all artists who are mindful of the lessons of the past. His admiration for the great geniuses whom he has known and studied aids him in avowing himself only an imitator of these giants ; he is their victim ; he is resigned to his fate. His important compositions in the chapel of Sainte-Geneviève at Saint-Sulpice are treated in the style of the beautiful Florentine frescos of the Brancacci chapel : the expressions are true, but the movements seem suppressed for the sake of a dignity which is not in the character of all the personages." — GEORGES BERGER, *Gazette des Beaux-Arts,* February, 1876.

Tissot, James. (*Fr.*) Born at Nantes. Medal in 1866. Pupil of H. Flandrin and L. Lamothe. This artist, French by birth and education, has now so long resided in England that he has become in effect a man of that country. His picture of the " Meeting of Faust and Marguerite " (1861) is in the Luxembourg. He exhibited at the Salon of 1870 (for the last time), " A Young Girl in a Boat " (belonging to Mr. W. H. Stewart) and " Partie Carrée " ; in 1869, " A Widow " and " Young Women examining some Japanese Articles " ; in 1868, " A Breakfast " and " The Retreat in the Garden of the Tuileries " ; in 1867, " A Young Woman singing with an Organ " and " Confidence " ; in 1866, " A Young Woman in Church " and " The Confessional " ; etc. At the Royal Academy Exhibition, London, in 1876, he exhibited " The Thames," " A Convalescent," an etching of " The Thames," and another etching, " Quarreling " ; in 1875, " A Bunch of Lilacs " and " Hush " ; in 1874, " London Visitors," " Waiting," and " The Ball on Shipboard " ; in 1873, " The Captain's Daughter," " The Last Evening," and " Too Early " ; in 1872, " An Interesting Story " and " Les adieux." At the Walters Gallery, Baltimore, is a " Marguerite," by Tissot. " Faust and Marguerite " (a remarkably fine work of its kind) is in the collection of Mrs. H. E. Maynard of Boston.

" Tissot is the declared enemy of aerial perspective, and be has sworn that by the force of talent and mind he will make us forget that there is an atmosphere which serves to unite the tones of color, to graduate them in their plane, and from them to bring out harmony. We will not stop before the large picture, which leaves us too much to desire in this direction, but we pass rather to the two delicious portraits of comedians. There Tissot, who had but one figure to paint, was obliged to renounce his monomania, and show himself that which he really is, a very skilful painter, and an artist full of spirit." — RENÉ MÉNARD, *Gazette des Beaux-Arts,* June, 1869.

" Both Alma Tadema and Tissot have wielded a large influence on contemporary English art." — BENJAMIN's *Contemporary Art in Europe.*

" The pictures of Tissot, Heilbuth, and Legros, hung side by side, suggest curious contrasts. The first sends five pictures, ' Spring ' and ' July,' full-length portraits in white, with knots of pale yellow riband, under skilfully managed reflected lights ; ' Croquet,' a graceful figure of a stripling girl, dressed in black, in a garden ; ' Evening,' the crush at the entrance to a West-end *soirée,* with a young lady in a daring ' arrangement,' in which yellow predominates in head-gear, fan, and dress, all of the most pronounced fashion of modern millinery, a figure worthy of Worth ; and a ' Study,' of which only a pretty simple head is finished. It is impossible to conceive art less unsophisticated, less in contact with nature, as far as its subject-matter gnes, than Tissot's. But it would be difficult to find in any contemporary painter's work more artistic thought and resource than have been lavished on these unsophisticated subjects. It is art brought to the doors and laid at the feet of the *monde,* if not sometimes of the *demi-monde,* with an almost cynical sincerity. Thus far it is French rather than English, alike in the ideas it suggests and the skill it shows." — *London Times,* May 2, 1878.

Tite, Sir William. (*Brit.*) (1802 – 1873.) He studied architecture under Laing, and was very prominent in his profession. He furnished plans for many fine buildings in London and elsewhere in Great Britain, the best known, perhaps, being the Royal Exchange in the metropolis. In 1862 he was elected President of the Institute of British Architects, and was knighted by the Queen in 1869. He was a member of Parliament for upwards of twenty years.

Tolles, Sophie Mapes. (*Am.*) Native of the city of New York. Began the study of art in Philadelphia, in 1864, under P. F. Rothermel. She was some time in the schools of the National Academy and of the Cooper Institute, New York, where she received two medals. Spending two years in Paris, she was a pupil of E. Luminais, painting and copying in that city and in Italy. She first exhibited at the National Academy, in 1876, a portrait ; in 1877, she exhibited " The Cottage Door," and several flower-pieces ; in 1878, " In Memoriam." Among her portraits is one of Linda Gilbert of Chicago. For several years she has been Vice-President of the Ladies' Art Association.

Tompkins, Clementina M. G. (*Am.*) A native of Washington, D. C. She has lived for some time in Paris, studying in the National Schools of Design there, and under Bonnat. Her specialty is portraits and figure-pieces. She exhibited at the Salon in Brussels in 1872, and has contributed regularly to the Paris Salons since 1873. To Philadelphia in 1876 she sent " The Little Musician," for which she received a medal ; to the Paris Exposition of 1878, " The Little Artist " and " Rosa, la fileuse."

Topham, Francis William. (*Brit.*) Born in Leeds (1808–1877). He began life as an engraver in his native city, removing to London about 1830. Shortly after joining the Institute of Painters in Water-Colors, he devoted himself to painting Spanish, Welsh, and Irish peasant life with marked success. Leaving the Institute, he became an active member of the Society of Painters in Water-Colors, contributing, among other sketches, " Irish Courtship," " Welsh Cabin," " Spanish Gypsies," " Reading the Bible," etc. Among his later works are, " Preparing for the Fight " and " Waiting by the Stile," exhibited in 1872 ; " The Bird's-Nest " and " Listening to the Love-Letter," in 1873 (sent to Philadelphia in 1876) ; " Wayfarers " and " A Welsh Stream," in 1875; and after his death, in 1877, " Blackberry-Gatherers " and " Haymaking." Two of his works, " Venetian Water-Carriers " and " The Eve of the Festa," were at the Paris Exposition of 1878. His death occurred in Spain.

Topham, Francis W. W. (*Brit.*) Born in London, 1838. Son of Francis W. Topham, from whom he received his first instruction in art, studying later at the schools of the Royal Academy. He has lived and painted in Italy and France, and is at present a resident of the suburbs of London. He exhibits frequently at the Royal Academy, the Society of British Artists, etc. Among his more important works are, "Relics of Pompeii," " The Fall of Rienzi, the last Roman Tribune," " Drawing for Military Service, Modern Italy " (R. A., 1878), "Refugees from Pompeii," etc.

His "Fall of Rienzi " was at the Philadelphia Exhibition of 1876. " The Winged Pensioners of Assisi," at Paris, in 1878.

" The cloister of Assisi has been carefully and literally studied in all but what is singular or beautiful in it. . . . . But there is more conscientious treatment of the rest of the building, and greater quietness of natural light, than in most picture backgrounds of these days [' The Sacking of Assisi by the Perugians in 1442 ']."— RUSKIN'S *Notes of the Academy*, 1875.

Torelli, Lot. (*Ital.*) Sculptor of Florence. At Philadelphia he exhibited " Eva St. Clair " (" Uncle Tom's Cabin ") and " A Good Housekeeper," and received a medal. At the London Academy in 1876 he exhibited a statuette in terra-cotta, " Fidelity," and " The Love-Message."

Toudouze, Édouard. (*Fr.*) Born at Paris. *Prix de Rome*, 1871. Medals, 1876 and '77. Pupil of Pils and A. Leloir. At the Salon of 1877 he exhibited " The Wife of Lot " ; in 1876, " Clytemnestra, — the Murder of Agamemnon "; in 1878, a portrait and " The Beach at Yport."

Toulmouche, Auguste. (*Fr.*) Born at Nantes. Chevalier of the Legion of Honor. Pupil of Gleyre. The works of this artist are well known. They are usually interiors, with Parisian women of our day. He holds a high place among painters of these subjects. At the Salon of 1876 he exhibited "Flirtation " and " Summer "; in 1874,

" The Serious Book " (a very pleasing picture) and " The Response." At the Latham sale, New York, 1878, " Why don't he come ? " (26 by 20) sold for $950. His " Waiting " belongs to Mr. S. Hawk of New York.

Tournemine, Charles Émile Vacher de. (*Fr.*) Born at Toulon (1814 – 1872). Chevalier of the Legion of Honor. Pupil of Eugène Isabey. At the Luxembourg is his " Elephants of Africa " (1861). Many of his pictures are of hunting-scenes, others of landscapes, and some illustrative of the customs of Eastern countries which he had visited.

Trautmann, Karl Friedrich. (*Ger.*) Born at Breslau (1804 – 1875). Studied at Berlin Academy. His small wood-scenes and groups of trees are very agreeable pictures. He was also a lithographer. At the National Gallery, Berlin, is " The Oak Wood."

Trigt, H. A. Van. (*Dutch.*) Of Hilversum. Medal at Philadelphia, where he exhibited " Norwegian Women bringing Children to be baptized." This picture is specially commended by Mr. John F. Weir in his report.

Triqueti, Henri de. (*Fr.*) Born at Conflans (1804 – 1874). This artist was a pupil of Hersent. He made his début at the Salon of 1831 with four pictures, and to the same Salon he sent also a sculptured group of the " Death of Charles le Téméraire," the success of which decided him to devote himself to sculpture. This work and some others led Thiers, then Minister of the Interior, to give him the commission for the doors of the Madeleine. One of his most speaking works is the " Resurrection of Lazarus," made for the tomb of the only son of the artist, who was killed by an accident in 1861. Lazarus has the face of the son. Triqueti received from Queen Victoria the order for the complete ornamentation of the chapel at Windsor, and the construction of the tomb of Prince Albert, which is there. Here he has employed both painting and sculpture. It is an immense work, and any proper description of it would demand more space than we can here give. Triqueti was also a writer on art matters. Among his writings is a volume called " Les Trois Musées de Londres."

Trotter, Newbold H. (*Am.*) A resident of Philadelphia. He devotes himself to pictures of animal life. His " On the Hills " and " Resting " were at the National Academy in 1874 ; his " Quiet Nook " and " California Valley Quail," in 1875. To the Centennial Exhibition of 1876 he sent " Wounded Buffalo pursued by Prairie Wolves."

[No response to circular.]

"Trotter's 'They know not the Voice of the Stranger ' [Phil. Acad. 1873] is a valuable specimen of animal painting. . . . . His 'Fading Race,' a herd of buffalo speeding towards the setting sun, is poetical in conception, and both in matter and manner is much the best work the artist has produced in a long time." — *Art Journal,* June, 1877.

Troyon, Constant. (*Fr.*) Born at Sèvres (1810 – 1865). Chevalier of the Legion of Honor, and member of the Academy of Amsterdam. His parents wished him to be a painter of porcelain, but after a time spent in the manufactory at Sèvres he studied under Riocreux, and became a painter of landscapes and animals. He was a hard worker, and determined to overcome the difficulties of his art. He cannot be positively called a literal painter, but he painted very little that was not apparent to an uneducated eye, and his representation of animals was the truth of nature, interpreted in a large sense and with freedom of touch. He seldom worked continuously on one subject, but kept a large number of pictures in progress at the same time. He traveled much in his own country, and made a journey to Holland, in which country, as well as in Belgium and England, his works were much admired. After his death, in the Exposition of 1867, the following pictures were exhibited, "A Landscape with Animals" (afterwards given to the Museum of the Luxembourg by the mother of Troyon), "Scotch Dogs," "A Dog and a Partridge," "A White Cow in a Field," and "A Seashore." Troyon first sent pictures to the Salon in 1833 ; he received medals in 1838, '40, '46, '48, and '55 ; he was decorated in 1849. Among his principal works are, "The Ferry-Boat" ; "Oxen going to Work" (1853), for which the city of Bordeaux paid 4,000 francs in 1860 ; "The Valley of the Toque in Normandy" (1853) ; views of Sèvres, Saint-Cloud, Argenton, and the environs of Vannes, of The Hague, and of Amsterdam ; etc. Many of his works have been engraved, such as "The Bathers," "The Poacher," "The Watering-Place," and some of the pictures mentioned above, etc. At the Laurent-Richard sale, Paris, 1873, "The Ford" sold for £2,480 ; "A Shepherd and his Flock," for £1,668 ; "Cows, — Sunset," for £1,082 ; "The Return of the Flock," for £1,020. At the Johnston sale of pictures, in 1876, the "Autumn Morning, — Landscape and Cattle" (28 by 42) was sold for $9,700, and a pastel, "Roadside Cottage" (12 by 15), brought $110. At the Norzy sale, Paris, 1860, "Cows in a Pasture, — Effect of a Storm" brought 3,000 francs. In Paris, in 1874, the "Plaine de la Toque, Normandie," sold for £1,840.

"He had, however. a more poetical mind than any other artist of the same class, and the poetry of the fields has never been more feelingly interpreted than by him. In the 'Oxen going to Work' we have a page of rustic description as good as anything in literature, — of fresh and misty morning air, of rough, illimitable land, of mighty oxen marching slowly to their toil ! Who that has seen these creatures work can be indifferent to the steadfast grandeur of their nature? they have no petulance, no hurry, no nervous excitability ; but they will bear the yoke upon their necks, and the thongs about their horns, and push forward without flinching from sunrise until dusk ! " — HAMERTON's *Contemporary French Painters.*

"A *mise en scène*, picturesque, and often with a rare magnificence of effect ; a color, sober, fine, distinguished, unfolding itself in sweet harmonies ; a bold and original modeling, a quick instinct for light, the magic of shaded or radiant horizons, —these are the attractive charms, the exceptionable qualities, which assure this artist an eternal place among the masters of the *genre.*" — LAROUSSE, *Dictionnaire Universel.*

Trübner, Wilhelm. (*Ger.*) Born at Heidelberg, 1852. Pupil of the Academy of Munich, of Dietz, and, later, of the great portrait-painter, Canon, at Stuttgart. In the spring of 1878 this young artist exhibited at Munich a full-length portrait which excited immense interest, and he is now engaged upon several other portraits, which, it is said by other artists, will give him a great reputation.

Trumbull, Gurdon. (*Am.*) Born at Stonington, Ct., 1841. Youngest son of Hon. Gurdon Trumbull. He studied art under F. S. Jewett of Hartford, Ct., and for a short time under James Hart of New York. His professional life has been spent in Hartford. Among the better known of his works are, "A Moorish Watch-Tower, Coast of Spain" and "A Critical Moment," a trout picture (both belonging to William C. Prime of New York). Hon. Charles M. Pond, Dr. E. K. Hunt of Hartford, Ct., and others, own his pictures of fish. His "Plunge for Life" and "Over the Falls," exhibited at Snedecor's Gallery, New York, in 1874, have been chromoed, and are very popular. The "Critical Moment" was at the Centennial Exhibition at Philadelphia in 1876.

"Mr. Trumbull's standing as an artist was long since assured by works of this class ['The Plunge for Life' and 'Over the Falls']. His work is distinguished for a somewhat uncommon union of characters, namely, accurate and finished detail joined to complete action and life in the whole picture. Viewed at a distance, his fish are living and moving, full of reality, while, as they are approached and examined, even with the aid of a glass, they are found to be minutely accurate in the rendering of even the texture of skin and the arrangement of scales." — *New York Sun*, March 19, 1874.

"The two pictures represent a trout and a black bass. The trout has the hook, has made his mad rush, has snapped the frail tackle, and is 'over the falls' with a plunge and a swirl, and you see him flash through the green water. . . . . This work shows the most astounding care, all those delicate, soft, pink points on the trout's side imitate nature, and the wondrous delicate gossamer fins absolutely undulate. The bass is quite as surprising as a picture. It is not only as a work of art that it is admirable ; it has the merit of being a perfect ichthyological study." — *Forest and Stream*, March 26, 1874.

Tryon, Benjamin F. (*Am.*) Born in New York City, 1824. Pupil of Richard Bengough and James H. Cafferty. His subjects are landscapes, and his works are in galleries in Boston (where he now resides) and other cities. He has exhibited at the Boston Art Club exhibitions, and at the Academy of Design in New York, since 1866. His "New England Scenery" was at the Mechanics' Fair, Boston, 1878. Among his works are "River St. Lawrence near the Thousand Islands," "Early Autumn Afternoon," "Conway Valley and Moat Mountain," "A Quiet Nook," etc. His "View of San Miguel Falls, San Juan Mountains," exhibited in Boston in November, 1878, excels his former work, and has been the means of attracting attention to this artist.

T'Schaggeny, Charles Philogène. (*Belgian.*) Born at Brussels, 1815. Chevalier of the Order of Léopold. Pupil of Eugène Verboeckhoven. His pictures represent animals and landscapes. At the Latham sale, New York, 1878, "Rest at a Blacksmith's Shop" (30 by

44) sold for $ 800. To the Exposition at Paris, in 1878, he sent " Before the Storm."

T'Schaggeny, Edmond. (*Belgian.*) Born at Brussels (1818 – 1873). Chevalier of the Order of Léopold. Brother of the preceding, and pupil of the same master. He has also chosen similar subjects for his pictures. At the Leipsic Museum there is a " Resting Herd " painted by him. At the Latham sale, a water-color, the " Shepherdess and Flock " (20 by 30) brought $ 275. At the Khalil Bey sale, 1868, " Shepherd and Sheep." brought £ 268, and in London, in 1872, a pair, " Returning to the Fold " and " Repose of the Flock," brought 232 guineas.

Tuckerman, S. S. (*Am.*) A native of Massachusetts. He paints marine views and landscapes, and studied under Hunt in Boston. He has also studied in Paris. At present (1878) he is a resident of London. In 1876 a collection of some forty of his works, chiefly autumnal views, and scenes of North Easton and Newburyport, Mass., was on exhibition in Boston, where many of them are owned. To Philadelphia, the same year, he sent " Beach at Hastings " and " The United States Frigate Constitution escaping from the British Fleet in 1812."

Turcan, Jean. (*Fr.*) Born at Arles. Pupil of Cavalier. Medal of the second class in 1878, when he exhibited " Ganymede," a group in plaster.

Turner, Joseph M. W., R. A. (*Brit.*) (1775 – 1851.) Displayed artistic talents at an early age, exhibiting at the Royal Academy, in 1787, two drawings. In 1788 he was in the office of an architect in London, entering the Royal Academy schools in 1789, subsequently making sketching-tours along the banks of the Thames, in Wales, and the North of England. He confined himself for a few years to water-color sketches, which were sent annually to the Academy. " Moonlight, — a Study at Millbank," was his first oil-painting at the Royal Academy in 1797. His " Battle of the Nile " appeared in 1799. He was elected an Associate of the Royal Academy in 1800, Academician in 1802. In 1807 he was elected Professor of Perspective. He visited Italy three times. He had no family, and left his pictures to the nation. Over a hundred of his paintings, and as many sketches and drawings, are in the National Gallery, London, dating from 1790 to 1850. Of all the artists of the nineteenth century, Turner was perhaps the most remarkable, and of no artist in any age has more been written. There is no space here for enumeration of his works, or further account of his career, with which so many volumes have been filled. His pictures now command fabulous prices. His " Antwerp, — Van Goyen looking for a subject," painted in 1833, was sold in London, in 1863, for 2,510 guineas ($ 16,000), its original price to the artist being perhaps less than one tenth of that sum ; some of his drawings at the same sale bringing $ 2,500 to $ 3,000.

His "Slave Ship" (36 by 48), exhibited at the Royal Academy in 1840, and purchased by John Taylor Johnston from Mr. Ruskin, was sold in 1876 for $10,000, to Miss Alice Hooper of Boston. One hundred and five of his drawings and pictures, at a sale in London, April, 1878, brought over £73,000, or $365,000. Turner's "Dolbadden Castle, North Wales," lent by the Royal Academy of London, was in the Philadelphia Exhibition of 1876.

"I believe if I were reduced to rest Turner's immortality upon any single work, I should choose 'The Slave Ship.' Its daring conception, ideal in the highest sense of the word, is based on the purest truth, and wrought out with the concentrated knowledge of a life. Its color is absolutely perfect, not one false or morbid hue in any part or line, and so modulated that every square inch of canvas is a perfect composition ; its drawing as accurate as fearless ; the ship buoyant, bending, and full of motion ; its tones as true as they are wonderful ; and the whole picture dedicated to the most sublime of subjects and impressions (completing thus the perfect system of all truth, which we have shown to be formed by Turner's works), — the power, majesty, and deathfulness of the open, deep, illimitable sea." — RUSKIN'S *Modern Painters.*

"Thackeray, when speaking of 'The Slave Ship' by the same amazing artist, says, with delightful *naïveté,* 'I don't know whether it is sublime or ridiculous.'" — DR. BROWN'S *Spare Hours.*

"Turner had three styles as a landscape-painter ; the first was highly elaborated, especially in his water-color drawings. The contrast of style between his early and latest works is remarkable ; in the best of his early works he shows a strong imitation of Wilson and a certain coldness of color ; the latest are distinguished for their excessive looseness of execution and extravagance of coloring. It is in his middle style that he is greatest, that he is himself. The middle period may date from 1802 to 1832. . . . . In the last ten years of his career and occasionally before, Turner was extravagant to an extreme degree ; he played equally with nature and with his colors. Light with all its prismatic varieties seems to have been the chief object of his studies ; individuality of form or color he was wholly indifferent to. The looseness of execution in his latest works has not even the apology of having been attempted on scientific principles; he did not work upon a particular point of a picture as a focus and leave the rest obscure, as a foil to enhance it, on a principle of unity; on the contrary, all is equally obscure and wild alike. These last productions are a calamity to his reputation ; yet we may, perhaps, safely assert that, since Rembrandt, there has been no painter of such originality and power as Turner." — WORNUM'S *Epochs of Painting.*

"No landscape-painter has yet appeared with such versatility of talent. His historical landscapes exhibit the most exquisite feeling for beauty of hues and effect of lighting, at the same time that he has the power of making them express the most varied moods of nature. . . . . I should therefore not hesitate to recognize Turner as the greatest landscape-painter of all times, but for his deficiency in an indispensable element in every work of art, viz. a sound technical basis." — DR. WAAGEN, *Treasury of Art in Great Britain.*

"Turner's great genius needs no panegyric ; his best monument is the great works bequeathed by him to the nation, which will be ever the most lasting memorial of his fame." — SMILES' *Self-Help.*

"That day [May 5, 1812], I saw at the Exhibition a picture by Turner, the impression of which still remains [written in 1849]. It seemed to me the most marvelous landscape I had ever seen, 'Hannibal crossing the Alps in a Storm.' I can never forget it." — *Diary of* HENRY CRABBE ROBINSON.

"I must request you to turn your attention to a noble river-piece by Turner, 'The Fighting Téméraire,' as grand a painting as ever figured on the walls of any academy, or came from the easel of any painter. . . . . It is absurd, you will say (and with a great deal of reason) for Titmarsh or any other Briton to grow so politically enthusiastic about a four-foot canvas representing a ship, a steamer, a river, and a sunset. But herein surely lies the power of the great artist. He makes you see and think of a great deal more than the objects before you ; he knows how to soothe or to intoxicate, to fire or to depress, by a few notes, or forms, or colors, of which we cannot trace the effect to the source, but only acknowledge the power." — THACKERAV, *in Fraser's Magazine*, 1839.

"The influence of Turner upon engraving might supply the subject for a separate essay. He educated a whole school of engravers, and a very remarkable school it was ; he educated them first by showing them the more subtle and delicate tonelity in his pictures, and afterwards by a strict supervision of their work as it proceeded. His best qualities as a teacher came from his union of extreme delicacy with force : his worst fault, his most evil influence, came from his reckless desire for brilliance, which made him always ready to destroy the tranquillity of a plate if he thought that it did not look effective enough. This was the same spirit acting in another direction which made him so determined to make his pictures brilliant at all costs, on the walls of the Academy ; but there he could achieve it with the help of chrome, and cobalt, and vermilion. On a dull plate he had no resource but that of glittering lights, which he scattered in profusion 'like stars on the sea.'" — P. G. HAMERTON, *in the Portfolio*, March, 1878.

"The following opinion, expressed by an intelligent and accomplished American artist, Mr. George Inness, is interesting for its frankness : 'Turner's "Slave Ship" is the most infernal piece of claptrap ever painted. There is nothing in it. It has as much to do with human affections and thought as a ghost. It is not even a fine bouquet of color. The color is harsh, disagreeable, and discordant.' This is severe, and I think its severity is partly due to reaction against Mr. Ruskin's eloquent praises. On the other hand, I have observed that some Americans seem to think it a sort of duty to admire Turner, and to become enthusiastic about even his least important works. May I venture to observe, both to American and English readers, that nobody is under any obligation to admire either the late or the early works of Turner ; that they are as much open to criticism as those of any other artist, and that the best way to judge them fairly is to look at them as if they had never been either praised or censured. The warm controversy at Boston about the 'Slave Ship' was caused by a feeling of rebellion in some minds, too independent to accept dictation from an English critic, whilst others defended the picture as the work of a man of genius who had been roughly treated by the press. An antagonism of this description is good for the fame of an artist, because it makes everybody talk about him, but truth disengages itself only when the noise has ceased and the smoke of battle has passed away. It is not of the least use to argue about color. From Mr. Ruskin the color of the 'Slave Ship' calls forth no harsher criticism than that he thinks 'the two blue and white stripes on the drifting flag of the "Slave Ship" in the last degree too purely cold,' and he elsewhere expressly approves of its strongest passages. It is one of these compositions in which Turner used the most brilliant of all his pigments. A lurid splendor was his purpose, and he hesitated at nothing for its attainment. It is hardly possible for any painter to deal with vermilion and lemon yellow, in any quantity, without falling into some degree of crudity. If you compare even the 'Téméraire' with the rich, deep harmonies of Titian and Giorgione you will feel it to be relatively crude. But are fiery sunsets never to be painted ?

"Form may be argued about more positively. The wave-forms in the slaver are original, but they are, I believe, carefully observed. The comparatively flat, or simply swelling space, between the ridges of broken sea I have often seen in nature, and the sudden leaping of the spray is no doubt also a reminiscence. The introduction of the sharks, manacles, and human hand and leg was artistically awkward to manage, and is so horrible that the mind revolts from these details. The thoroughness of study in the sky may be judged of by the rain-cloud engraved from it by Mr. Armitage under the title, 'The Locks of Typhon.' Our sense of the delicacy of this piece of work may be heightened by the exquisiteness of the engraver's performance ; but the painter must have worked delicately also." — P. G. HAMERTON, *The Portfolio*, 1878.

Turner, William Green. *(Am.)* Born àt Newport, R. I., 1833. He went abroad for the purpose of studying sculpture, and was for some time a pupil of the Academy of Fine Arts in Florence, spending his professional life there and in other Italian cities. He is a member of two of the Florentine Art Societies. Among his works may be mentioned, " Transition " ("There is no death ; what seems so is transition." *Longfellow*), which was exhibited at the Centennial at Philadelphia in 1876, and is now in charge or possession of Mr. Sartain of the Philadelphia Academy of Fine Arts ; with two medallions, " Night" and " Morning." His " Fisherman's Daughter," also at the Centennial Exhibition, was purchased by Mr. Wolverton, and is now in his collection at Philadelphia. In his studio (1878) are, " Rhoda," " The Herald of Peace " (an allegory to be cast in bronze), and " Sabrina " from " Comus " (still in clay).

" A most splendid figure, half life-size, now adorns Mr. Turner's studio ; it represents 'Rhoda' when she ran in and told how 'Peter stood before the Gate.' His 'Night' and 'Morning' (medallion busts), and his 'Incredulity' and 'Herald of Peace,' all give evidence of the original genius of the artist. His compositions show great originality, and are more distinguished for largeness and simplicity of masses than for secondary matters of fine detail." — *Swiss Times*, December, 1876.

Twachtman, J. H. *(Am.)* Born in Cincinnati, 1853. He began his art studies in the School of Design in Cincinnati, and spent the winter of 1874 and '75 in Duveneck's Life School and Painting Class in the same city. He went to Europe in the fall of 1875, entering the Art School at Munich, where his professional life so far has been spent. He is a member of the American Art Club of Munich, and exhibited for the first time in New York with the Society of American Artists, in 1878, two " Italian Scenes."

Ulivi, Pietro. *(Ital.)* Born at Pistoia, 1806. Professor in the Royal Lyceum, Forteguerra. He won many prizes in various cities of Italy. His portraits are celebrated for their fine coloring. Many of his best works are in his native city. His correctness in drawing is remarkable. Victor Emmanuel II. bought his picture of a " Father blessing his Son, who goes forth to be a Soldier." Ulivi was chosen to copy, for engraving, the frieze around the Hospital of Pistoia, containing the bassi-relievi of the Della Robbia.

Ulmann, Benjamin. *(Fr.)* Born at Blotzheim. Chevalier of the Legion of Honor. Pupil of Drölling and Picot. This artist paints many portraits. Among his other works are, " Remorse," " The Gitanos of Granada," " The Bell-Ringers of Nuremberg," etc. At the Luxembourg is his picture of " Sylla at the House of Marius " (1866). To the Paris Salon of 1878 he sent " The Lurlei."

Unger, Wilhelm. *(Ger.)* Born at Hanover, 1837. Professor at Vienna. Pupil of Keller and Thäter. Medal at Philadelphia, where he exhibited the following etchings : " Marine View," after Van der Capella ; " Portrait," after Velasquez ; " Portrait," after Palma

Vecchio ; " Landscape," after Hobbema ; " Jacob's Blessing," after Govaert Flinck ; " Catherine Cornaro," after Hans Makart ; " Katrina Fourment," after Rubens. Unger is one of the best living etchers, and his works are much sought for illustrations of books of luxury, etc. To the Paris Exposition, 1878, he sent " La ronde de nuit," after Rembrandt ; a portrait of Rembrandt, after his own picture ; and other etchings after Rubens, Snyders, and other ancient masters.

Uasi, Commander Stefano. (*Ital.*) Born at Florence, 1822. Medal at Paris, 1867, and at Vienna in 1873. Professor of Fine Arts at Florence. Pupil of Pollastrini, and a painter of the first rank. " The Expulsion of the Duke of Athens," an early work, won much fame for the artist, and gained the gold medal at the Paris Exposition in 1867. It is now in the Gallery of Modern Paintings in Florence. He went up the Nile, and brought back many valuable sketches. His " Departure of a Caravan for Mecca " was a commission from the Khedive of Egypt, who declared that the picture merited a frame of gold. It was much noticed at Vienna in 1873. One of his latest works is a fine painting of the " Last Day of Bianco Capello." His portrait is in the collection of autograph portraits in the Uffizi. To Paris in 1878 he sent " Bianca Capello at Poggio a Cajano attempts to poison the Cardinal de'Medici," and two Eastern scenes.

Uwins, Thomas, R. A. (*Brit.*) Born in London (1782 – 1857). He began life as an engraver, entering the schools of the Royal Academy. Later, he devoted himself to oil and water-color painting. He painted portraits for some time in Scotland and on the Continent. As early as 1811 he was Secretary of the Society of Painters in Water-Colors, contributing to its exhibitions for many years. He was elected Associate of the Royal Academy in 1833, on the strength of his " Interior of a Saint Manufactory at Naples." He was made Academician in 1839. He was Keeper of the National Gallery from 1847 to '55, and for some time Librarian of the Royal Academy. Among the more important of his many works are, " Taking the Veil," " Vintage in the Claret Vineyards, South of France," " Le Chapeau de Brigand," and " Sir Guyon fighting for Temperance " (the last three in the National Gallery). Uwins, during his long career, exhibited, in all, one hundred and two pictures at the Royal Academy. Many of his works have been engraved.

"Among the many artists either already eminent or rising to eminence, who made the acquaintance of Lady Blessington in Italy, was Mr. Uwins, the painter, who already [1824] had acquired celebrity by several works in which the glowing scenery and pictur-esque inhabitants of Rome and Naples were delineated, in a style of the highest excel-lence." — *Memoirs of the Countess of Blessington.*

Vaini, Pietro. (*Ital.-Am.*) Born in Rome (1847 – 1875). Studied and practiced art in Italy. In 1872 he settled in New York, where he painted portraits of a number of prominent people with considerable success. His large figure-pictures attracted much attention when exhibited, on account of the morbidly somber nature of the subjects, and the vivid, and sometimes horrible, realism of his treatment of them. His " Othello and the Handkerchief" (property of the Palette Club), his " First Grief," " After the War," and " Veronica gazing upon the Face of her Dead Rival," will not be quickly forgotten by those who saw them. These did not meet with ready sale in this country. His smaller ideal works, pleasanter in style, and generally pictures of fashionable life, were more popular. His death was startling and dramatic. While entertaining a party of friends at a picnic by the recitation of a tragic poem in his native language, he illustrated the narrative by taking his own life as described by the poet.

" As a colorist Valni had no superior in this country, and his style was fully in accord with that of the famous school in which he was educated. He was an indefatigable worker, and left a rare collection of studies as well as finished pictures." —*Art Journal,* October, 1875.

Valerio, Théodore. (*Fr.*) Born at Herserange, 1819. Chevalier of the Legion of Honor. Pupil of Charlet at Paris. This painter is remarked for his water-colors and etchings. Several of his pictures show the customs of the Montenegrins, Tsiganes, Hungarians, etc. At the Salon of 1876 he exhibited " The Beach at Tresmalouen in a Storm" and " Women near Carnac " ; in 1875, " A Well of Sweet Water, near Carnac," " The Departure for the Fields," " Saint Colombau," and a " Souvenir of the Rocks of Kermarie at Low Tide." [Died, 1879.]

Vallance, W. F. (*Brit.*) Born in Paisley. Went to Edinburgh in his youth, studying from the antique under Robert Scott Lauder, and, later, passing through the Life School of the Royal Scottish Academy. He first exhibited small figure-pieces, subsequently turning his attention to marine views. He is a resident of Edinburgh, and was elected an Associate of the Royal Scottish Academy in 1875. Among his works are, " Sunday Morning," " Leisure Hours," " Loch Fine," " Largo Bay," " A Fresh Breeze," etc.

Valles, Lorenzo. (*Span.*) Of Madrid. Medal at Philadelphia, where he exhibited the " Insanity of Donna Juana de Castille."

Van Elten, Kruseman. (*Dutch-Am.*) Born in Alkman, Holland, 1829. Chevalier of the Order of the Lion, of the Netherlands. Member of the Academies of Amsterdam and Rotterdam, and of the Belgian Water-Color Society ; Associate of the National Academy, New York ; and member of the American Society of Painters in Water-Colors. Medals at Amsterdam in 1860, and at Philadelphia in 1876. He was instructed in drawing in his native town, and in 1844 went to Haarlem and studied painting under C. Lieste and other masters. His professional life has been spent in Haarlem, Amsterdam, Brussels, and New York, and he has made sketches in Germany, Austria, Switzerland, France, and England.

To the National Academy, New York (in oil), Van Elten has contributed many pictures : "Summer Morning, Esopus Creek," in 1867 ; "Druidical Tombs, Holland," in 1869 ; "Peace" and "War," in 1870 ; "Morning in the Harz," in 1871 ; "Passing Shower near Pittsfield, Mass.," in 1875 ; "Cornfields," in 1876 ; "Landscape, Delaware," in 1877· "Summer Day, Winnockie River, N. J.," in 1878. To the Water-Color Society Exhibition, in 1867, he sent "Sunday Morning in Holland" ; in 1871, "Meadows near Farmington" ; in 1875, "Evening, Long Island Sound"; in 1876, "Landscape in Holland" ; in 1877, "Landscape near Torresdale, Pa.," "Chickens," and "Ducks" ; in 1878, "Home, Sweet Home,— Scene in Holland," "Morning near Gloucester, Mass.," and others. To the Centennial Exhibition of 1876 he sent, "Clearing Off, Adirondacks," "The Grove in the Heath," "Russell's Falls, Adirondacks" (in oil), and "Autumn in the White Mountains" (in water-colors).

Among his earlier works may be mentioned, "Early Morning in the Woods" (belonging to the Queen of Holland), "Sunday Morning," "Interior of the Woods," "Landscape in Gelderland" (in private collections in Haarlem and Amsterdam). His "Well in the Heath" belongs to Jay Cook of Philadelphia.

"To the earnest student of landscape art Mr. Van Elten's pictures furnish an agreeable surprise ; their originality of treatment raises them above the common art level, and their boldness and vigor of coloring are not reflected in the works of any of his contemporaries. In his pictures Van Elten rarely composes ; he selects his studies with the idea of making pictures, and hence when finished they are perfect and truthful portraits of the scenes they purport to represent. .... There is a calm sweetness about this picture ['Landscape on the Farmington River'], a depth of perspective, and conscientious elaboration of detail which will be appreciated by all lovers of the beautiful. In its composition it shows an harmonious tone which is in keeping with the scene in Nature." — *Art Journal,* November. 1877.

Van Hove, Victor. (*Belgian.*) Born at Renaix, 1825. Medals at Paris for sculpture and painting. Of later years this artist seems to have abandoned sculpture, and paints *genre* landscapes ; such as, "Fishermen's Daughters of the Coasts of Flanders," "Orphans going to Church, near Dordrecht," etc. His sculptures of the "Child playing with a Cat" and "A Slave after the Bastinado" were exhibited in Paris, and were well received.

Van Lerius, Joseph Henri François. (*Dutch.*) Born at Boom, near Antwerp (1823 - 1876). Professor of Painting in the Academy of Antwerp. Honorary Member of the Academies of Rotterdam, Amsterdam, and Saxony. Chevalier of the Order of Léopold. Pupil of the Academy of Brussels, schools of Antwerp, and of Baron Wappers. At first Van Lerius painted portraits, in which department he was successful. His first subject-picture was "An Interview between Leicester and Amy Robsart," followed by "Milton dictating to his Daughter" and "Paul and Virginia crossing the Stream," which last was in the collection of the Baroness Voykerstoot at Brussels. Among his later works are, "Esmeralda" (1848), in the Brussels Museum ; "Adam and Eve"

(1848); "The Four Ages"; "The First-Born," bought by Queen Victoria; "Volupté et Dénouement" (1857), bought by Prince Saxe-Colnrg of Gotha; "Cinderella"; "The Golden Age"; Joan of Arc"; "Venice"; "Portrait of a Swedish Girl"; etc. In 1877 the city of Antwerp bought the "Lady Godiva" for 18,000 francs. At the International Exposition at Munich, in 1869, he exhibited a melodramatic work called "Plutôt mourir"; it represented a young girl throwing herself from a window in order to escape dishonor.

Van Luppen, G. J. A. (*Belgian.*) Of Antwerp. Medal at Philadelphia, where he exhibited "After the Rain" and "Before the Storm." To Paris, in 1878, he sent the last-named picture and "La Flandre."

Van Marcke, Émile. (*Fr.*) Born at Sèvres. Chevalier of the Legion of Honor. Pupil of Troyon. At the Salon of 1877 he exhibited, "The Spring at Neslette, in Normandy," belonging to Mr. Brown of Philadelphia; in 1876, "The Cliff"; in 1875, "The Village Pasture, Normandy," "The River Morte at Tréport," and "A Bridge on the Bresles, Normandy." At the Johnston sale, New York, 1876, "A Herd of French Cattle" (38 by 59) sold for $5,100, and "Landscape with Cattle" (14 by 21) for $2,550. At the Walters Gallery is a large picture of cattle by Van Marcke; and a fine picture by the same artist is in the collection of Mrs. H. E. Maynard of Boston.

Vannutelli, Cavaliere Scipione. (*Ital.*) Born at Rome, where he resides. Medals at Paris in 1864 and '67. At the Paris Exposition of 1878 he exhibited "The Monferrina" (an Italian dance) and "The Night." At the Salon of the same year were "The Roman Campagna" and "An Agreeable Reading"; in 1877, "A Procession at Venice"; etc. [This artist merits a more extended notice, but no reliable information could be obtained.]

Varley, John. (*Brit.*) (1778 – 1842.) One of the early English artists in water-colors, and a founder of the Old Water-Color Society, in 1805. He painted many views in Wales and the valley of the Thames, and was the author of several text-books on drawing, some of which are still in use. Among his works are, "Holy Island," "Rochester Castle," "A Quiet Stream," "Old Inn on the Banks of the Thames," "Conway Castle," etc.

Varley, Cornelius. (*Brit.*) Born in London (1781 – 1873). Brother of John Varley. Artist in water-colors, devoting himself chiefly to Welsh and English landscapes and classical scenes. He was one of the original members of the Society of Painters in Water-Colors.

Varley, William Fleetwood. (*Brit.*) (1785 – 1856.) Younger brother of Cornelius and John Varley, studying under the latter. He painted landscapes in water-colors, teaching drawing at Oxford for some years before his death.

Varni, Santo. (*Ital.*) Born at Genoa. He is one of the first sculptors of the day, and one of whom Genoa is justly proud. His work is chiefly monumental. For Staglieno he made the fine monument of Marchese Donghi, with statues of "Prudence," "Eternity," and "Faith in God." At the same place, also, is the monument to Marchese Lomellini, with a beautiful statue of "Grief," a monument to Dufour, with a sleeping figure, and a very grand monument for the Cattanei family, with a seated figure of the Saviour, and the figures of St. John the Baptist and St. Matthew below. In Santa Croce in Florence is a monument to Giovanni Rossini, and in Pisa one to Luigi Canina. In the Hospital of Genoa are the statues of Merani and Tignago, by Varni, and the monument to Columbus begun by Pampaloni in Genoa was finished by this sculptor. The statues of Pagano Doria and Vittorio Pisani in Venice, and Emmanuel Fileberto in the Royal Palace in Turin, are by Varni.

Vasselot, Anatole Marquet de. (*Fr.*) Born at Paris, 1840. Medals in 1873 and '76. Pupil of Jouffroy and Bonnat. This sculptor was intended for a diplomatic career by his family, but his tastes so controlled him that at length he separated himself from all former surroundings, and after many difficulties made his début at the Salon of 1866. His bust of Balzac (1870) ornaments the grand staircase of the Comédie-Française, and is a truly fine work. In 1868 he made a good medallion portrait of Abraham Lincoln. His best work is the "Chloe" of 1869. In 1873 it was put in marble, and was medaled and bought by the government. His "Christ in the Tomb," in bronze (1876), received a second medal. His "Patrie" (1874) was purchased for the court of the palace of the Grande Chancellerie of the Legion of Honor. In 1875 he exhibited a bas-relief called "Honor to our Dead!" and in 1876, a "Theseus," also bought by the State. His portrait busts are excellent. This sculptor has received many medals and testimonials of honor in various cities of France, at Brussels, and at Philadelphia, where he exhibited a portrait of Monsieur Auzoux, and a figure of "Chloe," both in bronze. At the London Academy, in 1875, he exhibited "Chloe," in marble, and "Mlle. Sombreuil," and in 1878, at the Paris Salon, a statue of the "Young Greek Athlete" and a bust in bronze of Rose-Anais.

Vaudremer, Joseph-Auguste-Émile. (*Fr.*) Born at Paris, 1829. Chevalier of the Legion of Honor. This architect gained the *prix de Rome* in 1854. He has held various offices in Paris, and has been associated with important works there since 1859. He has also constructed some civil and funereal monuments, and has sent to the Salons very remarkable architectural drawings.

Vauréal, Henri de. (*Fr.*) Born at Paris. Pupil of Toussaint. Medal of third class in 1878, when he exhibited a plaster statue of "Perseus"; in 1877, he sent a bronze statue, "The Little Gleaner"; in 1876, a "Portrait of a Child" (a bust in bronze).

Vautier, Benjamin. (*Swiss.*) Born at Morges, 1830. Member of the Academies of Berlin, Munich, Antwerp, and Amsterdam. Medals at Berlin and Paris. Pupil of Rudolph Jordan at Düsseldorf. Painter of scenes from peasant home-life. His "First Dancing-Lesson" (village of the Black Forest) is in the National Gallery, Berlin; "A Courtier and Peasants of Würtemberg," in the Museum of Bâle; "After the Burial" (canton of Berne), in the Museum of Cologne. At the Johnston sale, New York, in 1876, "The Music-Lesson" (11 by 8) sold for $360. At the Walters Gallery is his "Consulting his Lawyer," well painted and full of humor; also, "Caught in the Act."

"The scenes which he places before us are never superficially treated; he never expects us to be satisfied with the costumes in place of the characters of the people he represents; on the contrary, his figures, in their faces and in every line of detail, express their peculiar individualities with marked force. . . . . The wine-merchant on the Rhine differs from the beer-merchant in Bavaria, and the Spiessbürger of a Westphalian middle city, who is happily placed between beer and wine, is again a different person. Vautier has so well hit this characteristic trait-painting, that he proves himself not only to have studied closely, but he has given rein to a natural genius for such conceptions. Moreover, he has a full vein of humor which is all his own, but he only gives way to this when it accords with the subject he represents. He is not one of those who, by reason of vanity, add to their representation their own conceits, like some actors who in side play act their own farces; but he is a true interpreter of the poet whom he represents. Just this beautiful moderation brings out the meaning of the composition as if in a concentrated light, so that the delight of originating and that of showing forth the intention must almost be united in one emotion." — W. L., *Zeitschrift für bildende Kunst*, 1866.

Vedder, Elihu, N. A. (*Am.*) Born in New York, 1836. As a child he showed decided talent for art, studying for a short time in his native city. Later, he became a pupil of T. H. Matteson at Sherbourne, N. Y. After some years spent in Italy he opened a studio in New York, but is at present a resident of Rome. He was elected a full Member of the National Academy of Design in 1865. Among Vedder's earlier works are, "The Lair of the Sea-Serpent," "The Monk upon the Gloomy Path," "Arab listening to the Great Sphinx," "The Crucifixion," and "The Lost Mind" (belonging to Mrs. Laura Curtis Bullard). He sent to the National Academy, in 1869, "The Death of Abel"; in 1871, "An Ideal Head"; in 1874, "A Scene on the Mediterranean" and "Une fête champêtre." He rarely exhibits, however, in America. His "Greek Actor's Daughter" was at Philadelphia in 1876; his "Old Madonna" (belonging to E. D Morgan), "Cumean Sibyl," and "Young Marsyas" were at the Pari Exposition of 1878. Martin Brimmer owns his "Genii." "A Pastoral" (belonging to E. B. Haskell) was at the Mechanics' Fair, Boston, in 1878.

"Vigor and independence in Vedder are allied to great ambition and general æsthetic instinct. While in Italy he manifested a keen appreciation of the best elements of its old art. A clever, indefatigable student, he never became a mere copyist, but, making notes of ideas and technical details, assimilated to himself much of the lofty feeling and strong manner of the world's masters in painting. . . . . Vedder is a painter of ideas. His style is naturalistic as relates to truth of illustration, but ideal and intellectual in motive.]

he were not so drawn to painting by delight of color, he could be eminent as a sculptor. That he would be the most original and inventive of our school, the dramatic force of expression and power of modeling shown in his recent bas-reliefs of the ' Arab Slave ' and ' Endymion ' sufficiently attest." — JARVES, *Art Idea,* 1866.

" Vedder is one of the most original of the American painters in Rome, distinguished especially for his quaintness, alike in his subjects and in their treatment." — MRS. TYTLER'S *Modern Painters.*

" Mr. Vedder sent his ' Greek Actor's Daughter,' a thoughtful and poetic conception, painted with rare feeling and learning." — PROF. WEIR'S *Official Report of the American Centennial Exhibition of 1876.*

Veit, Philip. (*Ger.*) Born at Berlin (1793 – 1878). This painter belonged to the school of Cornelius and Overbeck. His mother was the daughter of Mendelssohn, and the wife of Friedrich Schlegel. Veit was a devout Roman Catholic. At the National Gallery, Berlin, is his picture of the "Three Maries." His allegorical picture of "Germany," represented as a young matron, and his portraits of the Emperors of the Middle Ages made him much reputation.

Vela, Vincenzo. (*Ital.*) Born at Ligurnetto, in the Swiss canton of Tessin, 1822. Officer of the Legion of Honor. Son of poor peasants, he worked as a boy in quarries, and when fourteen went to Milan, where he was employed in the restoration of the Cathedral. His brother, who had become a sculptor, placed him in the studio of Cacciatori. He was often forced to work by night upon jewelers' models, in order to save himself from starvation. In 1848 he obtained a prize at Venice for his "Christ raising the Daughter of Jairus." In 1847 he went to Rome, but was called suddenly away to serve in the army. He was also a volunteer in the Italian army in 1848. His earlier works are, "Prayer," "Spartacus," for which he received a medal at Paris in 1855 (bought by the Duke Antonio Litta), and some busts. He was elected member of the Academy of Milan, but declined the honor. In 1855 he executed " Harmony in Tears," for the tomb of Donizetti. In 1863 he exhibited a group, " France and Italy," given by the ladies of Milan to the French Empress. His " Last Days of Napoleon," much remarked at the Exposition of 1867, was purchased by Napoleon III. in the name of the French people. A *replica* was sold at the Johnston sale, New York, for $ 8,100, and is now at the Corcoran Gallery, Washington. His " Christopher Columbus," " America," and " Springtime " are much admired. In 1873 he was commissioned by the Town Council of Geneva to execute the monument to the Duke of Brunswick, after the model of the Tomb of the Scaligers at Verona.

Vely, Anatole. (*Fr.*) Born at Ronsoy. Medal in 1874. Pupil of Signol. At the Paris Salon of 1876 he exhibited the " First Step " and a portrait ; in 1875, " Meditation " ; in 1874, " Lucia di Lammermoor." At the Corcoran Art Gallery, Washington, is his " Talking Well." The catalogue says : —

"This charming picture is by one of the leading figure-painters of France. The maiden is a model of rustic grace, and the coloring throughout is harmonious. Its sentiment is delicately expressed. The 'talk' may come from the well, but it is evident, from the arch glance and smile of the maiden, that she suspects the whisper to be somewhat human."

Vera, Alejo. (*Spanish.*) Medal at Philadelphia, where he exhibited "The Burial of San Lorenzo at Rome." Vera is one of the artists who have made the art of Spain known with favor in present times, and in the report upon the Fine Arts of the Philadelphia Exposition this picture is especially commended.

Verboeckhoven, Eugène Joseph. (*Belgian*). Born at Warneton (1799). Chevalier of the Legion of Honor, of the Orders of Léopold of Belgium and Michael of Bavaria and Christ of Portugal, and decorated with the Iron Cross. Member of the Academies of Belgium, Antwerp, and St. Petersburg. This artist devoted himself to the painting of animals, and his works are so well known in America as well as Europe that they need no description or praise. They are in many private galleries. At the Johnston sale, New York, 1876, "Flemish Landscape and Cattle" (23 by 28) sold for $ 875. At the Latham sale, New York, 1878, "A Frightened Bull" was purchased by J. J. Astor for $ 1,500, and "Sheep and Twin Lambs, Scotch Highlands" (44 by 34) for $ 3,400. This artist has made some portraits worthy of mention, and has also essayed sculpture. His statue of "Meditation" was far above most first attempts, and possessed a good degree of merit. A fine picture of "Sheep, — Interior" is in the collection of Mrs. H. E. Maynard of Boston. To the Paris Exposition in 1878 he contributed seven characteristic works.

Verboeckhoven, Charles-Louis. (*Belgian.*) Born at Warneton, 1802. Medals at Brussels. Brother and pupil of Eugène. This painter at first essayed animal subjects, but soon gave them up for marines, in which he has a reputable name.

Verhas, Jan. (*Belgian.*) Born at Termonde. Medal at Philadelphia, where he exhibited a "Seashore at Blankenberghe." In Paris, in 1877, were "The Inundation" and "The Studio"; in 1878, "The Master Painter" and "The Bouquet of Marguerites."

Verheyden, Isidor. (*Belgian.*) Of Brussels. Medal at Philadelphia, where he exhibited "A Landscape."

Verlat, Charles. (*Belgian.*) Born at Antwerp, 1824. Professor at the Antwerp Academy. Chevalier of the Legion of Honor. Pupil of the Antwerp Academy and of Nicaise de Keyser. He has painted a great variety of subjects, but his animal pictures are the best. His "Storming of Jerusalem" is in the Museum at Brussels. Some of his pictures have a comic vein, such as "Might is Right," in which a big monkey takes a nut from the jaws of a little monkey. Some of his portraits are good; among them, those of Frederick Preller and the Grand Duchess of Saxe-Weimar. At Paris, in 1869, he exhibited "A Dog at Bay"; in 1868, "A Holy Family" and "A Day of Mourning"; in 1866, "A Rabbit-Hunt." Among his works are, "The

Wolf-Hunt," "Mourning over the Body of Christ," "Madonna with Christ and John," "Shepherd Girl with her Flock," "Dogs waiting for the Start," "The First Snow," "Quarreling over the Booty," "Buffaloes attacked by a Tiger," "Renard in Hope," and "Renard Deceived." Verlat has also executed some admirable etchings ; his versatility and his certainty and celerity of touch are remarkable.

"As a painter of sheep and shepherd-dogs, Verlat is altogether without a superior, oven in Belgium, where Verboeckhoven has enjoyed a great reputation for many years." WILLIAM B. SCOTT, *Gems of Modern Belgian Art.*

Vernet, Émile-Jean-Horace. (*Fr.*) Born in the Louvre (1789 – 1863). Member of the Institute, 1826. Director of the French Academy at Rome, 1828. Grand Officer of the Legion of Honor. At fifteen years of age this artist was able to support himself by the sale of his drawings. He studied with Vincent, and sketched from the living model. At his father's desire he contended for the *prix de Rome*, but failed. He then painted his first military subject, "The Taking of a Redoubt," and afterwards devoted himself to that class of pictures. At twenty years of age he was married, and soon began to keep an account of receipts and expenditures, by means of which may be traced the gradual increase of his prices, from that of 24 sous for a sketch of a tulip up to 50,000 francs for the portrait of the Empress of Russia. In 1814 Vernet, with his father and Géricault, fought on the Barrière de Clichy, and for his gallant conduct there the Emperor gave him, with his own hand, the decoration of the Legion of Honor. In 1812 he had received commissions from the King of Westphalia, and, in 1813, from Maria Louisa. In 1817 his "Battle of Torlosa" was much praised. This was the beginning of his triumphs ; the picture was purchased for the Maison du Roi for 6,000 francs. He now desired to secure Royal commissions, but his political record had not been pleasing to the Bourbons, and after many experiences, the nature of which we have not space to relate, he became the protégé of the Duke of Orleans. In 1817 he painted a portrait of the Duke for which he received 3,000 francs ; he repeated this portrait in various costumes and characters, besides making other pictures for his patrons. Naturally those who made the little court of Orleans also became his patrons, and at this period he executed some fine works. At the Salon of 1819 he exhibited sixteen or more pictures ; it was the year when the "Medusa" of Géricault and the "Odalisque" of Ingres occupied all minds, yet Vernet also received much attention and praise. The Duke of Berry, in his rôle of patron of the Société des Amis des Arts, now commanded two pictures of Vernet ; he painted "The Dog of the Regiment" and "The Horse of the Trumpeter," for the two receiving 5,000 francs. Meantime Vernet made numerous sketches for lithographs, which were scattered among the people, the spirit of which was displeasing to the King, and it seemed wise for the artist to leave Paris. In 1820 he and his father went to Rome. At this time was painted the famous "Course des Barberi," or the departure of the horses for the carnival races. It was sold to M. de Blacas for 4,000 francs. After his return to Paris he painted for M. Odiot "The Defence of the Barrier of Clichy," which is by many considered his best work. Odiot paid him 4,000 francs for it, and gave it to the Chamber of Peers ; it is now at the Louvre. The year 1822 may be said to end the first period of his life ; he had made one of his very best pictures, but he had not been recognized at the Salon ; he had sent there the abovementioned work, also the "Battle of Jemmapes," painted for the Duke of Orleans, and a number of other works. They were refused, the only one exhibited being one that had been ordered by the government, and the subject chosen. It represented his grandfather, Joseph Vernet, lashing himself to the mast of a ship during a tempest. He received 6,000 francs for it. The public were indignant that he should have been excluded on account of the political sentiments he held, and he opened at his studio an exhibition of forty-five of his pictures, which embraced a great variety of subjects. Before this time he had relied on the court of Orleans ; but after this exposition he had the public for his friend. Money came now in plenty ; the dealer Schroth bought his small pictures, giving him from 700 to 2,000 francs each. The Société des Amis des Arts paid him 3,000 francs for one, and a Russian princess demanded some portraits of Napoleon at 1,000 francs each. In 1824 he received 51,850 francs. Among the works of that year was the equestrian portrait of the Duke of Angoulême, for which he was paid 9,950 francs, and before the year was out, Charles X. ordered his portrait at the same price. The following year he was overwhelmed with orders for portraits, but he found time to paint the "Bridge of Arcole," for which he received 10,000 francs, and the "Battle of Valmy," for the Duke of Orleans, which closed the series of four battles which the Duke wished for the Palais-Royal ; — they were Jemmapes, Hanau, Montmirail, and Valmy.

In 1826 Horace and his father were invited to Avignon to attend the opening of a gallery in the Museum, devoted to the Vernets, who had originated in that city. Carle Vernet sent his picture of the "Course des Barberi," and Horace sent his "Mazeppa pursued by Wolves." At Avignon they received every possible attention ; they were conducted to the home of their ancestors ; they piously saluted it, and inscribed their names on the door-posts. At the ceremony of opening the gallery, poems were read in their praise, and they were made members of the Athenæum. After they returned to Paris they received two urns of sculptured silver. They bore the two designs of the pictures which the father and son had sent to Avignon ; they were the work of a jeweler in that city, who refused to be paid for his labor on them ; they were presented to the artists by the city of

Avignon. The Gallery Vernet is still a sacred place in the old city of the Popes. There are works of Antoine, François, Joseph, Carle, and Horace Vernet. The first canvas of the "Mazeppa" was injured by a saber-stroke in the tumultuous studio of Vernet ; he made a second picture, and both are at Avignon ; beneath them are the busts of Joseph Vernet by Brian, and that of Horace by Thorwaldsen. After his election to the Institute in 1826 Vernet changed the style of his subjects. For the "Julius II.," a ceiling in the Museum of Charles X., he received 17,910 francs ; for "Philip Augustus before Bouvines," now at Versailles, 24,775 francs ; for the "Battle of Fontenoy," 30,000 francs. In 1828, when appointed to the French Academy at Rome, he established Salons every Thursday ; they were very gay, — they were attended by artists, travelers, and men of distinction, who danced and amused themselves as if the world of Paris had sprung up in Rome. Vernet now added new subjects to his list ; he painted Roman women, brigands, etc., and the year 1831 marks the end of his second period. In serious work he had not advanced. The "Arrest of the Princes" was the best picture sent from Rome, but it was not equal to the "Clichy" of ten years before. After the revolution of 1830, it was a trial to Vernet to wear his honors at the Villa Medici. The French army was making more subjects for pictures than ever before since the campaign in Egypt, and Vernet could not follow it. In 1833 he was relieved, and soon went to Algiers. At the time of his arrival military operations were suspended, but he occupied himself continually in sketching. He painted also the "Rebecca," for which the Duke of Rohan paid 1,000 crowns, and "Arabs conversing under a Fig-Tree," for Lord Pembroke, and duplicated it for Gourieff, receiving 16,000 francs for the two. In 1833 the King ordered the palace at Versailles to be used for an historical museum. From this time the two thoughts of Horace Vernet were the East and the Museum at Versailles. The few works that he executed, not connected with these two objects, are comparatively unimportant. Louis Philippe, who had ordered from him the four battle-scenes already mentioned, now required of him Friedland, Jéna, and Wagram. There was no room large enough to hold his immense canvases, and on that account one floor was removed, throwing two *étages* into one, and thus the grand Gallery of Battles was made. Bouvines and Fontenoy were added to the above-named works. At length the King wished the artist to paint the Siege of Valenciennes. It is related that on that occasion Louis XIV. with Mme. de Maintenon remained in a mill, where they could safely watch the combat ; the King wished this to be represented. Vernet refused to so paint it, and left Paris for St. Petersburg. He was received with open arms, flattered, fêted, and caressed. After a time the Czar desired him to paint the "Taking of Warsaw"; instead of refusing, Vernet replied, "Why not ? Does a Christian artist hesitate to paint the passion of

Christ ? " If the Czar had ever seen the picture which Vernet made, he would have been amazed at his audacity. Under a gloomy sky, in the midst of smoke, he painted a soldier, dressed in a white tunic with purple facings, fallen and fearfully wounded in the head ; upon his breast rested an eagle, decorated with the *cordon noir*, pressing hard upon the prostrate wretch with his frightful talons. Vernet was never willing to part with this picture, but guarded it as one cherishes the memory of a virtuous act.

He returned suddenly to Paris in order to see his father, who longed for him, and died a few months later. Vernet had no trouble in re-entering Versailles; he was as necessary there as he could wish to be; no one had been found who could satisfactorily fill his place. News came of the taking of Constantine, and Vernet was officially dispatched to take sketches on the spot for his three great paintings for the Salon of Constantine. When these were completed, they were surrounded by other works of his, until that Salon became a wonderful monument to his facility of design and execution. In 1839 Vernet went to Egypt, Syria, and Turkey. In 1842 he went again to Russia, where he made a long journey with the Czar, and others of high position. He was a great favorite with the Emperor, who liked him all the more that he did not always agree with His Majesty. On returning to St. Petersburg, he remained for some time, painted his portrait of the Empress, received many valuable presents, etc. After his return to Paris he took up portrait-painting, but still new battles were fought, and his old love resumed her sway over him. He left Marseilles for Aran in 1845. The army received him with great enthusiasm, and showed him unprecedented honors, hailing him as the great painter of its hardships, bravery, and victories. Upon this, and all the occasions of his life in which he was made the recipient of unusual honors, he conducted himself with most becoming modesty, and in this way, perhaps more than in any other, he manifested the sensible common-sense side of his character. The revolution of 1848 struck Vernet to the heart ; he still worked on, but his best and happiest days were gone. At the Exposition of 1855 he had a Salon entirely devoted to his works, and it was a great satisfaction to him to thus show to men from the four quarters of the globe upon what rested his claim to fame. He lived yet eight years more. He worked always; the Crimean war opened to him a new field, and he was much interested in it. He painted the battle of Alma, a portrait of Napoleon III., and other works, but he wrote of himself thus : " When time has worn out a portion of our faculties, we are not entirely destroyed, but it is necessary to know how to leave the first rank, and content one's self with the fourth."

" How can one judge with one word a career so long and full? At an age when so many only commence to feel their way, he was already a painter. He held the brush sixty years. Could he have held it without weaknesses? To expect it would not be loyal.

Is it necessary, on the other part, to place the prophetic trumpet at the lips and proclaim Horace Vernet the national painter of France? Without doubt he has recorded the history of France in pictures, but all the painters at Versailles have done the same. For us, leaving to foreigners the malign pleasure of judging us after their standards, we believe that we recognize in the French nation more depth and more height than Horace Vernet has known how to give it. But to what profit these useless debates? We have before us a man of incontestable value, an artist by right of birth, a skillful designer, who has cast to the wind of publicity more than two hundred lithographs : a skillful painter, whose pictures can be numbered to five hundred ; an amusing story-teller when he takes the pen ; a man who by his labors, his activity, his travels, has lived the measure of several lives, and has influenced his country and his age. Shall we attempt to lessen him by most incomplete criticisms, or aggrandize him without moderation by unreasonable eulogies? No ! Let us bow before this triumph of skill and genius, and without seeking outside his family for comparisons, let us salute him as the last and greatest of the Vernets." — Léon Lagrange, *Gazette des Beaux-Arts*, November, 1863.

" Vernet is the most direct offspring of the common taste and mind of France. He is the artist of the multitude. All is revealed at one look. His hand and eye are quick, memory retentive, and manner dashing, materialistic, and sensational. The love of excitement and adventure, a free camp-life, and brave deeds, are his special attractions. He tells his story rapidly and off-hand, freely emphasizing for effect, but, in the main, truth-telling. It is done by action, for he has no sentiment for color, and no higher intellectual aim than declamation. Vernet is a clever but not great artist. He rejects academic trammels, and makes himself a spirited reporter of history in its external look, the French soldier being his ideal man. In fine, he seems to be a sort of ' our own correspondent ' of the brush, after the stamp of the Times' Russell, very acceptable to those who care only for a lively-told story." — Jarves, *Art Thoughts*, 1869.

Vernon, Thomas. (*Brit.*) (1824 – 1871.) Studied art in Paris for some years. Well and favorably known in England as a line-engraver. Among his works are, " The Virgin Mother," after Dyce ; " Abundance," after Van Eycken ; " Olivia," after C. R. Leslie ; " The Novice," after A. Elmore ; Raphael's " Mother and Child," Cope's " First-Born," and Murillo's " Christ healing the Sick."

Veron, Alexandre René. (*Fr.*) Born at Montbazon. Pupil of M. Delaroche. At Philadelphia he exhibited " The Banks of the Seine," " Entrance to the Harbor of Boulogne,— a Storm," and a " Park at Senlis," and received a medal. At the Salon of 1878 he exhibited " After the Rain " and " A Fine Winter Day," both views at Argenteuil (Seine et Oise) ; and, in 1877, " The Park at Mont-l'Évêque " and " Evening in the same Park."

Vertunni, Achille. (*Ital.*) Born at Naples. Pupil of Fergola. A painter of landscapes. Medal at Philadelphia. Some of his views in Egypt are remarkable for their truthful rendering of the characteristic lighting of that country, and the grandeur and impressiveness of its ruins are told in the pictures of Vertunni as few artists have attempted to portray them. Our idea of Eastern pictures is too much associated with scenes in harems, mosques, etc., which are, strictly speaking, costume pictures, and give no idea of the great and grand wonders of that old world. Vertunni had shown his power in kindred subjects, in his fine representations of the Roman Campagna, before he saw the East, and he has well fulfilled the hopes which his admirers indulged regarding the manner in which he would interpret other scenery than that of Italy. At the Paris Salon of 1876 he exhibited "At Naples" and "A Pool, Roman Campagna." The works of Vertunni are sometimes seen in England, more rarely in America. His means are such that he has been able to surround himself with everything that artists love, and a visit to his studio, where salon after salon is filled with artistic treasures of past centuries, is one of the choicest pleasures a visitor to Rome can enjoy. But amid this little world of rich old tapestries, rugs, bronzes, statues, armor, porcelains, and flowers, amid all this deep-toned coloring and artistic richness, the pictures of the artist cannot be overlooked, though modestly placed, as if but a part of the elegant furnishing of the rooms. The eye may wander from them for a time, but it will return, and in the future these pictures are the distinctive feature in one's remembrance of that wonderful Roman studio. At Philadelphia his pictures were the "Ruins of Pæstum" and "The Pyramids of Egypt." To Paris, in 1878, he sent the last work, and three other Eastern and Italian scenes. Two of Vertunni's pictures belong to Mrs. J. H. Weeks of Boston. "At the Dudley Gallery," says the London Illustrated News, "are now exhibited some landscapes by Cavaliere Vertunni, a celebrated Neapolitan artist, usually resident in Rome. These works, like many others recently produced in Italy, afford very gratifying evidence of the rapid advance lately made by the modern Italian school."

"The landscapes of Vertunni are remarkable for almost exuberant power, for almost excessive daring in the application of the pigments, and for entire freedom from the conventionalities of 'classical,' as opposed to naturalistic, representation. They comprise five large and noble views, widely differing in subject and effect, and a smaller study for a picture ; the whole taken, with one exception, from the neighborhood of Rome or in Central Italy." — *Art Journal,* August 13, 1870.

Verveer, Samuel Leonidas. *(Dutch.)* Born at The Hague (1813 - 1876). Chevalier of the Order of Léopold, and of the Crown of Oak of Luxembourg. Member of the Art Societies of Brussels and Ghent. Medal at Philadelphia. This artist represented views of cities, such as Amsterdam, Rotterdam, Bruges, Dordrecht, etc. He also painted some *genre* subjects, such as "Salmon-Fishers," "Departure for the Market," etc. At Philadelphia he exhibited "The Village of Scheveningen."

Vetter, Jean Hégésippe. *(Fr.)* Born at Paris, about 1816. Chevalier of the Legion of Honor. Pupil of Steuben. Made his début at the Salon of 1842 with a portrait, but his subjects are those of anecdote, such as "Mascarilla presenting Jodelet to Cathos and Madelon" (1865); "Bernard Palissy" (1861), a work which made a great success, and was sold for 25,000 francs ; "The Quarter of an Hour of Rabelais" (1855) ; "Molière and Louis XIV.," at the Luxembourg ; "The Exquisite, — Time of Louis XIII." (1875) ; "The Flight into Egypt"

(1874) ; " Mazarin " (1872), purchased by the Ministry of the Beaux-Arts ; etc. In 1878 he exhibited a portrait and " The Letter."

Veyrassat, Jules Jacques. (*Fr.*) Born at Paris. Medal for etching in 1866 and '69, and for painting in 1872. The father of Veyrassat was a jeweler, and wished his son to follow the same occupation ; he placed the boy at the Drawing School in the Rue l'École de Médecine, which was intended to fit young men for trades which have some connection with art. .The young artist was very happy there, and drew and modeled arduously. His success in this school determined him to make art a profession. His father sought the advice of Decamps, who said that obstacles should be thrown in the way of the son, thinking that if he indeed had a vocation for art, he would overcome all difficulties, and if not he had best be discouraged. After the revolution of 1848 the father was too poor to aid the son in any case. Veyrassat then commenced making copies of works in the Louvre, and also some etchings for publishers. In this way he supplied his necessities, and as soon as he could afford it moved to Écouen, where he became the friend of Édouard Frère. Veyrassat paints pictures of country-life pure and simple. In 1877 he exhibited the " Passe-cheval " (a small boat for taking horses over a stream, etc.) and the " Stone Quarry " (Fontainebleau) ; in 1876, " The Little Bridge at Samois " and " A Relay of Horses for Tow-Boats " ; in 1875, " The Watering-Place," " The Well," and " Stone Carts " (Fontainebleau), etc. His subjects are often repeated. Veyrassat lives at Samois on the Seine, near the Forest of Fontainebleau, a place well suited to his studies. This artist also paints in water-colors ; " The Luncheon of the Harvesters " (1877) is a good specimen of his art in this direction. A picture by Veyrassat, " Barge Horses," is in the collection of Mrs. H. E. Maynard of Boston. To the Salon of 1878 he sent " The Fair of St. Catherine at Fontainebleau " and " A Relay for Horses of Tow-Boats."

Vibert, Jehan Georges. (*Fr.*) Born at Paris, 1840. Chevalier of the Legion of Honor, 1870. Pupil of l'École des Beaux-Arts, and of Barrias. Made his début at the Salon of 1863, seven years only before his decoration. During the siege of Paris he belonged to the Sharp-Shooters, and was wounded at the combat of Malmaison, October, 1870. At the Salon of 1877 he exhibited " The New Clerk " (purchased by Mr. Butler of New York) and " The Serenade," also four water-color sketches ; in 1876, a portrait and " The Antechamber of Milord " ; in 1875, " The Grasshopper and the Ant " and " The Repose of the Painter " ; in 1874, " The Reprimand " (belonging to Miss Wolfe), " A Monk gathering Radishes," and a portrait ; in 1873, " The Departure of the Bridegrooms " (Spain) and " The First-Born " (belonging to Mr. Stebbins) ; in 1870, " Gulliver fastened to the Ground and surrounded by the Army " and " The Importunate " ; etc. At the Johnston sale, the " Servant Reading " (water-color, 8 by

11) sold for $ 330 ; " The Knife-Grinder " (pen and ink, 7 by 5), for $ 200 ; and " The Offer of the Umbrella " (water-color, 18 by 13), $ 1,000. Besides his exhibits at the Salons, Vibert has painted more than one hundred easel-pictures. He has also executed an " Assumption of the Virgin " for the chapel of Saint-Denis in the church of Saint-Bernard. As an author he has produced a vaudeville, the " Tribune mécanique," two comic scenes for acting, called the " Chapeaux " and the " Portraits " ; also a comedy, the " Verglas." At a sale in Brussels, 1874, " Gulliver in Liliput " sold for £ 800. At the Latham sale, New York, 1878, " A Committee on Moral Books " sold for $ 4,100. It is 19 by 26 inches in size. At the Salon of 1878 he exhibited " The Apotheosis of Thiers." This is fully described in the following letter written from Paris, October, 1877, by Miss Brewster of Rome : —

" One of the most original artists that Le Roux introduced me to is Vibert ; he is truly an original man in every way. He is middle-sized, stout for his age, — for he seems only thirty-five, — has a full, merry, happy, but very shrewd, sensible face ; he loves work, and is, as are all these men, an indefatigable, untiring worker, but he loves also to take his play-hours. In the evening he goes to the theater, and among his friends and himself removes his thoughts from his work and his studio.

" And what a worker he is, not only in his studio, but all over his house ! From the moment you enter the *grille* of his handsome residence in Rue de Boulogne, up to the studio, you see you are in an artist's house. There are fine Japanese majolica monsters on the portico ; marble shells full of flowers ; the walls of the entrance-way are Pompeian ; the walls of the staircase are covered with India-straw matting, and the outside of the stair-balustrade has a deep fringe of rattan ; India plates of brass and India panelings are on the landing-places. His bedroom is Japanese, and he has painted the ceiling to imitate a great plaque of crackled porcelain ; it is deliciously done. He has inclosed all his garden and made a sort of Japanese court and salon ; there are skylights and gay friezes, and part of the ceiling he has decorated most skillfully with curious, grotesque, and gay-colored Japanese dragons and gilt diaperings. At the end of the court is to be a fountain of his own designing. I saw the photographs of it. There is a red marble basin, and on the top of the whole is a bronze bust of La Fontaine, the French fabulist. On the fountain front are bas-reliefs from some of the fables. One is of the stork's feast to the wolf, and at the side of the fountain 's the device Vibert has adopted from one of La Fontaine's fables, ' Travaillez, prenez de la peine.'

" Vibert's pictures are remarkable, as you know, for delicacy of touch and nice feeling for color. He, as all the other Parisian artists, studies nature constantly. He builds up his pictures, and copies accurately. His poetic imagination supplies the ideal. His studio is arranged for different compositions of pictures. On one side are two fine columns with gilt capitals, and draperies hanging between. On another side is a balustrade. There are all manner of accessories about.

" I have left to the last the description of the picture Vibert is painting for the coming Salon : it is already celebrated, although only a study as yet of the immense work it will be when completed. All Paris that is interested in art is talking of this picture, not only on account of its great cleverness but also because of its curious history. The subject is now called the ' Apotheosis of Thiers.' When Vibert designed the picture he asked Detaille to help him paint it. The two men worked on it most faithfully ; when it arrived at a certain point Detaille requested his master, Meissonier, to see it. Meissonier refused, and showed such displeasure that Detaille was obliged to give up all work upon it, as his master selfishly wished to keep the subject for himself. Vibert luckily, however, has no such feelings of delicacy toward Meissonier, and has resolved to finish the stupendous work alone and unaided.

"It is hardly an 'apotheosis,' for the ideas and works of Thiers, rather than his person, are deified in this noble design of Vibert's. I think I never felt so deeply before how difficult it is to explain or describe in words a picture ; it is always a thankless task, but in the present case the subject is so complex that language can do it no justice. There are an infinite number of details in the picture ; but the principal personage is expressed in a forcible, striking manner. The dead body of the great French debater, historian, and statesman lies on a bier, decorated with the grand cross of the Legion of Honor. Although the body and face have the cadaverous rigidity of death, there is likewise a noble expression, an elevated character given to this form of death that seems to make it grander and more dignified than in life ; and in the center of the immense composition, so original in its conception, this figure first arrests the attention ; this is the great difficulty of such a picture, and it has been overcome in a masterly manner. At the foot of the bier stands France, a beautiful, noble woman, weeping, draped in black crape ; she is laying gently the tricolored flag over the bier, and its folds are enveloping the body of the dead. At the head of the bier, to the right, almost in the center of the picture, is Glory, tall and beautiful, with a transparent Greek tunic ; she has just alighted ; the feet hardly touch the ground ; her wings (golden) are unfolded, and with a noble movement she points to the heavens, where you see displayed, as in cloud-visions, the works and ideas of the dead great man ; in one of her hands is an oak branch, the civic recompense she offers to the citizen of citizens, — he who triumphed so nobly over the horrors of the Commune and redeemed France.

"The Commune is represented by a sort of hybrid being that lies in the right corner of the picture on the ground in a death agony ; the red flag is in tatters beneath this creature, and in its hand is a burning torch. This torch rests against the shield of Paris, which is half charred. This is a most curious and impressive part of the remarkable picture.

"At the foot of the bier are heaped up laurels, wreaths and crowns and garlands, the memories of the numberless testimonies of sorrow that were sent by all classes of persons to the funeral of Thiers, and there is also the black standard of Belfort, dedicated to him who was able to save this city for France after the terrible Prussian-French war. To the right in the distance is represented the siege of Paris ; there is fighting and carnage ; the forts are defending the city. This is another testimony of gratitude to the dead statesman, for it was Thiers who fortified the city in 1840, when he was minister under Louis Phillppe. By these fortifications, it will be remembered, Paris was able to hold out so long, to the great astonishment of all Europe, when the formidable Prussian army invaded the city, for it was known that only some débris of regiments, collected in haste, had subdued the insurgents among the people, and were defending the place.

"To the left, back of the lovely figure of mourning France, we see the funeral cortége, soldiers, deputations, the funeral car or chariot, the immense crowd, the whole people — a million of men as it were — entering Père la Chaise, and behind this vast concourse is the great silhouette or outline of the city of Paris. This completes the various ground-plans of the picture.

"The artist then desires to express M. Thiers in the three great phases of his life, — a life that was singularly complete in each phase, — the orator, the historian, and the statesman. To give these three forms, he uses most happily the heavens of his picture, and, although the representations are multiplied, all is so well ordered, arranged with such clever ingenuity, that nothing is confused or troubled. Here, again, words are miserably weak. Each episode of the dead statesman's life is given with clearness and diversity in the moving messes of clouds, and the clouds lose none of their lightness. The varied actions, too, produce a happy effect to the eye, although in description the *mélange* may seem incredible and impossible. As M. Thiers first made himself known as a speaker, it is with that phase the cloud phantasmagoria begins. To the left, at the very summit of the clouds, is the Chamber of Deputies, with its tribune that was so often made illustrious by the speeches of Thiers ; 1830 is personified by the Column of July, when he be made part of the government. Below this rolls a mass of clouds that sweep across the canvas ; these contain the historian's phase, the works he wrote on the Revolution, the Consulate, and the First Empire.

" In the clouds we see first the Bastile, and the people destroying it in their fury. Then advance forward the soldiers of the Republic ; these are Jemapes, Fleuris, and the great wars of Italy. To these, follows mysterious Egypt, with its pyramids ; the banks of the Nile, covered with triumphant French armies, Kleber, Desaix ; here is the center of the canvas, and the heavens are brightly illuminated ; this glow is very harmonious, and unites well with the warm color of glory. To this center also is given part of the history of Napoleon at the summit of his glory and power : it is the brilliant period of the First Empire ; but the heavens gradually lose their brilliancy, as if to typify that it is no longer the people that is ruling ; there are battles and victories, but the imperial glory becomes obscured and somber ; Russia is represented by a routed army in the center of snow and ice. This wonderful historical epic is given with marvelous clearness and genius ; it traverses the canvas from left to right. Then at the right extremity the acts of M. Thiers are resumed. We see the grounds of Longchamps, where Thiers, as President of the Republic, held the grand review of the troops, which he reorganized when it was thought that France, crushed, humiliated, despoiled, could never rise from her terrible fall.' When I think how beautiful is this truly sublime picture, and how inefficient are words to give an idea of it, my attempt seems most audacious. Those of you who will see the picture next spring may forget my description, but those of you who cannot have that privilege and pleasure may accept my intentions indulgently, and probably be glad to have the result of them."

Vinck, Franz. *(Belgian.)* Of Antwerp. Medal at Philadelphia, where he exhibited "A Flemish Burgher's Wife in the Sixteenth Century" and "The Confederates in the Presence of Marguerite of Parma."

Vinton, Frederick Porter. *(Am.)* Born in Bangor, Me., 1846. This painter was brought up to mercantile pursuits, but turned his attention to art, and when seventeen years old the advice and influence of W. M. Hunt helped to fix his decision to become a painter. In 1875 Vinton went to Paris and studied seven months under Bonnat. He then went to Munich, and remained a year, studying under Duveneck and in the Academy under Professors Wagner and Diez. He returned to Paris, and was one of the early pupils in the school of Jean Paul Laurens. He returned to America in the autumn of 1878, and opened a studio in Boston. Before going to Europe Vinton exhibited his pictures at the Boston Art Club. "Celestina," one of his early works, belongs to Mrs. Dix of Boston. At the Paris Salon of 1878 Vinton exhibited the "Little Gypsy" or "Italian Girl," which was recently seen at Doll and Richards, Boston. To the Paris Exhibition, 1878, he sent "A Head of a Neapolitan Boy" and the "Head of an Old French Peasant-Woman." The former was sold for 1,200 francs. Vinton paints portraits, and is now engaged upon one of Mr. T. G. Appleton.

"Mr. Vinton's 'Celestina' is more to our mind than either Bouguereau or Duveneck. However, Mr. Vinton stands in an intermediate place, with a picture professing neither the actualness of Duveneck nor the idealized polish of Bouguereau, but merely the charming reality of art modifying and sweetening its subject, — a young Italian girl playing a mandolin, and clad in a faded blue kirtle, drab jacket, and a white kerchief yellow fringed. Green, gray, brown, and red are darkly interblended in the background, and the figure is defined by some bold and yet subdued spreading of lights on face, hair, and form." — *The Atlantic*, June, 1875.

" Mr. Frederick Vinton's ' Italian Girl,' which was exhibited in the Salon and received the generous praises of his brother artists in Paris, is the best representative of his work abroad, and affords an excellent opportunity for renewing our acquaintance with him. The picture made a good impression in Paris, and certainly will sustain before the Boston public the honor which is conferred upon a painting by its admission to the Salon. . . . . In Mr. Vinton's picture what charms most is the richness and harmony of the coloring. The flesh is very natural. It looks as though it would yield to the pressure of the finger, — there is nothing hard about it. To say that he has given the subject a new charm, is to say a great deal, when we remember how many times the subject has been treated and by what artists." — J. R. MILLET, *Boston Advertiser*, November 12, 1878.

Viollet-le-Duc, Étienne Adolphe. (*Fr.*) Born at Paris (1817 – 1878). Three medals at the Salons. Pupil of Léon-Fleury. This landscape-painter has exhibited at the Salons since 1844. Among his numerous works we may name the following : in 1877, " Cliff and Beach at Étretat " and the " Plateau of Amont, at Étretat " ; in 1876, " The Aqueduct of Buc, in the Valley of Jouy " and " The Calvary of Yport " ; in 1875, two pictures, the " Western and the Eastern Entrances to the Ferme du Mont," at Étretat ; in 1874, " The Environs of Cannes " and " The Isles of Hyères " ; in 1872, " The Valley of Jouy, taken from the Heights of Metz " ; in 1870, " The Valley of Jouy, — Morning," one of his best works. Two of his landscapes were sent to the Salon of 1878 after his death.

Viry, Paul. (*Fr.*) Born at Pocé. Pupil of Picot. At the Paris Salon of 1877 he exhibited " Music " and " A Falconer " ; in 1876, " The Duo " ; and in 1875, " The Return from the Hunt " and " The Aviary." At the Latham sale, New York, 1878, "Courtiers of Louis XIII." (32 by 40) sold for $ 1,800.

Vogel von Vogelstein, Karl Christian. (*Ger.*) Born at Wildenfels (1788 – 1868). Member of the Academies of Vienna, Munich, Berlin, and St. Petersburg. This artist studied at the Academy of Dresden, and went to Rome, where he passed seven years. In 1820 he was called to Dresden as a Professor. In 1842 he returned to Rome, remaining some time. He executed various decorative works, but his fame rests on his portraits. That of Tieck is at the Berlin National Gallery. After his death the government bought for the Museum of Dresden the entire collection left in his studio. The Leipsic Museum has two of his portraits. Among other honors he received letters of nobility.

Voillemot, André-Charles. (*Fr.*) Born at Paris. Chevalier of the Legion of Honor. Pupil of Drölling. Among his works are, " Twilight, — a Decorative Fantasy," " The Woman with Roses," " Spring," and " Innocence in Danger."

Volk, Leonard W. (*Am.*) Born at Wellstown, New York, 1828. He has spent his professional life principally in Chicago. He was for several years in Italy at work and at study, but under no particular master. In 1867 he was elected Academician of the Chicago

Academy of Design, and has been for eight years its president. He is also a member of the Chicago Academy of Sciences and of other Art associations and societies. Among his more important works are the Douglas Monument ; a bust of President Lincoln, from life, exhibited at Paris in 1867 ; life-sized statues of Lincoln and Douglas, in the Illinois State-House, executed from life studies ; the statuary in the Keep Monument in Watertown, N. Y.; the Erie County, N. Y., Soldiers' Monument, the first monument of this kind erected in this country ; the Soldiers' Monuments, with statues, at Rock Island and Cook County, Ill. ; etc.

Volk, Douglas. (*Am.*) Son of Leonard Volk. He has been a resident of Paris for some time, where he was a pupil of Gérôme. He has also studied in Rome. To the Paris Salon in 1878 he sent a portrait of Mlle. T. He contributed to the Centennial Exhibition at Philadelphia, in 1876, "Vanity" and "In Brittany"; to the Exhibition of the Society of American Artists in New York in 1878, two views of "Domestic Life in Normandy."

Vollon, Antoine. (*Fr.*) Born at Lyons, 1838. Chevalier of the Legion of Honor, 1870. Studied at the Academy of Lyons. He went to Paris and made his début at the Salon of 1864. So great was his success that he was decorated six years after his first exhibition. His subjects are mostly kitchen interiors, sea-fish, and portraits. In 1876 he exhibited at the Salon, "A Woman of Pollet at Dieppe " ; in 1875, "The Pig " and "Armures " (at the Luxembourg) ; in 1874, "A Bit of the Market "; in 1872, "New Year's Day " and "The Kettle " ; in 1870, "A Corner of my Studio" and "Sea-Fish" (in the Luxembourg); in 1869, "After the Ball"; in 1868, "Curiosities" (in the Luxembourg) and "Portrait of a Fisherman." In 1871 he exhibited at the Royal Academy, London, "Luncheon." At the Salon of 1878 he exhibited "The Helmet of Henry II." and "A Spaniard."

"Among the new names which the public has learned this year, I recommend to you especially that of Vollon.· The catalogue does not tell us under what masters he has worked, neither from what studio he emerges, armed at all points. If spiritualism was not a pure absurdity, I should believe that Chardin had come back at night to give lessons to this young man. He has exhibited two pictures, of which one represents the 'Interior of a Kitchen,' the other, a monkey surrounded with fruits and musical instruments. The two subjects are treated with decision, firmness, and a freedom already masterly. The tones are just and true. This young man is truly strong. If I saw in him only a hopeful pupil, I should not cry out to him the name of Chardin."— EDMOND ABOUT. *Salon de 1864.*

In the "Gazette des Beaux-Arts" of July, 1878, Roger Ballu praises the work of Vollon, "The Helmet of Henry II.," and finally says :—

"It is not an exact imitation, a faithful copy, made at the expense of patience by a minute and skillful brush : it is, so to speak, a portrait : yes, I am right, a portrait of the helmet of Henry II., represented with the physiognomy of an object of ancient art, and that charm so peculiar to the taste of the sixteenth century. In truth, the amount of real talent here bestowed is not to be appreciated, and I am convinced that in this still-life Vollon has equaled Chardin."

Voltz, Friedrich Johann. (*Ger.*) Born at Nördlingen, 1817. Member of the Academies of Berlin and Munich. Royal Bavarian Professor. Medals at Berlin, and the great Würtemberg Art Medal. Studied at the Academy of Munich. In 1843 be went to Italy, where he remained two years. His specialty is in representing idyllic animal pictures. He has been influenced in his manner and color by Schleich, Piloty, Spitzweg, and others of the Munich school. He has visited most of the art cities of Europe, and is *au fait* to the progress and interests of the art world. In later years Voltz has practiced etching and lithographing. At the National Gallery, Berlin, are his " Menagerie " and " Cows Drinking." At the Leipsic Museum there is a characteristic picture by Voltz. At Berlin, in 1876, he exhibited two cattle pictures and an " Idyl." At the Boston Museum there is now a fine picture by Voltz, belonging to Mr. H. P. Kidder. It represents a group of cattle coming over a hill. Mr. T. R. Butler of New York has in his collection a " Landscape with Cattle," by this artist.

Von Severdonck, J. (*Belgian.*) Born about 1825. A pupil of Verboeckhoven, with whom he has lived in Brussels, for many years. He occupies a studio with his master, and is said to do the greater part of the mechanical work of Verboeckhoven's pictures. Von Severdonck himself paints small landscapes with sheep, and sometimes fowls introduced as accessories ; they are painted with great care and tenderness, are agreeable in color, and truthful in drawing and action. They are in many fine collections in America. He has painted but few large works. He sent " A Cavalry Charge " to the Paris Exposition of 1878. One of his large pictures, a landscape with animals, belongs to Mr. Charles G. Woods of Boston.

Voss, Maria. (*Dutch.*) Of Oosterbeck. Medal at Philadelphia, where she exhibited " Still-Life." Mr. Weir calls her picture " quite superior to anything of its kind in the Exhibition."

Vriendt, Julian de. (*Belgian.*) Of Antwerp. At the Johnston sale in New York, 1876, " The Story of the Battle " (21 by 26) sold for $ 1,800. To the Paris Exposition of 1878 he contributed six portraits.

Vriendt, Albrecht de. (*Belgian.*) Knight of the Order of Léopold. Medals at London and Vienna. A resident of Brussels. At the Munich Exposition, in 1870, he exhibited " Episodes from the Life of Charles V." At Berlin, in 1876, " Charles V. in the Cloister of St. Just." To the Paris Exposition of 1878 he sent " Charles V. at Yuste," " Jacqueline of Bavaria imploring the Pardon of her Husband by Philip the Good," and " The Excommunication of Bouchard d'Anvers."

Wach, Karl Wilhelm. (*Ger.*) Born at Berlin (1787–1845). Royal Professor and member of the Academy of Berlin. Court painter. He studied at Berlin Academy. Especially excelled in knowledge of perspective. In the war of 1813 he served as an officer. Afterwards at Paris he studied under David and Gros. In 1817 he went to Italy. His power of application was remarkable, — in three months he made more than one hundred drawings from pictures, — but his individual style was not changed by this study. In 1819 he returned to Berlin, and established an atelier after the French manner, where he received large numbers of pupils, and became the most distinguished teacher of his time. He painted religious and historical subjects and portraits. He executed two altar-pieces for the Peter-Paul Church in Moscow. At the National Gallery, Berlin, are his "Psyche surprised by Cupid," "A Madonna," and "Studies of Heads."

Wagner, Ferdinand. (*Ger.*) Born at Schwabmünchen, 1820. Has received the freedom of the city of Augsburg. Studied under Cornelius and Schnorr. Paints historical subjects. He executed some frescos at the church of Königsbrunn, — others in the government buildings at Constance are quite famous. He has also painted decorative works in Augsburg, Breslau, Meiningen, Monaco, etc.

Wagner, Alexander. (*Hungarian.*) Born in Pesth, 1838. Professor at Munich. Medal at Philadelphia. Studied under Piloty at Munich. Was appointed professor when but twenty-eight years old. Among the more important works of Wagner are, "An Episode of the Siege of Belgrade" and a portrait of the Empress, both in the Museum at Pesth ; "Departure of Queen Isabella Zapolya," belonging to the Hungarian Academy ; "Baptism of Stephen I., King of Hungary " ; two frescos at the National Museum in Munich, called "Entrance of Gustavus Adolphus into Aschaffenburg " and the "Marriage of Otho the Illustrious " ; at Pesth, a fresco, "The Tournament of Matthias Corvinus," "Hussar-Life," and "Mädchenraub." Wagner is best known in America by his "Roman Chariot-Race," photographs of which were familiar before his second work, of the same subject, was seen at the Philadelphia Exposition. This is, by general consent, considered inferior to the first and smaller work, which was so admired at Vienna, and is now owned in England. "The Chariot-Race" was followed by "Racing among the Horse-Herders of Debreczin." This city is, next to Pesth, the leading one of Hungary, and the herders in that part of the country are famed for their skill in lassoing and taming the wild horses of the Putzta.

"Alexander Wagner loves his technique, but his ruling passion is to get at the mingled physical and spiritual life, the action, the soul of a conception, and he subordinates all else to its portrayal." — *Art Journal*, April, 1877.

Waldo, Samuel. (*Am.*) A native of Connecticut (1783 – 1861). He received his first instructions in art in his native State, but painted for some time in Charleston, S. C. In 1806 he went to London, and was admitted into the small but select circle of American artists then in the English metropolis. After painting portraits in London for three years, he returned to the United States in 1809 and opened a studio in New York, where the balance of his professional life was spent. He devoted himself to portrait-painting with marked success. The New York Historical Society owns his likeness of Peter Remsen, and several portraits of ex-mayors of the city of New York, by Waldo, are in the City Hall there.

Waldorp, Antoine. (*Dutch.*) Born at Basch (1803–1867). Chevalier of the Lion of the Netherlands, the Crown of Oak, and the Order of Léopold. He at first painted decorations, but devoted himself later to views of cities and marines.

Walker, Frederick, A. R. A. (*Brit.*) Born in London (1840–1875). Entered the office of an architect at the age of sixteen, beginning the study of art a year later, soon after which he entered the Royal Academy, London. His earliest efforts were made as a designer on wood, showing decided genius in his illustrations of current literature, furnishing the drawings for Thackeray's "Adventures of Philip," and other books. He first exhibited in colors, "The Lost Path," at the Royal Academy, in 1863. In 1864 he was elected an Associate of the Water-Color Society, and a full Member in 1867, making rapid progress in that branch of the profession, and exhibiting frequently such works as his "Fishmonger's Shop," "Spring," "Autumn," "Stream in Invernesshire," "Fate," "Well-Sinkers," etc. In oil, also, he was quite successful, sending to the Royal Academy, in 1868, "The Vagrants in the Glen "; in 1869, "The Old Gate "; in 1870, "The Plow "; in 1871, "At the Bar "; in 1872, "The Harbor of Refuge "; in 1875, "The Right of Way," his last picture. He was elected an Associate of the Royal Academy in 1870. About one hundred and fifty of his works in oil and water-colors were exhibited in London after his death in 1875.

"Mr. Walker is especially fond of out-door light, air, dew, sunshine, and the freshness of morning among spring leaves and flowers. The shrubs, annuals, and budding plants of an English garden have probably never before been painted with so much loving simplicity and harmonious freshness of color." — SIDNEY COLVIN, *in English Painters of the Present Day,* 1871.

"Walker's 'Right of Way' is a child frightened by sheep while crossing a meadow, full of charming expression of the poetry of nature, and softly and deftly handled The painter is one of considerable repute in this special line of art." — *Art Journal,* June, 1875.

"The predominating qualities of Walker's designs for book illustration are facility of invention combined with great tenderness and grace in drawing, and an innate perception of individual character. . . . . Of what may be termed idyllic painting Walker was unquestionably one of the ablest representatives. Defects of style were occasionally to be noticed, but they were in great measure redeemed by grace of composition." — *Art Journal,* November, 1876.

Wallace, William. (*Brit.*) Born in Falkirk (1801–1866). Portrait-painter. He practiced his profession in Edinburgh until 1833 or '34, when he opened a studio in Glasgow. His work is still highly regarded in his native country.

Waller, Frank. (*Am.*) Born in New York, 1842. He received his first lessons in drawing while a pupil of the New York Free Academy. Between the years 1863 and '68 he was in business in his native city, drawing with pen and ink, and painting in oil in his leisure hours. He went to Europe in 1870, when he entered the studio of J. G. Chapman in Rome, and first resolved to adopt art as a profession. In 1871 he returned to New York ; but again crossed the ocean in 1872, making many studies in Egypt for future works. On his Nile trip he was accompanied by the late Edwin White. Since 1874 he has studied at the Art Students' League, New York. He has been its Treasurer, and was its first President, still holding the latter office. Among his works are, "Temple at Biggeh Philæ in the Distance," "Tombs of the Califs, near Cairo," "On the Desert," "Santa Maria del Sasso, Lake Maggiore " (belonging to Parke Godwin), "Ruins near Cairo," "Interior of a Studio," etc., views of Egypt being a specialty with him. He exhibits frequently at the National Academy, New York.

Walter, Thomas N. (*Am.*) Born in Philadelphia, 1804. He studied architecture in his native city, under Strickland, and began the practice of the profession in 1830. Among the public buildings designed by Walter are the Philadelphia County Jail, in 1831 ; Girard College, in 1833 ; the extension of the Capitol at Washington, the iron dome of the Capitol, the new Treasury Building, the Congressional Library, and the wings of the Post-Office and the Patent Office. He was at one time Professor of Architecture in Franklin Institute.

Walton, Elijah. (*Brit.*) A contemporary English water-color painter, whose favorite subjects are mountain-tops wrapt in mist, and often covered with snow. There was an exhibition of his works, numerous drawings in water-colors, and a few pictures in oil, in London, in the summer of 1874, including "Dahabeah," "Valley of the Wandering," "Mount Sinai " (belonging to Dr. Blackie), "Bedouins and Dromedaries," etc.

"Elijah Walton has shown himself equally able to deal with the ruddy glow of the hot East, and with the sunlit aspect of the Western glaciers and snow-covered mountains, and while he is truthful in his delineation of the local characteristics of both the West and East, the unvarying sameness of his system of treatment establishes a strangely close connection between the two. In his Egyptian and Arabian scenes Mr. Walton's peculiarities are productive of the happiest effect ; and he seems to have entered into all of the associations of the scene with an unusual depth of feeling."— *Art Journal,* August, 1874.

Wappers, Egide-Charles-Gustave, Baron. (*Belgian.*) Born at Antwerp (1803 - 1875). Painter to Leopold I. Officer of the Legion of Honor. Pupil of the Academy of Antwerp, and of Herreyns and Van Bree. He went to Paris, and adopted the manner of the romantic school. From 1846 to '53 he was Director of the Academy of Antwerp, and resigned the office, in which he was followed by De Keyser. His pictures are mostly of historic subjects, such as "The

Devotion of the Burgomasters of Leyden," "Charles IX. during St. Bartholomew's Massacre," " Peter the Great with the Ship-Builders of Saardam," " The Defence of Rhodes by the Knights of Saint-John of Jerusalem " (for the Gallery of Versailles), " The Great Fishing at Antwerp " (for Queen Victoria), etc. He also made numerous portraits. Mr. Probasco of Cincinnati has in his collection the " Neuvaines of the Family of Count Egmont previous to his Execution by the Duke of Alva," painted in 1866.

Ward, Edward M., R. A. (*Brit.*) Born in London, 1816. He entered the schools of the Royal Academy in 1835. Went to Rome in 1836, studying in that city for three years, winning a medal in the Academy of St. Luke for historical composition in 1838. He returned to England in 1839, exhibiting his first picture, " Cimabue and Giotto," the same year. In 1840 he sent to the Royal Academy " King Lear," and in 1843, to the British Institution, " Napoleon in the Prison of Nice," which was subsequently the property of the Duke of Wellington. Among his early works are, " Dr. Johnson reading the Manuscript of the Vicar of Wakefield," " The Early Life of Goldsmith," "Dr. Johnson in the Antechamber of Lord Chesterfield's House," " Lord Clarendon's Disgrace," in 1846 ; " The South Sea Bubble," in 1847 ; " London during the Great Fire," in 1848 ; " Charles Second and Nell Gwynn," in 1849 ; " Daniel Defoe with the Manuscript of Robinson Crusoe," in 1850 ; " Isaac Walton Angling," in 1851 ; " The Royal Family of France in the Temple," in 1852 ; " Charlotte Corday going to Execution " and " The Execution of Montrose," in 1853 ; and " The Last Sleep of Argyle," in 1854. In 1856, when he was made Royal Academician, having been elected an Associate ten years previously, he exhibited " Marie Antoinette parting with her Son." In 1858, by Royal command, he painted " Victoria visiting the Tomb of Napoleon I." and " The Investment of the Garter upon Napoleon III." His " Antechamber at Whitehall during the Dying Moments of Charles II." was exhibited at the Royal Academy in 1861; "Charlotte Corday in Prison," in 1863 ; " Thackeray in his Study," in 1864 ; " The Night of Rizzio's Murder," in 1865 ; " Amy Robsart and Leicester," in 1866 ; " Juliet in Friar Lawrence's Cell," in 1867 ; "The Marriage of the Duke of York to Lady Anne Mowbray," in 1868 ; " Beatrice, Much Ado about Nothing," in 1869 ; " Judge Jeffreys and Richard Baxter," in 1870 ; " Anne Boleyn at the Queen's Stairs, Tower," in 1871 ; " The Quarrel between Captain Absolute and Lydia Languish," in 1872 ; " The Eve of St. Bartholomew " and " The Landing of Charles Second at Dover," in 1873 ; " Midsummer," " Christmas," and " Charles Second and Lady Rachel Russell," in 1874 ; " Lady Clara Vere de Vere " and " The Orphan of the Temple," in 1875 ; " A Normandy Fish-Market," in 1876 ; " Forbidden Fruit," " William Third at Windsor," and " Forgotten, — Court of Charles Second," in 1877. He contributed both to Philadelphia in 1876, and to Paris in 1878. Mr. Ward has been a very prolific painter, sending every year five or six elaborate works to the Royal Academy. Many of his paintings have been engraved. His "Dr. Johnson in the Ante-room of Lord Chesterfield," "The Disgrace of Lord Clarendon," "South Sea Bubble," and "James Second receiving the News of the Landing of the Prince of Orange" are the property of the nation, in the National Gallery. He contributed eight pictures in fresco for the corridor of the House of Commons. [Died, 1879.]

"In his 'Charlotte Corday' [R. A., 1863] Mr. Ward has attempted a subject which hardly any power in art could render pleasing ; and conscientiously as he has studied the period, one cannot help feeling that these decisively foreign historical subjects are dangerous ground. . . . . In his larger picture, 'The Foundlings visiting Hogarth's Studio,' the artist has selected what the result proves to be a better field for the exercise of his inventive powers. The execution is indeed hard and grating ; it is almost like wind-instruments played out of tune ; but the vivacity of the children, and the pretty, natural action, shown in some of their figures, would render the design attractive in print." — PALGRAVE's *Essays on Art.*

"This picture is a most masterly performance, 'Eve of St. Bartholomew' [R. A., 1873]. Never did Mr. Ward take up a subject which, according to our idea, had less promise, and never has he made more of a passage he has taken in hand." — *Art Journal,* June, 1873.

"The artist has made a touching picture [' William III. at Windsor,' R. A., 1877], like many others from his hands calculated to appeal to the common human heart. He has told the story very pleasantly. We need hardly say that the walls, near and remote, which include a portion of the chapel, and the costume of the guard of the King, are perfect. No painter takes greater delight and pains to ascertain the facts of history when he makes history his study. The whole scene is compact and wisely arranged." — *London Standard,* May, 1877.

"Mr Ward has realized an incident which actually took place, with convincing fidelity [' Last Interview between Napoleon I. and Queen Louisa of Prussia,' R. A., 1877]. Only the back of the Emperor is seen, but his unheroic figure, his head sunk between his shoulders, and his hands clasped behind his back, are very characteristic ; and the figure of Talleyrand, who looks over his shoulder at the Queen, with an air of exultation, is scarcely less good. The portraits have evidently been taken from authentic sources, and all the details of costume and accessories are scrupulously correct. The artist never spares either time or trouble to secure absolute accuracy in these matters." — *London Globe,* May, 1877.

Ward, Henrietta. (*Brit.*) Wife of Edward M. Ward, R. A., belonging by birth to an artistic family, her father being Raphael Ward, an engraver, and her grandfather, James Ward, R. A., one of the best animal-painters of England. Mrs. Ward, in late years, has been a regular contributor to the Exhibitions of the Royal Academy. In 1860 she sent "The First Step in Life" ; in 1862, "Despair of Queen Henrietta Maria at the Death of Charles I." ; in 1863, "Mary, Queen of Scots, quitting Sterling" ; in 1864, "The Tower, ay, the Tower!" ; in 1866, "Palissy the Potter" ; in 1867, "Scene from the Childhood of Joan of Arc" ; in 1868, "Lady Jane Grey" ; in 1869, "Scene from the Childhood of the Old Pretender" ; in 1870, "Going to Market, Picardy" ; in 1871, "The Fortunes of Little Fritz" ; in 1872, "The Queen's Lodge, Windsor, in 1786" ; in 1873, "Chat-

·terton"; in 1874, "The Defence of Latham House"; in 1875, "The Poet's First Love"; in 1876, "The Ugly Duckling"; in 1877, "Princess Charlotte of Wales"; in 1878, "One of the Last Lays of Robert Burns," several of which were at Philadelphia in 1876 and at Paris in 1878.

"Many traces of this artist's manner [E. M. Ward's] are naturally seen in Mrs. Ward's picture, 'Mary of Scotland giving her Infant to the Charge of Lord Mar' [R. A., 1863]. This work is finely painted, and tells its tale with clearness."— PALGRAVE'S *Essays on Art.*

"Mrs. Ward is a pleasantly gifted and accomplished painter of *genre*, especially in its relation to child-life. Her 'Little Fritz' and 'The First Interview between Josephine and the King of Rome' [R. A., 1871] are instances in point."— MRS. TYTLER's *Modern Painters.*

"'The Poet's First Love' [R. A., 1875], by Mrs. Ward, is an episode of child-life, painted with considerable artistic finish and care, and betokening many evidences of skill in the department of landscape-painting."— *Art Journal*, July, 1875.

Ward, John Q. A., N. A. (*Am.*) Born in the State of Ohio, 1830. Displayed a talent for plastic art at an early age. Studied under H. K. Brown, remaining his pupil for six years, 1850 – 56. He modeled in Washington during the sessions of Congress for two winters. In 1857 he made his first sketch for " The Indian Hunter," now in Central Park, New York ; subsequently visiting the Indian country in the far West in order to study his subject in the aboriginal state. In 1861 he opened a studio in New York, was elected an Associate of the National Academy in 1862, Academician in 1863, and President in 1874. In 1866 he executed the group of statuary (now in the Public Garden, Boston) in honor of the discovery of anæsthetics, and in 1867 he presented his design for the Shakspere statue in Central Park, N. Y. Among Ward's portrait busts are those of Alexander H. Stephens, Vice-President Hamlin, Dr. Valentine Mott, Joshua Giddings, James T. Brady, etc., and a full-length statue of Commodore Perry, erected by his son-in-law, August Belmont, in Newport, R. I. His "Indian Hunter" and " Freedman," both in bronze, were at the Paris Exposition of 1867, and in the National Academy, New York, the next winter. The " Freedman " is now on the steps of the Capitol at Washington. In the Capitol at Washington he has also a bronze statue of Putnam, executed for the State of Massachusetts, and he is the author of the Seventh Regiment statue in Central Park, New York.

"A naked slave has burst his shackles, and with uplifted face thanks God for freedom [Ward's 'Freedman']. It symbolizes the African race of America, the birth of a new people within the ranks of Christian civilization. We have seen nothing in our sculpture more soul-lifting or more comprehensively eloquent."— JARVES, *Art Idea.*

"Although Mr. Ward has never practiced modelling in an academy or foreign or famed studio, he has labored with rare assiduity to master the principles of his art. He understands proportion and anatomical conditions. His figure of Shakspere stands firmly and naturally on its feat, and is harmoniously true to the conditions and relations of the human form."— TUCKERMAN's *Book of the Artists.*

Ward, Edgar M., A. N. A. (*Am.*) Born at Urbana, Ohio. Younger brother of J. Q. A. Ward. He has studied in Paris, under

Cabanel, spending the better part of his professional life on the Continent. He painted in the studio of his brother in New York during the winter of 1876 and '77. He is an Associate of the National Academy, exhibiting there and in the Paris Salon. His " Brittany Washerwomen " (belonging to Robert Gordon) was at the Philadelphia Exhibition of 1876. His "Sabot-Maker," " Venetian Water-Carriers," and "Washing in Brittany " (the last belonging to J. H. Sherwood) were at Paris in 1878.

"Ward has studied conscientiously and in a severe school, and the character of his work, in almost every light in which it may be viewed, will stand the test of comparison with the pictures of the leading artists represented in the Exhibition. . . . . The coloring of the works [' Young Housekeepers in Brittany' and ' Washing in the Brook,' N. A., 1875] is quiet and unobtrusive, and it is evident the artist has simply painted what he saw, and has introduced no sensational features to secure momentary applause." — *Art Journal*, May, 1875.

Warner, Olin L. (*Am.*) Born at Suffield, Ct., 1844. He studied sculpture in l'École des Beaux-Arts, Paris, under Jouffroy, and afterwards in the studio of Carpeaux, spending his professional life in Paris and New York. He is a member of the Society of American Artists. Among his more important works are a statuette entitled " May," exhibited at the National Academy in 1873 (now owned by Archer and Pancoast, New York), a colossal medallion of Edwin Forrest (at the Centennial Exhibition of 1876), a bust of President Hayes (belonging to the Union League Club, New York), and a statuette in marble called " Night."

Warren, Henry. (*Brit.*) Born in London, 1798. He began his art studies as a sculptor, under Nollekens, about 1816 ; later, he turned his attention to painting, entering the schools of the Royal Academy. He exhibited for some years in oil, but joined the Institute of Painters in Water-Colors early in its organization, and has since devoted himself entirely to that branch of his profession, and with marked success. He was for some time President of the Institute, and has been Honorary President for many years. Among his drawings are, " Cottages at Linton, Cambridgeshire," painted in 1815, and many others, some of which have brought very large prices. He has exhibited rarely of late years. [Died, 1879.]

Warren, Edmond G. (*Brit.*) Son of Henry Warren, a pupil of his father, and for some years an active member of the Institute of Painters in Water-Colors, exhibiting, among others, " Summer Morning on the River Arun," " A Water Picnic," " Waiting at the Lock," "Epping Forest," " A Rural Home," " Getting in the Corn," and (in 1878) " Summer Shade," " A Forest Clearing," " Under the Shady Beeches," etc.

Wasson, George S. (*Am.*) Born at Groveland, Mass., 1855. He studied at the Royal Academy at Stuttgart from 1872 to '75, and received a medal for drawing. He paints marine views and landscapes, and exhibits at the Boston Art Club. He has a studio at present in Boston.

Waterhouse, Alfred, A. R. A. (*Brit.*) Born near Liverpool, 1830. Received his early training in the office of an architect in Manchester, where he began his professional career. Studied for some time on the Continent, and was the successful competitor for the Manchester Assize Courts in 1859, building also in that city the Salford Gaol, Owens College, and the Town Hall, commenced in 1866. Among his other public buildings are the new portions of Baliol College, Oxford, and of Caius and Pembroke Colleges, Cambridge; Lime Street Station Hotel, Liverpool; new National History Museum, South Kensington; new University Club, and many country-houses throughout England. In 1867 he was made a member of the Academy of Vienna, won the *Grand Prix* at the Paris International Exhibition the same year, has been for some time one of the Vice-Presidents of the Royal Institute of British Architects, and was elected an Associate of the Royal Academy in 1878.

Waterman, Marcus, A. N. A. (*Am.*) Born in Providence, R. I., and educated at Brown University. He worked at his profession for some time in New York, opening a studio in Boston in 1874. A collection of his works was exhibited and sold in Boston in the spring of 1878, previous to his departure for Europe. He is an Associate of the National Academy, and a member of the Artists' Fund and American Water-Color Societies. His "Gulliver in Liliput" was at the Centennial Exhibition at Philadelphia in 1876.

Watson, John D. (*Brit.*) Born in Yorkshire, 1832. He was a student of the Manchester Academy of Design, and, later, of the Royal Academy, London. He first exhibited at the Royal Academy, in 1853, "An Artist's Study," and his pictures since have frequently been seen on its walls; among others, "Woman's Work," "Thinking It Out," "Saved," "The Stolen Meeting," "The Plague of her Life," "The Old Clock," "The Gleaner's Harvest," etc. He has contributed also, regularly, to the exhibitions of the Society of Painters in Water-Colors, of which he was made an Associate in 1865, and a full Member in 1870. Among his drawings in this medium are, "The Duet," "The Cottage Door," "A Gentleman of the Road," "A Chat by the Way," "The Village Stream," "The Swineherd," "The Clandestine Marriage," and many more.

He received a medal at the Vienna Exposition of 1873, to which he sent "The Poisoned Cup." To Paris, in 1878, he sent "The Gleaner's Harvest," "Only Been with a Few Friends" (in oil), "Stolen Marriage," "Book Lore," etc. He has been successful as an illustrator of magazines and books, and has made drawings for holiday editions of such volumes as "Robinson Crusoe" and "The Pilgrim's Progress," which are very popular.

Watson, Thomas H. (*Brit.*) Born in 1839. Educated at the Royal Academy, he received several medals for architectural drawings, and was awarded the "first annual traveling studentship" in 1863.

He has furnished designs for several important public and private
buildings in Great Britain, and was elected President of the British
Architectural Association in 1871.

Watt, James Henry. (*Brit.*) (1799 – 1867.) A pupil and assistant of Charles Heath. Resided in London, and executed many well-
known plates after Landseer, Eastlake, Leslie, and other modern
painters.

Watter, Josef. (*Bavarian.*) An artist of the modern realistic
school of Munich. Among his works are, "In a Bavarian Stage-
Coach," "On the Edge of a Wood," "Ann, is it you ?" etc.

Watts, George F., R. A. (*Brit.*) Born, 1818. First exhibited at
the Royal Academy in 1837. Received a prize of £300 for a cartoon,
"Caractacus," and £500 for his "Alfred inciting the Saxons to Mari-
time Enterprise," from the Commissioners for the Decoration of the
Houses of Parliament in 1843. He painted also "St. George and the
Dragon," at Westminster Palace, and a large fresco in the new Hall
of Lincoln's Inn. Among his most successful portraits are those of
Tennyson (1862), Gladstone (1865), Duke of Argyle (1860), Dean of
Westminster (1867), J. E. Millais and Frederick Leighton (1871), Rev.
James Martineau and John Stuart Mill (1874). Among his ideal
and mythological works may be mentioned, "The Window-Seat"
and "Sir Galahad" at the Royal Academy in 1862; "Virginia" and
"Ariadne," in 1863; "Esau," in 1865; and "Thetis," in 1866. In
1867, when he was elected an Associate of the Royal Academy,
he contributed "A Lamplight Study"; and in 1868, when he was
raised to the rank of Academician, "The Wife of Pygmalion" and
"The Meeting of Jacob and Esau." In 1869 he sent "The Return of
the Dove" and "The Red Cross Knight and Una"; in 1870, "Daphne";
in 1873, "The Prodigal"; in 1875, "Dedicated to all the Churches";
in 1876, "By the Sea, — a Study"; in 1877, "The Dove"; in 1878,
"Britomart and her Nurse." He has contributed several portraits
and ideal figures to the Grosvenor Gallery. His "Love and Death,"
"Esau," and a portrait of Herr Joachim and one of Robert Browning
were at Paris in 1878.

"As a real master in tender coloring and admirable delicacy of touch, Mr. Watts does
his gifts better justice in the beautiful girl's head named 'Choosing' [R. A., 1864].
Surely a work like this, with the many charming specimens in the same style which we
have received from this artist, may be admitted as evidence in what direction his genius
really lies ; not force, thought, imagination, but refinement, grace, and fancy. It is his
work in the latter manner which will at any rate be preferred by all the world to his attempts in the *terribile via* of life-size allegories. ' — PALGRAVE's *Essays on Art.*

"But whether of distinguished men, or of men and women utterly unknown to the
world, the portraits of Mr. Watts stand out in strong relief from the portraits of the
painter's contemporaries, redeeming portrait-painting from the charge of decline in our
day." — MRS. TYTLER's *Modern Painters.*

"Mr. Watts has painted much, he has also thought much, and his works have come to
be regarded as the exponents of a principle, and the expression of a conviction. As a
painter, he has few followers, and no imitators, and yet the example he sets, if it have

alight visibla aign, is felt as a guiding power. . . . . It is well known that the use of fresco in domestic decoration, though still a novelty in England, finds abundant precedents in Rome, Florence, Bologna, and Genoa. Mr. Watts has perhaps done more than any other man to domesticate high art in the homes of England." — J. B. ATKINSON, *in English Painters of the Present Day*, 1871.

"Mr. Watts' portraits are all conscientious and subtle, and of great present interest, yet not realistic enough to last." — RUSKIN'S *Notes of the Academy*, 1875.

Wauters, Charles Augustin. (*Belgian.*) Born at Boom, 1811. Chevalier of the Order of Léopold. Two great medals at Brussels. Director of the Academy of Malines, where he had been a pupil under Van Bree. His subjects are religious and historical ; he has also painted portraits and a few *genre* scenes. Among his works are, " Peter the Hermit preaching the Crusade," " The Passage of the Red Sea," " The Martyrdom of Saint Lawrence," " Giotto," " Dante and Beatrice," " Death of Mary of Burgundy," " The Day after the Ball," " The Unhappy Family."

Wauters, Émile Charles. (*Belgian.*) Born at Brussels. Member of the Academies of Brussels and Vienna, and Knight of the Order of Léopold. Medals at Paris in 1875 and '76. Pupil of Portaels. He exhibited at the Paris Salon in 1877, " Mary of Burgundy sworn to respect the Privileges of the Commons, 1477 " (for the grand staircase of the Hotel de Ville at Brussels) ; in 1875, " The Madness of Hugh van der Goes " (belonging to the Belgian Government). His picture of " Mary of Burgundy before the Sheriffs of Ghent " was exhibited in London, and was much noticed. At Berlin, in 1876, he exhibited a portrait of Herr C. Somzée. At Paris, in 1878, three of the foregoing pictures were exhibited.

Way, A. J. H. (*Am.*) Born in Washington, D. C., 1826. He inherited his taste for art from his mother, who is said to have handled the pencil with no little skill. He began his studies under John P. Frankenstein in Cincinnati, at that time considered one of the strongest head-painters in the country. Later, he was a pupil of Alfred J. Müller of Baltimore. In 1850 he went to Paris, entering the atelier of Drölling ; in 1851 he was admitted to the Academy of Fine Arts in Florence. He spent four years in study in Europe, and the rest of his professional life in Baltimore. He was one of the four artists who organized the Maryland Academy of Fine Arts, and was for some time its Vice-President. His early efforts were directed to portraiture, but about 1859 he painted by chance a fruit-piece, which attracted the attention of Leutze, who advised him to devote himself to still-life, a branch of the profession he has since followed with marked success. He has exhibited for the last twenty years in the National Academy, and occasionally at the Royal Academy, London. Among the better known of his works are, " A Christmas Morning " (chromolithographed in Berlin, and well known in America). It was painted in 1870. His " Appetizer " has also been chromoed. Dr. H. F. Zollickoffer of Baltimore owns his " Purity " and " Flora and Pomona."

His "Prince Albert Grapes" (1874) is in the collection of W. T. Walters of Baltimore. To the Centennial Exhibition of 1876 he contributed two panels (grapes) belonging now to J. T. Williams of New York, for which he received a medal "for excellence in still-life."

"Perhaps Mr. Way is best known by 'A Christmas Memory.' It is a small picture, and represents a plate of Sèvres porcelain, with bunches of grapes and raisins, an orange, some ruddy apples, etc., all resting on a crimson and blue fruit napkin. Thus it would have made a charming dessert piece; but some sprigs of holly were twisted into a sort of wreath, giving warmth to the picture and suggesting the season." — *Washington, D. C., Capitol,* September 15, 1872.

"In all qualities of form, color, texture, and solidity, his grapes are admirable. He attains these fine results by conscientious portraiture of his models. He selects fine bunches of his favorite fruit, hangs them in the light that he desires, and against such background as best brings out their beauties, and then paints, with the most loving care, every detail. His treatment of this subject is most masterly." — *Baltimore Every Saturday,* November 10, 1877.

Weber, August. (*Ger.*) Born at Frankfort (1817 – 1873.) Studied under Rosenkranz, and, later, in Darmstadt under Schilbach. Settled at Düsseldorf, where he became a professor. His evening lights and moonlight effects are worthy of notice. Weber painted in water-colors and executed some lithographs. At the National Gallery, Berlin, is "A Westphalian Landscape" by him; at the Leipsic Museum, a "Moonlight Scene."

Weber, Paul. (*Ger.*) Born about 1823. Made his studies in Frankfort. In 1848 he went to the United States and settled in Philadelphia. In 1857 he traveled in Scotland and Germany, and returned to America. In 1858 he went to Darmstadt, and was there appointed court painter. Since then he has sometimes resided in Munich. "A Scene in the Catskills" (painted in 1858) is a good example of his work, and is now in the Corcoran Gallery at Washington. One of his most important pictures, called "Morning," is in the Gallery of the Pennsylvania Academy of Fine Arts. A large, fine picture by Weber, "Lake Chiemsee, in the Bavarian Highlands," belongs to Mrs. E. D. Kimball of Salem, Mass. Several works of this artist were exhibited at the National Academy, New York, in 1869.

Weber, Otto. (*Ger.*) Born at Berlin. Killed in the war of 1870. Medals at Paris in 1864 and '69. Pupil of Steffeck and Coutnre. At the Salon of 1870 he exhibited "Springtime" and "Annunziata,— the Spinner and her Cow"; in 1869, "An Ox-Team"; in 1868, "The Deer Quarry" and "La rentrée du bois de chauffage"; in 1867, "The Plowing" and "Under the Chestnut-Trees"; in 1864, "A Wedding at Pontaven, Brittany" and "Cattle in a Wood." At the Walters Gallery, Baltimore, are "The Hay-Gathering" and a large representation of a "Fête in Brittany," by this artist. The whole work, figures and landscapes, is worthy of praise. Two of his pictures are in the Luxembourg.

"The first picture by Otto Weber that proved his claim to high position was exhibited in the Salon of 1866, and afterward in Mr. Wallis' exhibition, in the Suffolk Street Gallery. It was entitled ' La première neige sur l'Alm (Bavière),' and represented Bavarian peasants bringing their cattle down from the mountains. The cattle and figures were admirable for perfect freedom of movement and truth of design. There is a certain point in animal painting which is not easily passed, but which is well known to all who have practically attempted that branch of art. You may be able to paint a cow or a horse quite respectably in some very common attitude, which the animal can be induced to retain for several minutes at a time, but it does not follow that you are able to put the animal in one of those highly expressive and *living* postures which do not remain unaltered for one second. To do this you must have some memory and imagination, and a knowledge of the animal far surpassing any ordinary accuracy. All the great animal-painters have this power and continually use it, the great amount of life which all recognize in their pictures being mainly due to it. Otto Weber has it in the same degree as Troyon and the Bonheurs, and he has all the other accomplishments necessary to the production of a first-rate cattle-picture ; his color is delicate and agreeable, though he is not a colorist in the great and peculiar meaning of the word ; and his chiaroscuro is fairly good, although he is not in any way remarkable as a master of tonality. His sense of the values of local colors, as lights and darks, is, however, exceptional, the effect of the picture above mentioned being altogether due to it, and very powerful. His landscape is always excellent, and was shown to the greatest advantage in that picture, where the whole country, from the snows on the high mountains to the vegetation in the immediate foreground, was admirably studied and most faithfully rendered. The photograph . . . . is from a picture of Highland cattle just going to pass a ferry, and it will be seen that Otto Weber, in spite of his foreign origin, has entered as completely into the character of our glorious little Highland breed as the best of our native painters. I have seen several other pictures by the same painter, and a few etchings of his, which confirm my favorable opinion, but, on the whole, consider ' La première neige sur l'Alm ' his most complete and masterly work."— HAMERTON's *Painting in France.*

Webster, Thomas, R. A. (*Brit.*) Born, 1800. He entered the Royal Academy at the age of twenty, receiving in 1825 the gold medal of the Academy. He exhibited at the Royal Academy as early as 1823, and among his earlier works sent to that gallery and to the British Institution may be mentioned, "The Gunpowder Plot," "The Sick Child," "Returning from the Fair," "The Love-Letter," "Reading the Scriptures," "The Village School," "Anticipation," "Punch," "The Smile," "The Frown," "Contrary Winds," "The Dame's School," "Dotheboy's Hall," "The Battle of Waterloo," "Good Night," "The Village Choir," "See-Saw," "Village Gossips," etc., many of which have been engraved. In 1840 he was elected an Associate of the National Academy, and Academician in 1846. He still contributes regularly to its exhibitions, sending, in 1869, "Politicians" ; in 1871, "Volunteers at Artillery Practice" ; in 1872, "Odd or Even" ; in 1873, "An Interested Adviser" ; in 1874, "The Wreck Ashore" ; in 1876, "Youth and Age" ; in 1877, "The Letter" ; in 1878, a portrait of himself. His "Going into School" and "Dame's School " are at the National Gallery.

He was placed on the list of Honorary Retired Academicians in 1877.

Weeks, Henry, R. A. (*Brit.*) Born in Canterbury (1807 – 1877). Studied under Chantrey and Behnes. Was elected an Associate of the Royal Academy in 1850, and Academician in 1863. In 1852 he received the gold medal of the Society of Arts for the best treatise on the Fine Art section of the Great Exhibition. He was appointed Professor of Sculpture at the Royal Academy in 1869. He made the first portrait bust of Queen Victoria executed after her accession. Among his works are colossal statues of Cranmer, Latimer, and Ridley, which form part of the Martyrs' Monument at Oxford; a statue of Lord Bacon, at Trinity College, Oxford; Dr. Goodale, at Eton; Marquis of Wellesley, at the India House; Lord Auckland, at Calcutta; and one of the groups of the Albert Memorial.

Weeks, E. L. (*Am.*) Born in Boston, 1849. He studied in l'École des Beaux-Arts, in Paris, and in the ateliers of Gérôme and Bonnat, spending his professional life in his native city and in Cairo (Egypt), Jerusalem, Damascus, and Tangiers. He is a member of the Boston Art Club, elected in 1874, and has exhibited at the Paris Salon and at the Paris Société des Amis des Arts. Among his works are, "A Cup of Coffee in the Desert," a group of Arabs and camels (belonging to Ole Bull), "Pilgrimage to the Jordan" (owned in Albany, N. Y.), "A Scene in Tangiers" (in the collection of T. G. Appleton), "Jerusalem from the Bethany Road," an early picture (belonging to Rev. E. L. Clark of New York), "A Moorish Camel-Driver" (in the Paris Salon of 1878), "Alhambra Windows" (belonging to J. B. Richmond, Boston), "An Arab Story-Teller" (at the Centennial Exhibition of 1876), "They toil not, neither do they spin" (exhibited in Boston), etc.

"The illustrations of Eastern life by E. L. Weeks are striking and full of merit. One of them — camels and their riders on the desert, with a boy marching along playing the flute — has the charm of simplicity, and much good color. The camels are drawn with understanding, and are well planted on their feet, while the figure of the boy is *naïve* and in good action. Mr. Weeks has made immense strides the last season, and promises to rank high in the branch of art he has chosen to follow." — *Boston Advertiser*, January 17, 1876.

"The one thing to be noticed in all the paintings of this artist is the remarkable skill he displays in keeping the individuality of the colors. By this he produces most charming effects of color, where a less skillful artist would fail to make the picture more than interesting. There is a decided out-of-door look about this picture ['Midsummer'], too, which tells the beholders that the artist painted Nature just as he found her." — *Boston Advertiser* November 20, 1877.

"Mr. Weeks has taken up a field for study in which he finds himself almost alone, and has given every effort to the increase of his knowledge of the life and character of these people who toil in the field. For years Mr. Weeks has traveled in the East, filling his sketch-book with scenes with which to illustrate his experience there." — *Boston Advertiser*, February 16, 1878.

Wegener, Johann Friedrich Wilhelm. (*Ger.*) Born at Dresden, 1812. Under the greatest difficulties and with no instructor he became a portrait-painter, by which means he supported himself, and as soon as possible took up animal painting. At length he was able to go to the Dresden Academy for a short time. He also made a student's journey in the German mountains and Upper Italy. As an historical painter he has executed altar-pictures for the churches in Gröss-Gmehlen and Lichtenstein. At the National Gallery, Berlin, is his " Wild Buck."

Weir, Robert W., N. A. (*Am.*) Born at New Rochelle, N. Y., 1803. He became a professional artist at the age of twenty. For several years he painted in New York, and spent a long time in study in Florence and Rome. In 1829 he was elected a member of the National Academy, and Professor of Drawing in the Military Academy at West Point in 1832, a position he held for many years. Among Professor Weir's earlier works are, " The Bourbons' Last March," " Landing of Henry Hudson," " Indian Captives," " Christ and Nicodemus," " Child's Evening Prayer," " Pier at Venice," " View on the Hudson," " Taking the Veil," etc. In 1867 he sent to the National Academy, " Heaving the Lead," in water-color, and " The Evening of the Crucifixion " ; in 1869, " Virgil and Dante crossing the Styx " ; in 1874, " The Portico of the Palace of Octavia, Rome " ; in 1877, " The Belle of the Carnival " and " Our Lord on the Mount of Olives " ; in 1878, " Indian Falls." Professor Weir is an Associate Member of the Water-Color Society, but not a frequent contributor to its exhibitions. He has at present (1878) a studio near Hoboken, on the Hudson, in which are " Christ in the Garden," " Titian in his Studio," and a nearly completed picture, " Columbus before the Council of Salamanca." His " Taking the Veil " (belonging to A. C. Alden) was in the Centennial Exhibition of 1876 ; his " Pæstum by Moonlight" and " Last Communion of Henry Clay " (water-color) were in the Johnston Collection. His " Embarkation of the Pilgrims " is in the rotunda of the Capitol at Washington.

" Weir excels in cabinet *genre* pictures. We recall one representing a child saying its evening prayers at its grandmother's knee ; a most graceful, simple, expressive little work, the still-life of Flemish authenticity. Some of his landscapes and portraits are excellent." — TUCKERMAN's *Book of the Artists.*

Weir, John F., N. A. (*Am.*) Son of Robert W. Weir. Born at West Point, N. Y., 1841. He received his education under the instructors of the Military Academy there, and began painting in the studio of his father. In 1861 he took a studio of his own in the Tenth Street Building, New York. He was elected a member of the Artists' Fund Society in 1864, and full member of the National Academy in 1866. He went to Europe in 1868, remaining about a year in the different art-centers. In 1869 he was elected by the Corporation of Yale College to fill the chair of Director of the Yale School of Fine Arts, a position which he still holds. In 1876 he was appointed Judge of the Fine Arts at the Centennial Exhibition at Philadelphia, and wrote the official report of the same, which is so frequently quoted in these pages. His professional life has been spent in New Haven and New York. His first work was a " Sunset at West Point," painted at the age of seventeen. Among the better known of his pictures are,

"The Culprit Fay," "The Christmas Bell," "The Gun Foundry" (belonging to R. P. Parrott), which was exhibited at the National Academy, New York, the Paris Exposition of 1867, and Philadelphia in 1876. "Forging the Shaft" (at the National Academy, New York) was burned while in the possession of H. W. Derby. "The Confessional" (belonging to Justus Hotchkiss of New Haven) was at Philadelphia in 1876; "Venice" is in the collection of Jno. W. Jewett; "Tapping the Furnace" and "An Artist's Studio" belong to Cyrus Butler. A *replica* of "Forging the Shaft," painted in 1868, was sent to the Paris Exposition of 1878.

"Weir's 'West Point Foundry,' representing the casting of a gun, is his best-known and most successful work. He has spared no pains to render it authentic, the figures are modeled from some of the athletes of the establishment, the details are exact, and the extremely difficult task of eliminating all the light on the picture from the molten metal passing from the caldron into the mold has proved a complete success." — TUCKERMAN's *Book of the Artists.*

"Professor Weir contributes a forest interior [Artists' Fund Exhibition of 1878], excellent in what may be termed its ideal reality, details being not sacrificed to sentiment, nor sentiment to objective force ; excellent also in the pleasantness of the light that creeps and glows through the foliage or on the pearly bark of the trees, and in the quiet harmony and delicious purity of the tints." — *New York Evening Post,* January 15, 1878.

Weir, Julian Alden. (*Am.*) Son of Robert W. Weir, N. A., and younger brother of John F. Weir, N. A. Inheriting much of the family talent for art, he has a studio in New York, devoting himself particularly to portrait-painting. He exhibits at the National Academy, is a member of the Society of American Artists, and sent to its first exhibition several portraits and "An Interior." He sent from Paris to the National Academy, New York, in 1875, "A Brittany Interior"; in 1877, "At the Water-Trough," "Brittany Peasant-Girl," "Brittany Washerwomen," and "Study of an Old Peasant." He sent "A Breton Interior" to the Paris Exposition of 1878.

[No response to circular.]

"Mr. Weir has a wonderful delicacy in the flesh tones, where the highest light graduates into the slightest half-tints with singular purity. An instinctive feeling has a great deal to do with the softness and purity of the colors, but his knowledge is also very unusual. . . . . His heads have attracted great attention in Paris, and the look of individuality in his faces, together with his other good qualities, promises for him great success as a portrait-painter." — *Art Journal,* April, 1878.

Wells, Henry T., R. A. (*Brit.*) Born in London, 1828. He began his career as a painter of miniatures, in which branch of art he won decided distinction, exhibiting at the Royal Academy as early as 1845. About 1860 he began the execution of larger canvases, contributing regularly to the Royal Academy, and numbering among his sitters many distinguished people. He was elected an Associate of the Royal Academy in 1866, and Academician in 1870. Several of his portraits and portrait groups were at the Centennial Exhibition at Philadelphia in 1876, and at Paris in 1878.

" We are glad to see that Mr. Wells varies the practice of portraits by landscapes, a union of styles for which he can easily find great precedents. His 'Farmyard at Evening' [R. A., 1865] has an impressive sobriety of tone which wants more gradation to achieve the effect aimed at by the artist. The trees are well discriminated." — PAL-GRAVE'S *Essays on Art.*

" H. T. Wells always employs sound taste in arrangement, and is often very success-ful in management of color." — *Art Journal,* July, 1873.

Wells, Johanna Mary. (*Brit.*) Wife of Henry T. Wells (*née* Boyce). (1831 – 1861.) She received her art education in London, and later, for a short time, under Couture in Paris. She studied also in Italy, and was married in Rome in 1858. " Elgiva," her first pic-ture, was exhibited at the Royal Academy in 1855 ; " The Boys' Crusade," in 1860 ; " Bo-Peep," "The Heather Gatherers," and " Do I like Butter ?" in 1861.

Wencker, Joseph. (*Fr.*) Born at Strasbourg. *Prix de Rome,* 1876. Medal in 1877. Pupil of Gérôme.' At the Salon of 1877 he exhibited a portrait of Mlle. Marthe G. ; in 1876, " Stoning of St. Stephen."

Werner, Anton von. (*Ger.*) Born at Frankfort-on-Oder, 1843. Director of the Royal Academy of Berlin. Court painter. Officer of the Order of the Crown of Italy, Knight of various orders, and the recipient of many medals. Member also of the Academies of Venice and of Caraccas (Venezuela). At the Royal Academy of Berlin, in 1876, he exhibited " The Festival," "Schneewittchen, die 7 Raben " (all sketches of decorative works), and a portrait of a man. Among his pictures are, " Luther at the Diet of Worms," " Moltke before Paris," " Moltke at Versailles," " Proclamation of the German Em-pire in the Galerie des Glaces at Versailles," " Irregang," and "Don Quixote at the Goatherd's." He has illustrated the works of T. V. von Scheffel. For the " Trumpeter of Seckengen " he made thirty-nine drawings ; these are much admired, and well represent the spirit of the time they illustrate.

"Anton von Werner, although still a young man, is already Director of the Royal Academy at Berlin. He is one of the first of living historical painters. To a correct eye for color and drawing, he adds a grandeur of style very appropriate in an artist who is court painter for the Germanic Empire. Some of his decorative works are character-ized by a happy combination of breadth, harmonious color, and energetic action. But the work that has added most to his celebrity is a picture which illustrates the procla-mation of the German Empire in the sumptuous Galerie des Glaces at the Palace of Versailles." — BENJAMIN'S *Contemporary Art in Europe.*

West, Peter B. (*Brit.-Am.*) Born at Bedford, 1833. Studied in his native city, and in the Lees School of Arts in London. Was also a pupil of his father, Robert West, considered one of the best judges of painting in the midland counties of England. He followed his father's profession, that of picture-restorer, in New Orleans and other American cities, finally turning his attention to animal painting with considerable success. His studio at present (1878) is in Cleve-land, Ohio, where he has painted many of the fine horses of that section of the country. Among his works may be mentioned, " Portrait of Lady Kate," a trotting-horse owned by F. Rockefellow; " Bull-Fight," owned by Dr. D. H. Beckwith, and " Group of Game," the property of J. H. Clark, all of Cleveland. To the Centennial Exhibition at Philadelphia, in 1876, he contributed a *genre* picture, still-life, now owned by Mr. Grant of Foxburg, Pa.

Westmacott, Richard, R. A. (*Brit.*) (1799–1872.) Son of Sir Richard Westmacott, R. A., from whom he inherited his artistic talent, and received his first instruction in art. He entered the schools of the Royal Academy in 1818. In 1820 he went to Italy for the purpose of study, remaining six years. In 1826 he sent his first work to the Royal Academy, a marble statue of a girl holding a bird. He exhibited " The Reaper " in 1831, and the " Cymbal-Player " (belonging to the Duke of Devonshire) in 1832. About this time he executed in bas-relief, " Narcissus," " Venus and Ascanius," " Venus instructing Cupid," and " Bluebell and Butterfly." In 1838 he was elected an Associate of the Royal Academy, and Academician in 1849. Among his later works are, " David," " Resignation," " Prayer," " Angel Watching," and busts of Earl Russell, Sydney Smith, etc. Westmacott was the author of several valuable works upon art subjects, one of the most important being his "Hand-Book of Ancient and Modern Sculpture," published in 1864.

" As a sculptor, Richard Westmacott's works generally must rank below those of his father. Yet they are by no means without merit, graceful rather than powerful, but manifesting careful study and untured knowledge. He was learned in his art, and accepted as an authority on all matters connected with it." — *Art Journal*, June, 1872.

Wharton, P. F. (*Am.*) Born at Philadelphia, 1841. Received his art education in the Pennsylvania Academy of Fine Arts, later, going abroad and studying in Dresden and in the Atelier Suisse in Paris. Many of his earlier works are in the possession of Mrs. John Lardner and Joseph W. Drexel of Philadelphia, where the better part of his professional life has been spent. To the Centennial Exhibition of 1876 he sent his most important work, for which he received a medal. It is entitled " Perdita at the Sheep-Shearing Festival," a scene from " Winter's Tale." His last picture (1878), " Waiting for the Parade," belongs to D. C. W. Smith of Philadelphia. Smaller and less elaborate works are owned in New York and elsewhere.

Whistler, James Abbott M'Neill. (*Am.*) According to the register of St. Anne's Church, Lowell, Mass., he was born in that city in 1834, but was taken when a child to Russia, where his father was employed as an engineer. When twelve years old this artist returned to America, and was educated at West Point. About 1855 he removed to England. Later, he studied two years under Gleyre in Paris. He next went to London, where he settled. He has exhibited his works at the Royal Academy, the Dudley and Grosvenor Galleries, the Paris Salons, and at The Hague. He made an exhibition of his works in Lon-

15 *

don in 1874, which attracted much attention. To the Academy he sent, in 1863 (in oils), " The Last of Old Westminster " and " Westminster Bridge " ; in 1864, " Wapping " ; in 1865, " The Golden Screen," "Old Battersea Bridge," and "The Little White Girl " ; in 1867, "Symphony in White, No. 3 " and " Sea and Rain " ; in 1870, " The Balcony " ; etc. In 1877 he exhibited at the Grosvenor Gallery, eight pictures, — a portrait of Mr. Carlyle, " A Nocturne in Blue and Gold," " A Nocturne in Blue and Silver," " A Nocturne in Black and Silver," " An Arrangement in Black " (representing Mr. Irving as Philip II.), " A Harmony in Amber and Black," and " An Arrangement in Brown." To the Grosvenor Gallery, in 1878, he sent " Variations in Flesh-Color and Green," and others. One of his earlier works, " Mère Gerard," belongs to A. C. Swinburne.

There has been of late (November, 1878) a decision in a suit for damages brought by Mr. Whistler against Mr. Ruskin. It was grounded upon the following passage, which appeared in " Fors Clavigera," which Mr. Ruskin edits : —

" For Mr. Whistler's own sake, no less than for the protection of the purchaser, Sir Coutts Lindsay ought not to have admitted works into the gallery in which the ill-educated conceit of the artist so nearly approached the aspect of willful imposture. I have seen and heard much of cockney impudence before now, but never expected to hear a coxcomb ask 200 guineas for flinging a pot of paint in the public's face."

Mr. Ruskin claimed this to be a fair and bona-fide criticism upon a painting which had been exposed to public view. The decision of the court gave Mr. Whistler one farthing damages and no costs. The following is a portion of Mr. Whistler's testimony before the court : —

" Before the Nocturnes entered the Grosvenor Gallery they were sold, except one. One was sold to the Hon. Percy Wyndham for 200 guineas. I had a commission for one of 150 guineas, and another I sold for 200 guineas. Since the publication of this criticism I have not been able to sell my pictures at the old price. As to the name of ' Nocturne,' it means an arrangement of lines, form, and color, with some incident or object of nature in illustration of my theory. The ' Nocturne in Blue and Gold ' I knocked off in a couple of days. I painted the picture in one day, and finished it off the next day. I do not ask 200 guineas for a couple of days' work ; the picture is the result of the studies of a lifetime. . . . . I do not put my pictures in a place to mellow, but I expose them in the open air to dry as I go on with my work ; I think that is a good thing, and if I were a Professor I would recommend it to my pupils."

The " Arrangement in Black and Gold," the artist explains as a night view of Cremorne Gardens with the fireworks, — hence its name. The " Nocturne in Blue and Silver" is "A View of the Thames at Old Battersea Bridge." During the entire career of this artist he has been in the habit of etching. He received a gold medal at The Hague for works in this manner. A collection of his etchings is in the library of Her Majesty at Windsor Castle, and another collection is in the hands of the authorities of the British Museum. The portrait of Mr. Carlyle has been engraved, and the mass of the artist's proofs were sold by subscription.

" ' Old Battersea Bridge,' with a mud shore and a river-side group, boats ready for launching, a gray sky, a grayer river, the sidelong bridge crossed by carts and passengers, shows one way of treating these simple materials to perfection, whether composition, tone, truth, or originality is in demand. 'Lange Lizen of the Six Marks' is the most delightful piece of color on the walls of the Academy this year." — WILLIAM M. ROSSETTI, in 1874.

"Whistler's freaks of coloring were original, and his Tiepolo-like touch effective; but his pictures were rather suggestive of power than complete art." — JARVES, *Art Thoughts.*

" Every touch here has been struck in apparently with that directness which has long made Velasquez the envy of all artists; the colored paper labels on the right, above the figure, should be especially noticed; and we may fairly suppose that if, in this picture ['Die Lange Lizen'] and in the 'View of Wapping' near it, the figures had been free from some obvious negligences, Mr. Whistler might have obtained from a jury of oil-painters the first prize for mastery over the technicalities of his profession." — PALGRAVE'S *Essays on Art,* 1864.

" Whistler is known by his etchings and his paintings; the former receive nearly unqualified praise, the latter have been alternately abused and landed, but even his severest critics seem inclined in these days to allow Whistler exceptional achievements, however fitful or marred in color." — MRS. TYTLER's *Modern Painters,* 1873.

"Whistler as a painter has the rare faculty of true oil-sketching, selecting with certainty the most essential truths. . . . . He seems insensible to beauty, which is a grievous defect in any artist; but his work is redeemable from vulgarity by strange sensitiveness to color and character. It is audacious, almost impudent in manner; but it is not effective, although it looks so at first; and even its audacity is based on directness and simplicity of color." — HAMERTON's *Thoughts about Art.*

"The most finished and perfect specimens of Mr. Whistler's artistic powers are to be found in the collection of etchings and engravings in dry point. For some time amateurs in this branch of art have been acquainted with the views of the Thames executed by Mr. Whistler. We can think of no work in which genius, of a certain kind, is more decisively manifested. The views of shipping and river-bank reveal the closest study of the effects to be seen in and about London." — *Art Journal,* August, 1874.

" 'The Girl in White,' exhibited in Baltimore in 1876, is especially marked by Whistler's idiosyncrasies. . . . . It cannot be doubted that his mannerisms, which have the appearance of affectation, are not in unison with the spirit of true art." — *Art Journal,* March, 1876.

"Whistler's 'Nocturnes,' 'Variations,' and 'Arrangements' are all, we have not the slightest doubt, brimful of talent, but it is talent applied to the interpretation of a school of art which we confess ourselves utterly unable to comprehend. Napoleon I. said of Goethe that he was a great genius who had something to say, but who had not succeeded in making himself understood. Mr. Whistler is assuredly gifted with genius, but he has scarcely to our thinking become articulate." — *London Daily Telegraph,* May 6, 1878.

" Mr. Whistler has his own abilities, his own aims, and his own admirers, and it is no use denying the one, arguing about the second, or abusing the third. He has a right to his place among the originals of his time; and it is well he should find room and verge enough in the Grosvenor Gallery." — *London Times,* May 2, 1878.

White, John Blake. (*Am.*) Born in South Carolina (1781 – 1859). He studied art in London for four years in the early part of the century under Benjamin West. Returning to America, he settled in Charleston, S. C., where he studied and practiced Law, painting only as an amateur. He received, while still a young man, from the South Carolina Institute, a medal for the " Best Historical Painting in Oils." Many of Mr. White's pictures are still in the possession of various members of his family. Dr. Octavius A. White of New York owns his " General Marion inviting the British Officer to Dinner in the Pedee Swamp" (engraved by the Apollo Association of New York), his "Poverty and Love," "The Arrival of the Mail," "Macbeth and Banquo on the Heath," and "The Brand of Sweet Water." Col. T. G. White of Beaufort, S. C., owns his "Grave-Robbers" and "Mrs. Motte urging General Marion to burn her Residence in order to dislodge the British." A. J. White of Charleston owns "The Taking of the White Veil"; J. E. Holmes of South Carolina, "The Interior of Old St. Philip's Church, Charleston" and "The Burning of Old St. Philip's Church." Elias Ball of South Carolina owns his "Conrad and Gulnare"; J. J. B. White of Mississippi, "The Battle of Fort Moultrie." Among his other works are, "The Rescue of the American Prisoners by Sergeant Jasper and John Newton" (engraved by the Apollo Association), "Massacre of American Prisoners by the English and Indians at Frenchtown" (painted in 1813), "The Battle of Eutaw Springs" (presented to the State of South Carolina), "The Martyrdom of Hayne," "General Marion and his Men fording the Pedee," "The Battle of New Orleans" (painted in 1816), "Death of Osceola," "The Capture of André," and "The Unfurling of the United States Flag in the City of Mexico" (presented to Andrew Jackson, and mentioned by him in his will). Among the more important of Mr. White's portraits are those of Col. Charles C. Pickney (owned by John W. Chandler, New York), Dr. Matthew O. Driscoll (owned by the Charleston Medical College), Hon. Keating Simmons, Josiah Smith, Edward R. Rutledge, South Carolina, and other prominent men.

Mr. White was also distinguished for his literary attainments, having written several successful dramas, essays, etc. He was regarded as the pioneer of Southern literature and art, and called by Tuckerman "the old American master."

White, Edwin, N. A. (*Am.*) (About 1817 – 1877.) He began to paint when not more than twelve years of age. Studied in Paris, Rome, Florence, and Düsseldorf, going abroad for that purpose in 1850 and '69. His works are largely historical in character. Among them may be mentioned, "Washington resigning his Commission" (purchased by the State of Maryland for $6,000, and now at Annapolis), "Washington reading the Burial Service over the Body of Braddock," "The Requiem of De Soto," "Pocahontas informing Smith of the Conspiracy of the Indians" (painted for General Kearney), "Age's Reverie" (belonging to the West Point Military Academy), "Luther's Vow," "The Death-Bed of Luther," "Milton's Visit to Galileo," "The Old Age of Milton" (bought by the Art Union), "Giotto sketching the Head of Dante," "The Evening Hymn of the Huguenot Refugees," "The First New England Thanksgiving," "The First Printing of the Bible," "Sabbath of the Emigrants," "Major Anderson raising the Flag at Fort Sumter," "Country Studio," "Fisher-Boy," "Strawberry-Girl," etc. By his will he left to the New York

Metropolitan Museum of Art "The Antiquary"; "Leonardo da Vinci and his Pupils" he bequeathed to Amherst College; and his last and unfinished work, "The Signing of the Compact on the Mayflower," to Yale College.

"White has good taste, pure sentiment, industry, and a correct intellectual apprecia- tion of historical subjects. There is, however, nothing great or original in his art, al- though as a whole it is truer and more effective than much of that of his German teachers, owing, perhaps, to his studies in Italy ; as a colorist he decidedly excels them." — Jarves, *Art Idea.*

"White's knowledge of art was very great, and he was an assiduous student. His aim was the illustration of historical subjects, and if he was not always successful none can dispute the earnestness of his effort." —*Art Journal,* August, 1877.

Whitehorne, James, N. A. (*Am.*) Born at Wallingford, Vt., 1803. He began the study of art about 1826, having no regular mas- ter, but receiving occasional instruction from Alexander Roberston, Colonel Trumbull, Professor Morse, and William Dunlap. When a student of the schools of the National Academy, in 1827, the silver medal for the best drawing from the antique was awarded him. He never had the advantage of foreign study. He was elected a full member of the National Academy in 1833, and has spent his pro- fessional life in the city of New York, painting in Washington, D. C., in the winters of 1844–46. He has devoted himself to por- trait-painting, executing perhaps a larger number of works of that kind than any other living American artist. His portrait of Silas Wright, now in the Governor's Room, City Hall, New York, taken after death, and under many difficulties, attracted much atten- tion when completed. He made the design for the mezzotint engrav- ing, "Henry Clay addressing the Senate," published by Anthony, Edwards & Co. about 1846, and well known throughout the United States.

Whittredge, Worthington, N. A. (*Am.*) Born in the State of Ohio, 1820. He followed mercantile pursuits in Cincinnati, but soon abandoned business for the profession of art. Was at first a portrait- painter in Cincinnati. In 1850 he went to Europe, studying in the galleries of London and Paris. In Düsseldorf he became a pupil of Andreas Achenbach, living in that city for three years. He studied, later, in Belgium and Holland, and went to Rome in 1855, remaining until he finally settled in New York, in 1859, being elected National Academician the same year. In 1866 he made a sketching-tour to the Far West of America, his "View of the Rocky Mountains from the River Platte," belonging to the Century Club, being one of the results of this trip. In 1874 he was elected President of the Acad- emy of Design, holding the office for three years. Among Whit- tredge's works are, "Trout Brook at Milford" (belonging to J. H. Sherwood, seen in the National Academy, 1869) ; "Trout Brook" (belonging to H. G. Marquand) ; and "Sangre di Christo Mountains, Colorado" (belonging to W. B. Shattuck) ; in 1870, "Evening on the Delaware " ; in 1871, " On the Hudson " ; in 1872, " A House by the Sea " and "Christmas Eve, Italy " ; in 1874, " The Camp-Meeting," " The Morning Stage," and " After the Rain " ; in 1875, " Autumn on the Delaware "; in 1876, " Morning in the Woods " and " Evening in the Woods " ; in 1877, "Paradise," Newport, R. I. " The Window," by Whittredge, belongs to R. L. Stuart ; " A Hundred Years Ago," to R. M. Olyphant ; " The Pilgrims of St. Roche," to W. B. Smith. His " Old Hunting-Ground," the property of J. W. Pinchot, and his " Rhode Island Coast," the property of A. M. Cozzens, were at the Paris Exposition of 1867. To the Paris Exposition of 1878 he sent "A Forest Brook " and " The Platte River."

" Whittredge is a progressive artist. He acquired with the dexterity some of the mannerism of the Düsseldorf school ; but constant and loving study of nature since he return from abroad has modified this habitude. He is more original, and applies his skill with deeper sentiment. Conscientiously devoted to his art, for manly fidelity to the simple verity of nature, no one of our painters is more consistently distinguished than Worthington Whittredge."—TUCKERMAN's *Book of the Artists.*

" Mr. Whittredge contributed his ' Rocky Mountains from the Platte River,' ' A House by the Sea,' ' A Hundred Years Ago,' ' Twilight on the Shawangunk Mountains,' and ' The Old Hunting-Grounds,'—the latter are especially admirable examples of his free nervous style, and of his felicitous treatment of wood interiors. Mr. Whittredge's pictures of forest solitudes, with their delicate intricacies of foliage, and the sifting down of feeble rays of light into depths of shade are always executed with rare skill and feeling. His style is well suited to this class of subjects ; it is loose, free, sketchy, void of all that is rigid and formal. It evinces a subtle sympathy with the suggestive and evanescent qualities of the landscape. But in his treatment of the open sky this artist is less happy. There is sometimes apparent a slight crudeness in his rendering of this feature of nature that is open to unfavorable criticism. His pictures, however, always express a sincere and true motive."—PROF. WEIR's *Official Report of the American Centennial Exhibition of* 1876.

Wichmann, Ludwig-Wilhelm. (*Ger.*) Born at Potsdam (1785 – 1859). Member of the Academies of Berlin and St. Luke at Rome. Member of the Institute of France. Pupil of Boye, Unger, and the painter Schadow. This sculptor made a reputation by his busts, which are numerous. He became Professor and Member of the Senate of the Academy of Berlin. Several groups executed by him are seen in public places in Berlin.

Wichmann, Otto Gottfried. (*Ger.*) Born at Berlin (1828 – 1858). Studied at Paris under Robert-Fleury. Went to Italy, where he died. At the National Gallery, Berlin, are his " Paul Veronese at Venice " and " Catherine de' Medici in the Apartment of a Poisoner."

Wieder, Wilhelm. (*Ger.*) Born at Sepnitz, 1818. Pupil of Otto at Berlin. Has spent much time in foreign countries, England, Russia, France, and Italy. Returned to Berlin in 1873. At the National Gallery, Berlin, is his " Mass at Ara Cœli at Rome."

Wiegmann, Marie Elisabeth (*née* **Hancke**). (*Ger.*) Born at Silberberg, 1826. She received the small gold medal at Berlin. Studied at Düsseldorf under Sohn. Paints *genre* subjects and portraits. At the National Gallery, Berlin, is her portrait of Karl

Schnasse. At Berlin, in 1876, she exhibited "A Venetian Lady," "A Young Girl with Roses," and "A French Woman of 1792."

Wight, Moses. (*Am.*) Born in Boston, 1827. He began the practice of art as a profession in 1845, in his native city, devoting himself chiefly to portrait-painting. In 1851 he went to Europe, spending three years in study on the Continent. During this visit he painted Von Humboldt from life, a picture which was highly praised and exhibited at the Grand Hall of the Art Union at Berlin. He made a second trip to Europe in 1860, and a third in 1865, settling in Paris, where he has since lived. Among the better known of his portraits are those of Agassiz, Sumner, Everett, and Josiah Quincy ; and among his composition pictures may be mentioned, "The Confidants," "Lisette," "The Sixteenth Century," "The Old Cuirassier," "Pet's First Cake," and "John Alden and Priscilla." Many of his works are owned in Boston. He has rarely exhibited in public of late years.

Wight, Peter B. (*Am.*) Born in New York, 1838. He studied architecture under Thomas R. Jackson, and furnished the designs for the New York Academy of Design in 1862. He is the architect of the Brooklyn Mercantile Library, the School of Fine Arts connected with Yale College, and other buildings, public and private, throughout the country, particularly in Chicago, where he resided for some years.

Wiles, Lemuel M. (*Am.*) Born in Wyoming County, N. Y., 1826. Between 1848 and '51 he studied under William Hart, in the Albany Academy, and under J. F. Cropsey in New York ; drawing later from nature, the only American school of painting available to the landscape-artist. He taught and worked at his profession in Washington, D. C., Albany, and Utica, N. Y., until 1864, when he opened a studio in the metropolis, where he still resides. In the year 1873 - 74 he went to Panama, California, and Colorado, where he executed a large number of painted studies, upon which he drew for his more ambitious works ; these are valuable as the only studies in color yet obtained of the old mission churches and cathedrals of those regions. He spends the summer months in Ingham, N. Y., delivering annually a course of lectures and conducting the drawing classes in the College of Fine Arts there. His specialty is landscape and figure-painting. Among the more important of his works are, "A Blustering Day" (storm with cattle, now in the possession of John C. Baker, near Montreal), "Mt. San Jacinto" (belonging to James L. Morgan of Brooklyn), "The Vale of Elms" (at Ingham University), "Reminiscences of Travel" (a miniature gallery of twenty-eight pictures, belonging to A. R. Frothingham of Brooklyn), "The Bridal Veil, Yosemite" (belonging to Mrs. E. J. Staunton, Le Roy, N. Y.), "Long Pond, Seneca Lake" (belonging to J. C. Lord, N. Y.), and "Moonrise" (the property of Cardinal McCloskey).

"L. M. Wiles exhibited several pictures ; among them was a large canvas giving a view of Washington, D. C., from the Soldiers' Home, and taking in its sweep a section of the city extending from Arlington Heights to the Navy Yard. Another fine subject was entitled 'A Snow-Squall,' which shows the figure of a woman carrying a baby, and a boy with his hands in his pockets plodding along, and apparently hurried by the cold wind. The figure of the woman is well drawn, and the action is admirable. This picture was very attractive." — *New York Evening Post.*

Wilkie, Sir David, R. A. (*Brit.*) Born in Fifeshire (1785 – 1841). Educated at the Trustees Academy in Edinburgh, and in the Royal Academy, London. He exhibited at the Royal Academy, London, for the first time, in 1806, " The Village Politician," a work which at once established his reputation. This was followed by " The Blind Fiddler," " The Card-Players," " Rent-Day," " Jew's-Harp," " Cut Finger," " Village Festival," " Rabbit on the Wall," " Penny Wedding," "Whisky Still," " Reading of the Will," "Parish Beadle," " Cotter's Saturday Night," etc., many of which are familiar to both hemispheres through the medium of engraving. He was elected an Associate of the Royal Academy in 1809, and Academician in 1811. He went to the Continent in 1825, spending three years there. Was made Painter in Ordinary to George IV. in 1830, and was knighted in 1836. He was also a member of the Royal Scottish Academy, and the King's Limner for Scotland. Many of his works are in the National Gallery, London. He stood in the first rank of his profession. He died on a vessel off Gibraltar and was buried at sea.

Willems, Florent. (*Belgian.*) Born at Liège, 1824. Officer of the Legion of Honor. Officer of the Order of Léopold. Pupil of the Academy of Malines. When very young he worked for a dealer in Brussels as a restorer of pictures. Before he was eighteen he found a friend and patron in Sir Hamilton Seymour, who commissioned him to paint the portraits of his wife and children. In 1842 he exhibited at Brussels " Le Corps-de-Garde " and the " Music-Lesson " (purchased by the late King of Belgium), and received a medal. From this time he gained a succession of medals, both at home and abroad. He sent to the Paris Exposition of 1855 " The Interior of a Silk-Mercer's Shop in 1660 " (purchased by Napoleon III.) and " Coquetry " (purchased by the Empress). In 1877 he exhibited " Aux armes de Flandre " ; in 1864, " L'Accouchée" and " Going Out " ; in 1863, " The Widow" and " The Presentation of the Future" ; in 1861, " Au Roi ! " At the Johnston sale, 1876, " The Reading " (26 by 21) sold for $ 1,975. At the Latham sale, New York, 1878, " No Song, no Supper " (24 by 19) sold for $ 1,150, and " Jealousy " (28 by 21), for $ 1,550. At the Walters Gallery is his picture of " The Health of the King."

"In that particular department of art to which Willems has almost entirely limited his practice, he certainly takes rank with the foremost men of the modern continental schools. His pictures are much in request, and find their way into the best collections, both in his own country and in France. Subjects of a character so generally pleasing, and placed with such artistic skill and such persuasive beauty on the canvas, can never fail of finding patrons in men of taste and judgment." — JAMES DAFFORNE, *Art Journal,* August, 1866.

"Men of taste have almost worn mourning for Willems. He made his début with a pretty picture representing a blond woman in a white satin dress ; an amateur fell in love with the woman and the dress, — a hundred others wished to place in their galleries the same woman and the same dress. The public who do not buy, but who judge, have ended by imagining that Willems exhibited always one and the same picture : they noticed it no more. Happily for us the commands have ceased, and the artist, who is, after all, an excellent painter, has felt the need of doing something else. His two pictures of this year [' L'Accouchée ' and ' La Sortie '] show a true advance. The artist has not only regained his commercial value but also a large part of his legitimate popularity. He paints well, he has good taste, he possesses a *faire miraculeux*, he knows to the end of his fingers the reign of Louis XIII. I should counsel him to vary the heads of his personages, and not to become captivated by such and such a model. It is little to paint well the frippery of an age : if Meissonier had stopped at that he would have been only a quarter of Meissonier." — EDMOND ABOUT, *Salon de* 1864.

Willenich, Michel. (*Fr.*) Born in Egypt of French parents. Pupil of G. Boulanger, J. Lefebvre, and Kuwasseg. To the Salon of 1878 he contributed " La passerelle de la plage de Granville (Manche), à marée haute " (in oil) and an engraving of the " Roadstead of Brest " ; in 1876, " The Transatlantic Steamer, La Ville de Paris, entering the Port of Havre in the Storm of October, 1875."

Williams, Penry. (*Brit.*) Born in Wales, 1798. Exhibited for the first time at the Royal Academy in 1824. Went to Italy in 1827, settling in Rome, where he has since resided, exhibiting, however, frequently in England, Italian landscapes and studies of Italian character, such as " The Campagna of Rome," " Ferry on the Nimfer," " The Procession to the Christening," " The Fountain," " The Convalescent," and others. His " Italian Girl with a Tambourine," " Italian Peasants resting by the Roadside," and " Neapolitan Peasants resting at a Fountain," are in the National Gallery, London.

Williams, Isaac L. (*Am.*) Born in Philadelphia, 1817. He studied drawing under John R. Smith, afterwards practicing painting with John Neagle in his native city, where his entire professional life has been spent, with the exception of a visit to Europe in 1866 - 67. He was elected a member of the Artists' Fund Society of Philadelphia in 1860, and a full member of the Philadelphia Academy in 1865. Until about 1844 he devoted himself exclusively to portrait-painting ; since then he has given equal or greater attention to landscapes, confining himself to moderate-sized cabinet pictures, which are owned in Philadelphia and elsewhere. His " October " and " View near Meriden, Ct." were at the Centennial Exhibition of 1876.

"Mr. Williams' pictures are generally in a low key, and they therefore frequently escape the notice of visitors to exhibitions or galleries filled with brighter-colored works. But carefully examined they will be found to better repay inspection than some performances that appear more striking at first sight. Mr. Williams excels in the rendition of the delicate pearly effects that are characteristic of some of the most poetical phases of nature." — *Philadelphia Evening Telegraph.*

Williams, Frederick D. (*Am.*) Born in Boston. He was at one time a professor of drawing in the public schools of Boston, but has lived for a number of years in Paris. He sent to the Paris Salon in 1878, " Farmyard at Finistère " and a scene at Pont Nien. He devotes himself to landscapes and figures, and has exhibited at the Boston Art Club, at the Academy, New York, and elsewhere. Many of his works are owned in his native city, where they meet with a ready sale. To the Paris Exposition of 1878 he sent " The Marne " ; to the Exhibition of the Society of American Artists, the same year, " The Shepherdess and her Flock."

Williams, Mrs. Frederick D. (*née* Lunt). (*Am.*) Born in Boston. Wife of the foregoing. She drew in crayon the " Past," " Present," and " Future," familiarly known throughout the United States by the lithograph copies, which are the same size as the originals. Since her marriage she has occupied a studio in Paris, with her husband, painting cattle and figure-pieces in oil.

Williamson, Daniel Alexander. (*Brit.*) Born in Liverpool, 1823. A landscape-painter in water-colors. He first exhibited at the Royal Academy in 1850, living for some years in London. About 1861 he left the metropolis, painting since then, to a great extent, in the open air. Among his works may be mentioned " Plowing " and " Broughton Moor."

Williamson, John, A. N. A. (*Am.*) Born in Scotland, 1826. Taken to America by his family. Resident of Brooklyn, L. I. Member of Brooklyn Art Association, and its secretary for some years. Associate of the National Academy, and member of the Artists' Fund Society. Among his earlier works are, " American Trout," " Trout-Fishing," " Summit of Chocorua, — Twilight," and " Autumn in the Adirondacks." In 1867 he sent to the National Academy, " The Hanging Hills from Wallingford, Ct." ; in 1869, " A Passing Shower, Connecticut Valley," and " Bread and Cheese " ; in 1870, " Hook Mountains, Hudson River " (belonging to William M. Tweed) ; in 1871, " The Return of the Hunters " ; in 1873, " A Reminiscence of Berkshire County " ; in 1874, " The Daniel Drew " and " The C. Vibbard " ; in 1876, " From Glenwood, Hudson River " ; in 1877, " After the Storm, Blue Ridge " ; in 1878, " In the Mohawk Valley " and " Sugar-Loaf Mountain."

Willis, Henry Brittan. (*Brit.*) Born in Bristol. Was a pupil of his father, a landscape-painter in his native town. The younger Willis, after painting for some years in Bristol, spent a year in America, but returned to England in 1843, and settled in London, where he still resides. He is an active member of the British Society of Painters in Water-Colors, and has contributed to its gallery of late years, among others, " Harvest-Time in the South of Sussex," " A Welsh Homestead," in 1872; " Sheep-Pastures near Ballachulish " and " Early Morning Effect on Ben Nevis," in 1873 ; " A Cloudy Day in the Highlands " and " Snow in Harvest," in 1875 ; " A Harvest Scene near Broadstairs, Kent," " Plowing-Time, Sussex," in 1877 ; " Group of Cattle near Burnham " and " A Scene on the Wye," in 1878. In 1861 he sent to the Royal Academy " A Rest on the Road to the Fair " and " Cattle on the Sands, North Wales," but his name has not been seen in the Royal Academy Catalogue since that year. Two of Willis' water-colors were at the Centennial Exhibition of 1876, " A Group of Cattle on the Banks of the Hamble " and " A Group of Highland Cattle in Glen Nevis," the latter belonging to the Marchioness of Lorne.

" ' Evening Effect on the Wye ' [London, 1877] is a very beautiful piece of cattle-painting and landscape by Brittan Willis, a little opaque and over-smooth, but full of light and color." — *Art Journal,* February, 1877.

Willmore, James T., A. R. A. (*Brit.*) (1800 – 1863.) He began his professional life in Birmingham under William Radcliffe, a well-known engraver there. About 1825 he went to London, working for some time with Charles Heath. He executed many plates after Turner, Eastlake, Landseer, and others, and his work is highly regarded by connoisseurs. He was an Associate of the Royal Academy for twenty years before his death.

Willmore, A. (*Brit.*) Native of Birmingham. Younger brother of James T. Willmore, A. R. A., with whom he was associated for some years. Among his plates are, " Agrippina landing the Ashes of Germanicus," after Turner ; " The Royal Volunteer Review, Edinburgh," after Samuel Bough ; " The Word of God," after H. L. Roberts ; " The Pleasant Walk," after J. C. Hook ; " Old Churchyard, Bettws-y-coed," after Creswick ; " A Calm Evening" and " A Squally Morning," after David Cox ; " Dutch Boats landing Fish," after E. W. Cooke ; " Wreck off Whitby," after E. Duncan; etc.

Wilmarth, Lemuel E., N. A. (*Am.*) Born in Massachusetts. In his youth he was a watchmaker in Philadelphia, studying art from life and the antique in the Academy of Fine Arts of that city. In 1859 he went to Munich, where he entered the Antique School, then under the direction of Kaulbach, remaining until his return to America in 1862. In 1864 he went to Paris, became an inmate of the atelier of Gérôme, and sent several important works to the National Academy, New York, " Sparking in the Olden Time," " Playing Two Games at Once," " Little Pitchers have Big Ears," " The Last Hours of Captain Nathan Hall," etc. In 1867 he returned to New York ; in 1868 he took charge of the schools of the Brooklyn Academy of Design, and in 1870 he was appointed Professor of the free schools of the National Academy, a position he held for some years. Wilmarth sent to the National Academy, in 1869, " The Home Missionary" ; in 1871, when he was elected Associate, " An Afternoon at Home " ; in 1873, " Guess what I 've brought you," a picture which insured his election as an Academician ; in 1874 he exhibited " Left in Charge " ; in 1875, " Ingratitude " ; in 1876, " There 's Music in all Things if Men have Ears " ; in 1877, " A Study of Peaches." His " Ingratitude " was at the Paris Exposition of 1878.

"Mr. Wilmarth is one of the most painstaking artists belonging to the National Academy. His historical pictures show deep thought and study in their composition; and every detail is worked out with conscientious care. His subjects relating to every-day life are generally invested with pleasing fancy, and their story is always plainly expressed. His style of coloring is brilliant, and in his manner of manipulation his pictures are suggestive of the French school in which he was educated, but suggestion in no wise impairs their individuality." — *Art Journal,* September, 1875.

Wilms, Peter Josef. (*Ger.*) Born at Bilk, near Düsseldorf, 1814. Studied at Düsseldorf Academy. In 1848 he went to Amsterdam and remained a year. At the National Gallery, Berlin, is a picture of "Still-Life" by Wilms.

Winne, Lievin de. (*Belgian.*) Born at Ghent. Chevalier of the Legion of Honor. Pupil of Devigne. At the Salon of 1877 he exhibited a portrait of "Leopold II. King of Belgium," belonging to the King of Belgium. In 1872 his portrait of Mr. Sanford, the American minister at Brussels, was much admired. This artist has painted many notable persons, and his pictures are characterized by simple elegance and agreeable color.

Winter, L. de. (*Dutch.*) At the Johnston sale, New York, 1876, "Moonlight on the Dutch Coast" (27 by 36) sold for $560.

Winter, Pharaon-Abdon-Léon de. (*Fr.*) Born at Bailleul. Pupil of Cabanel. To the Salon of 1878 he sent "An Old Woman in Prayer" and "The Return of the Hop-Picker, — Saturday Evening"; in 1877, a portrait and "Judith"; and in 1876, "The Prodigal Son."

Winterhalter, François Xavier. (*Ger.*) Born at Baden (1806–1873). Officer of the Legion of Honor. Studied at Munich and Rome, where he spent several years, and settled in Paris in 1834. He also traveled frequently, and visited Germany, England, and Spain, and left, wherever he went, numerous portraits. His *genre* pictures are not numerous, and he executed a few engravings and lithographs. He was a favorite portrait-painter in the circles of royalty and high life. His composition and arrangement of his pictures was very happy. Among his portraits are those of Louis Philippe and his Queen and all the members of the family of Orleans, Prince Wagram, Napoleon III. and the Empress Eugénie and their son, the Grand Duchess Helen of Russia, etc. A few days before his death this artist made his will, in which he desired that twelve pictures which he had allowed no one to see should not be given to the public until fifty years after his death. He did this in order that at last a judgment should be formed of him as an artist without the influence of personal prejudice. He says: "Many painters are praised to the skies during their lifetime, and yet several years after they have passed away few will care to look at the works they have left. Especially is this the case with those painters who enjoy the favor of kings and emperors. It is unjust that they should be made to suffer for it. To my own lot has it fallen to be treated with extreme kind-

ness by such exalted personages. Should I be on that account denied
the position in art for which I have striven so long and zealously ?"
The wishes of Winterhalter were disregarded ; the heirs obtained
leave from the court to open the boxes, and found a portrait of Prince
Clement Metternich, walking in his splendid garden at Johannisberg;
attached to it was a parchment with these words : "I painted this
portrait in 1858. I was so pleased with it that I resolved to keep it."
There were also two battle-scenes from the Austro-German war of
1866, both very spirited, four landscapes, three flower-pieces, a portrait of Pauline Viardot Garcia, of whom Winterhalter was an
admirer, and another of Queen Caroline of England, painted from a
miniature in the Art Museum at Brunswick. This last was painted
in 1869, and was much admired by those who were present at the
opening of these boxes ; it is a masterpiece. Of the landscapes, two
were views in the Isle of Wight, of which Winterhalter was very
fond. One of the remaining two was called "Stubbenkammer, on
the Island of Rügen"; the other, "The Tannus Valley."

"I take first of all the portrait of the Prince Imperial. Certainly Winterhalter ought
not to be considered as an ordinary artist ; the favor which he enjoys with the princes
of Europe and even with the good public should not be attributed to a universal mistake. Twenty-five or thirty millions of individuals do not agree upon the same foolish-
ness at the same moment. Winterhalter has talent ; he has proved it more than once ;
he excels often in rendering the elegance and brilliancy of a pretty woman. He knows
how to pose, to adjust, to dress magnificently certain models ; he has made some portraits which can bear comparison with Lawrence and all of the most aristocratic painting which England has produced ; but his exposition this year is below mediocrity. He
cannot throw the fault on his models. He had to paint a beautiful child whom all Paris
knows, whom nearly twenty thousand babies saw last Sunday in the garden with
his father and mother ; he has made of him a cold doll, without blood, the eye dimmed,
the physiognomy dull, badly adjusted ; moreover, no one walks in the costume of the
city with a musket, since the *bisets* are excluded from the National Guard. The other
portrait is not in the Salon of Honor. . . . . It is the crime of treason to beauty, no
more nor less. One is able, I believe, without being a flatterer to render justice to the
figure of a truly beautiful, elegant, and graceful woman. What above all distinguishes
the amiable model sacrificed by the brush of Winterhalter is an incredible fineness of
skin, a mother-of-pearl flesh, a general tone of exquisite delicacy. One thinks, in spite
of himself, of those goddesses of Homer who bled ambrosia when the sharp metal
grazed their delicate members. Correggio alone, or our Prud'hon, could express in
color this fine flower of feminine sweetness. Winterhalter has taken, I know not whence,
some tones of washed flesh. — rewashed and soaked in water. His picture is almost like
a painting on porcelain; it has not even the compensation of the freshness and the
smile of enamel." — EDMOND ABOUT, *Salon of* 1864.

Wintz, Guillaume. (*Prussian.*) Born at Cologne, naturalized
Frenchman. Pupil of A. Rolland. At the Paris Salon of 1878 he
exhibited "Troupeau de moutons rentrant par une barrière" and
"Cows in a Barnyard, in Lorraine"; in 1877, "A Flock of Sheep";
and in 1876, "A Pasture near Saint-Arnold, — Morning Effect."

Wislicenus, Hermann. (*Ger.*) Born at Eisenach, 1825. Studied
under Professor Müller and at the Dresden Academy. His first
work, "Abundance and Poverty," is in the Gallery of Dresden. The

Grand Duke of Saxony assisted him to go to Italy, where he remained from 1854 to '57. After his return he settled at Weimar until, in 1868, he was called as Professor to Düsseldorf. When the Academy there was burned Wislicenus lost a large part of the result of his life's labors. At the Roman House in Leipsic are some of his wall-paintings, illustrating scenes from Roman history. Some of his decorative works of a religious character are in the Castle Chapel of Weimar, and in other churches. At the National Gallery, Berlin, are his pictures of the "Four Seasons" ; in the Leipsic Museum are some of his sketches for his large works.

Witherington, William Frederick, R. A. (*Brit.*) (1785 – 1865.) Brought up to mercantile pursuits, but early displayed a taste for art, studying diligently in his leisure moments. He finally devoted himself to painting as a profession, and sent his first picture to the Royal Academy, "Going out in the Morning," in 1812, contributing regularly thereafter to its exhibitions for over forty years. He was elected an Associate of the Royal Academy in 1830, and Academician in 1840, and was placed on the list of Honorary Retired Academicians in 1863. Among his earlier works are, "The Soldier's Wife," "Don Quixote and Sancho Panza," "John Gilpin," and many views of English scenery. Among his later productions may be mentioned, "Gleaners Returning," "Resting by the Way," "Harvest-Time, — Noon," "Lynmouth, North Devon," "Harvesting in the Vale of Conway," "Stacking Hay, North Wales," "The Way to the Village," etc. His "Hop Garden" is in the Sheepshanks Collection ; the "Hop Garland" and "The Stepping-Stones" are in the National Gallery, London, bequeathed by Mr. Vernon.

Wittig, Hermann Friedrich. (*Ger.*) Born at Berlin, 1819. Studied at the Berlin Academy and under Tieck. Has visited Paris and Rome. Lives in Berlin. His works are numerous, both idèal subjects and portraits. At the National Gallery, Berlin, there is a group called "Germany protecting the Arts," executed by Wittig after a model by Schultz. In Berlin, in 1871, he exhibited "A Listening Nymph," and in 1876, "Mignon."

Wittig, Friedrich August. (*Ger.*) Born at Meissen, 1826. Member of the Academies of Düsseldorf and Carrara. Medals at Berlin and Vienna. Studied under E. Rietschel at Dresden. He has visited Rome. In 1864 he went to Düsseldorf to act as director of a school of sculpture. His subjects are mostly mythological, or taken from the Old Testament. He loves purely classical art, and endeavors to show this in his works. At the National Gallery, Berlin, are his "Hagar and Ishmael" and a colossal bust of "Peter Cornelius." Some of his works are in the Museum of Leipsic.

Wolf, Emil. (*Ger.*) Born at Berlin, 1802. President of the Academy of St. Luke at Rome. This sculptor studied under J. G. Schadow. He went to Rome in 1822, where he occupied the studio of Rudolf Schadow, and completed many of the works left unfinished at the death of that artist. Wolf is a follower of Thorwaldsen, but has also some traits like Gottfried Schadow. He affects representations of female beauty. At the National Gallery, Berlin, is his "Judith." At Berlin, in 1871, he exhibited, "A Young Roman Matron taking off her Jewels to give them for her Country."

Wood, John. (*Brit.*) (1801–1870.) Son of an artist, from whom he received his first lessons in drawing. He entered the schools of the Royal Academy in 1819, and exhibited his first picture, "Adam and Eve lamenting over the dead Body of Abel," in 1823. In 1825 he gained the Royal Academy gold medal for a picture called "Joseph expounding the Dreams of Pharaoh's Butler and Baker." Among his earlier works may be mentioned, "The Orphans," "The Dream of Endymion," "Elizabeth in the Tower after the Death of Queen Mary," etc. His later pictures were chiefly of a religious character.

Wood, George B., Jr. (*Am.*) Born in Philadelphia, 1832. His entire professional life has been spent in his native city. He was educated at the Pennsylvania Academy of Fine Arts, of which he is now an active member. He is also a member of the Artists' Fund Society of Philadelphia. Among his works may be mentioned, "Early Spring" (belonging to G. C. Thomas), "Freddy Flechtenstein's Shop" (belonging to D. Haddock, Jr.), the "Interior of G. W. Childs' Private Office" (belonging to Mr. Childs), "Interior of the Philadelphia Library" (belonging to George Whitney), and "The Hunter in Luck" (the property of Mr. Harrison).

"The subdued but rich colors which abound in this room [' Office of G. W. Childs '] have afforded the artist abundant opportunities for the employment of all the resources of his palette, and he has produced a picture which is highly interesting in itself, and apart from its subject. This is, in fact, one of the best of Mr. Wood's very excellent representations of interiors. It is painted with great conscientiousness throughout, and it has evidently had an immense amount of labor and skill expended upon it." — *Philadelphia Evening Telegraph,* December 21, 1877.

Wood, Marshall. (*Brit.*) This sculptor is a resident of London. He exhibits at the Royal Academy. His marble bust of a woman, called "The Song of the Shirt," was exhibited in Boston some years ago and sold there. It was considered as very characteristic of the English school. Of it, the "Gazette des Beaux-Arts" says, "The production of the English sculptor is finely featured, in truth, almost captivating. After a cry of anguish Marshall Wood has made a sweet ballad." Among his works of an ideal character are, "The Siren" (1871), "Hebe" (a group), and "Musidora" (1870). His statue of the Queen was unveiled in Victoria Square, Montreal, by Earl Dufferin. His "Nymph at the Bath" sold for 330 guineas. He has made several busts of the Prince of Wales. One of these, of colossal size, is in the Guildhall, London.

Wood, Thomas W., N. A. (*Am.*) Born at Montpelier, Vt.

Studied from nature in the neighborhood of his native city, and painted portraits there until 1857, when he went to Boston, entering the studio of Chester Harding. Here he remained but a few months, when he went to Paris and there opened a studio. He made short trips to Italy and Switzerland, and returned to America in 1860. He painted portraits in Louisville, Ky., and Nashville, Tenn., until 1867, when he settled in New York. He was made an Associate of the National Academy the same year, Academician in 1871, and was one of the early members of the Water-Color Society. In 1867 he sent to the National Academy, "The Sharp-Shooter," "The Recruit," "The Veteran," a series of war-sketches ; in 1868, "The Contraband Volunteer" and "Politics in the Workshop" ; in 1869, "The Country Doctor" (belonging to J. R. Osgood) ; in 1870, "Return of the Flag" ; in 1871, "Cogitation" (bought by Fletcher Harper) ; in 1874, "The Wood-Sawyer" ; in 1875, "The Weekly Paper" and "A Quiet Smoke" ; in 1876, "Truants" ; in 1877, "Sunday Morning" and "Grandma's Bonnet" ; in 1878, "Not a Drop too Much." To the Water-Color Exhibition of 1874 he sent "A Poor White" ; in 1875, "Nominated" and "Style" ; in 1876, "Shine," "Waiting for a Job," and "No Smoking Allowed" ; in 1877, "Arguing the Question" and "Hospitality" ; in 1878, "The Stolen Glance" and "Crossing the Ferry." "The Veteran," "The Recruit," and "The Contraband" (belonging to C. S. Smith), and "The Leader's Call" (in water-color) were at the International Exhibition at Philadelphia in 1876 ; and "The Veteran," "The Recruit," and "The Contraband," at the Paris Exposition of 1878.

"Wood's pictures of the different phases of war-life of the Southern negro during the Rebellion, cleverly executed, tell their own story and appeal to the popular taste." — TUCKERMAN'S *Book of the Artists.*

"As a colorist Wood is forcible, and as a delineator of character he never accepts the ideal, but goes direct to nature for his models. In the composition of a picture every object is clearly drawn, and he secures attention by the directness of his story." — *Art Journal,* April, 1876.

Woodington, William F., A. R. A. (*Brit.*) Born near Birmingham, 1806. At the age of twelve he was articled to Robert Lievier, engraver, under whom he studied drawing, etc. Later, when his master became a sculptor, Mr. Woodington also turned his attention to that branch of the art, studying from life at evening schools for years. At the age of fourteen he gained a silver medal from the Society of Arts, and he received a prize of £500 in the competition for the Wellington Monument after the death of that statesman. Mr. Woodington has spent his professional life in London, and has been an Associate of the Royal Academy since 1876.

· He executed bas-relievos for the Nelson Monument, in bronze ; bas-relievos, in marble, for the decoration of the chapel in St. Paul's Cathedral, in which the Wellington Monument is placed ; statue of James Steele, editor of the Carlisle Journal, now in Carlisle ; statues of Captain Cook, Sir Walter Raleigh, Columbus, Drake, Mercator, Galileo (each eight feet in height), and other sculptures for the Royal Exchange at Liverpool ; colossal bust of Paxton, at the Crystal Palace ; two statues of the Old Barons, for the House of Lords ; etc.

Woolner, Thomas, R. A. (*Brit.*) Born, 1825. Among the better known of his works are a statue of Macaulay, at Cambridge ; statues of the Prince Consort and Lord Bacon, at Oxford ; of Palmerston, Palace Yard ; William III., in the House of Parliament ; busts of Darwin, Tennyson, Cobden, Gladstone, Dickens, Carlyle, Charles Kingsley (in Westminster Abbey), and many more ; also, " Puck," " Love," " Death of Boadicea," " Constance and Arthur," " Virgilia," " Ophelia," " In Memoriam," " The Lord's Prayer," and other ideal works.

He was elected an Associate of the Royal Academy in 1871, Academician in 1874, and Professor of Sculpture in 1877.

" The sculptor among ourselves who has the best insight into the conditions and needs of his art is Woolner. He sends to the Royal Academy this year [1873] a remarkably fine statue, representing Dr. Whewell of Trinity College, Cambridge. The molding of the head is massive and grand ; the expression of the face individual without narrowness. With the force and intellect of a portrait, the whole composition would seem to take also something of ideal influence." — *Art Journal,* September, 1873.

" Mr. Woolner's portraits are alive and energetic (perhaps in some cases a little to excess). We see a mouth that will open, an eyelid whose upper line is not a boundary but a movable fold. In the eye of Tennyson there is rapt attention that more than sees. In Gladstone, with scholarly refinement, there is indomitable will ; and in Carlyle the poetry of introspection." — JOHN L. TUPPER, *in English Artists of the Present Day.*

Worms, Jules. (*Fr.*) Born at Paris, 1837. Chevalier of the Legion of Honor. Pupil of Lafosse. Made his début at the Salon of 1859. One of his first pictures foretold his success in the humorous vein. It was called " A Dragoon making Love to a Nursery-Maid on a Bench in the Place Royale." In 1861 he exhibited " Arrested for Debt." He afterwards traveled in Spain, and collected many sketches of the life, manners, and costumes there. The water-colors of this painter are much prized by amateurs. In 1877 he exhibited " The Fountain of the Bull at Granada " (belonging to Miss Wolfe of New York), " The Chosen Flower," and four water-colors (a portrait, " The Cage," " The Well," and " The Toilette of a little Danseuse ") ; in 1876, " The Dance of the Vito at Granada " (belonging to the late Mr. Stewart) and " The Departure·for the Review " ; in 1875, " Une nouvelle à sensation " and " A Vocation " ; in 1874, " The Horse-Jockey, Granada " and " The Little Cabinet-Maker " ; in 1873, " Une tante à succession " and a " Portrait of Mlle. Priston " ; in 1872, " The Shearers at Granada " ; in 1870, " The Sale of a Mule " and a " Letter-Box." At the Johnston sale his " Waiting at the Rendezvous " (16 by 12) sold for $ 400. His " Romance à la Mode " (1868) is in the Luxembourg.

Worth, Thomas. (*Am.*) Born in New York, in 1839. He studied drawing in the school of Mr. Wells in New York, and has spent his professional life in that city. He was first brought into public notice as a caricaturist in 1862, when he furnished the illustrations for a humorous work entitled "Plutarch Restored," published and edited by G. W. Nichols. Mr. Worth drew the pictures on stone, and the descriptive articles were written by John R. Brady, James T. Brady, and other distinguished men. During the past ten years he has made many comic designs for the periodicals of the Harpers and other publishing-houses, besides drawing designs of horses of a humorous character for colored lithographs. His more elaborate water-colors and pen-and-ink drawings are owned by Judge Brady, Judge Noah Davis, George Watson, David Leavitt, Jr., Fletcher Harper, Nathaniel Jarvis, and others.

" . . . . Is it not then time to say or do something about the hoary old historian Plutarch? Mr. T. Worth has thought it worth his while to do something ; and as he recognizes the power of the pencil rather than the pen, he has undertaken in 'Plutarch Restored' to illustrate the illustrious of Greece and Rome. He furthermore calls his book 'An Anachronatic Metempsychosis,' which sounds resonant and classical, even if it conveys no very definite meaning. . . . . The drawings of Mr. Worth prove that we have among us a caricaturist possessing abilities of no ordinary character. Mr. Worth's style is original. He imitates neither Cruikshank, Leech, nor Doré, and, indeed, the subject chosen is one which they have never taken up. While preserving in these sketches the old Grecian costumes, architecture, and 'properties,' Mr. Worth gives to his figures the faces and forms of the good folks of the present century, — and it is to this amusing incongruity that one of the great charms of the book exists. What can be more witty (wit, says Burnet, is an assimilation of remote ideas oddly or humorously collected) in the picture line, than the 'Guide of the Elephant' (No. 13), a figure in Roman dress, with the head of an Irishman, a shocking bad hat, a shillelah, and a pipa stuck in the belt ; or the slouchy street boys gazing at 'Theseus taking his Evening Walk' (No. 17), who, though in classic dress, are suggestive of Center street and the Five Points in face and form ? Excellent, too, is the 'Frightened Senator' (in No. 14), seated before the Senate in a rocking-chair, his spectacles pushed up on his forehead and an old-fashioned black stock encircling his neck. Perhaps the best picture in the book is, however, that of Pelopidas in prison, — the very picture of abject seediness. Alcibiades (the text tells us he was a military man descended from the Telemonian Ajax, one of whose latest descendants was Andrew Jackson, — a modern refinement upon Ajax Son) looks like Barili the singer ; and, indeed, this artist seems to have copied not a few of his characters from the style of the Academy of Music." — *New York Evening Post,* April 12, 1862.

Wright, Rufus. (*Am.*) Born near Cleveland, O., in 1832. He received his art education in the schools of the National Academy, New York, and was for some time a pupil of George A. Baker. His professional life has been spent in New York, Washington, D. C., and Brooklyn. In 1866 he was made a member of the Brooklyn Academy of Design, and was for five or six years a teacher in its schools. Among the more important of his portraits are those of Chief Justice Taney and Chief Clerk Carrol, of Secretary Stanton, Secretary Seward, Father McGinn, Colonel Isaac H. Read, late President of the Produce Exchange, New York, etc. He turned his attention to the painting of composition pictures in 1875 or '76, exhibiting at the National Academy in New York in 1876, "The Morning Bouquet" and " The Inventor and the Bánker " ; in 1877, " Thank you, Sir ! "; in 1878, " Concerned for his Sole."

" ' The Inventor end the Banker ' is a strong composition, and one which not only shows thought, bnt also high artistic genius." — *Art Journal*, May, 1876.

Wright, F. H. (*Am.*) Born in South Weymouth, Mass., 1849. Studied in Paris for some time under T. L. Bonnat, Chapu, Boulanger, and Lefebvre. His professional life has been spent in Boston, where his portraits are popular and are generally owned.

Wyant, A. H., N. A. (*Am.*) Born in Ohio, 1839. Early manifested a taste for art, and began his professional career as a landscape-painter in Cincinnati. He spent some years in Düsseldorf, where he studied under Hans Gude ; subsequently he studied in London, and returned to America, settling in New York in 1864 or '65. His first picture, exhibited in New York, " A View of the Valley of the Ohio River," was at the National Academy in 1865. He was elected an Associate in 1868, Academician in 1869, and was one of the early members of the American Society of Painters in Water-Colors. Among his pictures in oil are, " Staten Island from the Jersey Meadows," in 1867 ; " Scene on the Upper Susquehanna," in 1869 ; " The Bird's-Nest" and " A Changeful Day," in 1870 ; " Shore of Lake Champlain " and " A Pool on the Ausable," in 1871 ; " Fort at New Bedford," in 1874 ; " A View on Lake George " and " A Midsummer Retreat," in 1875 ; " Macgillicuddy's Reeks " and " The Wilds of the Adirondacks," in 1876 ; " An Old Clearing," in 1877; " An Old Road,— Evening," and " Pool in the North Woods." To the Water-Color Exhibition he contributed, in 1867, " Scene on the Upper Little Miami " ; in 1869, " A Reminiscence of West Virginia " and " Trees and Stuff in New Jersey " ; in 1870, " New Jersey Meadows " ; in 1872, " Gathering Shells " ; in 1876, " Late Autumn, Ausable River " ; in 1877, " Scene in Massachusetts " and " An Irish Lake Scene " ; in 1878, " Reminiscences of the Connecticut," " Mountains in Kerry," and others. His " Sunset on the Prairie," in water-color (belonging to R. M. Schuyler), was in the Philadelphia Exhibition of 1876. His " Reminiscence of the Connecticut," in water-colors, and " New England Landscape," in oil, were at the Paris Exposition of 1878.

" As a painter of the wild and rugged scenery of the northern wilderness of New York, Wyant has but few equals in the Academic ranks." — *Art Journal*, December, 1876.

Wyatt, Sir Matthew Digby. (*Brit.*) Born in Wiltshire (1820 – 1877). A pupil at the Royal Academy, and subsequently of several Continental Academies. His first important work as an architect was the Crystal Palace in London in 1851, and in 1852 to '54 he was superintendent of the decorations and Fine Art Department of the same building on its erection in Sydenham. In 1856 he received the appointment of Surveyor to the British East India Company, furnishing the designs for many fine structures in India and in Great Britain. He was knighted in 1869. Among the more important works published by him are, "The Industrial Arts of the Nineteenth Century" (1851), "Art Treasures of the United Kingdom" (1857), "Fine Art" (1870), "An Architect's Note-Book in Spain" (1872). In 1869 he was appointed Slade Professor of Fine Arts at the Cambridge University.

Wyburd, Francis John. (*Brit.*) Born in London, 1826. Educated at Lille, France. On his return to England he was placed as a pupil with the late Thomas Fairland, a clever lithographic artist. In 1845 Wyburd received a silver medal from the Society of Arts for a drawing, and in 1848 he entered the schools of the Royal Academy, exhibiting for the first time at the Royal Academy the next year. In 1853 he sent "Beatrice," a small study which was highly praised. Among his other works may be mentioned, "Lalla Rookh," "The Kiosk" (painted for the Glasgow Art Union), "Hinda," "Amy Robsart and Janet Forster," "The Convent Shrine" (at the British Institution in 1862), "Immortelles" (painted for the Duchess of Cambridge, exhibited at the Royal Academy in 1862, and subsequently engraved). In 1863 he sent to the Royal Academy, "Christmas Time"; in 1864, "The Offering" and "The Private View"; in 1865, "The Church Door"; in 1867, "The Last Day in the Old Room"; in 1868, "The Confessional"; in 1869, "The Birthday Visit"; in 1872, "The Harem"; in 1874, "Nadira"; in 1875, "Breakfast-Time"; in 1876, "Life in the Old Manor-House."

"The characteristics of Wyburd's art are principally a perfect realization of female beauty, an attractive manner in setting out his figures, and a refinement of finish which is sometimes carried almost to excess." — *Art Journal*, June, 1877.

Wylie, Robert. (*Am.*) Native of the Isle of Man. Taken to America by his parents when a child. Died in Brittany, 1877, aged about forty years. He began his art studies in the Pennsylvania Academy of Fine Arts. Was a carver of ivory, but soon turned his attention to painting, and went to Europe in 1865. In the Paris Salon of 1869 he exhibited his "Reading the Letter from the Bridegroom," and received a medal for his "Breton Fortune-Teller" in the Salon of 1872. His works were little known in America.

"Wylie was one of the most brilliant members of the American Colony of Artists in Paris. Nearly all of his pictures represent peasant-women and rustic scenes, and there is a truthfulness shown that is in the highest degree interesting." — *Art Journal*, April, 1877.

"The characteristic of Wylie's genius was his strength. The slightest sketch from his pencil shows a vigorous and intelligent grasp of the subject. . . . . He transferred to canvas the life that was around him, the Breton peasant, the fisherwoman, the sturdy toilers of the sea and of the shore. His coloring and his style were all his own." — LUCY HOOPER, *Paris Letter*, March, 1878.

Wyllie, W. L. (*Brit.*) Born in London, 1851. He studied art in the Royal Academy, London, gaining in 1869 the Turner gold medal for landscape-painting. He has a studio in London, but spends much of his time upon the sea, making marine and coast views a specialty, and introducing frequently the figures of sailors and fishermen. He is a member of the Society of British Artists, exhibiting there and at the Royal Academy. Among his works are, "Northern Lights," "Tracking in Holland," "The Silent Highway," "Summer Clouds," "At the 'Good Intent,'" "A Dutch Canal," etc. To the Paris Exposition of 1878 he contributed "Sea-Birds."

"W. L. Wyllie has made a study of a wreck on the Goodwin Sands [R. A., 1874]. About a large ship stranded in calm weather the sea-birds are flying. The surface of the water just ripples with a fresh breeze, and across a stormy sky the bright tints of a rainbow pass and lighten the scene. Mr. Wyllie gives always a very genuine impression of reality to his sea-pictures." — *Art Journal*, August, 1874.

Wynfield, David W. (*Brit.*) Born, 1837. Grand nephew of Sir David Wilkie. Studied for the Church, but finally entered the studio of T. M. Leigh in 1856, devoting himself generally to historical subjects and such as are of a tragic nature. He first exhibited in 1859. In 1863 he sent to the Royal Academy, "The Meeting of Edward IV. and Elizabeth Woodville"; in 1864, "The Rival Queens"; in 1865, "The Last Days of Elizabeth"; in 1867, "The Death of Cromwell"; and in 1872, "Murdered Buckingham." Among his works of a less somber character are, "The Rich Widow" and "My Lady's Boudoir," in 1869; and "Round the Fountain" and "Confidences," in 1871. In 1872 he exhibited "The Arrest of Anne Boleyn"; in 1873, "The Ladye's Knight"; in 1874, "Instructions in Deportment" and "The Visit from the Inquisitors"; in 1875, "At·last, Mother!" and "Queen Elizabeth and Essex"; in 1876, "The New Curate" and "Market Morning"; in 1877, "Harvest Decorations," "The Discovery of Gold in Australia," and "David playing before Saul"; in 1878, "Sunny Hours" and "Joseph making himself known to his Brethren." His "New Curate" and "Death of Buckingham" were at Paris in 1878.

"The technical characteristics of Mr. Wynfield indicate carefulness and completeness of finish carried throughout the work, but with due subordination determined by the relative importance of objects ; great attention to correctness of costume and conformity to the best authority in faces and all other facts ; an absence of all bravado or display of skill in the manner of painting, leading sometimes into the vice of over-labor and heaviness of hand resulting in opacity. For the rest his work is solid and simple, and seems to stand well." — TOM TAYLOR, *in English Artists of the Present Day.*

"There is no elaborateness of beautiful detail, no trace of the rich symbolism which characterizes the true. Good sound workmanship the picture ['The Ladye's Knight,' R. A., 1873] does contain, however, and sufficient mastery of expression to render the scene intelligible and interesting. The color, as is usual with this painter, fails of brilliancy, but it is consistent throughout with a quiet and sober effect." — *Art Journal*, August, 1873.

Xylander, W. (*Ger.*) Of Schleissheim. Medal at Philadelphia, where he exhibited "The Mouth of the Thames," which was especially commended.

Yarz, Edmond. (*Fr.*) Born at Toulouse. At the Paris Salon of 1878 he exhibited "Vignes, aux environs de Toulouse" and "La berge du guichet du Louvre"; in 1876, "Under the Apple-Trees" (belonging to M. Aignette) and "A Cross-Road."

Yeames, William Frederick, R. A. (*Brit.*) Born in Southern Russia in 1835. He was educated in Dresden from 1843 to '48, when he went with his family to London. In 1849 he began the study of drawing, attending the anatomical classes of the University of London, and went to Florence in 1852, studying art and painting there for two years; he then spent some time in Rome, and settled finally in London in 1858. He first exhibited in the Royal Academy, in 1859, "The Stanch Friend." In 1860 he sent the "Trystinge House" to the British Institution. In 1861 he had, at the Royal Academy, "Sonnetto" and "The Toilette"; in 1862, "Rescued"; in 1863, "The Meeting of Sir Thomas More and his Daughter"; in 1864, "Arming the Young Knight" and "La reine malheureuse." In 1867, when he was elected an Associate of the Royal Academy, he exhibited "The Dawn of the Reformation" and "Bread and Water"; in 1868, "The Chimney-Corner"; in 1869, "The Fugitive Jacobite"; in 1870, "Maundy Thursday" and "Love's Young Dream"; in 1871, "Dr. Harvey and the Children of Charles I."; in 1872, "Old Parishioner" and "A Rest by the River-Side"; in 1873, "The Path of Roses" and "Pleading the Old Cause"; in 1874, "Flowers for Hall and Bower"; in 1875, "The Suitor"; in 1876, "The Last Bit of Scandal"; in 1877, "Waking," "Amy Robsart," and "The Fair Royalist" (a pastel study); in 1878, when he was elected Academician, "When did you last see your Father?" To Paris, in 1878, he sent several works.

"In this carefully studied work ['The Meeting of Sir Thomas More and his Daughter,' R. A., 1863] the attendant figures, sympathizing with or officially indifferent to the pathos of the situation, are more satisfactory than the daughter. More himself, however, is well imagined, although the expression of his features might have been strengthened." — PALGRAVE'S *Essays on Art,* 1863.

"Yeames is a conscientious and earnest artist; his gravity of conception and sobriety of style he owes mainly no doubt to his character and temperament, but it has been strengthened by his art education, the best part of which was carried on in Florence." — TOM TAYLOR, *in English Artists of the Present Day,* 1877.

"Considering how much of Yeames' art education was received in continental schools, one is surprised to see so little of foreign influence in his pictures. His subjects are essentially English, and his mode of treating them is generally analogous to that practiced in our own school. He is an earnest, intelligent, vigorous, yet painstaking artist, whose works merit the favor they receive from our best collectors." — *Art Journal,* April, 1874.

Yelland, R. D. (*Am.*) Born in London in 1848. He has lived in America since 1851, spending his professional life in New York and San Francisco, where his studio now is. He studied in the schools of the National Academy, and under William Page, L. E. Wilmarth, and J. R. Brevoort. He was elected an Associate of the San Francisco Art Association in 1874, and Assistant Director of the California School of Design in 1877. He devotes himself to landscapes and coast scenery; among his more important works being "Seal Rocks, Golden Gate, California" and "Half-Moon Beach, Gloucester Harbor, Mass.," both owned in San Francisco.

Yewell, George H., A. N. A. (*Am.*) American painter, living for some years in Rome. He studied in New York under Thomas Hicks, and in Paris under Couture. He is an Associate of the National Academy of Design. His works rarely come to America. He sent, however, to the National Academy, "Venice," in 1871 ; "A Country Girl," in 1872 ; and "The Interior of St. Mark's, Venice" and "The Interior of the Ducal Palace, — Senate Chamber," in 1877. His "Carpet Bazaar, Cairo" and "Mosque of Kait-Bey, Cairo" were at the Paris Exposition of 1878.

"Yewell paints landscapes and interiors; the latter with great fidelity and accuracy." — MRS. TYTLER's *Modern Painters.*

"In Yewell's 'First Communion' the architectural details of the church and the surrounding houses are painted with elaborate care." — TUCKERMAN's *Book of the Artists.*

"'The Senate Chamber in the Ducal Palace, Venice' is a large and brilliant example of Yewell's work. The architectural drawing is admirable, and every detail of pictorial ornamentation, for which the palace is so famous, is painted with conscientiousness and force." — *Art Journal,* June, 1875.

Yon, Edmond-Charles. (*Fr.*) Born at Paris. Medals (for painting) in 1875, (for engraving on wood) '74 and '72. He exhibited at the Salon of 1878 (in oils), "A Little Branch of the Marne, at Isle-lès-Villenoy" and "Avant la pluie" ; in 1877, "Le Morin, à Villiers" and "Le Bas-de-Villiers" ; in 1876, "A Summer Day" and "The Seine, near Gravon" ; in 1875, "A Branch of the Seine" and "Le Petit-Flot," two views near Montereau. Among his engravings are, "La carte à payer," after Leroux ; "The Fountain of Poul-Goïn," after Anastasi ; "La gardeuse d'oies," after F. Millet ; and a very large number after his own pictures and designs.

Young, James Harvey. (*Am.*) Born in Salem, Mass., 1830. He studied under John Pope, a portrait-painter of Boston, and at the age of fourteen opened a studio of his own in that city, painting portraits at five dollars each. After an experience of a few years in mercantile pursuits, he became a professional artist in Boston in 1858, where he has since lived. He devotes himself to portrait-painting, but seldom exhibits in public. He was for some years a member of the Boston Art Club, and from 1861 to '71 was Director of the Fine Art Exhibitions at the Boston Museum. Among his better known works are portraits of Edward Everett (belonging to Mrs. E. B. Everett), William Warren, W. H. Prescott and Horace Mann (in the Salem Normal School), Ellsworth and Brownell (belonging to the Salem Independent Cadets), General Townsend (Soldiers' Home, near Washington), Thatcher Magoun (for the town of Medford), Barnas Sears, Professor Whitney (in the Newton Theological Seminary), several of the Secretaries of State of the United States (now in the State Department, Washington), and of many private individuals. Mrs. George Livermore of Cambridge owns a half-length cabinet-sized portrait of Everett, and a head of the same statesman is in the Boston Public Library.

Young, Harvey. (*Am.*) A native of Vermont. He studied in Paris under Carolus Duran, sending to the Salon of 1878 "Spring" and "The Environs of Greg." His specialty is landscapes, and he has painted many scenes in California, where part of his professional life has been spent.

Yvon, Adolphe. (*Fr.*) Born at Eschwiller, 1817. Officer of the Legion of Honor. Pupil of Paul Delaroche. This painter made his début at the Salon of 1842, when he exhibited his portrait of Mme. Ancelot. The next year he went to Russia, and from there sent several pictures to the Salons. He received his first medal in 1848, and gradually ascended the scale of honors until, in 1867, he was made an Officer of the Legion of Honor. He was the only artist sent officially to the Crimea, and his picture of the "Taking of the Tower of Malakoff" (seen at the Exposition of 1867) holds an honorable place among the representations of modern battles in the Gallery at Versailles. His principal works are, "Portrait of General Neumayer" (1844) ; "The Remorse of Judas" (1846) ; "Battle of Koulikowo" (1850); "A Fallen Angel" (1852); "The First Consul descending the Alps" (1853), at the palace of Compiègne; "Marshal Ney supporting the Rear-Guard in Russia" and "The Seven Capital Scenes," illustrations of Dante (1855) ; "Battle of Solferino" and a "Portrait of the Prince Imperial" (1861); "The United States of America" (1870), an allegorical picture, purchased by the late Mr. Stewart of New York ; "A Street in Constantinople" and "Secrets of State" (1873) ; "Portrait of the Countess of Caen" (1875) ; and several portraits in 1876 and '77.

"His [Yvon's] pictures are full of movement, and the painting is sober and straightforward, quite free from every kind of affectation ; it has, however, very little interest derived from intellect or feeling." — HAMERTON's *Contemporary French Painters.*

"Another series of cartoons, in a grand style of model drawing, and daring in the vigor of their design, is Rage, Lust, Avarice, Gluttony, Envy, Idleness, and Pride, after Dante, by M. Yvon. The same artist's enormous oil-picture of 'Marshal Ney heading the Rear-Guard of the Grand Army in the Retreat from Russia' is one of those nightmare displays of physical energy and horror which the French painters affect, and in which the Englishman scarcely knows whether most to wonder at the display of force or reprobate the unalloyed and valueless monstrosity." — WILLIAM MICHAEL ROSSETTI, *Fine Art, chiefly Contemporary,* 1867.

Zacharie, Philippe-Ernest. (*Fr.*) Born at Radepont. Pupil of M. G. Morin. At the Salon of 1878 he exhibited "The Good Samaritan" ; in 1877, "The Punishment of Caiaphas" and "The Young Amateur" ; in 1876, "The Evening of the Epiphany" and "Field-Flowers" ; and in 1875, "Un vieux bouquiniste."

Zamacoïs, Édouard. (*Span.*) Born at Bilboa (about 1840 – 1871). Medal at Paris, 1867. Pupil of Meissonier. Made his début at the Salon of 1863, with the "Enlisting of Cervantes" and "Diderot and D'Alembert." In 1864 he exhibited "Conscripts in Spain" ; in 1866, "The Entrance of the Toreros" (painted in part by Vibert) and "The First Sword"; iñ 1867, "A Buffoon of the Sixteenth Century," "Indirect Contribution" (purchased by Mr. Matthews), and a water-color of "A Jester of the Sixteenth Century"; in 1868, "The Favorite of the King" (purchased by Mr. Stewart) and the "Refectory of the Trinitaires at Rome"; in 1869, "The Entrance to the Convent" (being a monk urging on an obstinate ass, loaded with provisions) and "A Good Pastor" (a priest in the confessional giving indulgences to the pretty girls kneeling about him, to the disgust of an ugly one near by); in 1870, "Platonic Love" (a negro making a declaration to the marble bust of a woman) and "The Education of a Prince" (which represents a Spanish prince of three years seated on a rug, playing with toy soldiers, while the king, cardinal, bishop, and priests, with the courtiers, look on admiringly). A "Figure" by this painter is in the collection of Mrs. H. E. Maynard of Boston. At the Johnston sale, New York, 1876, "The Puzzled Musician" (6 by 5) sold for $ 900, "The Two Confessors" (18 by 25) for $ 6,500, and a water-color, "Waiting at the Church Porch" (14 by 10), for $ 900. Mr. Walters of Baltimore has a good picture by Zamacoïs, which he purchased from the widow of the artist. Mr. H. P. Kidder of Boston owns his "Faust and Marguerite."

"This picture ['The Education of a Prince'] of Zamacoïs is a painted recitation, a page of memory taking on bustle and life. His keen, expressive brush is brilliant without false glitter; a mocker without grimace, it traces characters as would the pen of the most skillful chronicler. The spirit of touch, sharpened by the spirit of observation, could not speak better, or better represent itself." — PAUL DE SAINT-VICTOR, *in Dictionnaire Universel* (LAROUSSE).

"Of the recent men in French art who have distinguished themselves by novelty of subject and elaboration of manner, Zamacoïs is not the least noteworthy; he, in fact, holds the attention best, and, with Vibert, excites the most lively interest among amateurs of painting. Vibert and Zamacoïs are to the Parisian picture-fanciers, to-day, what Meissonier and Gérôme were yesterday, — the novelty and the perfection of art. If one can reproach Meissonier with a want of wit, if one can assert unrebuked that his carefully wrought casket is empty, or at best holds trivial stuff, such is not the reproach one can make to Zamacoïs. Zamacoïs, with a manner almost as perfect as Meissonier's, is a satirist; he is a man of wit, whose means of expression is comparable to a jeweled and dazzling weapon, — so much so that, to express his rich and intense color, his polished style, he has been said to embroider his coarse canvas with pearls, diamonds, and emeralds. I should suggest the form and substance of his works as a painter, by saying that he has done what Browning did as a poet when he wrote the 'Soliloquy of the Spanish Cloister'; what Victor Hugo has done in portraying dwarfs and hunchbacks; but with this difference, that what is *en grand* and awful in Hugo is small, elaborated, and amusing in Zamacoïs. Zamacoïs seeks his subjects in the sixteenth and seventeenth centuries, and in the life of monks and friars and priests in modern Italy. It is manifest that Zamacoïs admires Molière, that he appreciates the picturesque side of Victor Hugo's genius. He may be said to enamel the hardy creations of the poet of the incongruous, and to reduce them in a style so delicate and precious that one's admiration and curiosity are in amiable conflict over the novelty of the subject and the perfection of the representation. For it was novel to see a group of hunchbacks and dwarfs in the antechamber of a king, all clad in sheeny vesture, intense of hue like the plumage of tropical birds, in clear and glowing colors like carbuncles and emeralds and rubies, and rendered in a manner fine and elaborate enough to represent

16 *   x

the white skin, and pretty round arms, and perfect hands of the Marquise de Pompadour; it was a novelty to see a group of deformed beings, painted with as much care and clothed with as much splendor as a group of fair women. The pictures of Zamacoïs had the attraction of the *bizarre* and the perfect. The picturesque, the grotesque, the elaborate, all in one frame; this was more than the severe Gérôme gave in his studied sensualities, more than the dry and prosaic Meissonier gave in his studies of costume and character. . . . . Zamacoïs may be said to understand art not as a grand and noble means of expression, but as a fine and perfect and precious expression. He does with form and color what Tennyson does with words, — that is to say, he combines them in a studied and jeweled style, to express his pleasure in intense and brilliant things. But the French painter has wit, and no one would accuse Tennyson of that Gallic trait. Therefore, to make you acquainted with Zamacoïs, I must say he has a suspicion of malice that must be delightful to the compatriote of Voltaire, that he is bold and positive in his conceptions, and fine and elaborate in his expressions. But he is a painter of character rather than a creator of the beautiful; he is a comic artist and not an idealist; he puts a farce before your eyes in a setting of jewels. Zamacoïs is kindred to Molière. If you could suppose something of Molière's genius embodied in a series of sonnets, you would have a just literary expression of Zamacoïs as a painter. One is surprised to find so much of the comic in a style so finished and brilliant, and it is this which is the distinction of Zamacoïs; it is this which separates him from a crowd of skillful and talented French painters of *genre*. The purity and intensity of his color, of which I have spoken, are so remarkable that they suffice to distinguish him from all his contemporaries, and even make him the superior of Vibert. . . . . Such art as Zamacoïs' comes very close to a cultivated man without placing in his mind one suggestion of the noble or the beautiful. In this respect it is contemporary, and far from Greek sculpture and Italian painting. Instead of the ideal, it gives the exquisite; instead of the noble the comical. It is the difference between a comedy of Molière and a tragedy of Euripides. We enjoy the comedy; it gratifies our curiosity, — the most universal passion; but we are impressed by the tragedy; it holds our imagination brooding over the despotic and fatal evolution of human passion. I prefer the pagan idea of art to the latest contemporary French idea of art, as illustrated by Zamacoïs, because I prefer Medea to Tartuffe. It may be said of Zamacoïs, that he has been more successful in treating seventeenth-century subjects than the more widely celebrated Gérôme, who has repeatedly sought to pluck artistic honors from the contemporaries of Molière." — EUGENE BENSON, *Art Journal,* 1869.

Zetterström, Mme. M. (*Swede.*) Born at Gèfle. Pupil of the Academie des Beaux-Arts of Stockholm. At the Salon of 1878 she exhibited "A Prelude" and "A Swedish Peasant-Woman"; in 1877, "A Swedish Song"; in 1876, "Une visite en passant, — intérieur laponais"; and in 1875, "A Lapland Interior."

Zezzos, Alessandro. (*Ital.*) Pupil of the Academy of Venice. This artist sent to the Paris Exposition, 1878, "The Pigeons of Saint Mark," and to the Paris Salon, same year, "El-Mazrama (mouchoir du Sultan)"; and in 1877, "Les saltimbanques" and "A Venetian, — a Daughter of the People."

Ziem, Felix. (*Fr.*) Born at Beaune, about 1822. Chevalier of the Legion of Honor. Studied in Paris. Traveled in the East, and made his début at the Salon of 1849. His "View of Venice" (1852) is in the Luxembourg; "Evening at Venice" (1854) was purchased by the Duke de Morny; "View of Antwerp" (1855) was purchased by the government. In 1868 he exhibited "Venice, — a Party of Pleasure" and "Marseilles, — View at the Old Port"; in 1867, "The

Bucentaur adorned for the Ceremony of the Marriage of the Doge with the Adriatic, Venice, 1426," and "Carmagnola, accused of High Treason by the Venetians and beheaded under the Lion of St. Mark, Venice, 1422"; in 1866, "Venice, — a September Evening after a Rain" and "Constantinople,—Setting Sun." Ziem repeats his subjects over and over again. He has made some sketches, water-colors, fruit-pieces, etc. At the Johnston sale, "Venice at Sunset, — Entrance to the Grand Canal," from the Wolfe sale (27 by 42), sold for $1,510. At the Norzy sale, Paris, 1860, "View of the Grand Canal" sold for 3,880 francs. At the Laurent-Richard sale, Paris, 1873, "Stamboul" and "Venice" sold for £480 each. At the Corcoran Gallery is "Constantinople from the Golden Horn," 1874.

"Ziem is obliged to conceal the insufficiency of his design in an agreeable vapor. He has grace without firmness : his earth and his monuments undulate in the wave ; he has never known how to fix a silhouette. His pictures are like some of the works of Isabey the *chatoyant*, a little strengthened and refined by the example of Canaletto. It is not that Ziem is a mediocre artist. He excels in mirroring the most brilliant colors in a canal.

> 'Le moindre vent qui d'aventure
> Fait rider la face de l'eau '

('The least wind which perchance ruffles the face of the water') furnishes a delicious matter for his brush. His marines give us that delectable little shivering with which we are seized when we step on a boat. But Ziem would give us more durable and deeper pleasures if he would design only like Jayant." — EDMOND ABOUT, *Nos Artistes au Salon de* 1857.

"Among the artist travelers who have known how to conquer public favor, Ziem occupies a place apart. He sees with indifference the rocks, the plains, or the forests, and is arrested by choice in the great maritime cities which mirror in the water their edifices gilded by the sun of the South. He is a painter of architecture as well as a painter of marines, who willingly takes a siesta at noonday, and wishes to see nature only as twilight approaches. The two pictures in the Laurent-Richard Collection are among his most important works, and are sufficient to justify the rank which he holds in art.

"Here is Constantinople unrolling itself in an amphitheater, while the sun appears like a brilliant disc which is reflected in the waters of the Bosphorus, and bathes in a luminous vapor the domes and minarets of the great city. On one side we see the point of the Seraglio, the ancient kiosque of the Janissaries, the mosque of Bajazet, and the great walls which inclose the Golden Horn. On the other hand, we catch a glimpse of the coast of Asia and the first buildings in Scutari. A white sail, and some long-boats manned with rowers, lose themselves on a ruddy beach in the first plane.

"Lost in the midst of the lagunes of the Adriatic, Venice, the city of enchantments, so dear to poets and travelers, has such a fascination for Ziem, that in contemporaneous art it has become a sort of monopoly for his talent, so much so that one experiences an involuntary astonishment upon seeing a view of Venice not signed with his name. But his interpretation of Venice is so personal that one could not deceive himself long concerning it. In the Collection Laurent-Richard, Venice appears to us in an autumn evening. It has rained all day ; but the sky, now cleared, is only traversed by some light clouds of an orange tint, which the movement of the waves reflects, mingling it with the purple shades of the setting sun. The grand Campanile of St. Mark raises itself in the distance above the horizon, and the edifices of the quay mark their silhouettes in a golden light, while gondolas thread their way over the grand canal, and some fishers' barks are placed in order to throw the nets." — RENÉ MÉNARD, *Gazette des Beaux-Arts*, April, 1873.

Zier, Édouard. (*Fr.*) Born at Paris. Pupil of his father and of Gérôme. Medal at Philadelphia, where he exhibited "Julia." At Paris, in 1877, were "The Departure of Judith" and "Acis and Galatea."

Zimmermann, Albrecht. (*Ger.*) Professor of landscape-painting at Vienna. A picture of a "Waterfall" is in the Munich Pinakothek ; also, "A Fine, Rocky Landscape, with Centaurs Wrestling." Among his works are, "The Mountain Precipice" and several fine pictures from the vicinity of the Obersee. His pictures illustrative of Faust and his Biblical subjects are fine, and he succeeds in giving the warm tone to Southern scenes and the cold feeling to Northern climes with equal truth and happiness of effect.

Zocchi, Emilio. (*Ital.*) Of Florence. Professor of the Academy of Fine Arts. At Philadelphia he exhibited "Michael Angelo sculpturing the Head of a Faun," "Benjamin Franklin in his Youth," "Columbus in his Youth," "Bacchus," and "The Youth of Michael Angelo," and received a medal.

Zuber, Jean-Henri. (*Alsatian.*) Born at Rixheim. Pupil of Gleyre. Medal of the second class in 1878, when he exhibited "Dante and Virgil" and an "Autumn Evening, — Ille-et-Vilaine" ; in 1877 he exhibited "A Flock of Geese at Seppois-le-Haut" and "The Banks of the Ill at Fislis, Upper Alsace" ; in 1876, "Evening on the Heath, near Dinard," and "Les chercheurs de marne, marée basse dans l'anse de Dinard."

Zuber-Buhler, Fritz. (*Swiss.*) Born at Locle. Pupil of Picot and Gros-Claude. At Philadelphia he exhibited "The Dew," and received a medal. At the Salon of 1877 he exhibited "The Birth of Venus."

Zuccoli, Luigi. (*Ital.*) Born at Milan. Died, 1876. Member of the Academy of Milan. A painter of scenes from popular life in Italy. He composed with taste, drew well, and showed a fine, delicate fancy. His works were admired in Italian, French, and Belgian Salons. In 1870 he exhibited at the Paris Salon, "A Wedding Present" ; in 1869, "Breakfast of the Poor" and "A Wedding Banquet, — Roman Campagna"; in 1867, "A Card-Party at an Inn." At the London Academy in 1871 he exhibited "Peasantry relating a Dreadful Scene of the Neapolitan Brigands."

Zügel, Heinrich Johann. (*Ger.*) Born at Murrhardt, 1850. Studied at the Art School at Stuttgart, and in 1873 was for some months in Vienna. He resides in Munich. At the Berlin National Gallery is his "Sheep in an Alder Grove."

Zuliani, Jean. (*Ital.*) Born at Verona. To the Paris Exposition of 1878 he sent "A Marriage of State," and to the Paris Salon of 1876, "The Rehearsal," a scene in the palace of Cardinal Richelieu.

Zumbusch, Caspar. (*Ger.*) Of Vienna. At Philadelphia he exhibited "A Marble Bust of the Emperor of Austria," and received a medal.

Zwirner, Ernest Frederic. (*Silesian.*) Born at Jacobswald (1802 – 1861). President of the Council of Architecture for the Province of Cologne, and Councilor of the Prussian Government. In 1824 he went to the Academy of Berlin to study architecture ; he was there remarked by Schinkel, who attached him to himself and his interests for several years. In 1853 Zwirner was named architect of the Cathedral of Cologne, and entered into his work with such a spirit that he inspired King William IV. and the people at large with a desire that this magnificent edifice should be completed, for which he merits, and will receive, the gratitude of this and future generations.

INDEX TO AUTHORITIES QUOTED.

INDEX OF PLACES.

GENERAL INDEX.

CPSIA information can be obtained
at www.ICGtesting.com
Printed in the USA
BVHW031204050919
557659BV00002B/472/P